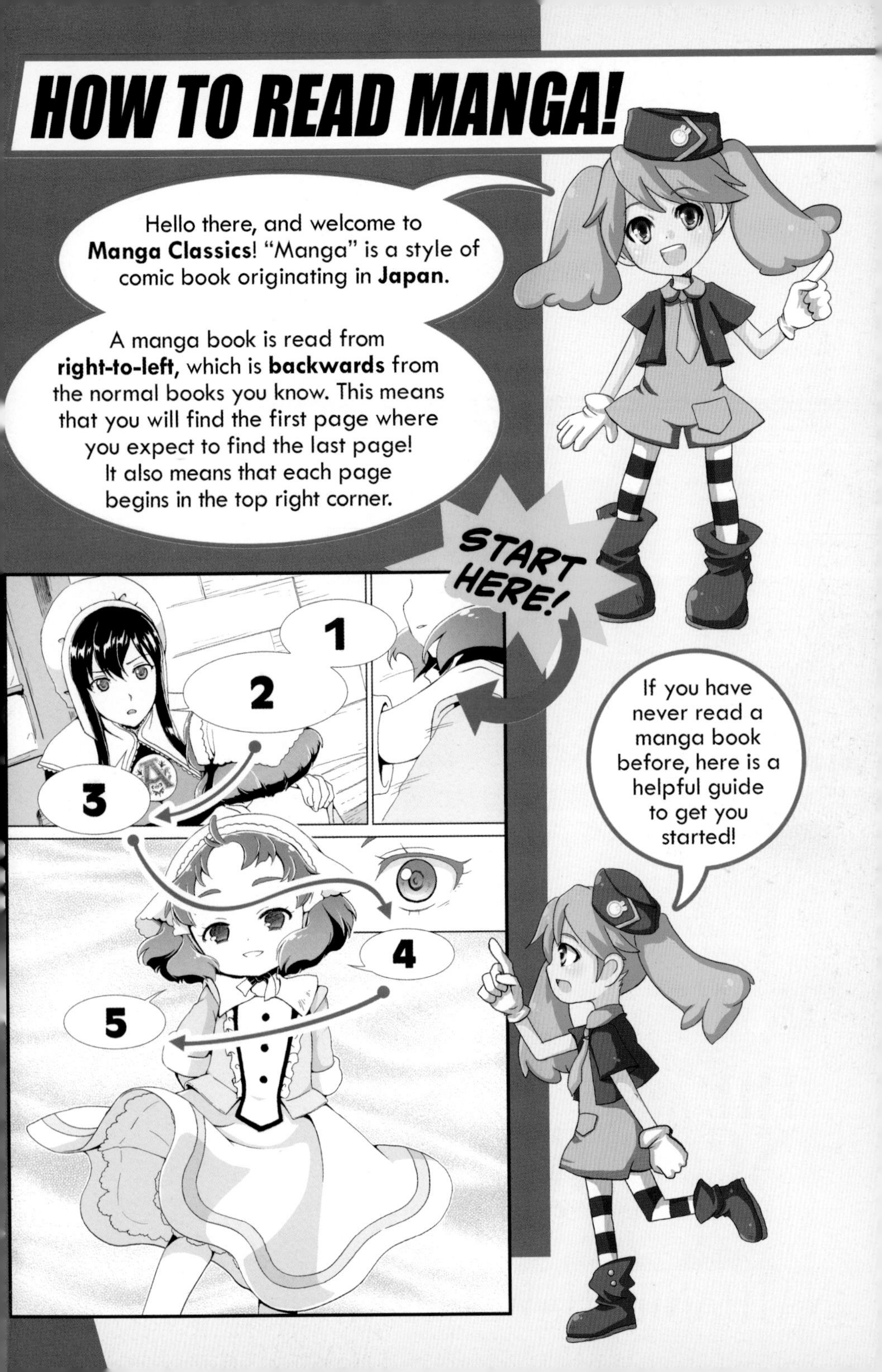
HOW TO READ MANGA!
Hello there, and welcome to Manga Classics! "Manga" is a style of comic book originating in Japan.
A manga book is read from right-to-left, which is backwards from the normal books you know. This means that you will find the first page where you expect to find the last page! It also means that each page begins in the top right corner.
If you have never read a manga book before, here is a helpful guide to get you started!
START HERE!
1
2
3
4
5

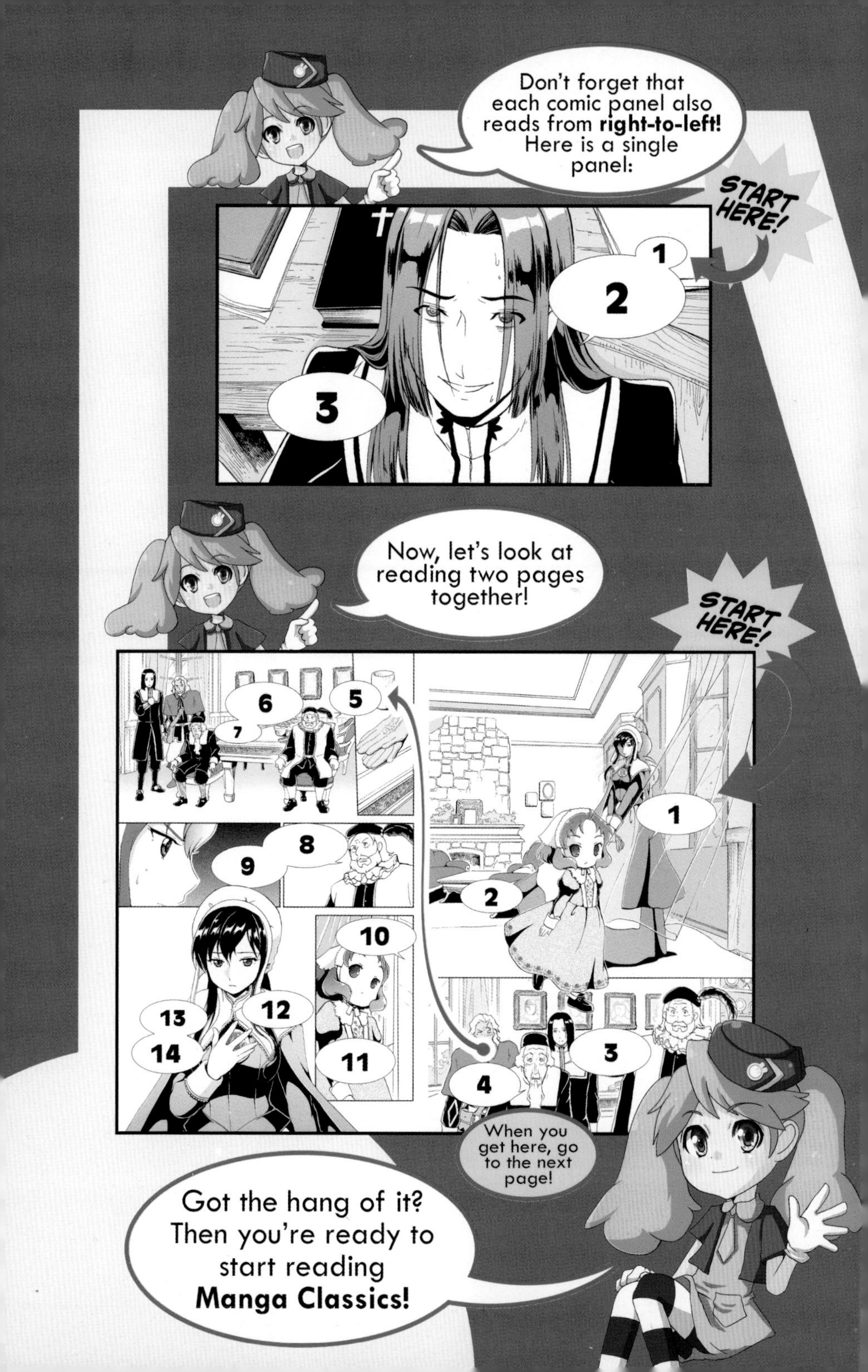
Don't forget that each comic panel also reads from **right-to-left!** Here is a single panel:
START HERE!
Now, let's look at reading two pages together!
START HERE!
When you get here, go to the next page!
Got the hang of it? Then you're ready to start reading **Manga Classics!**

CONTENTS:

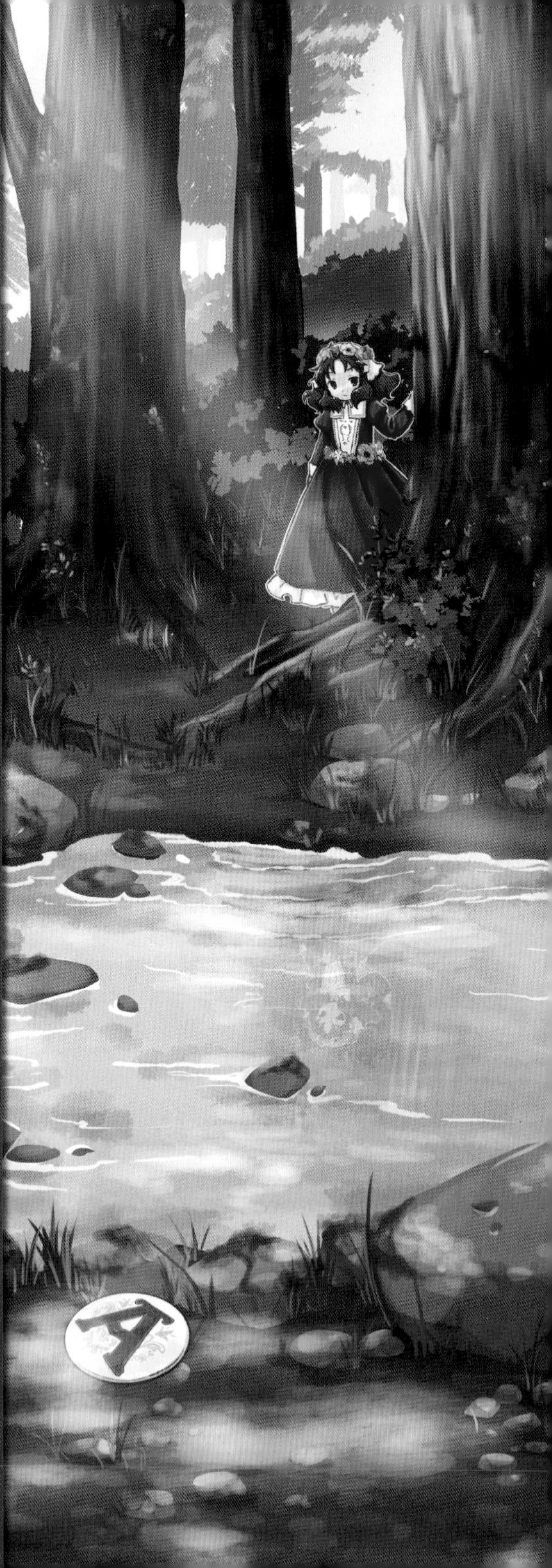

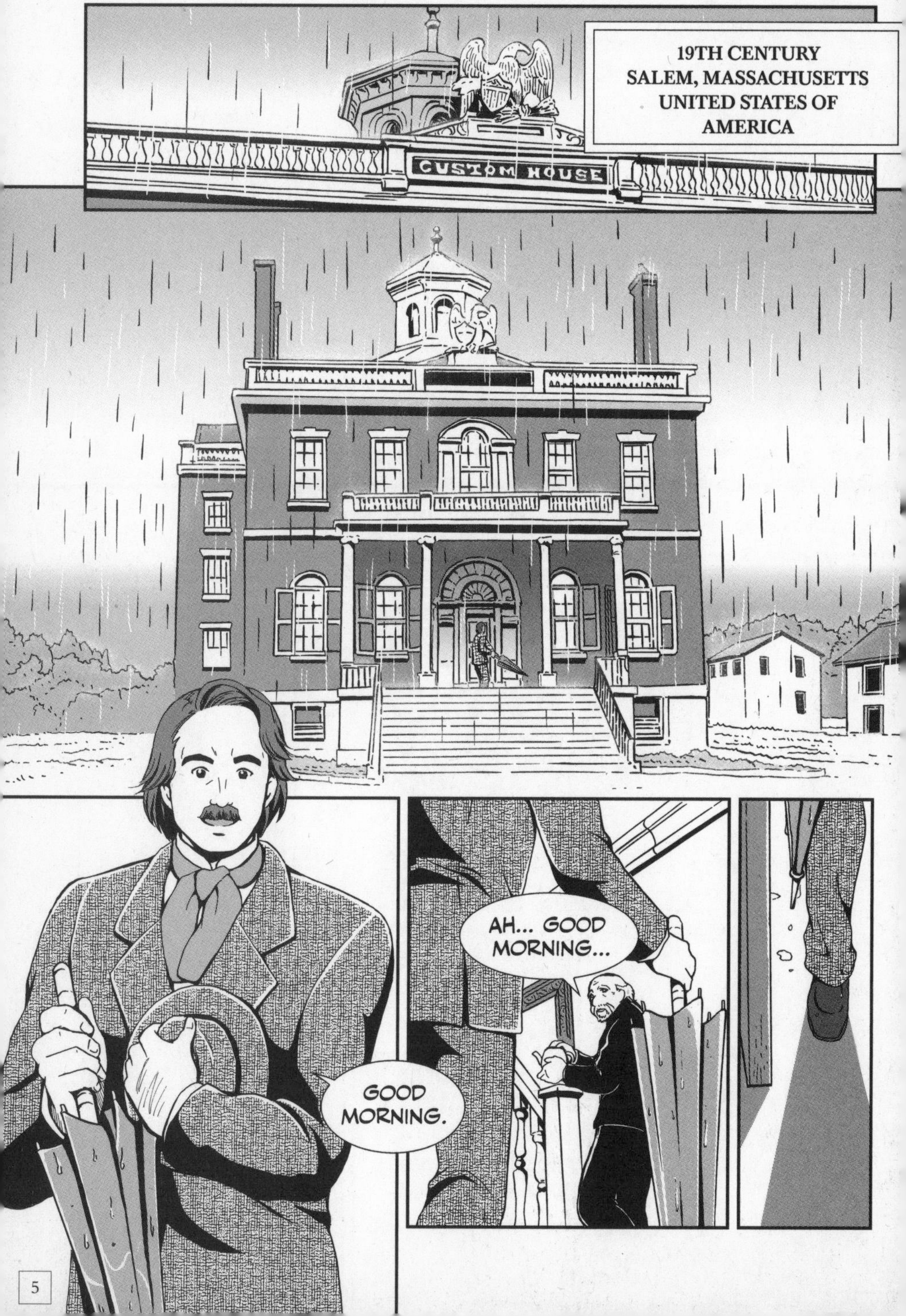
19TH CENTURY SALEM, MASSACHUSETTS UNITED STATES OF AMERICA
CUSTOM HOUSE
AH... GOOD MORNING...
GOOD MORNING.

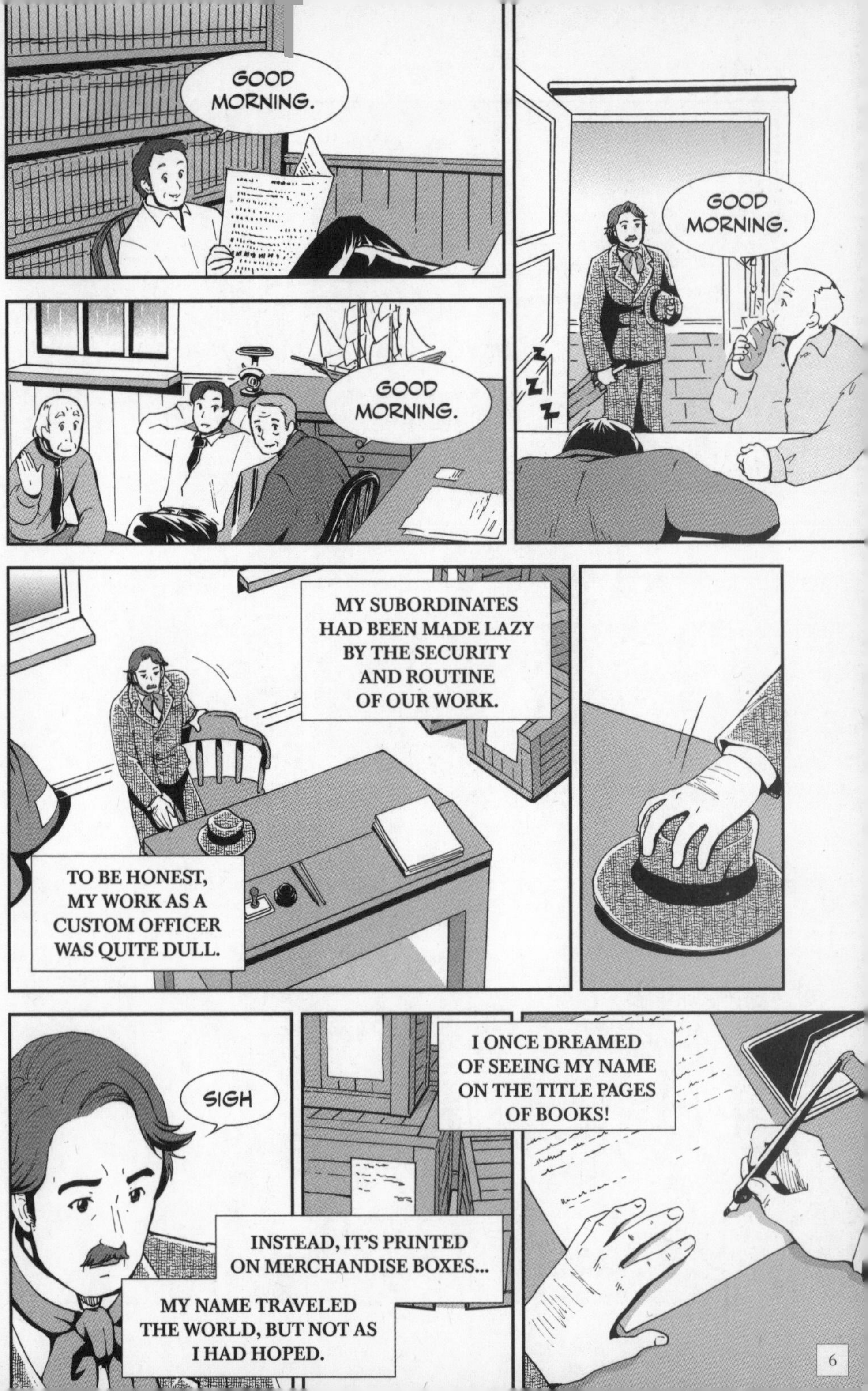
GOOD MORNING.
GOOD MORNING.
GOOD MORNING.
MY SUBORDINATES HAD BEEN MADE LAZY BY THE SECURITY AND ROUTINE OF OUR WORK.
TO BE HONEST, MY WORK AS A CUSTOM OFFICER WAS QUITE DULL.
I ONCE DREAMED OF SEEING MY NAME ON THE TITLE PAGES OF BOOKS!
SIGH
INSTEAD, IT'S PRINTED ON MERCHANDISE BOXES...
MY NAME TRAVELED THE WORLD, BUT NOT AS I HAD HOPED.

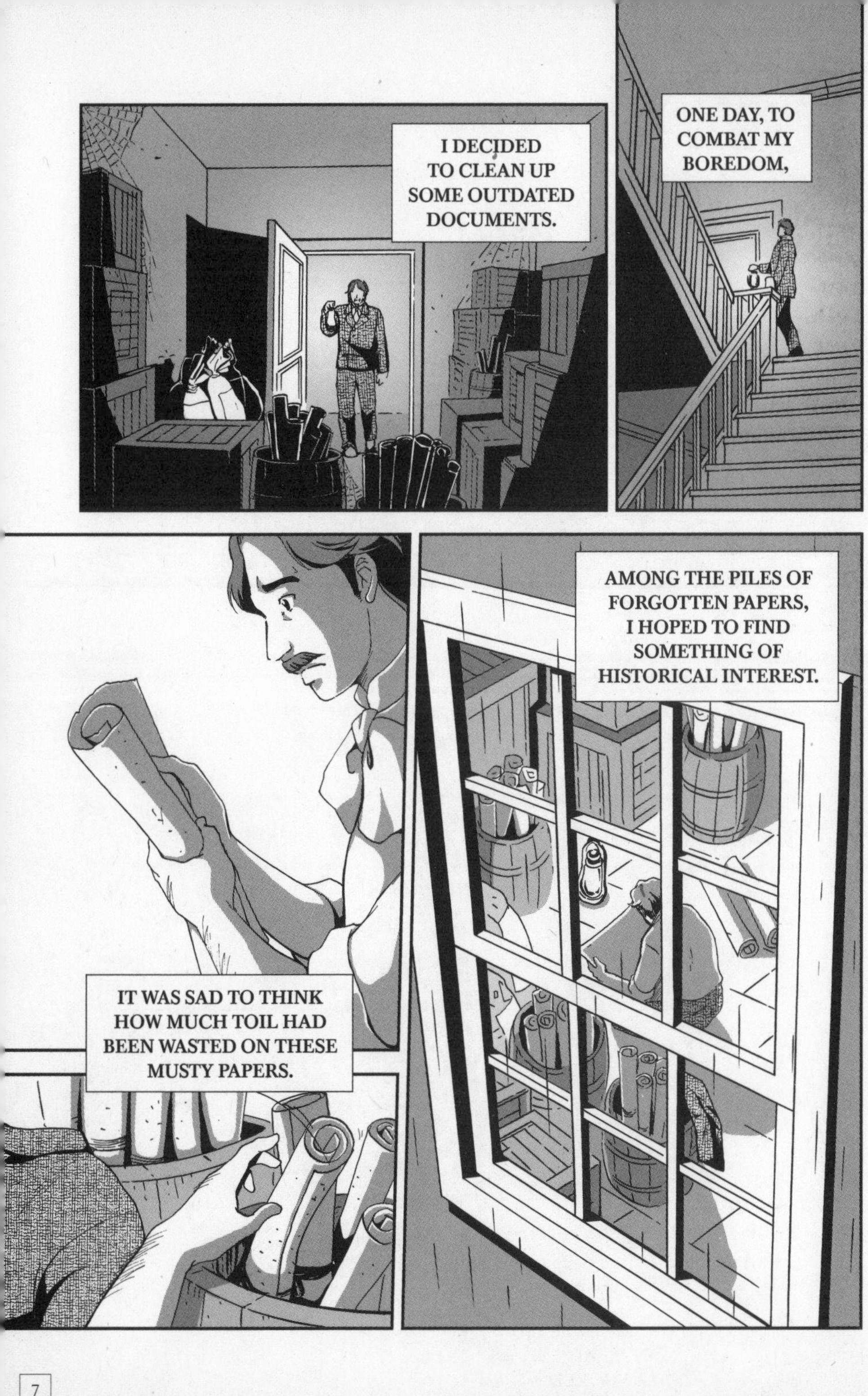
ONE DAY, TO COMBAT MY BOREDOM,
I DECIDED TO CLEAN UP SOME OUTDATED DOCUMENTS.
AMONG THE PILES OF FORGOTTEN PAPERS, I HOPED TO FIND SOMETHING OF HISTORICAL INTEREST.
IT WAS SAD TO THINK HOW MUCH TOIL HAD BEEN WASTED ON THESE MUSTY PAPERS.

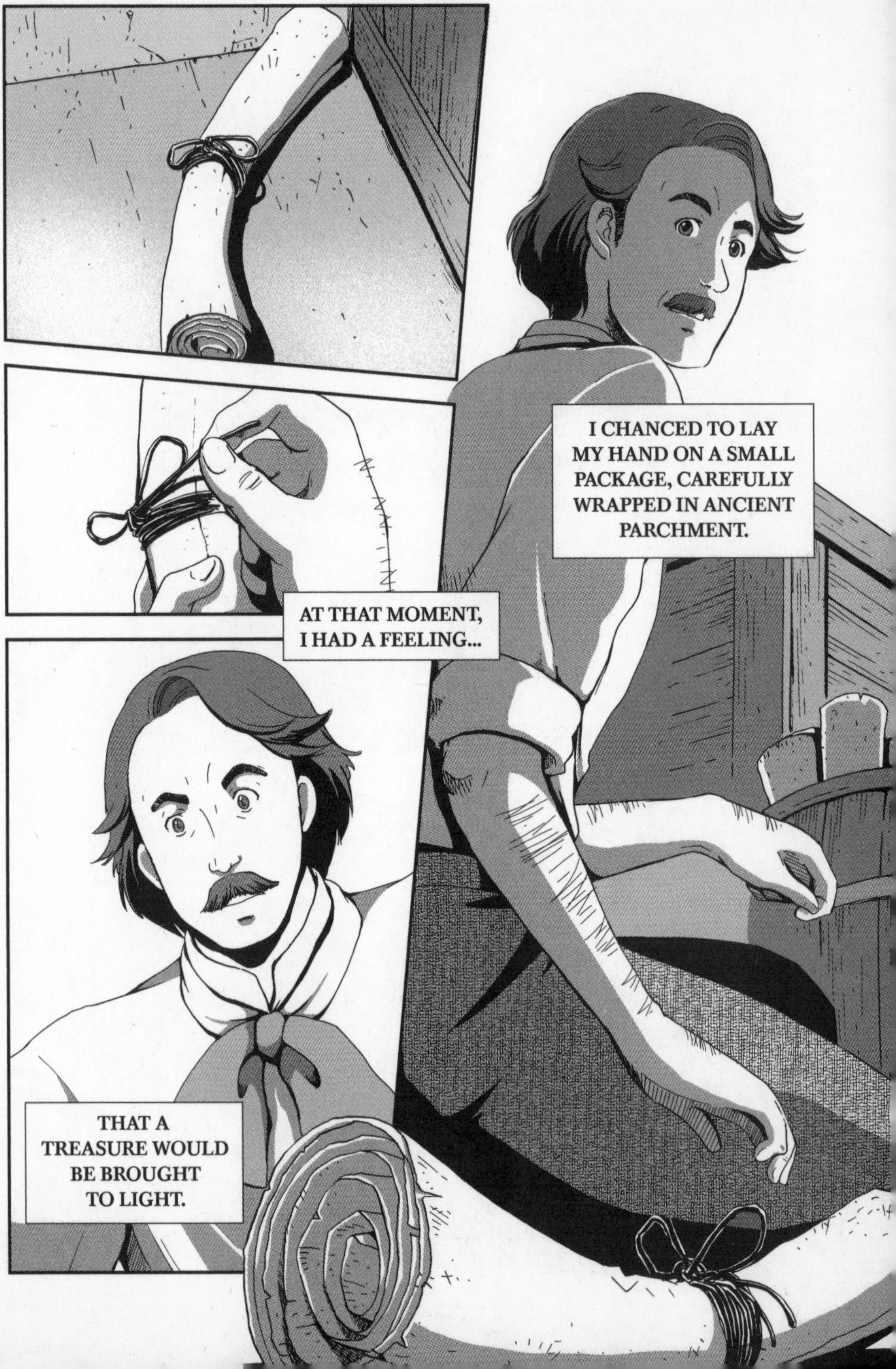
I CHANCED TO LAY MY HAND ON A SMALL PACKAGE, CAREFULLY WRAPPED IN ANCIENT PARCHMENT.
AT THAT MOMENT, I HAD A FEELING...
THAT A TREASURE WOULD BE BROUGHT TO LIGHT.

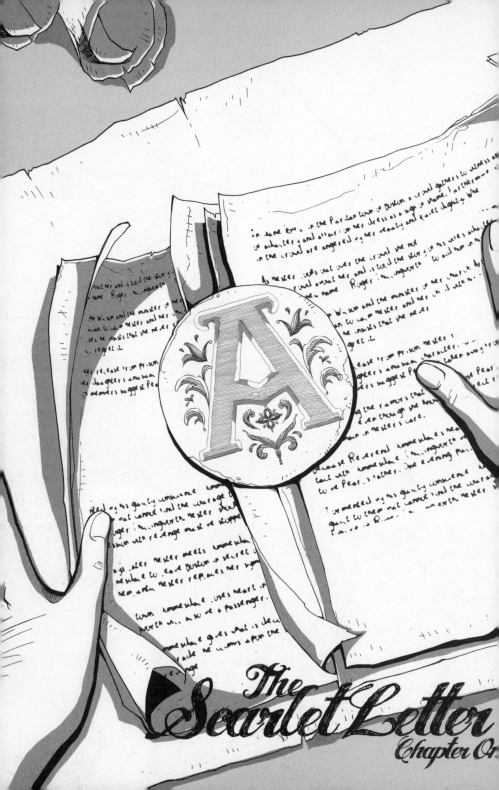

The Scarlet Letter
Chapter One

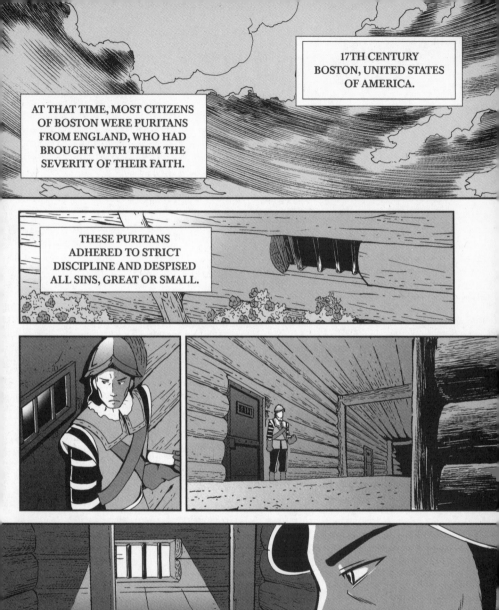

17TH CENTURY BOSTON, UNITED STATES OF AMERICA.

AT THAT TIME, MOST CITIZENS OF BOSTON WERE PURITANS FROM ENGLAND, WHO HAD BROUGHT WITH THEM THE SEVERITY OF THEIR FAITH.

THESE PURITANS ADHERED TO STRICT DISCIPLINE AND DESPISED ALL SINS, GREAT OR SMALL.

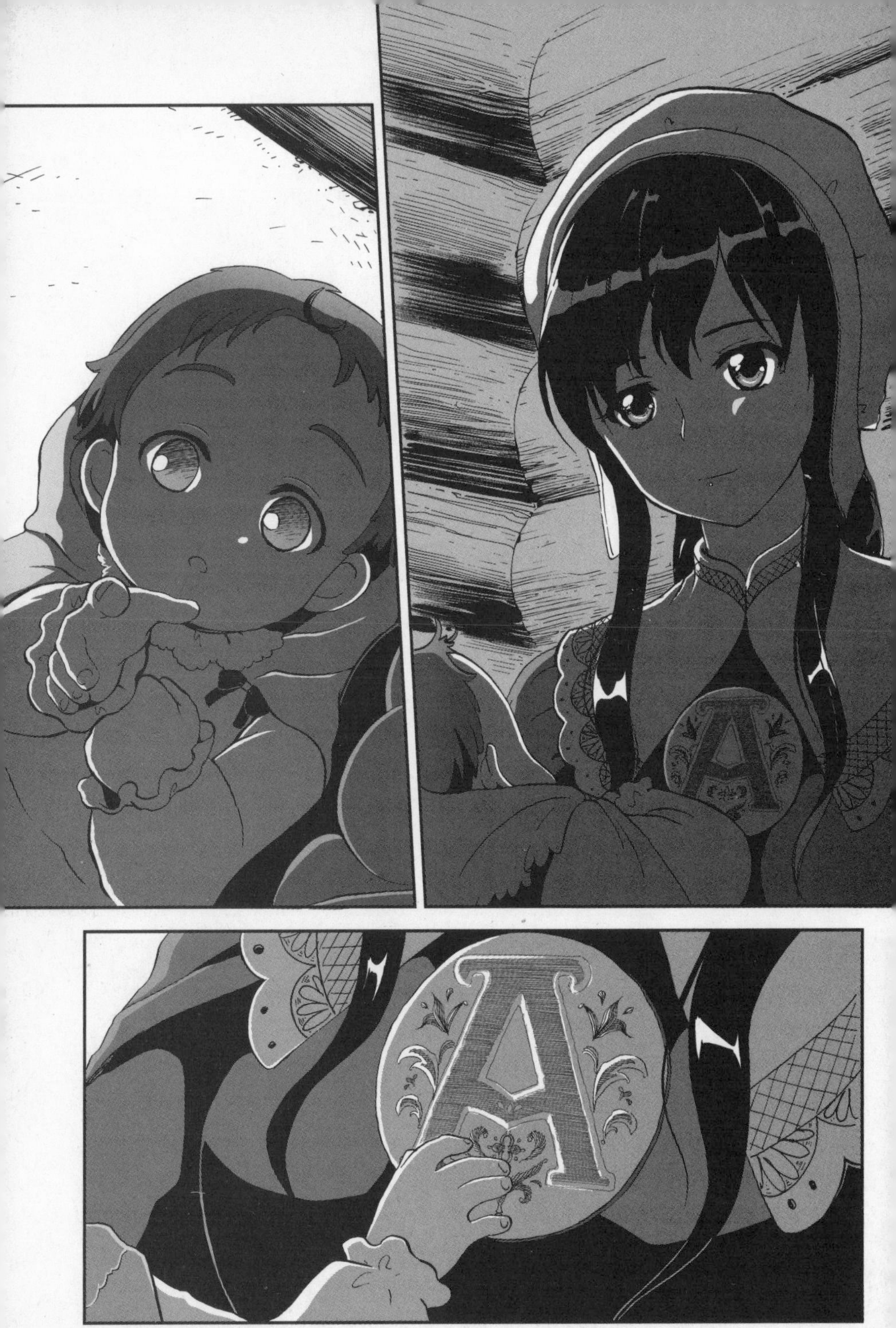

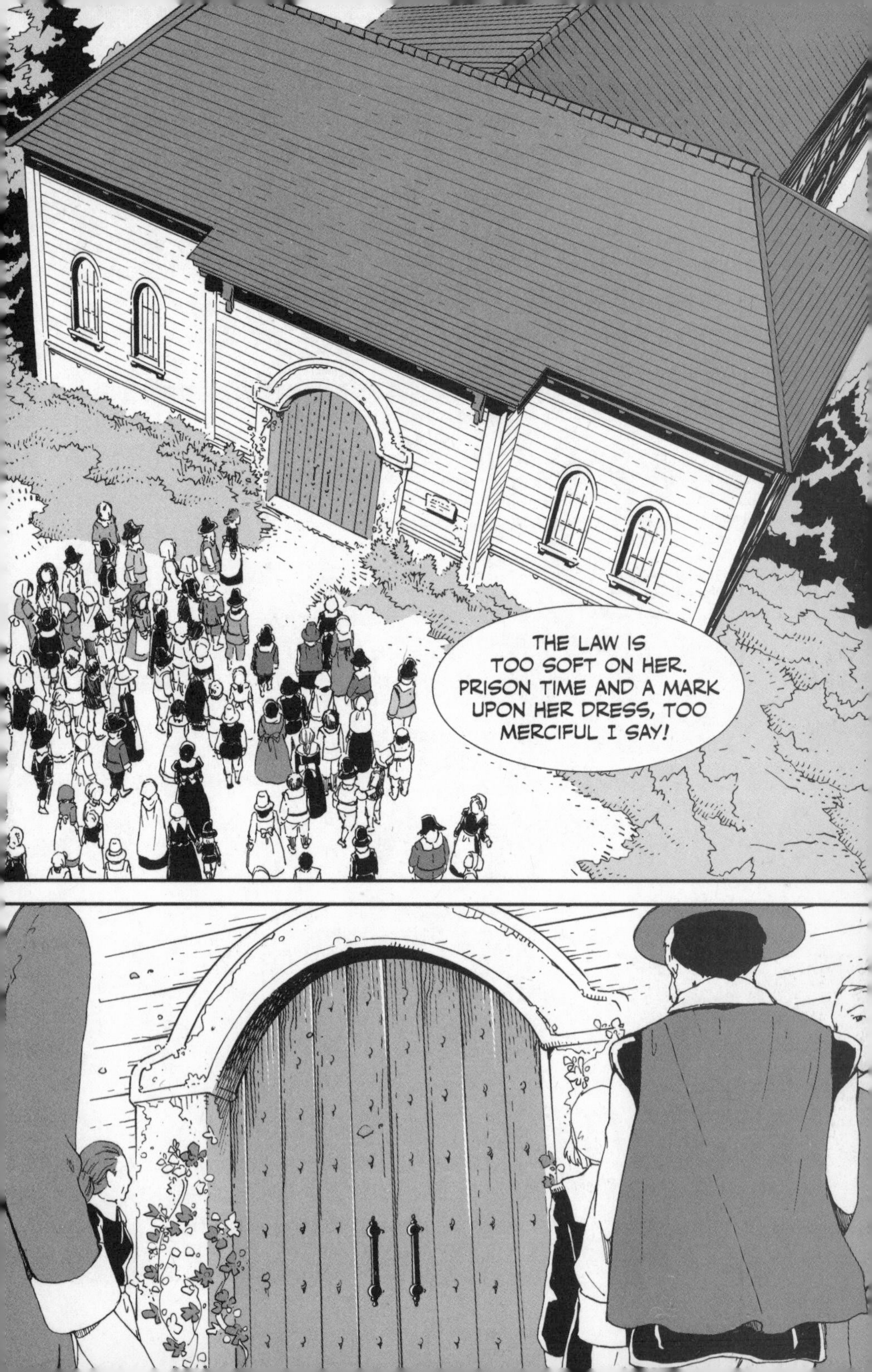
THE LAW IS TOO SOFT ON HER. PRISON TIME AND A MARK UPON HER DRESS, TOO MERCIFUL I SAY!

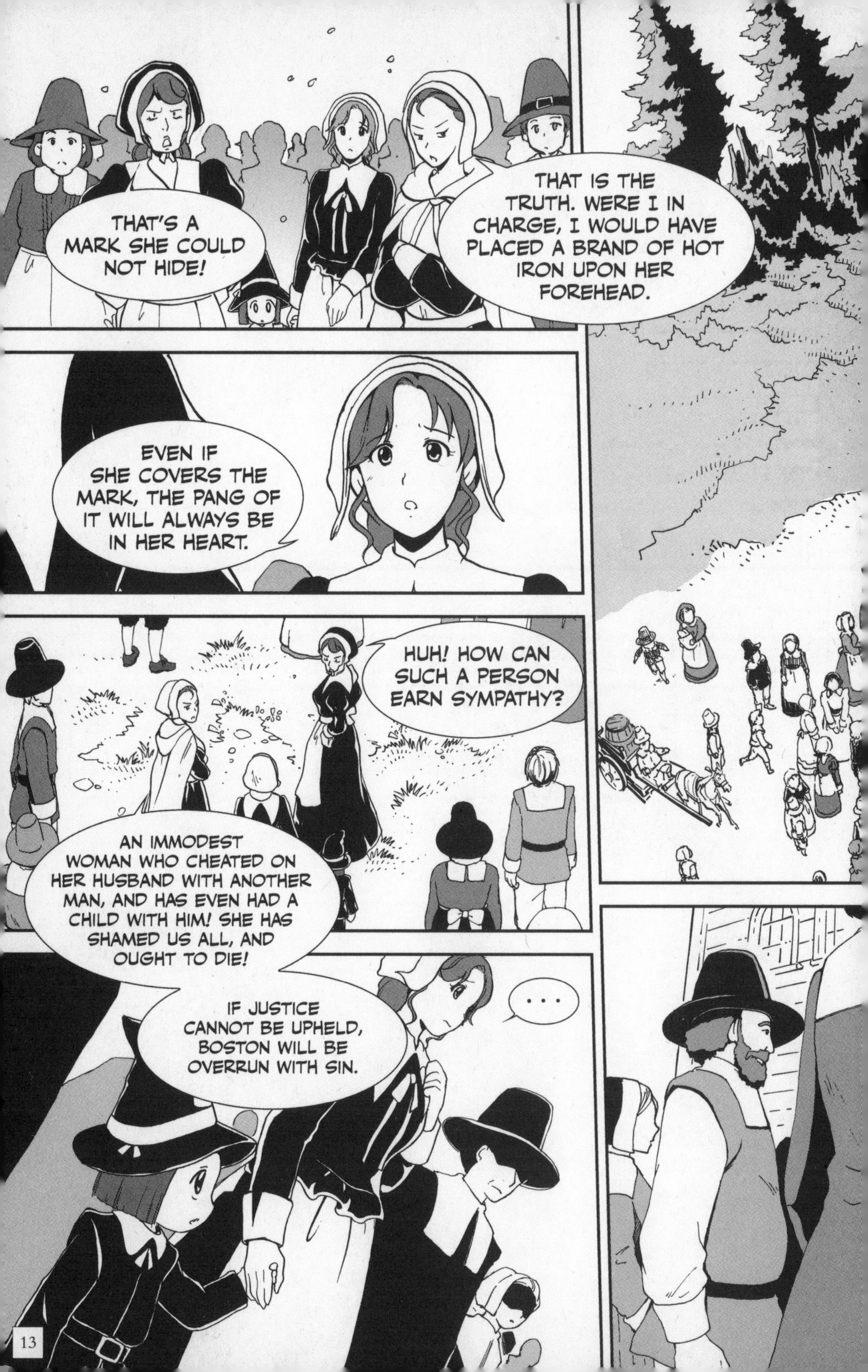
THAT IS THE TRUTH. WERE I IN CHARGE, I WOULD HAVE PLACED A BRAND OF HOT IRON UPON HER FOREHEAD.
THAT'S A MARK SHE COULD NOT HIDE!
EVEN IF SHE COVERS THE MARK, THE PANG OF IT WILL ALWAYS BE IN HER HEART.
HUH! HOW CAN SUCH A PERSON EARN SYMPATHY?
AN IMMODEST WOMAN WHO CHEATED ON HER HUSBAND WITH ANOTHER MAN, AND HAS EVEN HAD A CHILD WITH HIM! SHE HAS SHAMED US ALL, AND OUGHT TO DIE!
. . .
IF JUSTICE CANNOT BE UPHELD, BOSTON WILL BE OVERRUN WITH SIN.

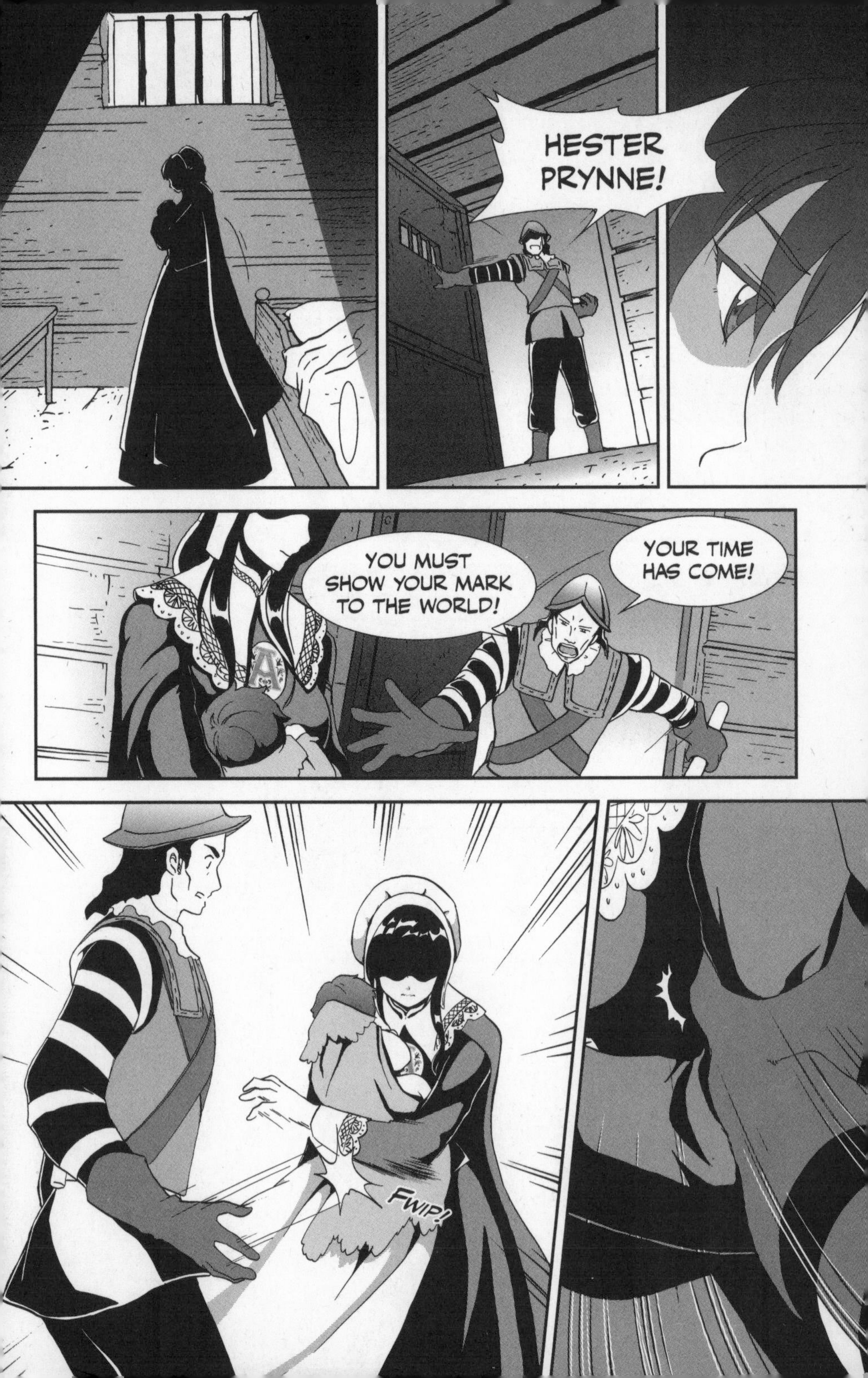
HESTER PRYNNE!
YOUR TIME HAS COME!
YOU MUST SHOW YOUR MARK TO THE WORLD!
FWIP!

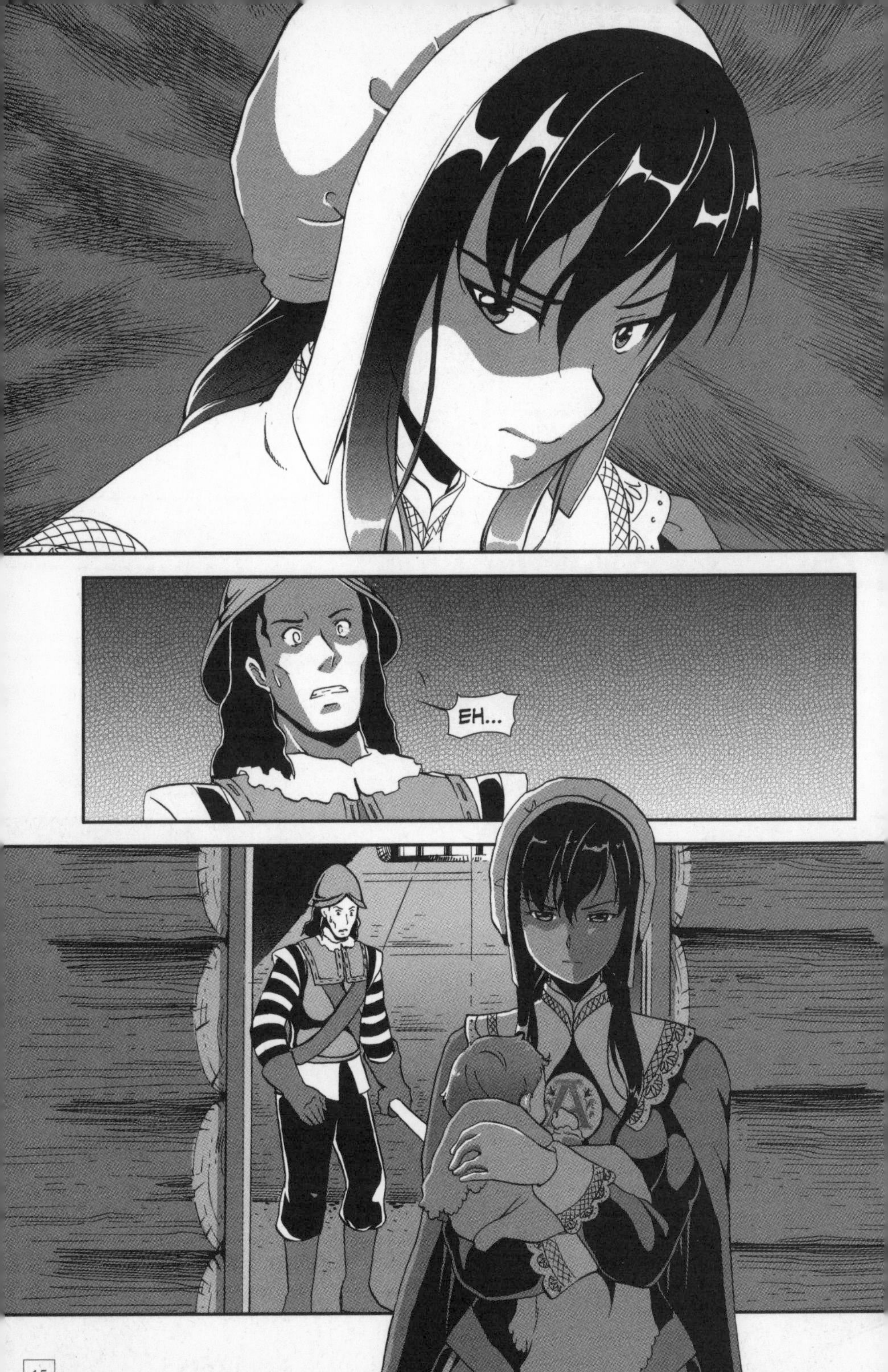
EH...

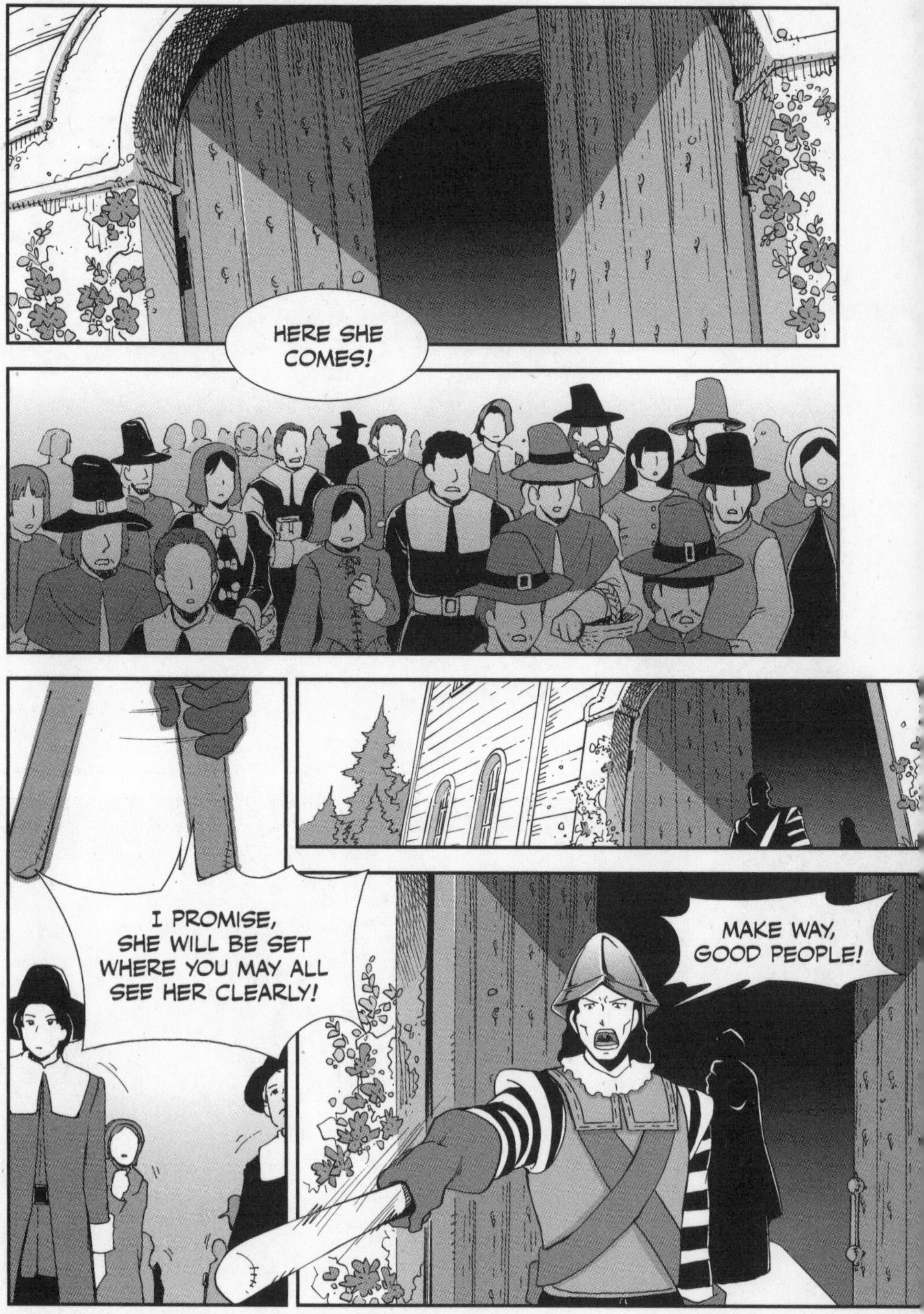
HERE SHE COMES!
MAKE WAY, GOOD PEOPLE!
I PROMISE, SHE WILL BE SET WHERE YOU MAY ALL SEE HER CLEARLY!

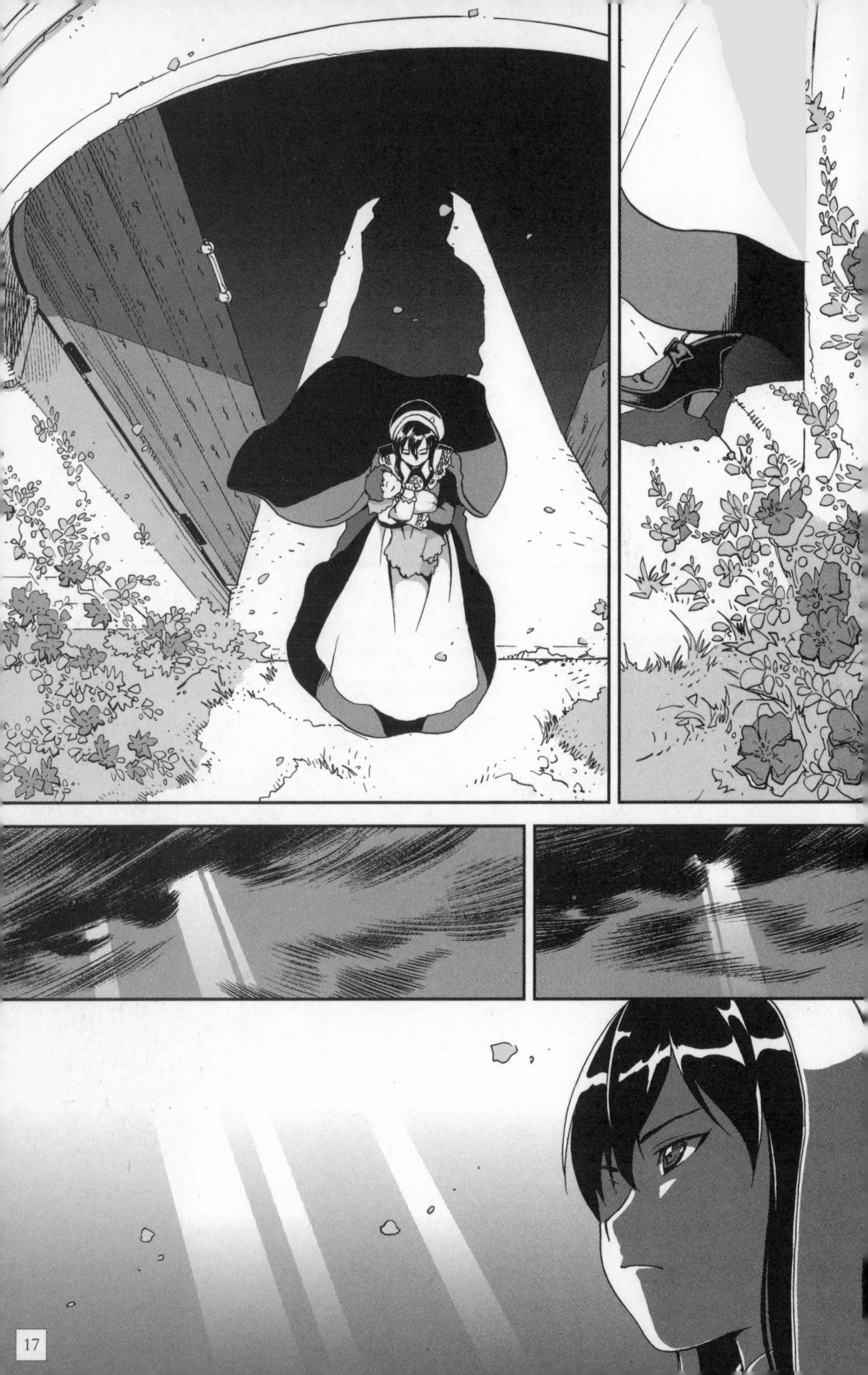

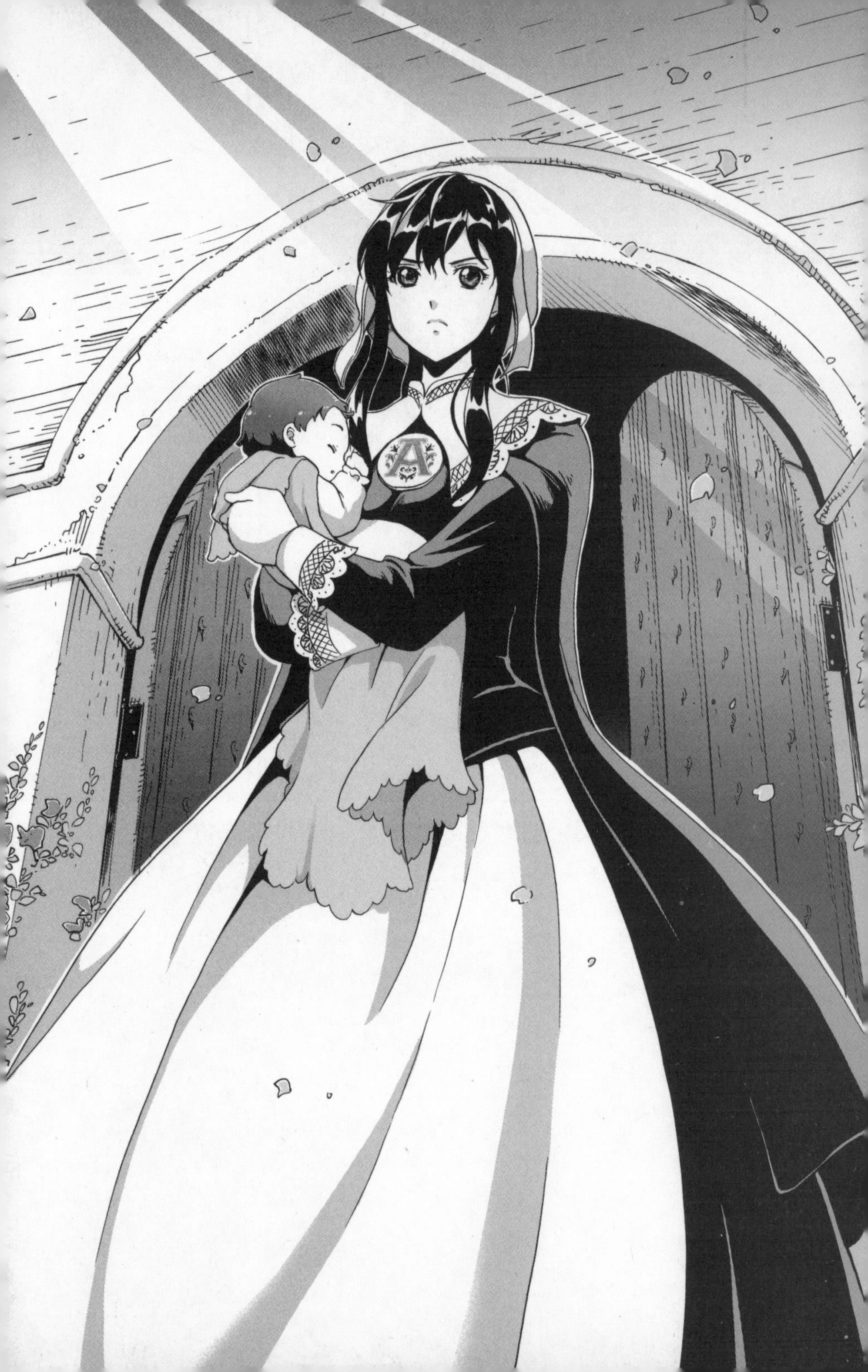

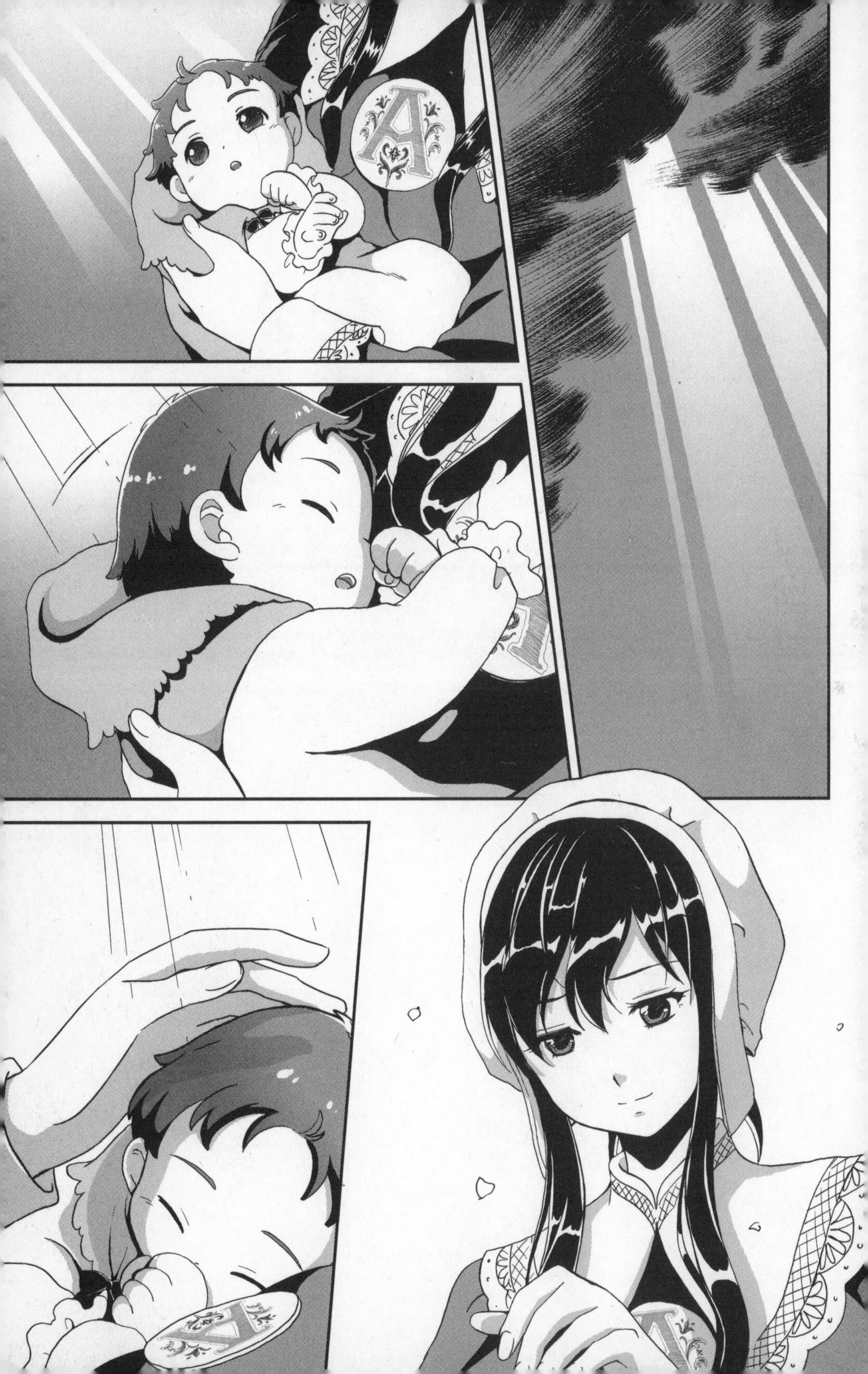

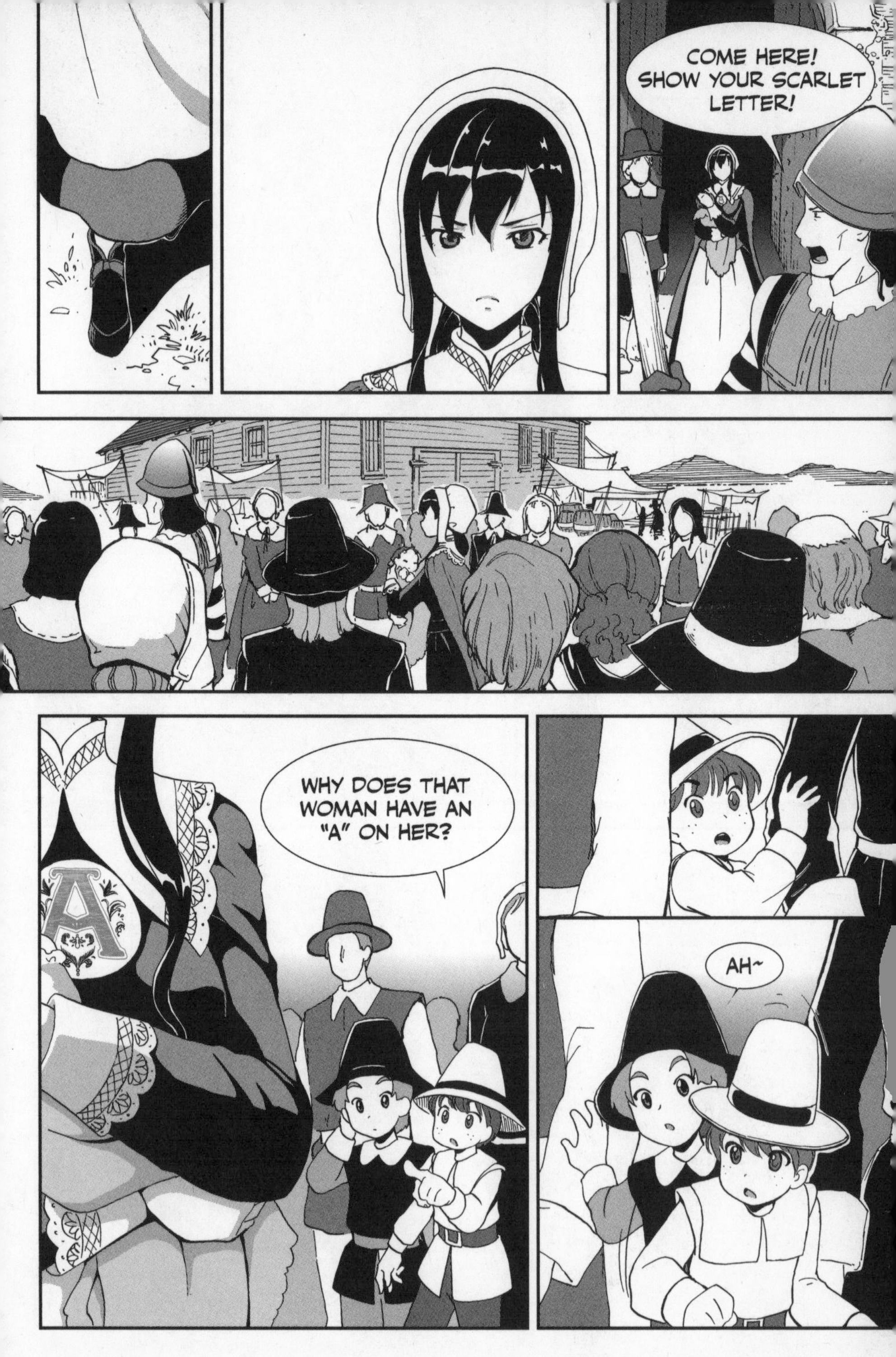
COME HERE! SHOW YOUR SCARLET LETTER!
AH~
WHY DOES THAT WOMAN HAVE AN "A" ON HER?

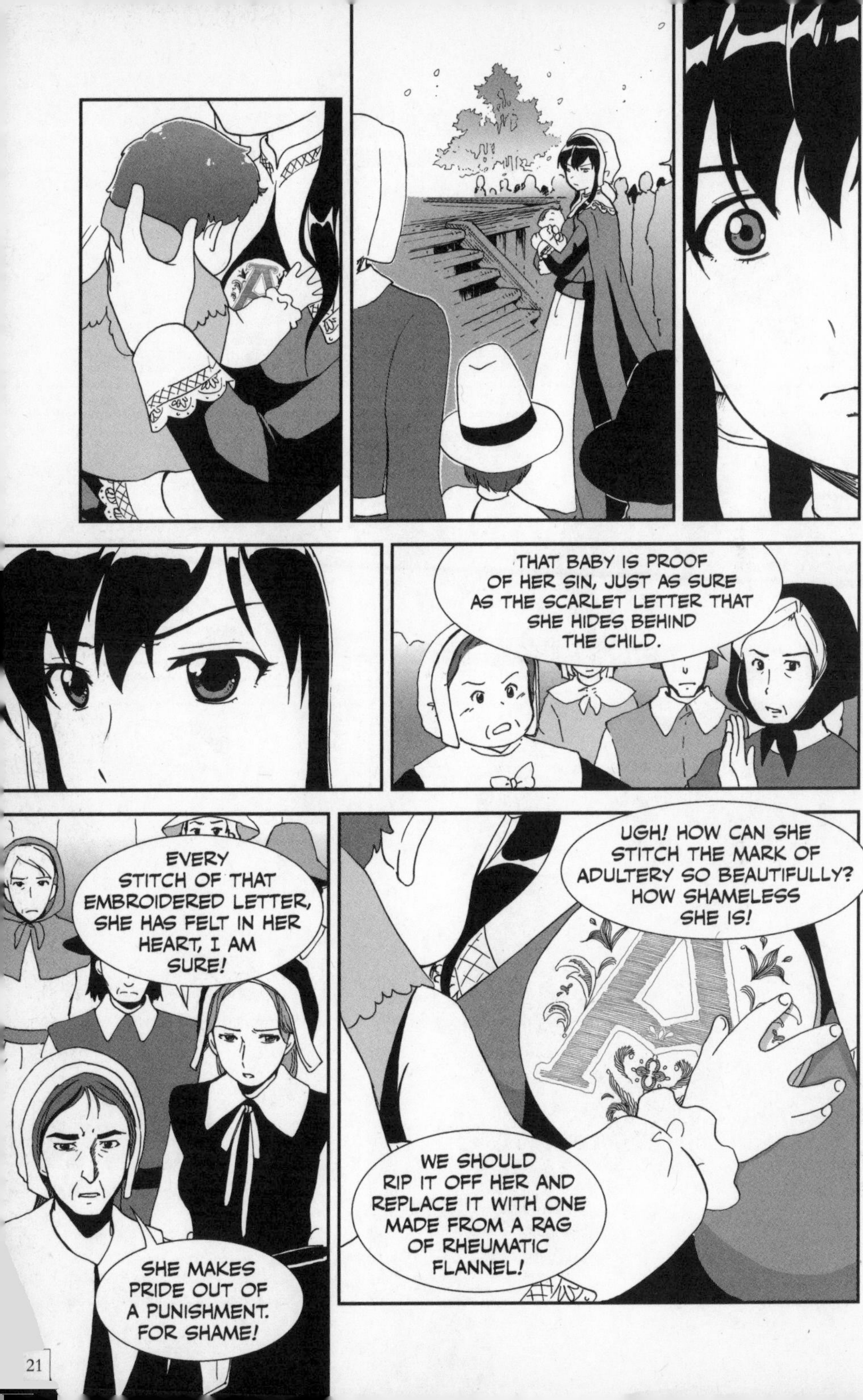
THAT BABY IS PROOF OF HER SIN, JUST AS SURE AS THE SCARLET LETTER THAT SHE HIDES BEHIND THE CHILD.
UGH! HOW CAN SHE STITCH THE MARK OF ADULTERY SO BEAUTIFULLY? HOW SHAMELESS SHE IS!
WE SHOULD RIP IT OFF HER AND REPLACE IT WITH ONE MADE FROM A RAG OF RHEUMATIC FLANNEL!
EVERY STITCH OF THAT EMBROIDERED LETTER, SHE HAS FELT IN HER HEART, I AM SURE!
SHE MAKES PRIDE OUT OF A PUNISHMENT. FOR SHAME!

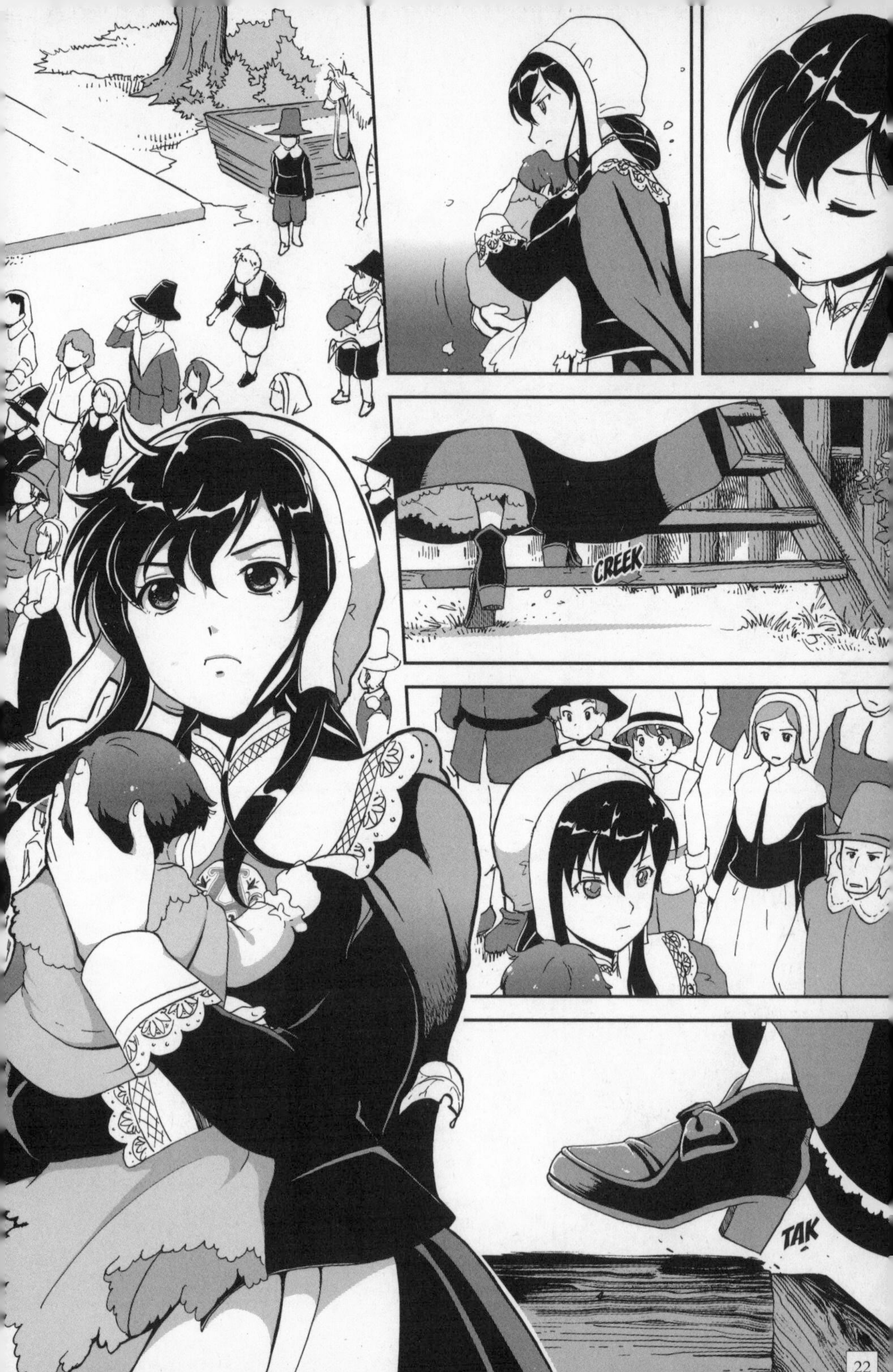
CREEK
TAK

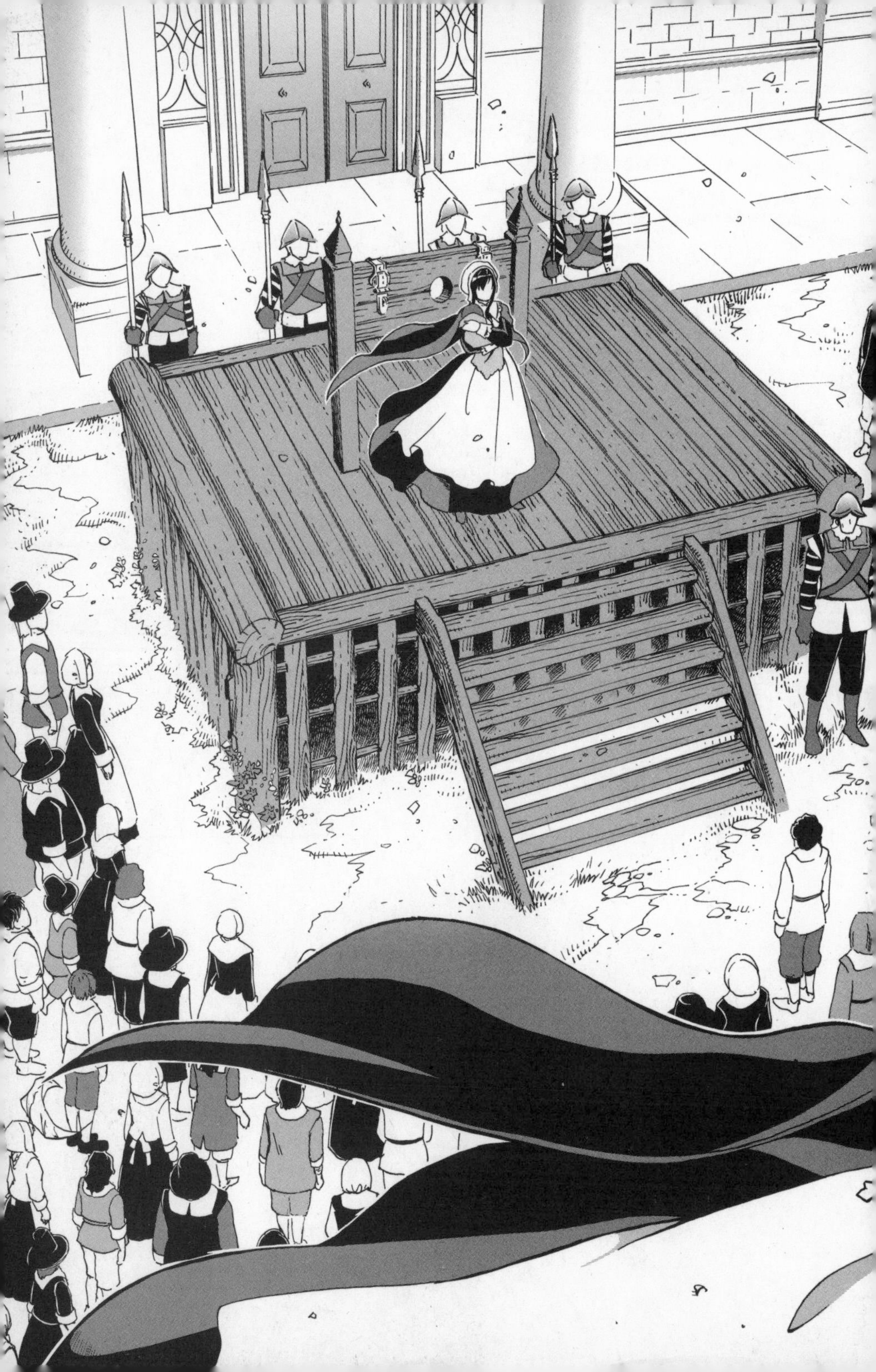

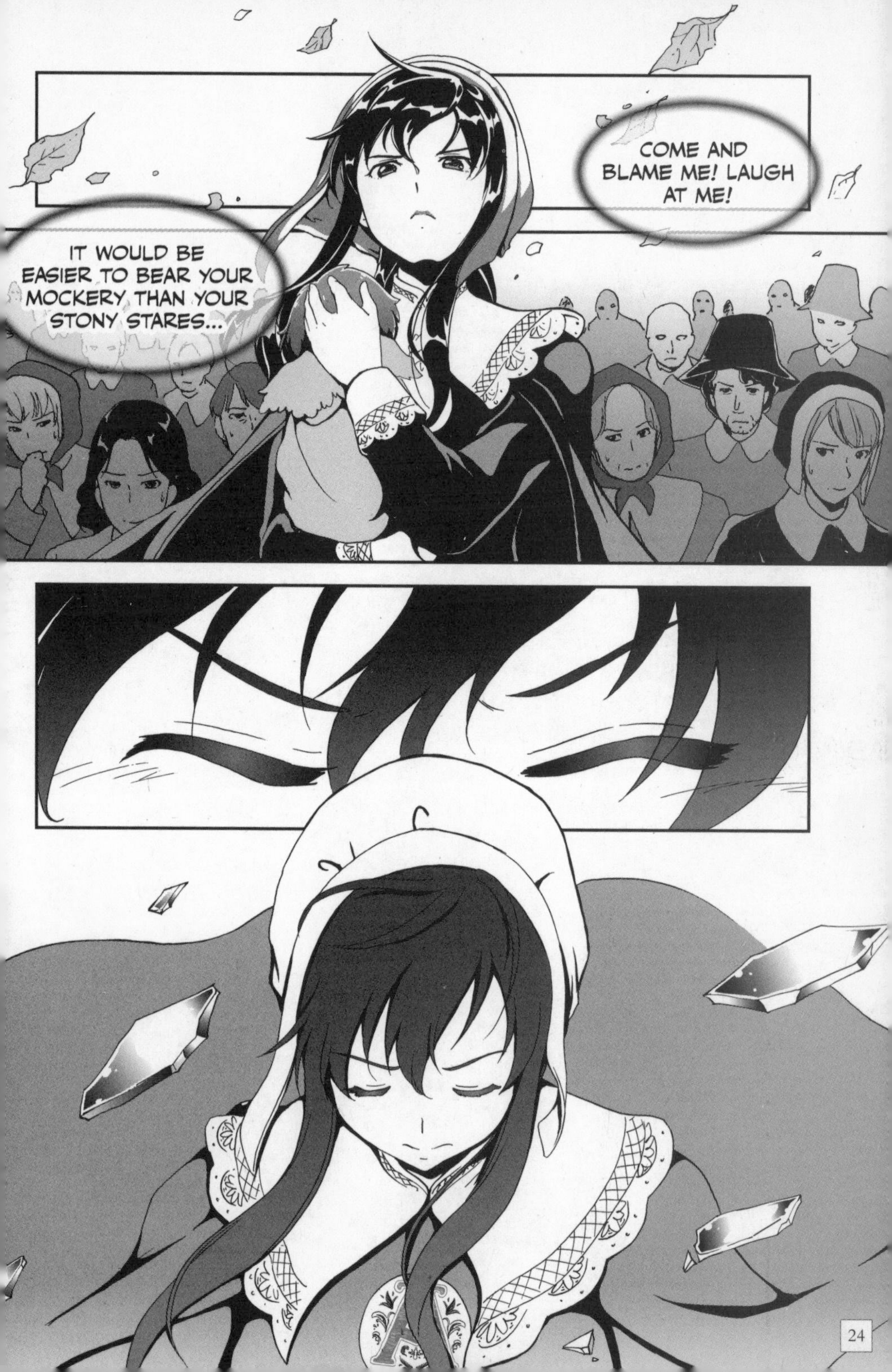
COME AND BLAME ME! LAUGH AT ME!
IT WOULD BE EASIER TO BEAR YOUR MOCKERY THAN YOUR STONY STARES...

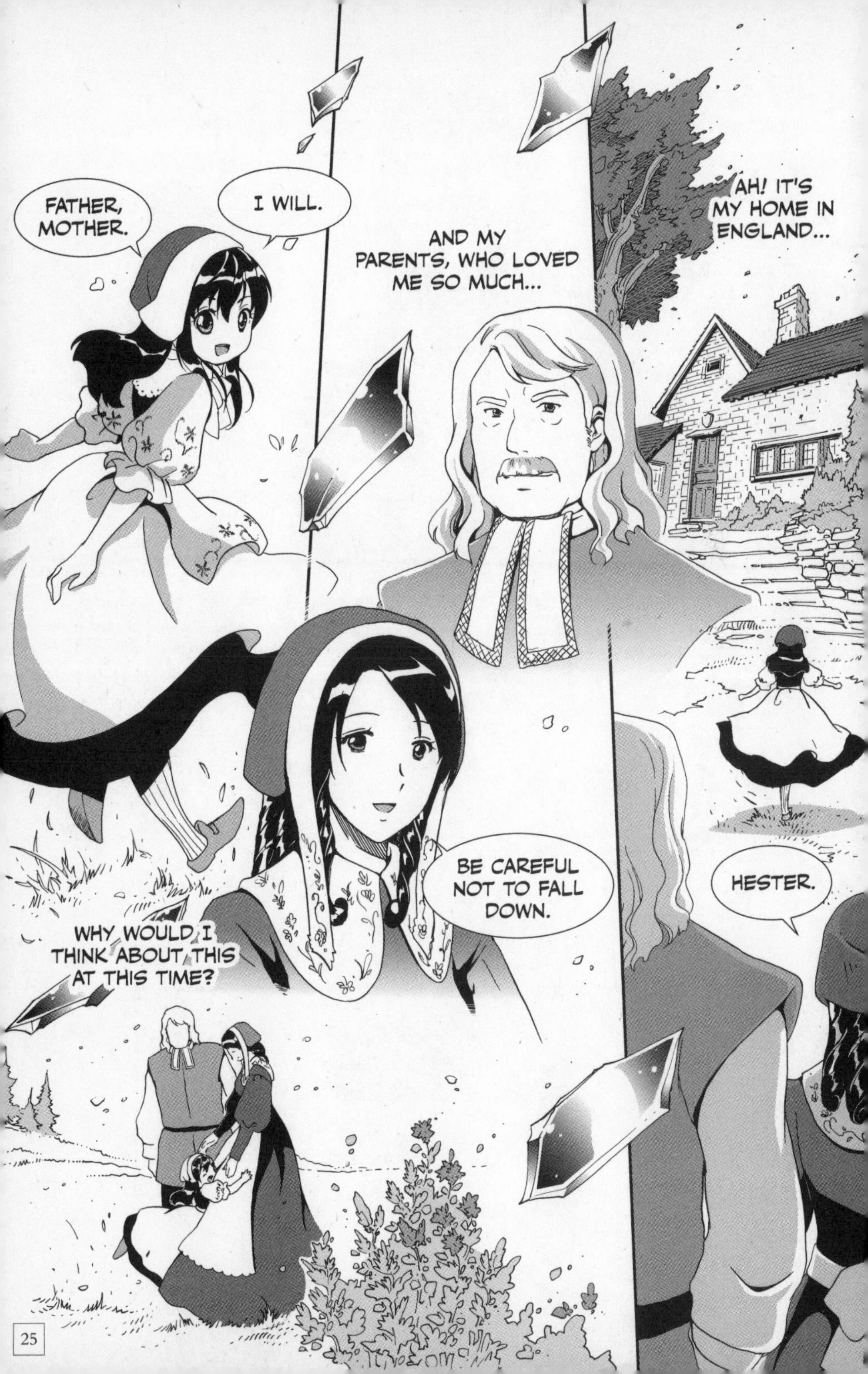
AH! IT'S MY HOME IN ENGLAND...
HESTER.
AND MY PARENTS, WHO LOVED ME SO MUCH...
BE CAREFUL NOT TO FALL DOWN.
I WILL.
FATHER, MOTHER.
WHY WOULD I THINK ABOUT THIS AT THIS TIME?

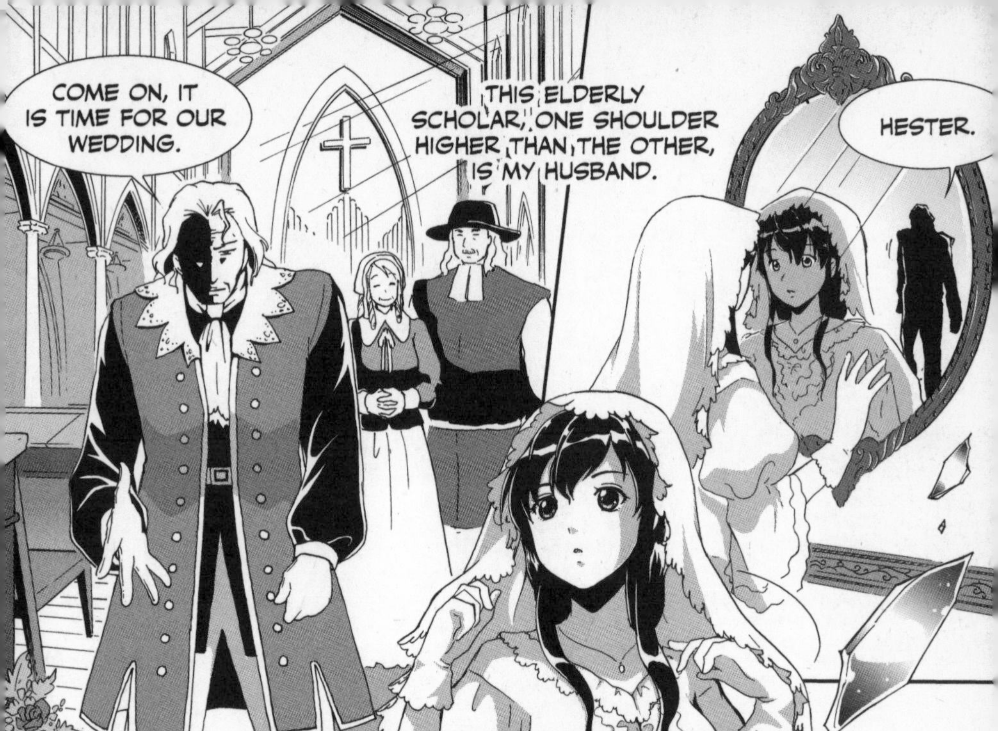
HESTER.
THIS ELDERLY SCHOLAR, ONE SHOULDER HIGHER THAN THE OTHER, IS MY HUSBAND.
COME ON, IT IS TIME FOR OUR WEDDING.
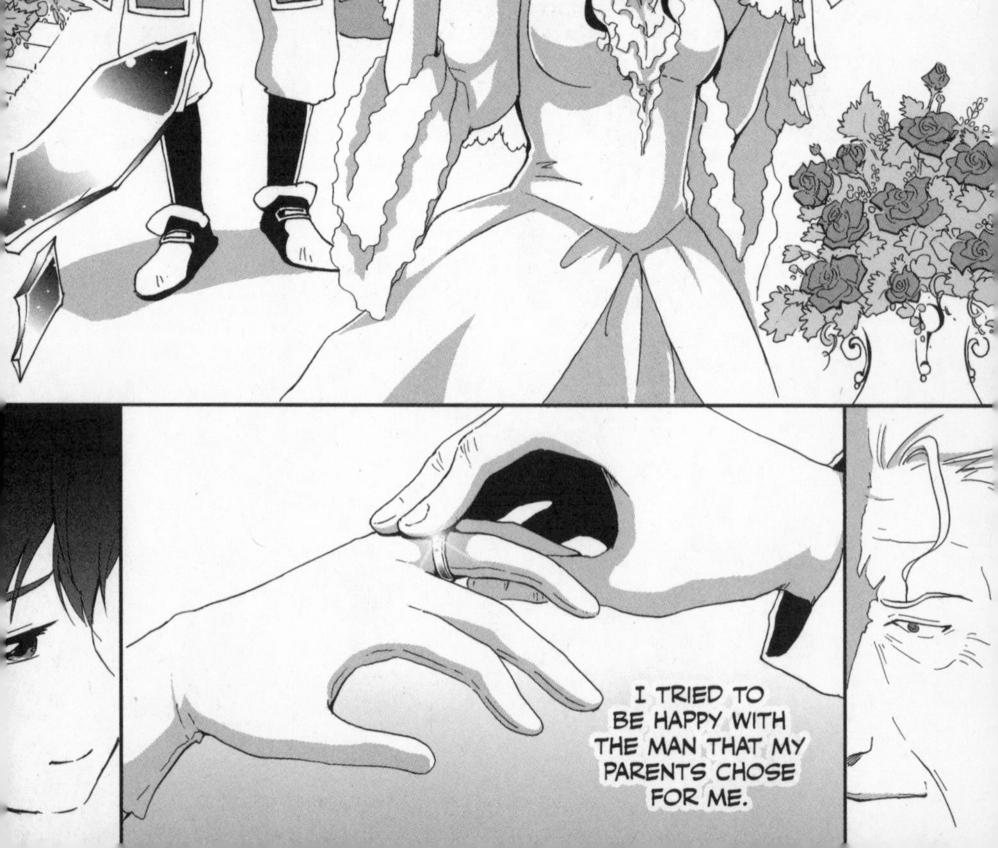
I TRIED TO BE HAPPY WITH THE MAN THAT MY PARENTS CHOSE FOR ME.

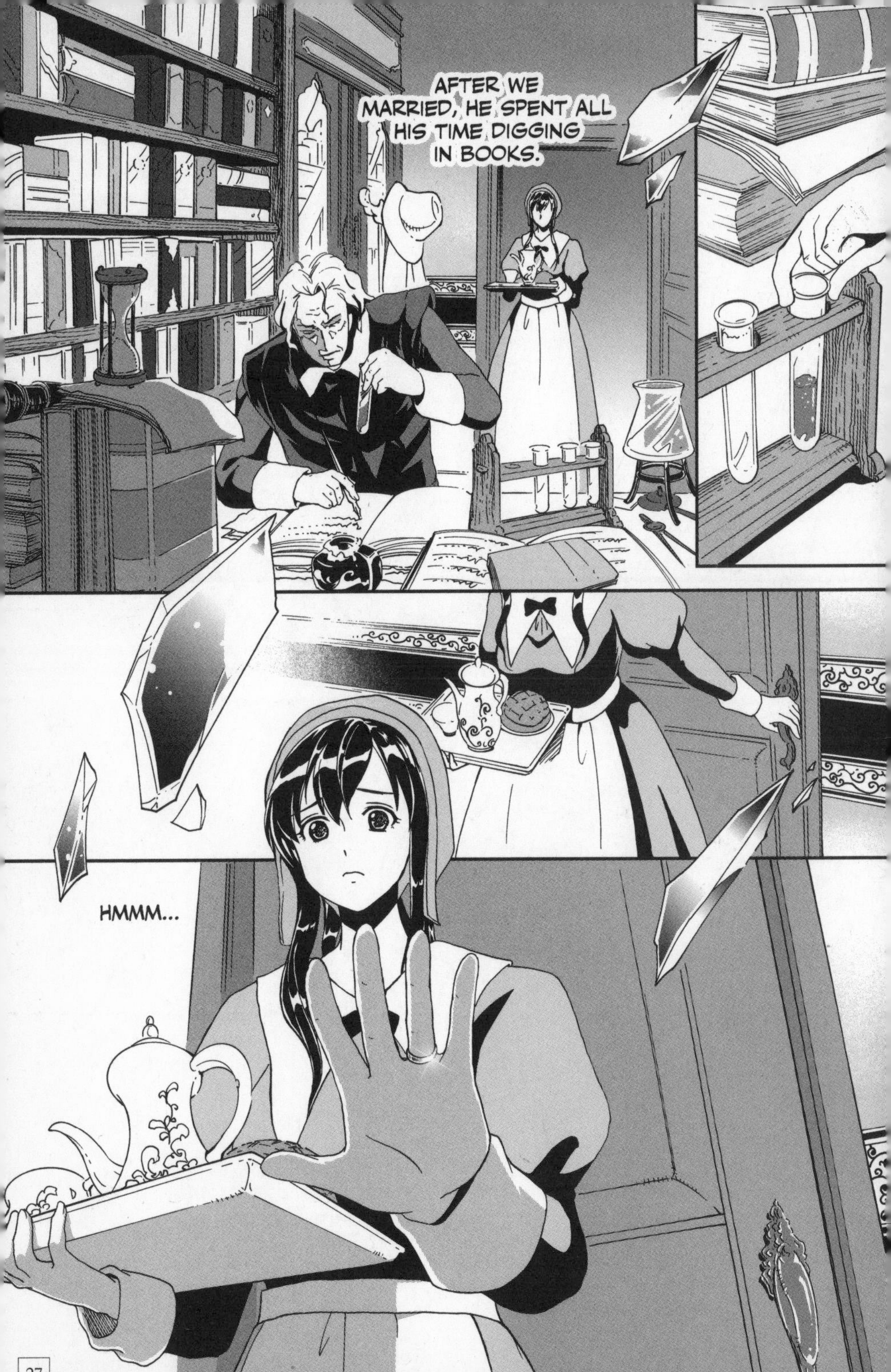
AFTER WE MARRIED, HE SPENT ALL HIS TIME DIGGING IN BOOKS.
HMMM...

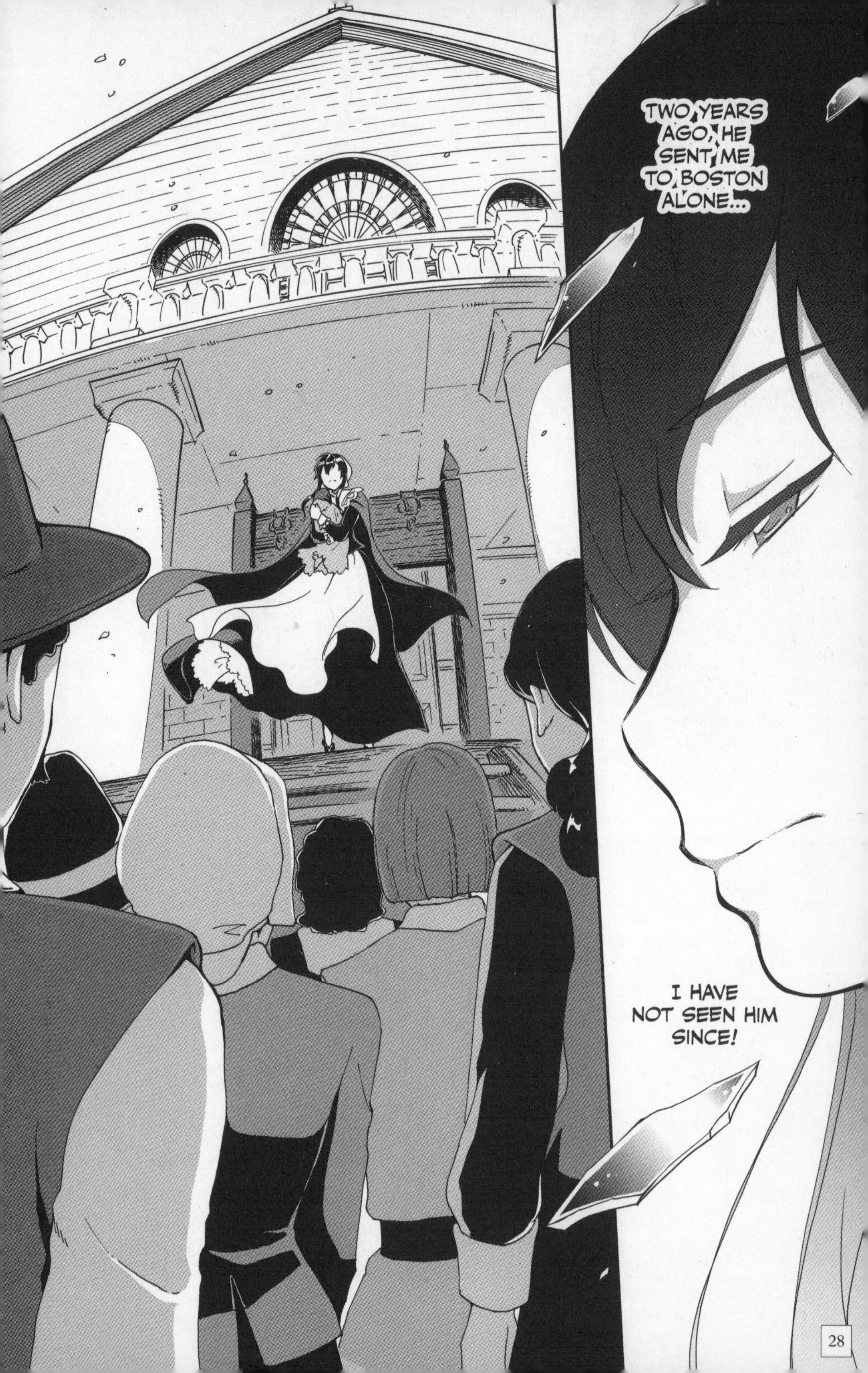
TWO YEARS AGO, HE SENT ME TO BOSTON ALONE...
I HAVE NOT SEEN HIM SINCE!

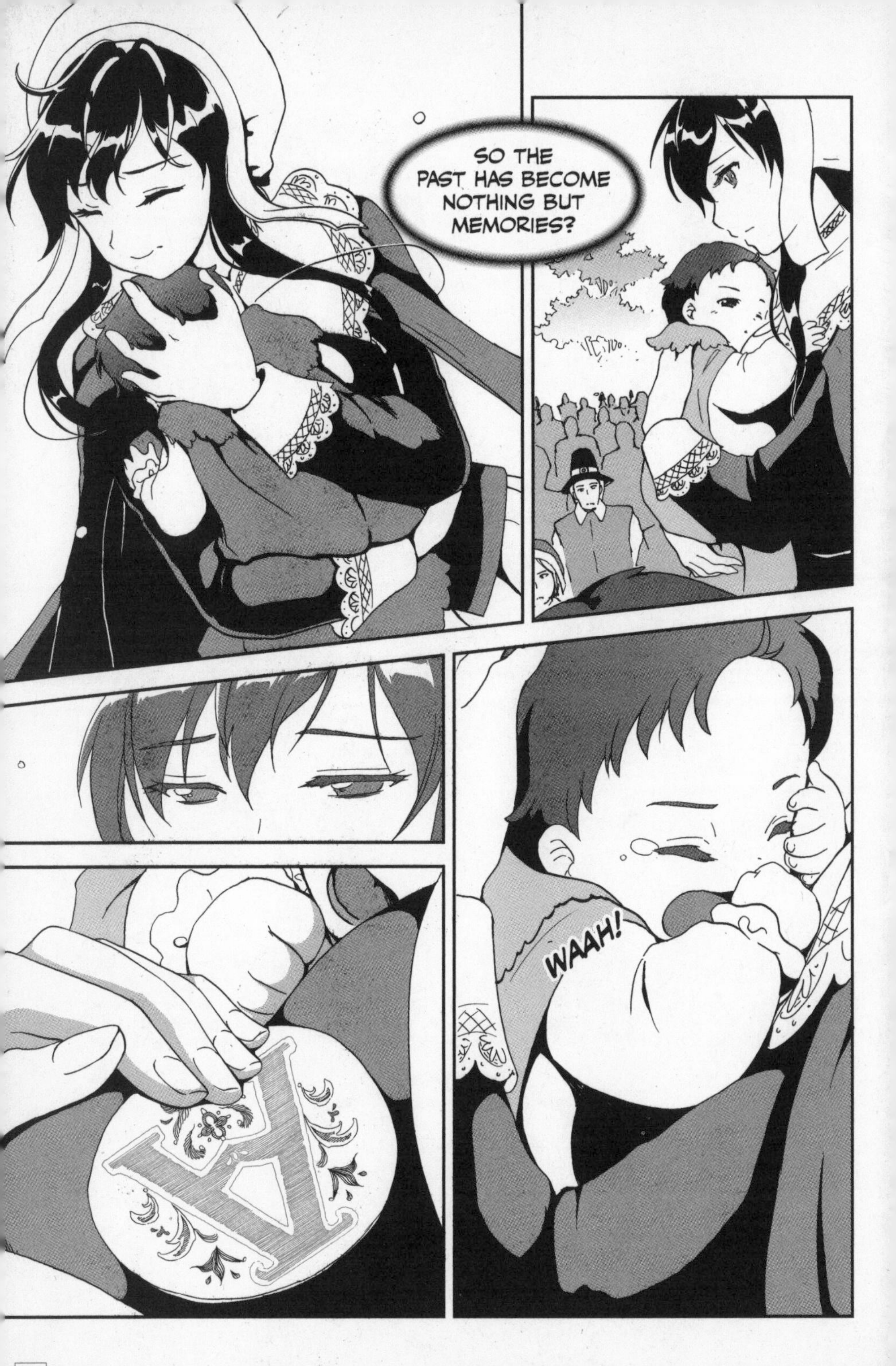
SO THE PAST HAS BECOME NOTHING BUT MEMORIES?
WAAH!

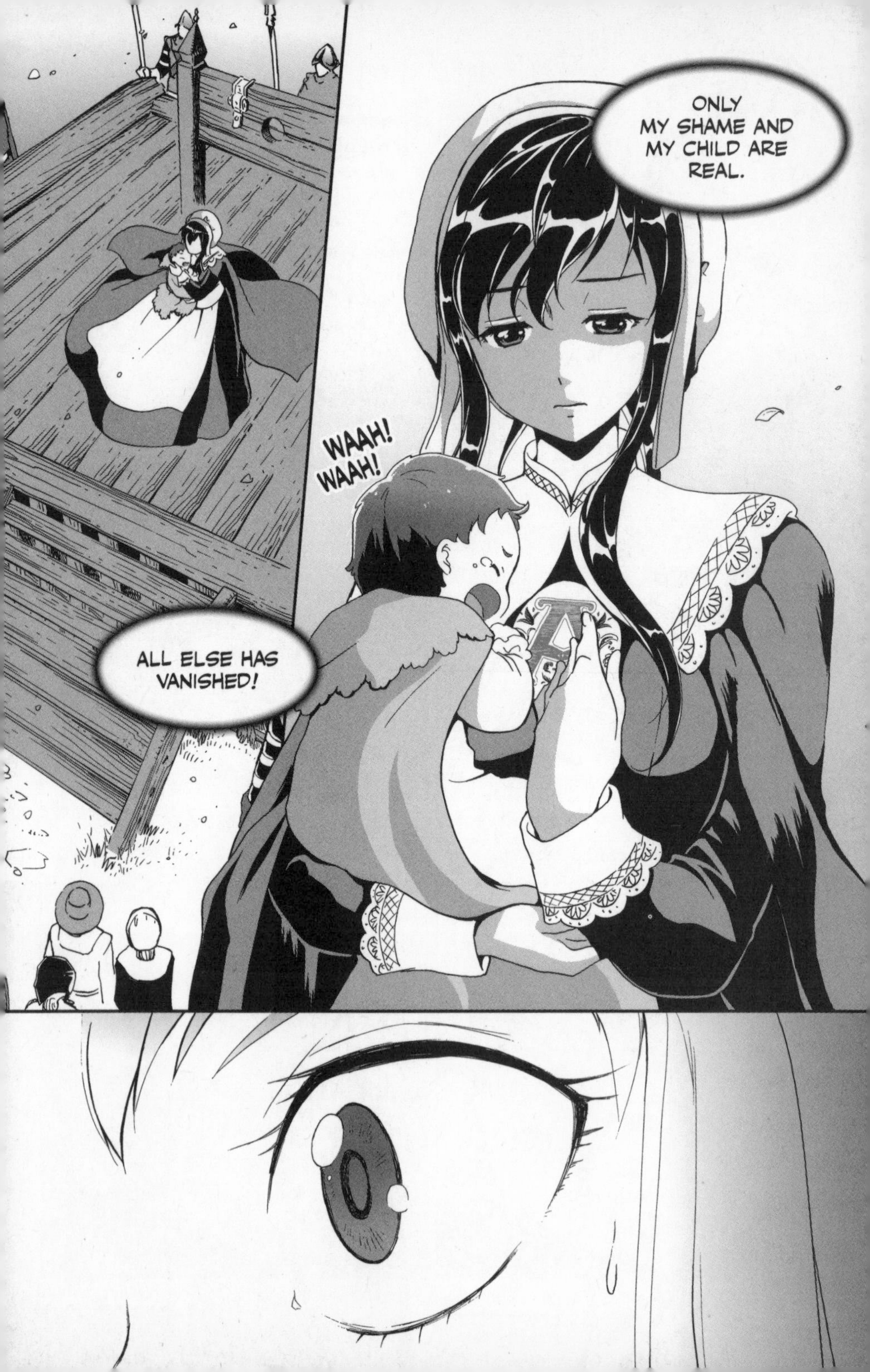
ONLY MY SHAME AND MY CHILD ARE REAL.
WAAH! WAAH!
ALL ELSE HAS VANISHED!

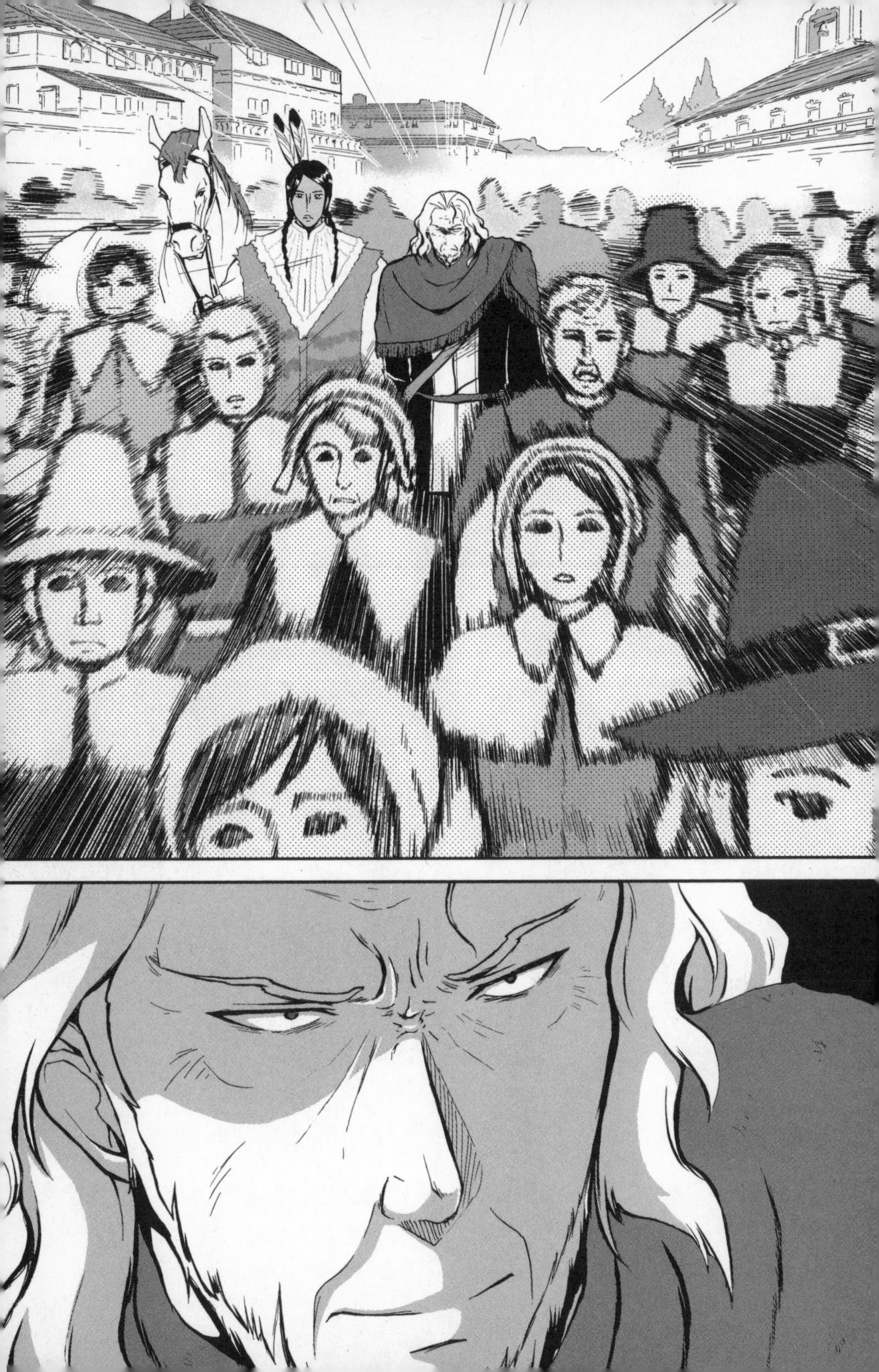

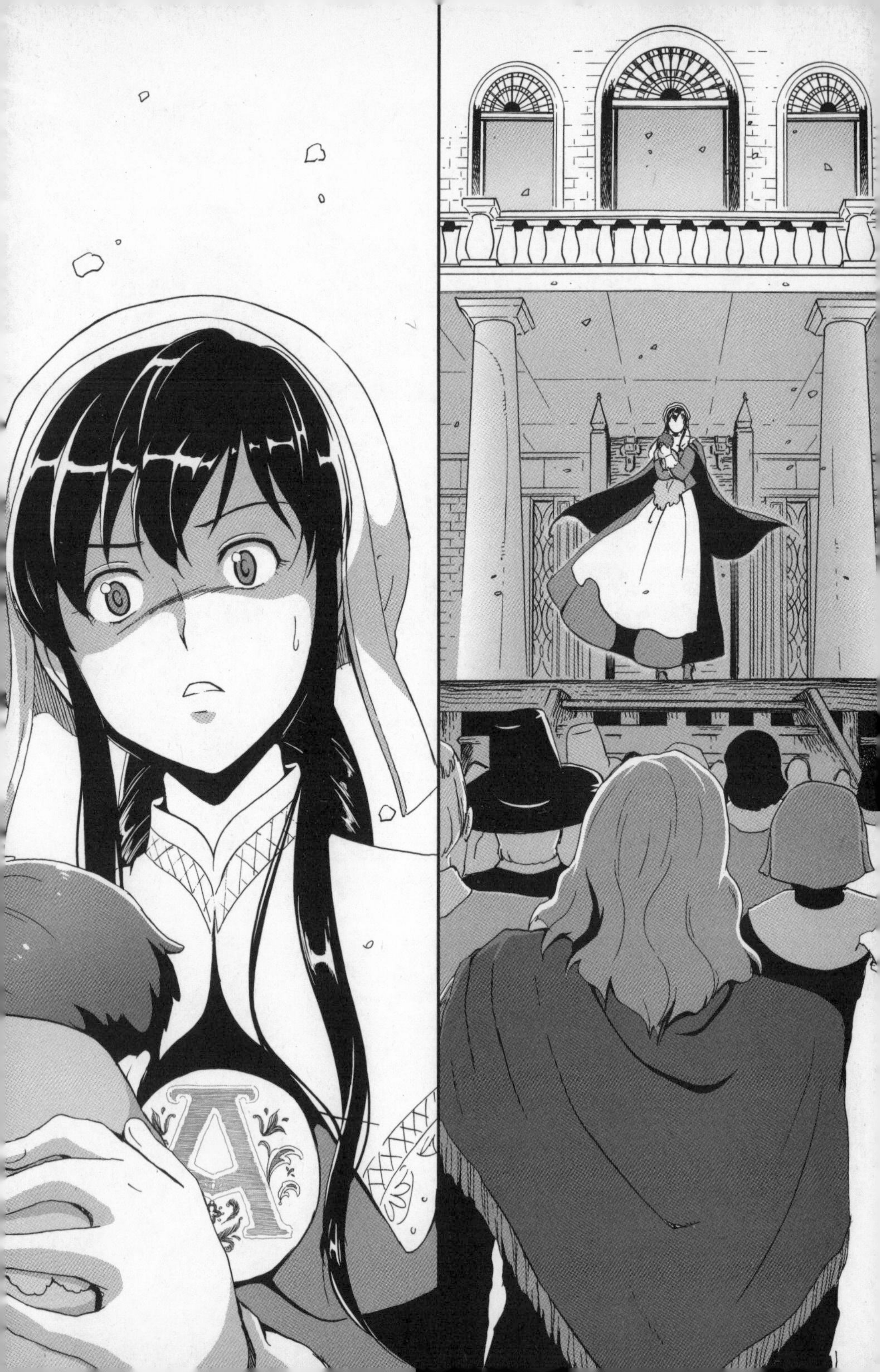

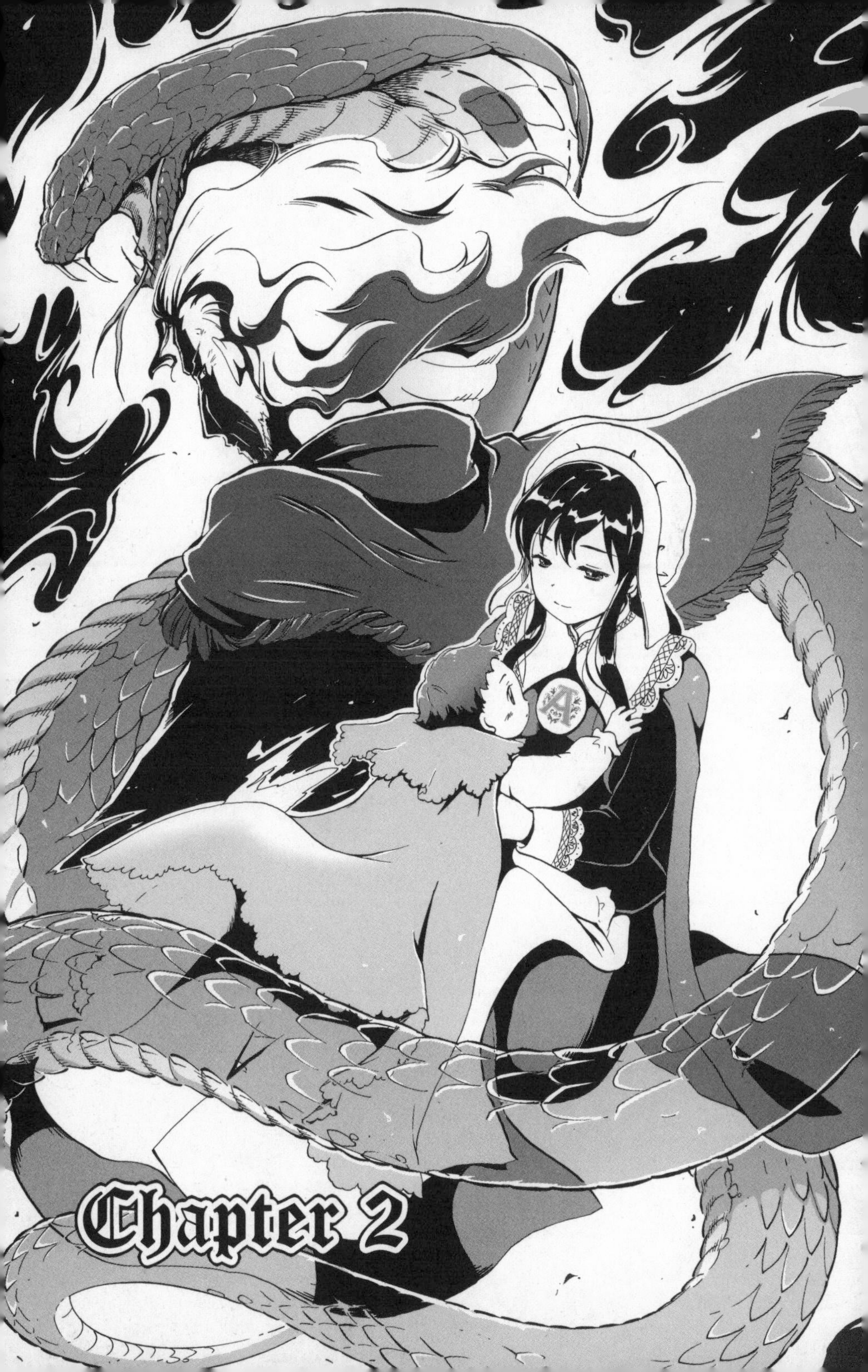
Chapter 2

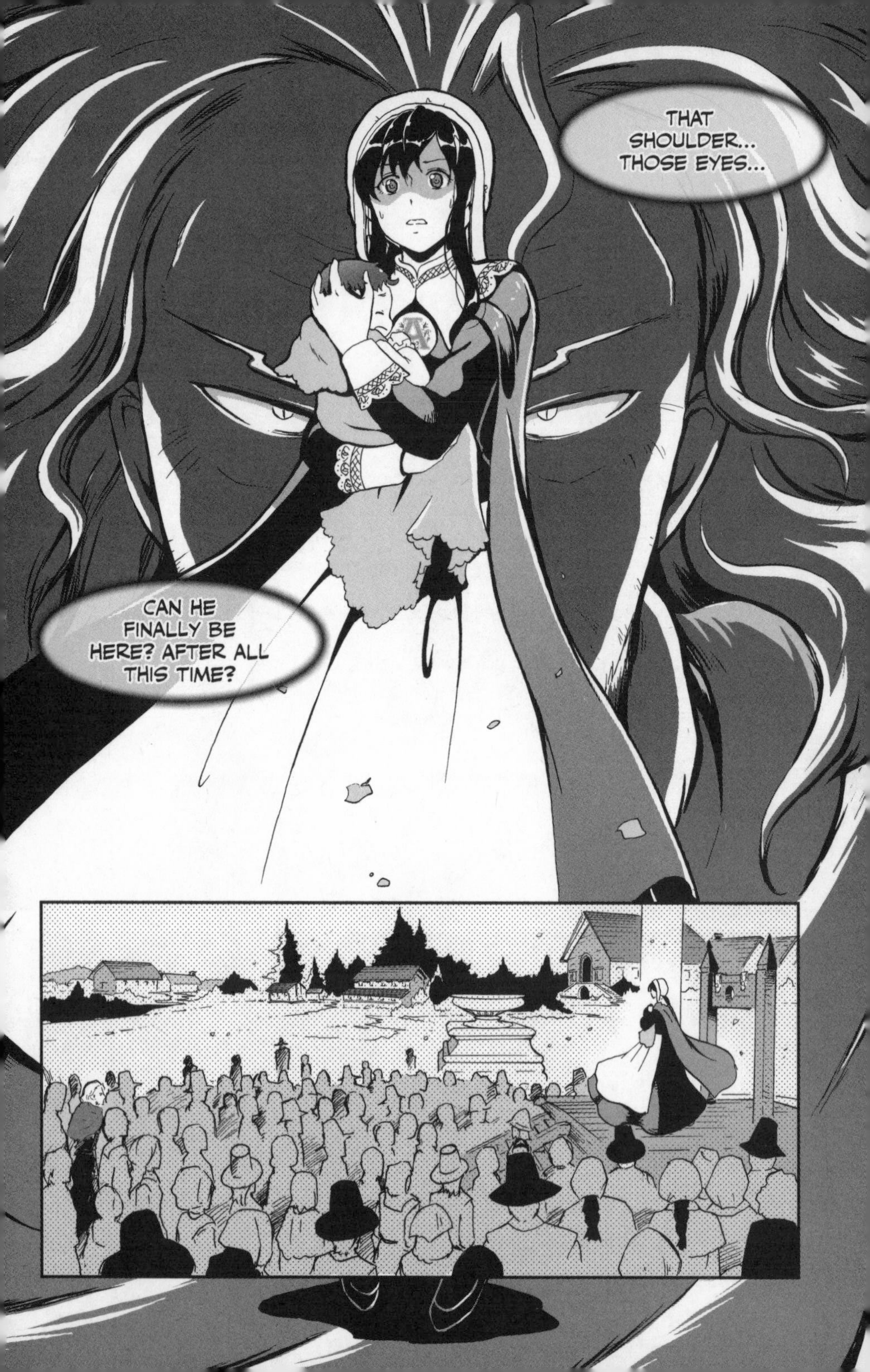
THAT SHOULDER... THOSE EYES...
CAN HE FINALLY BE HERE? AFTER ALL THIS TIME?

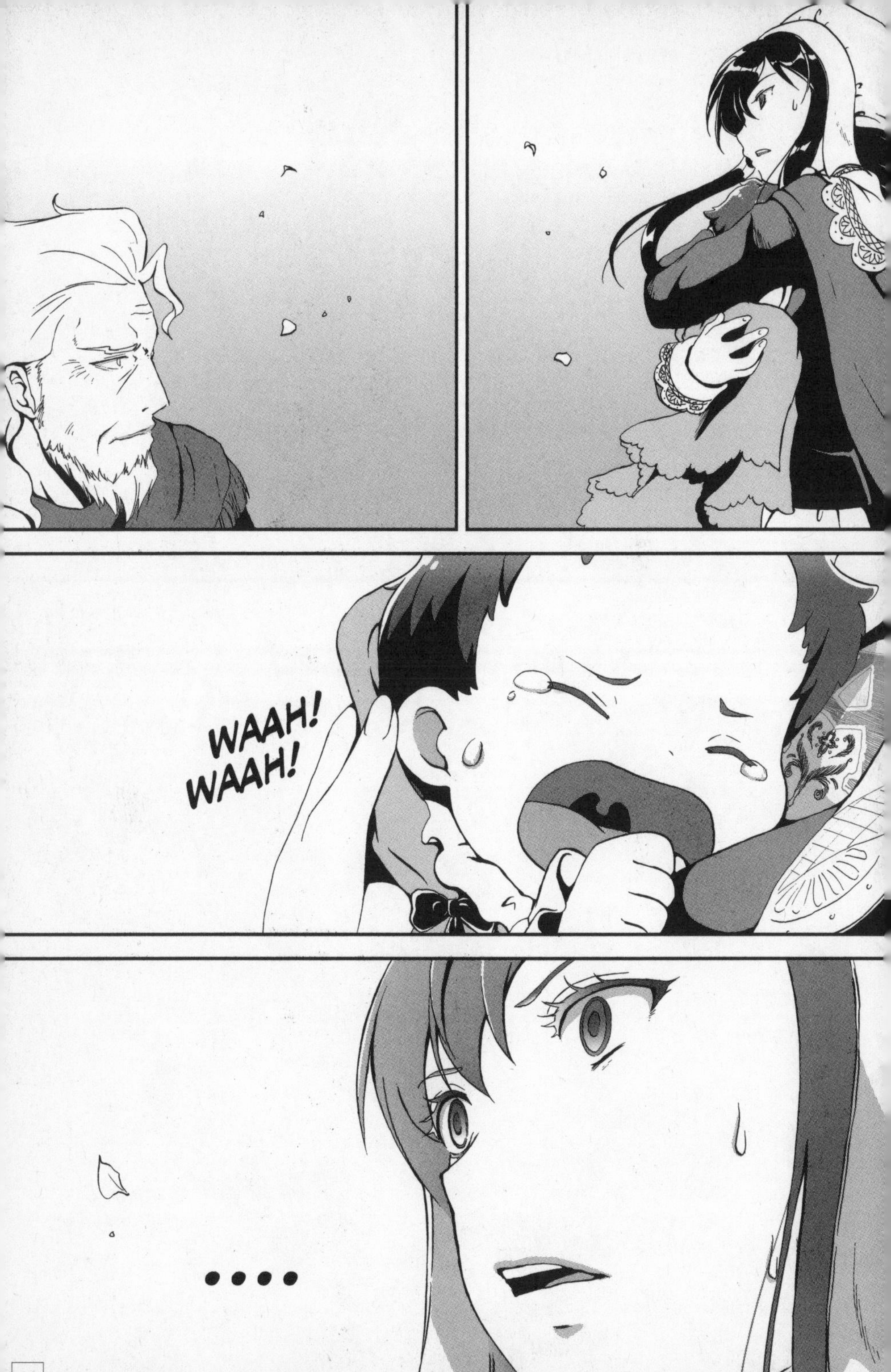
WAAH!
WAAH!
....

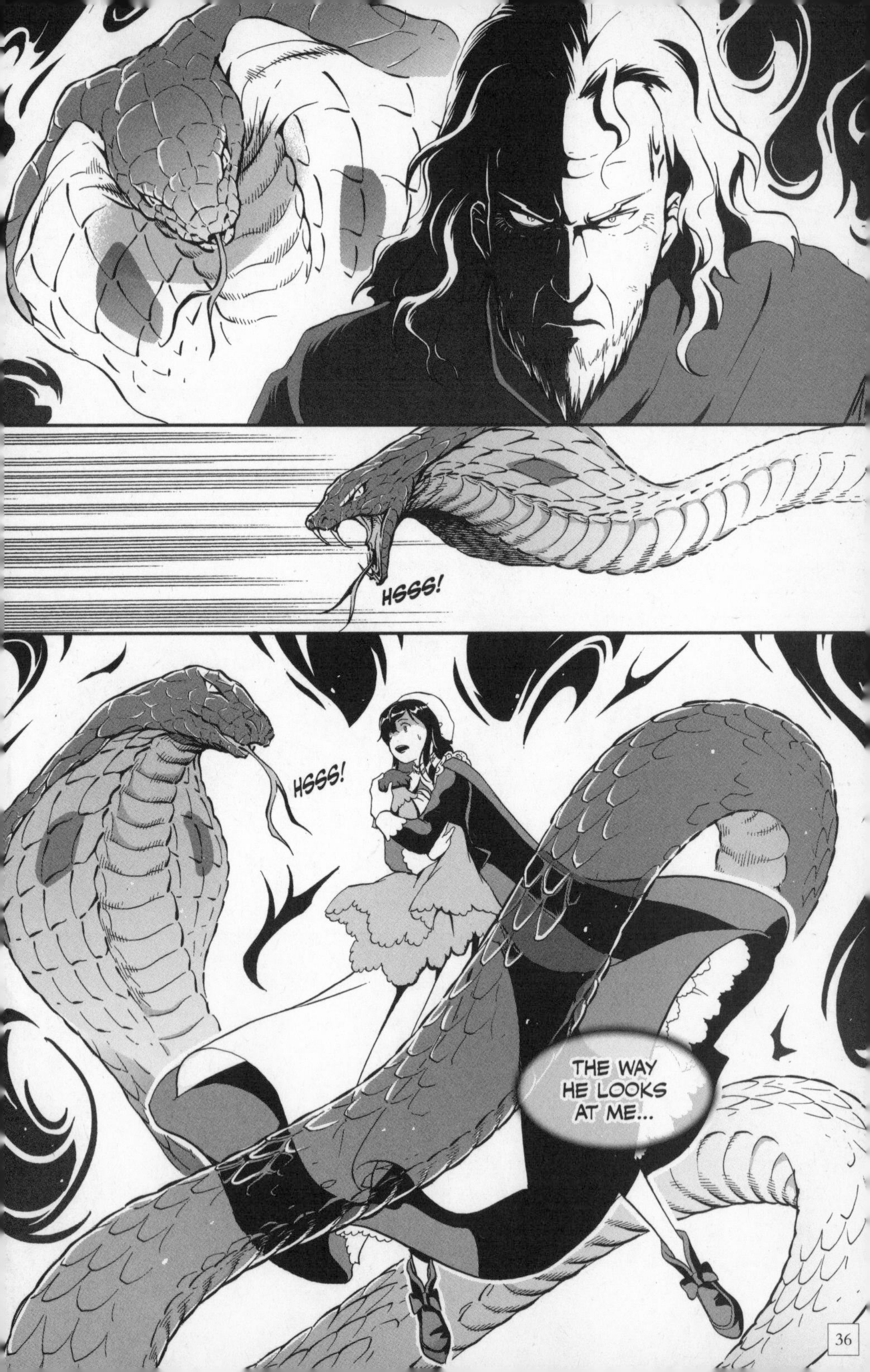
HSSS!
HSSS!
THE WAY HE LOOKS AT ME...

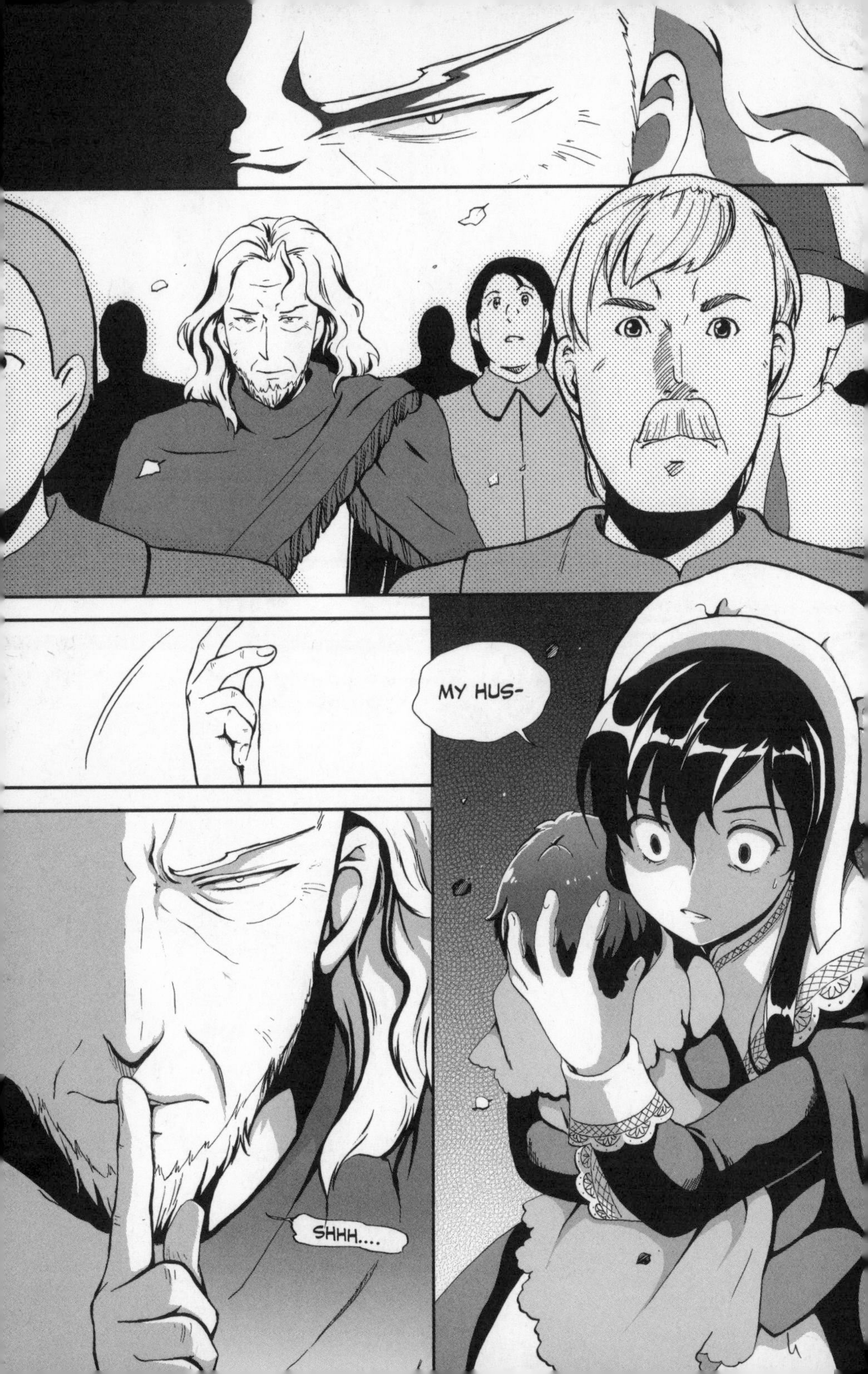
MY HUS-
SHHH....

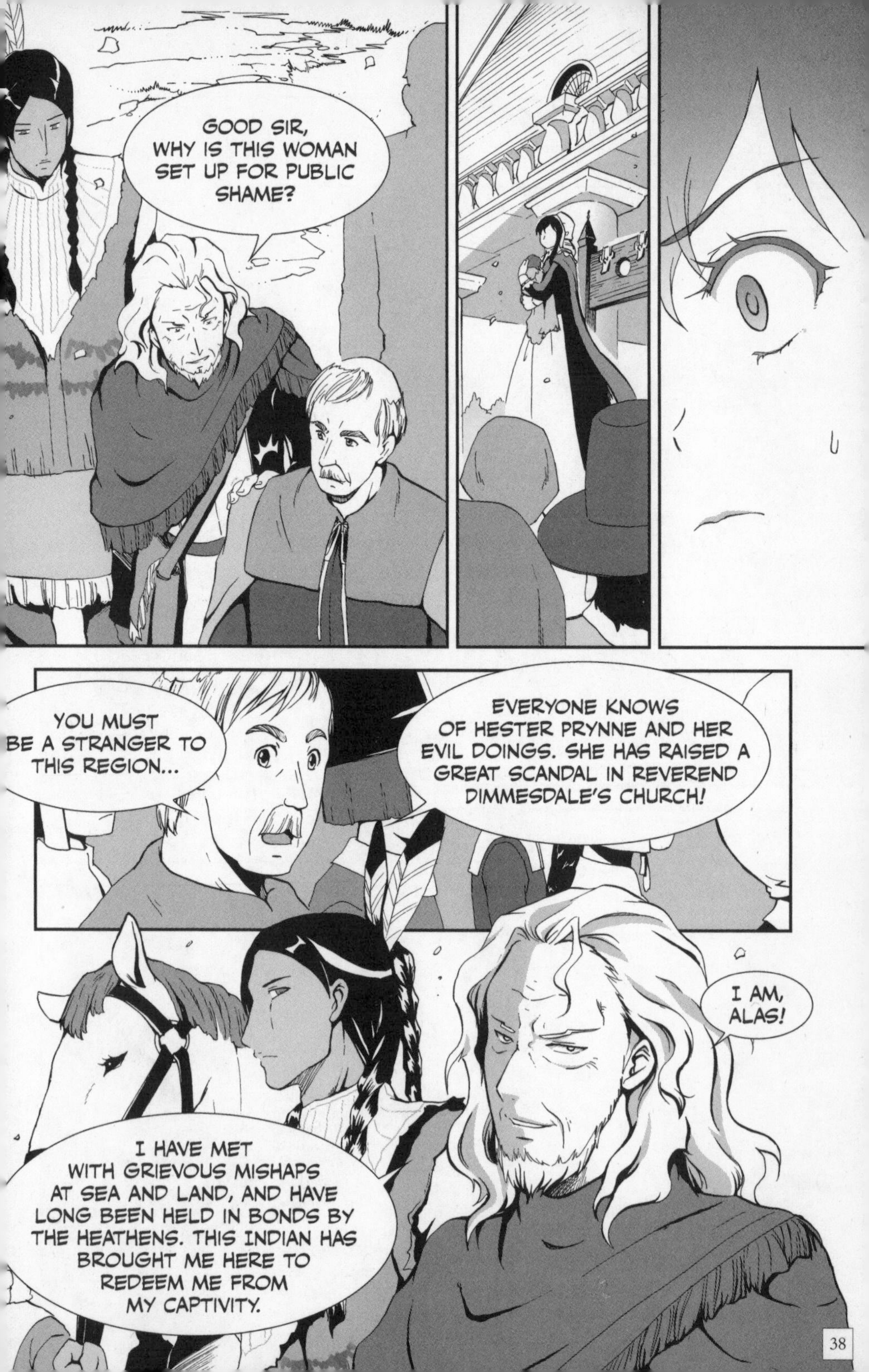
GOOD SIR, WHY IS THIS WOMAN SET UP FOR PUBLIC SHAME?
EVERYONE KNOWS OF HESTER PRYNNE AND HER EVIL DOINGS. SHE HAS RAISED A GREAT SCANDAL IN REVEREND DIMMESDALE'S CHURCH!
YOU MUST BE A STRANGER TO THIS REGION...
I AM, ALAS!
I HAVE MET WITH GRIEVOUS MISHAPS AT SEA AND LAND, AND HAVE LONG BEEN HELD IN BONDS BY THE HEATHENS. THIS INDIAN HAS BROUGHT ME HERE TO REDEEM ME FROM MY CAPTIVITY.

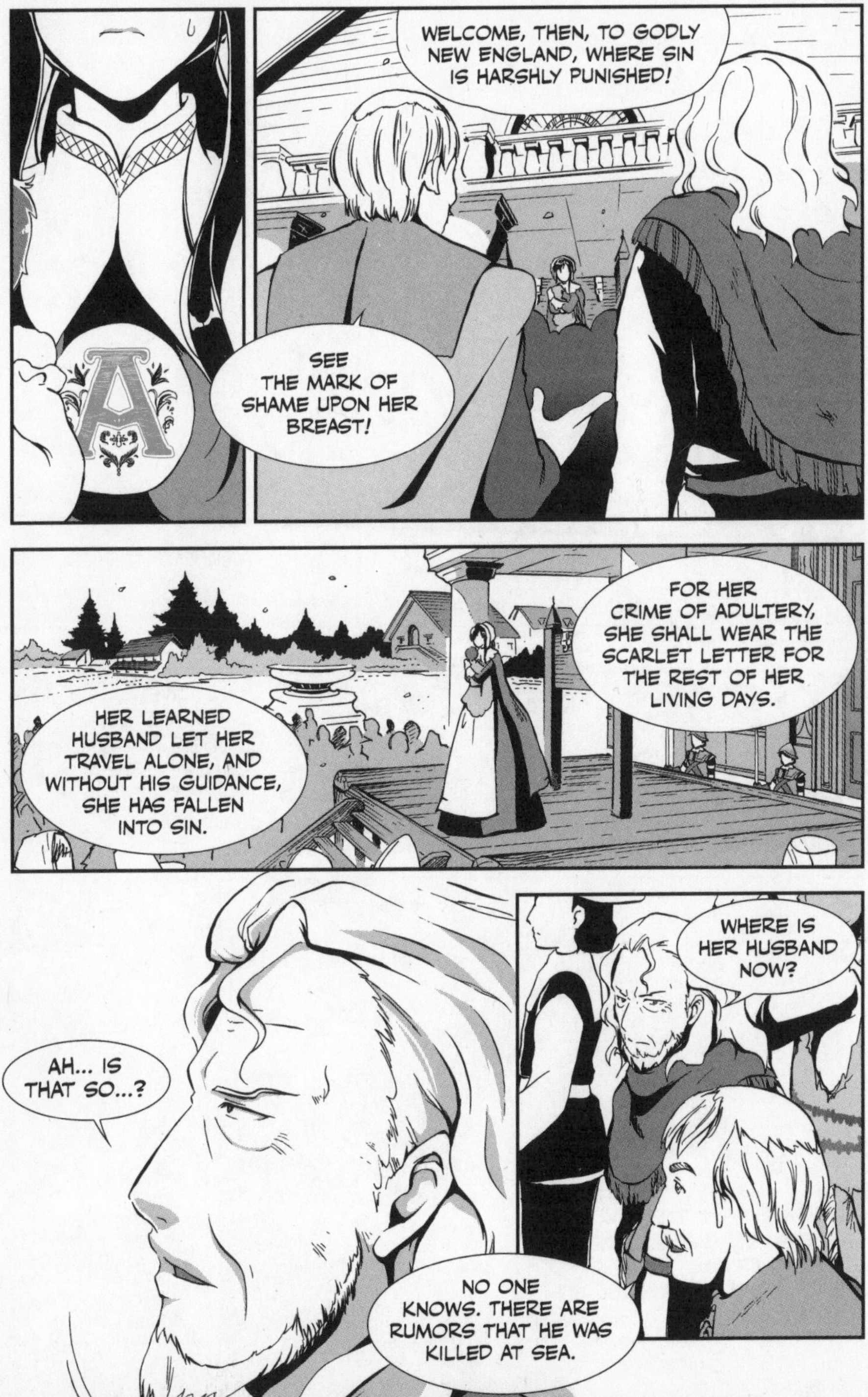
WELCOME, THEN, TO GODLY NEW ENGLAND, WHERE SIN IS HARSHLY PUNISHED!
SEE THE MARK OF SHAME UPON HER BREAST!
FOR HER CRIME OF ADULTERY, SHE SHALL WEAR THE SCARLET LETTER FOR THE REST OF HER LIVING DAYS.
HER LEARNED HUSBAND LET HER TRAVEL ALONE, AND WITHOUT HIS GUIDANCE, SHE HAS FALLEN INTO SIN.
WHERE IS HER HUSBAND NOW?
NO ONE KNOWS. THERE ARE RUMORS THAT HE WAS KILLED AT SEA.
AH... IS THAT SO...?

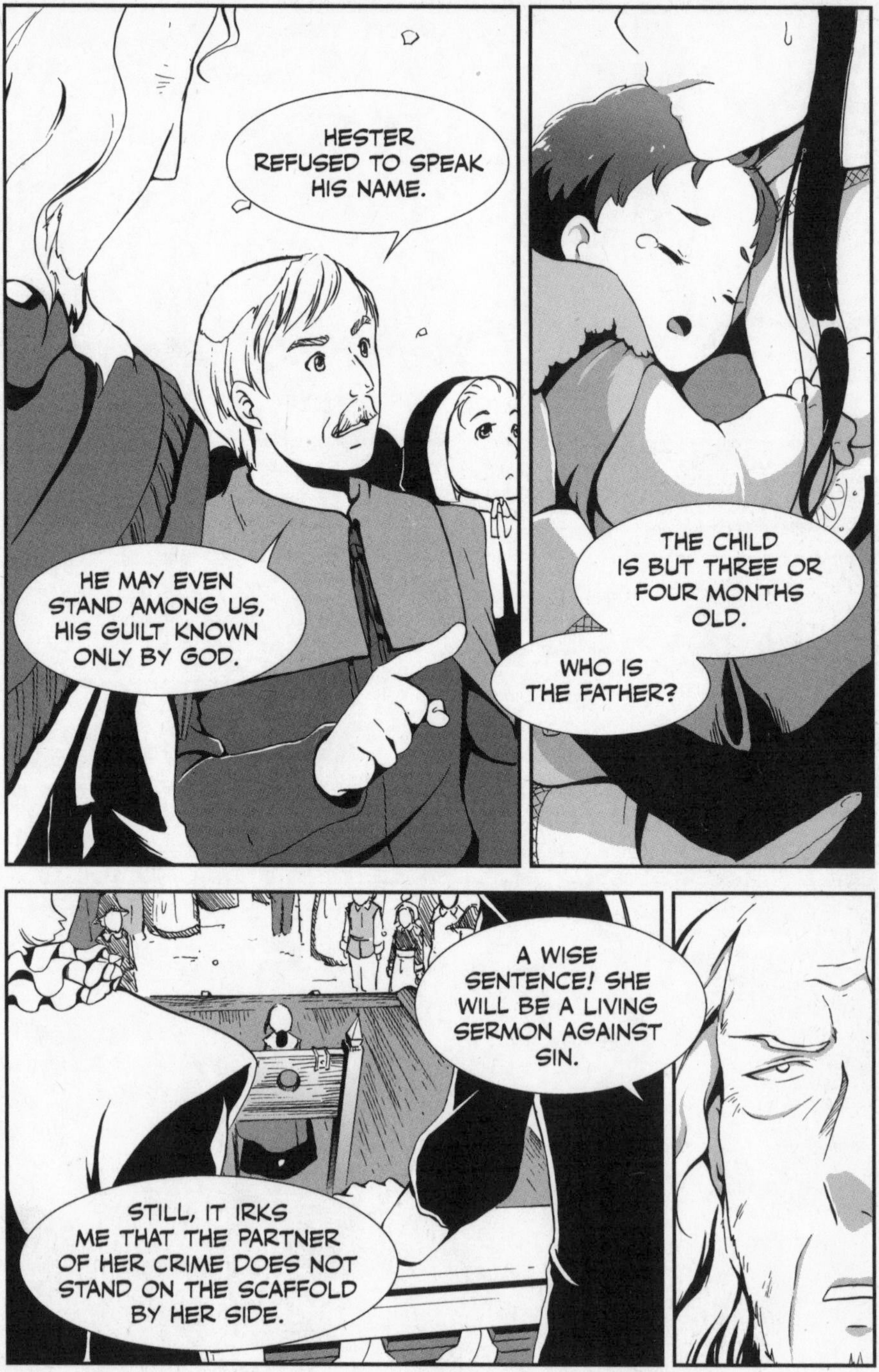
THE CHILD IS BUT THREE OR FOUR MONTHS OLD.
WHO IS THE FATHER?
HESTER REFUSED TO SPEAK HIS NAME.
HE MAY EVEN STAND AMONG US, HIS GUILT KNOWN ONLY BY GOD.
A WISE SENTENCE! SHE WILL BE A LIVING SERMON AGAINST SIN.
STILL, IT IRKS ME THAT THE PARTNER OF HER CRIME DOES NOT STAND ON THE SCAFFOLD BY HER SIDE.

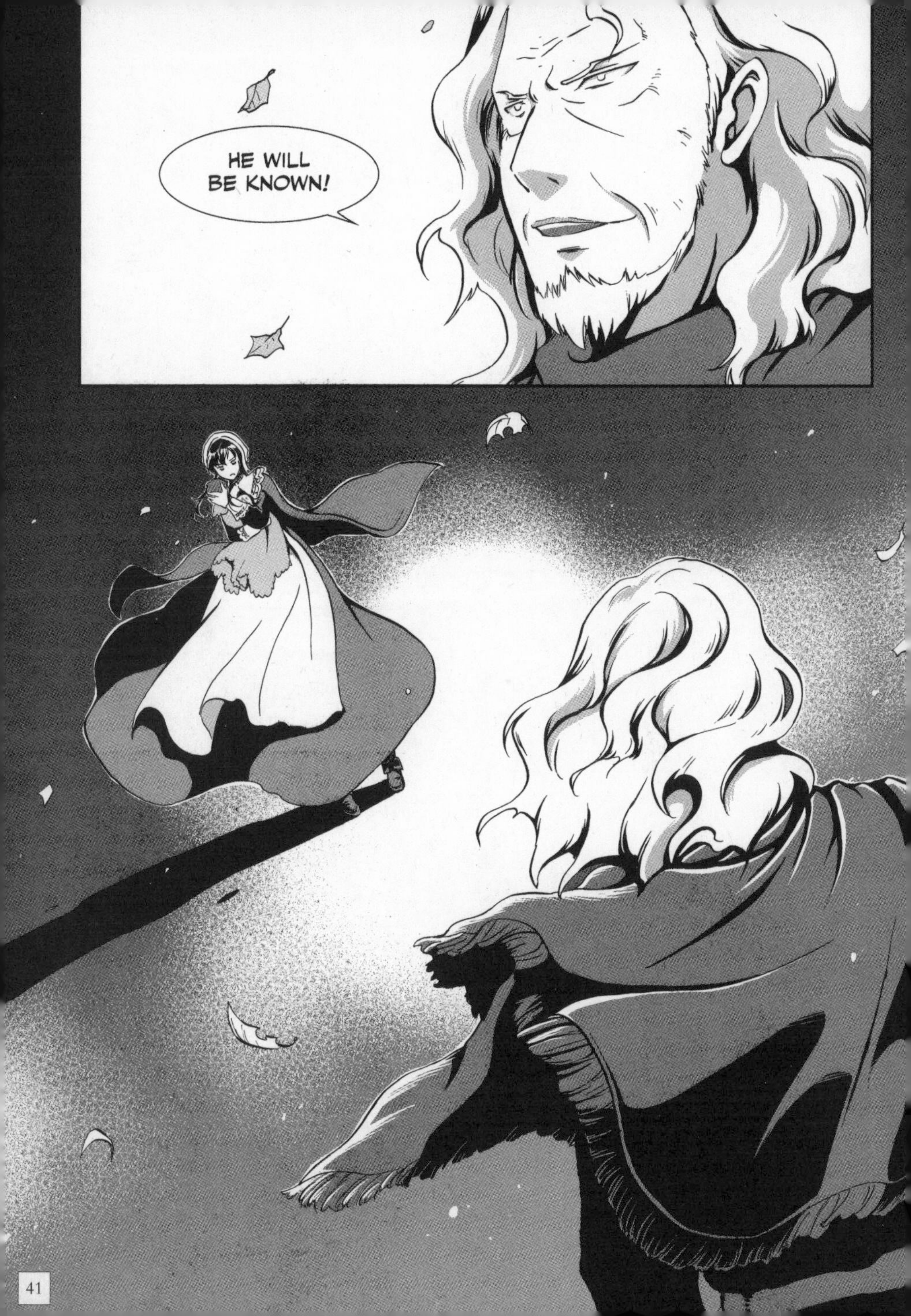
HE WILL
BE KNOWN!

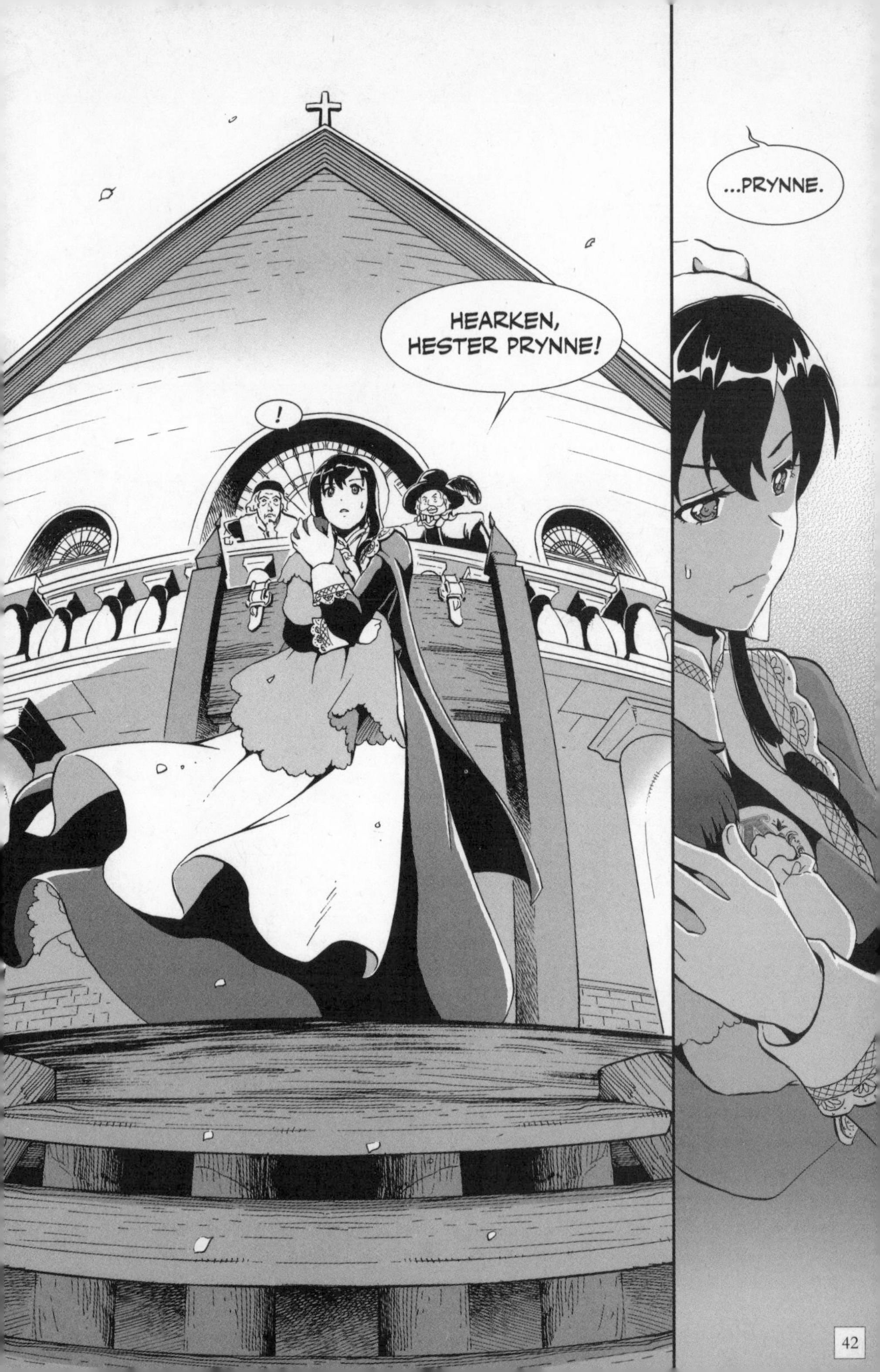
...PRYNNE.
HEARKEN, HESTER PRYNNE!
!

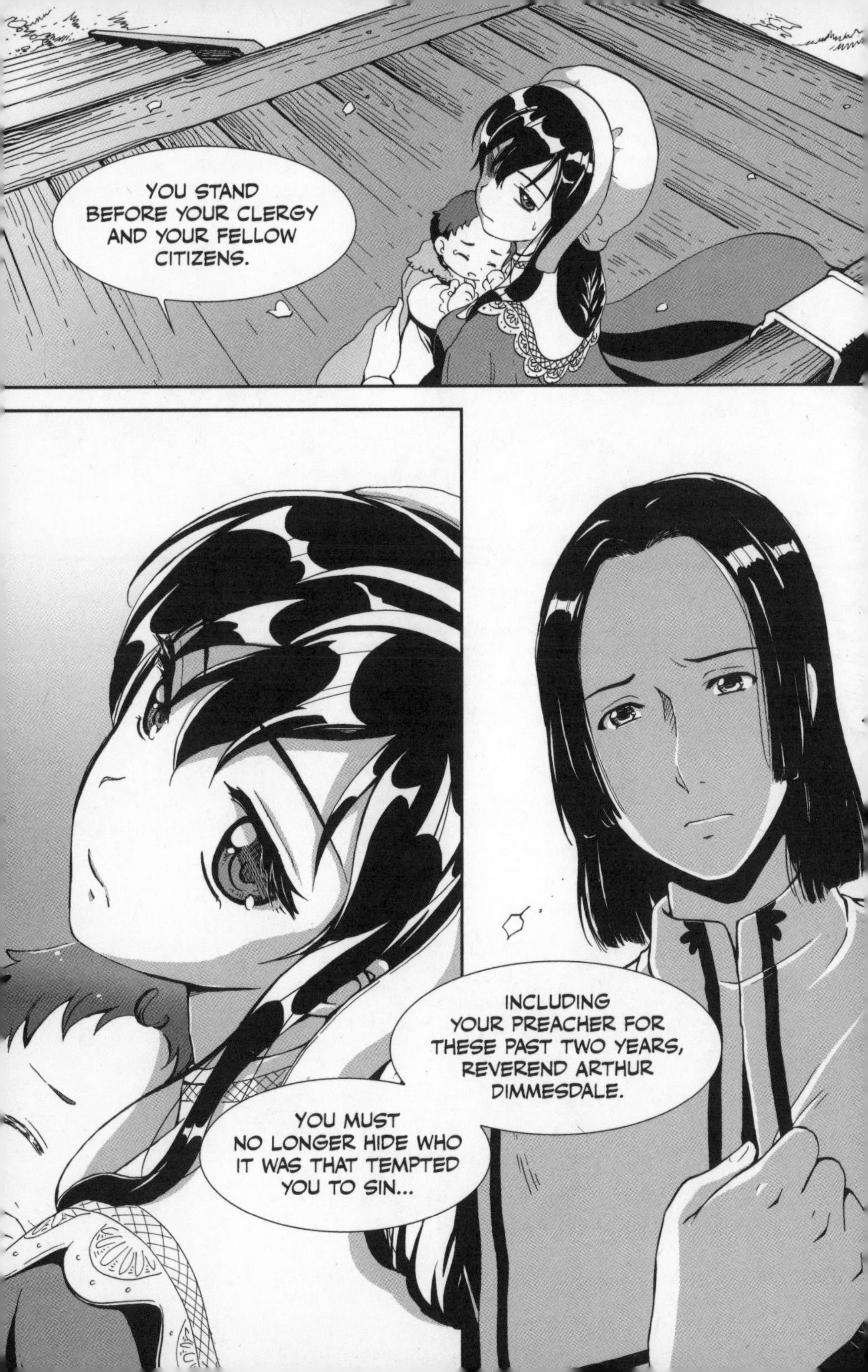
YOU STAND BEFORE YOUR CLERGY AND YOUR FELLOW CITIZENS.
INCLUDING YOUR PREACHER FOR THESE PAST TWO YEARS, REVEREND ARTHUR DIMMESDALE.
YOU MUST NO LONGER HIDE WHO IT WAS THAT TEMPTED YOU TO SIN...

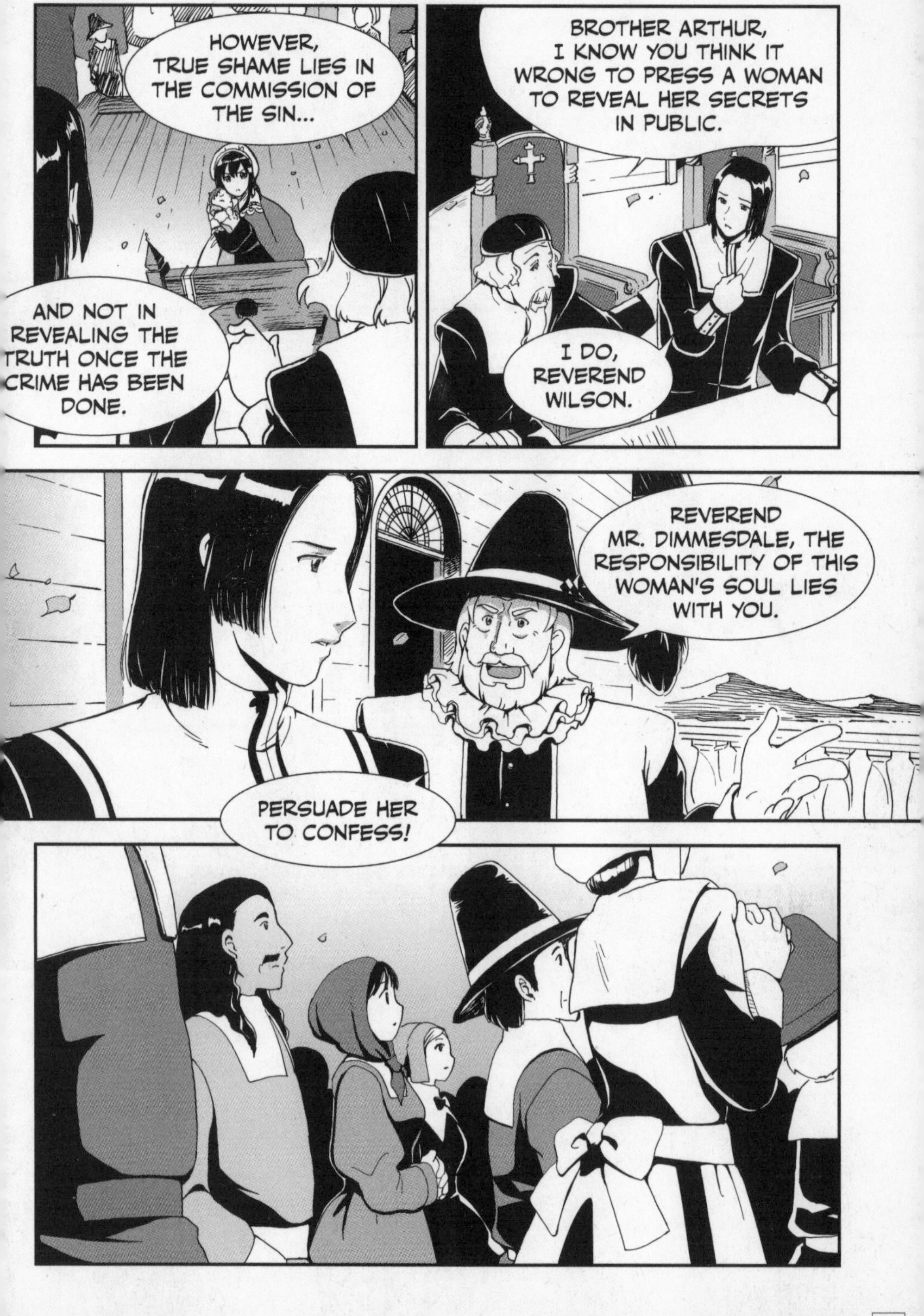
BROTHER ARTHUR, I KNOW YOU THINK IT WRONG TO PRESS A WOMAN TO REVEAL HER SECRETS IN PUBLIC.
I DO, REVEREND WILSON.
HOWEVER, TRUE SHAME LIES IN THE COMMISSION OF THE SIN...
AND NOT IN REVEALING THE TRUTH ONCE THE CRIME HAS BEEN DONE.
REVEREND MR. DIMMESDALE, THE RESPONSIBILITY OF THIS WOMAN'S SOUL LIES WITH YOU.
PERSUADE HER TO CONFESS!

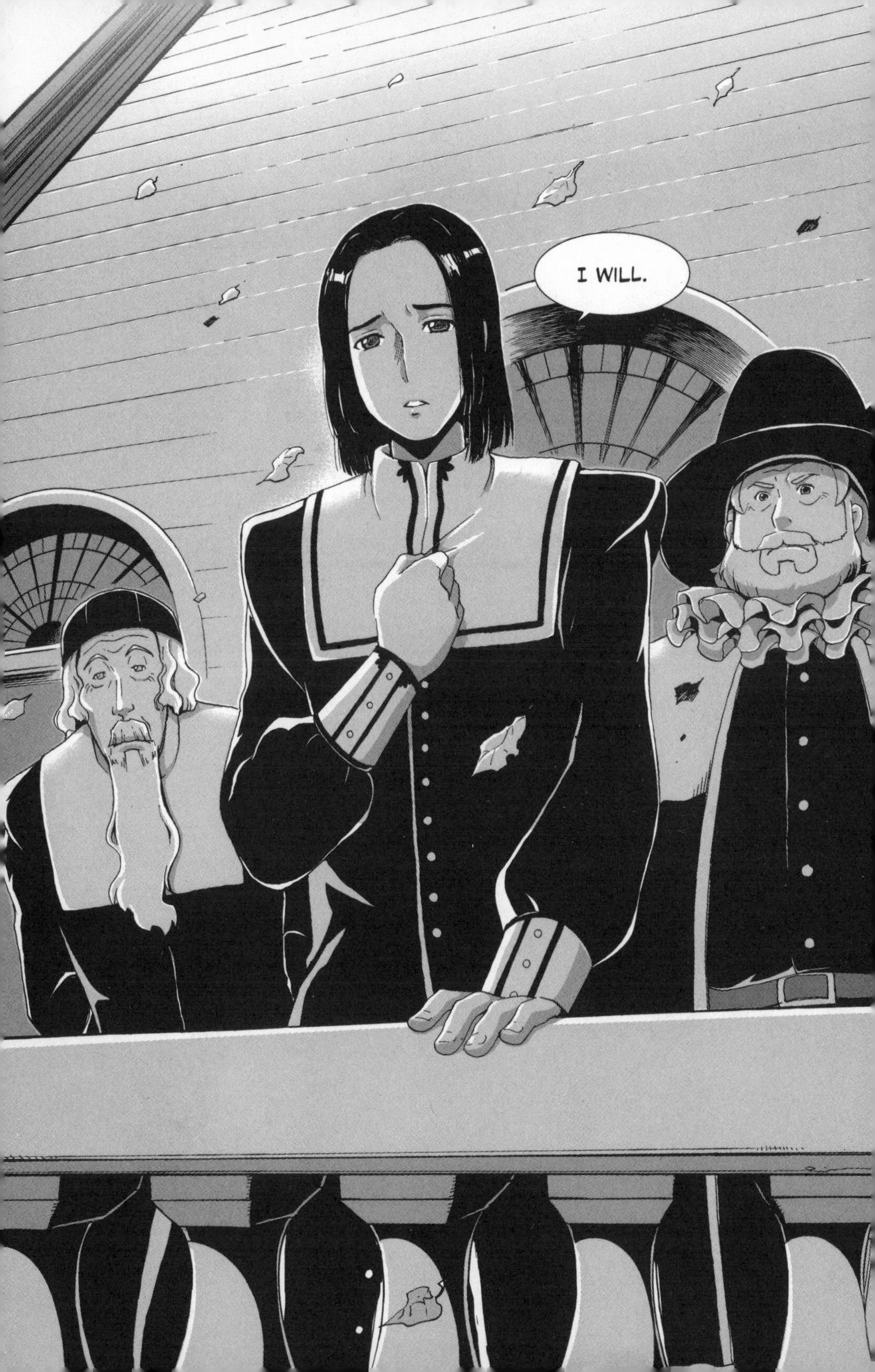
I WILL.

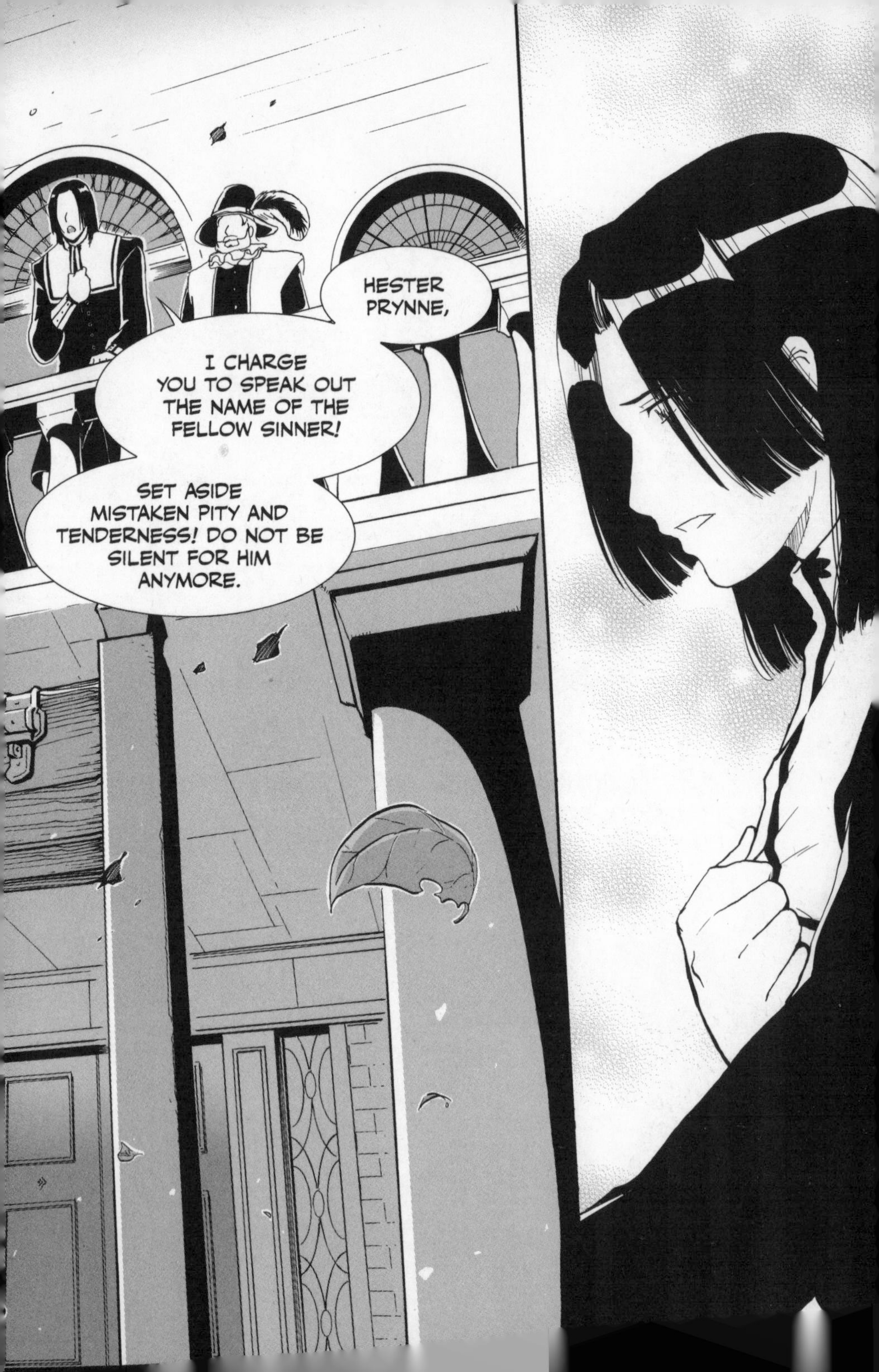
HESTER PRYNNE,
I CHARGE YOU TO SPEAK OUT THE NAME OF THE FELLOW SINNER!
SET ASIDE MISTAKEN PITY AND TENDERNESS! DO NOT BE SILENT FOR HIM ANYMORE.

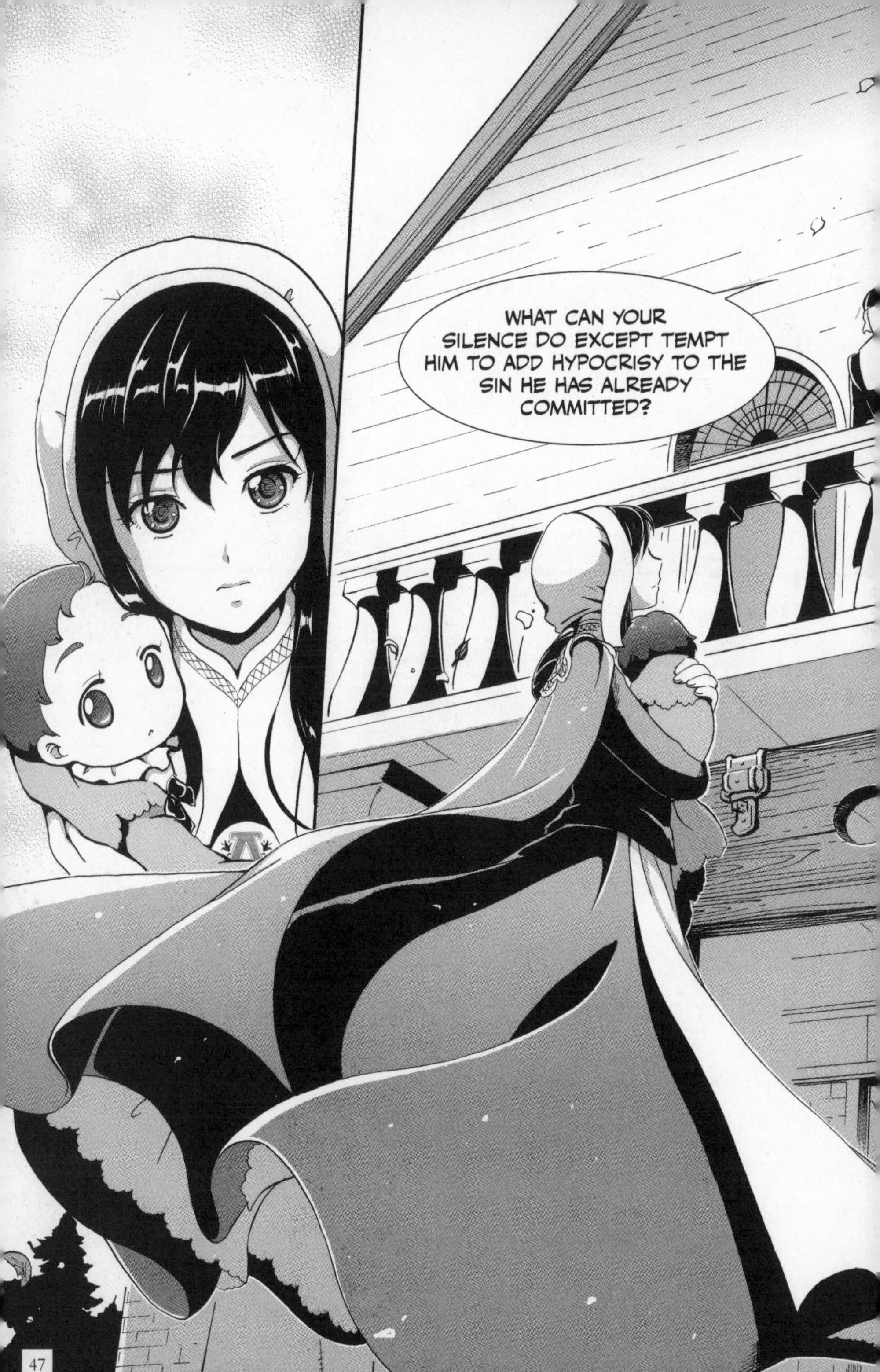
WHAT CAN YOUR SILENCE DO EXCEPT TEMPT HIM TO ADD HYPOCRISY TO THE SIN HE HAS ALREADY COMMITTED?

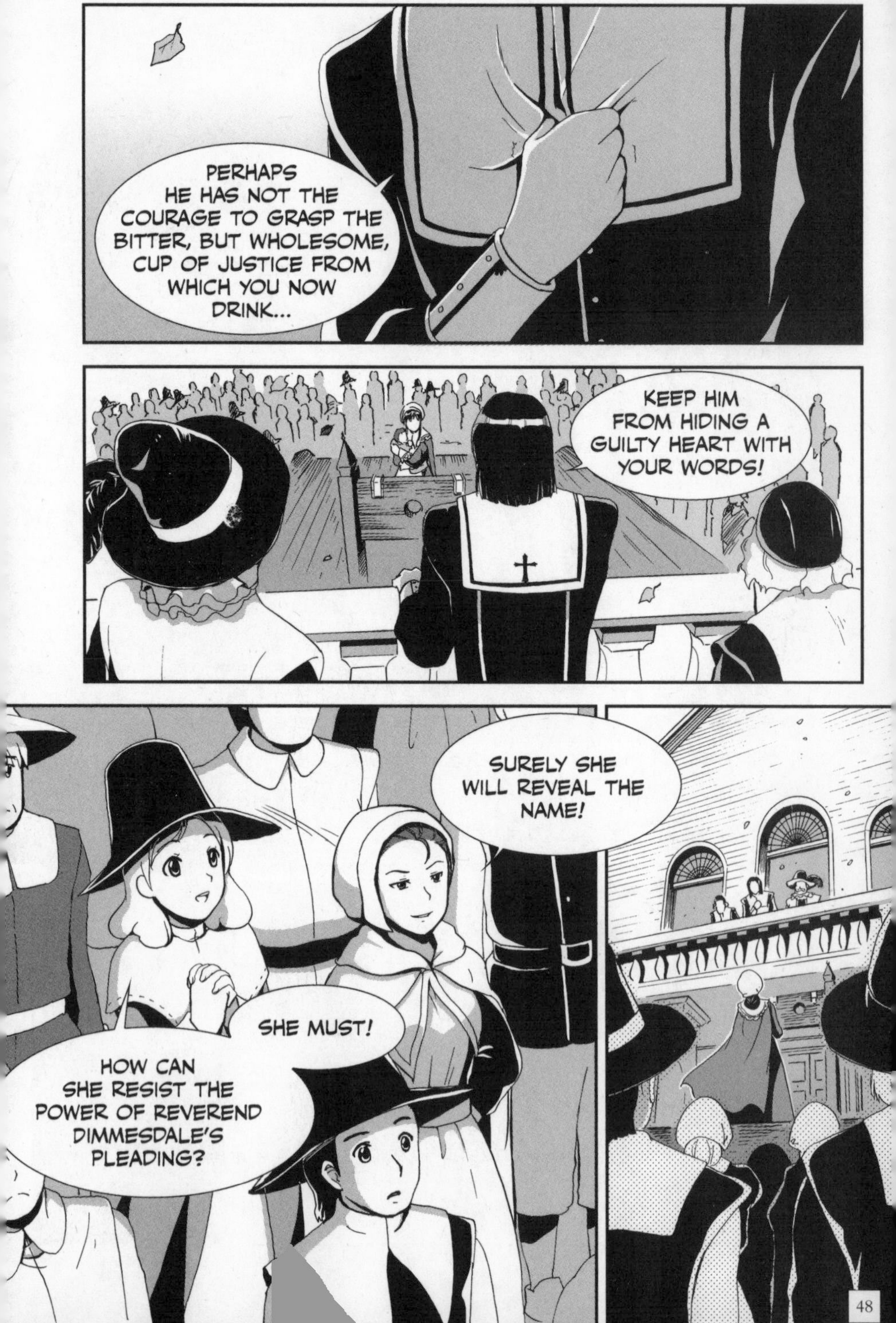
PERHAPS HE HAS NOT THE COURAGE TO GRASP THE BITTER, BUT WHOLESOME, CUP OF JUSTICE FROM WHICH YOU NOW DRINK...
KEEP HIM FROM HIDING A GUILTY HEART WITH YOUR WORDS!
SURELY SHE WILL REVEAL THE NAME!
SHE MUST!
HOW CAN SHE RESIST THE POWER OF REVEREND DIMMESDALE'S PLEADING?

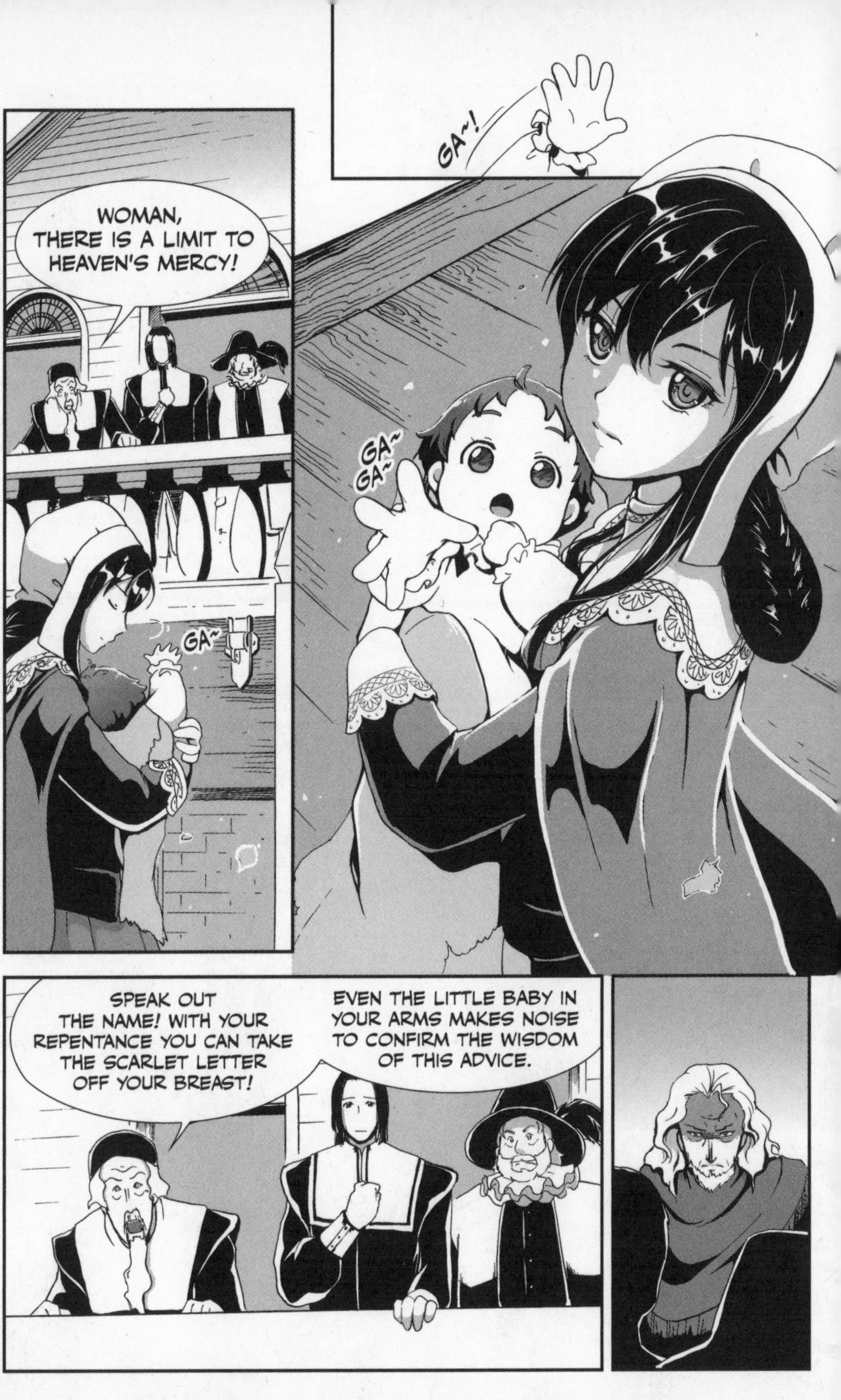
GA~!
GA~ GA~
WOMAN, THERE IS A LIMIT TO HEAVEN'S MERCY!
GA~
EVEN THE LITTLE BABY IN YOUR ARMS MAKES NOISE TO CONFIRM THE WISDOM OF THIS ADVICE.
SPEAK OUT THE NAME! WITH YOUR REPENTANCE YOU CAN TAKE THE SCARLET LETTER OFF YOUR BREAST!

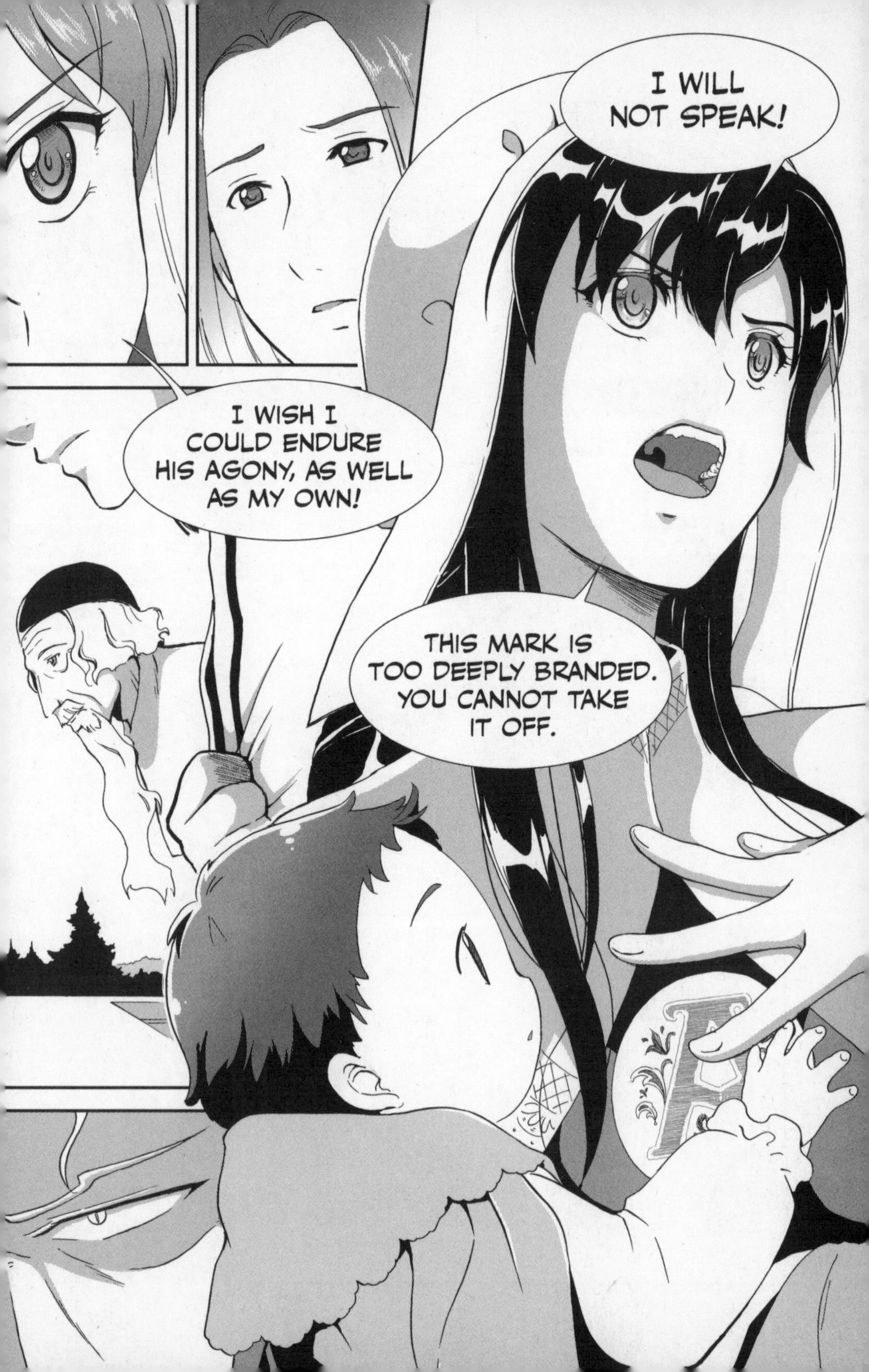
I WILL NOT SPEAK!
THIS MARK IS TOO DEEPLY BRANDED. YOU CANNOT TAKE IT OFF.
I WISH I COULD ENDURE HIS AGONY, AS WELL AS MY OWN!

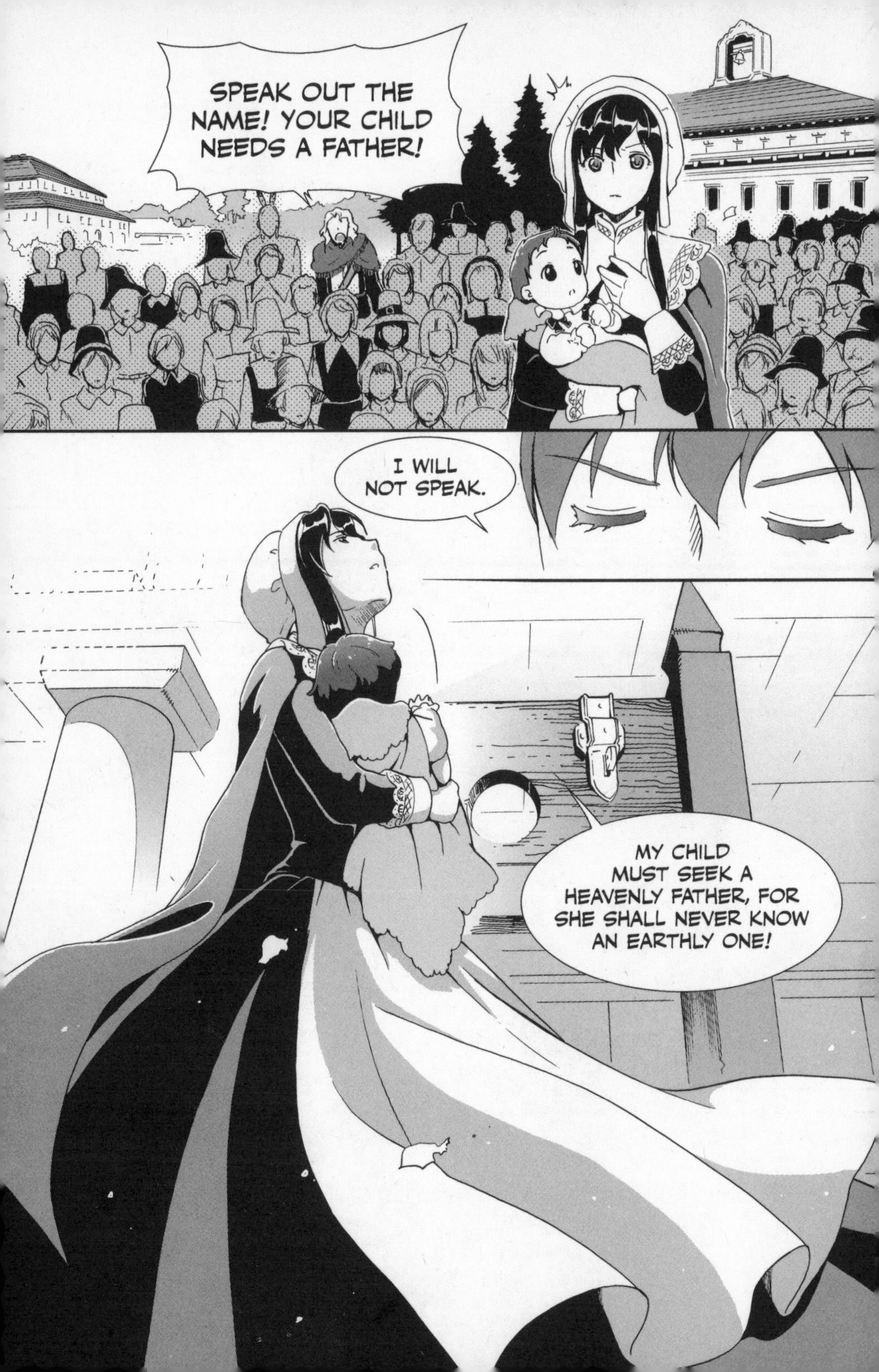
SPEAK OUT THE NAME! YOUR CHILD NEEDS A FATHER!
I WILL NOT SPEAK.
MY CHILD MUST SEEK A HEAVENLY FATHER, FOR SHE SHALL NEVER KNOW AN EARTHLY ONE!

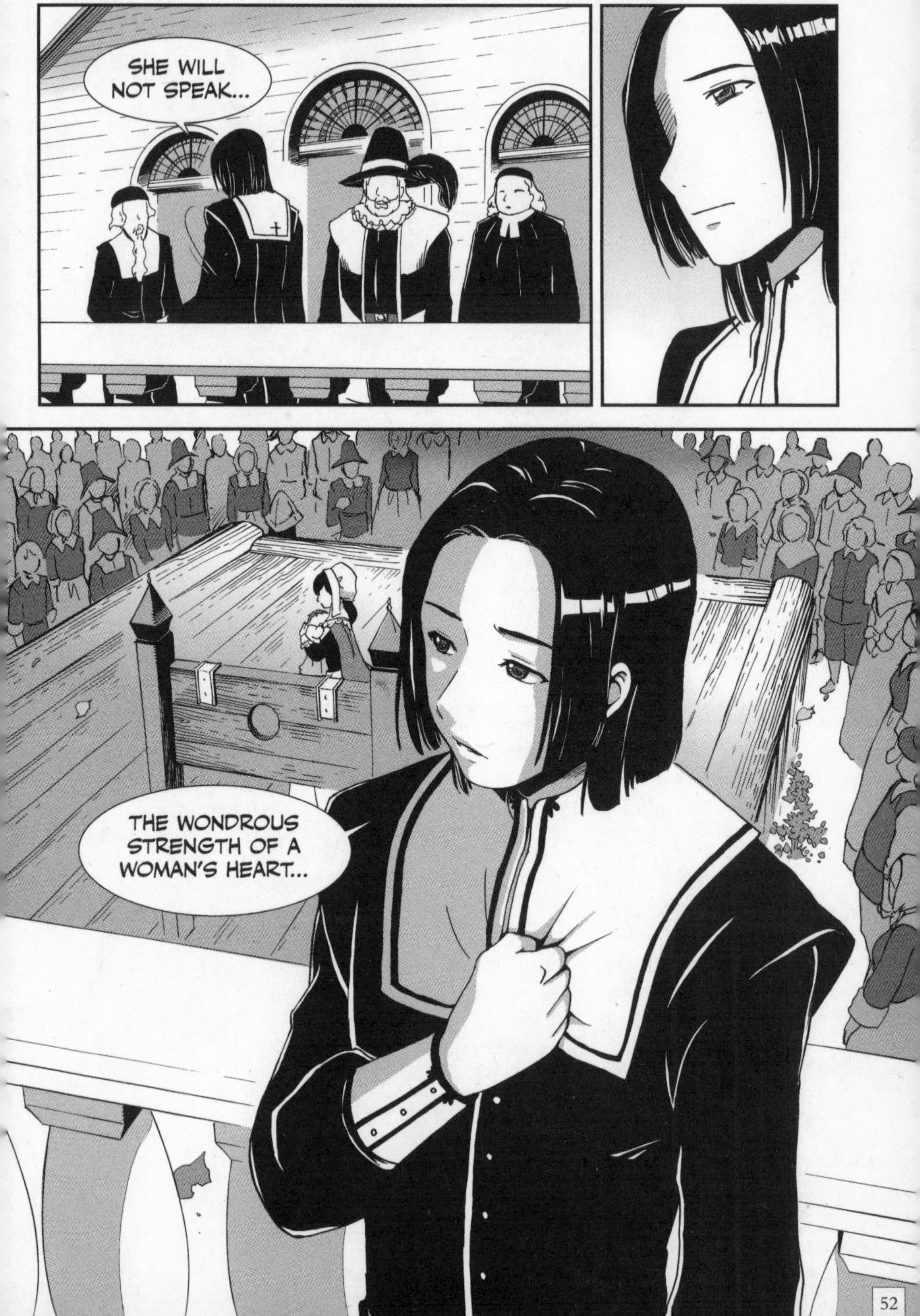
SHE WILL NOT SPEAK...
THE WONDROUS STRENGTH OF A WOMAN'S HEART...

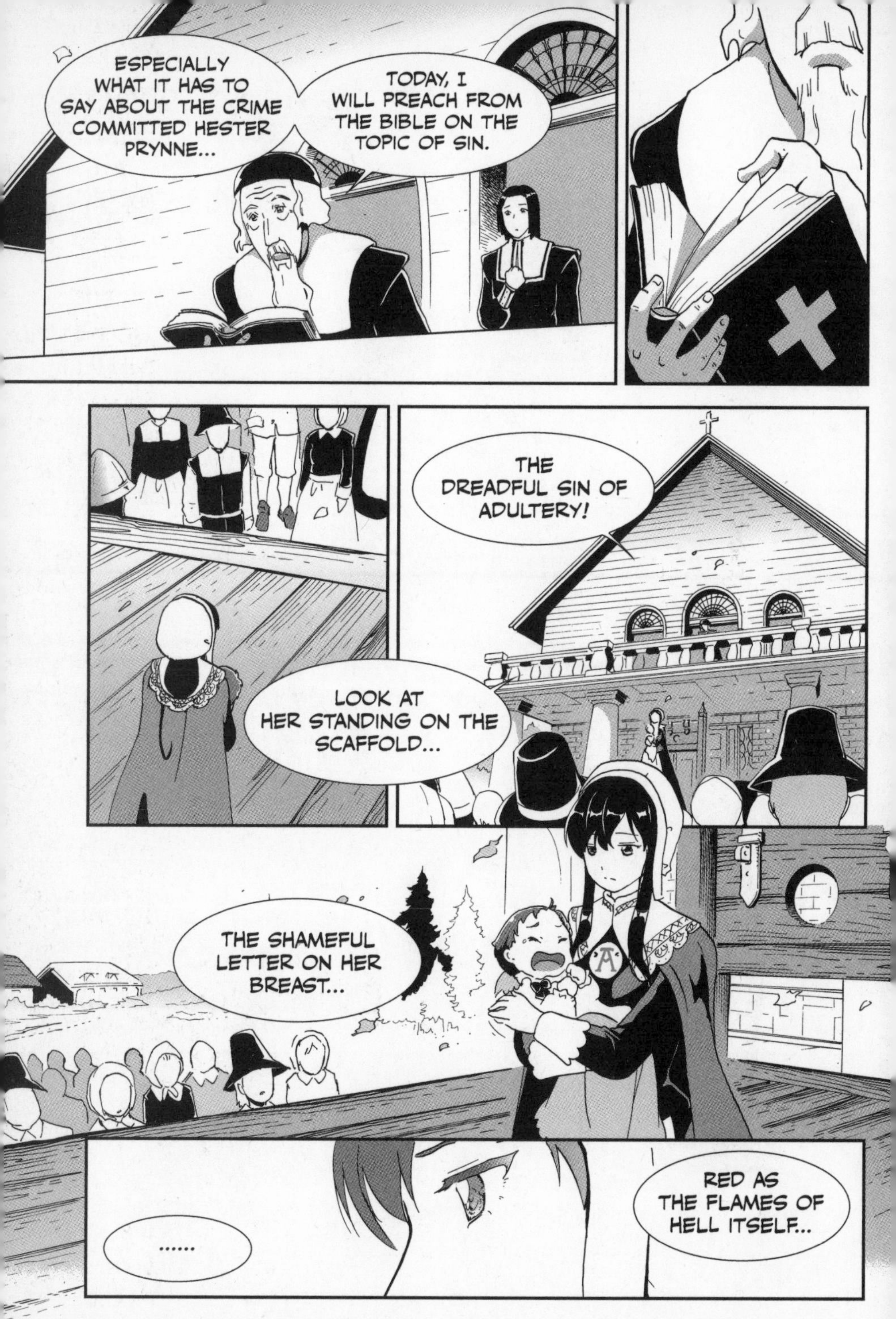
TODAY, I WILL PREACH FROM THE BIBLE ON THE TOPIC OF SIN.
ESPECIALLY WHAT IT HAS TO SAY ABOUT THE CRIME COMMITTED HESTER PRYNNE...
THE DREADFUL SIN OF ADULTERY!
LOOK AT HER STANDING ON THE SCAFFOLD...
THE SHAMEFUL LETTER ON HER BREAST...
RED AS THE FLAMES OF HELL ITSELF...
......

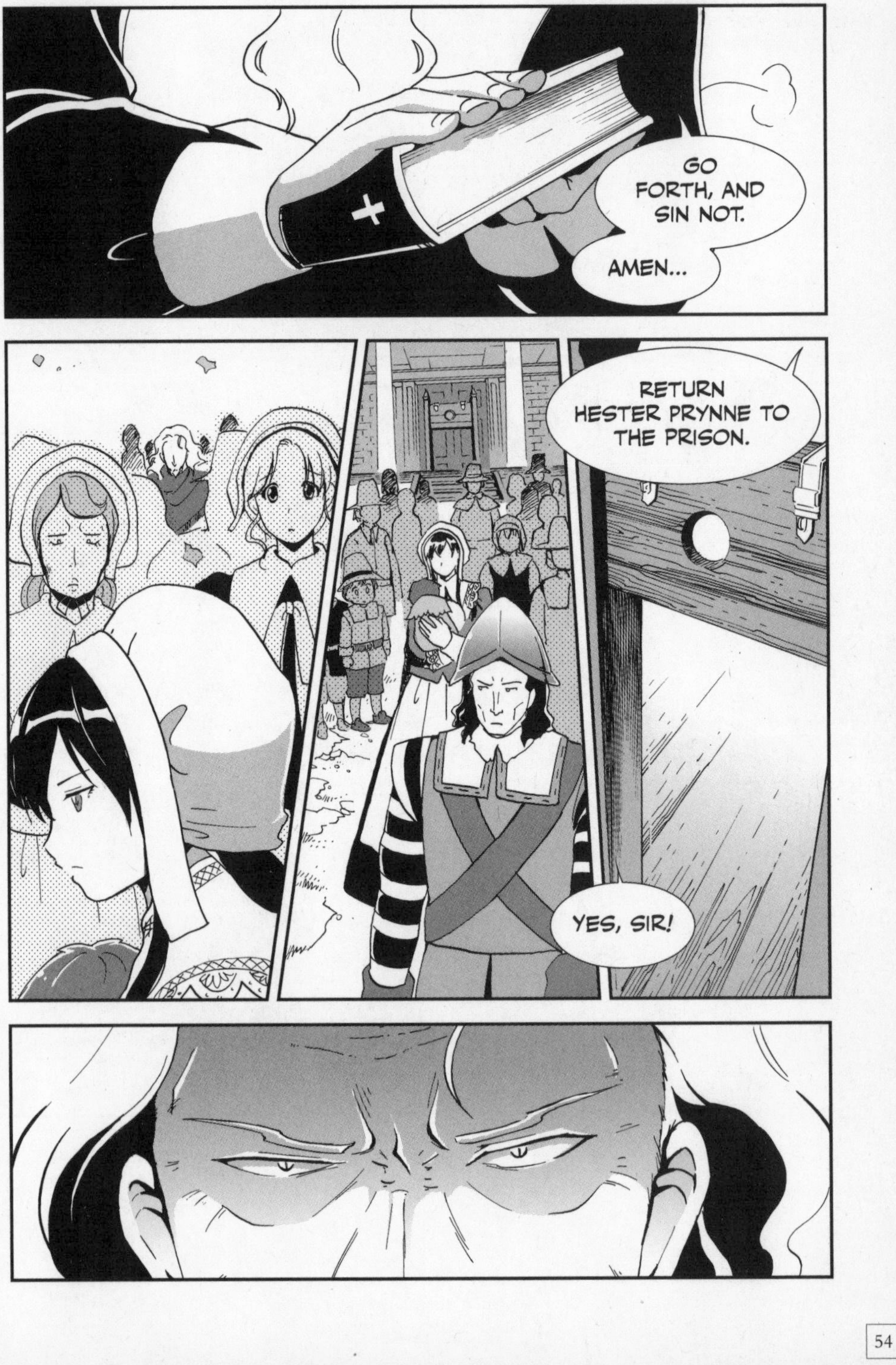
GO FORTH, AND SIN NOT.
AMEN...
RETURN HESTER PRYNNE TO THE PRISON.
YES, SIR!

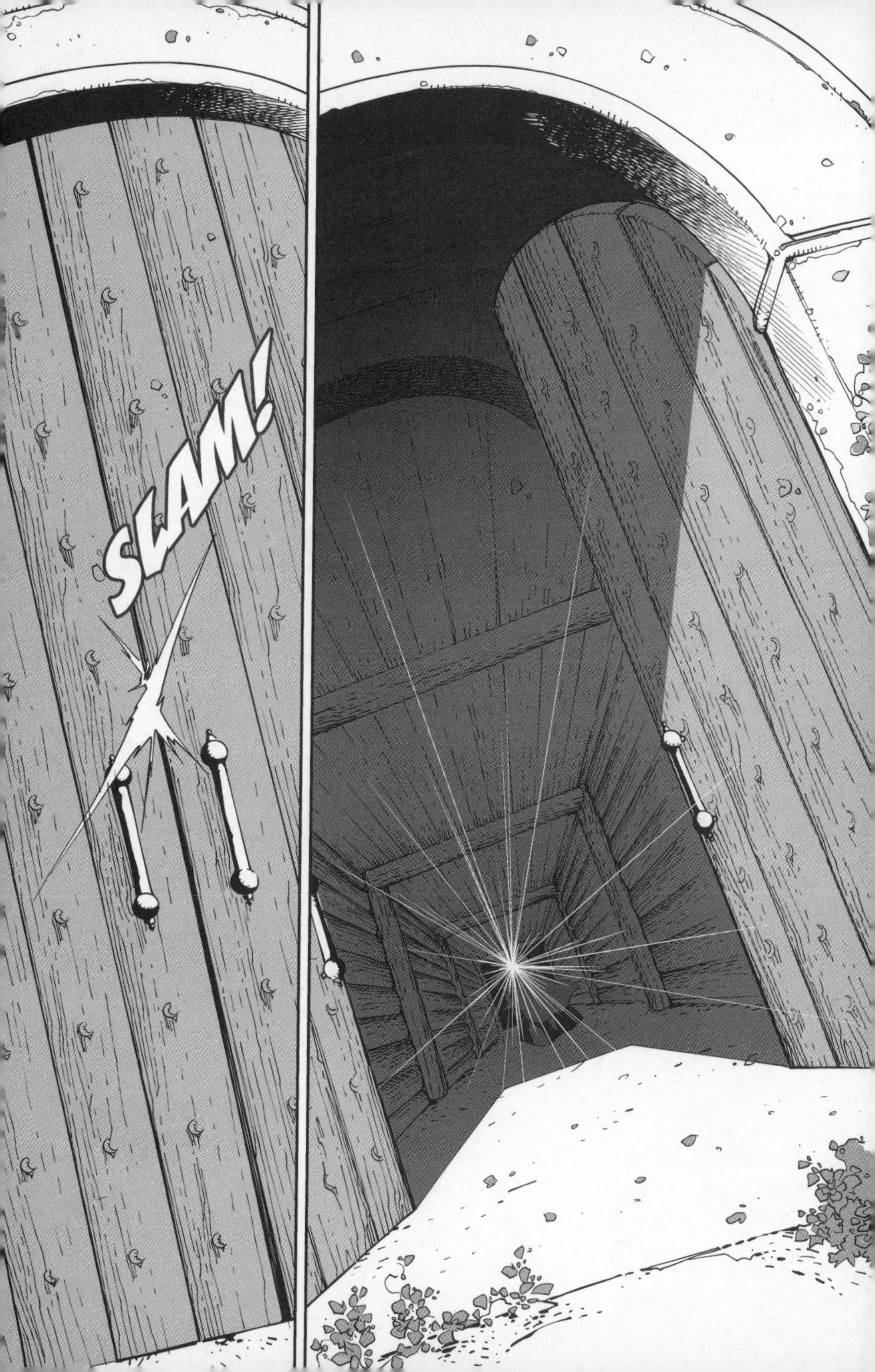
SLAM!

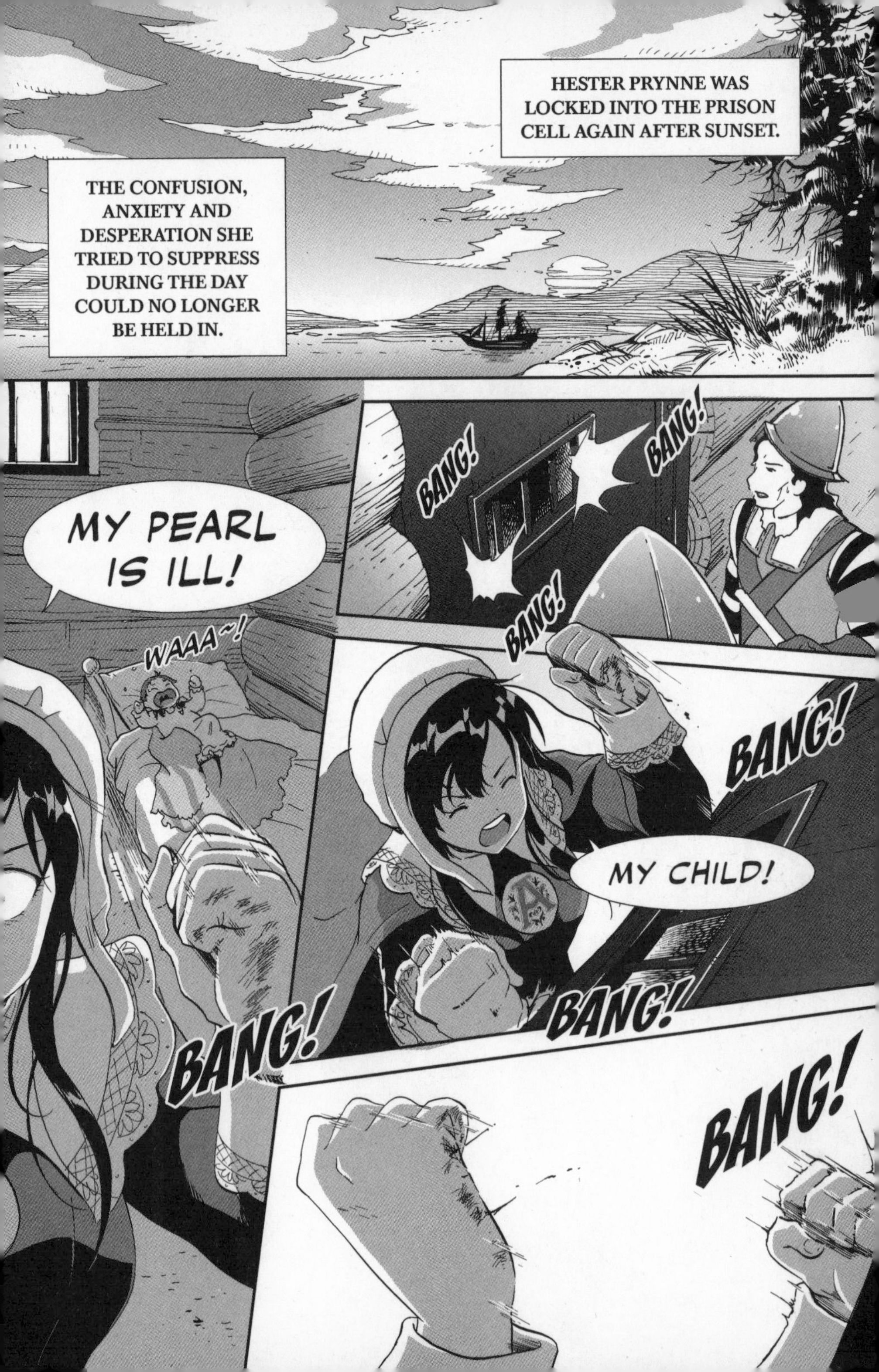
HESTER PRYNNE WAS LOCKED INTO THE PRISON CELL AGAIN AFTER SUNSET.
THE CONFUSION, ANXIETY AND DESPERATION SHE TRIED TO SUPPRESS DURING THE DAY COULD NO LONGER BE HELD IN.
BANG!
BANG!
BANG!
BANG!
MY CHILD!
BANG!
BANG!
MY PEARL IS ILL!
WAAA~!
BANG!

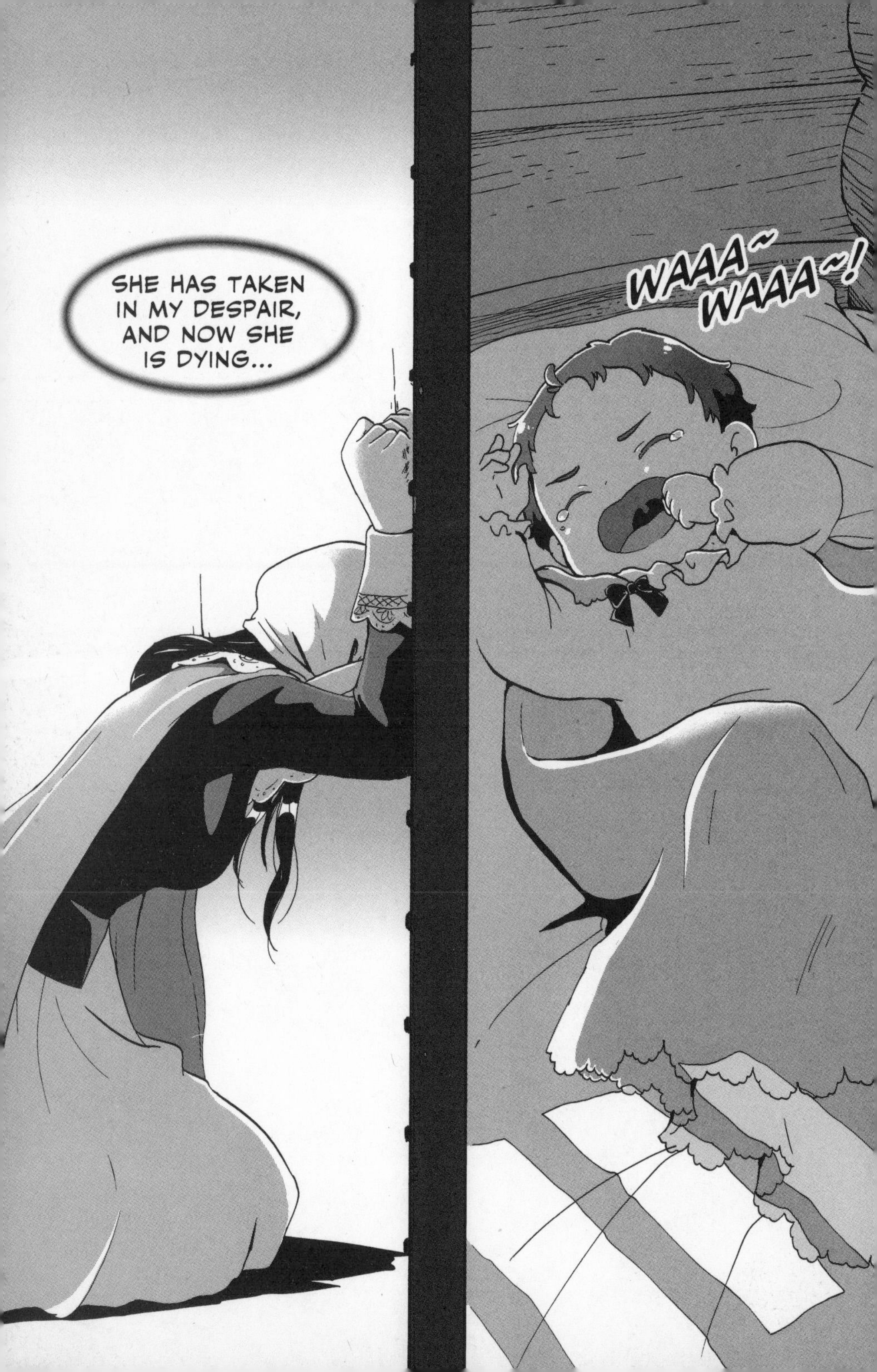
WAAA~ WAAA~!
SHE HAS TAKEN IN MY DESPAIR, AND NOW SHE IS DYING...

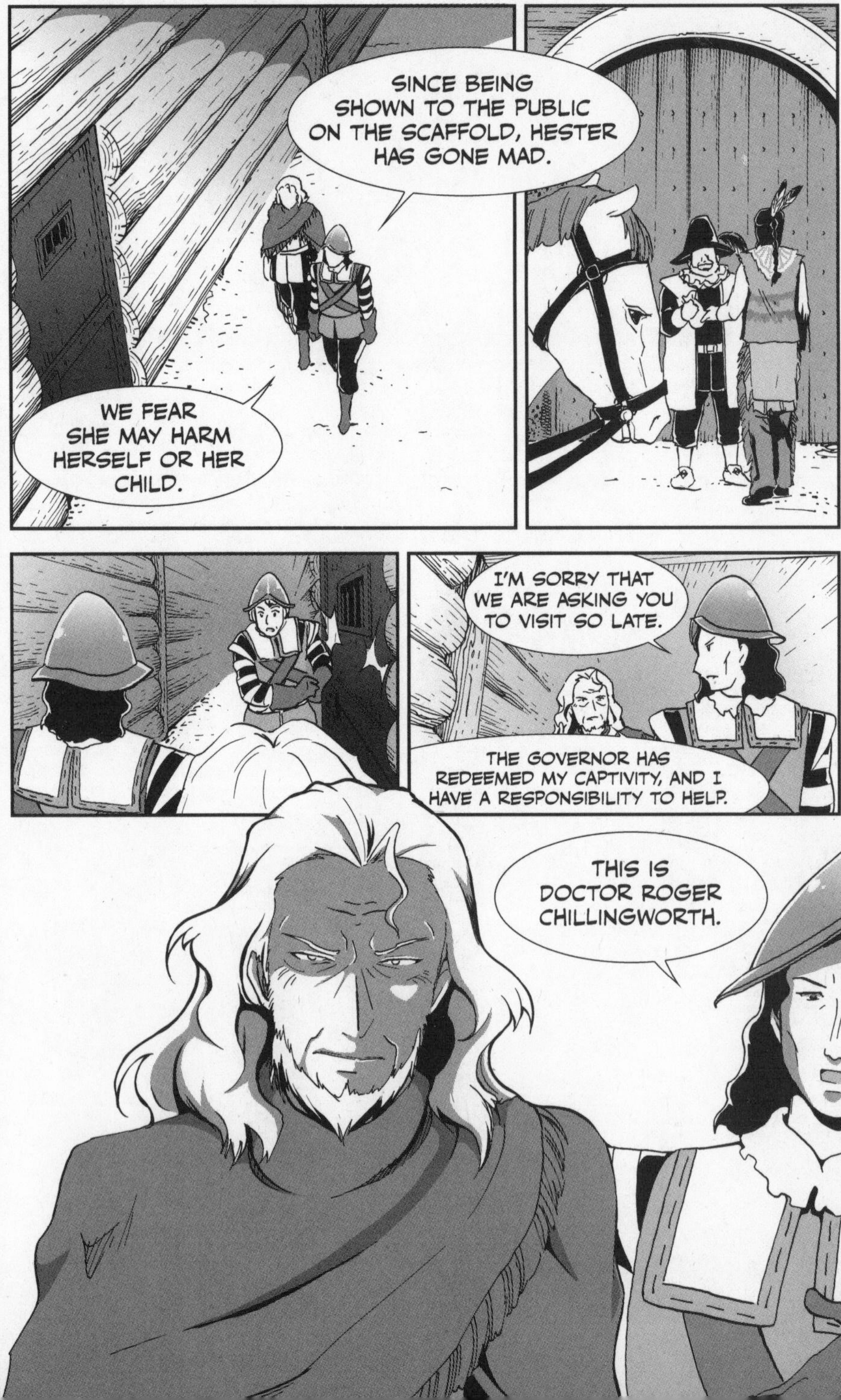
SINCE BEING SHOWN TO THE PUBLIC ON THE SCAFFOLD, HESTER HAS GONE MAD.
WE FEAR SHE MAY HARM HERSELF OR HER CHILD.
I'M SORRY THAT WE ARE ASKING YOU TO VISIT SO LATE.
THE GOVERNOR HAS REDEEMED MY CAPTIVITY, AND I HAVE A RESPONSIBILITY TO HELP.
THIS IS DOCTOR ROGER CHILLINGWORTH.

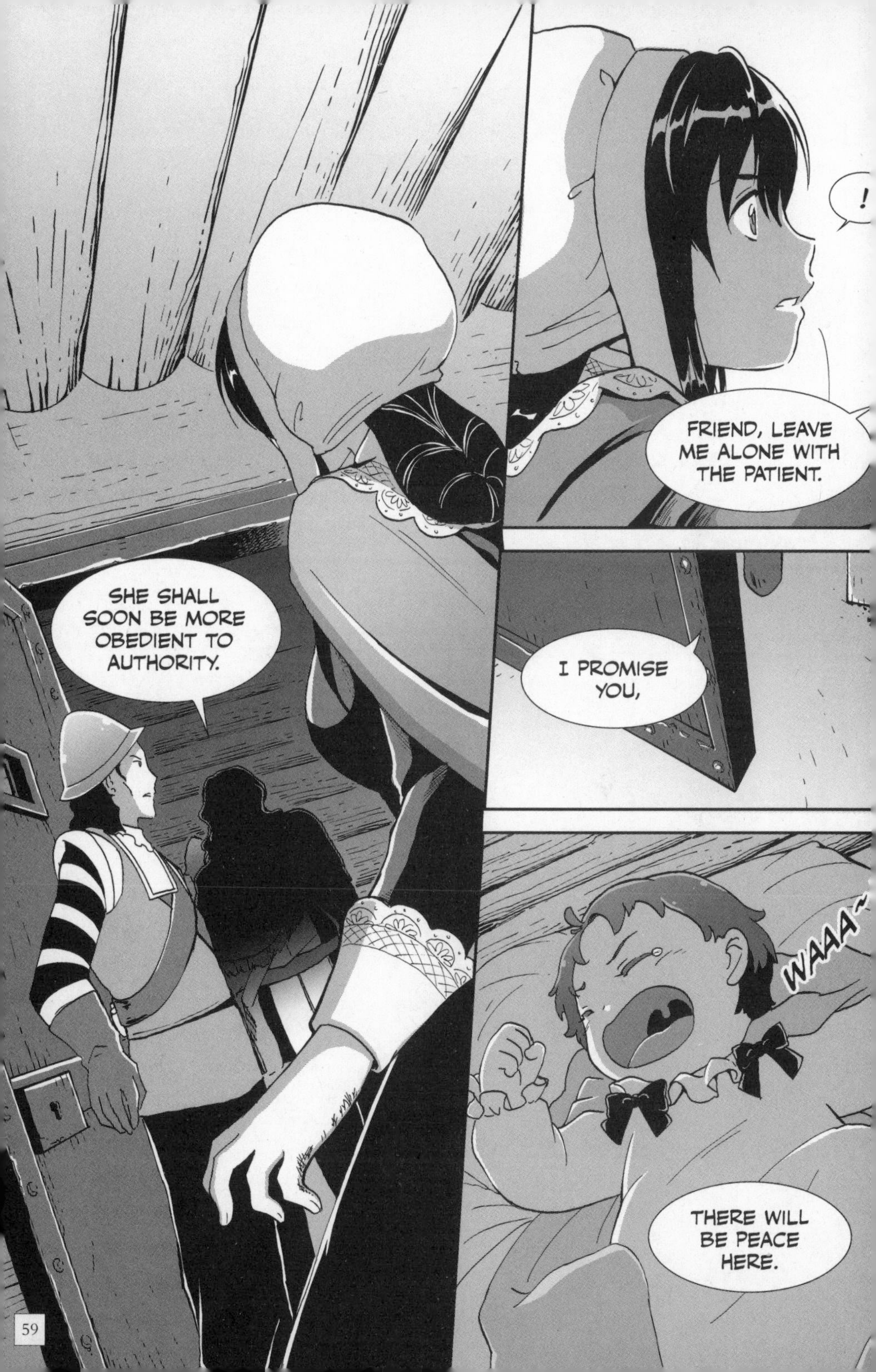
!
FRIEND, LEAVE ME ALONE WITH THE PATIENT.
I PROMISE YOU,
WAAA~
THERE WILL BE PEACE HERE.
SHE SHALL SOON BE MORE OBEDIENT TO AUTHORITY.

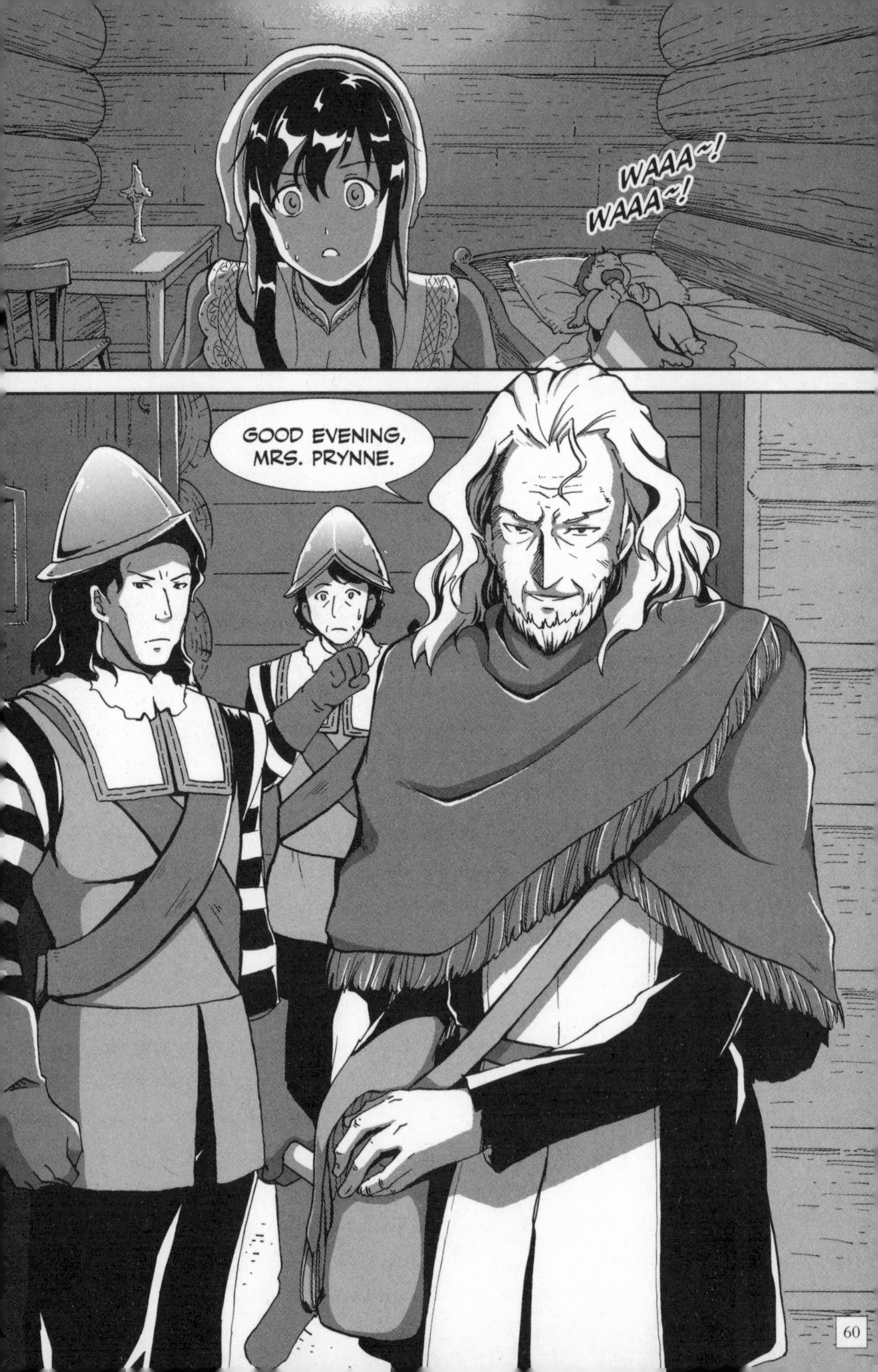
WAAA~!
WAAA~!
GOOD EVENING, MRS. PRYNNE.

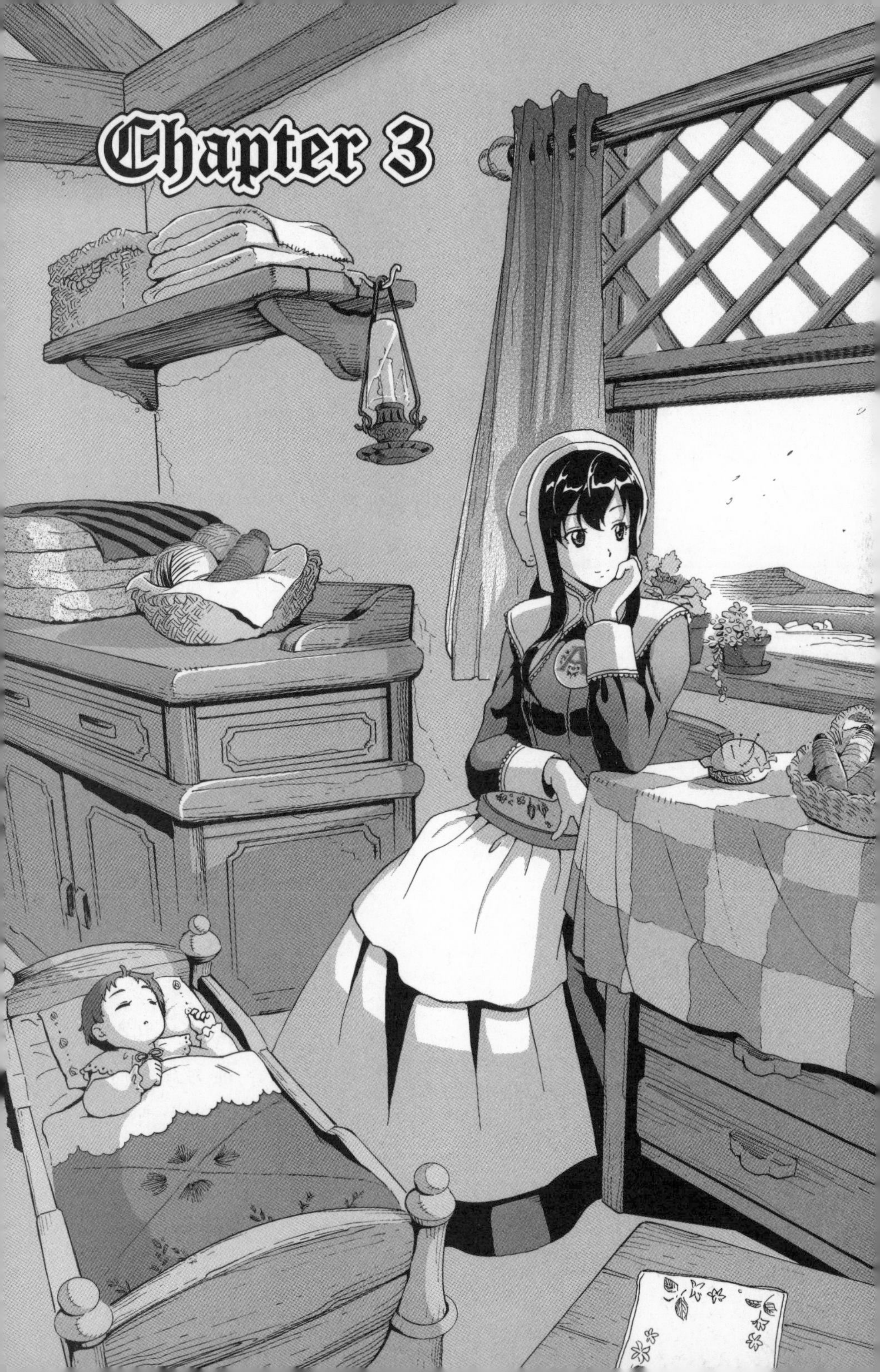
Chapter 3

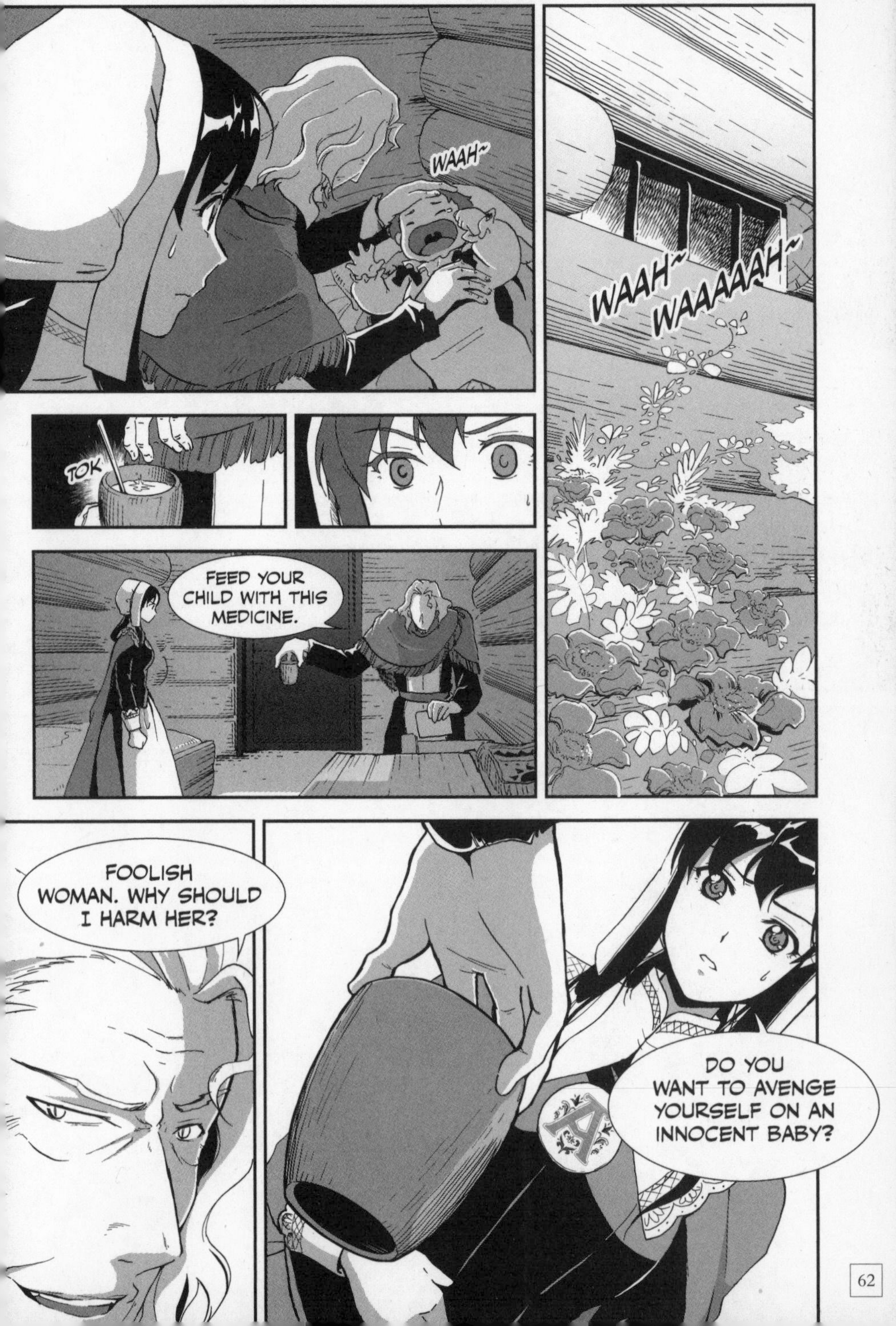
WAAH~
WAAAAAH~
WAAH~
TOK
FEED YOUR CHILD WITH THIS MEDICINE.
DO YOU WANT TO AVENGE YOURSELF ON AN INNOCENT BABY?
FOOLISH WOMAN. WHY SHOULD I HARM HER?

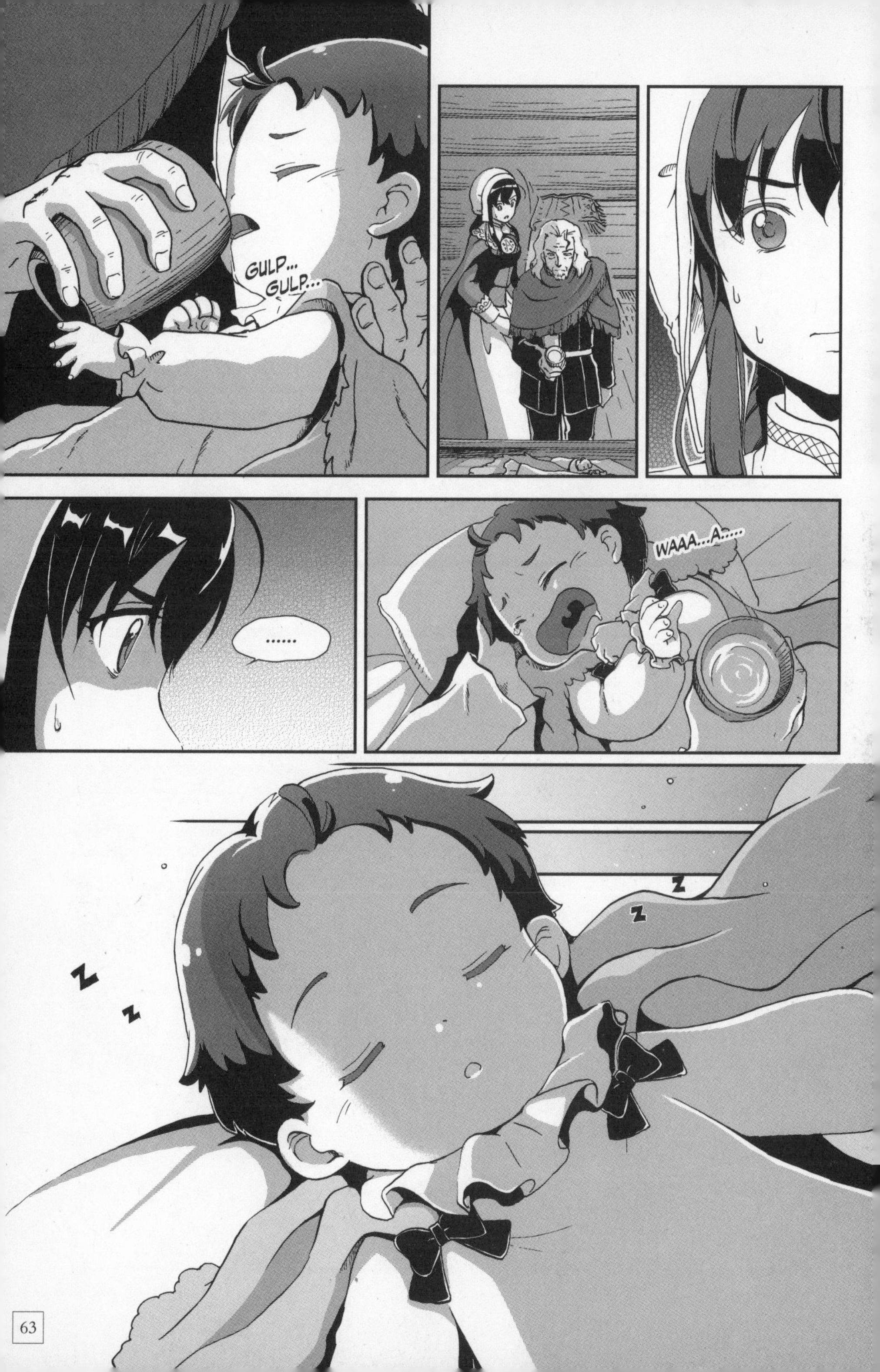
GULP... GULP...
WAAA...A.....
......
Z
Z
Z
Z

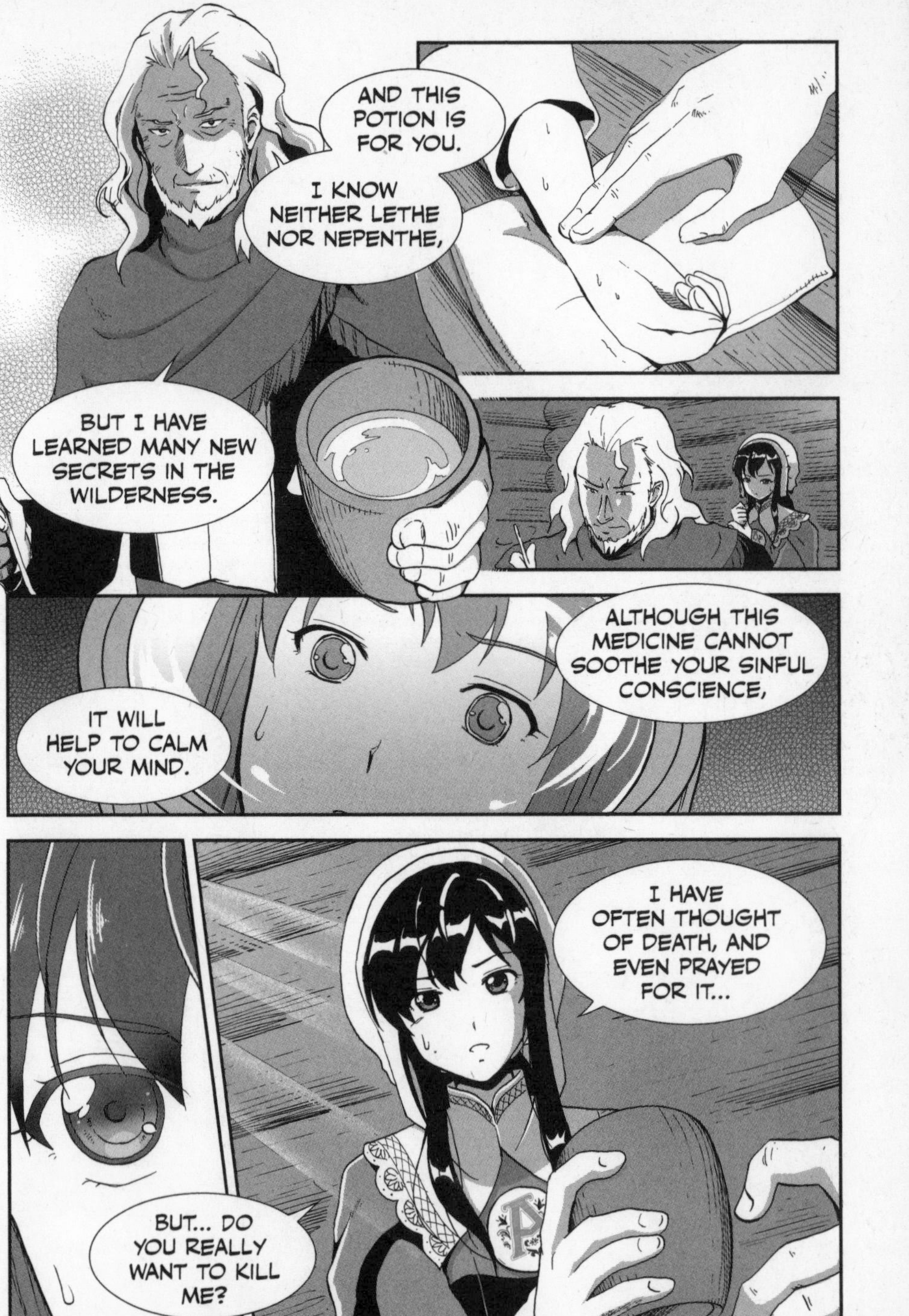
AND THIS POTION IS FOR YOU.
I KNOW NEITHER LETHE NOR NEPENTHE,
BUT I HAVE LEARNED MANY NEW SECRETS IN THE WILDERNESS.
ALTHOUGH THIS MEDICINE CANNOT SOOTHE YOUR SINFUL CONSCIENCE,
IT WILL HELP TO CALM YOUR MIND.
I HAVE OFTEN THOUGHT OF DEATH, AND EVEN PRAYED FOR IT...
BUT... DO YOU REALLY WANT TO KILL ME?

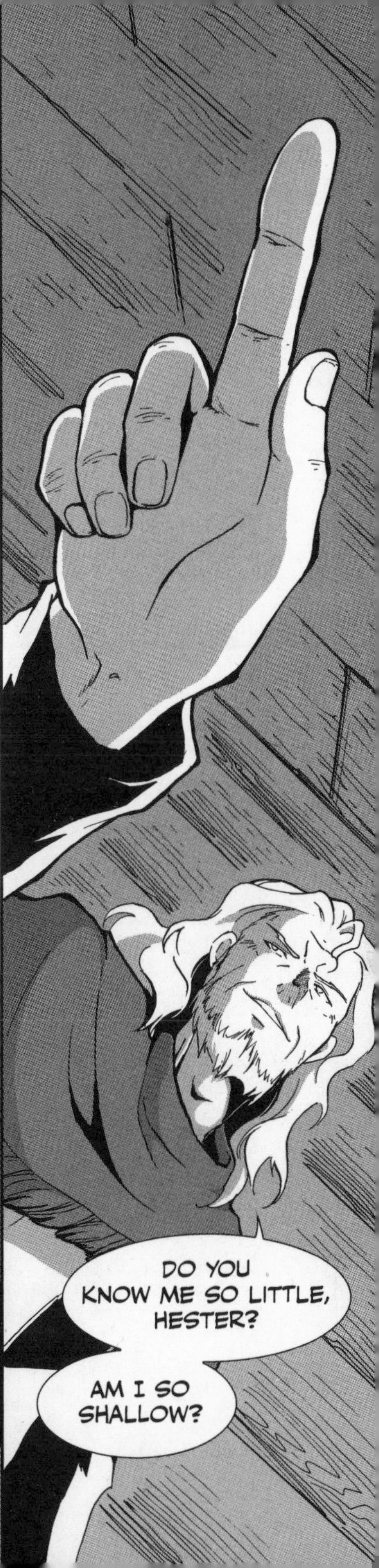
DO YOU KNOW ME SO LITTLE, HESTER?
AM I SO SHALLOW?

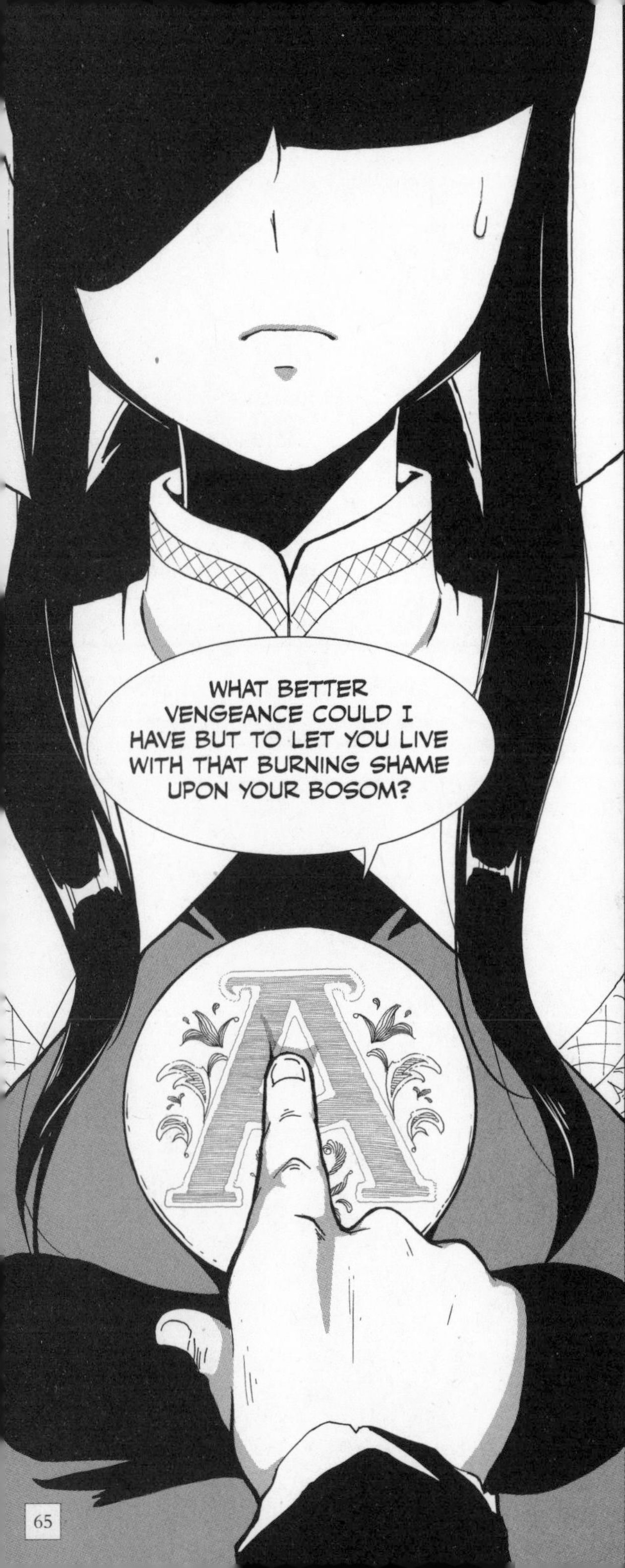
WHAT BETTER VENGEANCE COULD I HAVE BUT TO LET YOU LIVE WITH THAT BURNING SHAME UPON YOUR BOSOM?

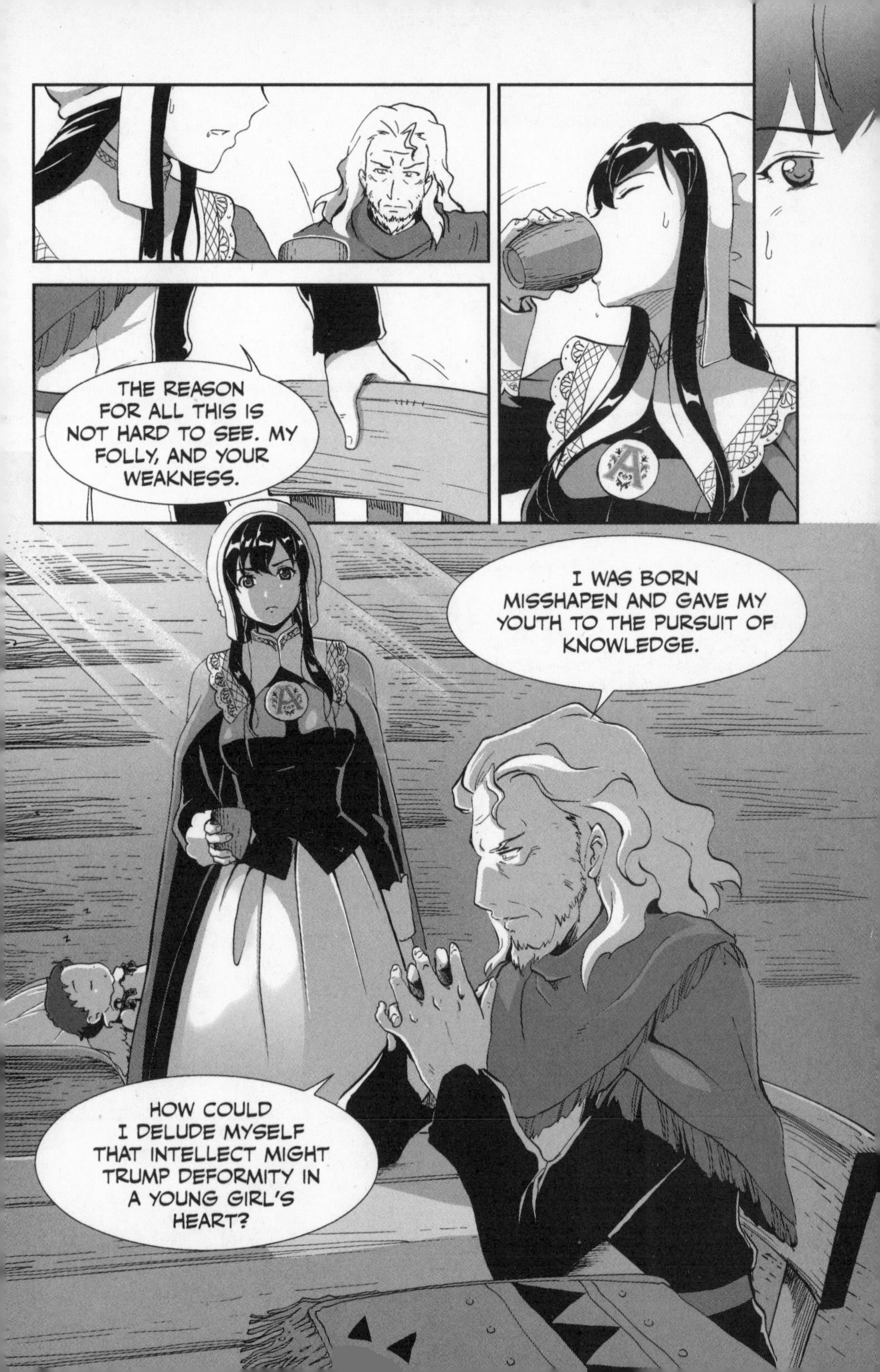
THE REASON FOR ALL THIS IS NOT HARD TO SEE. MY FOLLY, AND YOUR WEAKNESS.
I WAS BORN MISSHAPEN AND GAVE MY YOUTH TO THE PURSUIT OF KNOWLEDGE.
HOW COULD I DELUDE MYSELF THAT INTELLECT MIGHT TRUMP DEFORMITY IN A YOUNG GIRL'S HEART?

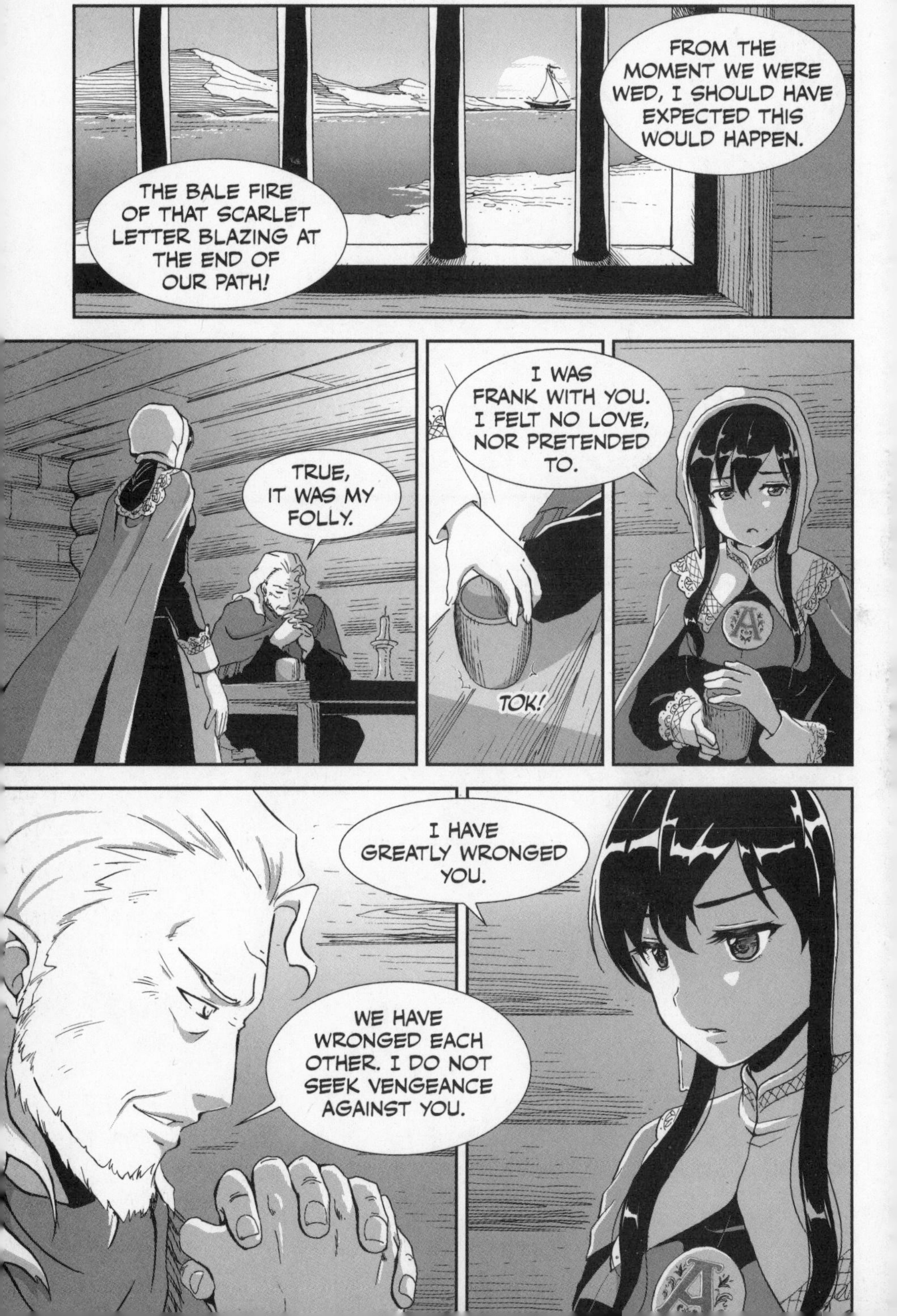
FROM THE MOMENT WE WERE WED, I SHOULD HAVE EXPECTED THIS WOULD HAPPEN.
THE BALE FIRE OF THAT SCARLET LETTER BLAZING AT THE END OF OUR PATH!
I WAS FRANK WITH YOU. I FELT NO LOVE, NOR PRETENDED TO.
TOK!
TRUE, IT WAS MY FOLLY.
I HAVE GREATLY WRONGED YOU.
WE HAVE WRONGED EACH OTHER. I DO NOT SEEK VENGEANCE AGAINST YOU.

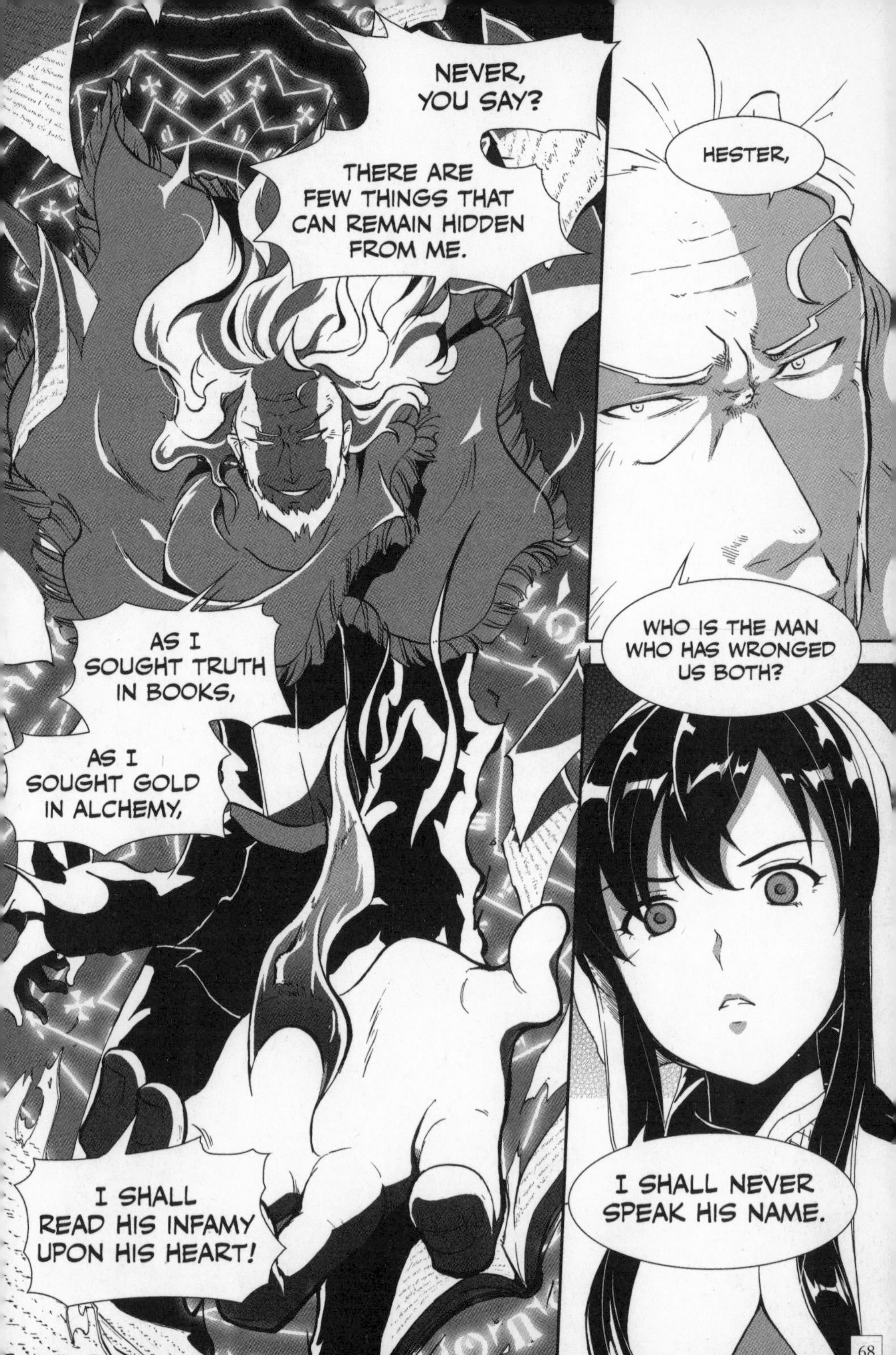
HESTER,
WHO IS THE MAN WHO HAS WRONGED US BOTH?
I SHALL NEVER SPEAK HIS NAME.
NEVER, YOU SAY?
THERE ARE FEW THINGS THAT CAN REMAIN HIDDEN FROM ME.
AS I SOUGHT TRUTH IN BOOKS,
AS I SOUGHT GOLD IN ALCHEMY,
I SHALL READ HIS INFAMY UPON HIS HEART!

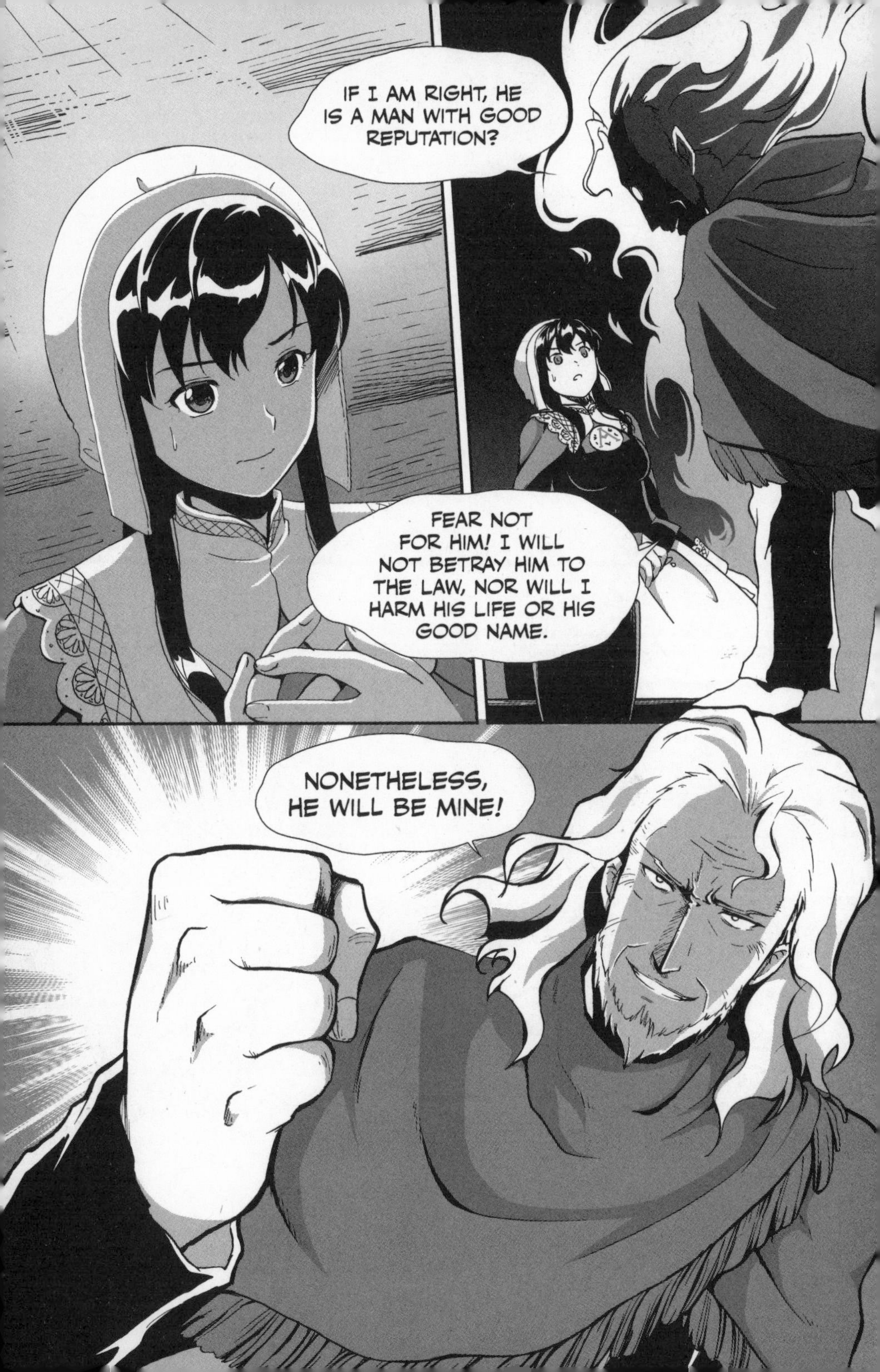
IF I AM RIGHT, HE IS A MAN WITH GOOD REPUTATION?
FEAR NOT FOR HIM! I WILL NOT BETRAY HIM TO THE LAW, NOR WILL I HARM HIS LIFE OR HIS GOOD NAME.
NONETHELESS, HE WILL BE MINE!

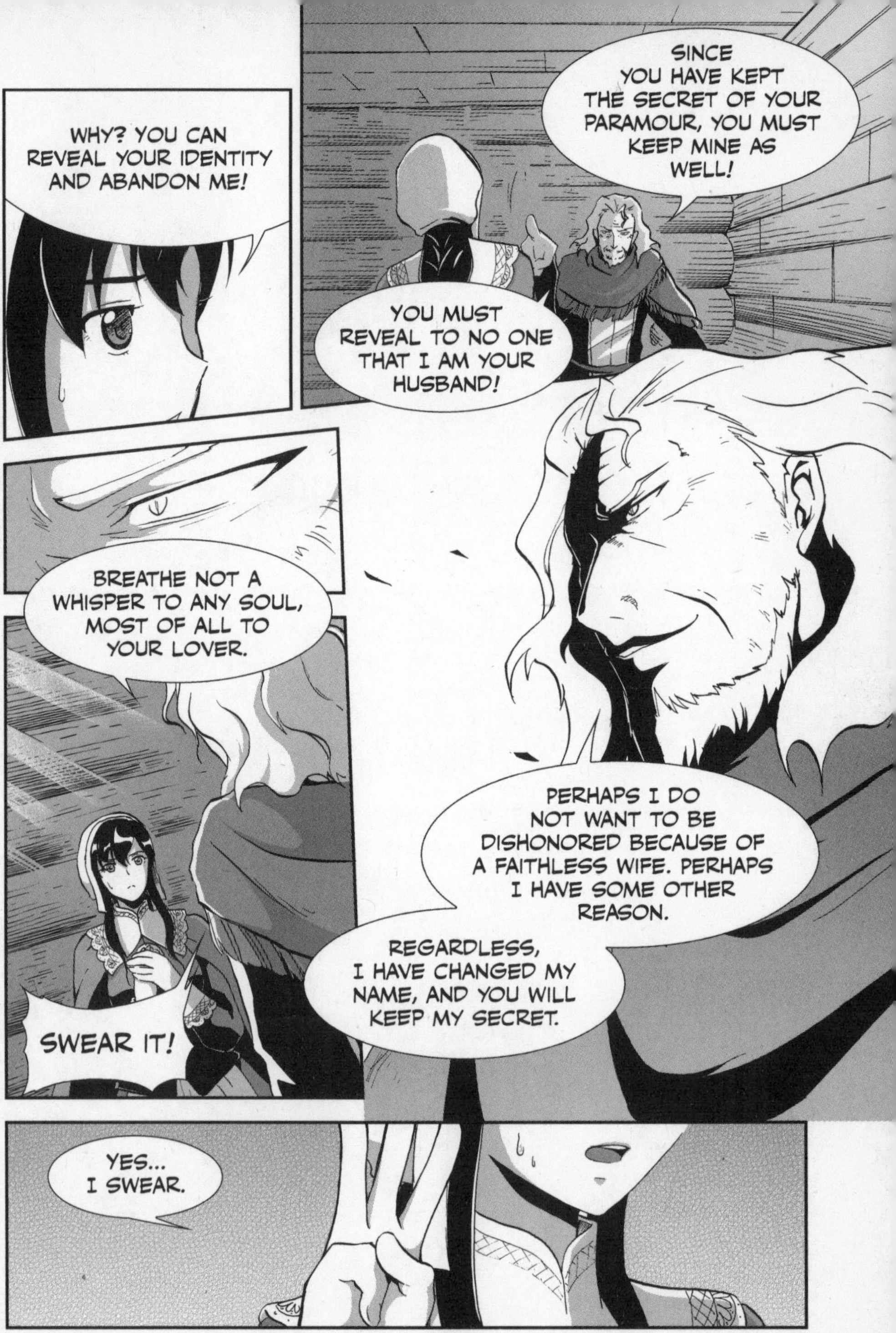
SINCE YOU HAVE KEPT THE SECRET OF YOUR PARAMOUR, YOU MUST KEEP MINE AS WELL!
YOU MUST REVEAL TO NO ONE THAT I AM YOUR HUSBAND!
WHY? YOU CAN REVEAL YOUR IDENTITY AND ABANDON ME!
PERHAPS I DO NOT WANT TO BE DISHONORED BECAUSE OF A FAITHLESS WIFE. PERHAPS I HAVE SOME OTHER REASON.
REGARDLESS, I HAVE CHANGED MY NAME, AND YOU WILL KEEP MY SECRET.
BREATHE NOT A WHISPER TO ANY SOUL, MOST OF ALL TO YOUR LOVER.
SWEAR IT!
YES... I SWEAR.

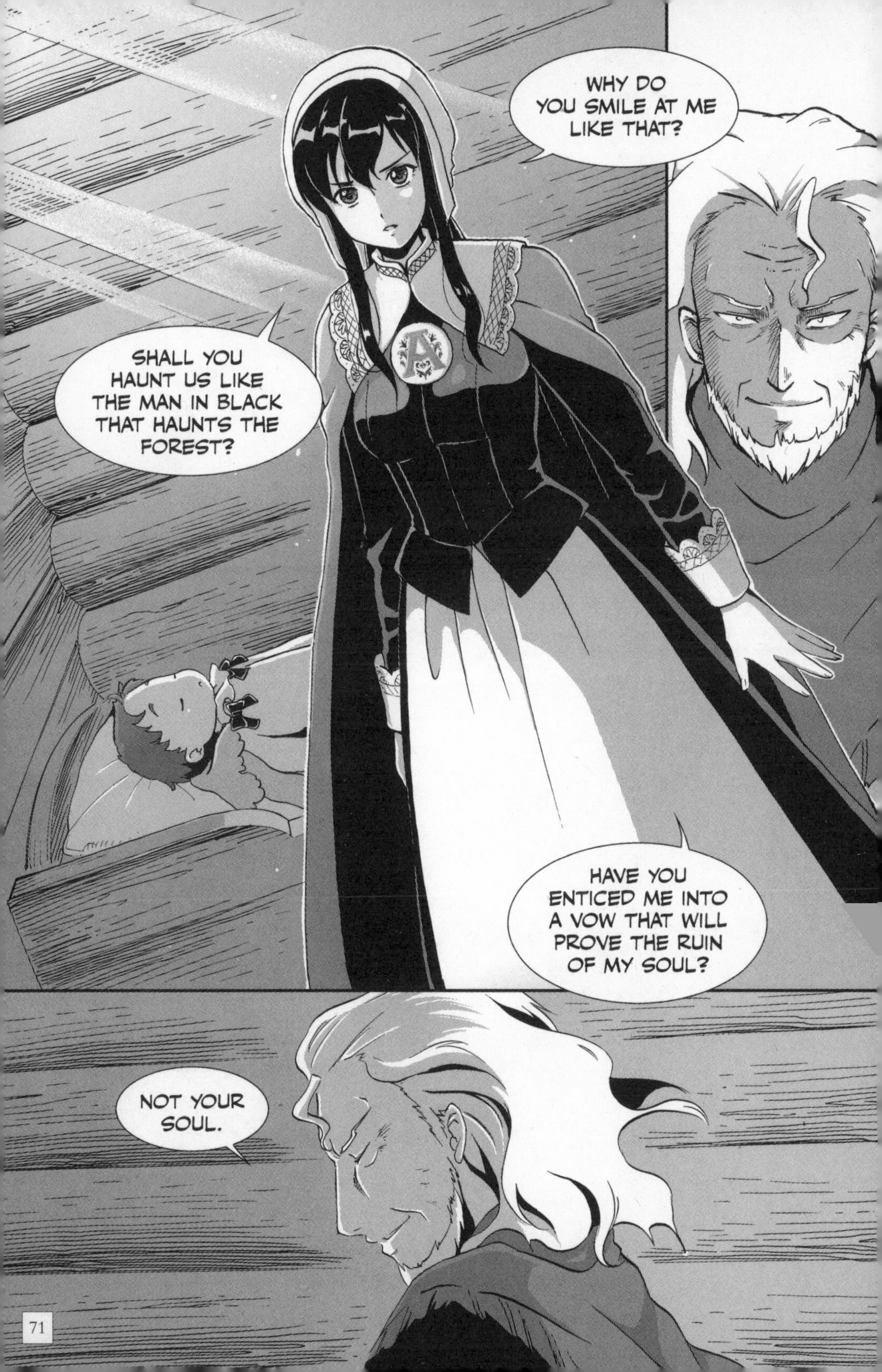
WHY DO YOU SMILE AT ME LIKE THAT?
SHALL YOU HAUNT US LIKE THE MAN IN BLACK THAT HAUNTS THE FOREST?
HAVE YOU ENTICED ME INTO A VOW THAT WILL PROVE THE RUIN OF MY SOUL?
NOT YOUR SOUL.

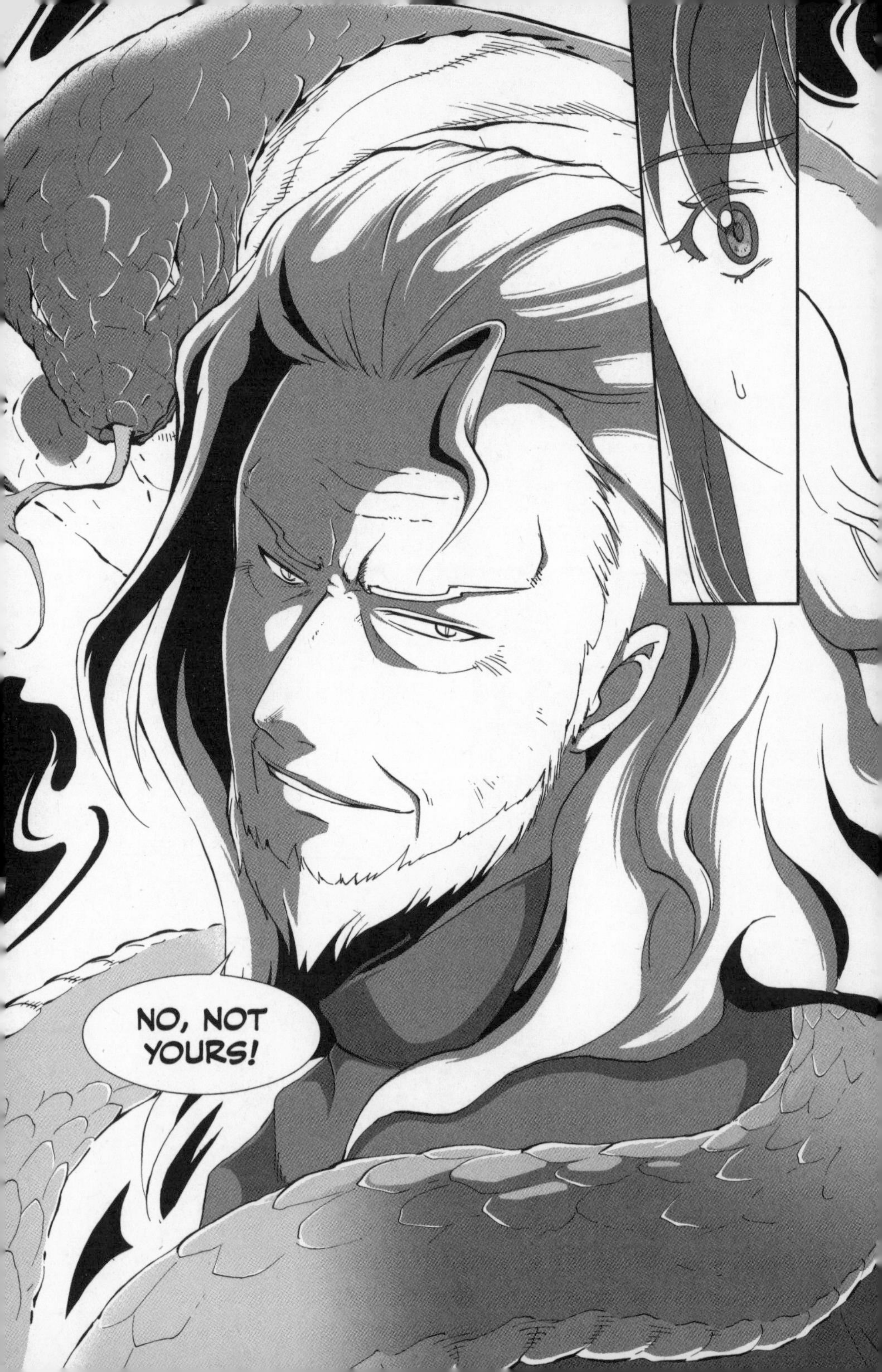
NO, NOT YOURS!

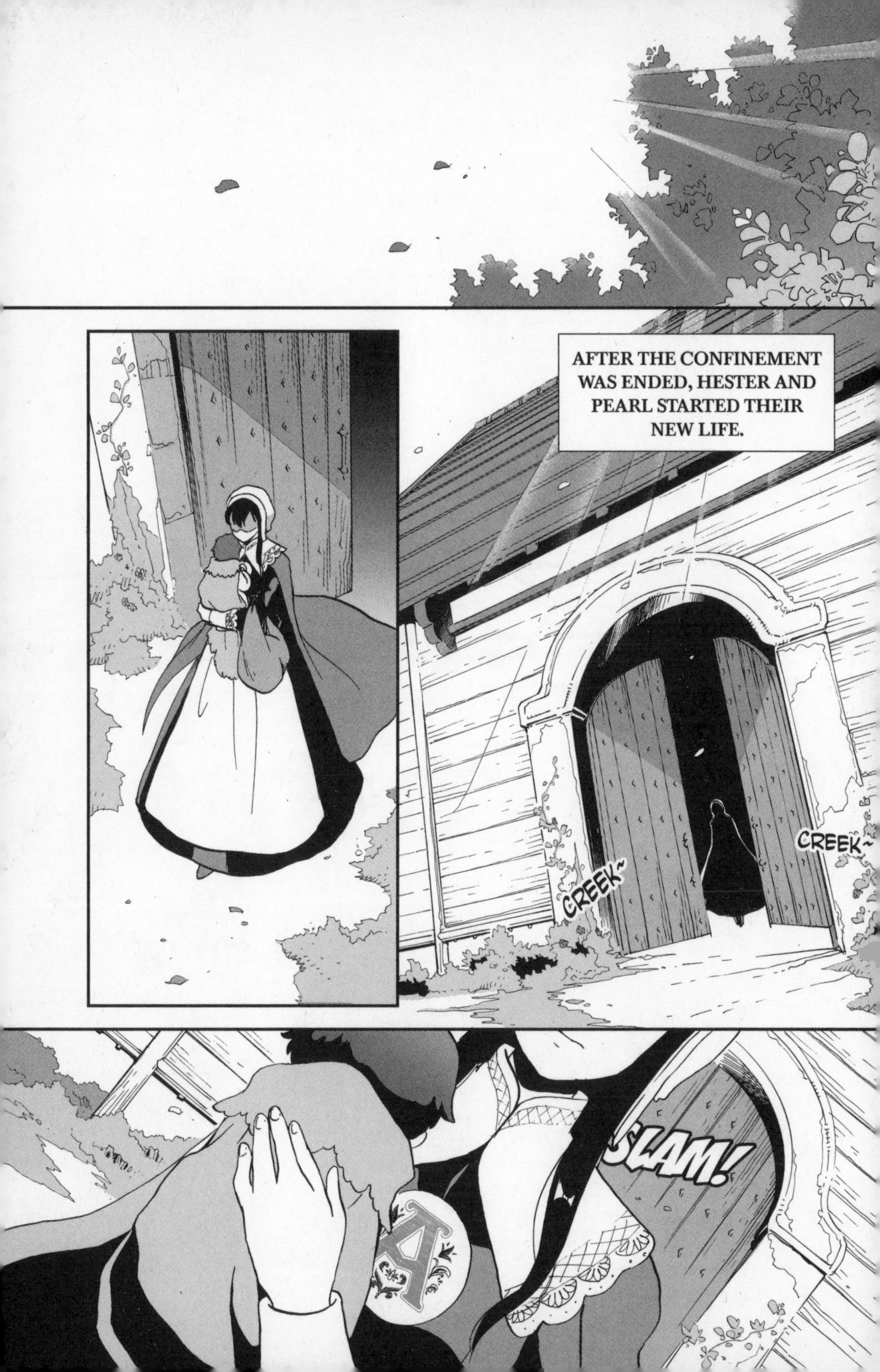
AFTER THE CONFINEMENT WAS ENDED, HESTER AND PEARL STARTED THEIR NEW LIFE.
CREEK~
CREEK~
SLAM!

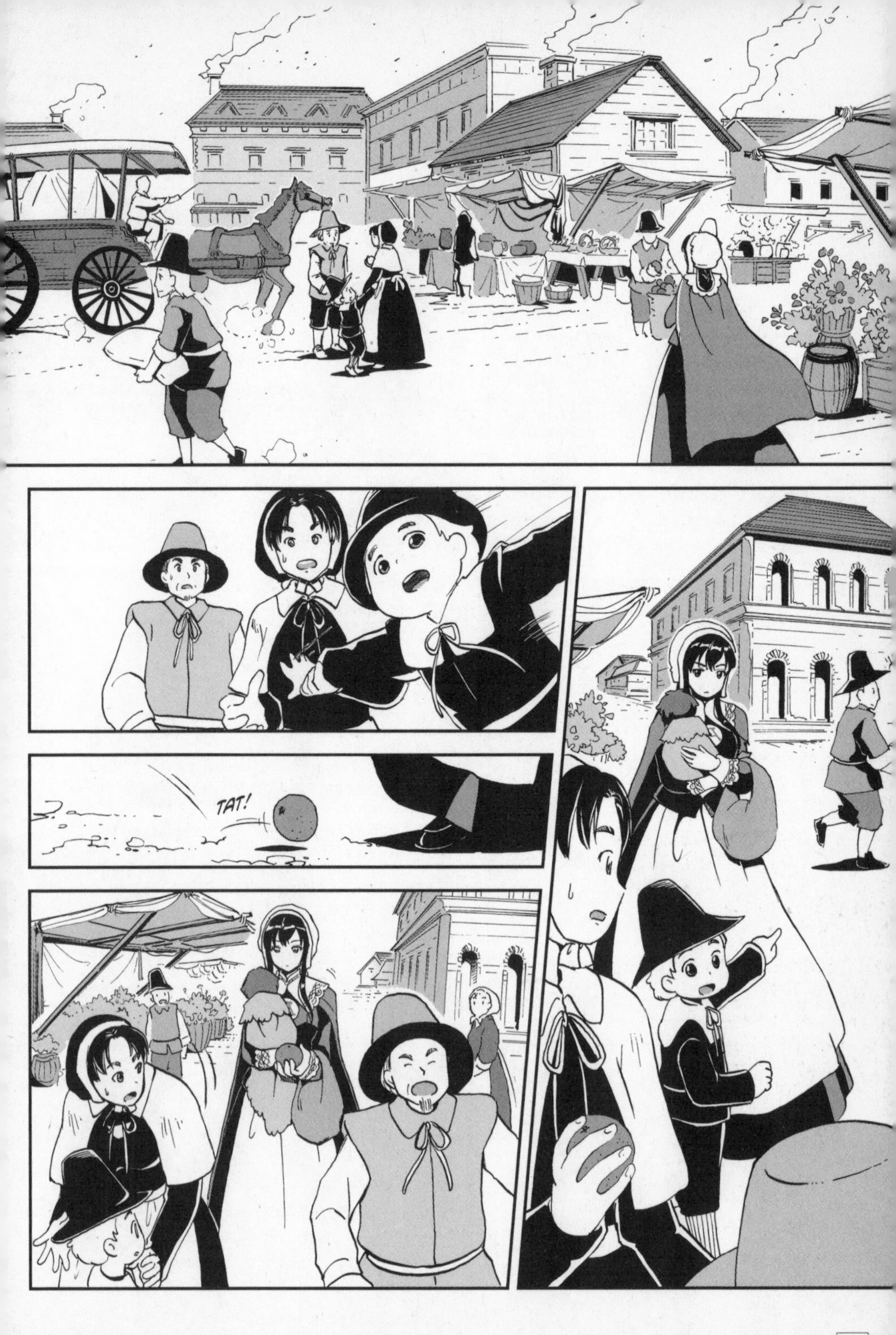
TAT!

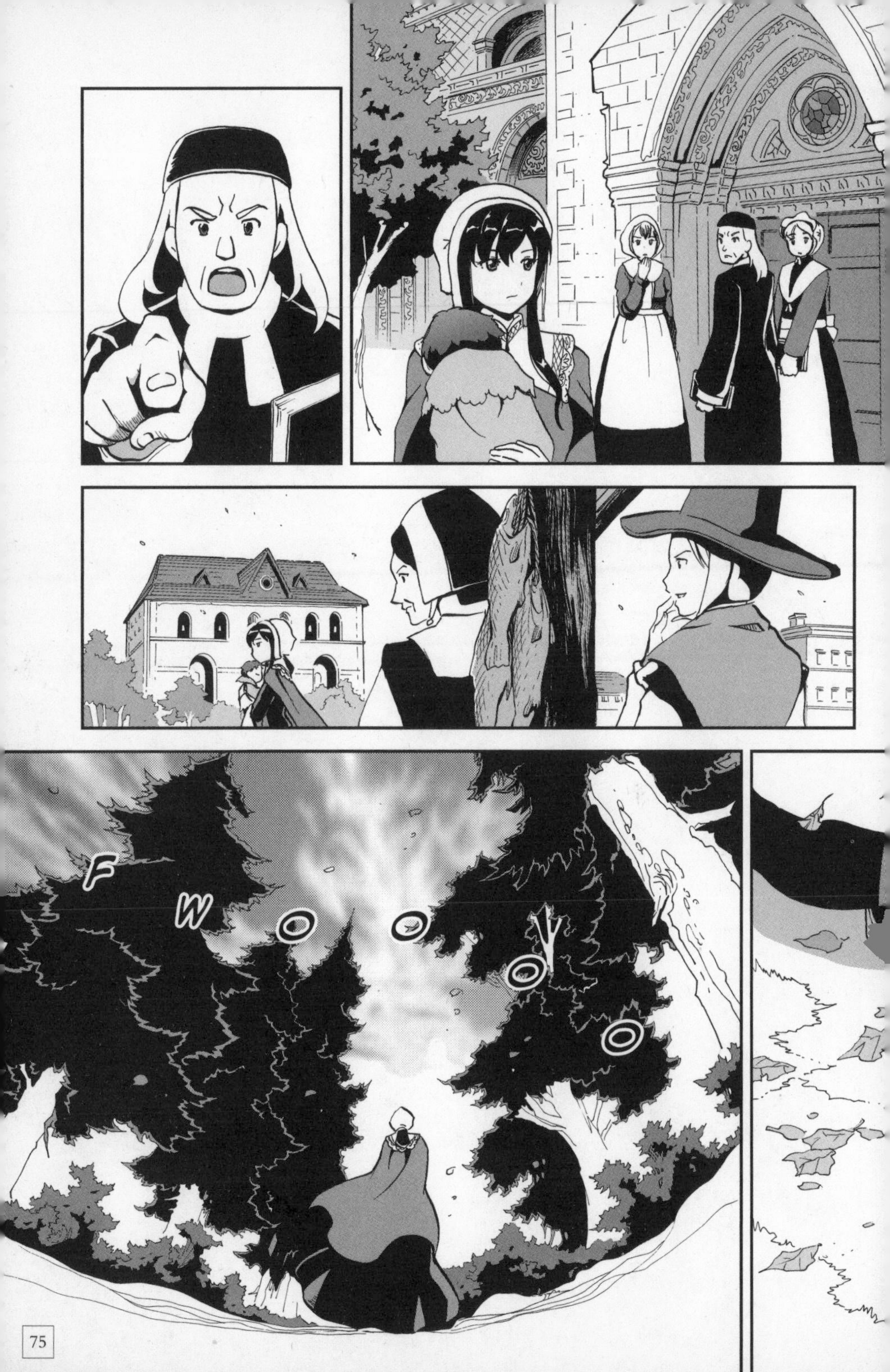
FWOOOO

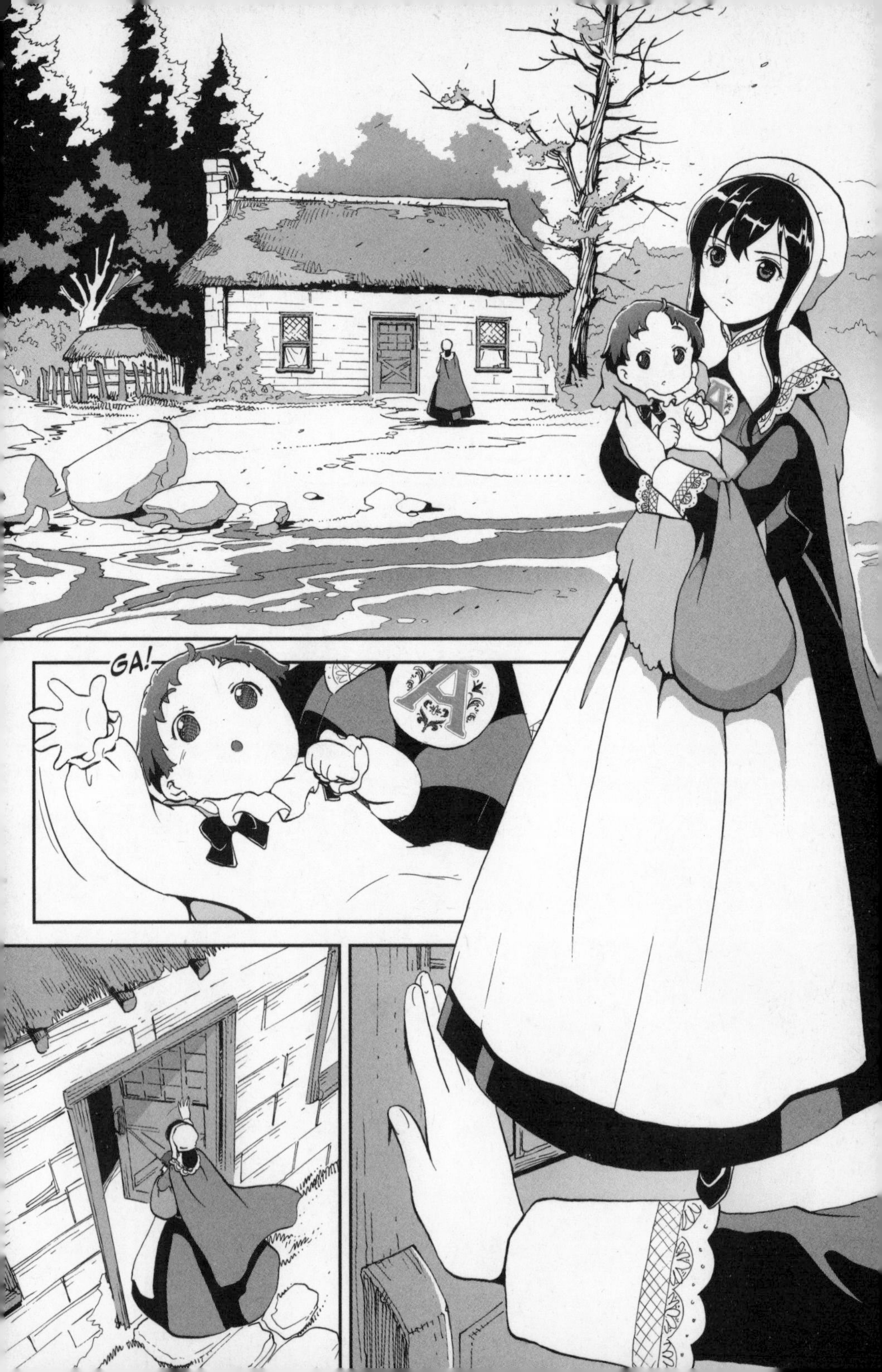
GA!

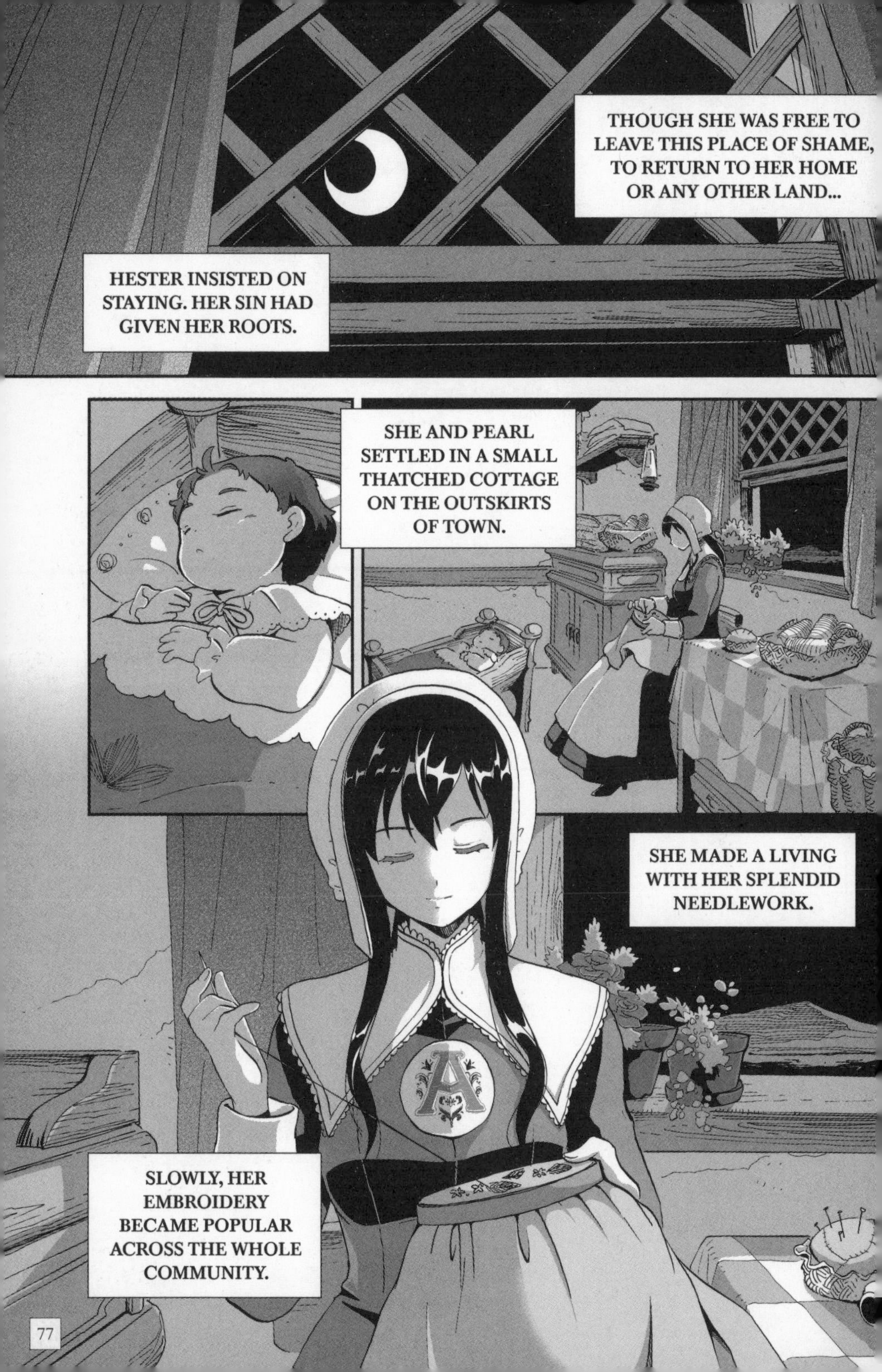
THOUGH SHE WAS FREE TO LEAVE THIS PLACE OF SHAME, TO RETURN TO HER HOME OR ANY OTHER LAND...
HESTER INSISTED ON STAYING. HER SIN HAD GIVEN HER ROOTS.
SHE AND PEARL SETTLED IN A SMALL THATCHED COTTAGE ON THE OUTSKIRTS OF TOWN.
SHE MADE A LIVING WITH HER SPLENDID NEEDLEWORK.
SLOWLY, HER EMBROIDERY BECAME POPULAR ACROSS THE WHOLE COMMUNITY.

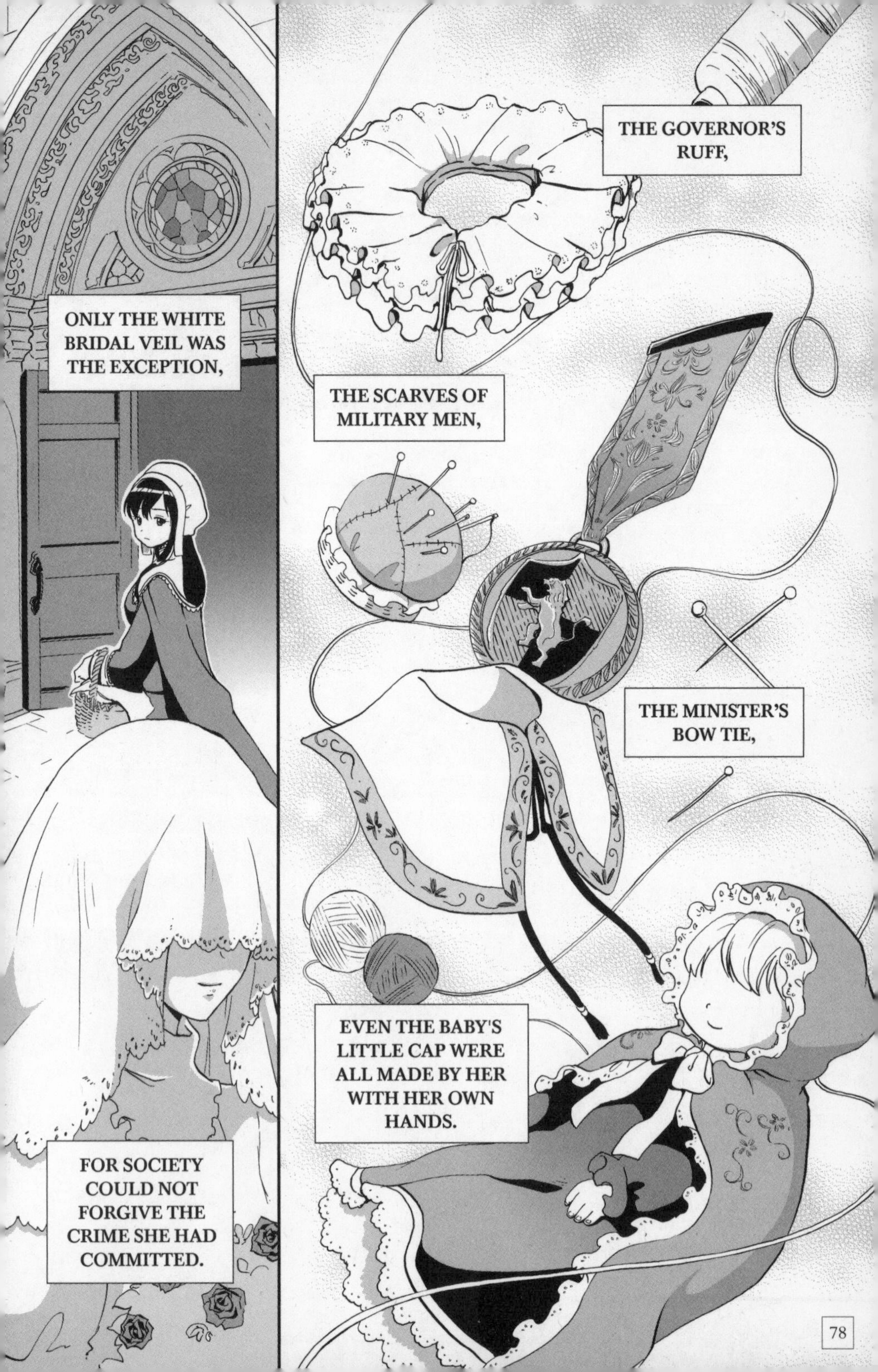
THE GOVERNOR'S RUFF,
THE SCARVES OF MILITARY MEN,
THE MINISTER'S BOW TIE,
EVEN THE BABY'S LITTLE CAP WERE ALL MADE BY HER WITH HER OWN HANDS.
ONLY THE WHITE BRIDAL VEIL WAS THE EXCEPTION,
FOR SOCIETY COULD NOT FORGIVE THE CRIME SHE HAD COMMITTED.

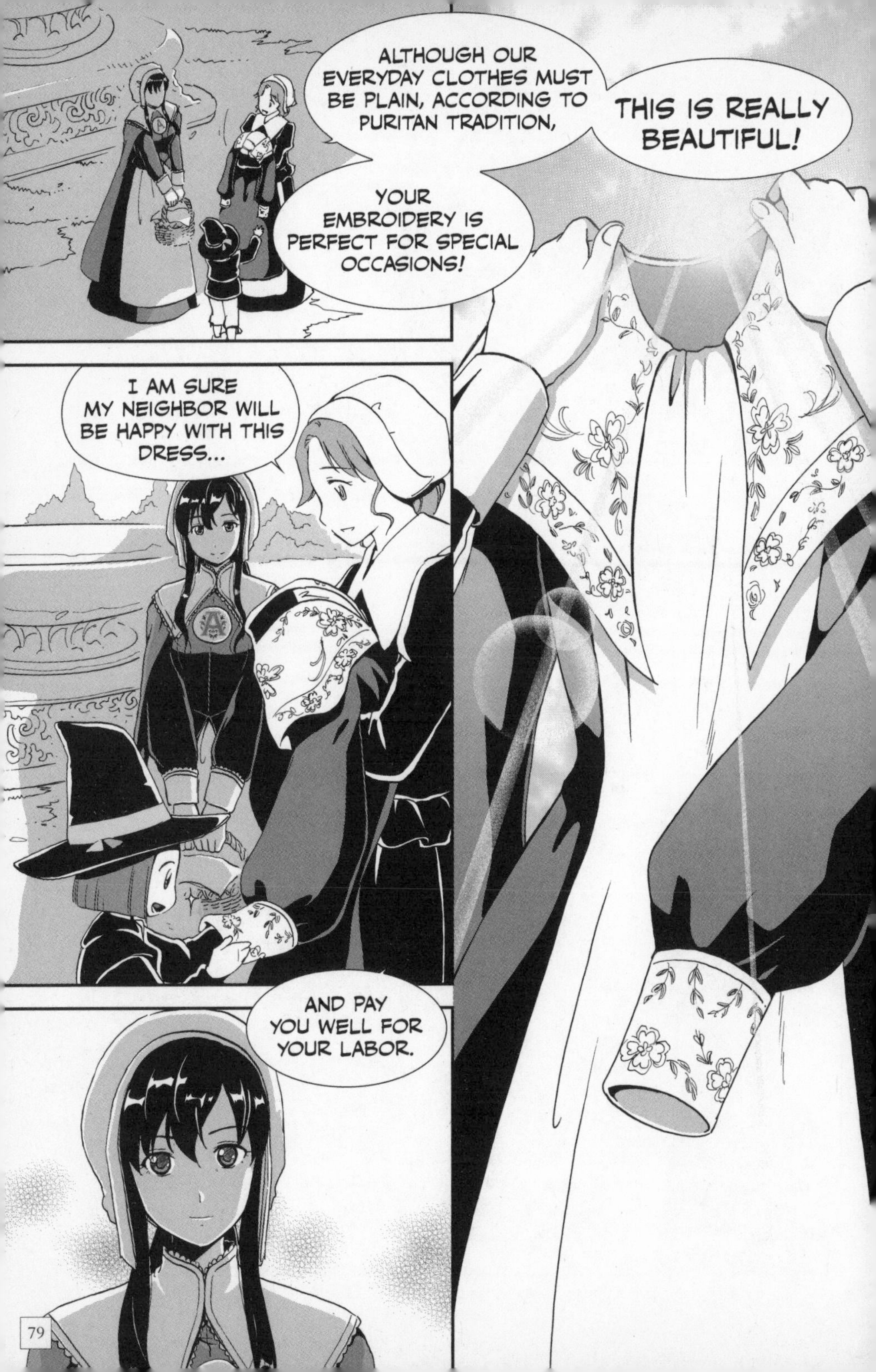
THIS IS REALLY BEAUTIFUL!
ALTHOUGH OUR EVERYDAY CLOTHES MUST BE PLAIN, ACCORDING TO PURITAN TRADITION,
YOUR EMBROIDERY IS PERFECT FOR SPECIAL OCCASIONS!
I AM SURE MY NEIGHBOR WILL BE HAPPY WITH THIS DRESS...
AND PAY YOU WELL FOR YOUR LABOR.

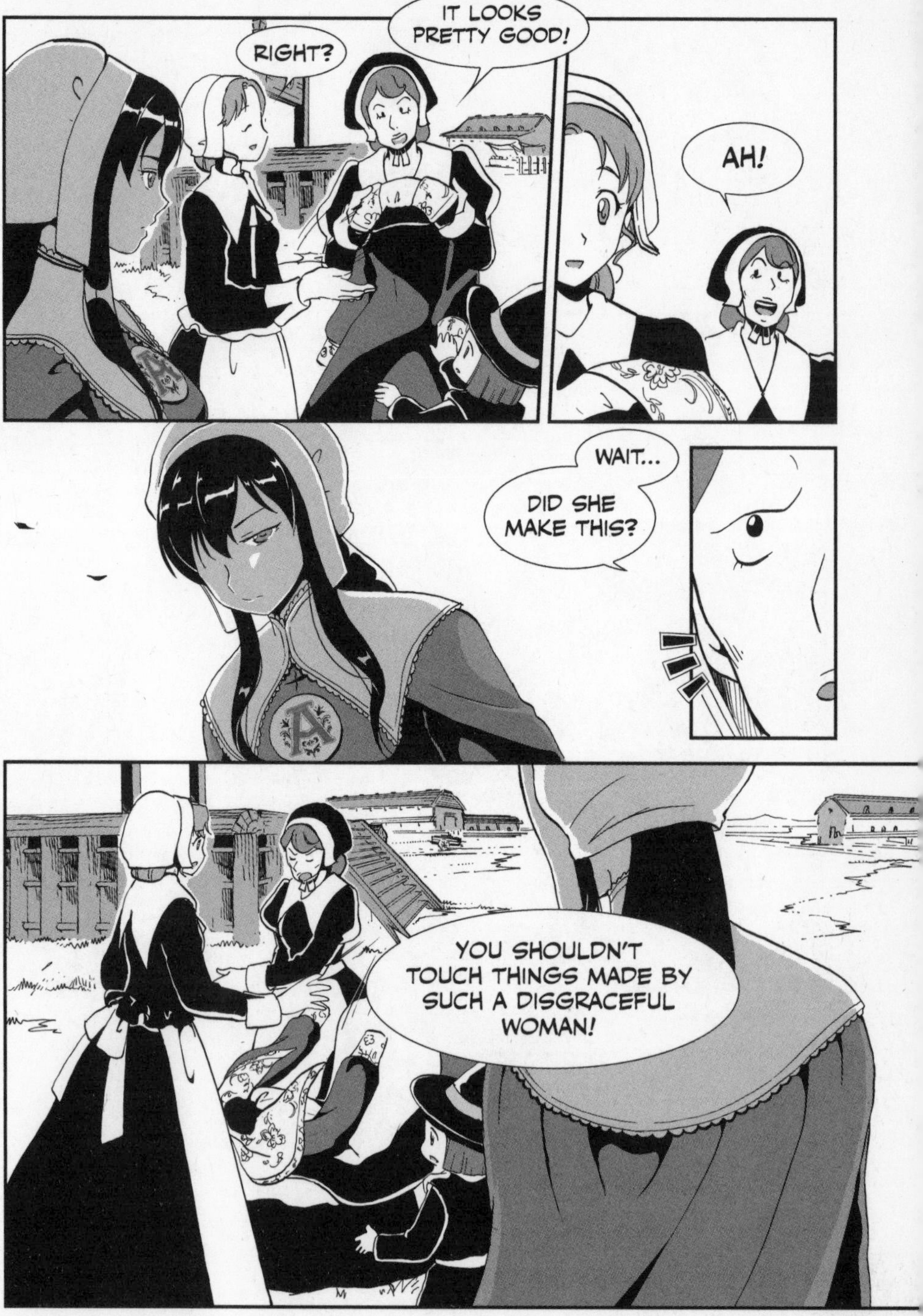
AH!
IT LOOKS PRETTY GOOD!
RIGHT?
WAIT...
DID SHE MAKE THIS?
YOU SHOULDN'T TOUCH THINGS MADE BY SUCH A DISGRACEFUL WOMAN!

HOW UNLUCKY THAT I SHOULD MEET THAT SINFUL WOMAN TODAY!

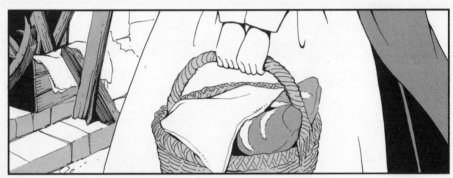

MOMMY, I'M HUNGRY...

WE WON'T TAKE CHARITY FROM A SINNER!

THUD!

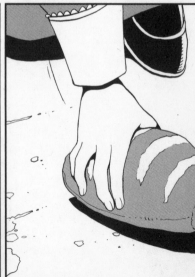

THUD!

...

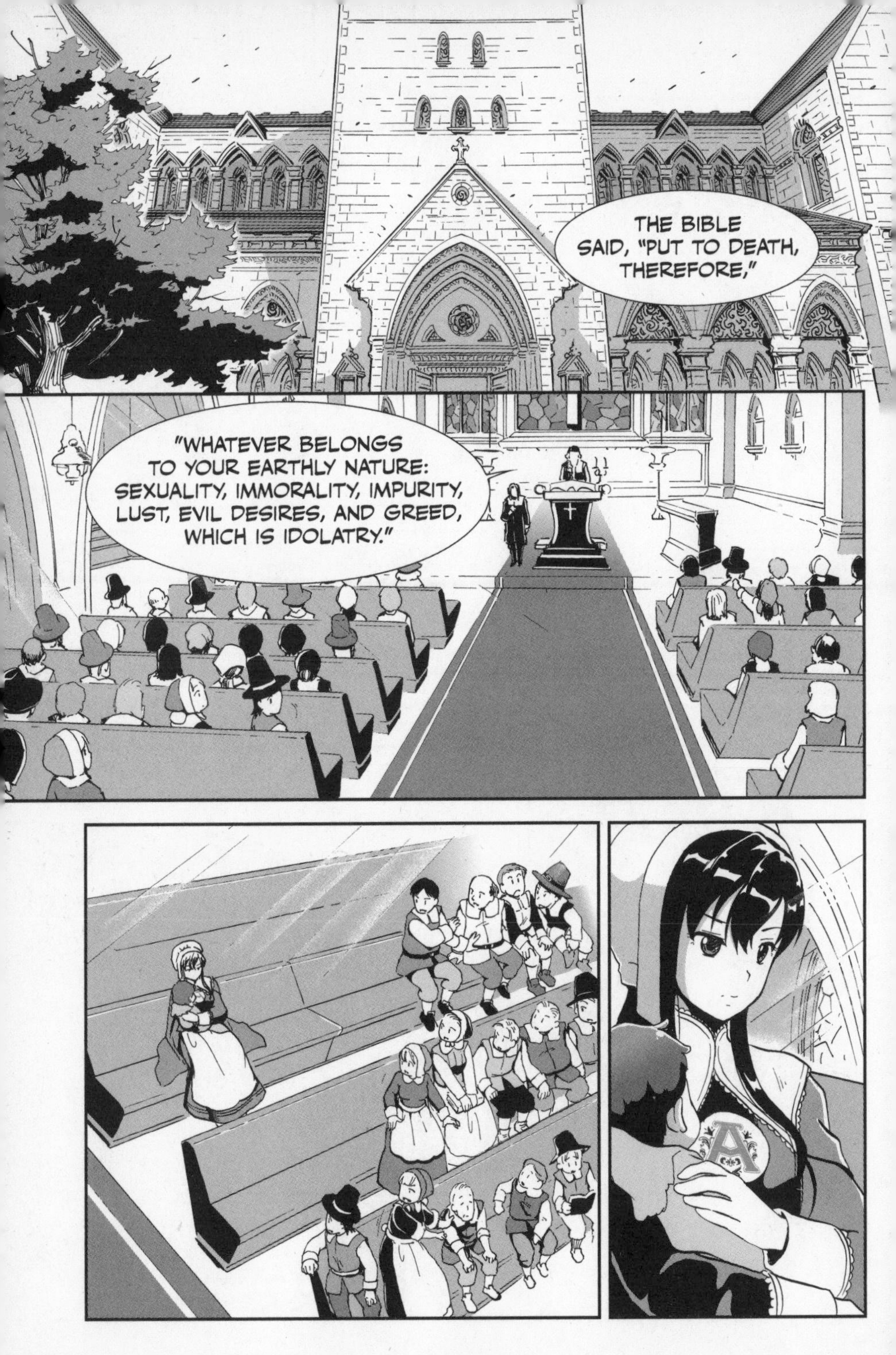
THE BIBLE SAID, "PUT TO DEATH, THEREFORE,"
"WHATEVER BELONGS TO YOUR EARTHLY NATURE: SEXUALITY, IMMORALITY, IMPURITY, LUST, EVIL DESIRES, AND GREED, WHICH IS IDOLATRY."

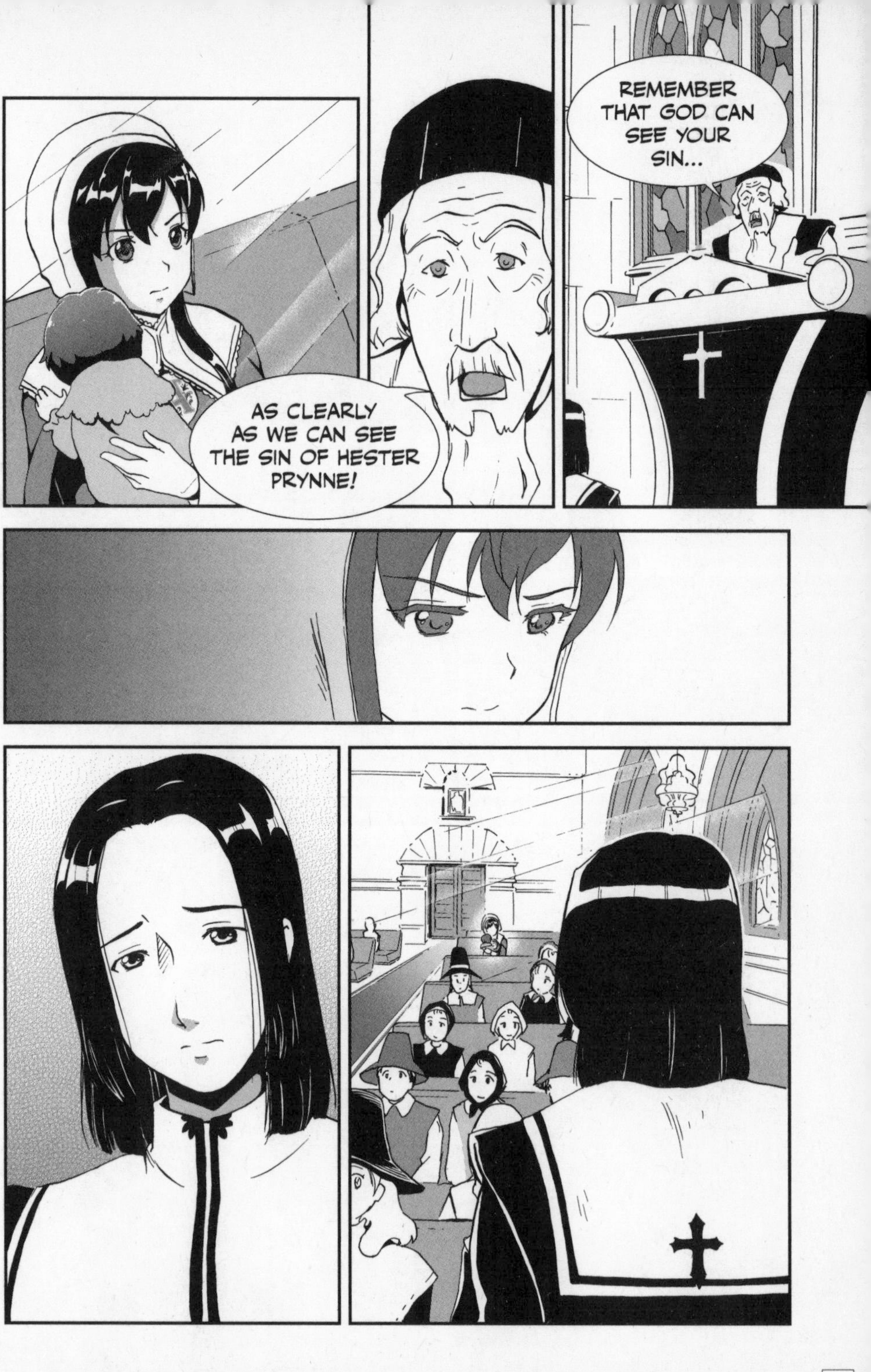
REMEMBER THAT GOD CAN SEE YOUR SIN...
AS CLEARLY AS WE CAN SEE THE SIN OF HESTER PRYNNE!

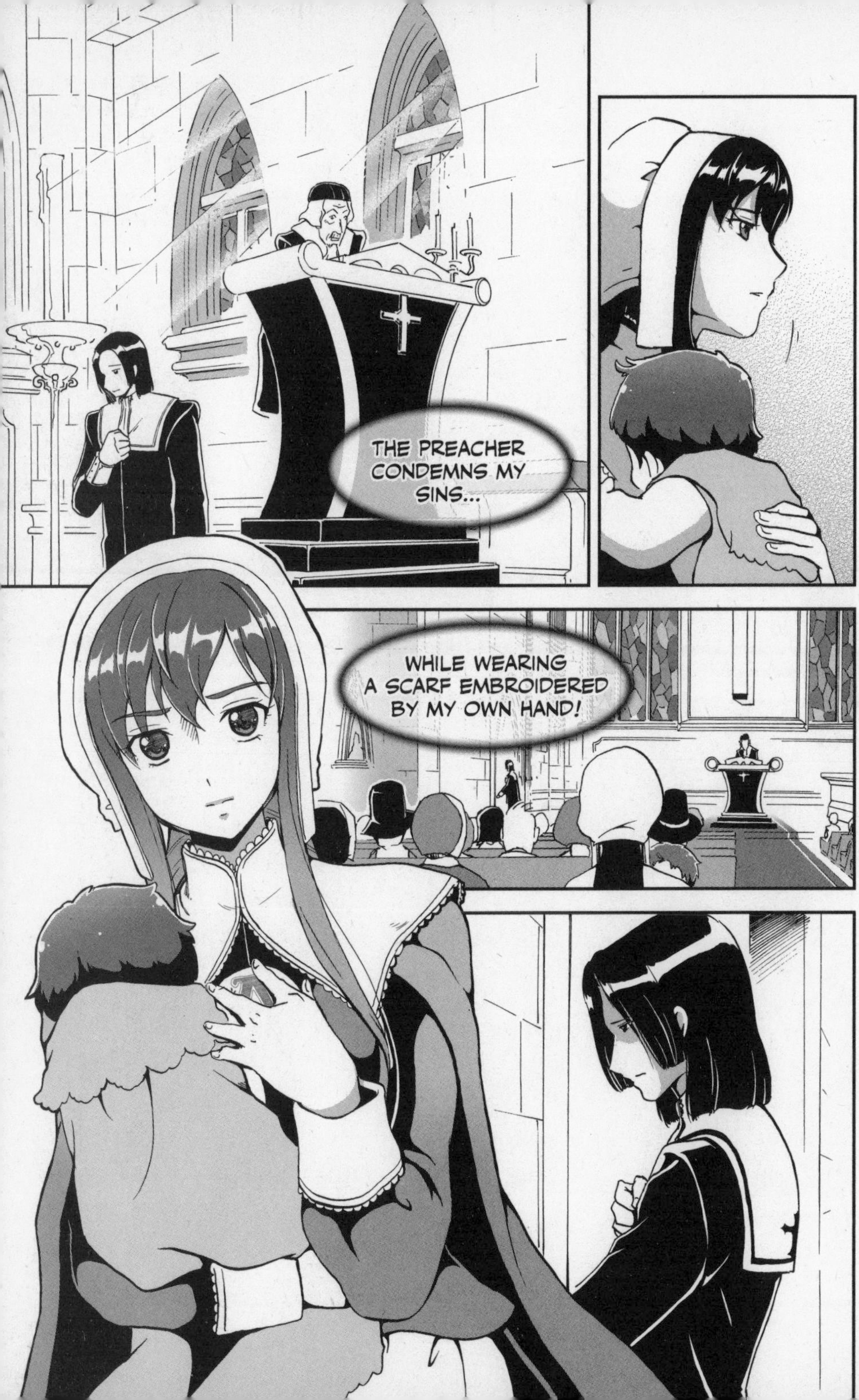
THE PREACHER CONDEMNS MY SINS...
WHILE WEARING A SCARF EMBROIDERED BY MY OWN HAND!

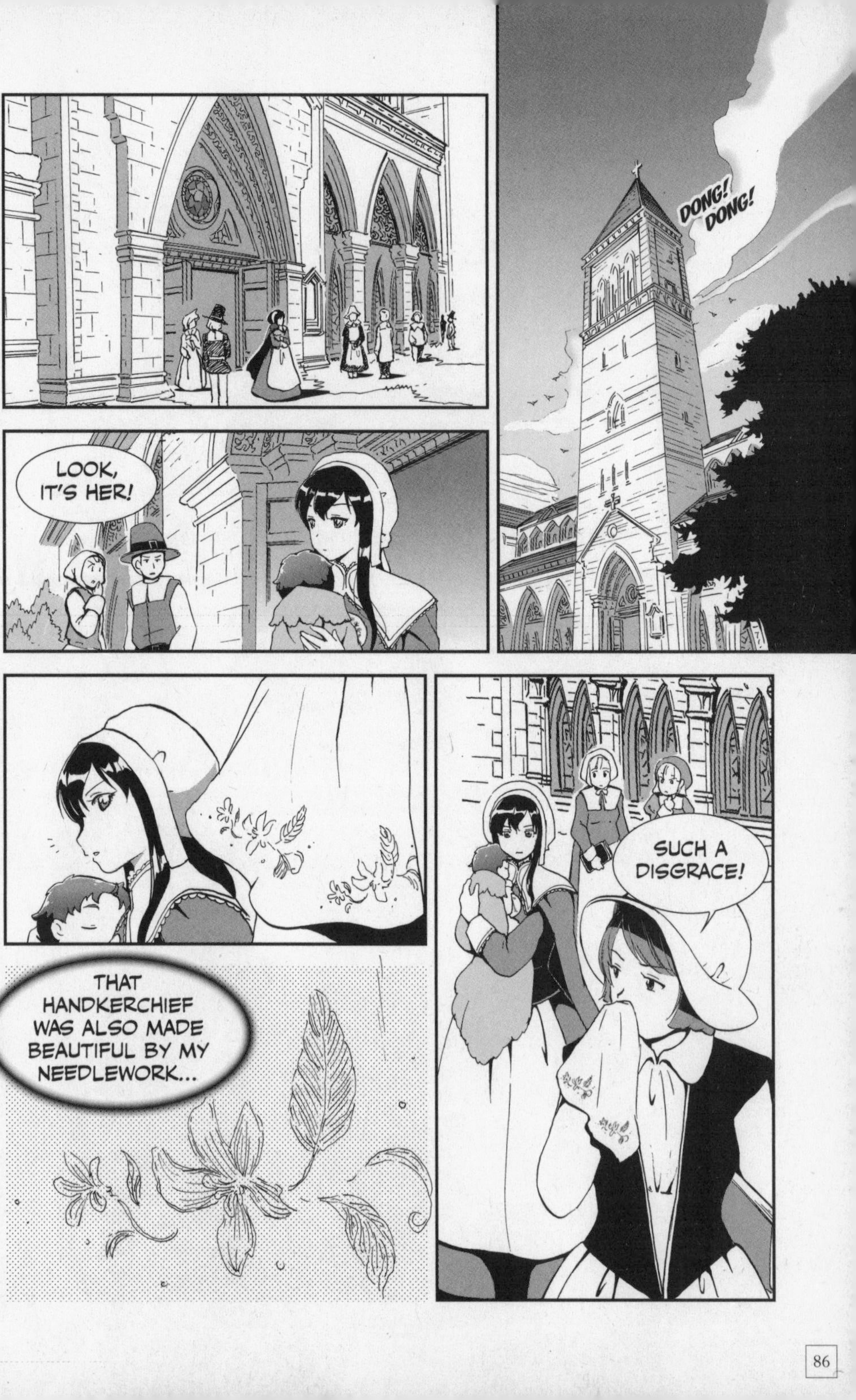
DONG! DONG!
LOOK, IT'S HER!
SUCH A DISGRACE!
THAT HANDKERCHIEF WAS ALSO MADE BEAUTIFUL BY MY NEEDLEWORK...

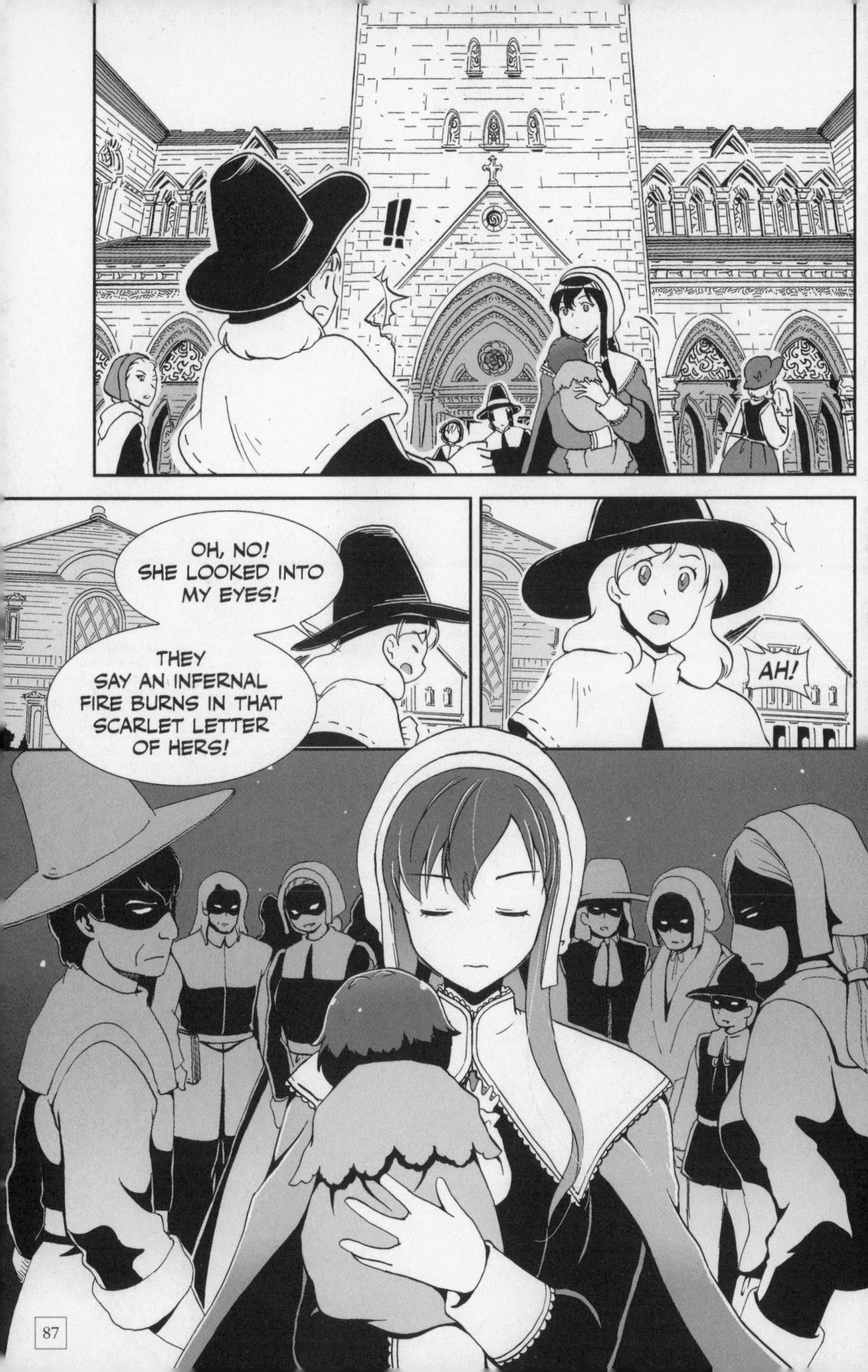
!!
AH!
OH, NO! SHE LOOKED INTO MY EYES!
THEY SAY AN INFERNAL FIRE BURNS IN THAT SCARLET LETTER OF HERS!

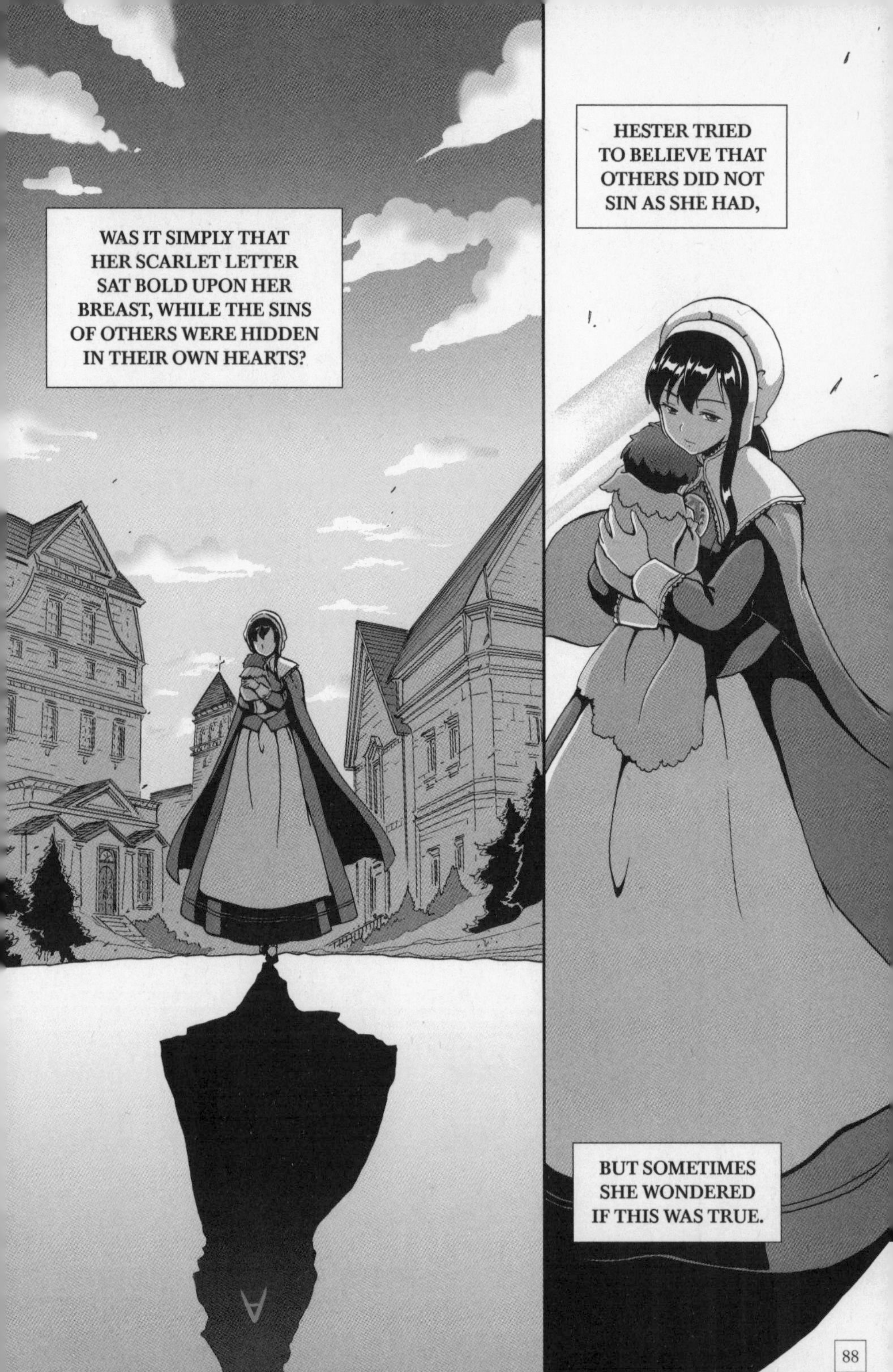
HESTER TRIED TO BELIEVE THAT OTHERS DID NOT SIN AS SHE HAD,
BUT SOMETIMES SHE WONDERED IF THIS WAS TRUE.
WAS IT SIMPLY THAT HER SCARLET LETTER SAT BOLD UPON HER BREAST, WHILE THE SINS OF OTHERS WERE HIDDEN IN THEIR OWN HEARTS?

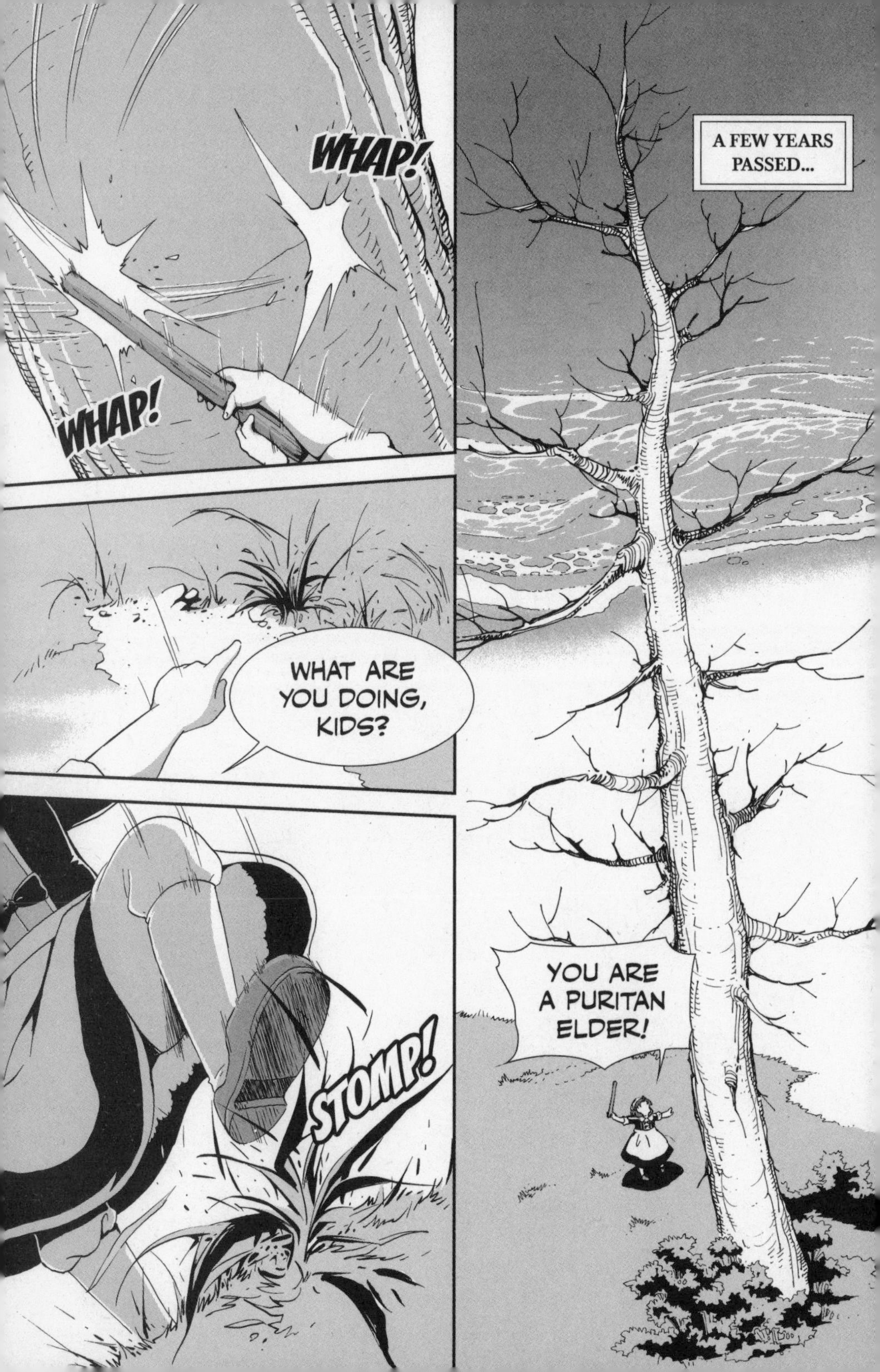
A FEW YEARS PASSED...
YOU ARE A PURITAN ELDER!
WHAP!
WHAP!
WHAT ARE YOU DOING, KIDS?
STOMP!

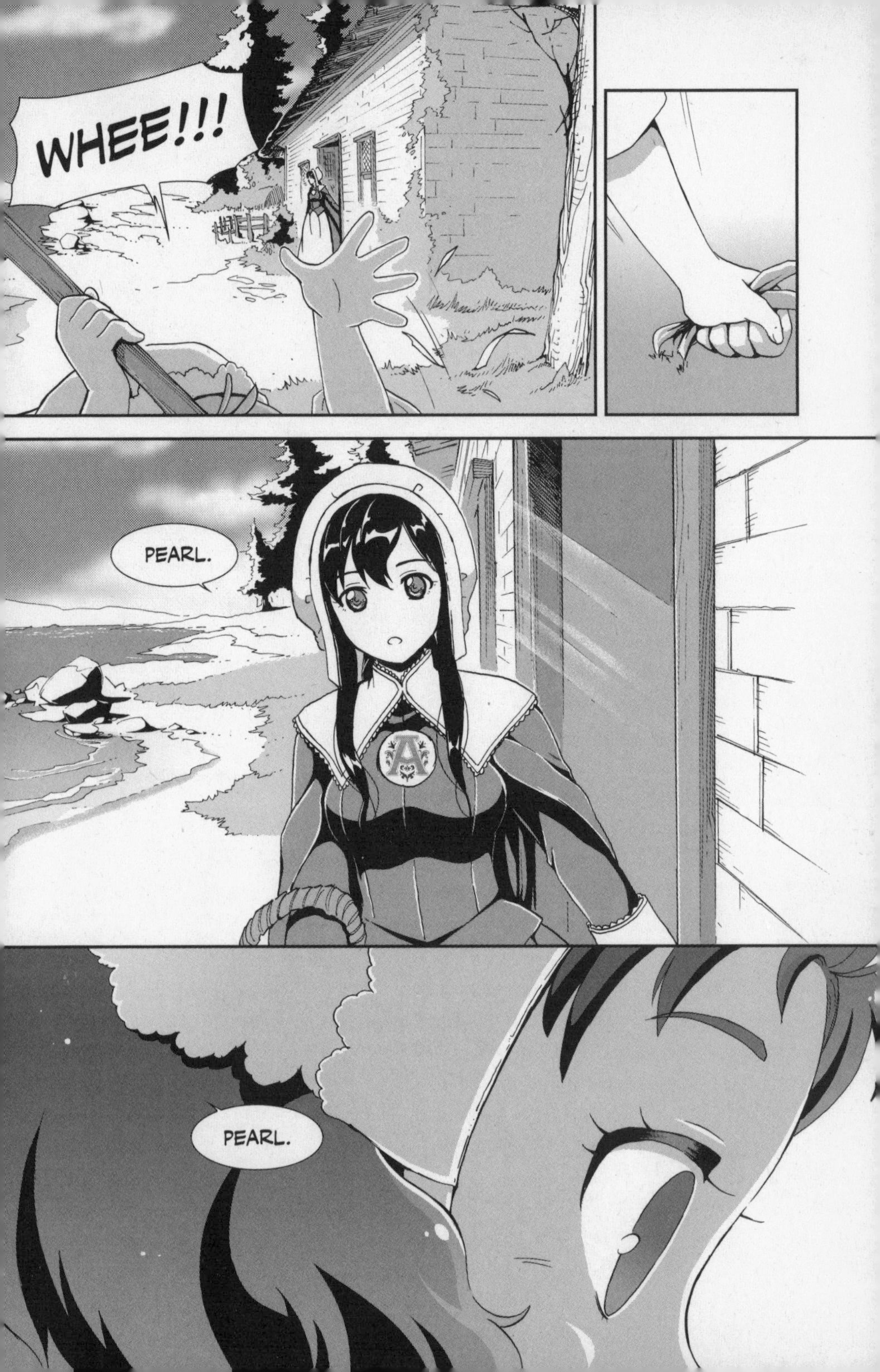
WHEE!!!
PEARL.
PEARL.

Chapter 4

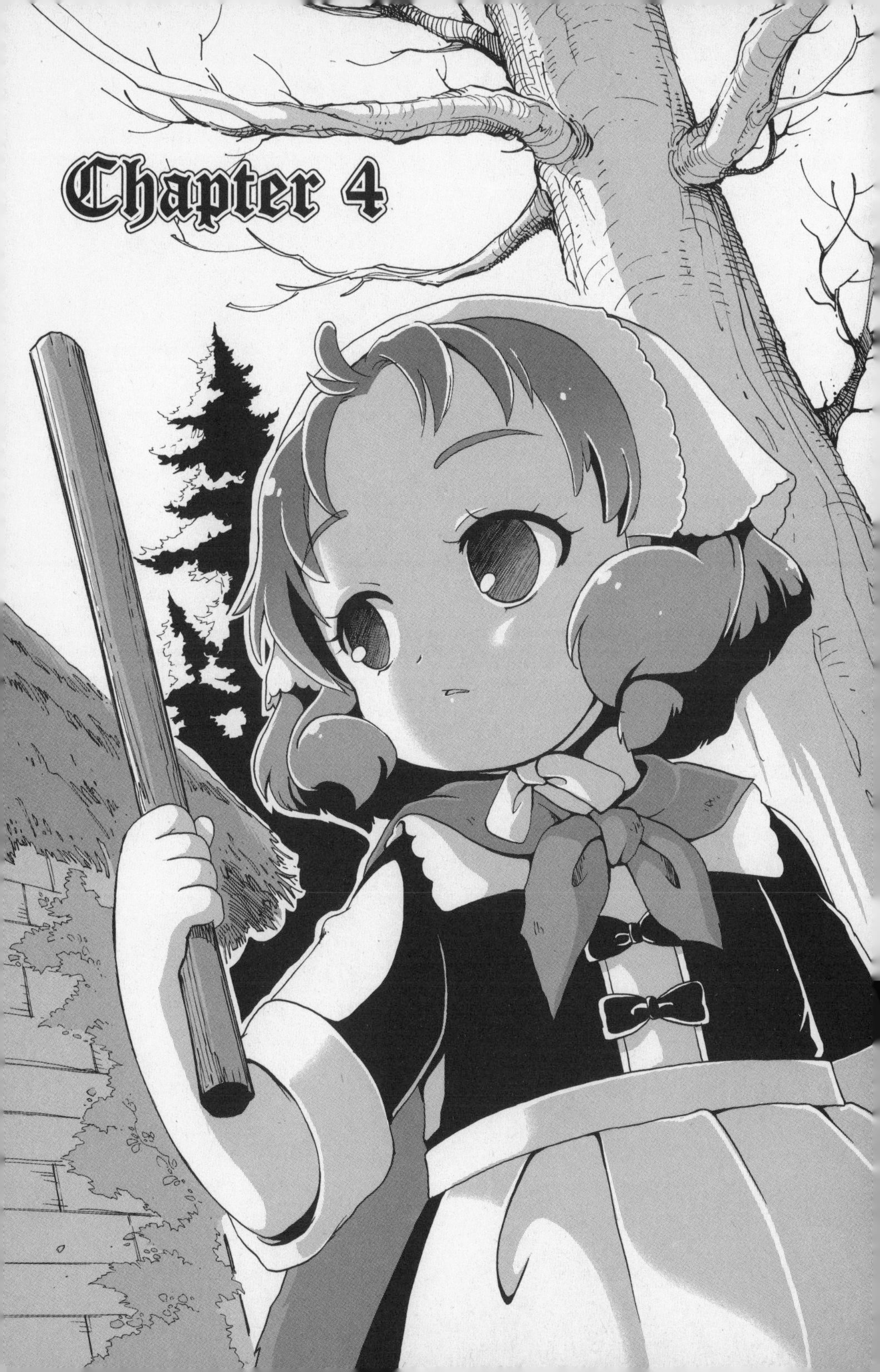

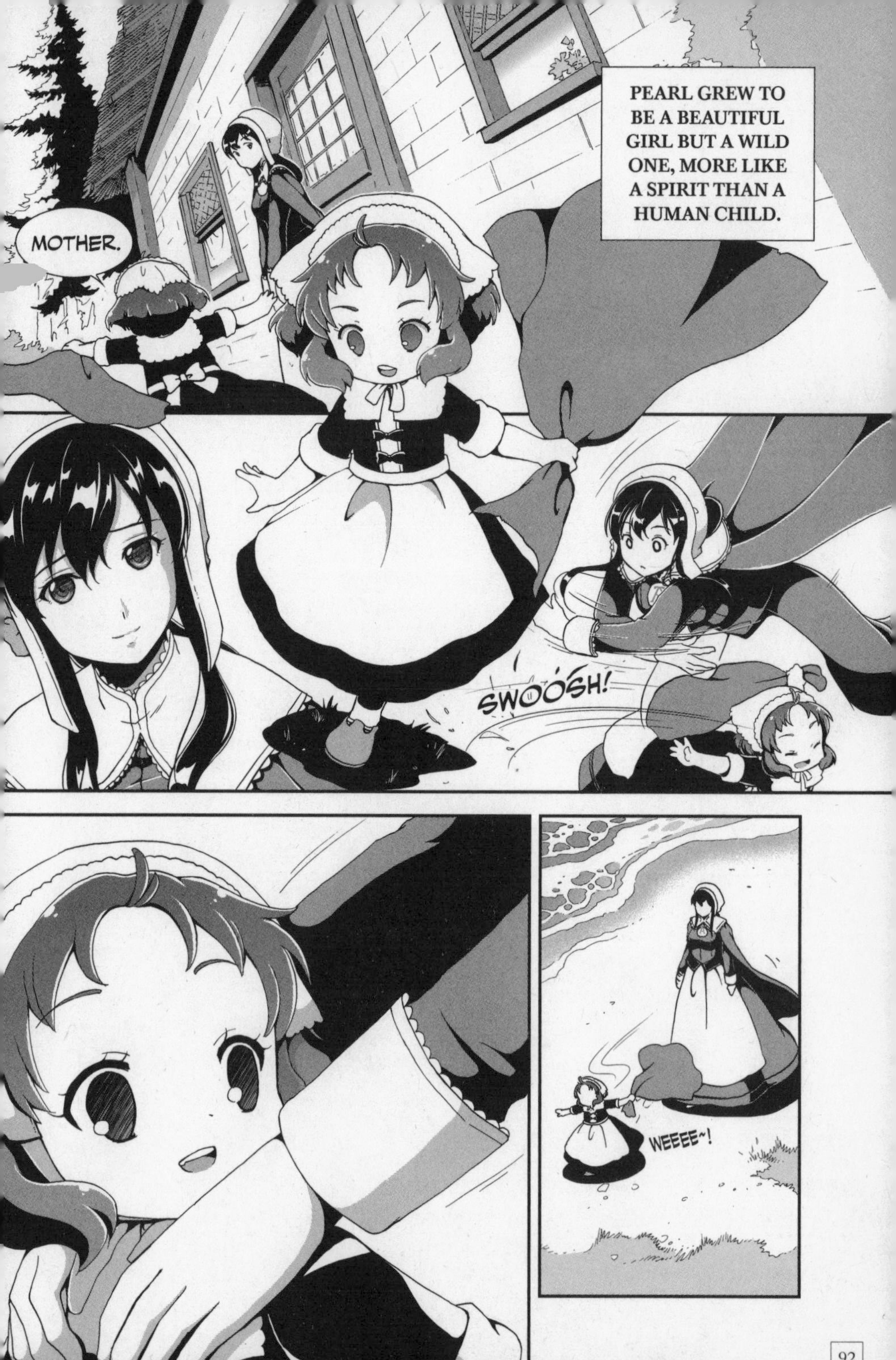
PEARL GREW TO BE A BEAUTIFUL GIRL BUT A WILD ONE, MORE LIKE A SPIRIT THAN A HUMAN CHILD.
MOTHER.
SWOOSH!
WEEEE~!

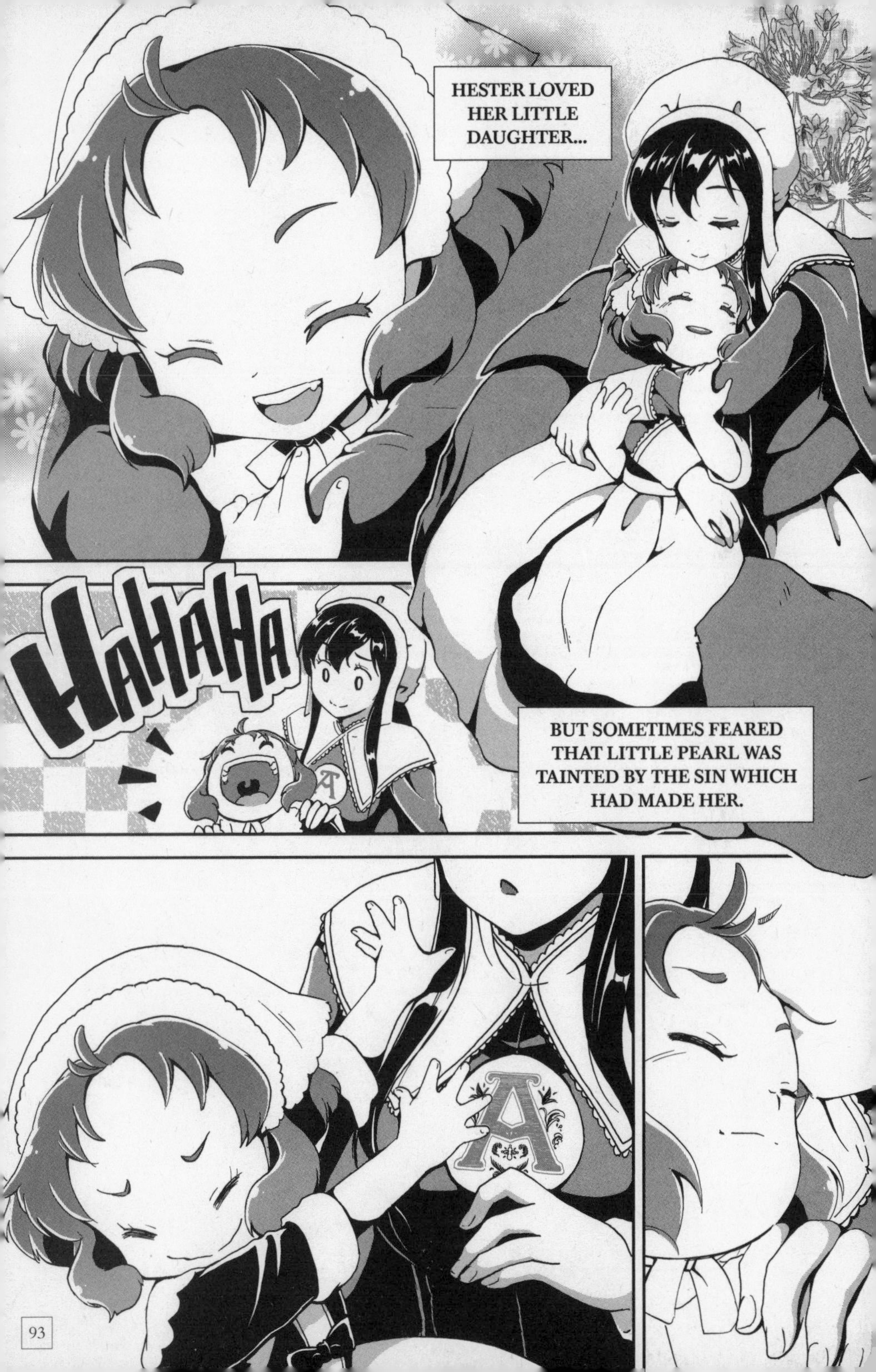
HESTER LOVED HER LITTLE DAUGHTER...
BUT SOMETIMES FEARED THAT LITTLE PEARL WAS TAINTED BY THE SIN WHICH HAD MADE HER.
HAHAHA

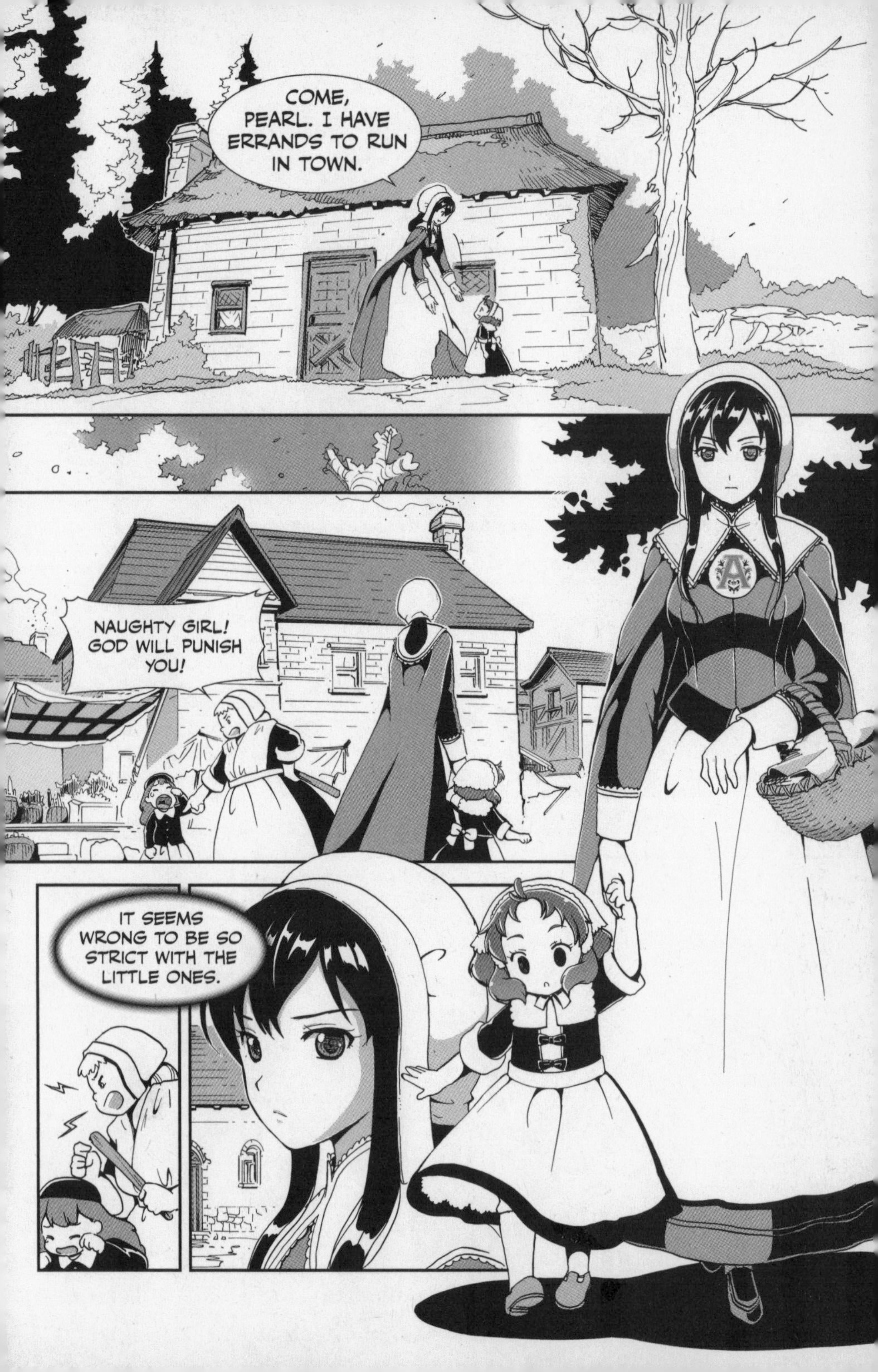
COME, PEARL. I HAVE ERRANDS TO RUN IN TOWN.
NAUGHTY GIRL! GOD WILL PUNISH YOU!
IT SEEMS WRONG TO BE SO STRICT WITH THE LITTLE ONES.

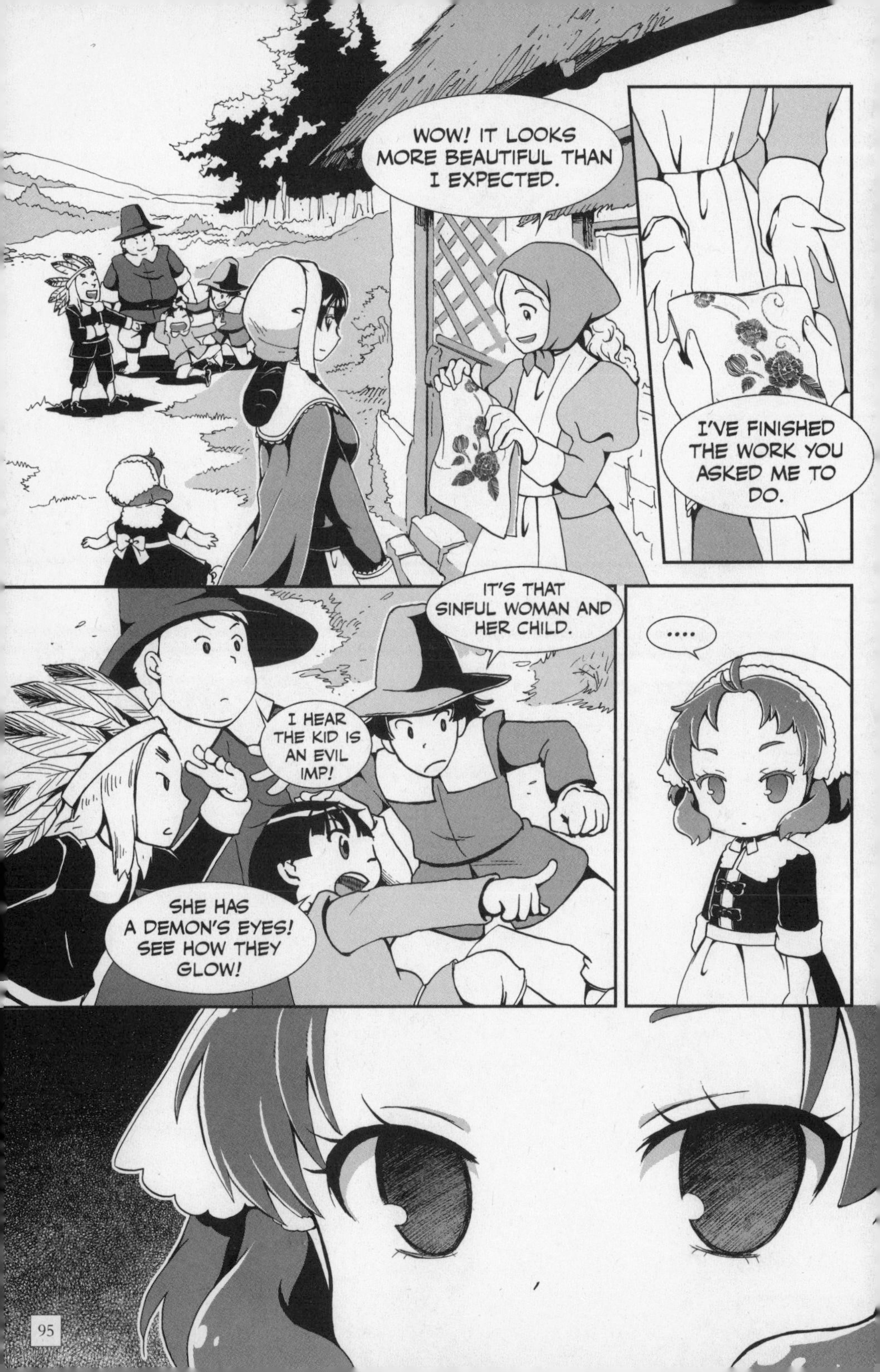
I'VE FINISHED THE WORK YOU ASKED ME TO DO.
WOW! IT LOOKS MORE BEAUTIFUL THAN I EXPECTED.
....
IT'S THAT SINFUL WOMAN AND HER CHILD.
I HEAR THE KID IS AN EVIL IMP!
SHE HAS A DEMON'S EYES! SEE HOW THEY GLOW!

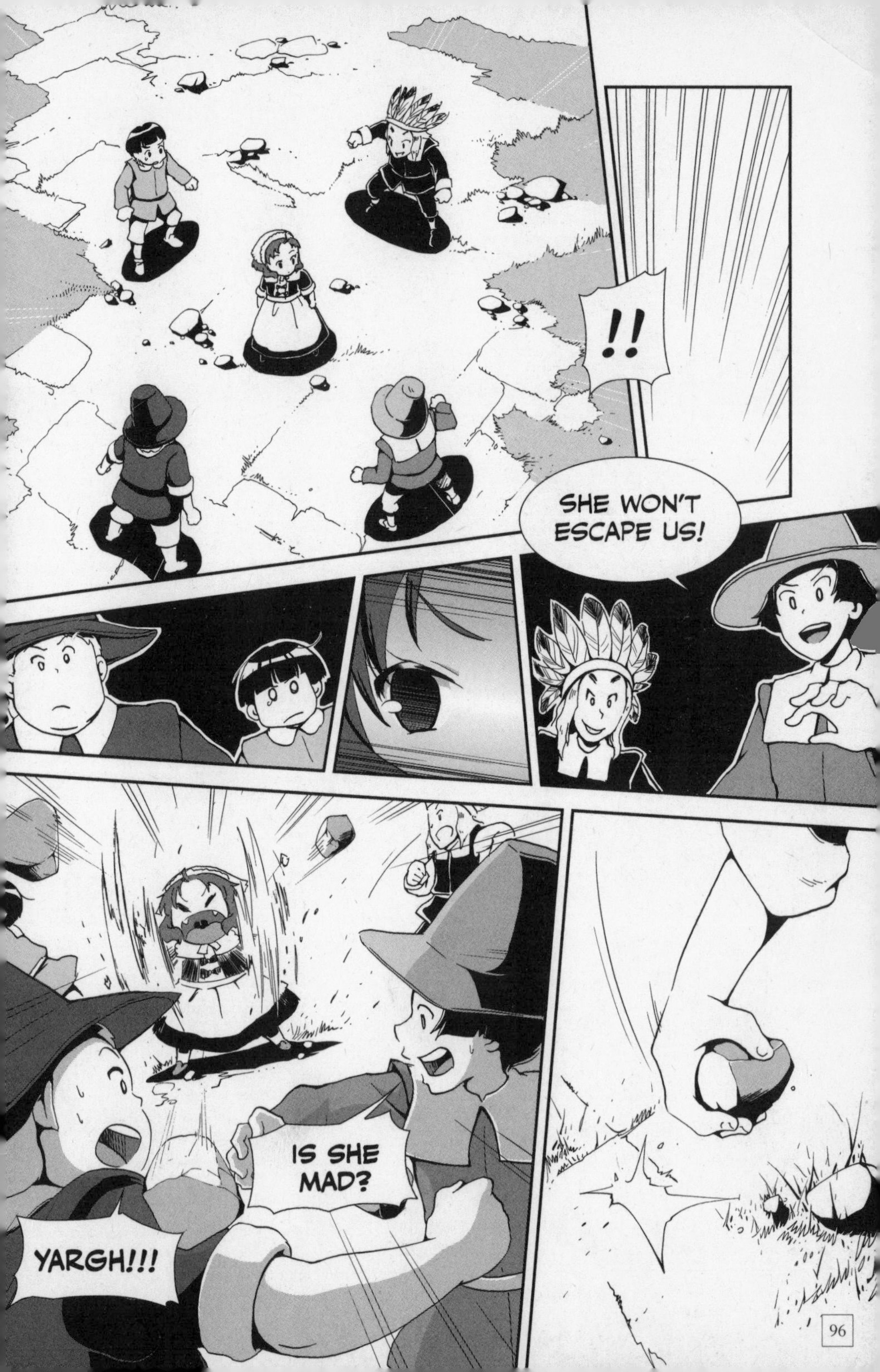
!!
SHE WON'T ESCAPE US!
IS SHE MAD?
YARGH!!!

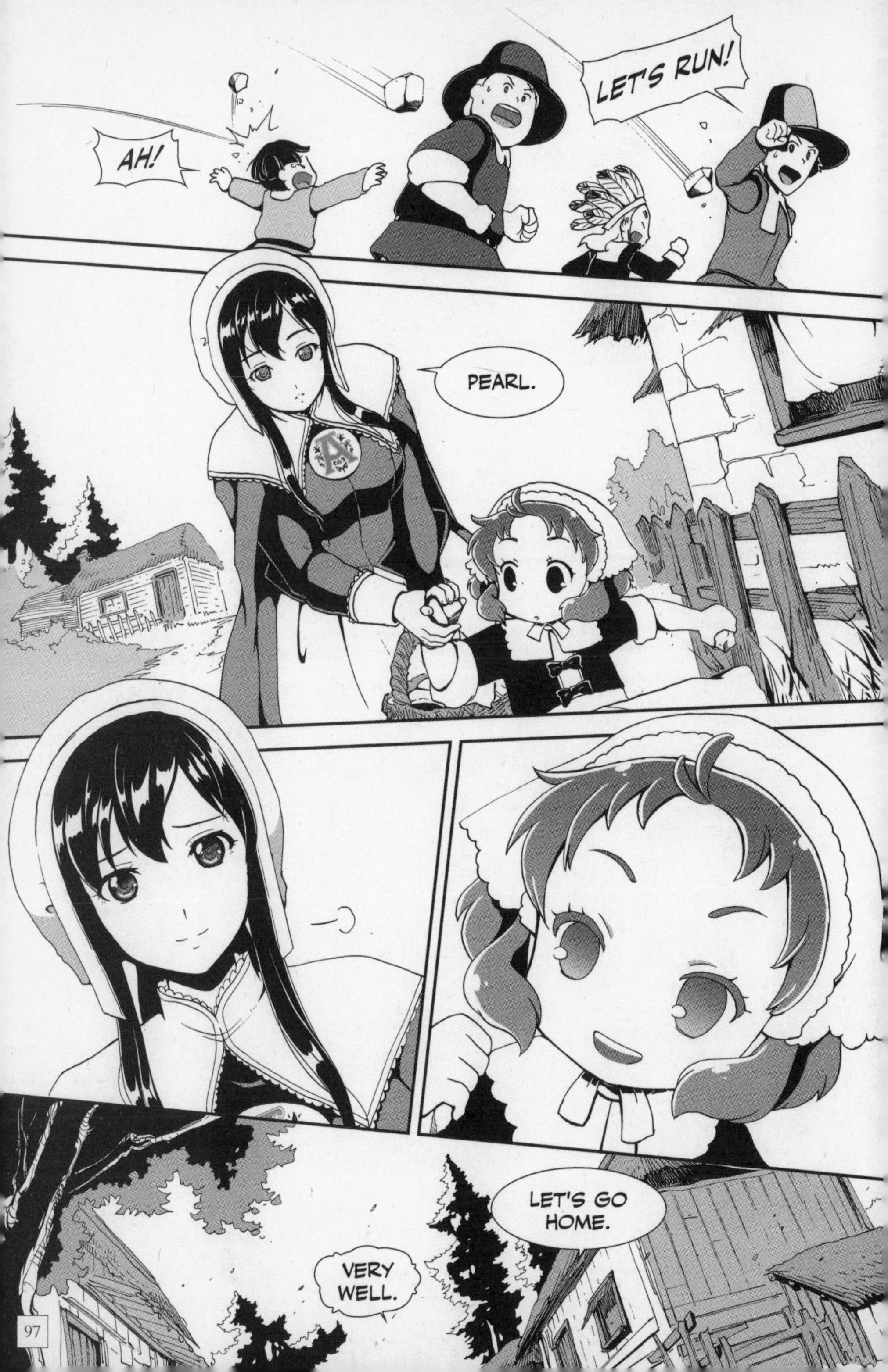
LET'S RUN!
AH!
PEARL.
LET'S GO HOME.
VERY WELL.

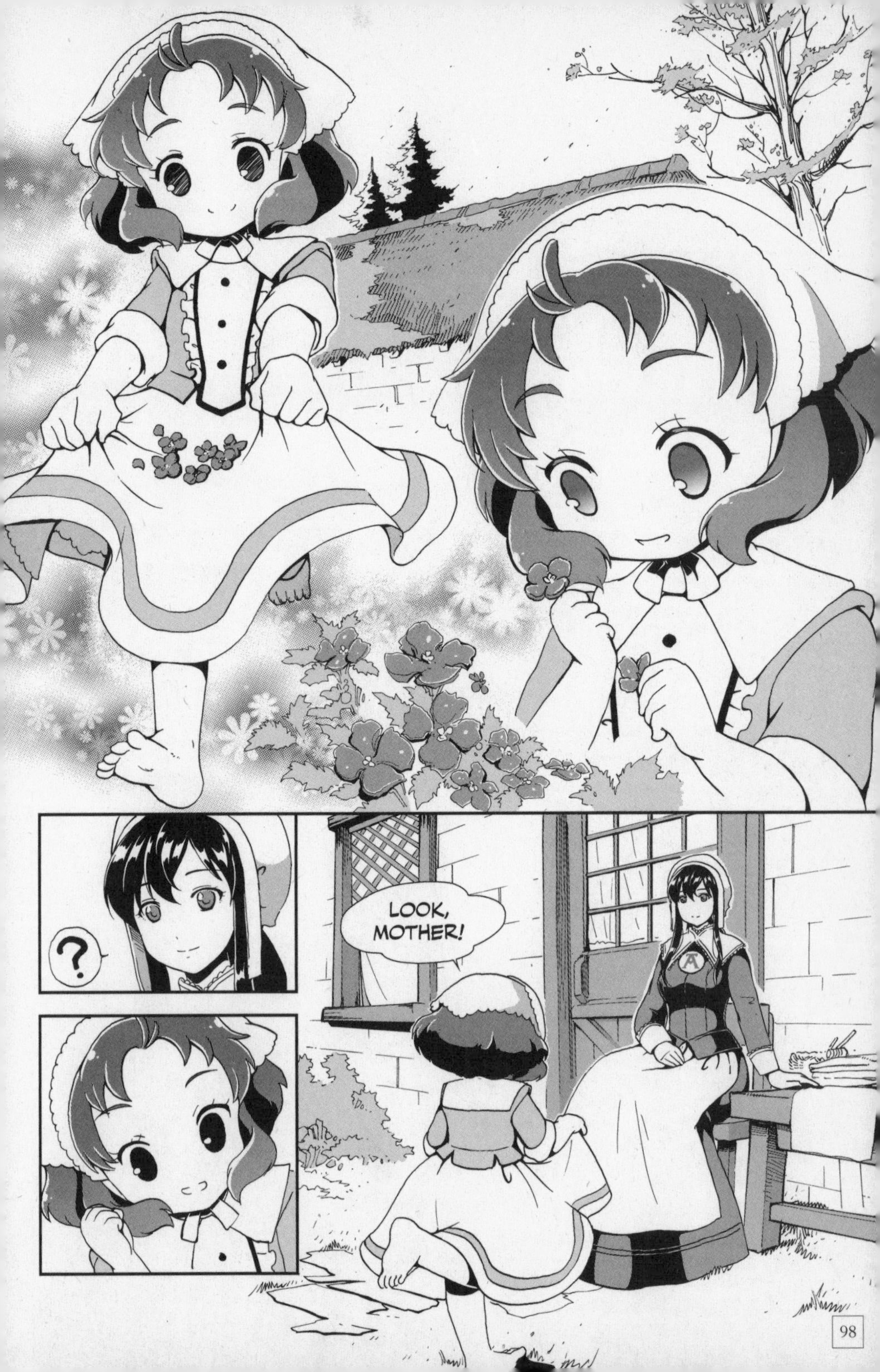
LOOK, MOTHER!
?

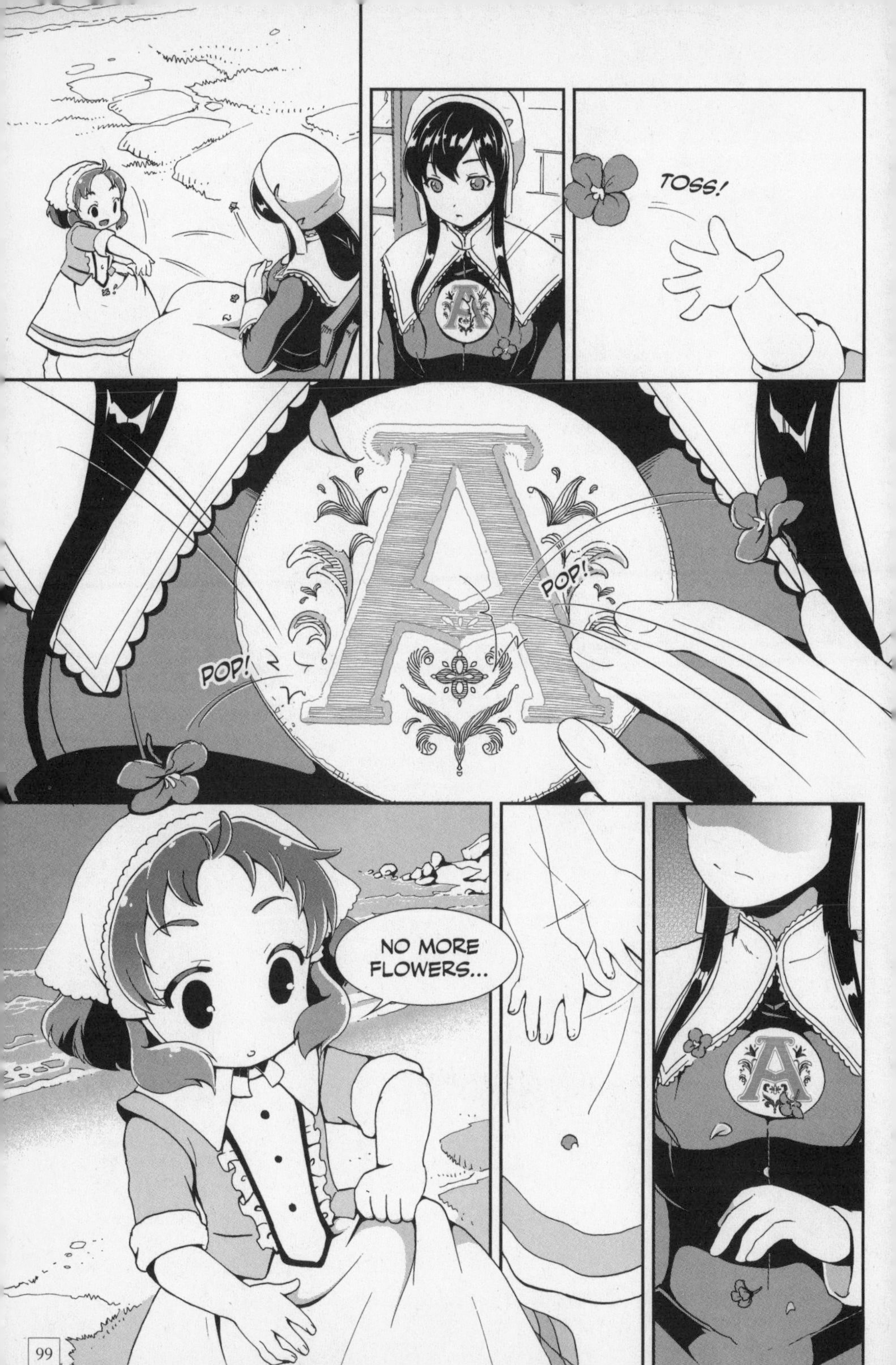
TOSS!
POP!
POP!
NO MORE FLOWERS...

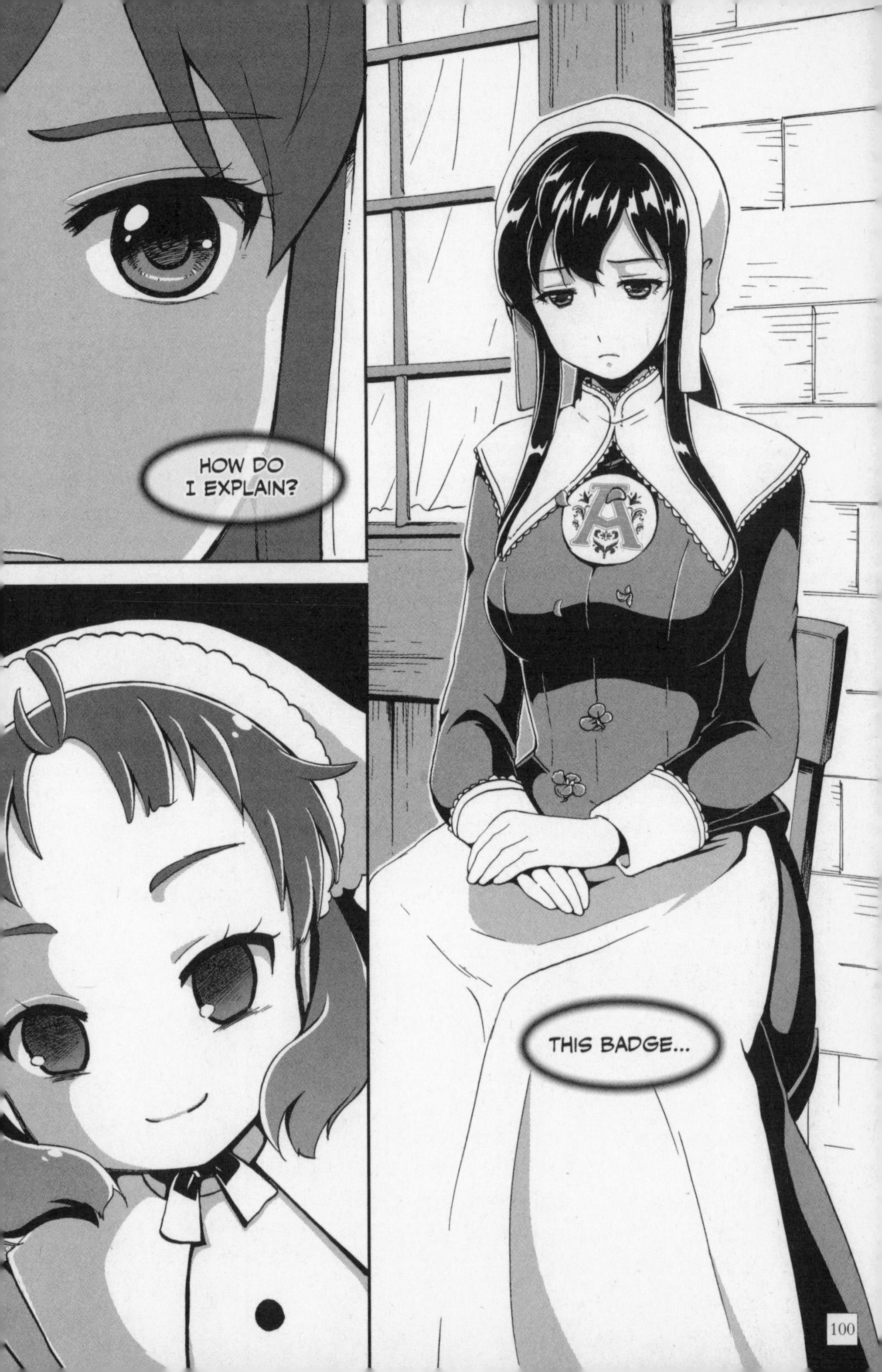
THIS BADGE...
HOW DO I EXPLAIN?

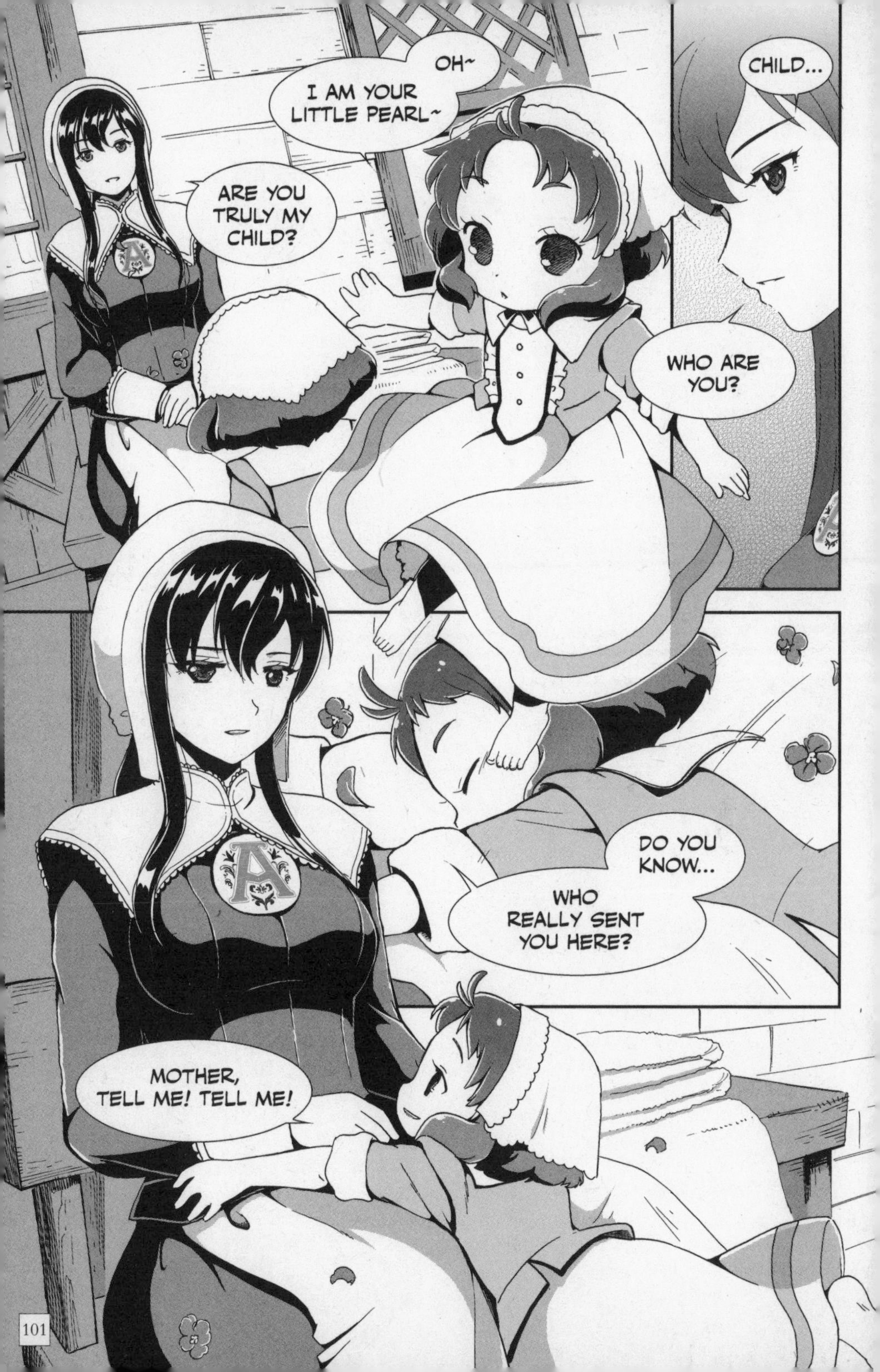
CHILD...
WHO ARE YOU?
OH~
I AM YOUR LITTLE PEARL~
ARE YOU TRULY MY CHILD?
DO YOU KNOW...
WHO REALLY SENT YOU HERE?
MOTHER, TELL ME! TELL ME!

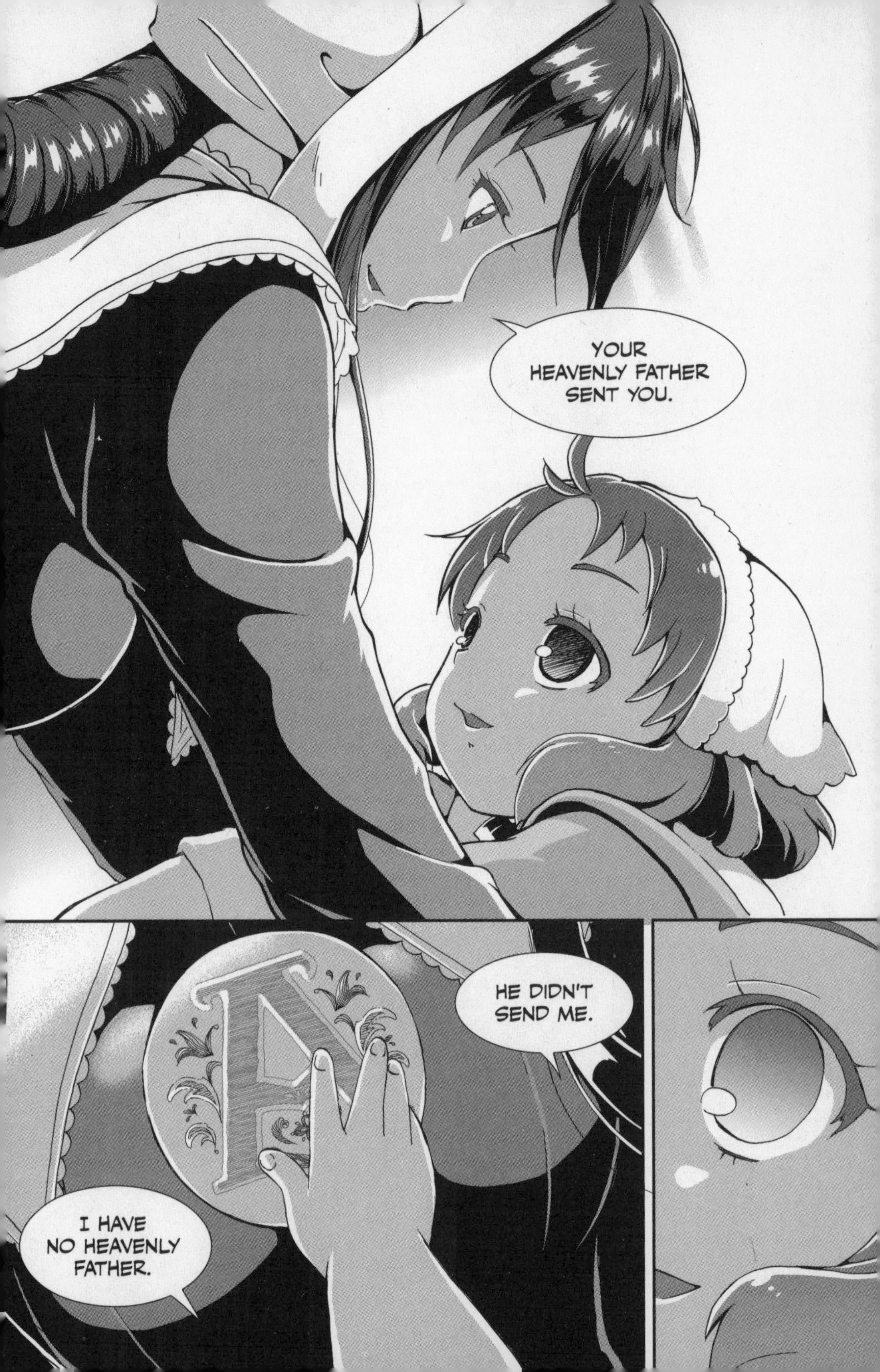
YOUR HEAVENLY FATHER SENT YOU.
HE DIDN'T SEND ME.
I HAVE NO HEAVENLY FATHER.

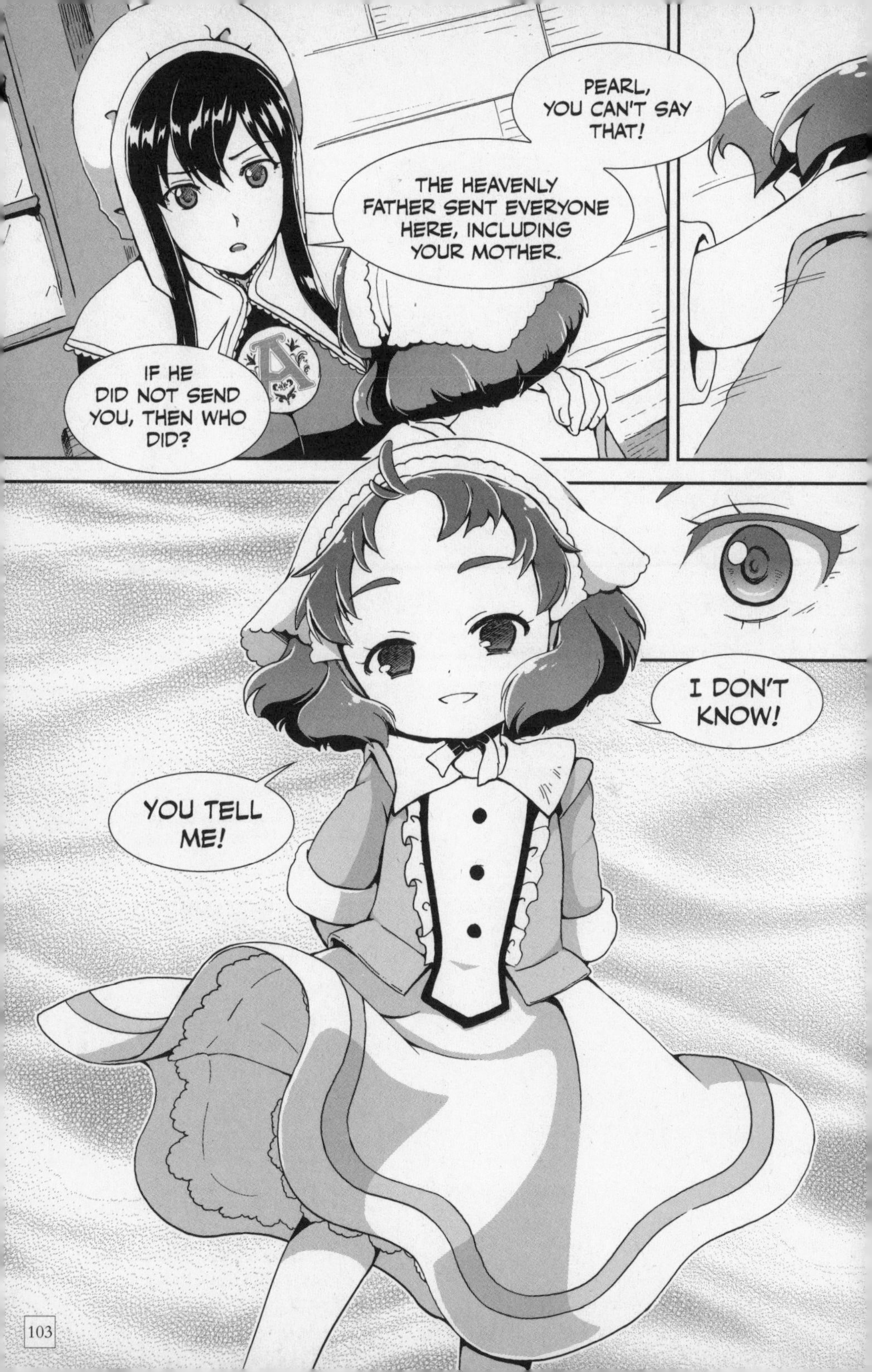
PEARL, YOU CAN'T SAY THAT!
THE HEAVENLY FATHER SENT EVERYONE HERE, INCLUDING YOUR MOTHER.
IF HE DID NOT SEND YOU, THEN WHO DID?
I DON'T KNOW!
YOU TELL ME!

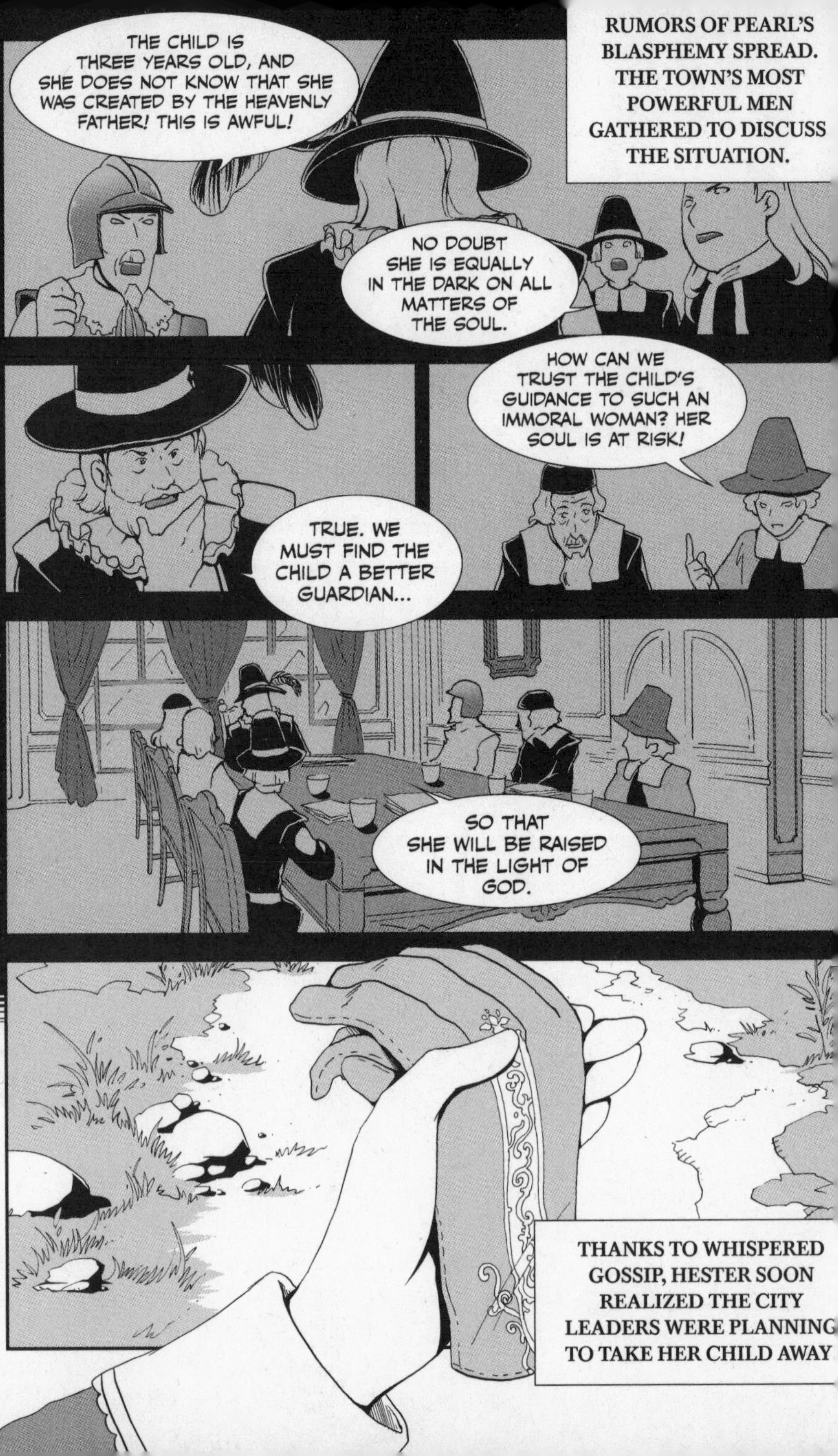
RUMORS OF PEARL'S BLASPHEMY SPREAD. THE TOWN'S MOST POWERFUL MEN GATHERED TO DISCUSS THE SITUATION.
THE CHILD IS THREE YEARS OLD, AND SHE DOES NOT KNOW THAT SHE WAS CREATED BY THE HEAVENLY FATHER! THIS IS AWFUL!
NO DOUBT SHE IS EQUALLY IN THE DARK ON ALL MATTERS OF THE SOUL.
HOW CAN WE TRUST THE CHILD'S GUIDANCE TO SUCH AN IMMORAL WOMAN? HER SOUL IS AT RISK!
TRUE. WE MUST FIND THE CHILD A BETTER GUARDIAN...
SO THAT SHE WILL BE RAISED IN THE LIGHT OF GOD.
THANKS TO WHISPERED GOSSIP, HESTER SOON REALIZED THE CITY LEADERS WERE PLANNING TO TAKE HER CHILD AWAY

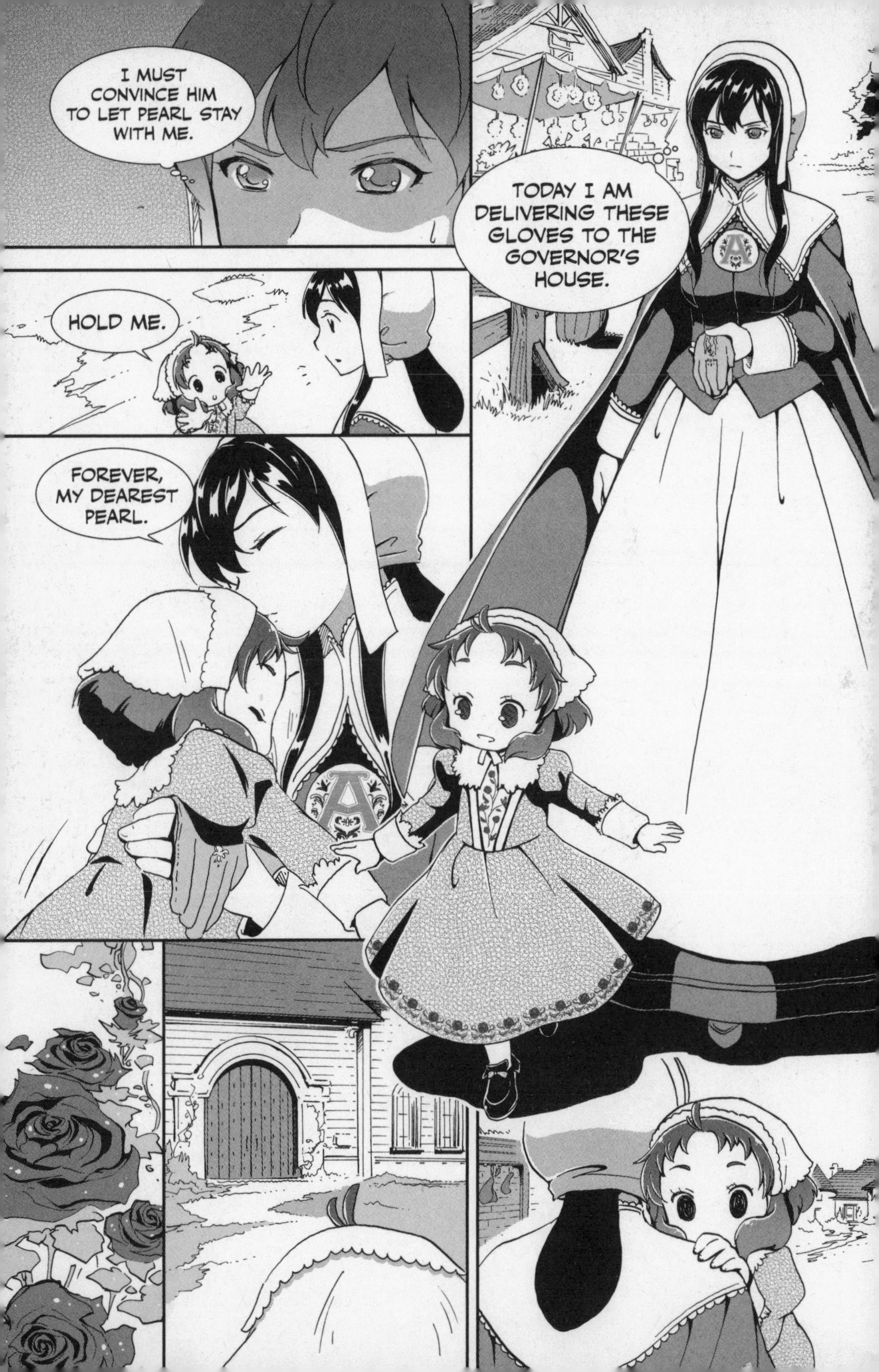
TODAY I AM DELIVERING THESE GLOVES TO THE GOVERNOR'S HOUSE.
I MUST CONVINCE HIM TO LET PEARL STAY WITH ME.
HOLD ME.
FOREVER, MY DEAREST PEARL.

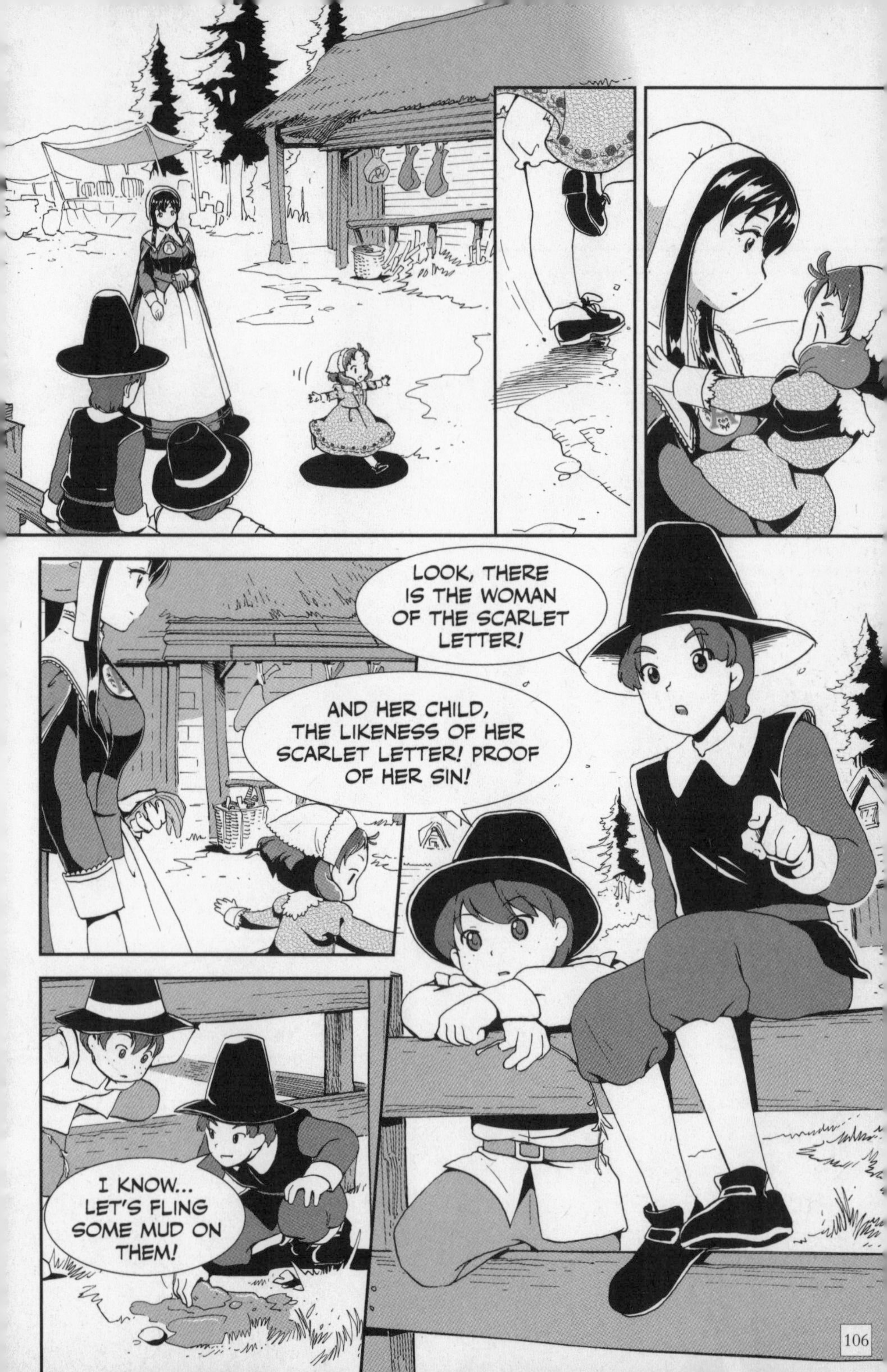
LOOK, THERE IS THE WOMAN OF THE SCARLET LETTER!
AND HER CHILD, THE LIKENESS OF HER SCARLET LETTER! PROOF OF HER SIN!
I KNOW... LET'S FLING SOME MUD ON THEM!

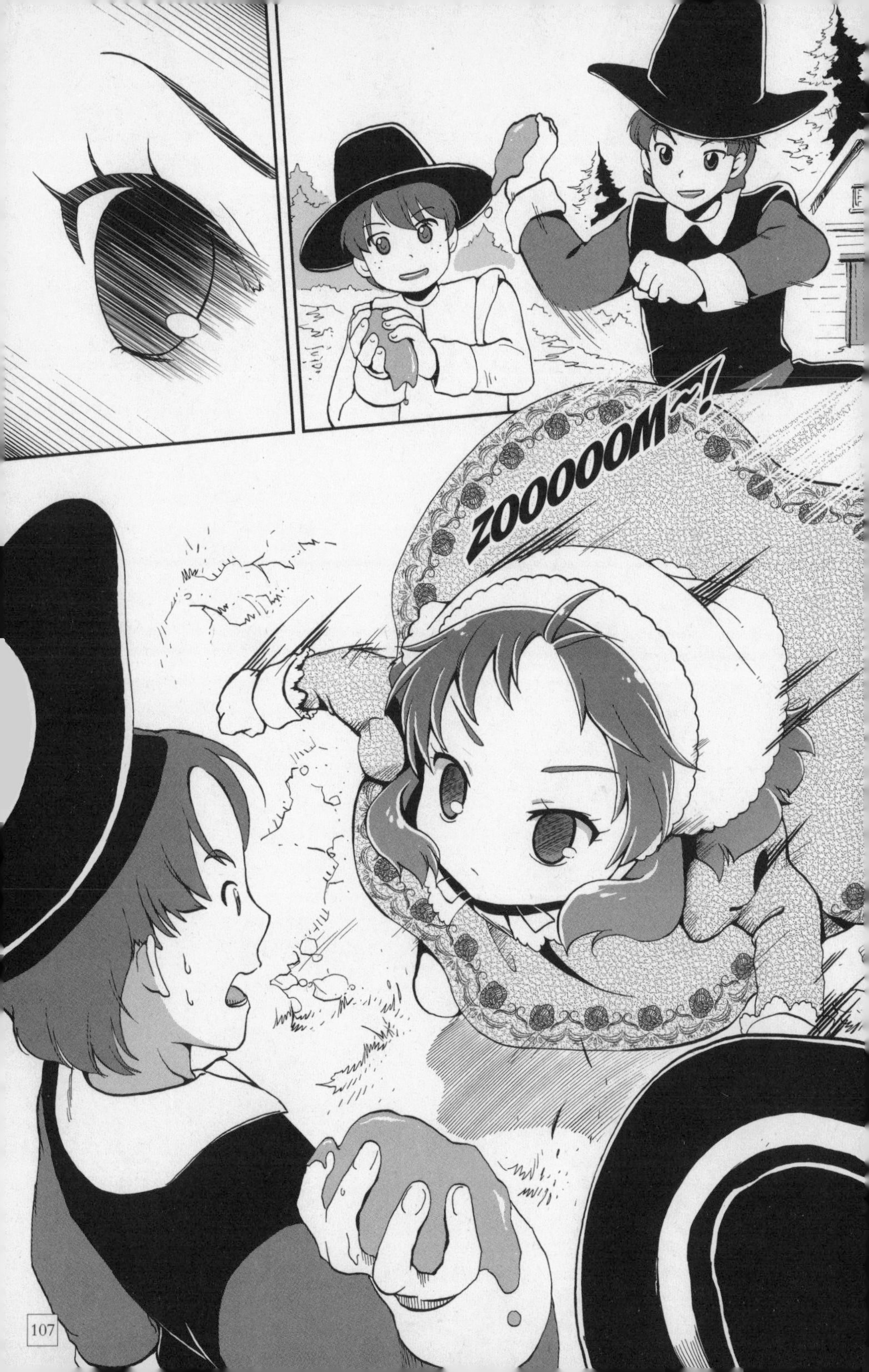
ZOOOOOM~!

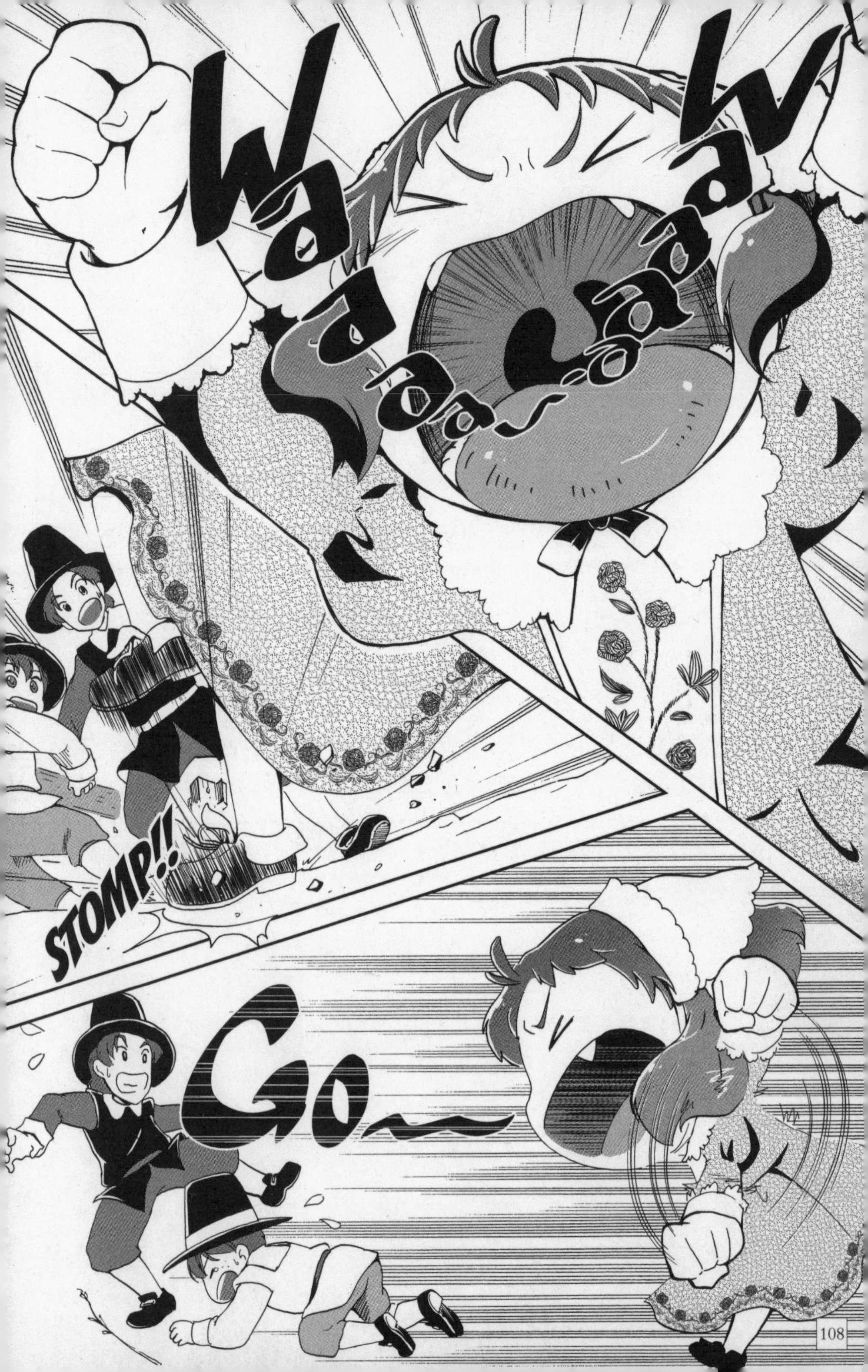
Waaaa~
Waaaa~
STOMP!!
Go~

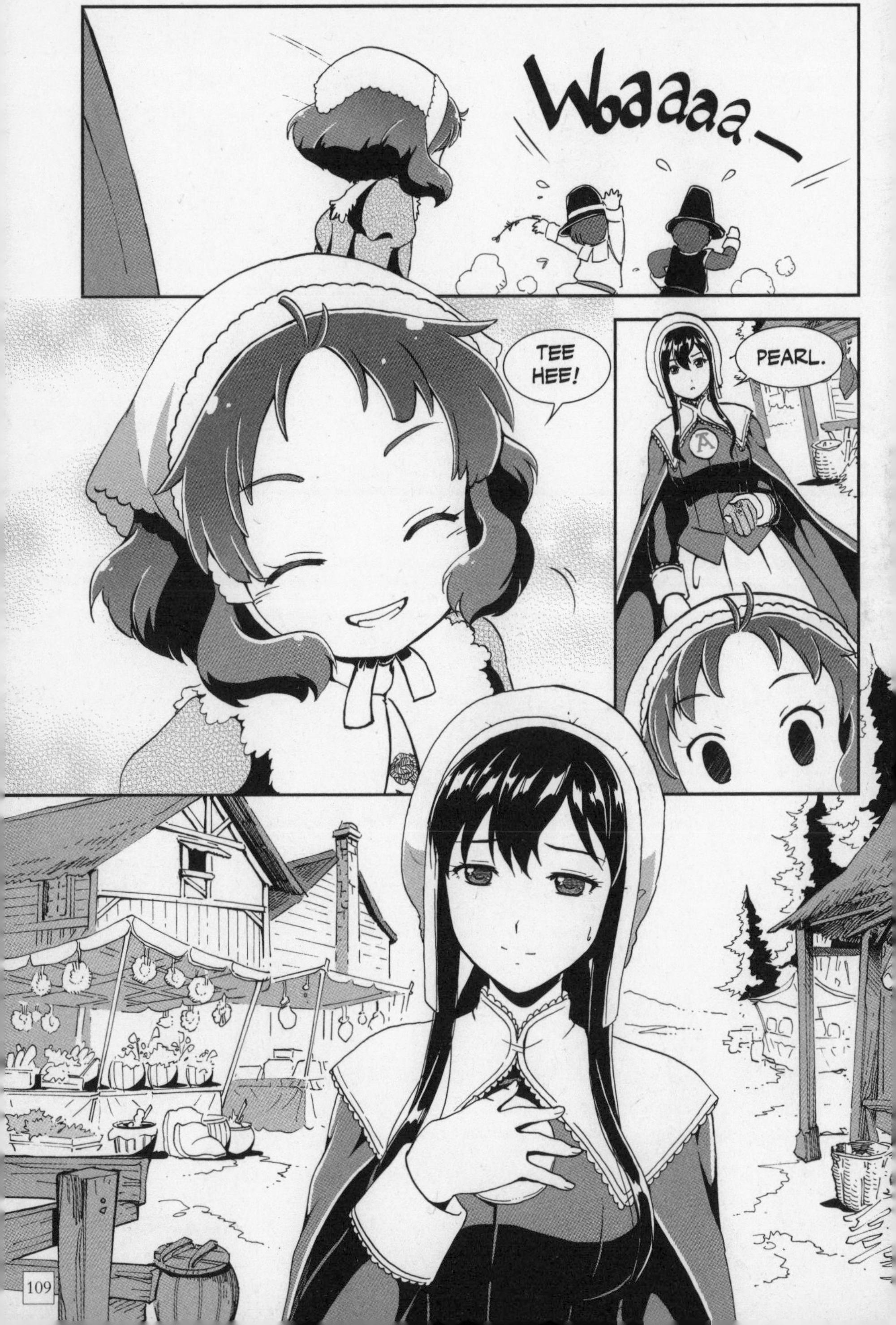
Waaaaa—
PEARL.
TEE HEE!

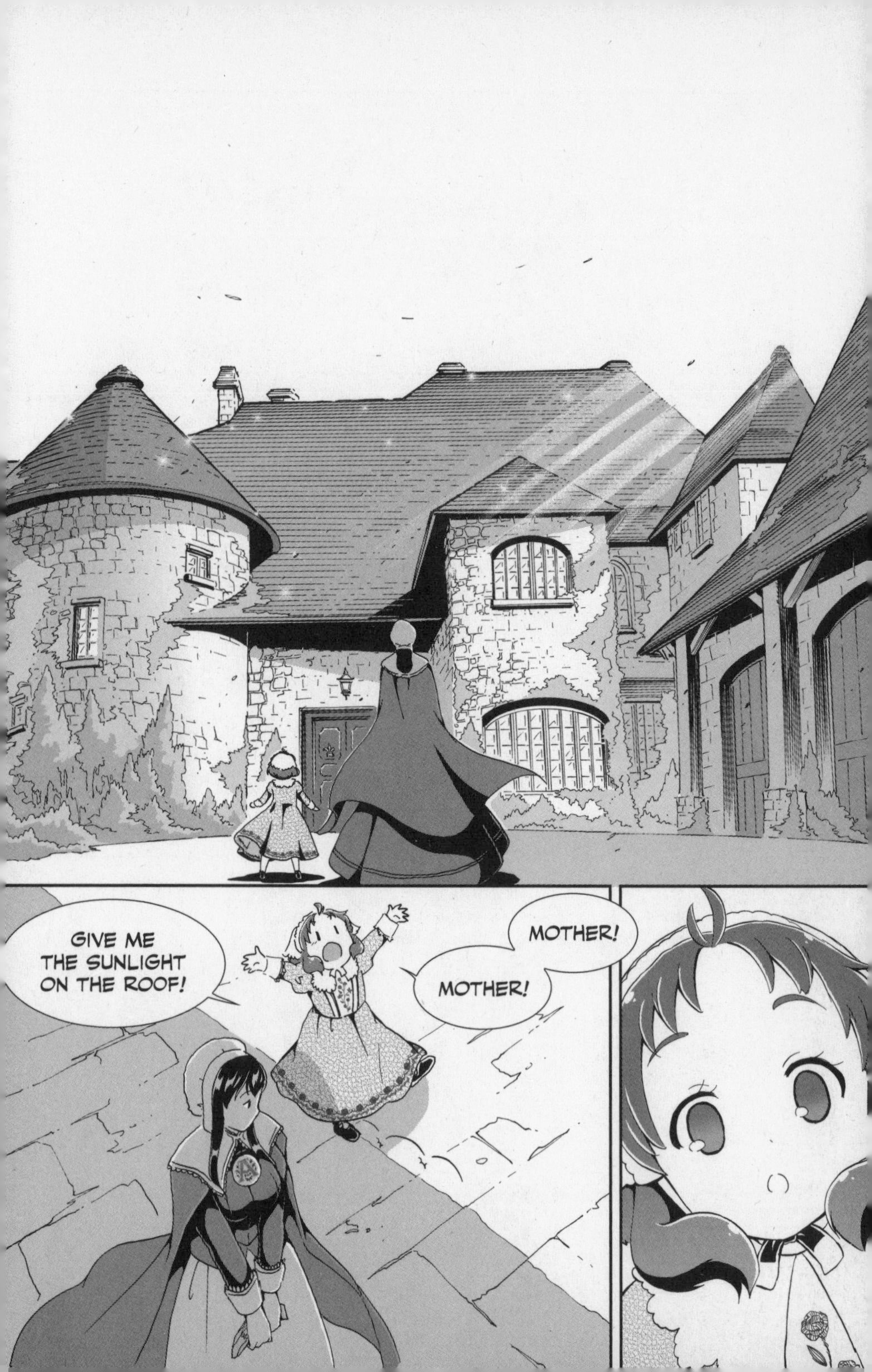
MOTHER!
MOTHER!
GIVE ME THE SUNLIGHT ON THE ROOF!

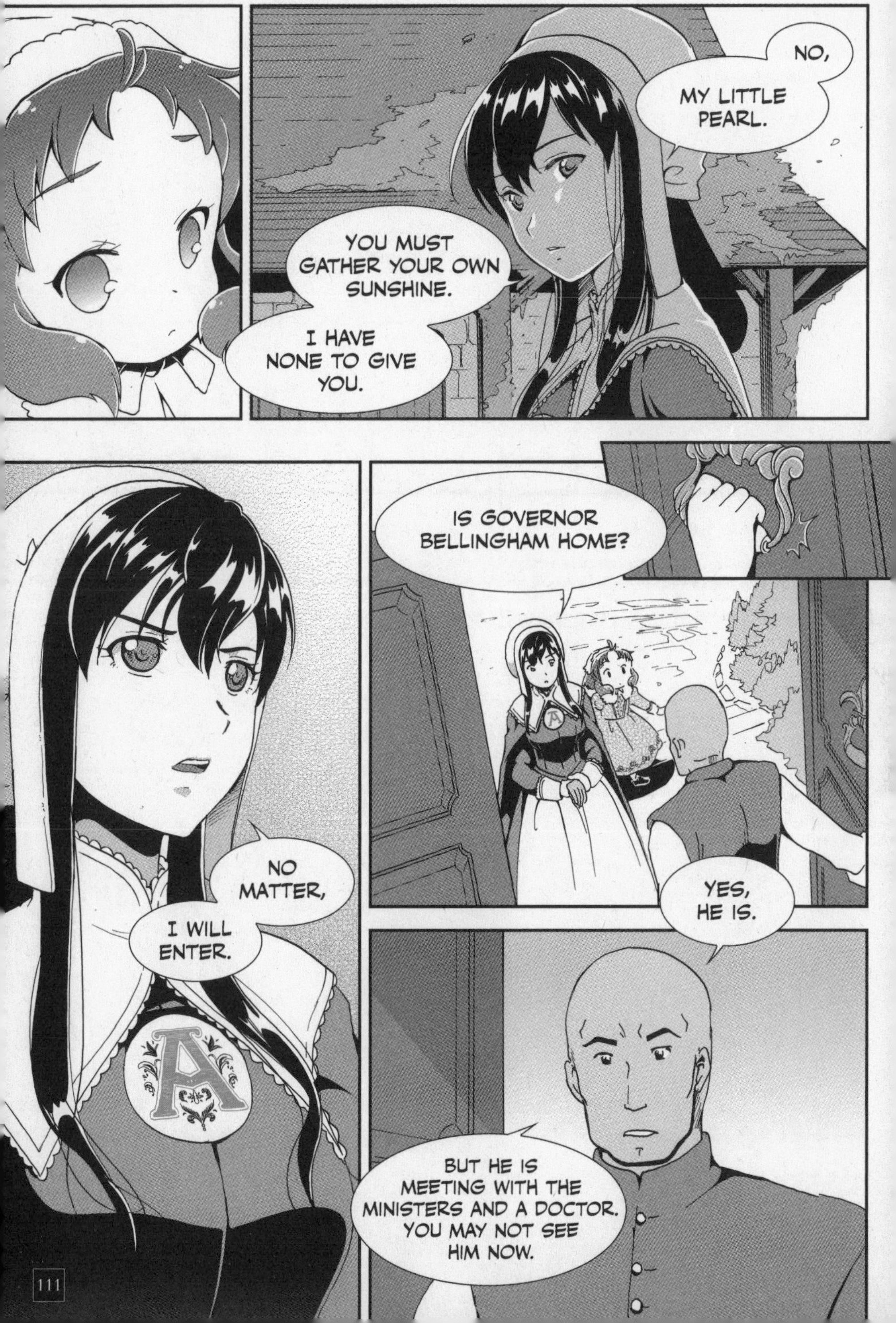
NO,
MY LITTLE PEARL.
YOU MUST GATHER YOUR OWN SUNSHINE.
I HAVE NONE TO GIVE YOU.
IS GOVERNOR BELLINGHAM HOME?
YES, HE IS.
BUT HE IS MEETING WITH THE MINISTERS AND A DOCTOR. YOU MAY NOT SEE HIM NOW.
NO MATTER,
I WILL ENTER.

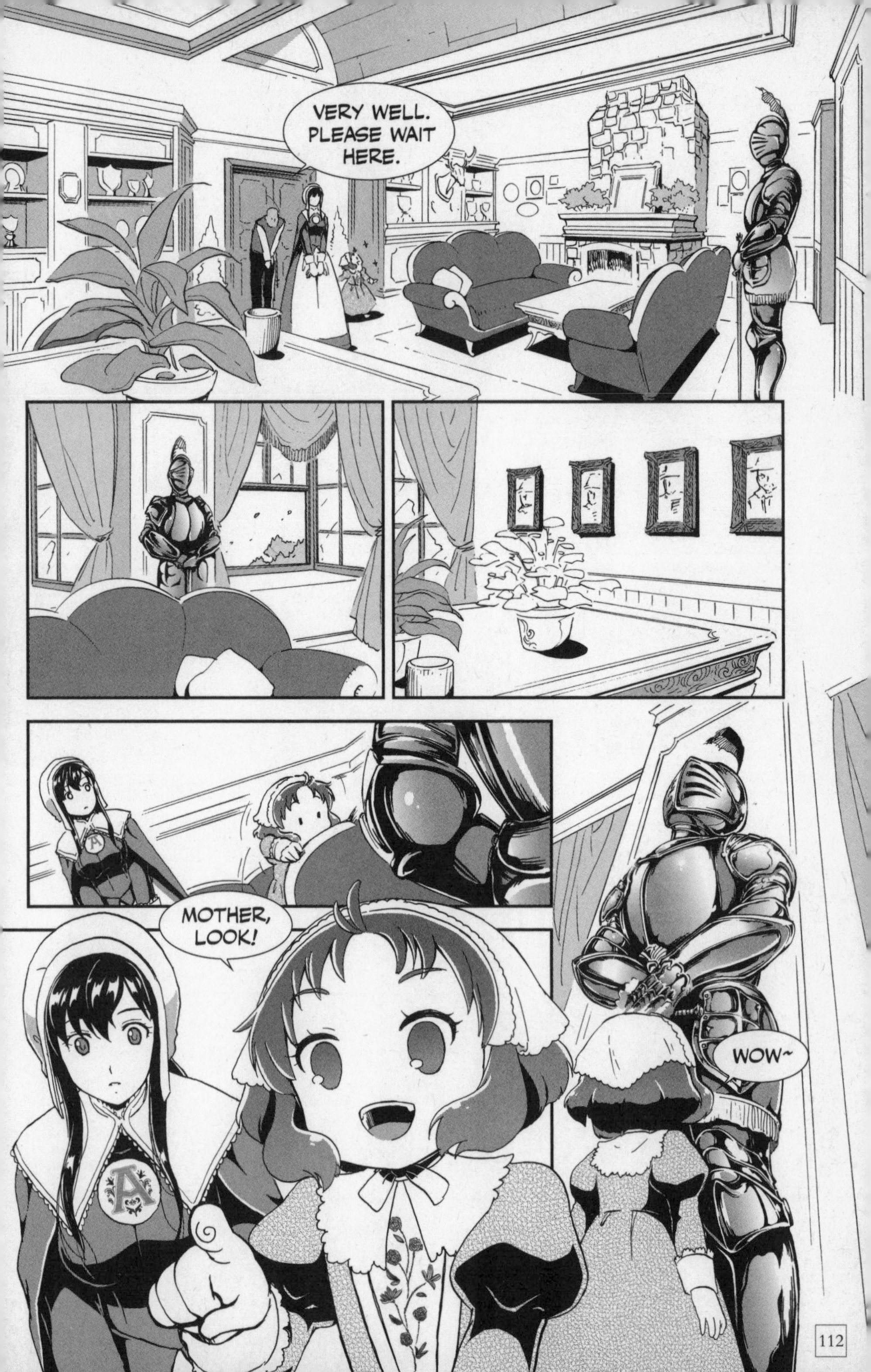
VERY WELL. PLEASE WAIT HERE.
WOW~
MOTHER, LOOK!

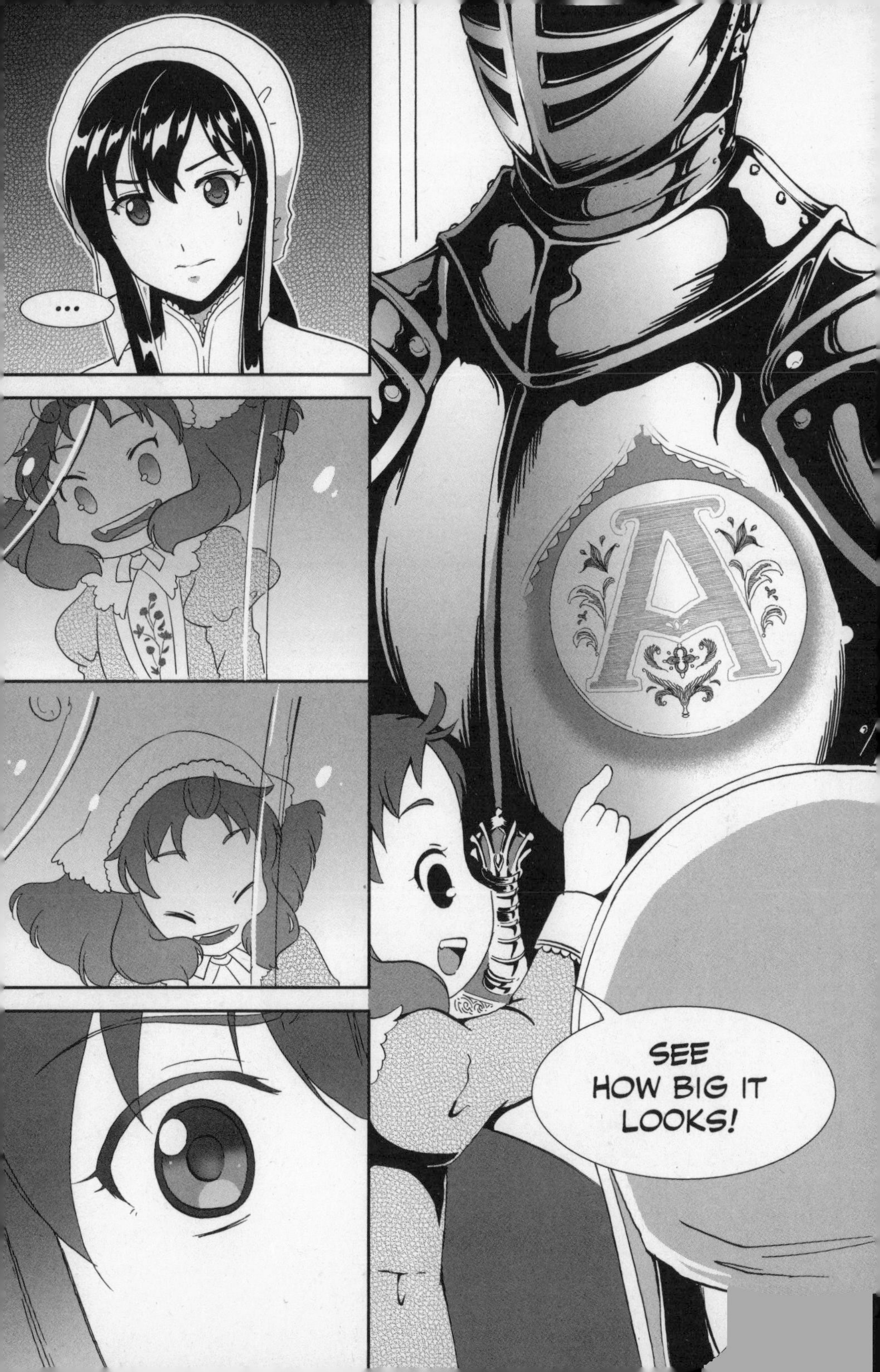
SEE HOW BIG IT LOOKS!
...

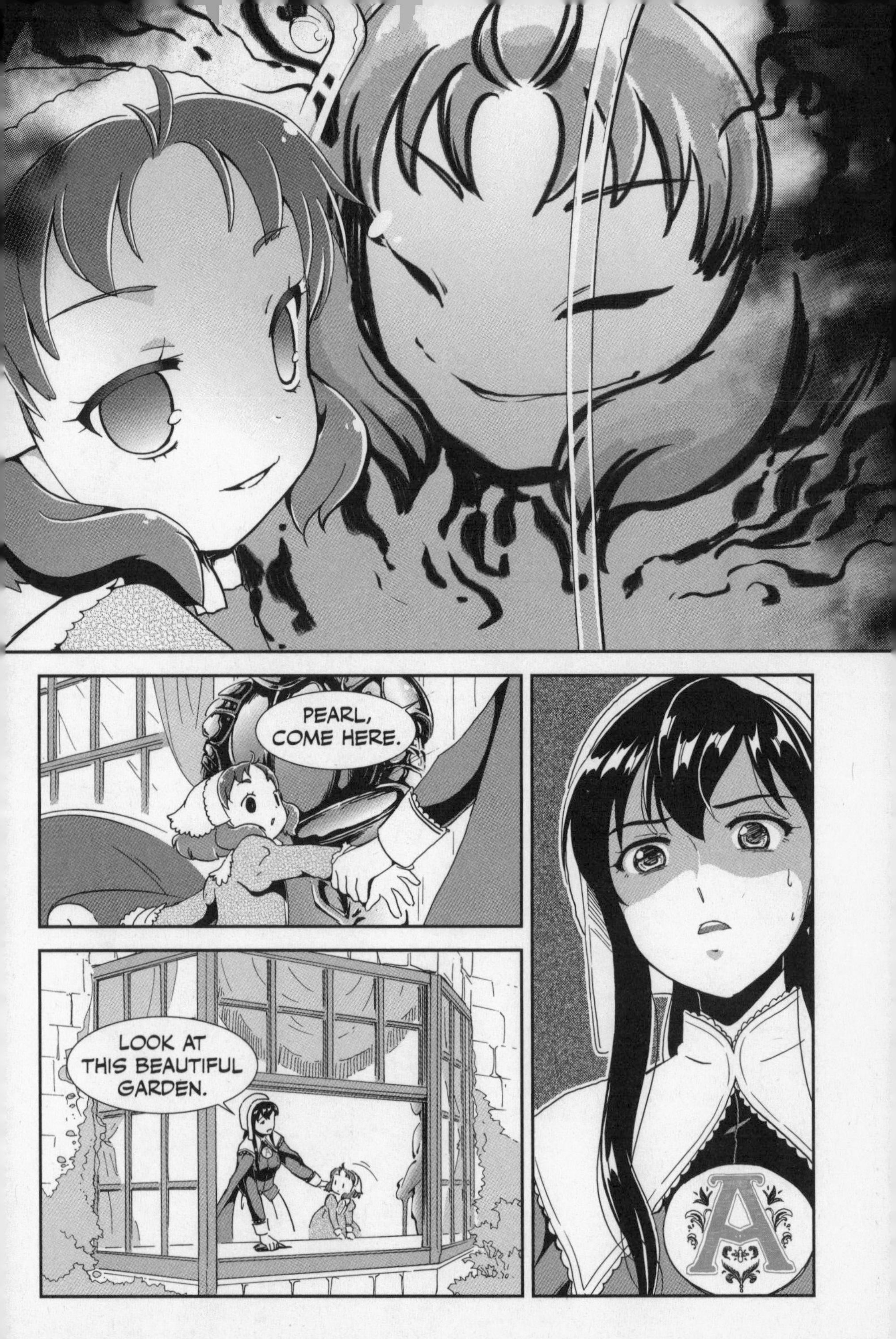
A
PEARL, COME HERE.
LOOK AT THIS BEAUTIFUL GARDEN.

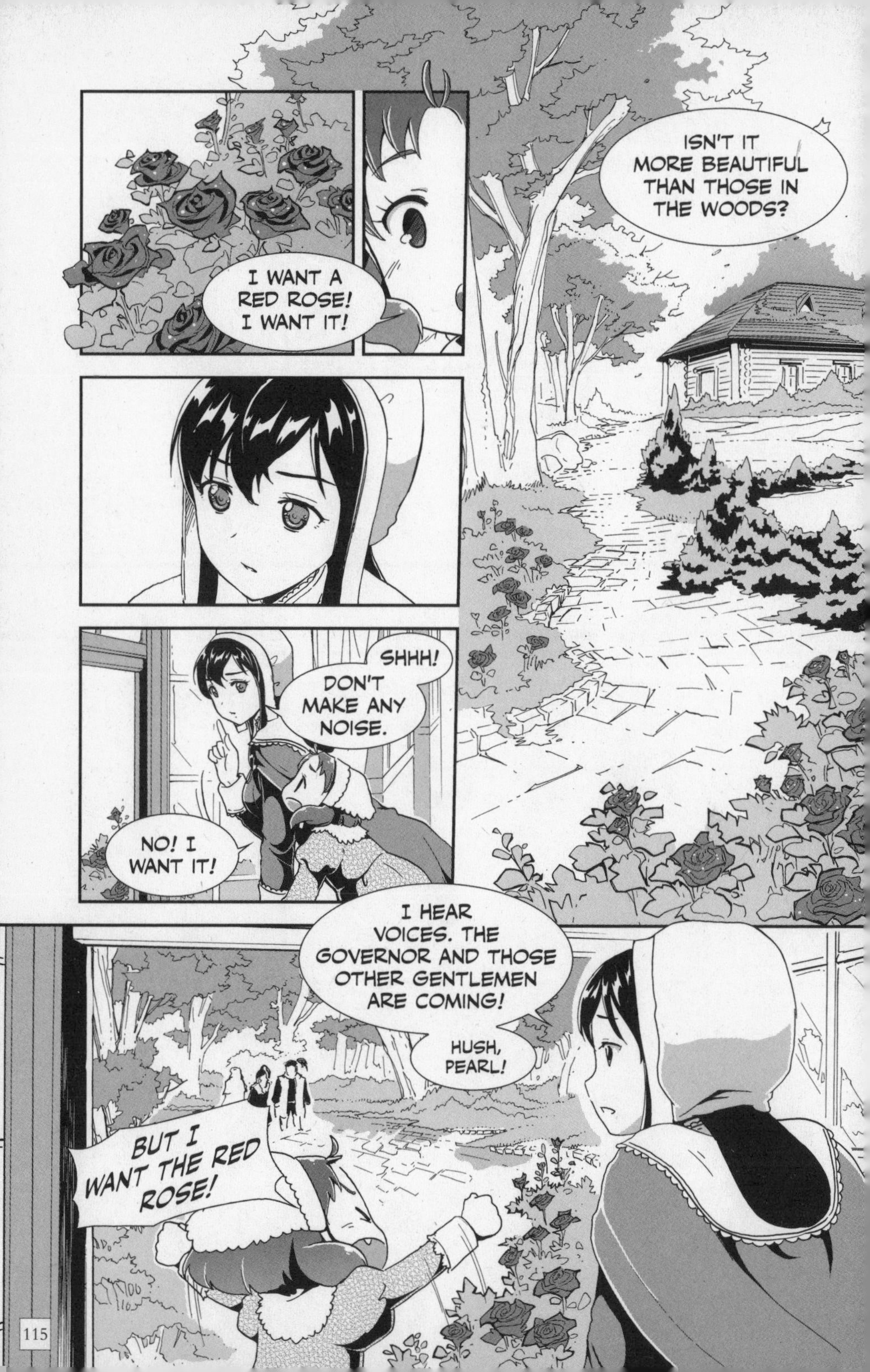

ISN'T IT MORE BEAUTIFUL THAN THOSE IN THE WOODS?
I WANT A RED ROSE! I WANT IT!
SHHH!
DON'T MAKE ANY NOISE.
NO! I WANT IT!
I HEAR VOICES. THE GOVERNOR AND THOSE OTHER GENTLEMEN ARE COMING!
HUSH, PEARL!
BUT I WANT THE RED ROSE!

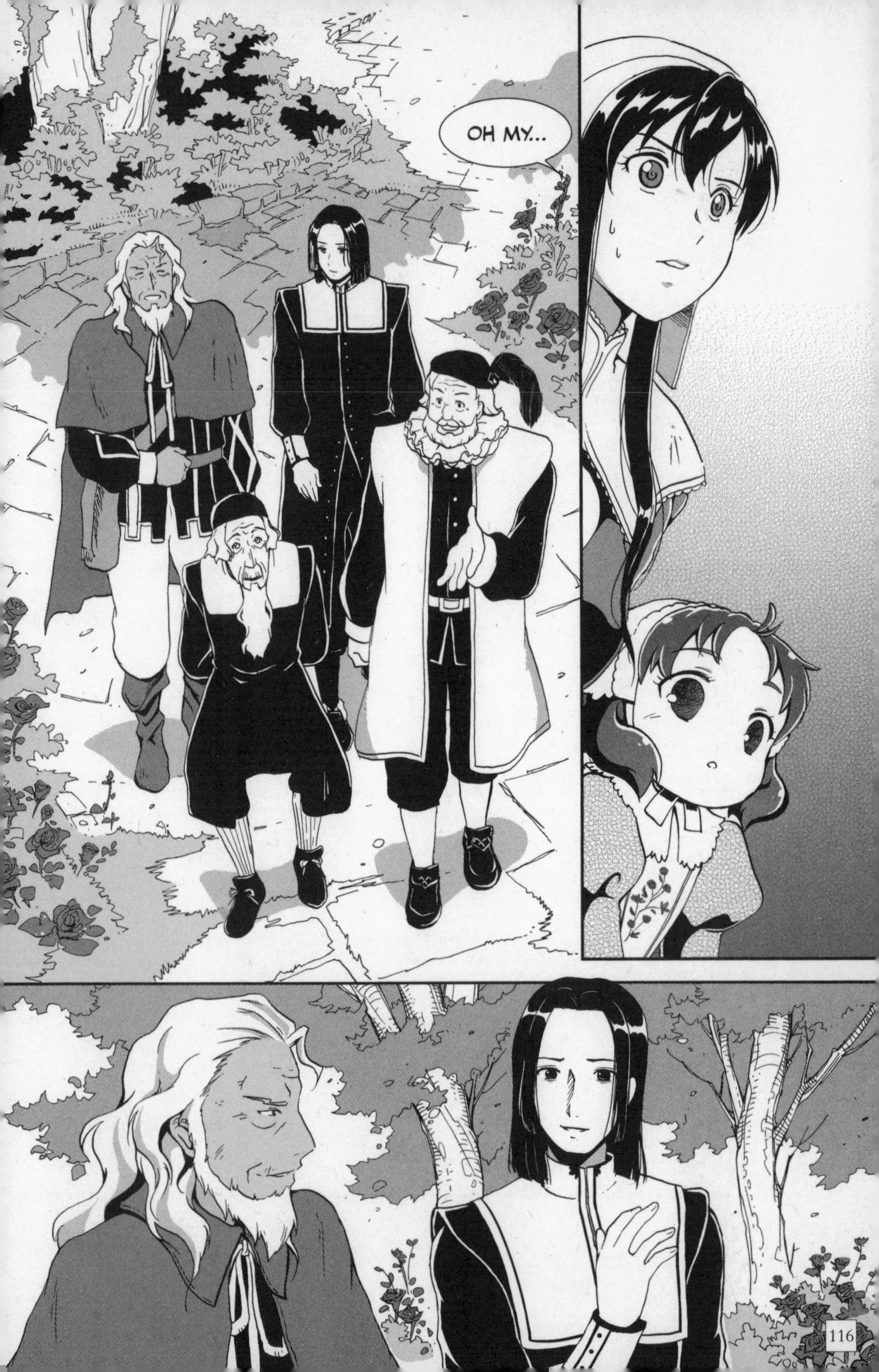
OH MY...

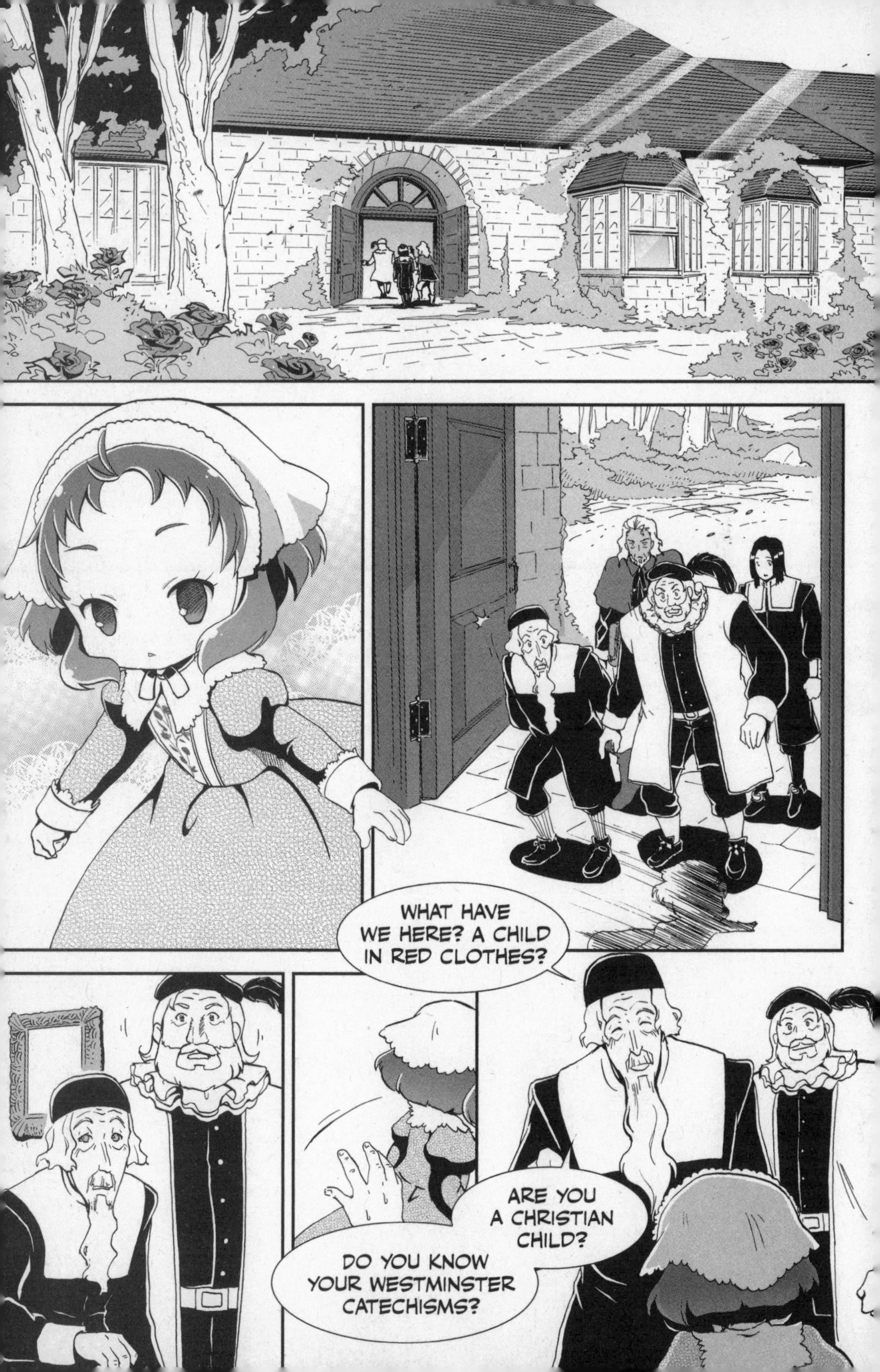
WHAT HAVE WE HERE? A CHILD IN RED CLOTHES?
ARE YOU A CHRISTIAN CHILD?
DO YOU KNOW YOUR WESTMINSTER CATECHISMS?

Chapter 5

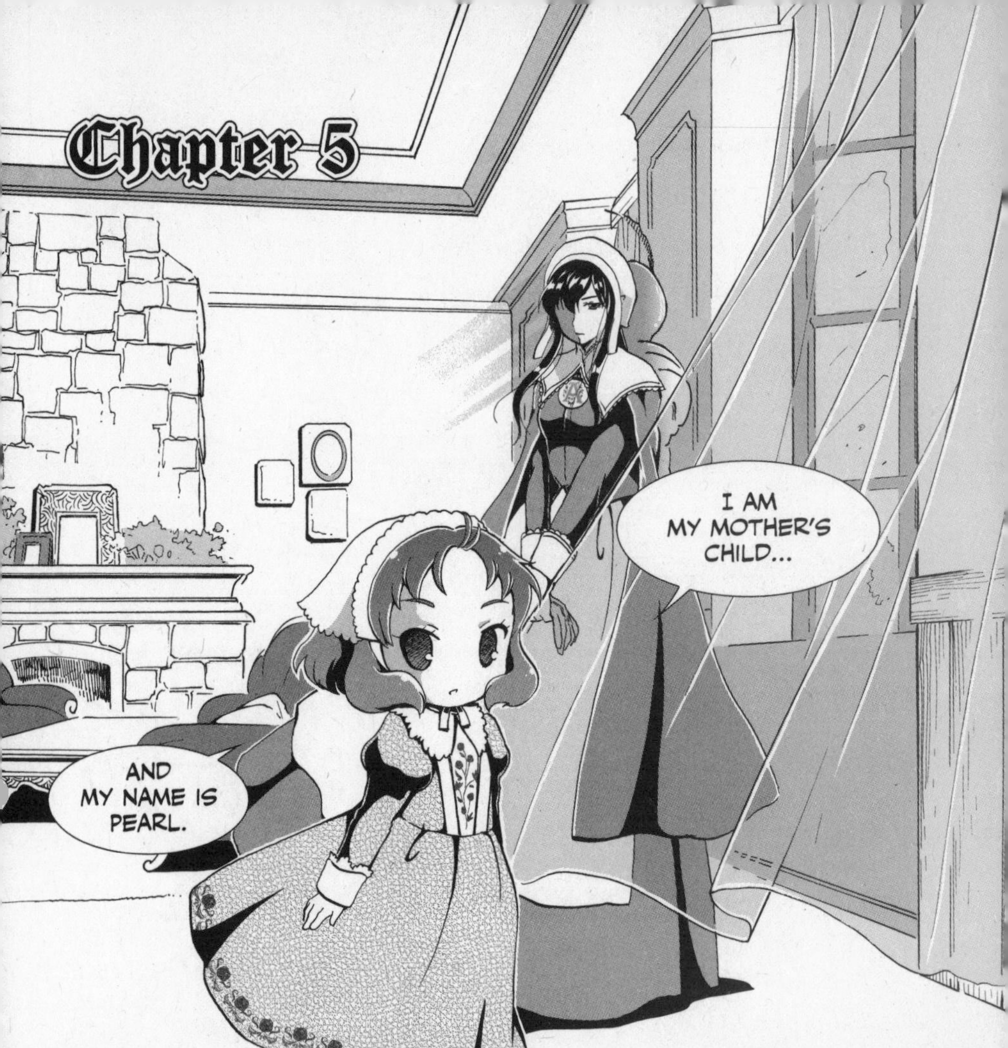
I AM MY MOTHER'S CHILD...
AND MY NAME IS PEARL.

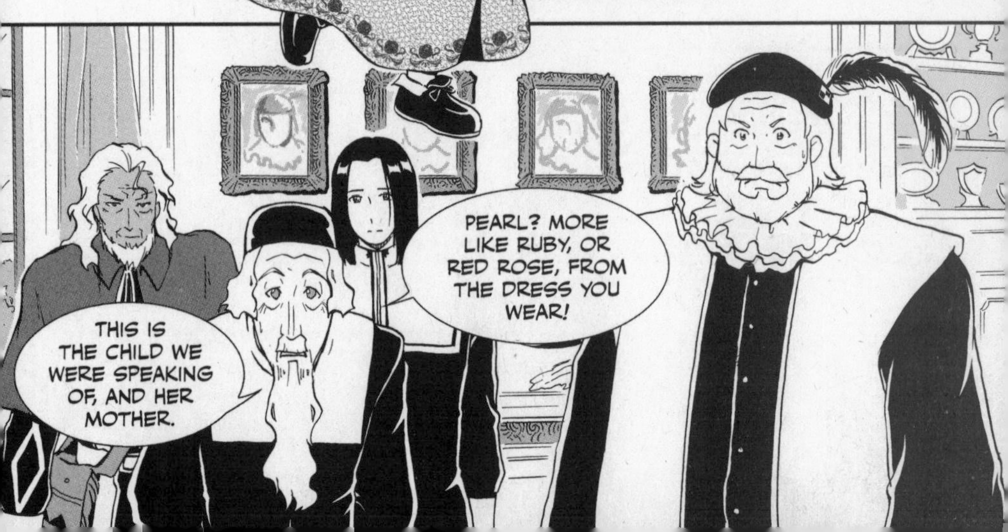
PEARL? MORE LIKE RUBY, OR RED ROSE, FROM THE DRESS YOU WEAR!
THIS IS THE CHILD WE WERE SPEAKING OF, AND HER MOTHER.

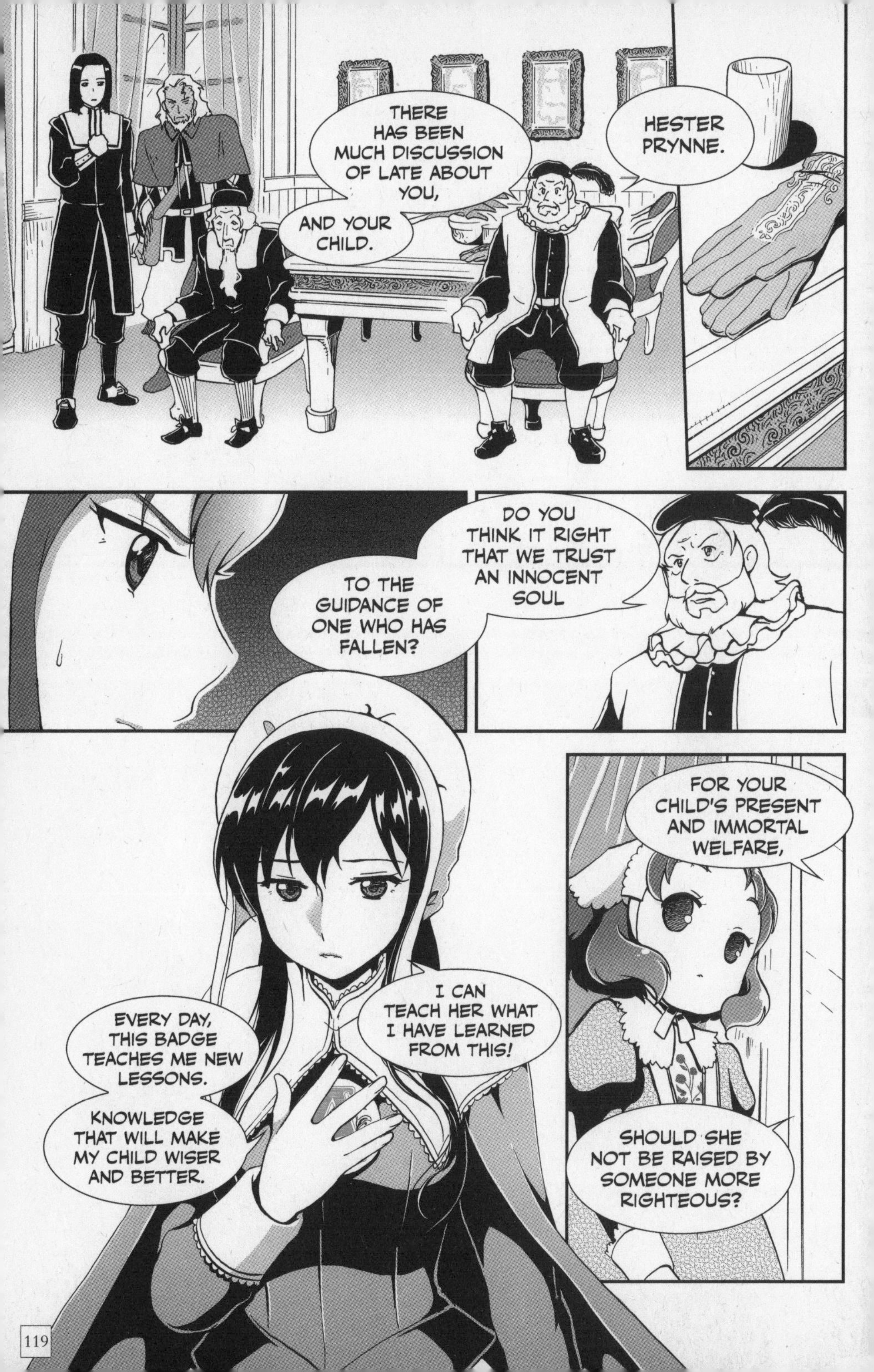
HESTER PRYNNE.
THERE HAS BEEN MUCH DISCUSSION OF LATE ABOUT YOU,
AND YOUR CHILD.
DO YOU THINK IT RIGHT THAT WE TRUST AN INNOCENT SOUL
TO THE GUIDANCE OF ONE WHO HAS FALLEN?
FOR YOUR CHILD'S PRESENT AND IMMORTAL WELFARE,
SHOULD SHE NOT BE RAISED BY SOMEONE MORE RIGHTEOUS?
I CAN TEACH HER WHAT I HAVE LEARNED FROM THIS!
EVERY DAY, THIS BADGE TEACHES ME NEW LESSONS.
KNOWLEDGE THAT WILL MAKE MY CHILD WISER AND BETTER.

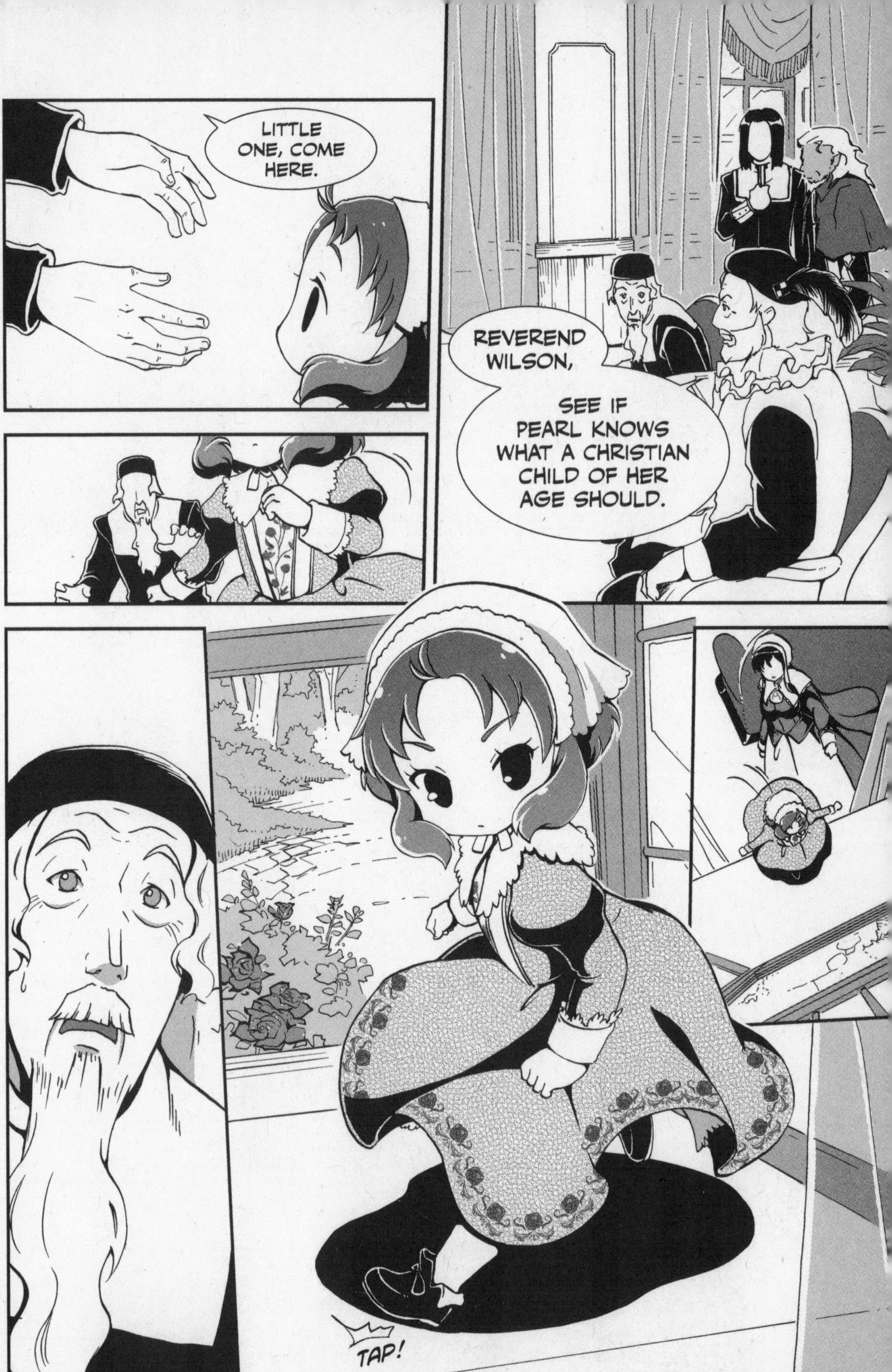
REVEREND WILSON,
SEE IF PEARL KNOWS WHAT A CHRISTIAN CHILD OF HER AGE SHOULD.
LITTLE ONE, COME HERE.
TAP!

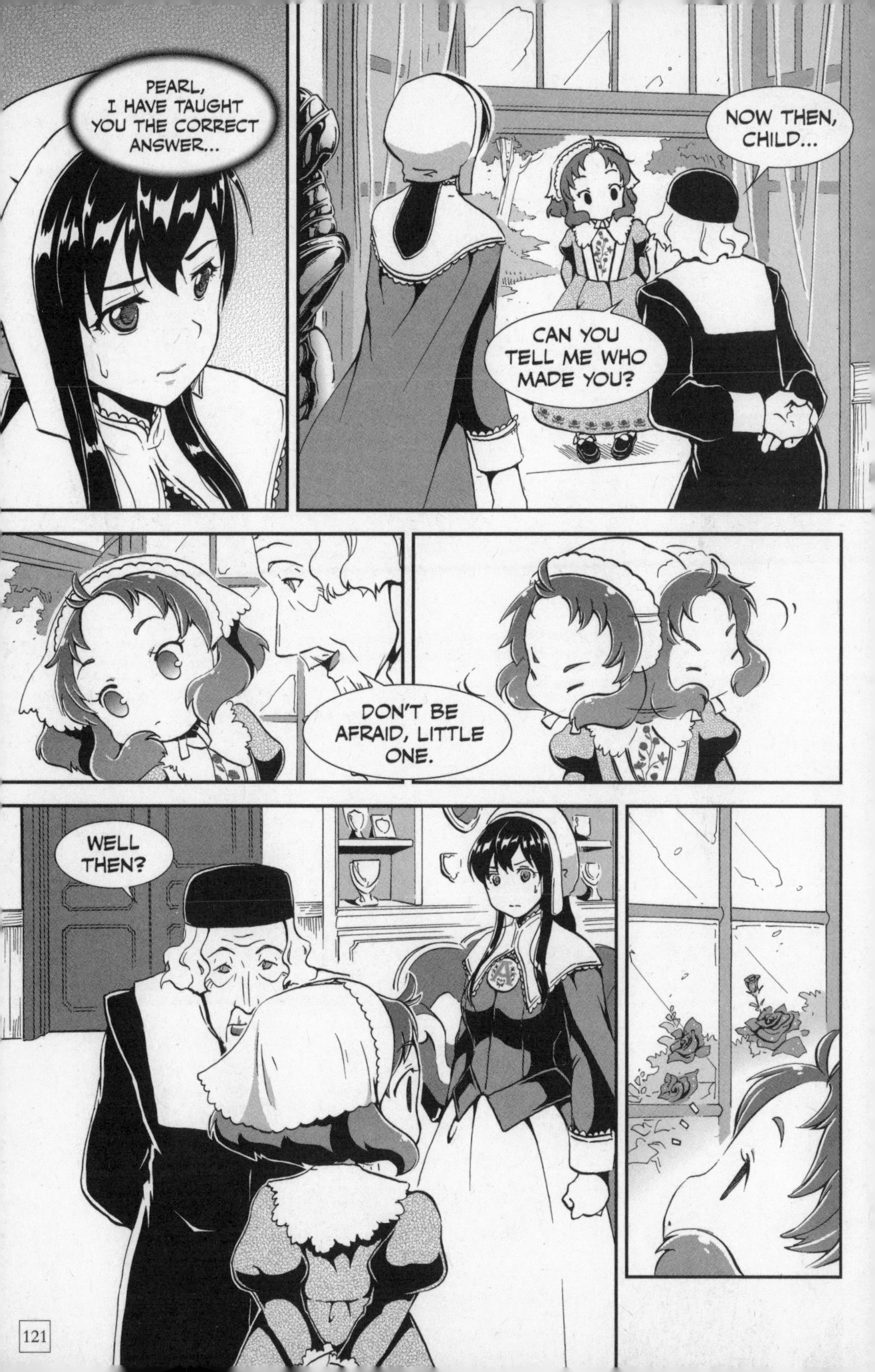
NOW THEN, CHILD...
CAN YOU TELL ME WHO MADE YOU?
PEARL, I HAVE TAUGHT YOU THE CORRECT ANSWER...
DON'T BE AFRAID, LITTLE ONE.
WELL THEN?

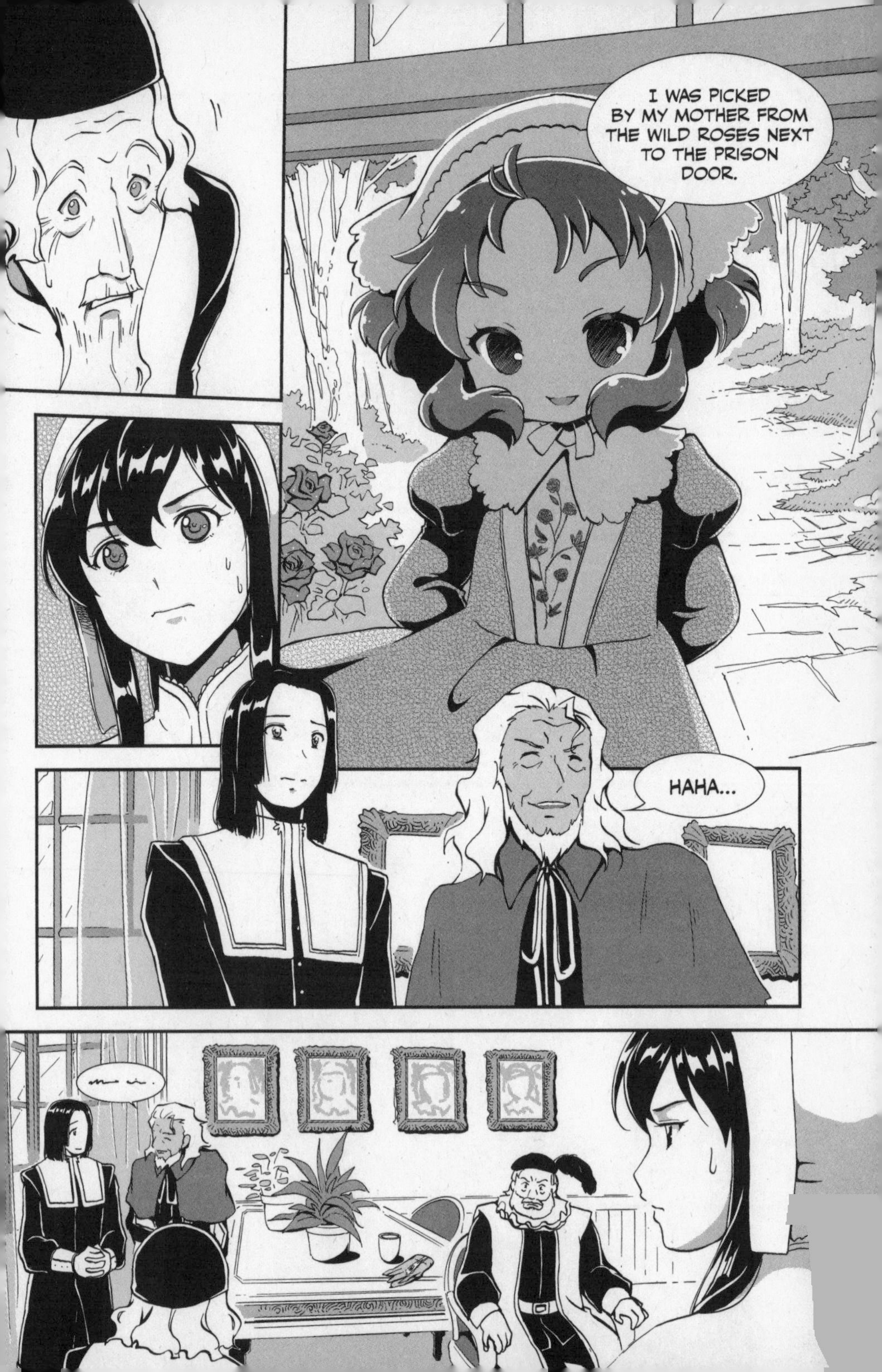
I WAS PICKED BY MY MOTHER FROM THE WILD ROSES NEXT TO THE PRISON DOOR.
HAHA...

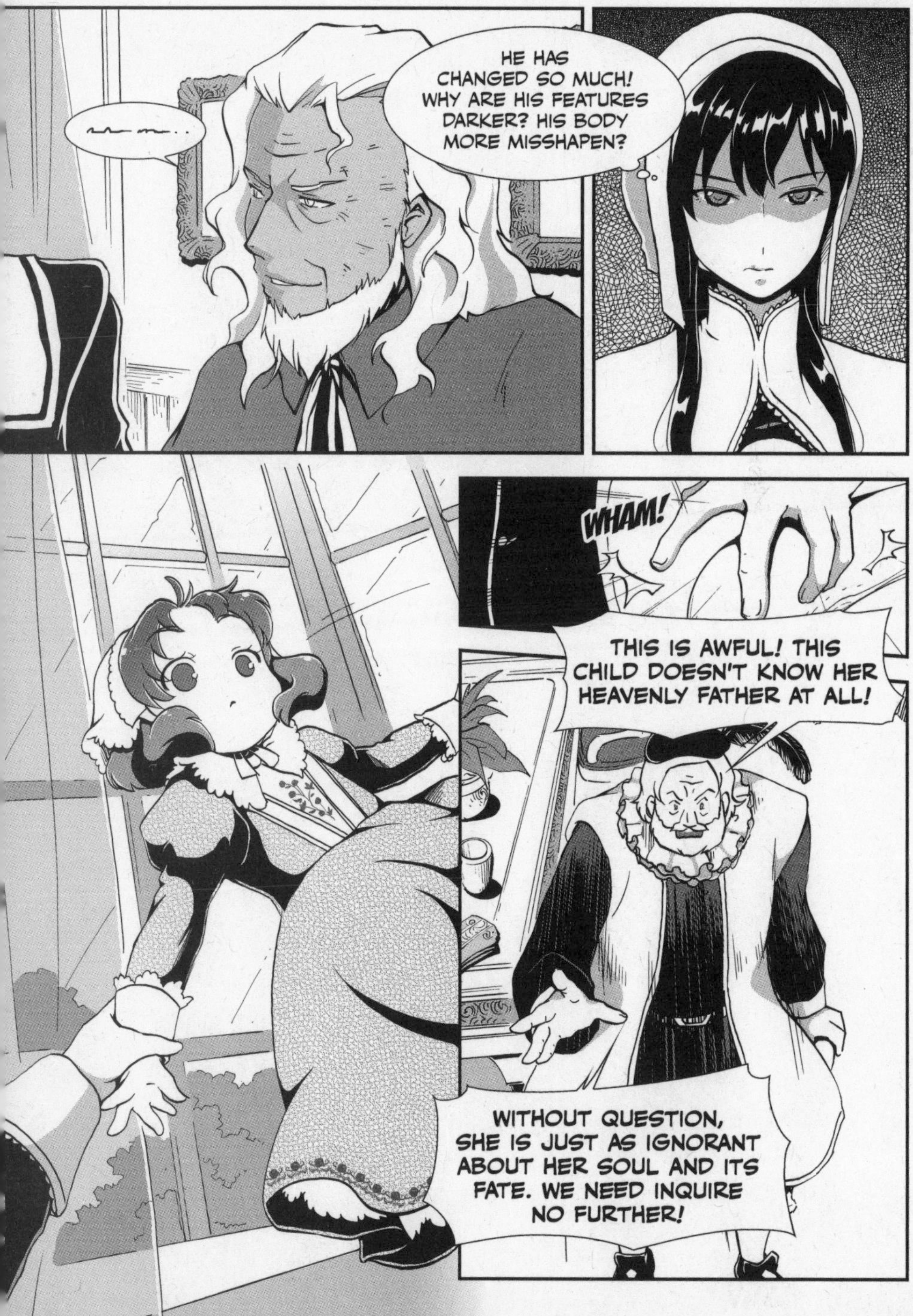
HE HAS CHANGED SO MUCH! WHY ARE HIS FEATURES DARKER? HIS BODY MORE MISSHAPEN?
WHAM!
THIS IS AWFUL! THIS CHILD DOESN'T KNOW HER HEAVENLY FATHER AT ALL!
WITHOUT QUESTION, SHE IS JUST AS IGNORANT ABOUT HER SOUL AND ITS FATE. WE NEED INQUIRE NO FURTHER!

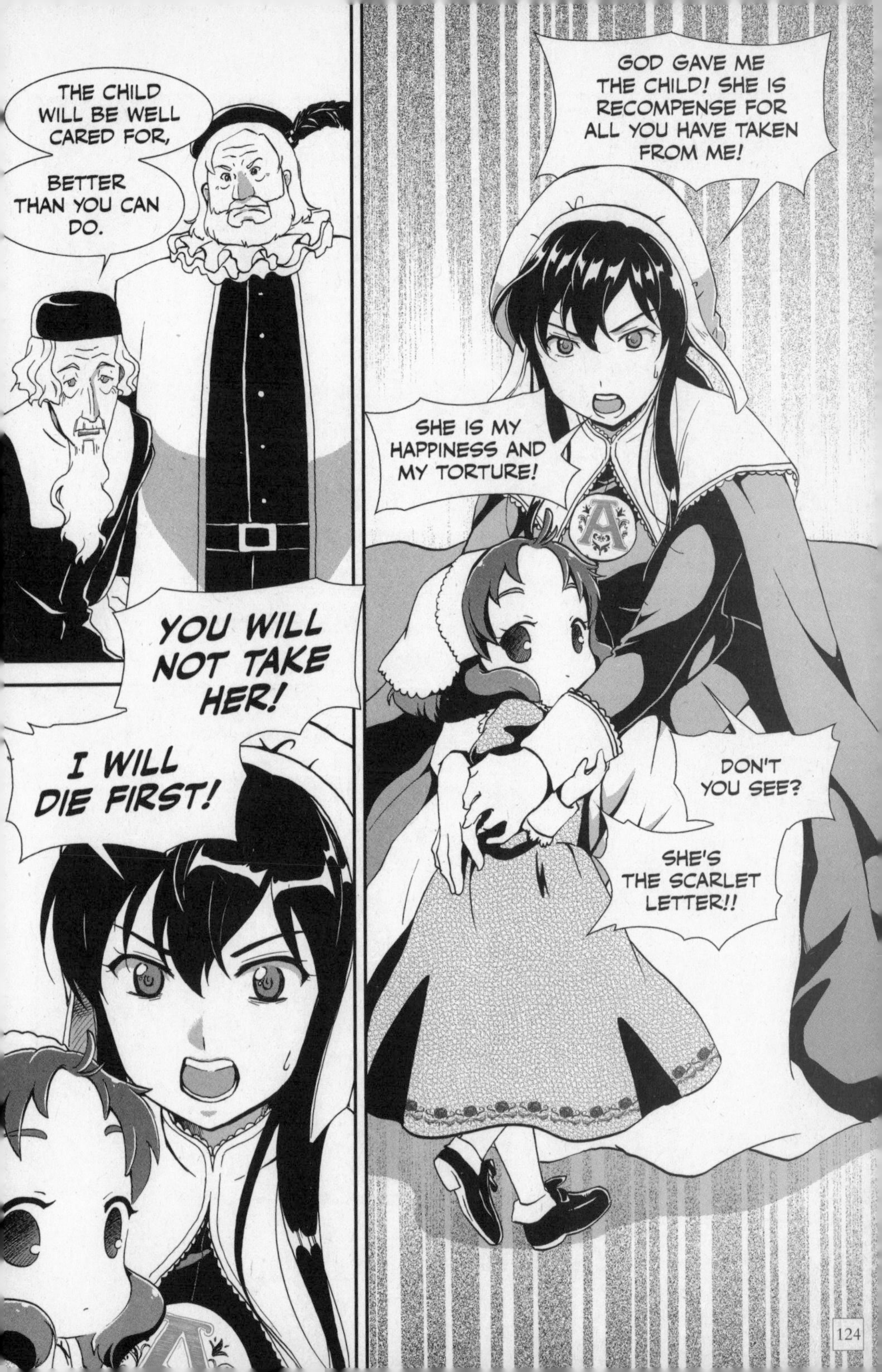
GOD GAVE ME THE CHILD! SHE IS RECOMPENSE FOR ALL YOU HAVE TAKEN FROM ME!
SHE IS MY HAPPINESS AND MY TORTURE!
DON'T YOU SEE?
SHE'S THE SCARLET LETTER!!
THE CHILD WILL BE WELL CARED FOR,
BETTER THAN YOU CAN DO.
YOU WILL NOT TAKE HER!
I WILL DIE FIRST!

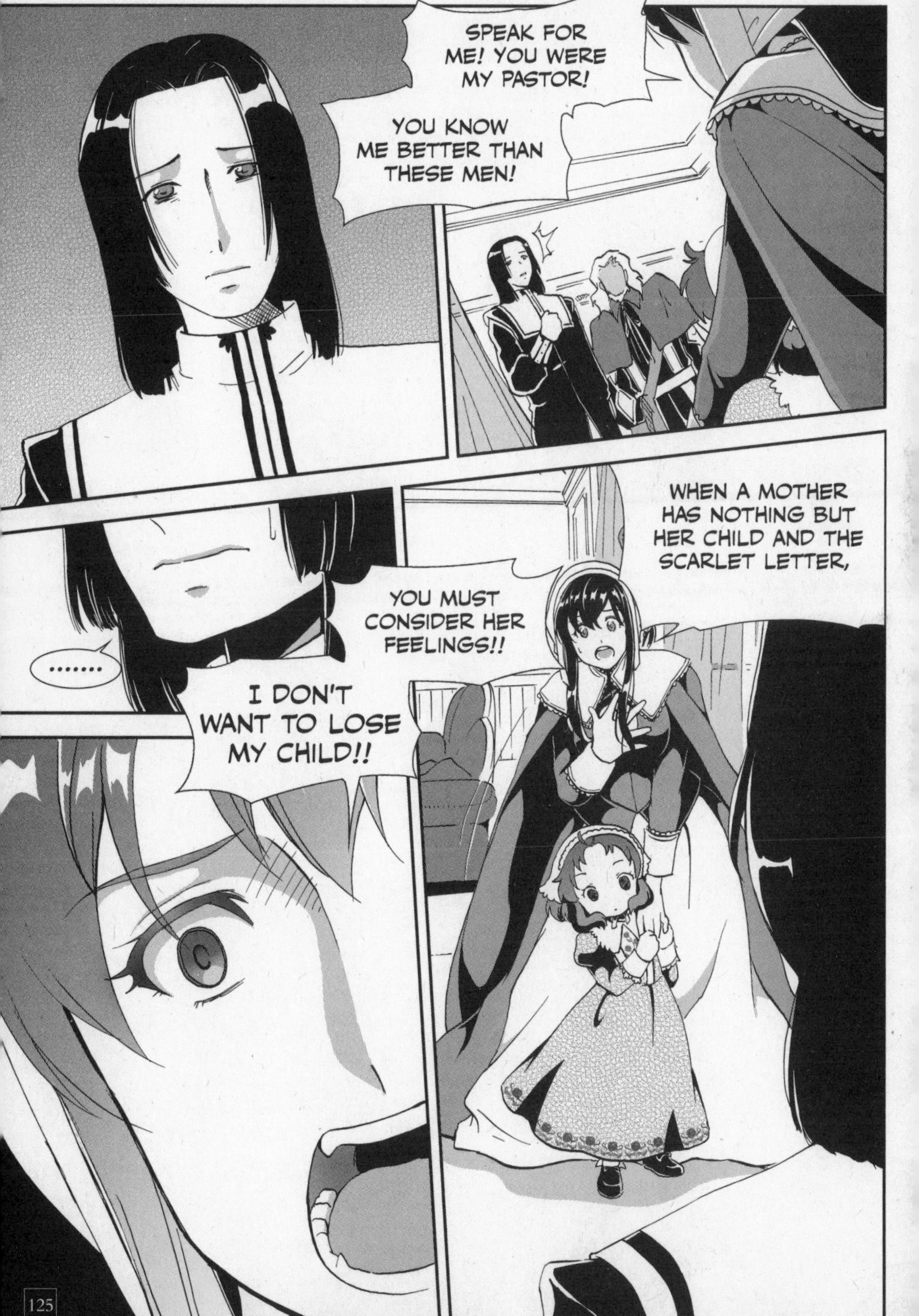
SPEAK FOR ME! YOU WERE MY PASTOR!
YOU KNOW ME BETTER THAN THESE MEN!
WHEN A MOTHER HAS NOTHING BUT HER CHILD AND THE SCARLET LETTER,
YOU MUST CONSIDER HER FEELINGS!!
....
I DON'T WANT TO LOSE MY CHILD!!

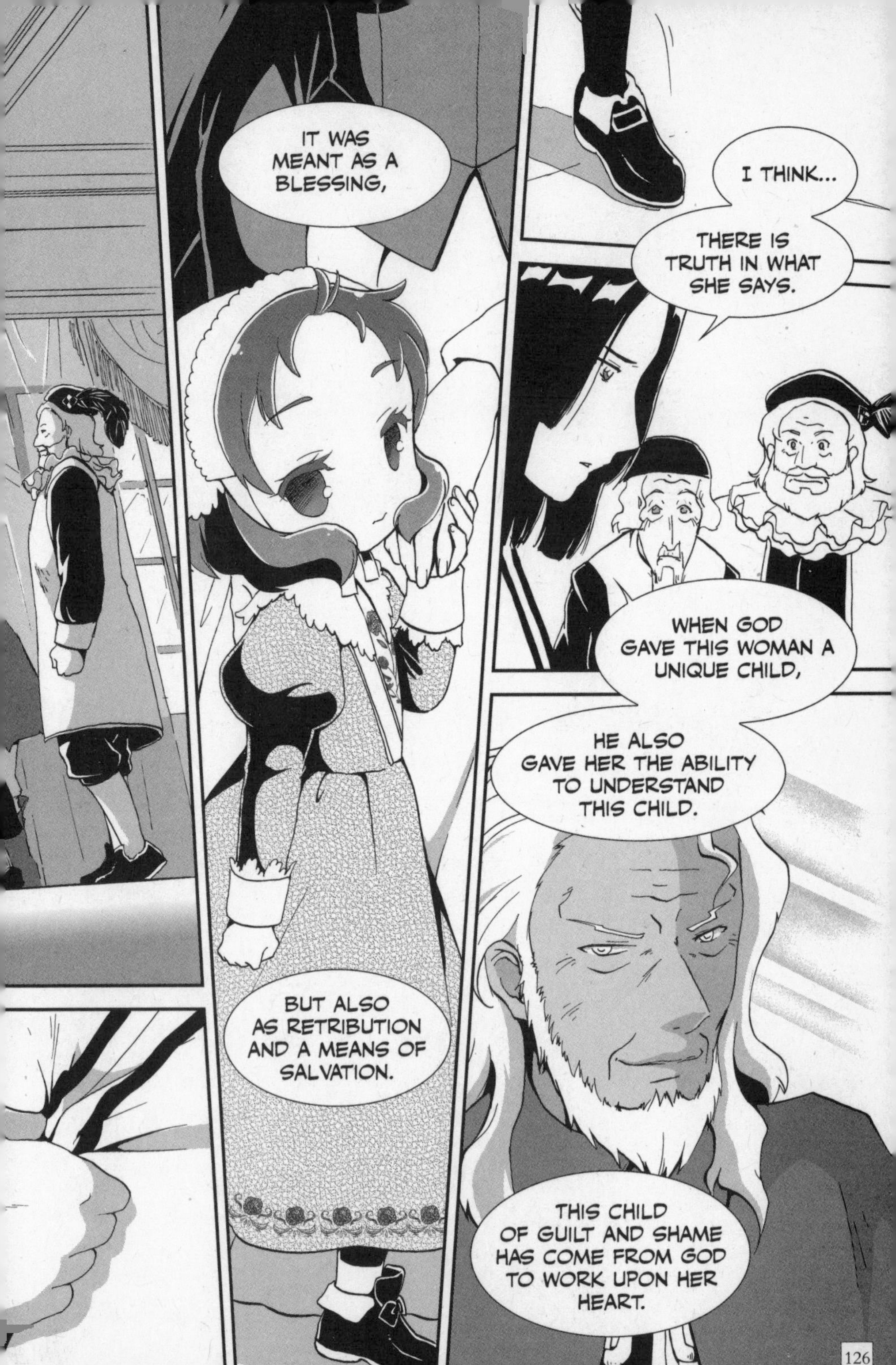
I THINK...
THERE IS TRUTH IN WHAT SHE SAYS.
WHEN GOD GAVE THIS WOMAN A UNIQUE CHILD,
HE ALSO GAVE HER THE ABILITY TO UNDERSTAND THIS CHILD.
THIS CHILD OF GUILT AND SHAME HAS COME FROM GOD TO WORK UPON HER HEART.
IT WAS MEANT AS A BLESSING,
BUT ALSO AS RETRIBUTION AND A MEANS OF SALVATION.

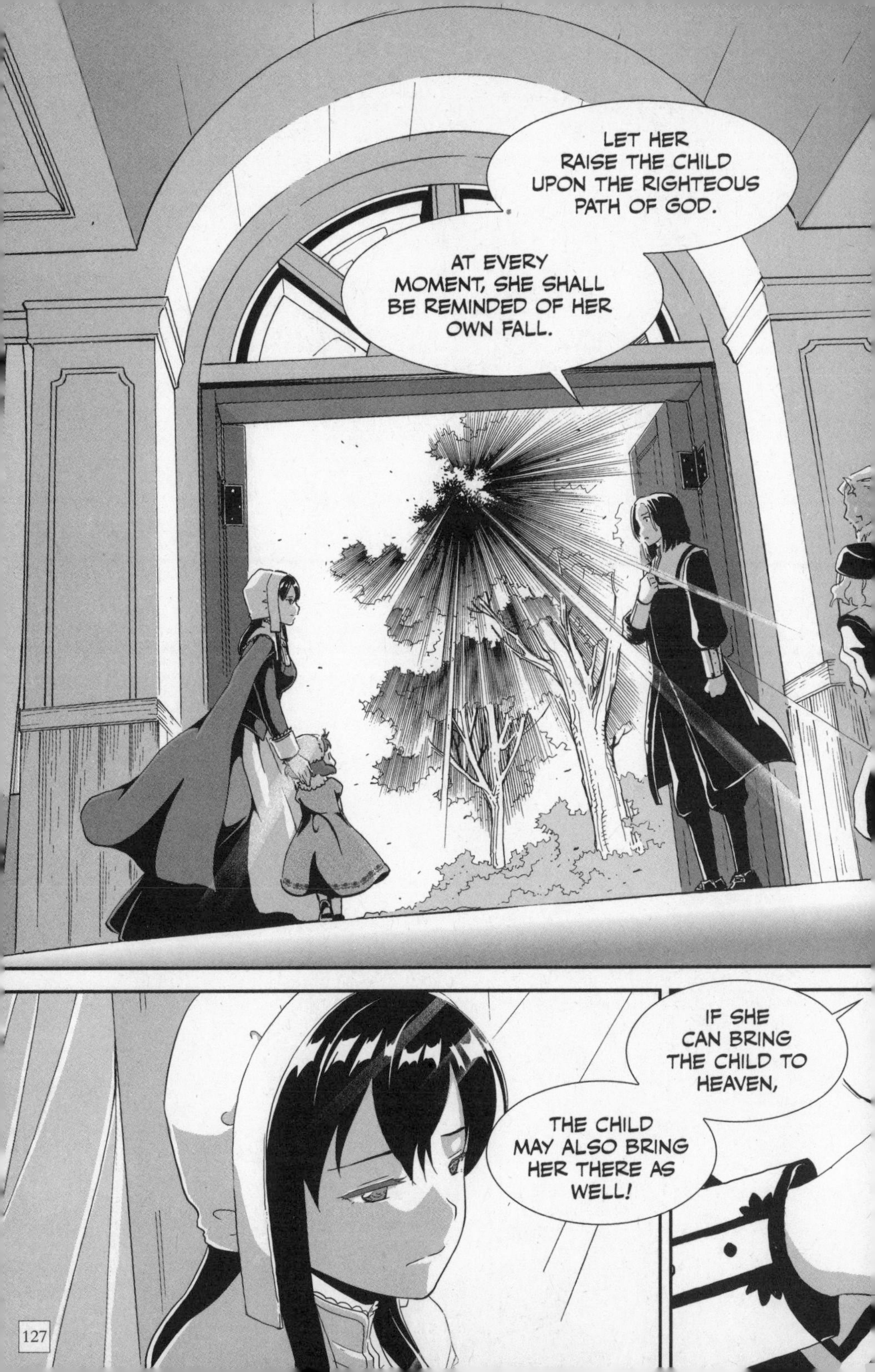
LET HER RAISE THE CHILD UPON THE RIGHTEOUS PATH OF GOD.
AT EVERY MOMENT, SHE SHALL BE REMINDED OF HER OWN FALL.
IF SHE CAN BRING THE CHILD TO HEAVEN,
THE CHILD MAY ALSO BRING HER THERE AS WELL!

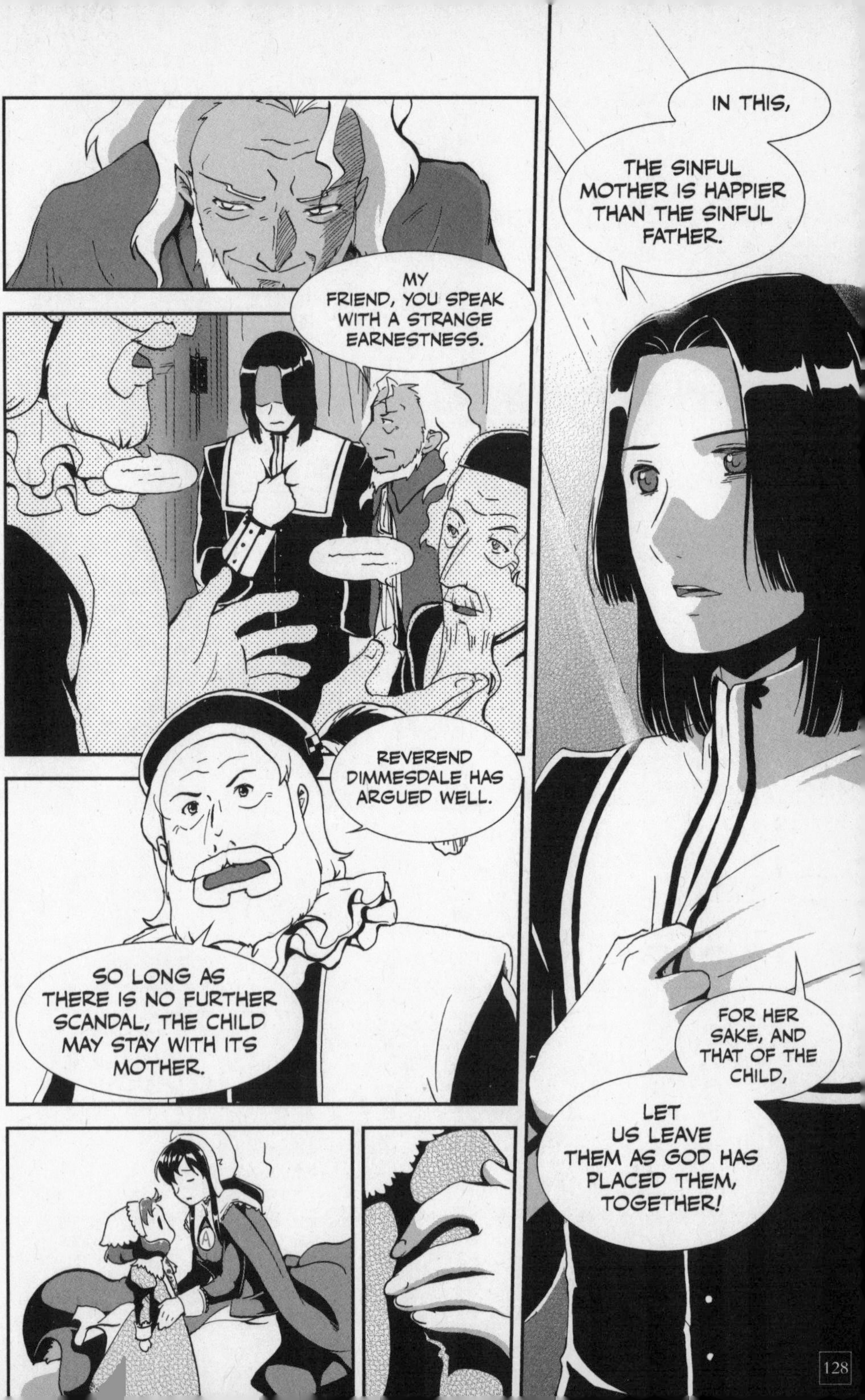
IN THIS,
THE SINFUL MOTHER IS HAPPIER THAN THE SINFUL FATHER.
FOR HER SAKE, AND THAT OF THE CHILD,
LET US LEAVE THEM AS GOD HAS PLACED THEM, TOGETHER!
MY FRIEND, YOU SPEAK WITH A STRANGE EARNESTNESS.
REVEREND DIMMESDALE HAS ARGUED WELL.
SO LONG AS THERE IS NO FURTHER SCANDAL, THE CHILD MAY STAY WITH ITS MOTHER.

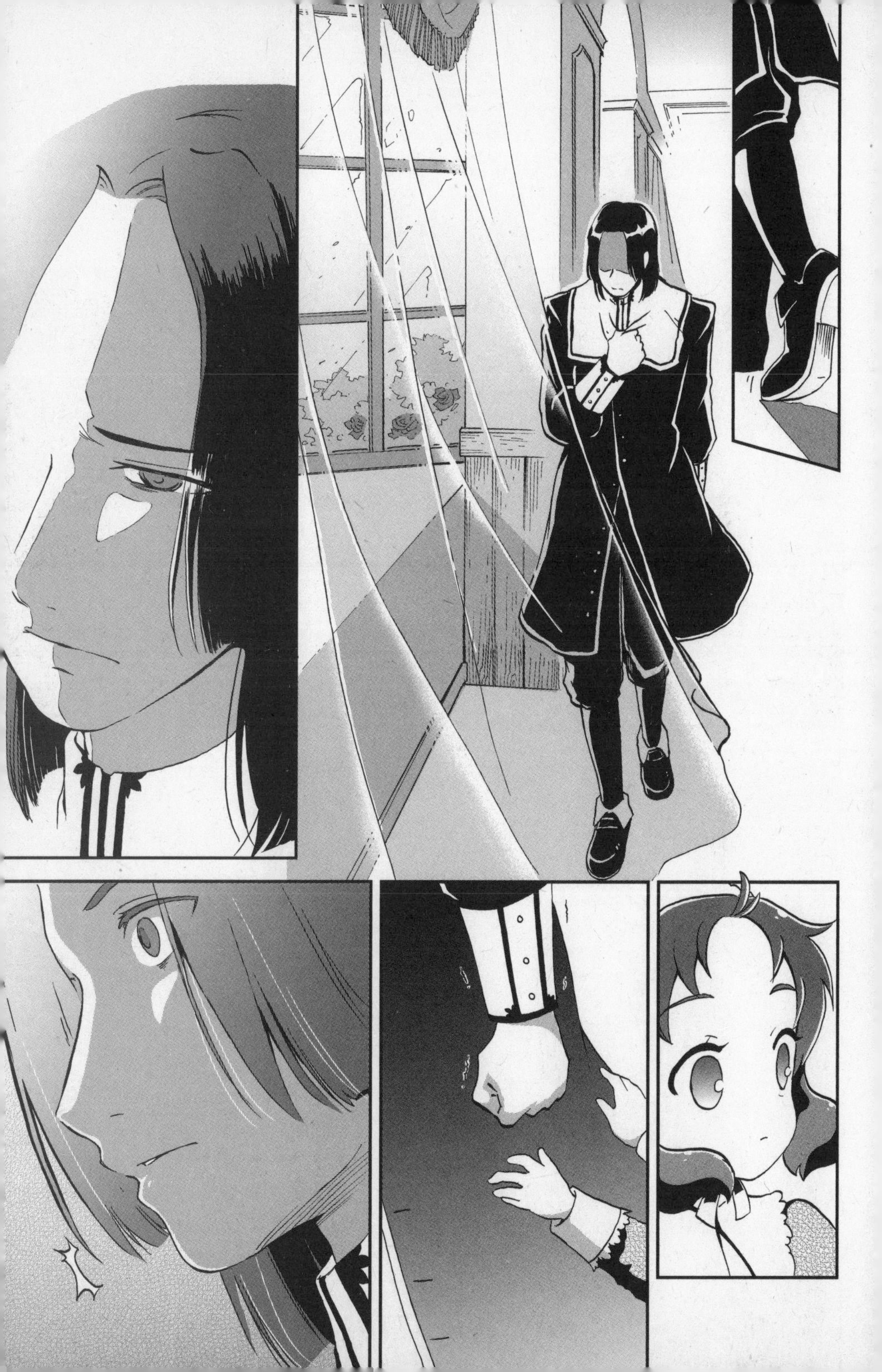

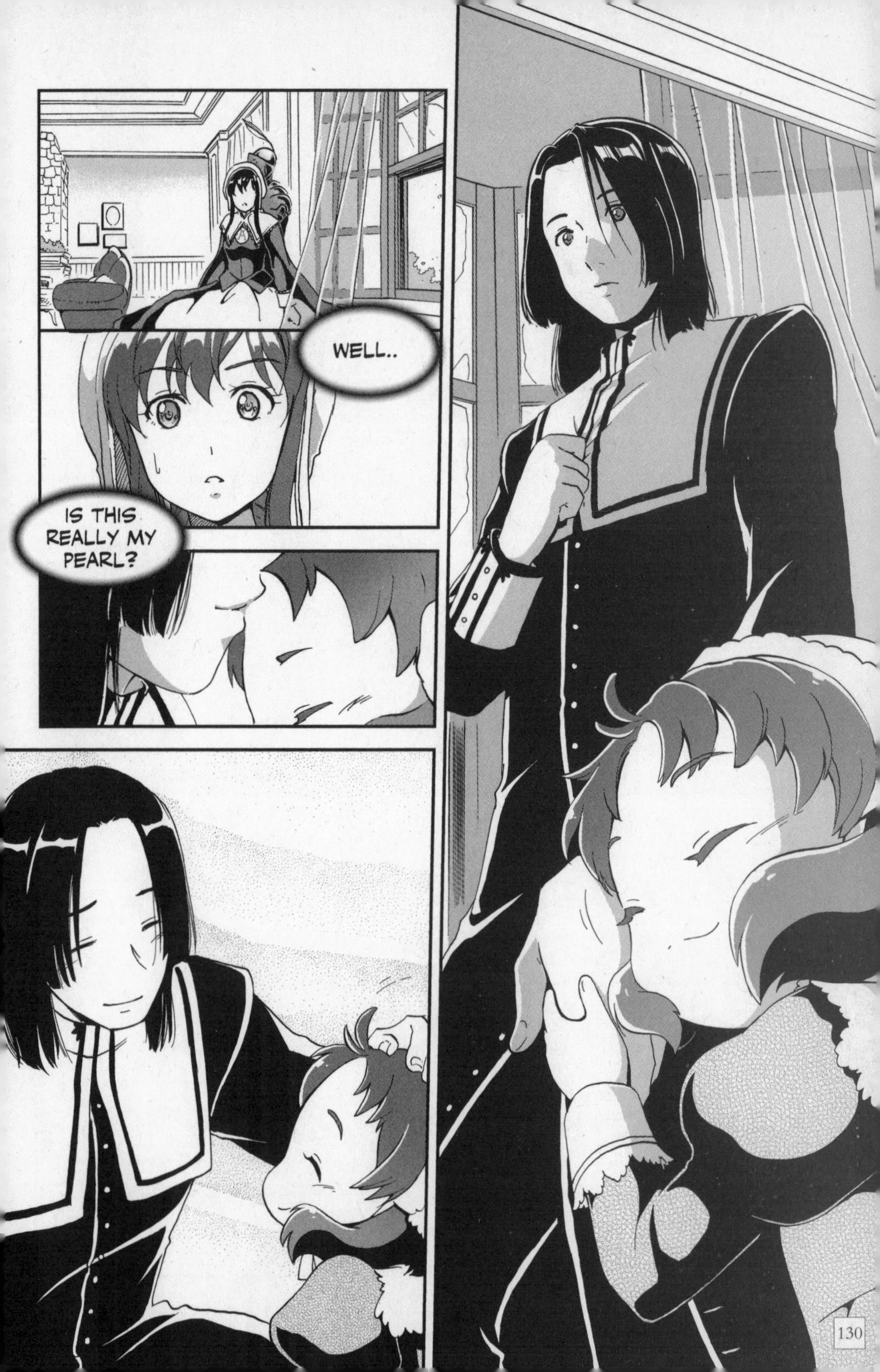
WELL..
IS THIS REALLY MY PEARL?

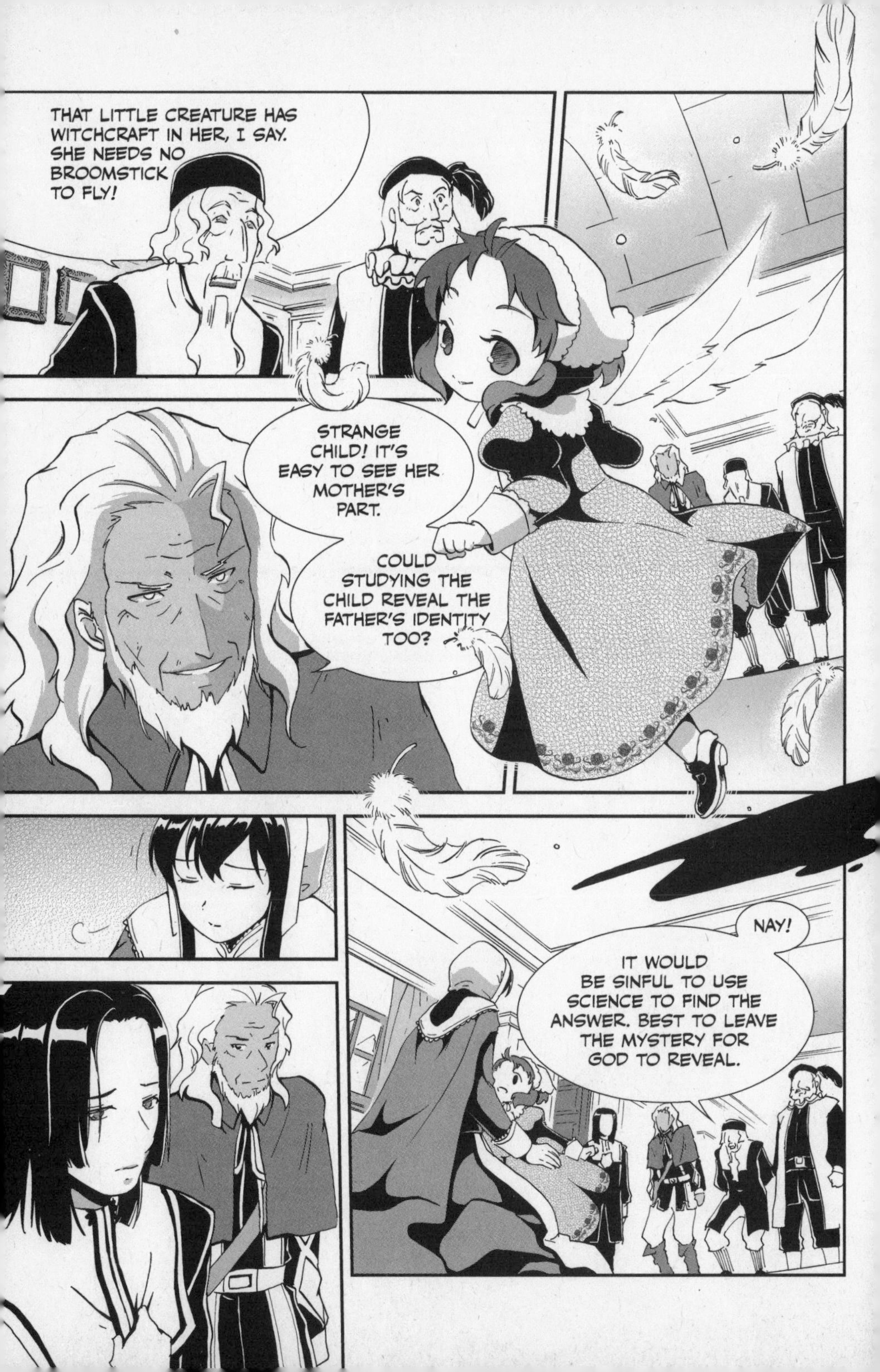
THAT LITTLE CREATURE HAS WITCHCRAFT IN HER, I SAY. SHE NEEDS NO BROOMSTICK TO FLY!
STRANGE CHILD! IT'S EASY TO SEE HER MOTHER'S PART.
COULD STUDYING THE CHILD REVEAL THE FATHER'S IDENTITY TOO?
NAY!
IT WOULD BE SINFUL TO USE SCIENCE TO FIND THE ANSWER. BEST TO LEAVE THE MYSTERY FOR GOD TO REVEAL.

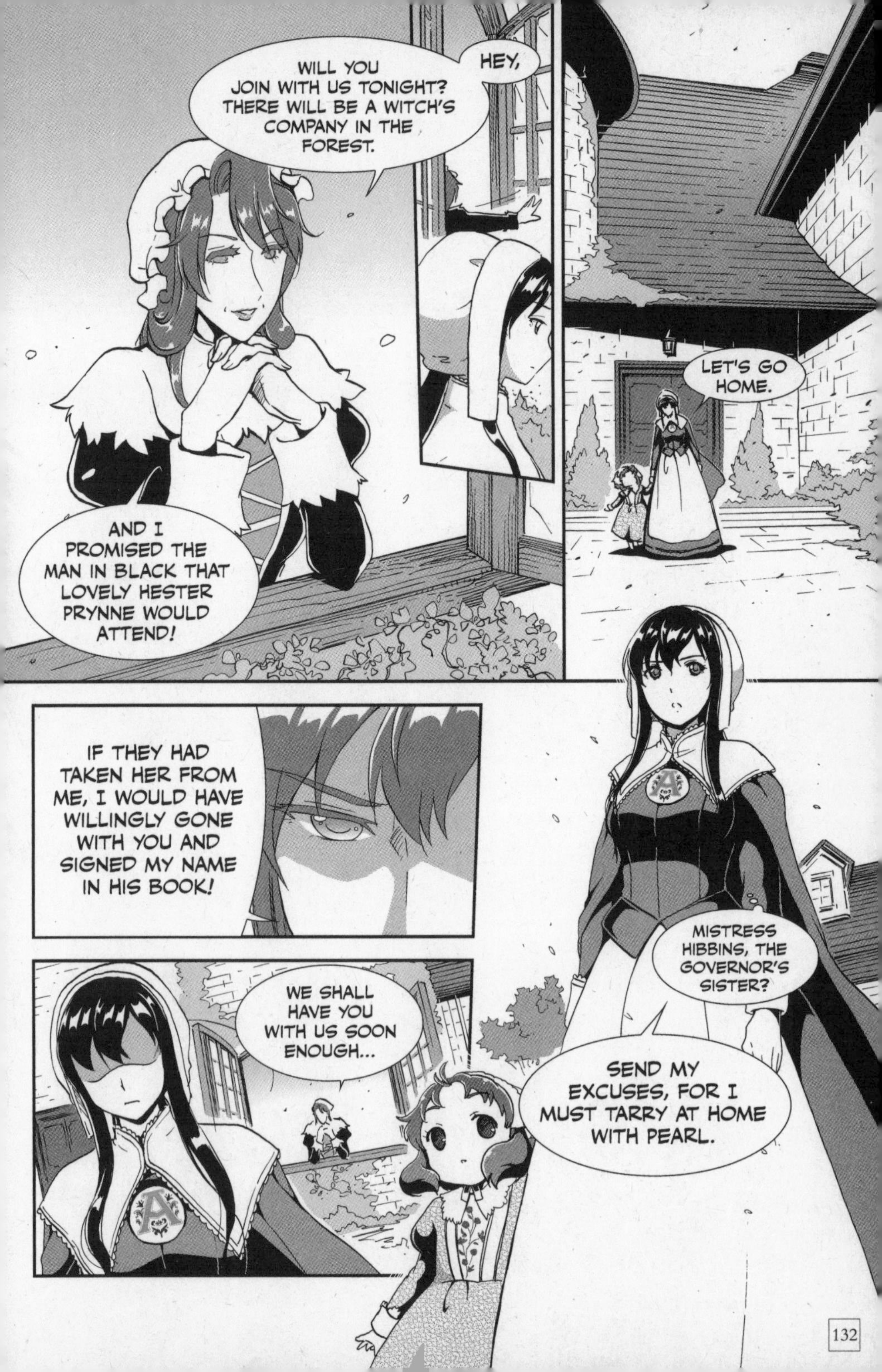
LET'S GO HOME.
HEY,
WILL YOU JOIN WITH US TONIGHT? THERE WILL BE A WITCH'S COMPANY IN THE FOREST.
AND I PROMISED THE MAN IN BLACK THAT LOVELY HESTER PRYNNE WOULD ATTEND!
MISTRESS HIBBINS, THE GOVERNOR'S SISTER?
SEND MY EXCUSES, FOR I MUST TARRY AT HOME WITH PEARL.
IF THEY HAD TAKEN HER FROM ME, I WOULD HAVE WILLINGLY GONE WITH YOU AND SIGNED MY NAME IN HIS BOOK!
WE SHALL HAVE YOU WITH US SOON ENOUGH...

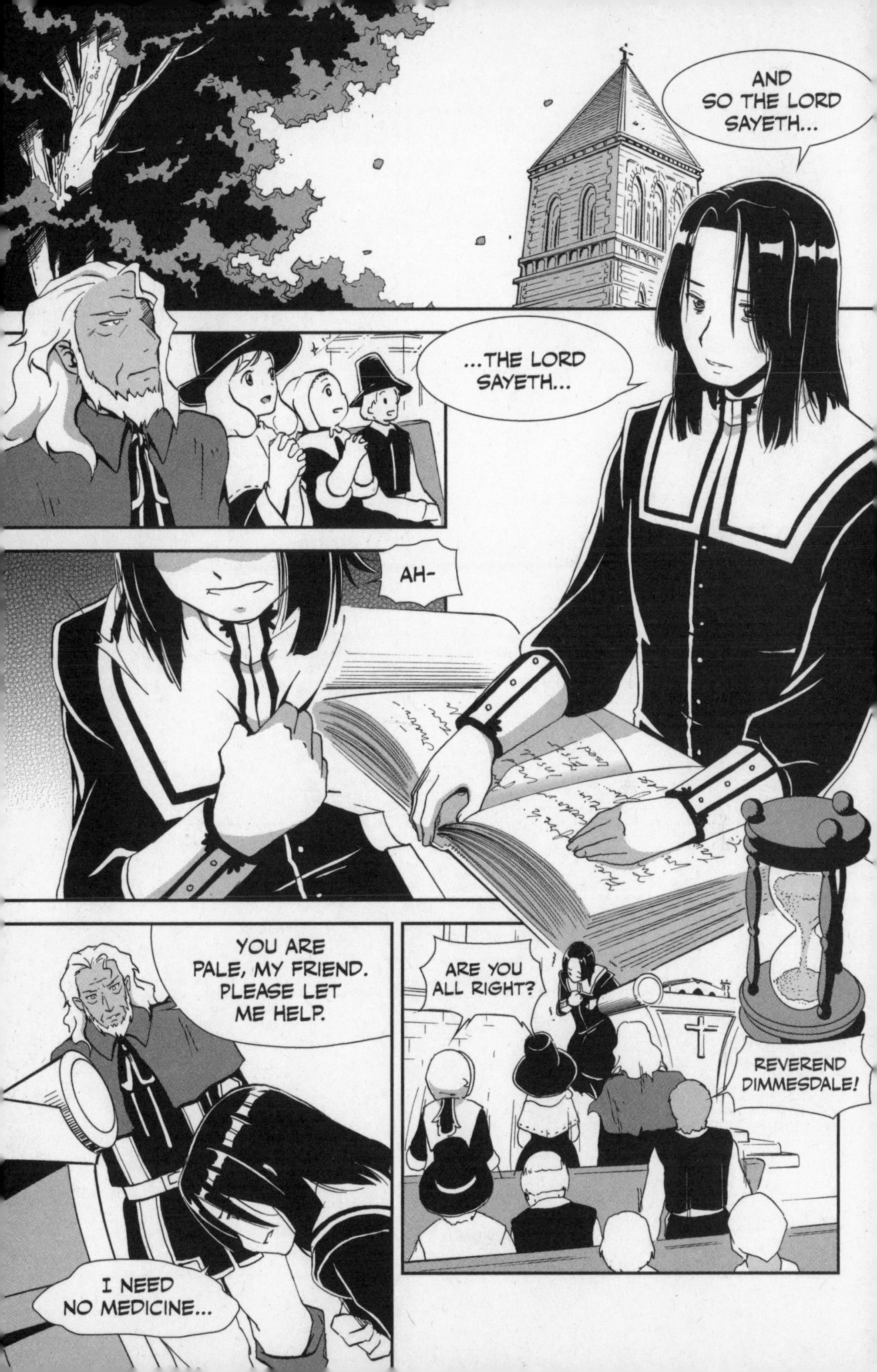
AND SO THE LORD SAYETH...
...THE LORD SAYETH...
AH-
REVEREND DIMMESDALE!
ARE YOU ALL RIGHT?
YOU ARE PALE, MY FRIEND. PLEASE LET ME HELP.
I NEED NO MEDICINE...

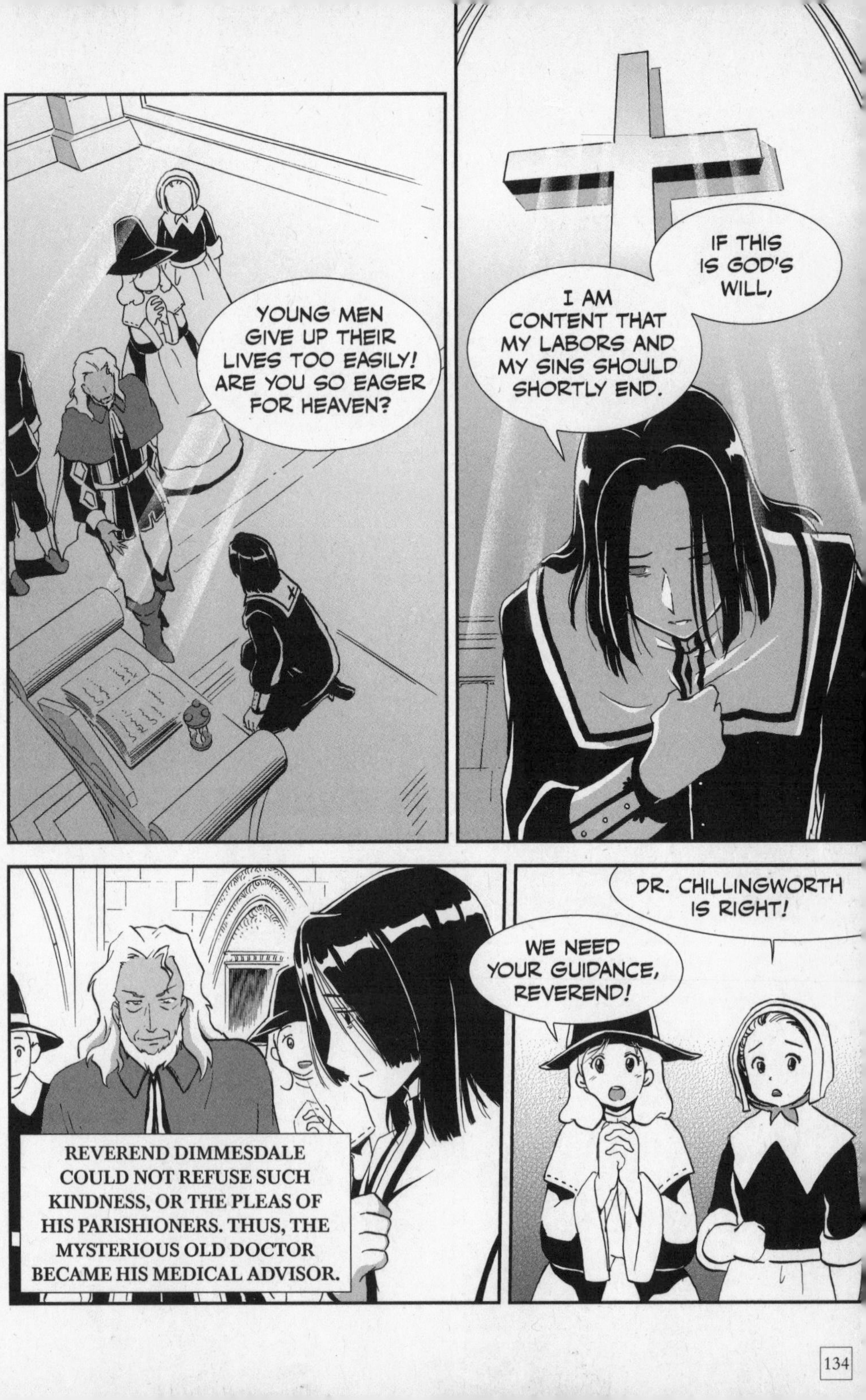
IF THIS IS GOD'S WILL,
I AM CONTENT THAT MY LABORS AND MY SINS SHOULD SHORTLY END.
YOUNG MEN GIVE UP THEIR LIVES TOO EASILY! ARE YOU SO EAGER FOR HEAVEN?
DR. CHILLINGWORTH IS RIGHT!
WE NEED YOUR GUIDANCE, REVEREND!
REVEREND DIMMESDALE COULD NOT REFUSE SUCH KINDNESS, OR THE PLEAS OF HIS PARISHIONERS. THUS, THE MYSTERIOUS OLD DOCTOR BECAME HIS MEDICAL ADVISOR.

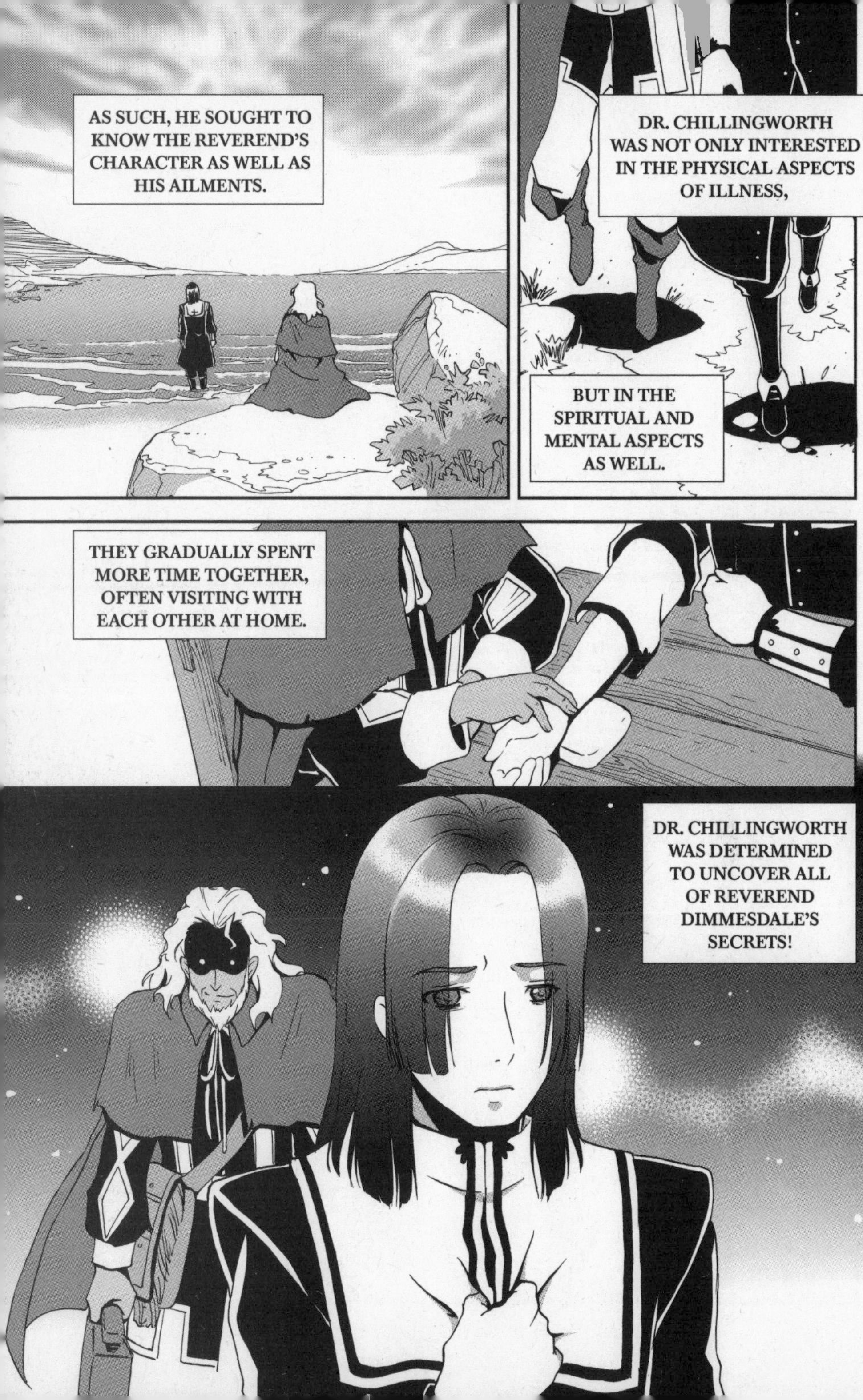
DR. CHILLINGWORTH WAS NOT ONLY INTERESTED IN THE PHYSICAL ASPECTS OF ILLNESS,
BUT IN THE SPIRITUAL AND MENTAL ASPECTS AS WELL.
AS SUCH, HE SOUGHT TO KNOW THE REVEREND'S CHARACTER AS WELL AS HIS AILMENTS.
THEY GRADUALLY SPENT MORE TIME TOGETHER, OFTEN VISITING WITH EACH OTHER AT HOME.
DR. CHILLINGWORTH WAS DETERMINED TO UNCOVER ALL OF REVEREND DIMMESDALE'S SECRETS!

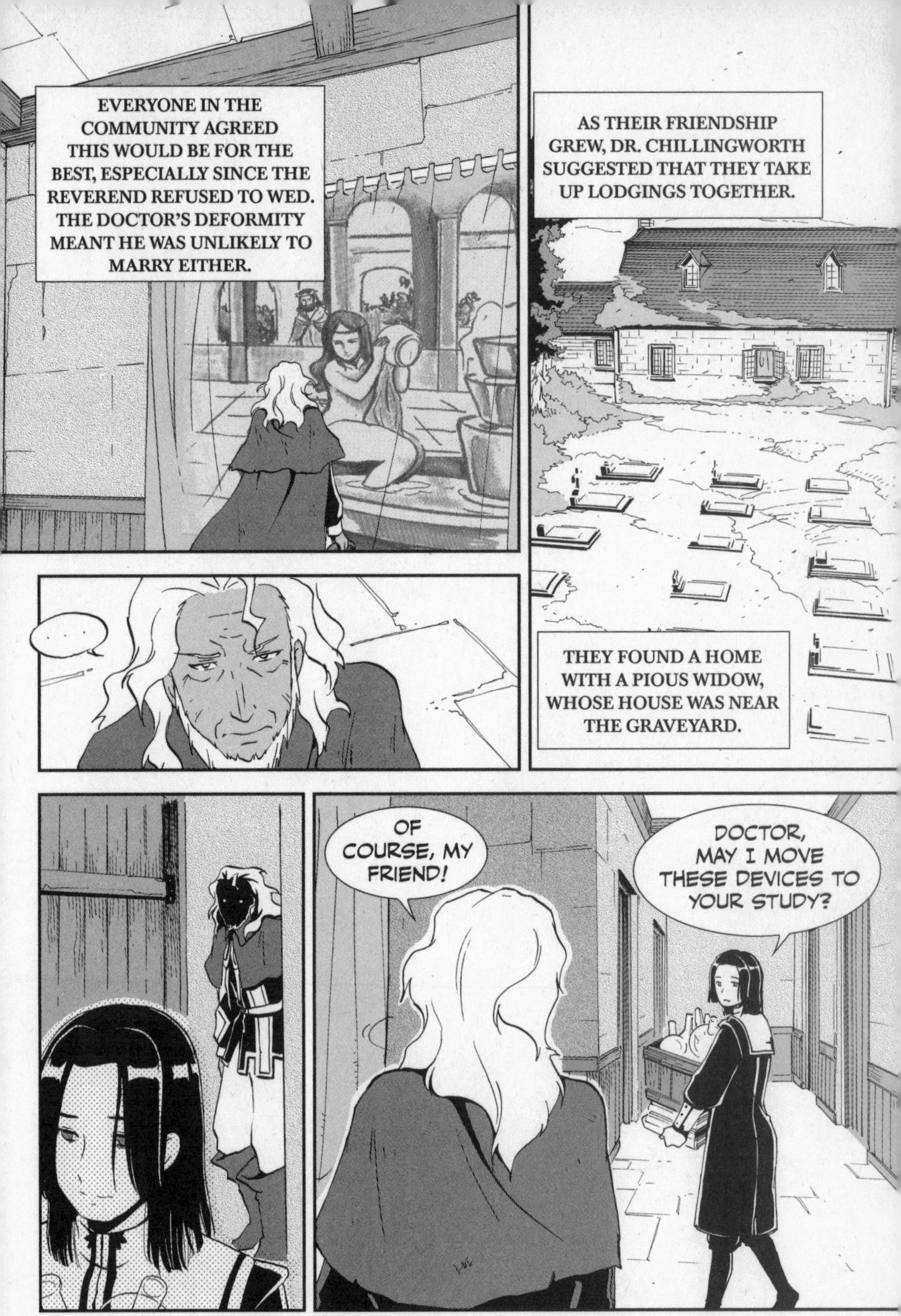
AS THEIR FRIENDSHIP GREW, DR. CHILLINGWORTH SUGGESTED THAT THEY TAKE UP LODGINGS TOGETHER.
THEY FOUND A HOME WITH A PIOUS WIDOW, WHOSE HOUSE WAS NEAR THE GRAVEYARD.
EVERYONE IN THE COMMUNITY AGREED THIS WOULD BE FOR THE BEST, ESPECIALLY SINCE THE REVEREND REFUSED TO WED. THE DOCTOR'S DEFORMITY MEANT HE WAS UNLIKELY TO MARRY EITHER.
. . .
DOCTOR, MAY I MOVE THESE DEVICES TO YOUR STUDY?
OF COURSE, MY FRIEND!

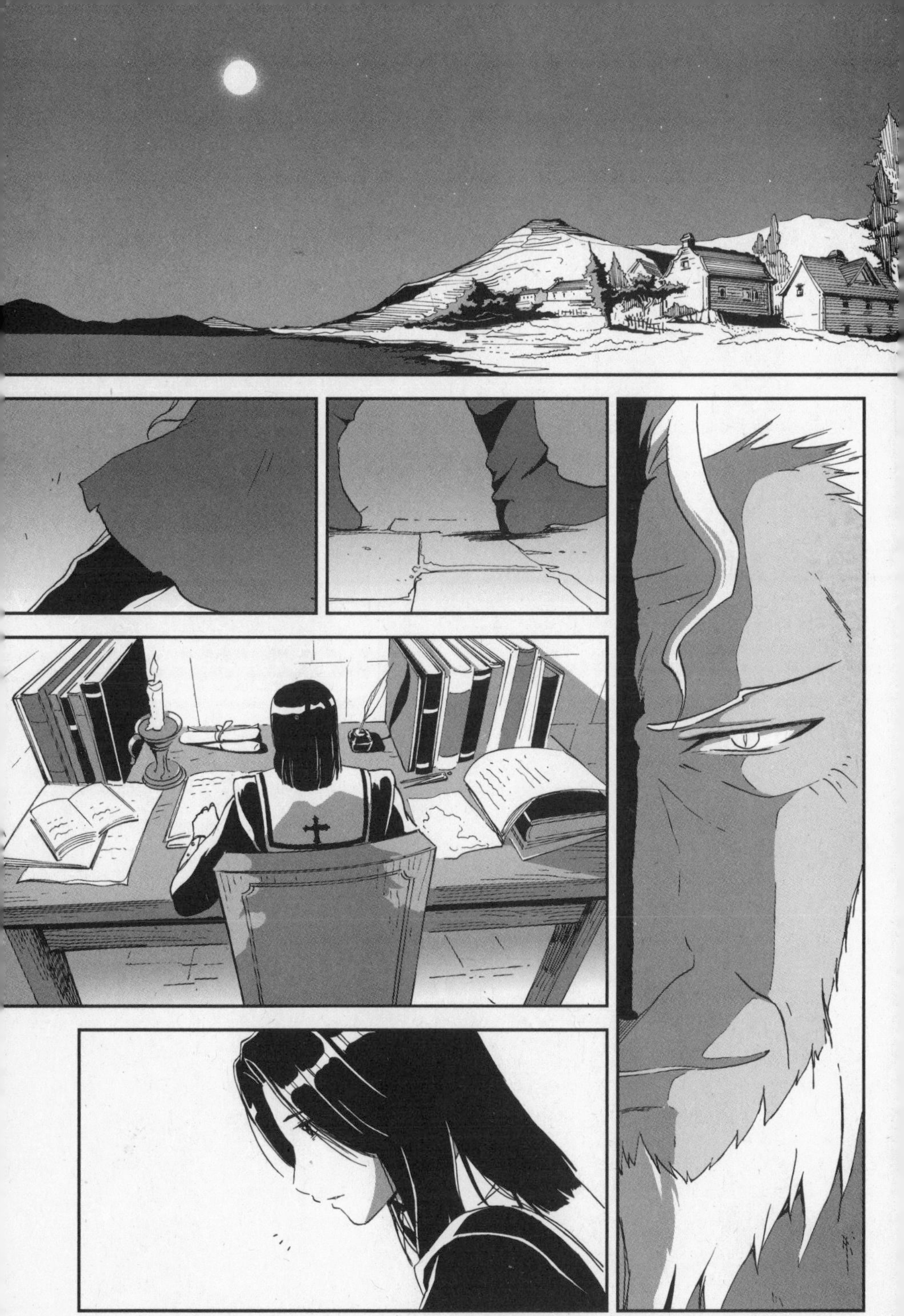

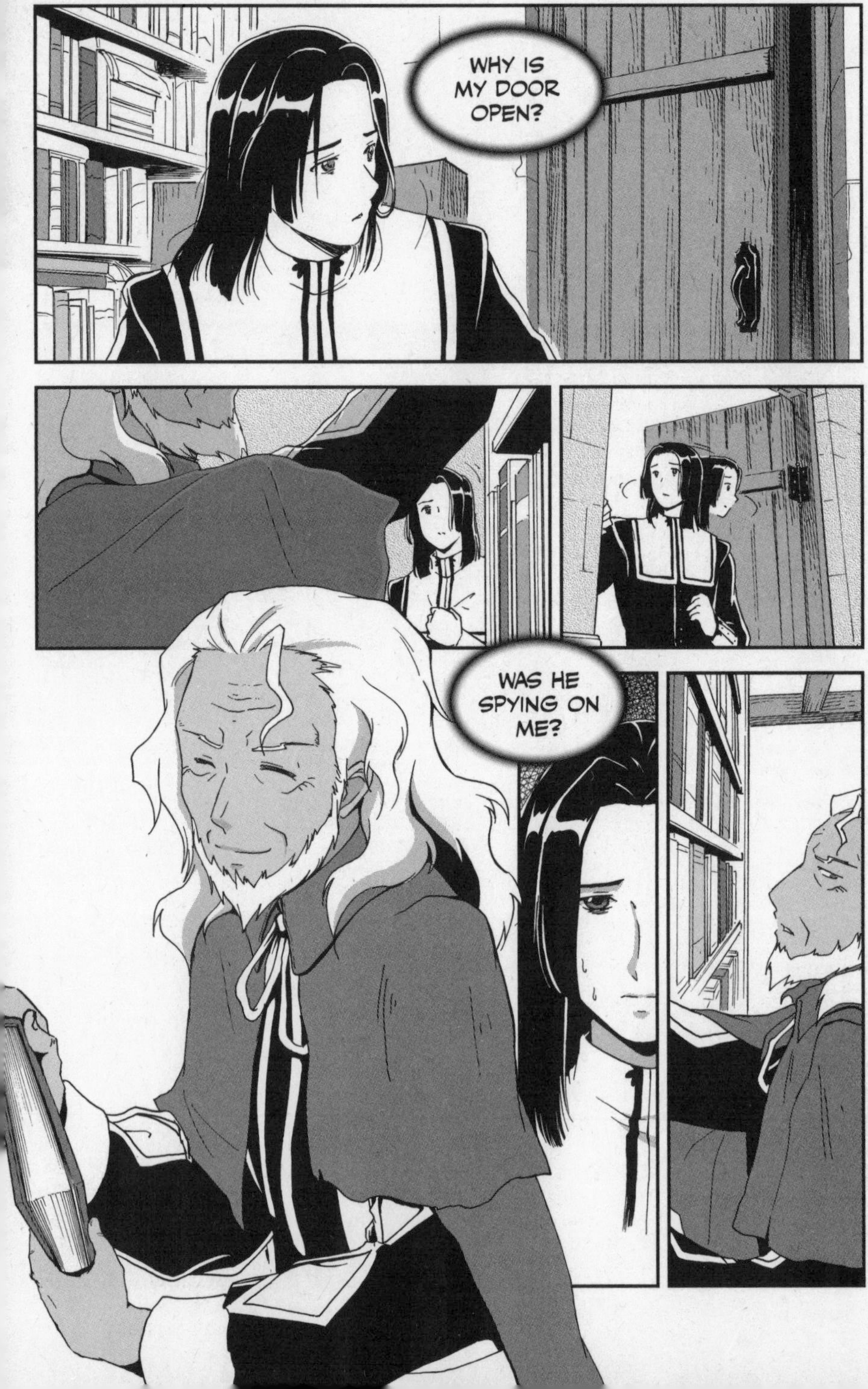
WHY IS MY DOOR OPEN?
WAS HE SPYING ON ME?

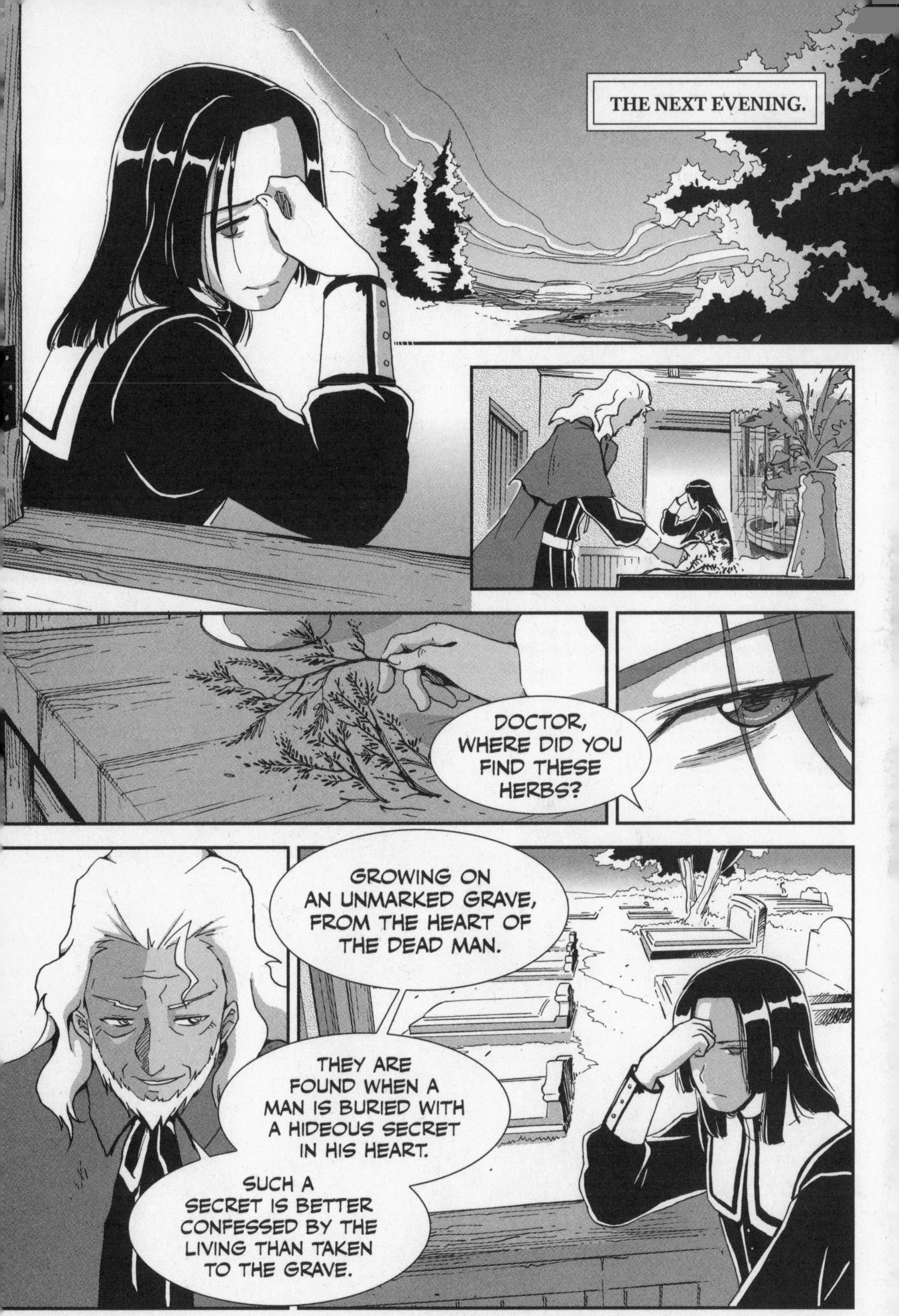
THE NEXT EVENING.
DOCTOR, WHERE DID YOU FIND THESE HERBS?
GROWING ON AN UNMARKED GRAVE, FROM THE HEART OF THE DEAD MAN.
THEY ARE FOUND WHEN A MAN IS BURIED WITH A HIDEOUS SECRET IN HIS HEART.
SUCH A SECRET IS BETTER CONFESSED BY THE LIVING THAN TAKEN TO THE GRAVE.

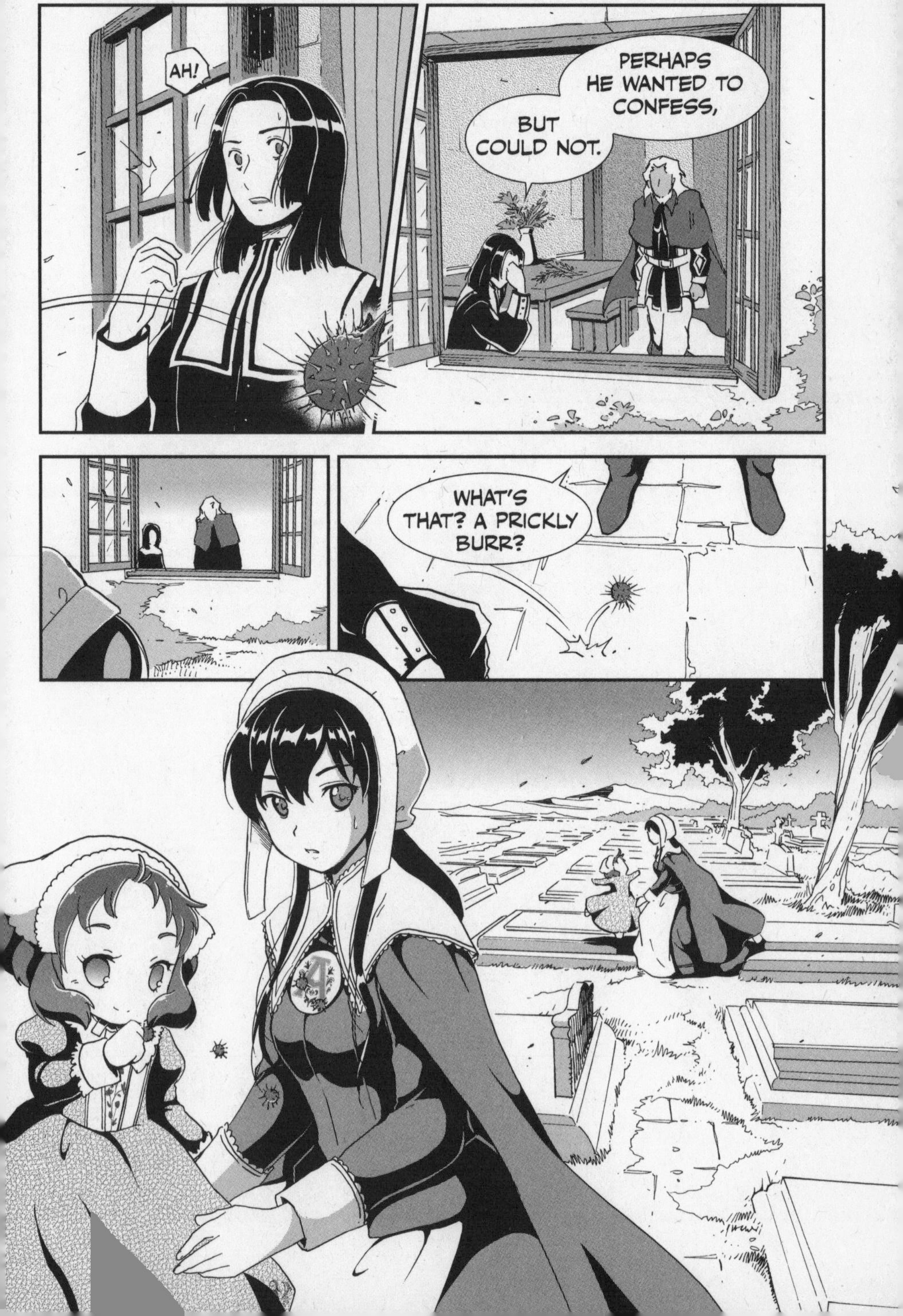
PERHAPS HE WANTED TO CONFESS,
BUT COULD NOT.
AH!
WHAT'S THAT? A PRICKLY BURR?

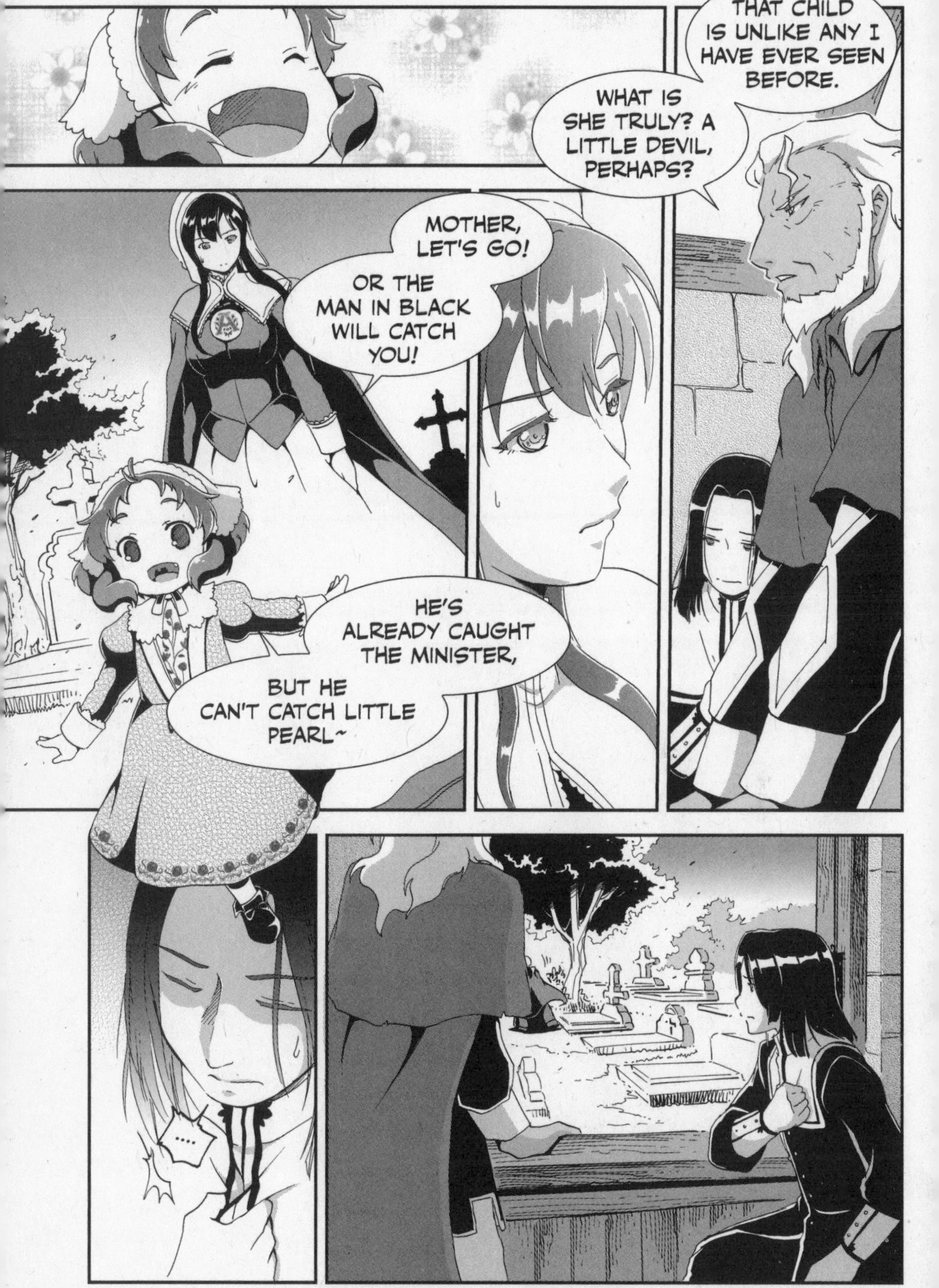
THAT CHILD IS UNLIKE ANY I HAVE EVER SEEN BEFORE.
WHAT IS SHE TRULY? A LITTLE DEVIL, PERHAPS?
MOTHER, LET'S GO!
OR THE MAN IN BLACK WILL CATCH YOU!
HE'S ALREADY CAUGHT THE MINISTER,
BUT HE CAN'T CATCH LITTLE PEARL~
....

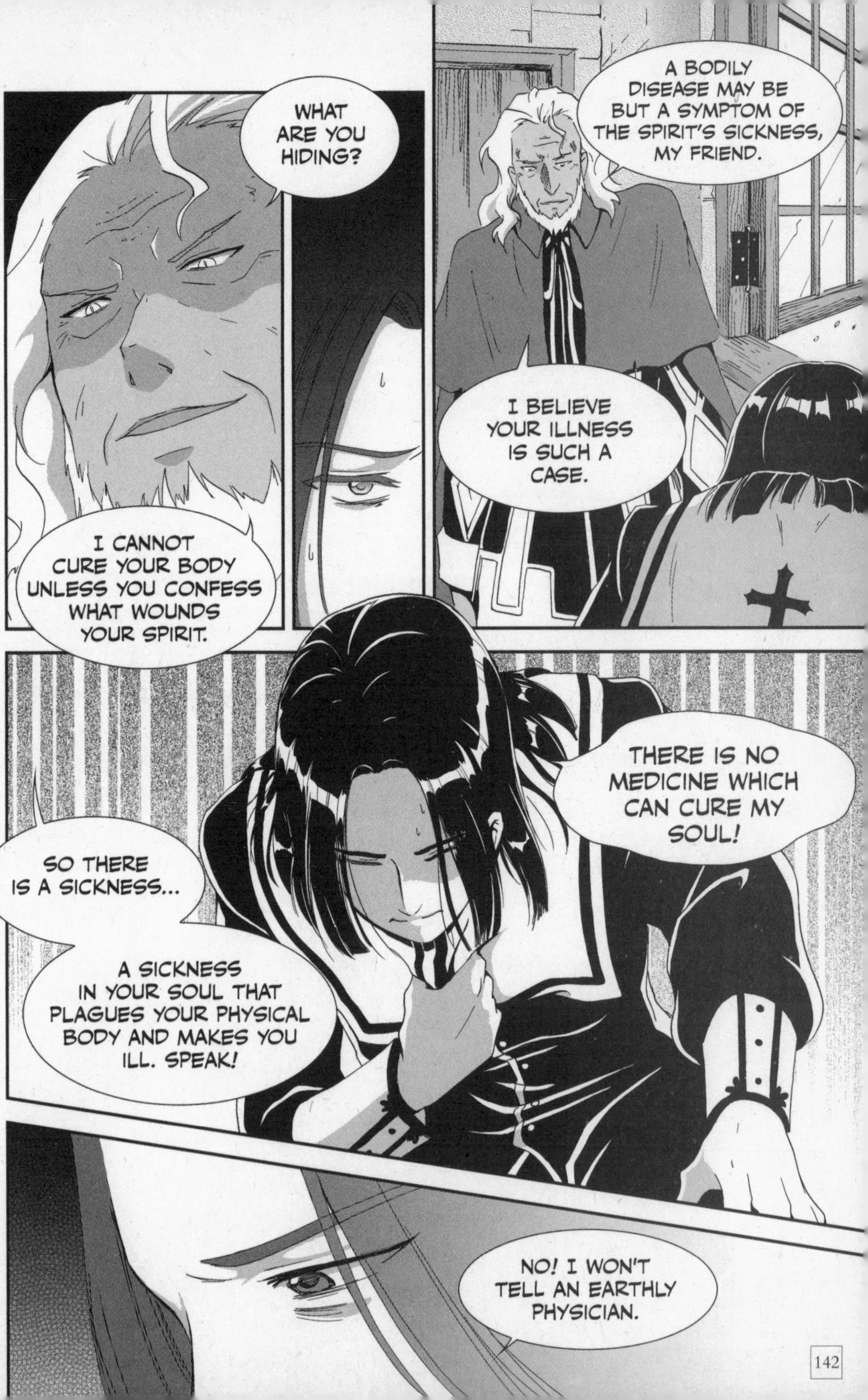
A BODILY DISEASE MAY BE BUT A SYMPTOM OF THE SPIRIT'S SICKNESS, MY FRIEND.
I BELIEVE YOUR ILLNESS IS SUCH A CASE.
WHAT ARE YOU HIDING?
I CANNOT CURE YOUR BODY UNLESS YOU CONFESS WHAT WOUNDS YOUR SPIRIT.
THERE IS NO MEDICINE WHICH CAN CURE MY SOUL!
SO THERE IS A SICKNESS...
A SICKNESS IN YOUR SOUL THAT PLAGUES YOUR PHYSICAL BODY AND MAKES YOU ILL. SPEAK!
NO! I WON'T TELL AN EARTHLY PHYSICIAN.

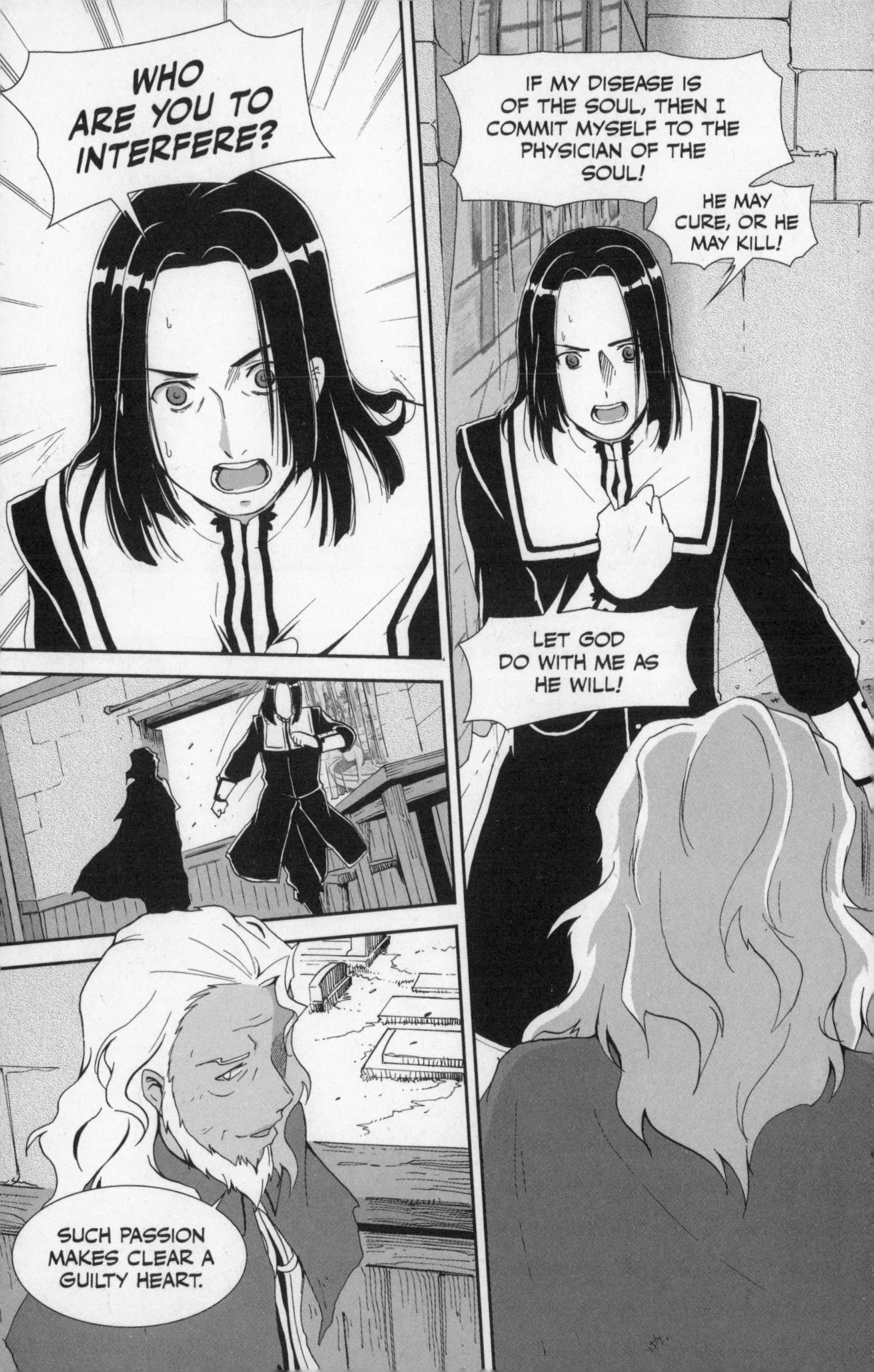
IF MY DISEASE IS OF THE SOUL, THEN I COMMIT MYSELF TO THE PHYSICIAN OF THE SOUL!
HE MAY CURE, OR HE MAY KILL!
LET GOD DO WITH ME AS HE WILL!
WHO ARE YOU TO INTERFERE?
SUCH PASSION MAKES CLEAR A GUILTY HEART.

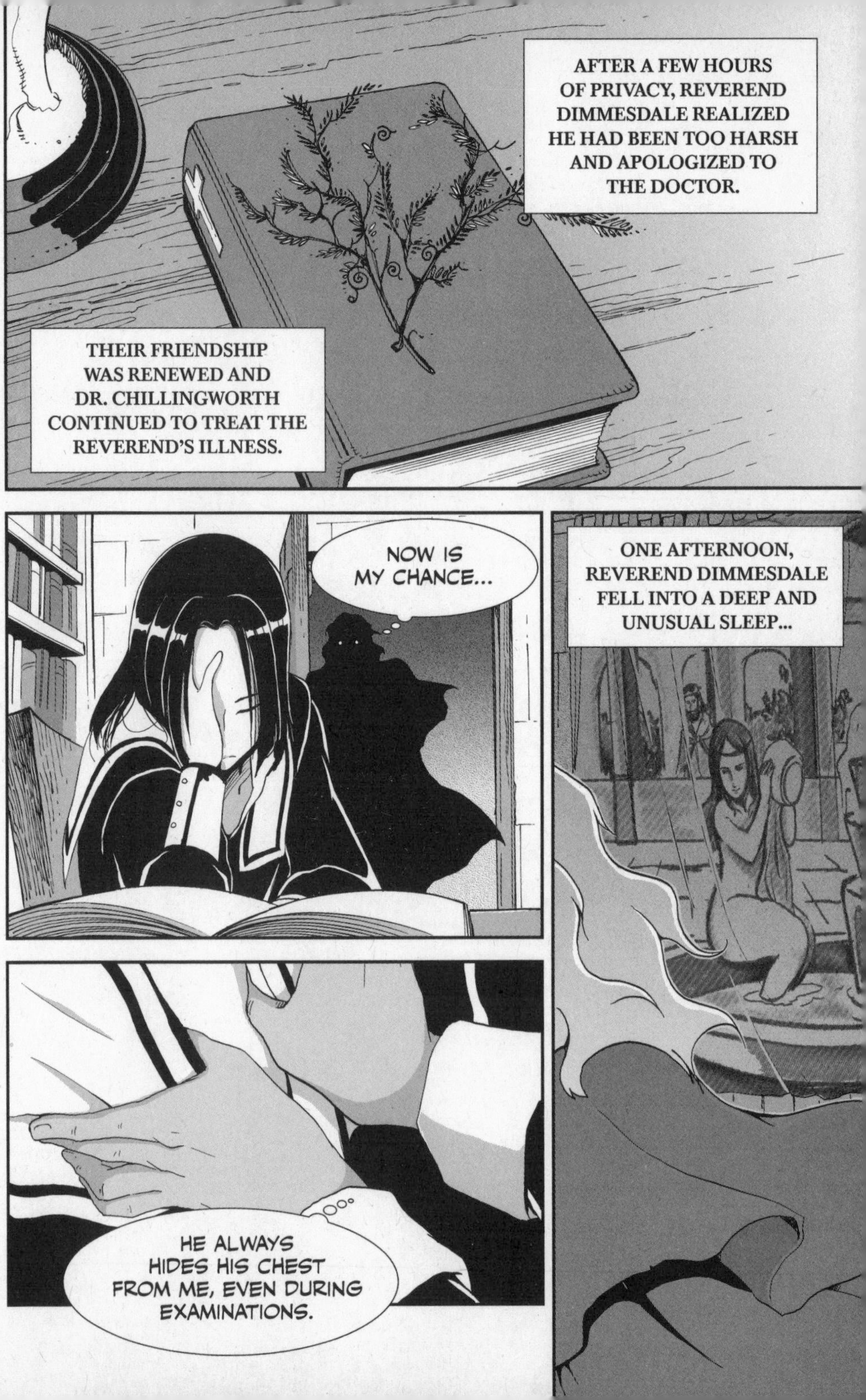
AFTER A FEW HOURS OF PRIVACY, REVEREND DIMMESDALE REALIZED HE HAD BEEN TOO HARSH AND APOLOGIZED TO THE DOCTOR.
THEIR FRIENDSHIP WAS RENEWED AND DR. CHILLINGWORTH CONTINUED TO TREAT THE REVEREND'S ILLNESS.
ONE AFTERNOON, REVEREND DIMMESDALE FELL INTO A DEEP AND UNUSUAL SLEEP...
NOW IS MY CHANCE...
HE ALWAYS HIDES HIS CHEST FROM ME, EVEN DURING EXAMINATIONS.

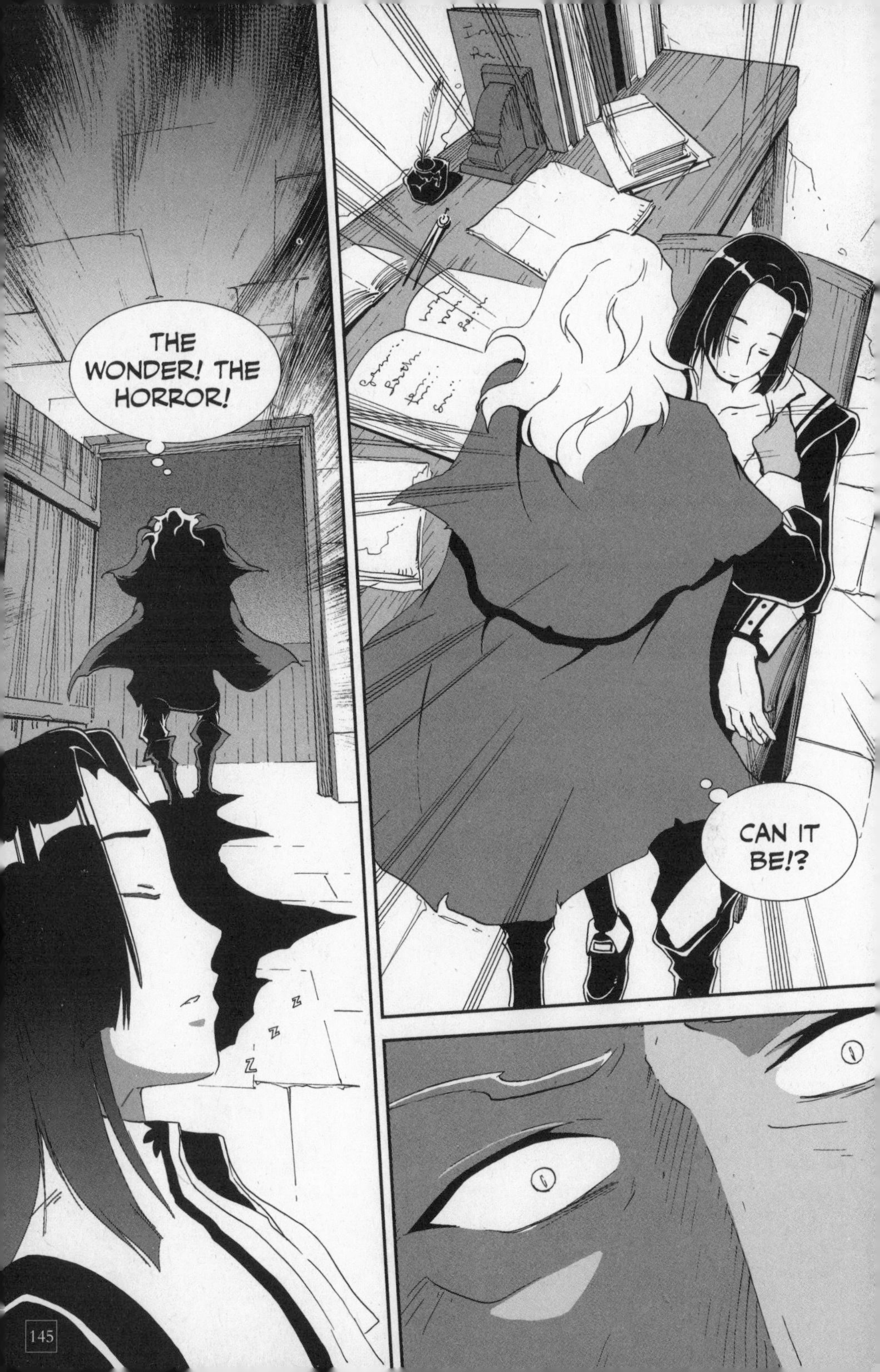
CAN IT BE!?
THE WONDER! THE HORROR!
Z Z Z

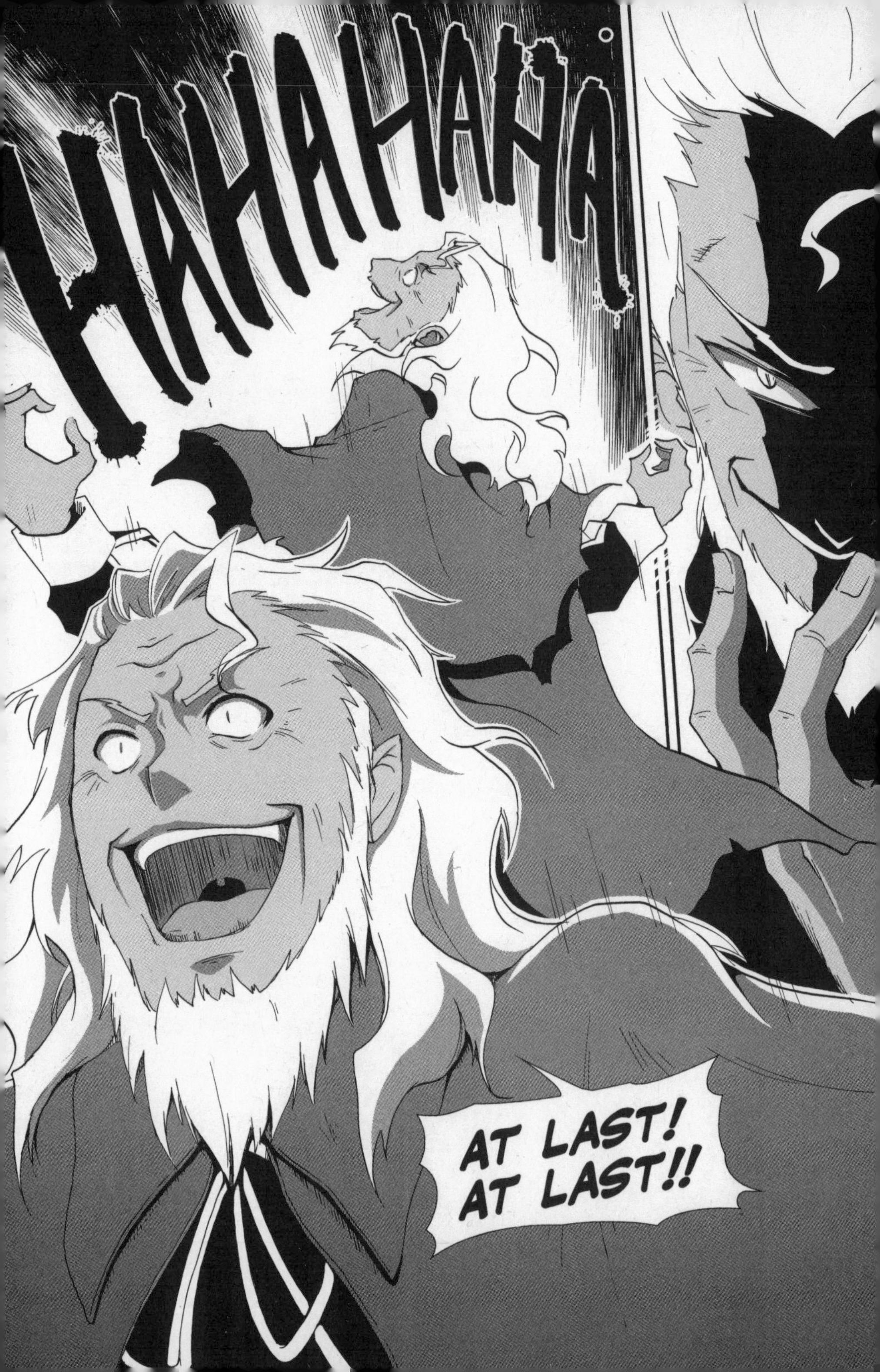
HAHAHAHAHA
AT LAST! AT LAST!!

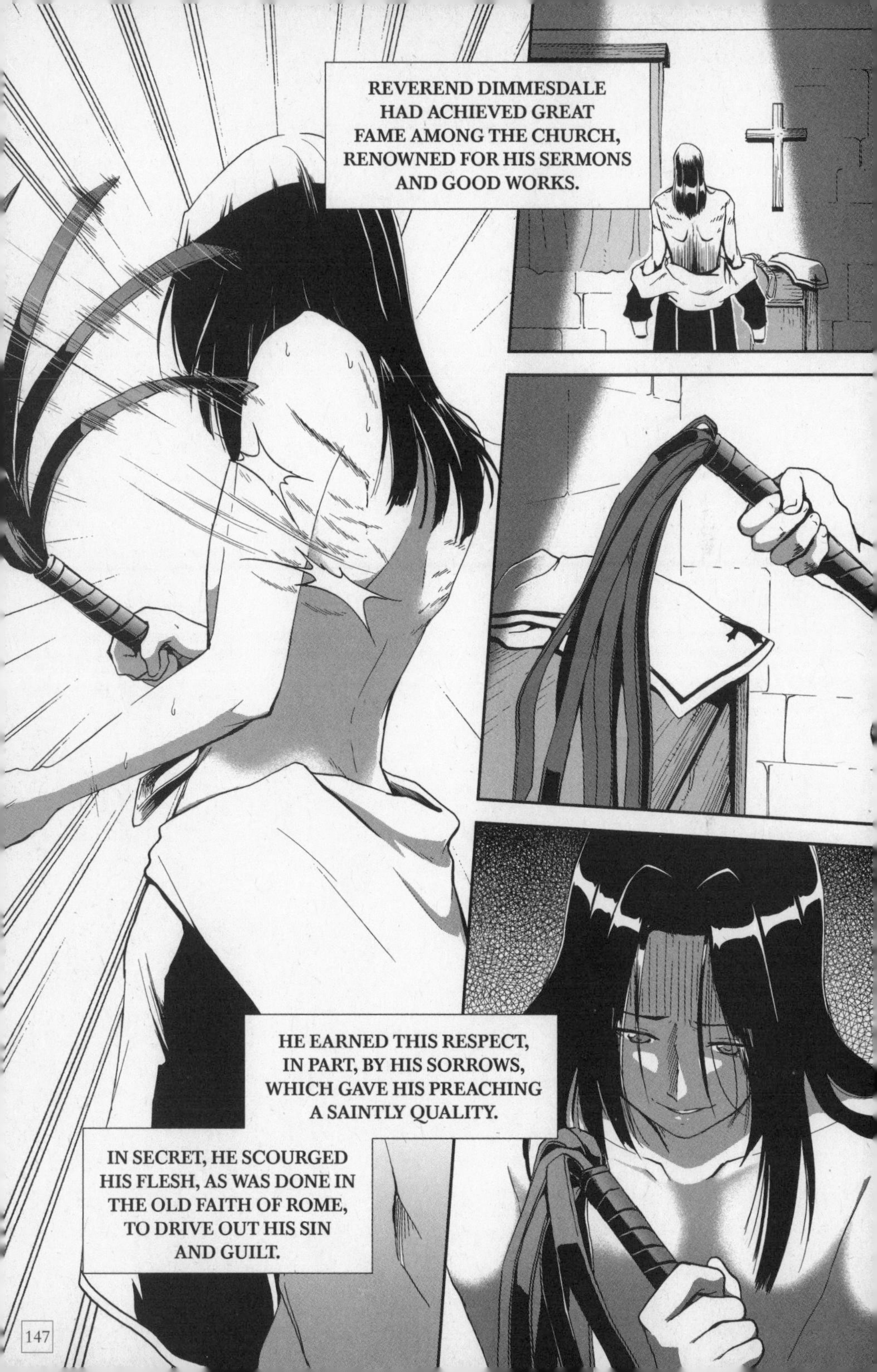
REVEREND DIMMESDALE HAD ACHIEVED GREAT FAME AMONG THE CHURCH, RENOWNED FOR HIS SERMONS AND GOOD WORKS.
HE EARNED THIS RESPECT, IN PART, BY HIS SORROWS, WHICH GAVE HIS PREACHING A SAINTLY QUALITY.
IN SECRET, HE SCOURGED HIS FLESH, AS WAS DONE IN THE OLD FAITH OF ROME, TO DRIVE OUT HIS SIN AND GUILT.

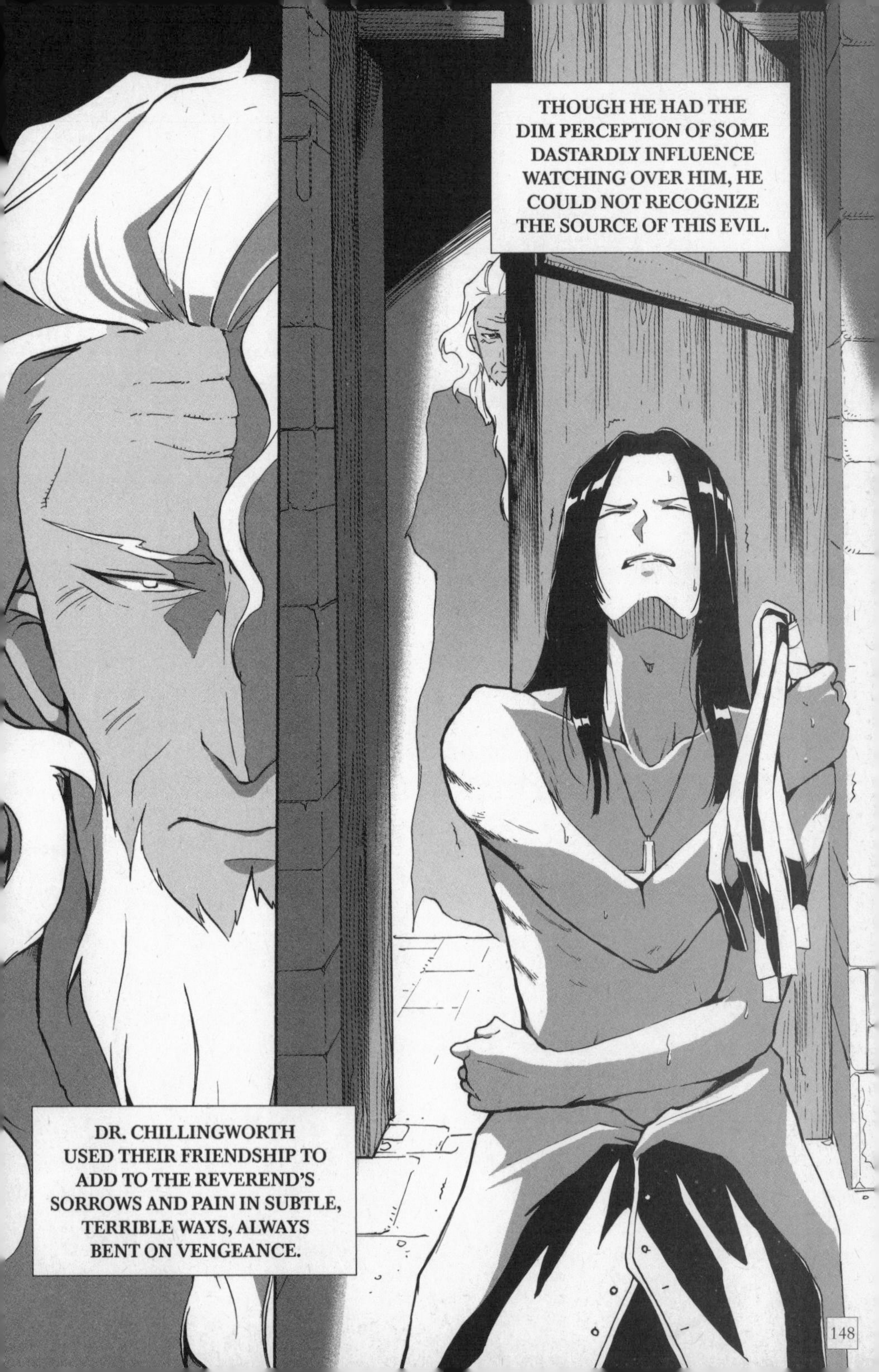
THOUGH HE HAD THE DIM PERCEPTION OF SOME DASTARDLY INFLUENCE WATCHING OVER HIM, HE COULD NOT RECOGNIZE THE SOURCE OF THIS EVIL.
DR. CHILLINGWORTH USED THEIR FRIENDSHIP TO ADD TO THE REVEREND'S SORROWS AND PAIN IN SUBTLE, TERRIBLE WAYS, ALWAYS BENT ON VENGEANCE.

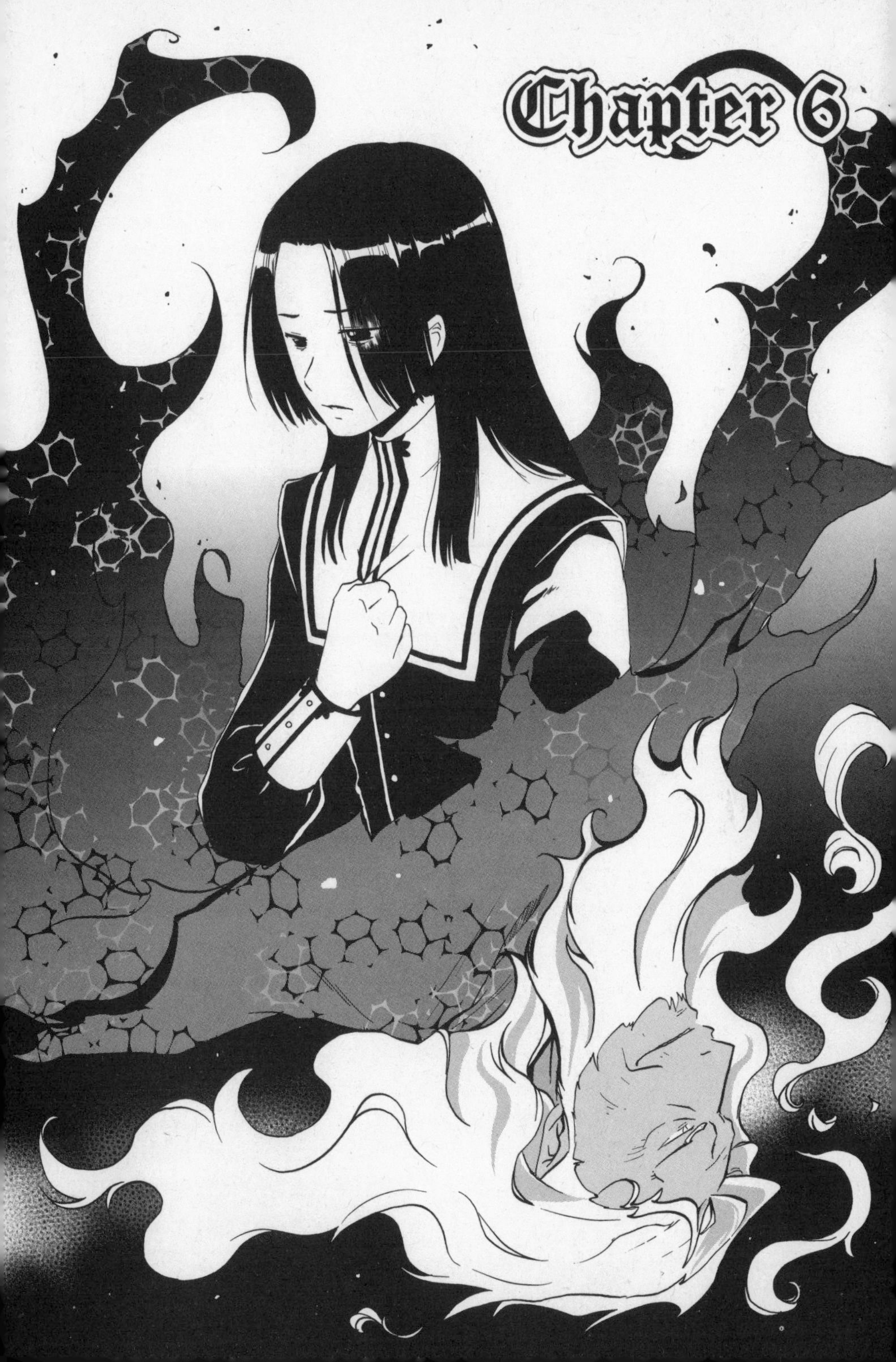
Chapter 6

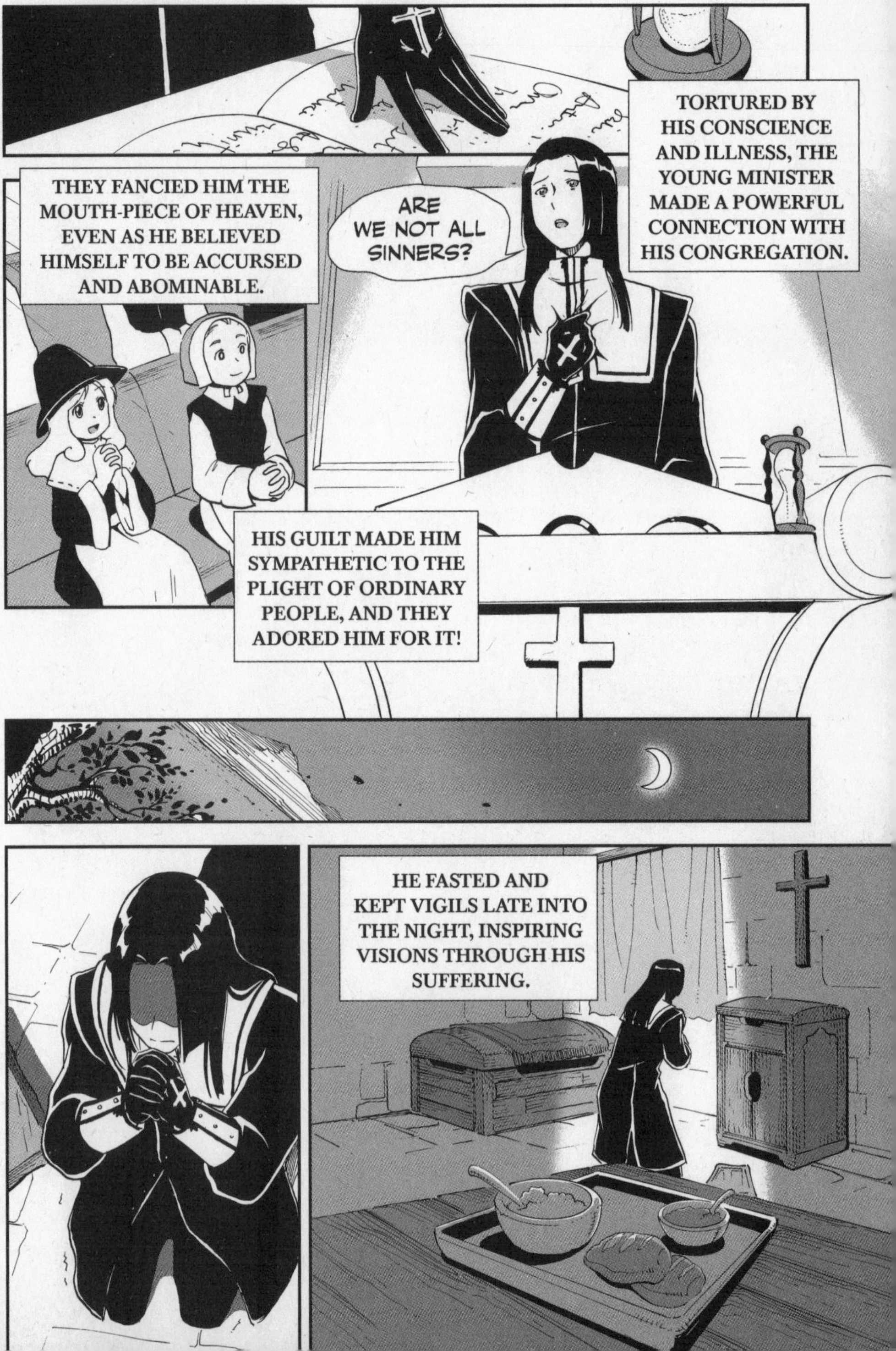
TORTURED BY HIS CONSCIENCE AND ILLNESS, THE YOUNG MINISTER MADE A POWERFUL CONNECTION WITH HIS CONGREGATION.
ARE WE NOT ALL SINNERS?
THEY FANCIED HIM THE MOUTH-PIECE OF HEAVEN, EVEN AS HE BELIEVED HIMSELF TO BE ACCURSED AND ABOMINABLE.
HIS GUILT MADE HIM SYMPATHETIC TO THE PLIGHT OF ORDINARY PEOPLE, AND THEY ADORED HIM FOR IT!
HE FASTED AND KEPT VIGILS LATE INTO THE NIGHT, INSPIRING VISIONS THROUGH HIS SUFFERING.

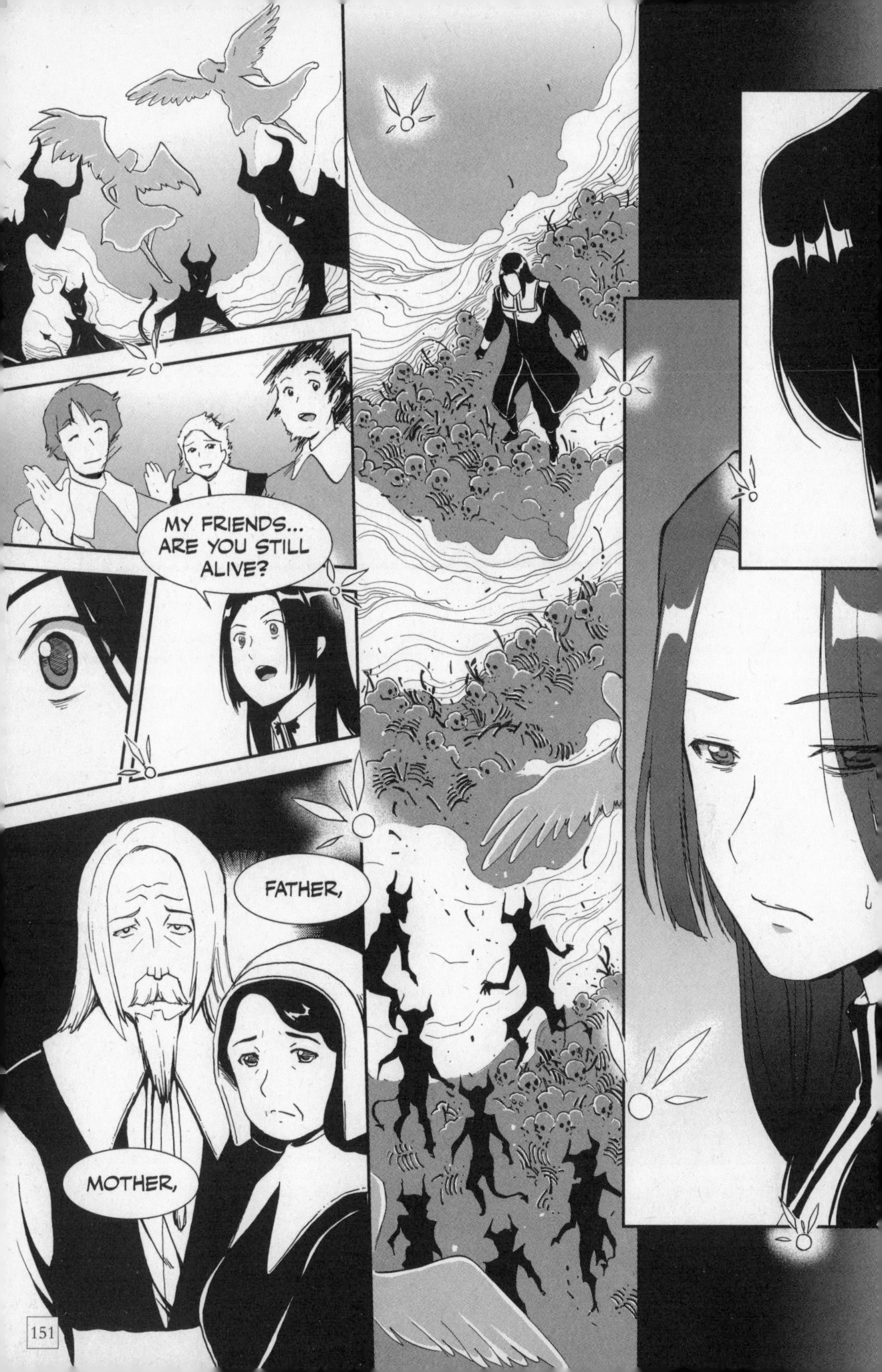
MY FRIENDS... ARE YOU STILL ALIVE?
FATHER,
MOTHER,

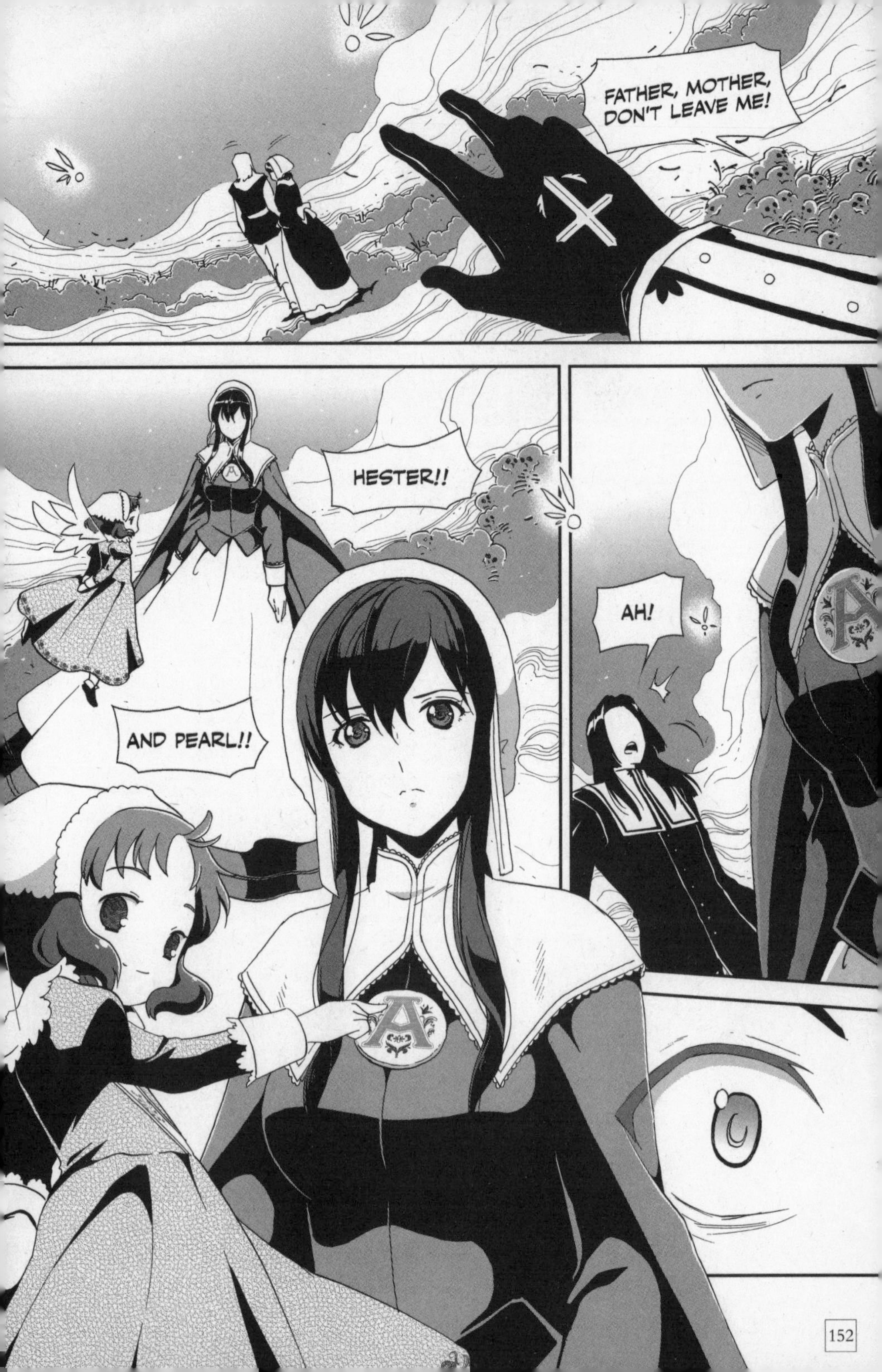
FATHER, MOTHER, DON'T LEAVE ME!
AH!
HESTER!!
AND PEARL!!

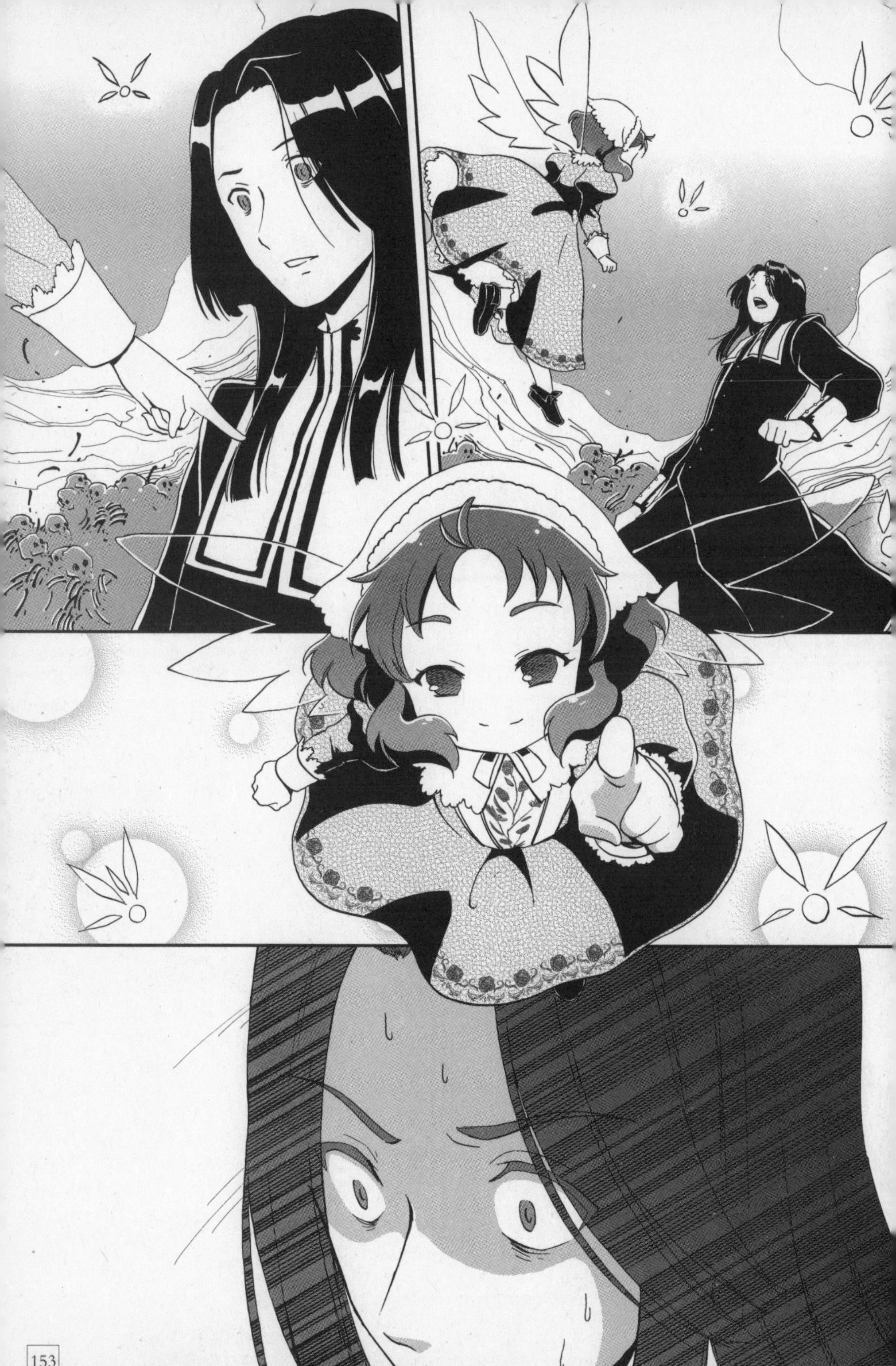

THESE VISIONS...

ARE THEY A MESSAGE FROM GOD?

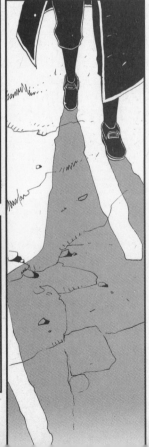

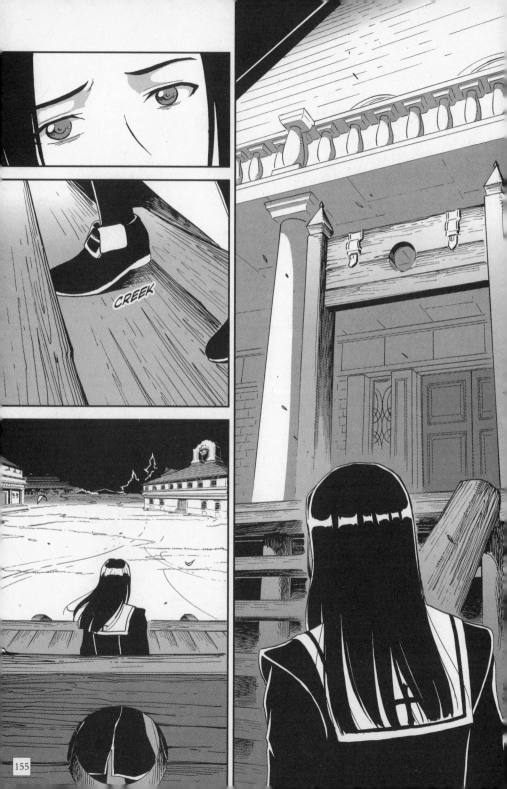

CREEK

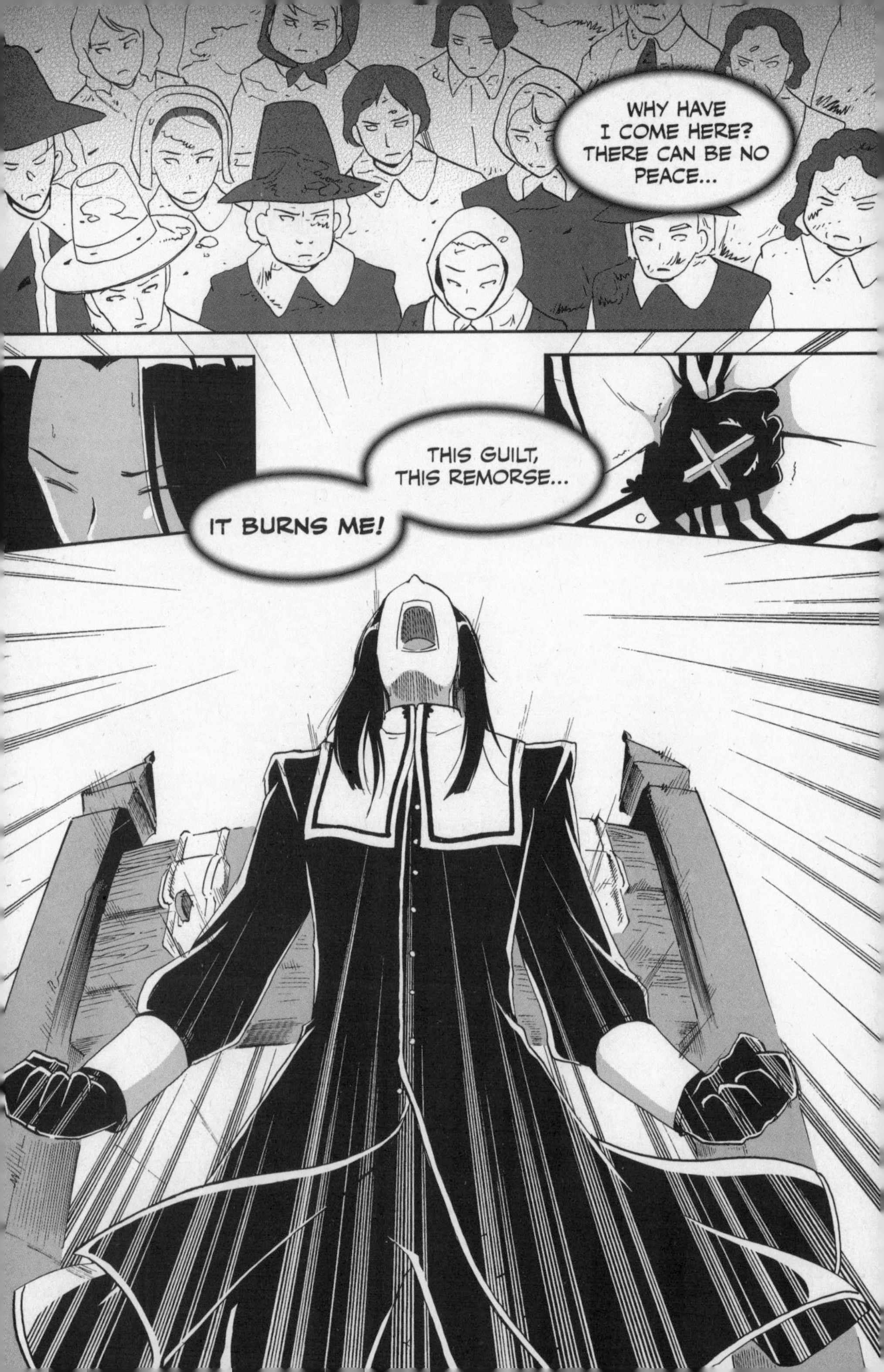
WHY HAVE I COME HERE? THERE CAN BE NO PEACE...
THIS GUILT, THIS REMORSE...
IT BURNS ME!

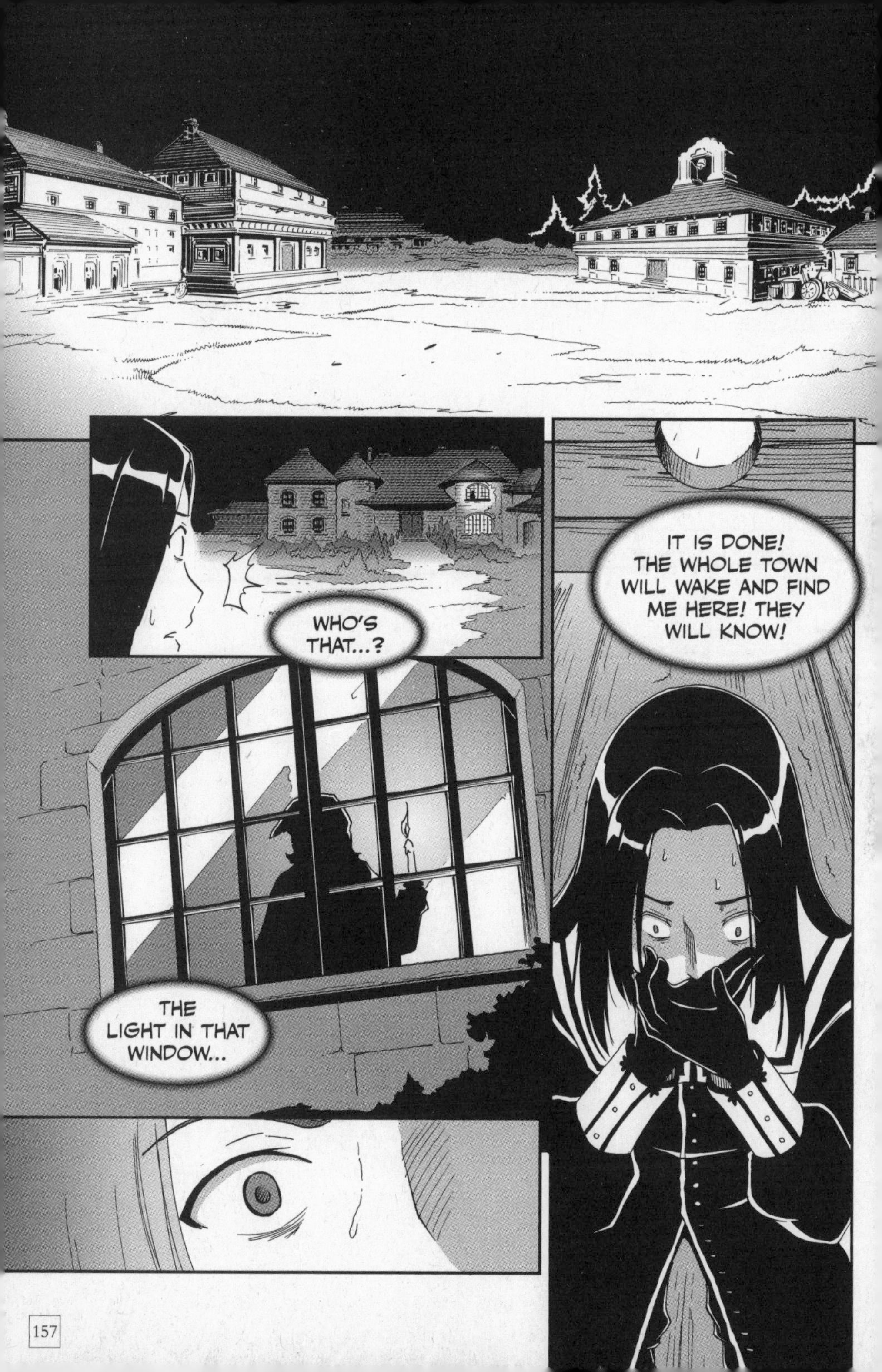
IT IS DONE! THE WHOLE TOWN WILL WAKE AND FIND ME HERE! THEY WILL KNOW!
WHO'S THAT...?
THE LIGHT IN THAT WINDOW...

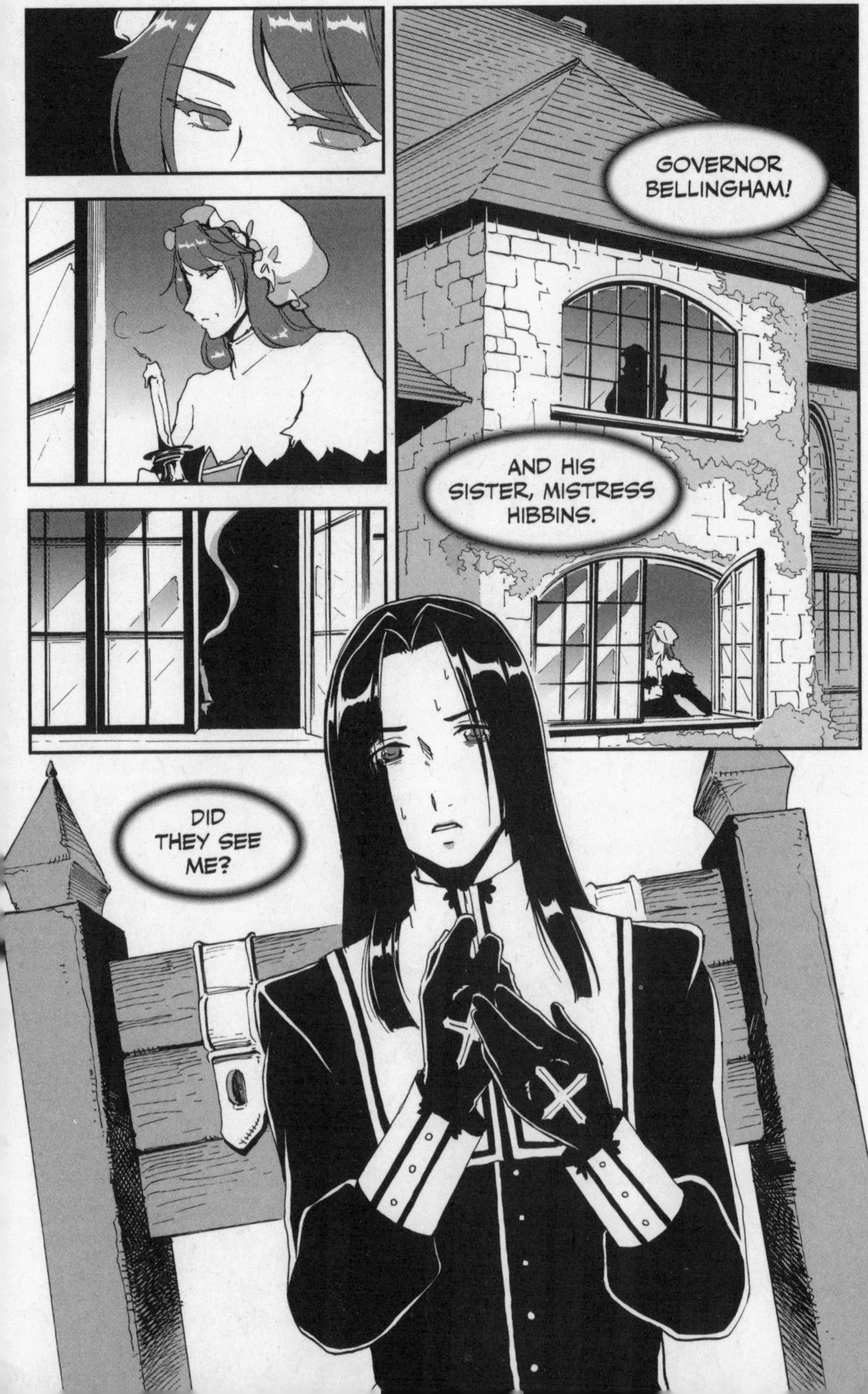
GOVERNOR BELLINGHAM!
AND HIS SISTER, MISTRESS HIBBINS.
DID THEY SEE ME?

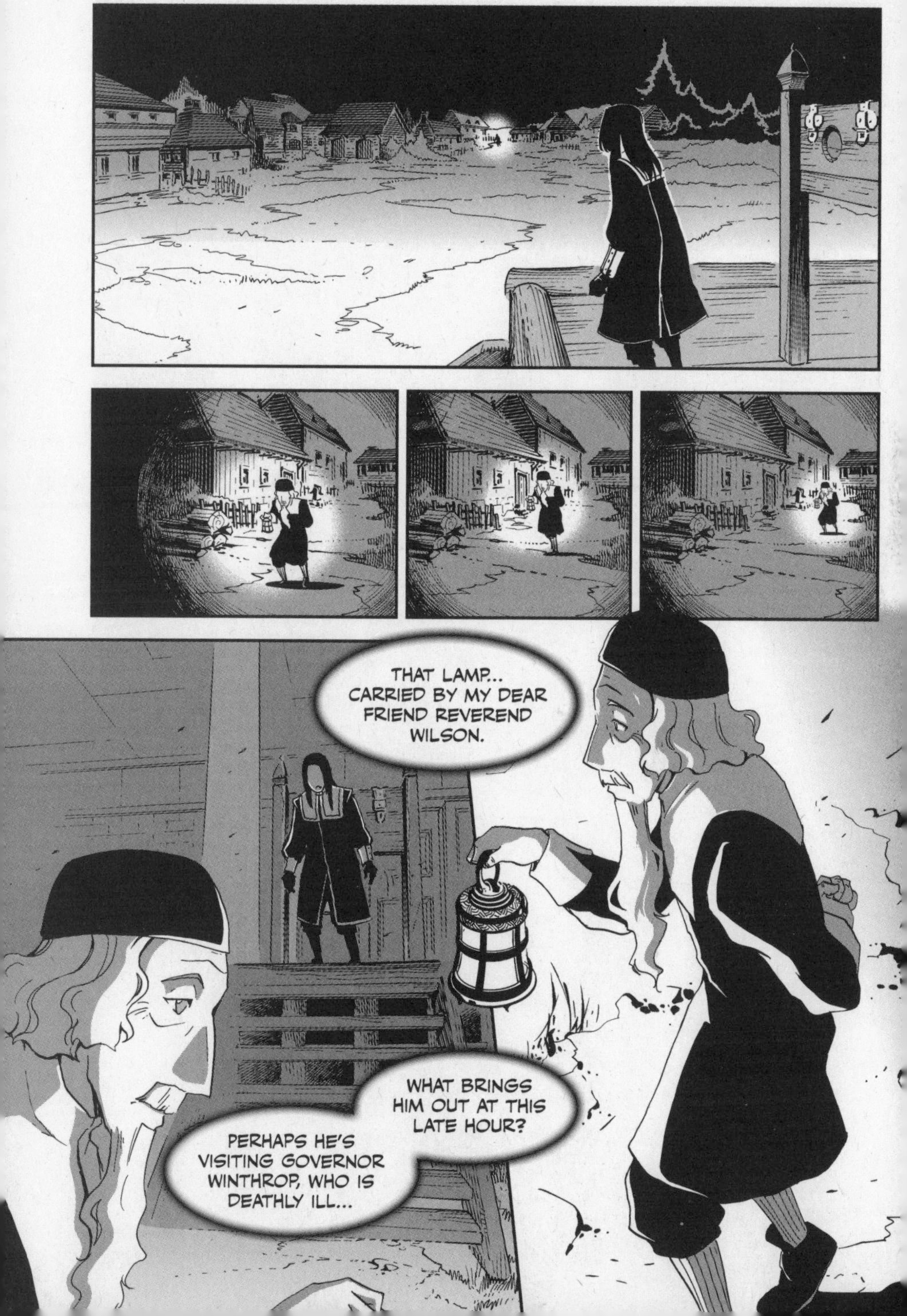
THAT LAMP... CARRIED BY MY DEAR FRIEND REVEREND WILSON.
WHAT BRINGS HIM OUT AT THIS LATE HOUR?
PERHAPS HE'S VISITING GOVERNOR WINTHROP, WHO IS DEATHLY ILL...

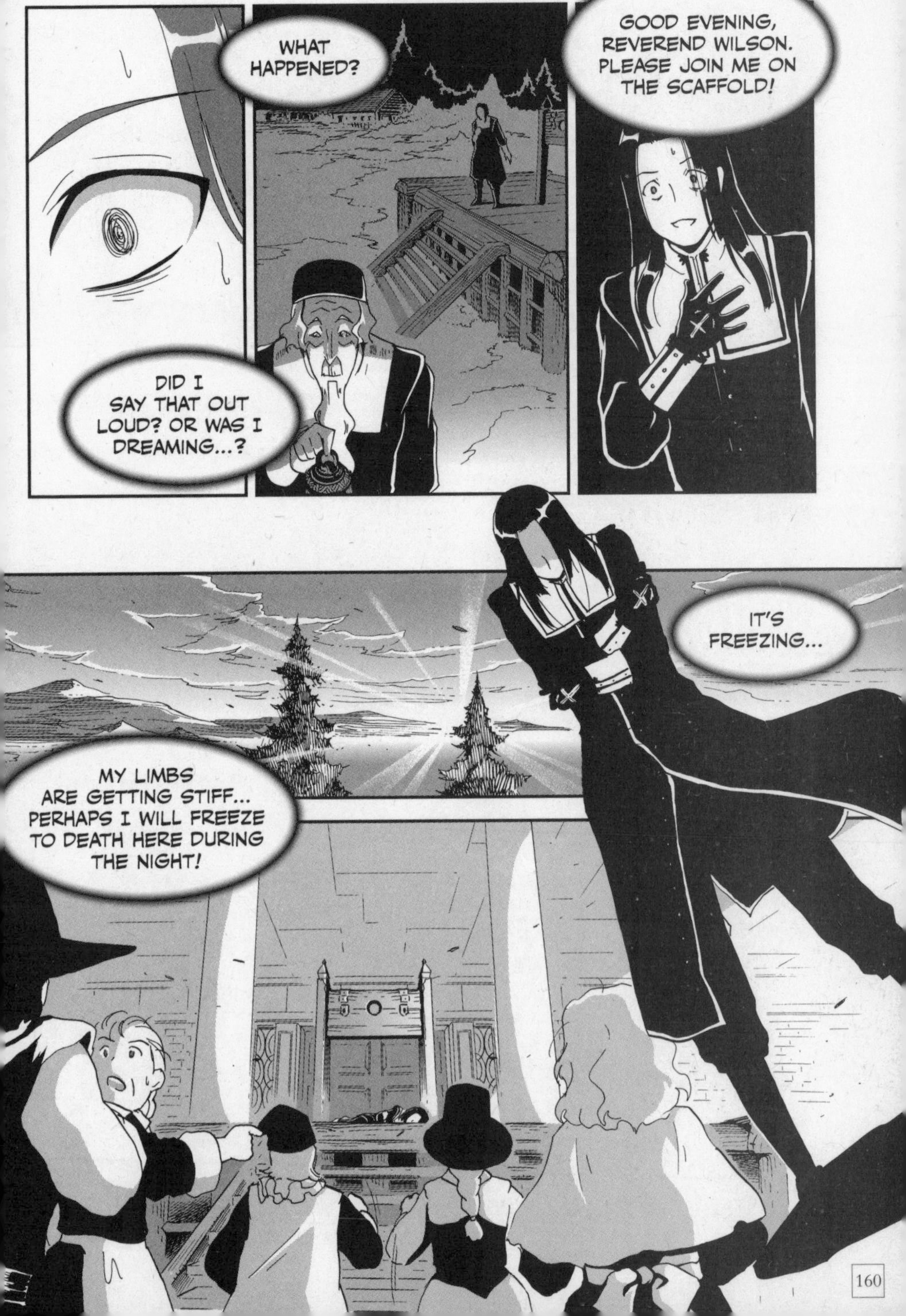
GOOD EVENING, REVEREND WILSON. PLEASE JOIN ME ON THE SCAFFOLD!
WHAT HAPPENED?
DID I SAY THAT OUT LOUD? OR WAS I DREAMING...?
IT'S FREEZING...
MY LIMBS ARE GETTING STIFF... PERHAPS I WILL FREEZE TO DEATH HERE DURING THE NIGHT!

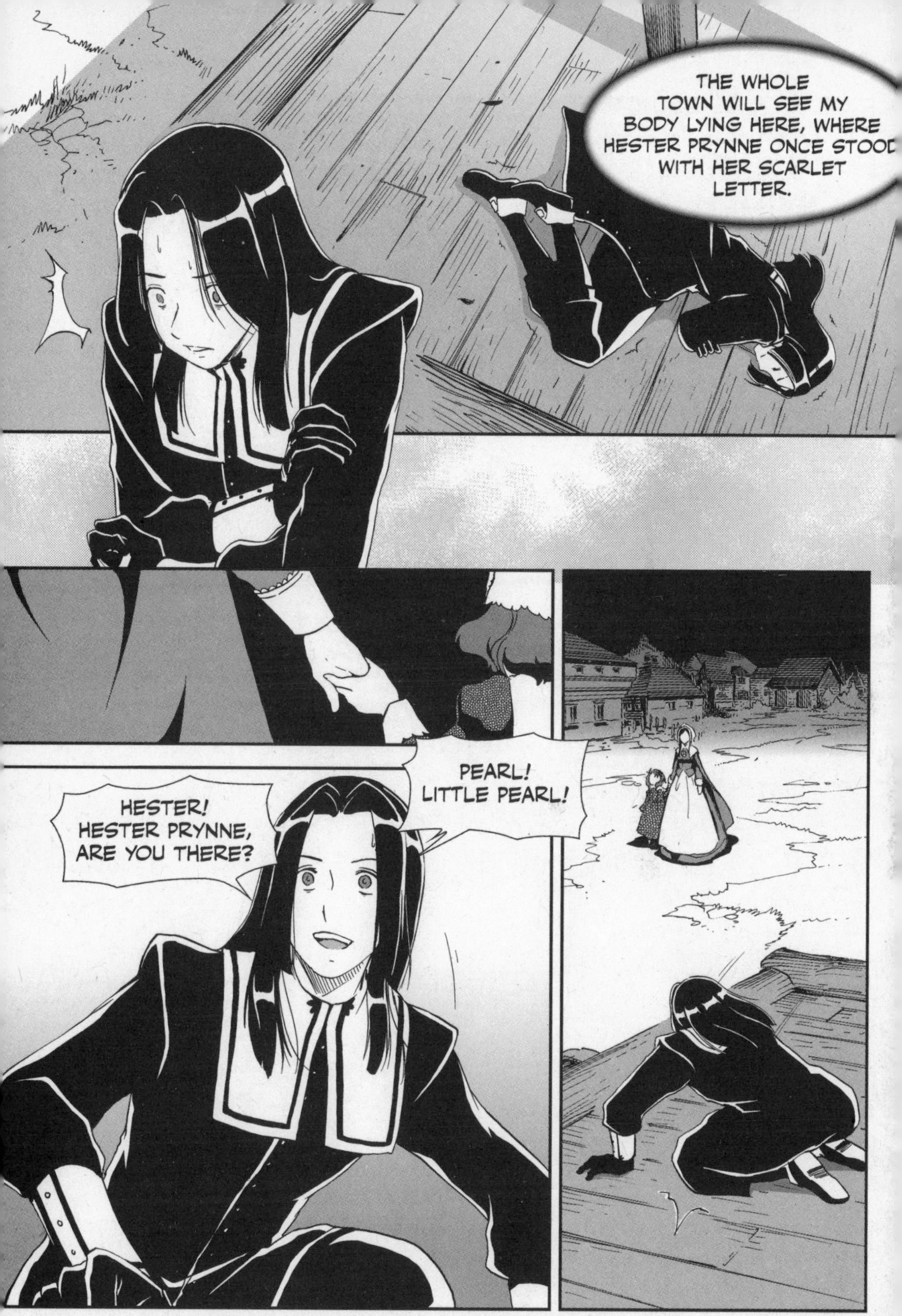
THE WHOLE TOWN WILL SEE MY BODY LYING HERE, WHERE HESTER PRYNNE ONCE STOOD WITH HER SCARLET LETTER.
PEARL! LITTLE PEARL!
HESTER! HESTER PRYNNE, ARE YOU THERE?

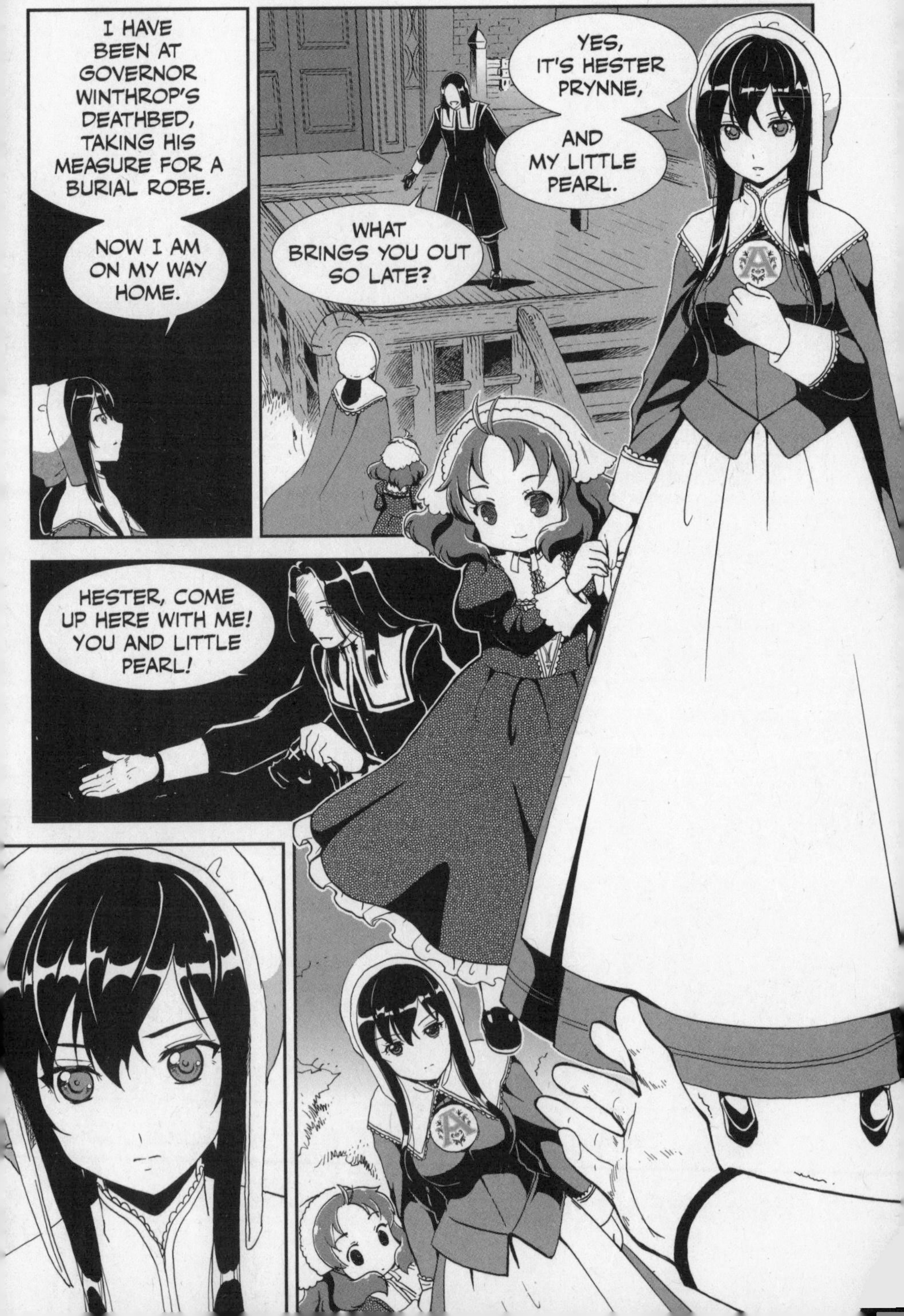
YES, IT'S HESTER PRYNNE,
AND MY LITTLE PEARL.
WHAT BRINGS YOU OUT SO LATE?
I HAVE BEEN AT GOVERNOR WINTHROP'S DEATHBED, TAKING HIS MEASURE FOR A BURIAL ROBE.
NOW I AM ON MY WAY HOME.
HESTER, COME UP HERE WITH ME! YOU AND LITTLE PEARL!

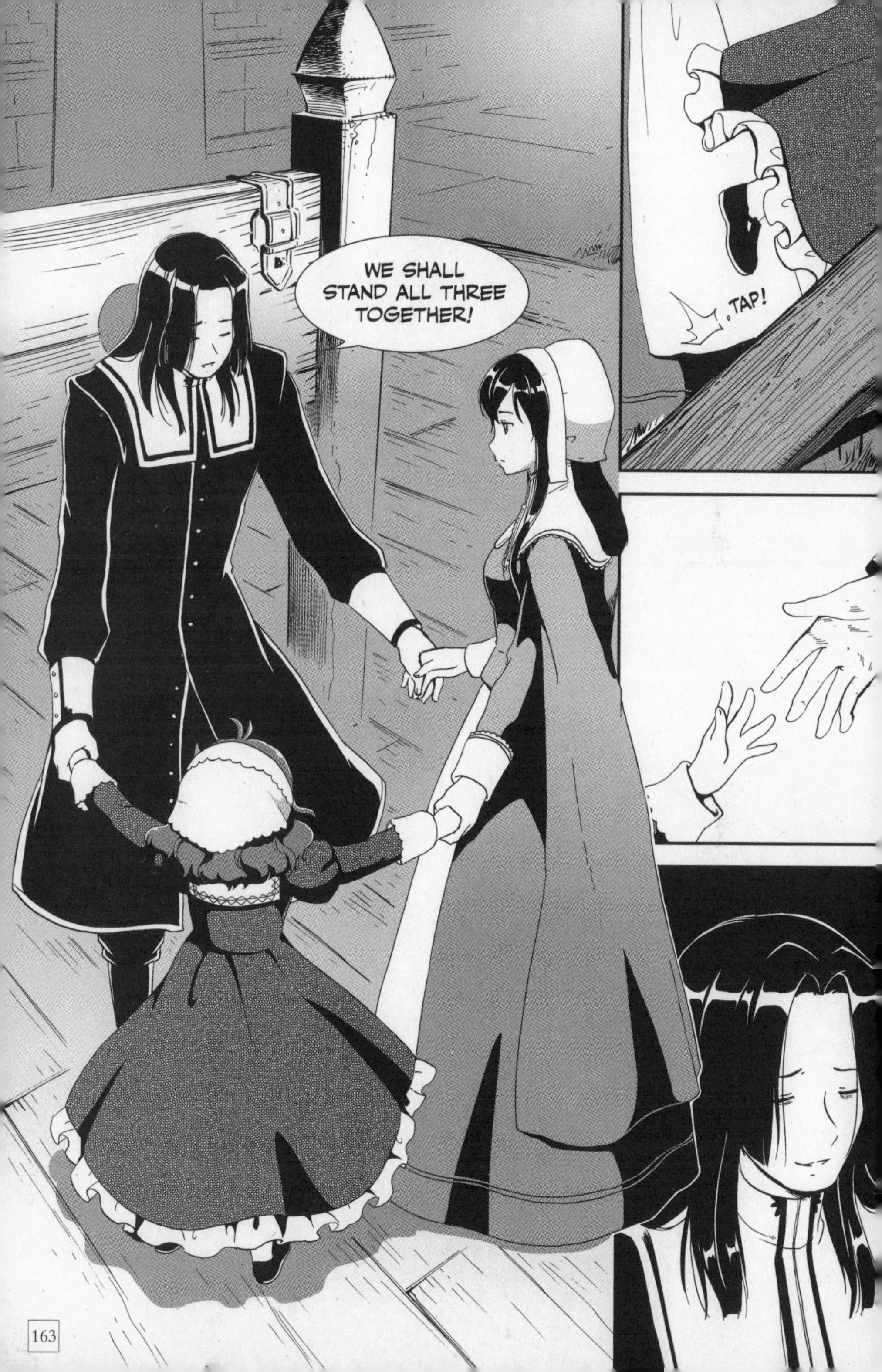
TAP!
WE SHALL STAND ALL THREE TOGETHER!

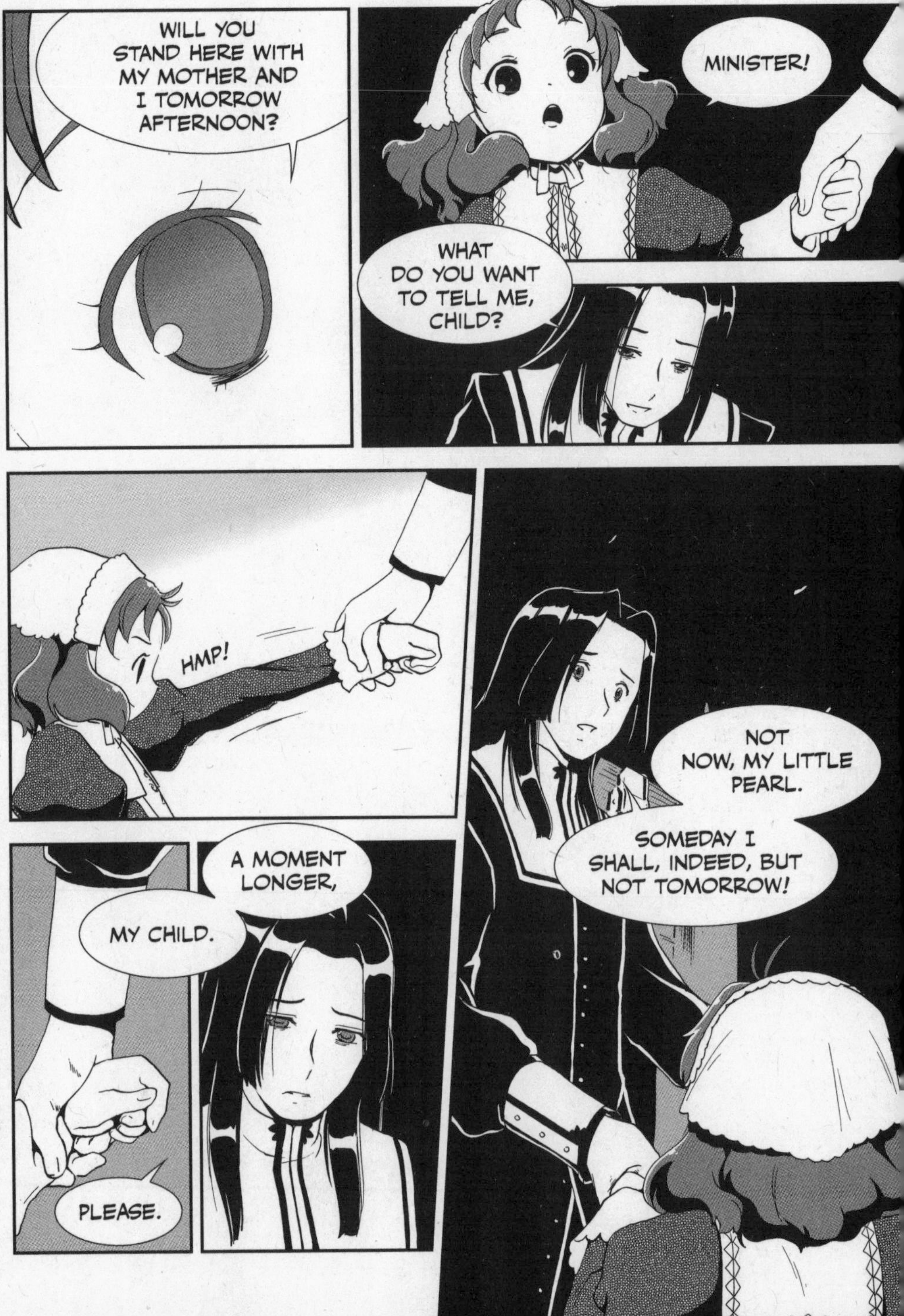
MINISTER!
WHAT DO YOU WANT TO TELL ME, CHILD?
WILL YOU STAND HERE WITH MY MOTHER AND I TOMORROW AFTERNOON?
NOT NOW, MY LITTLE PEARL.
SOMEDAY I SHALL, INDEED, BUT NOT TOMORROW!
HMP!
A MOMENT LONGER,
MY CHILD.
PLEASE.

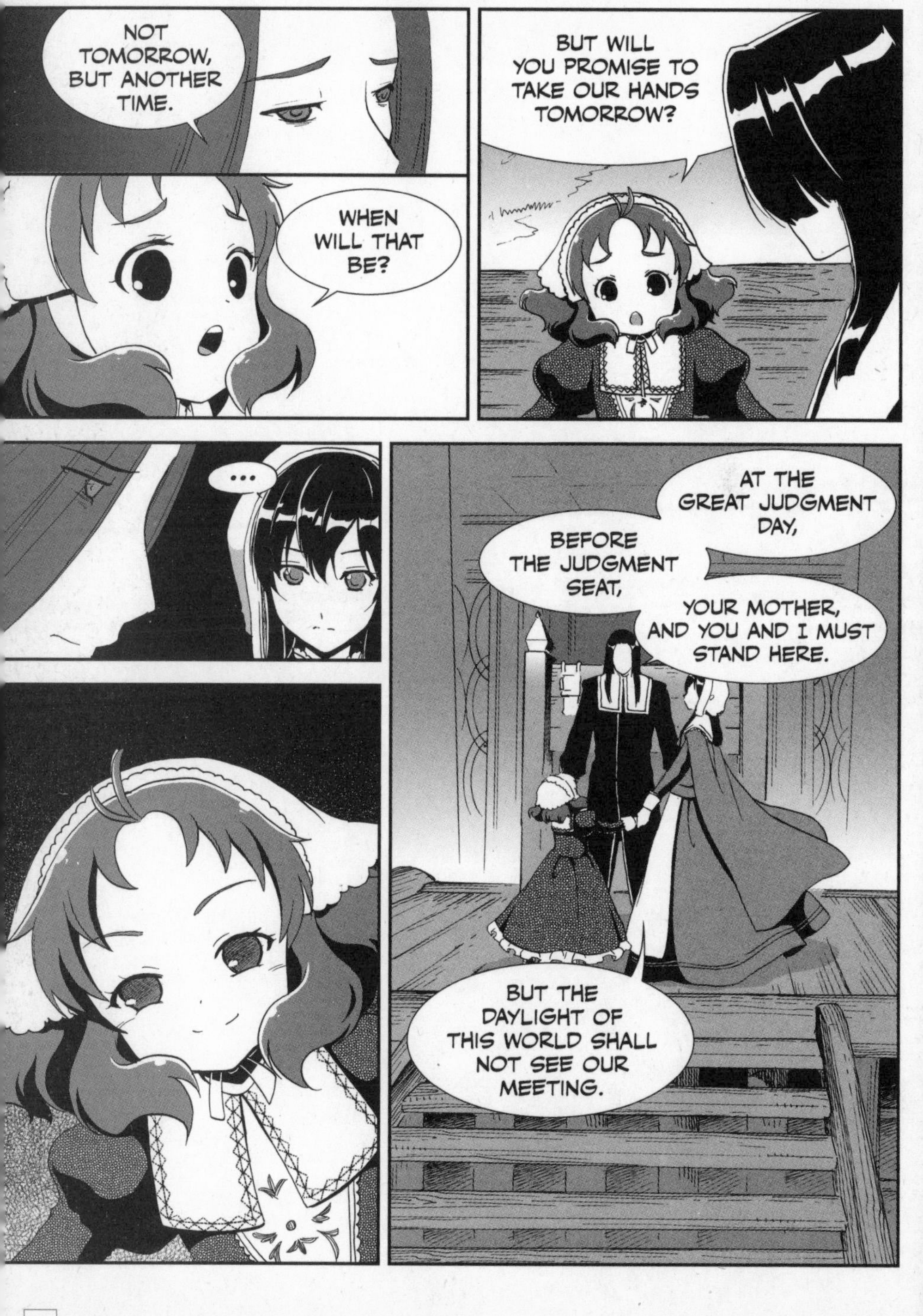
BUT WILL YOU PROMISE TO TAKE OUR HANDS TOMORROW?
NOT TOMORROW, BUT ANOTHER TIME.
WHEN WILL THAT BE?
AT THE GREAT JUDGMENT DAY,
BEFORE THE JUDGMENT SEAT,
YOUR MOTHER, AND YOU AND I MUST STAND HERE.
BUT THE DAYLIGHT OF THIS WORLD SHALL NOT SEE OUR MEETING.
...

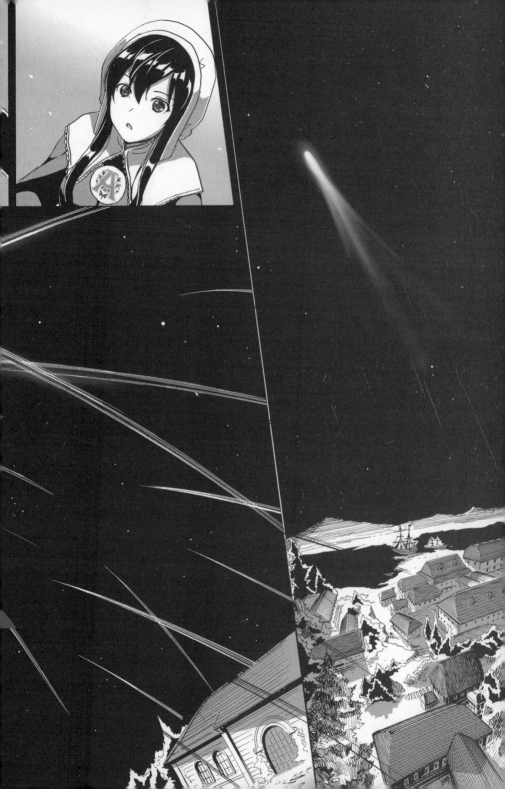

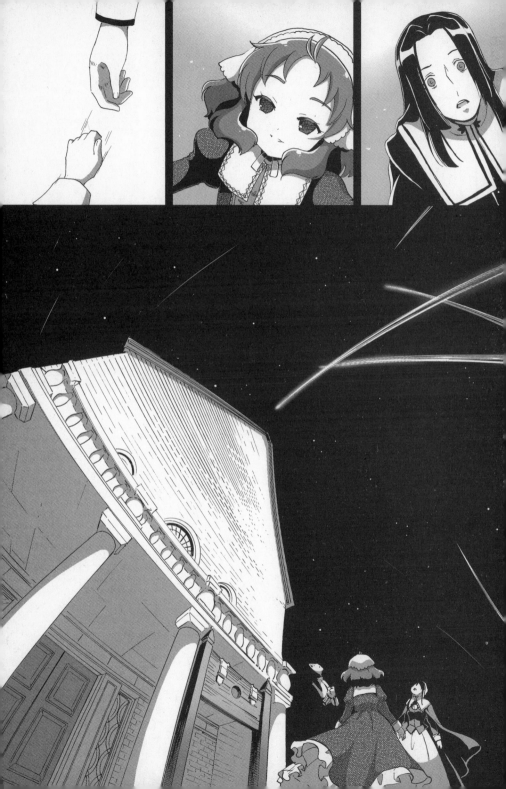

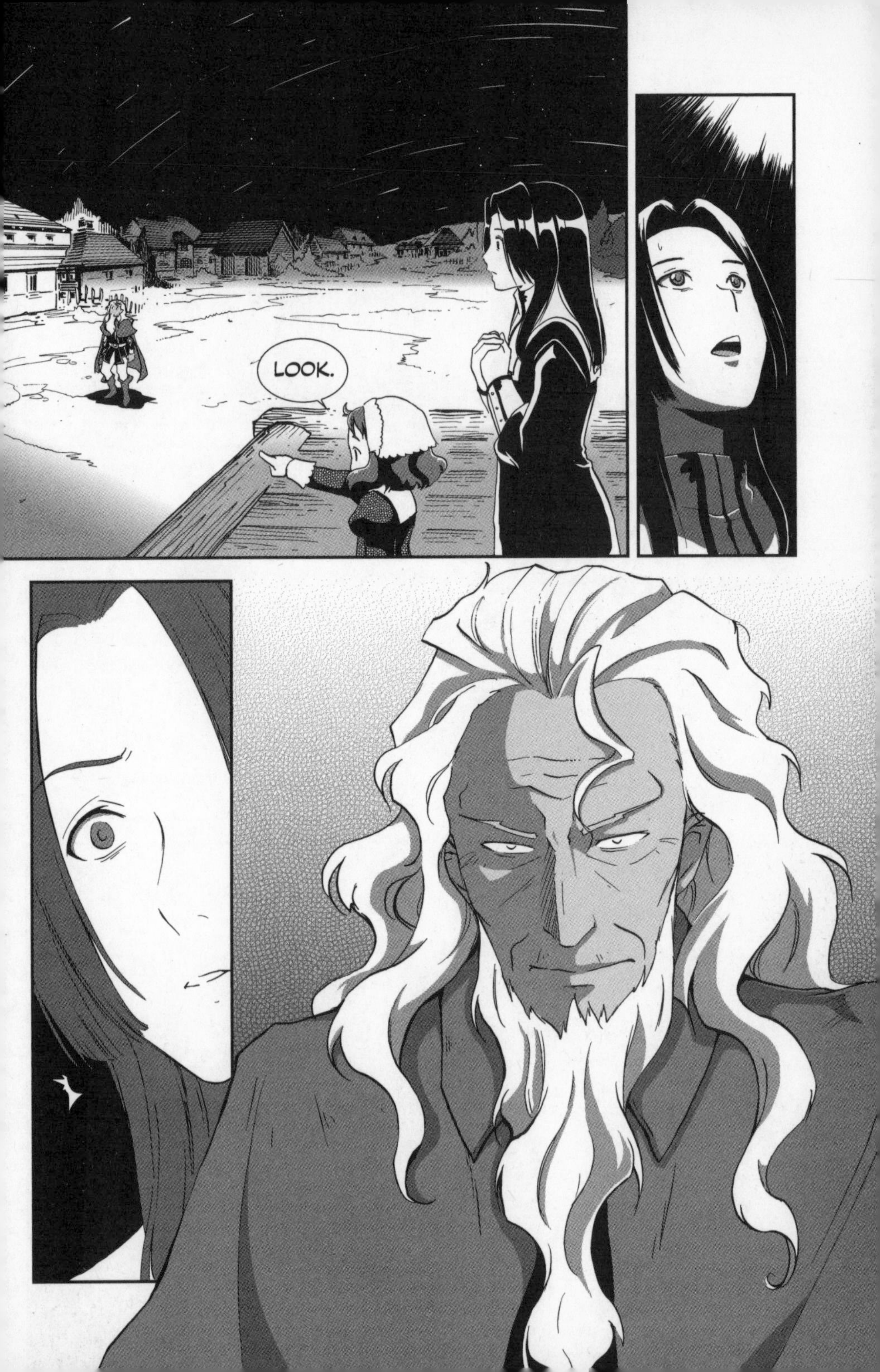
LOOK.

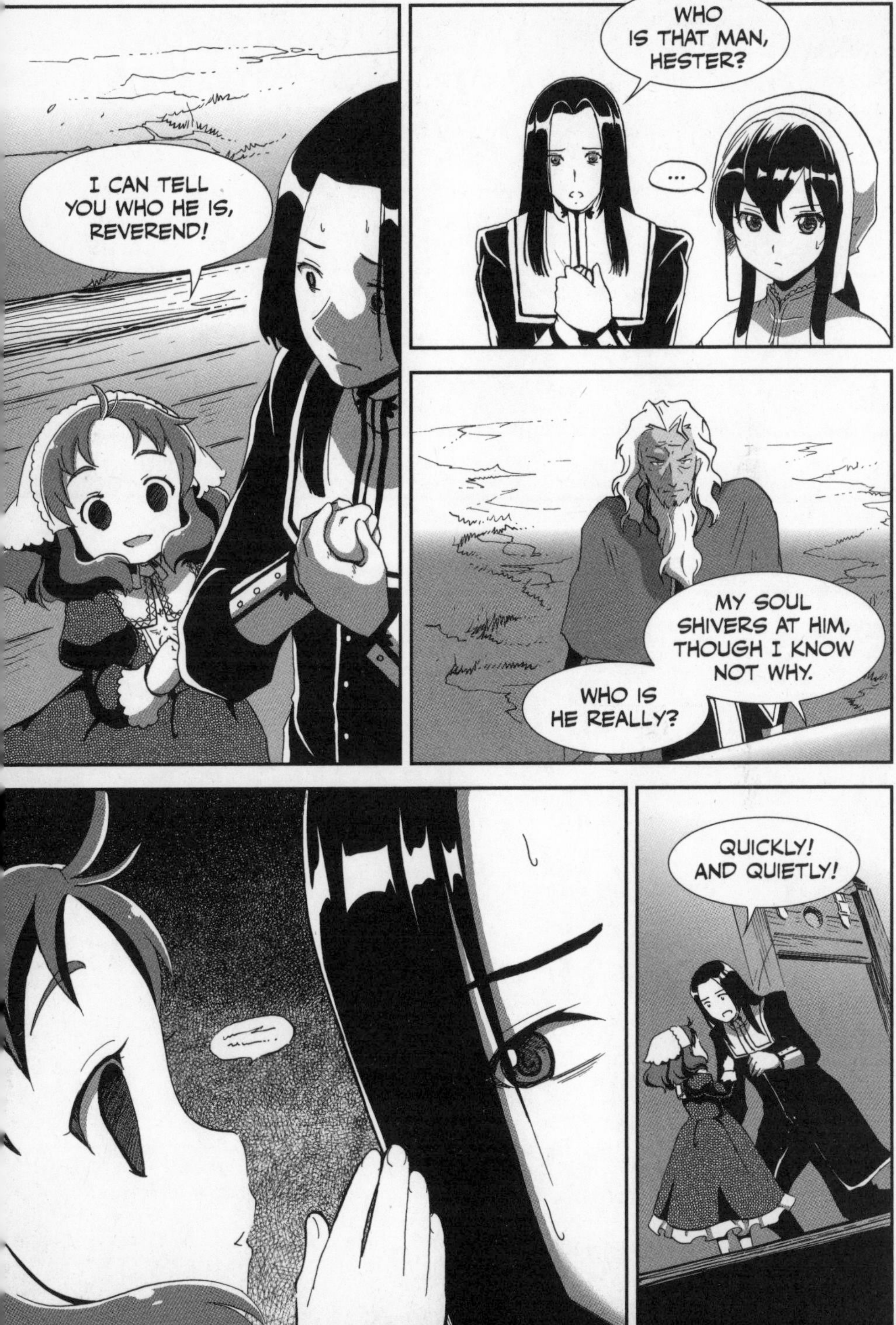
WHO IS THAT MAN, HESTER?
...
MY SOUL SHIVERS AT HIM, THOUGH I KNOW NOT WHY.
WHO IS HE REALLY?
I CAN TELL YOU WHO HE IS, REVEREND!
QUICKLY! AND QUIETLY!

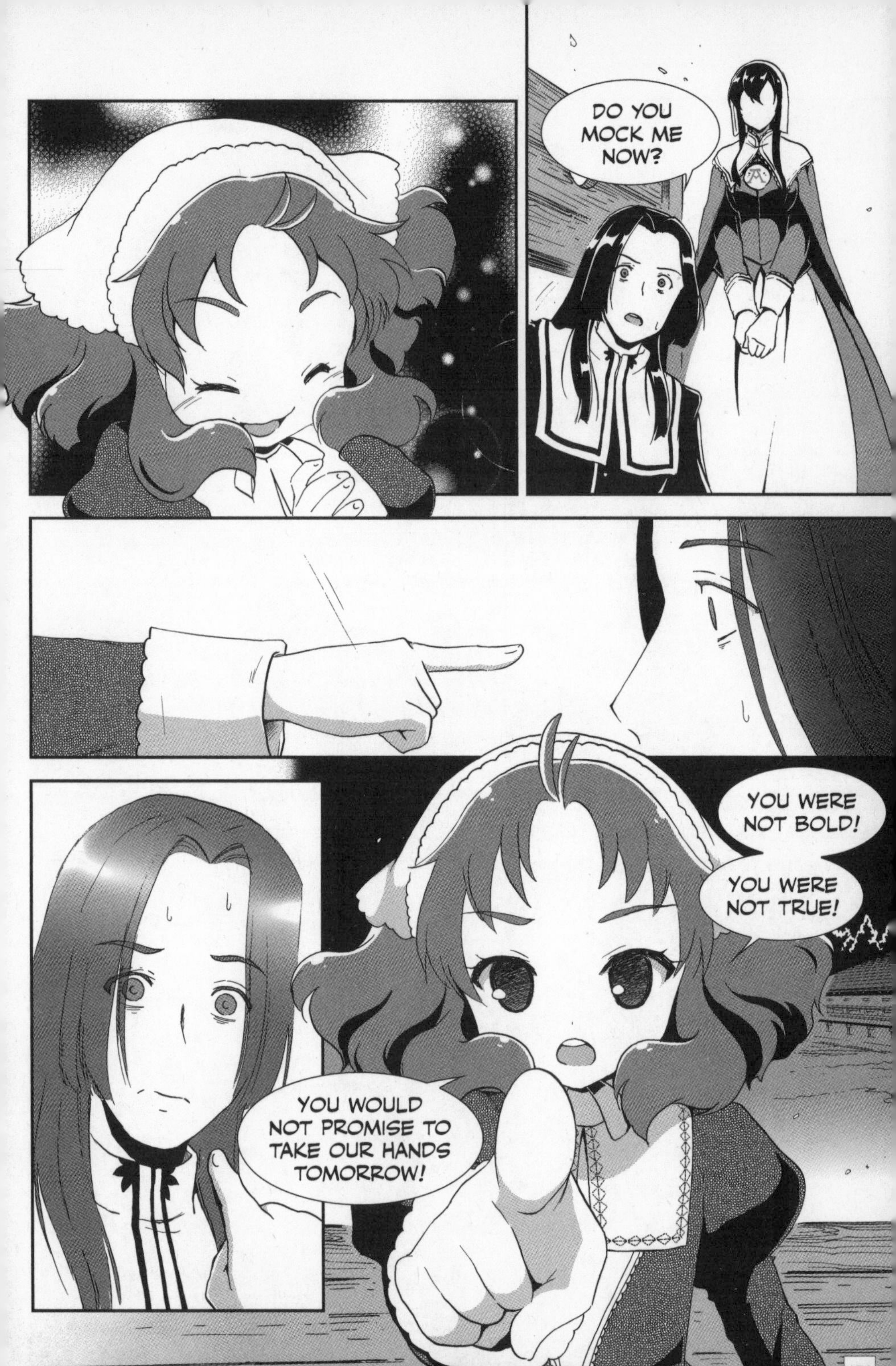
DO YOU MOCK ME NOW?
YOU WERE NOT BOLD!
YOU WERE NOT TRUE!
YOU WOULD NOT PROMISE TO TAKE OUR HANDS TOMORROW!

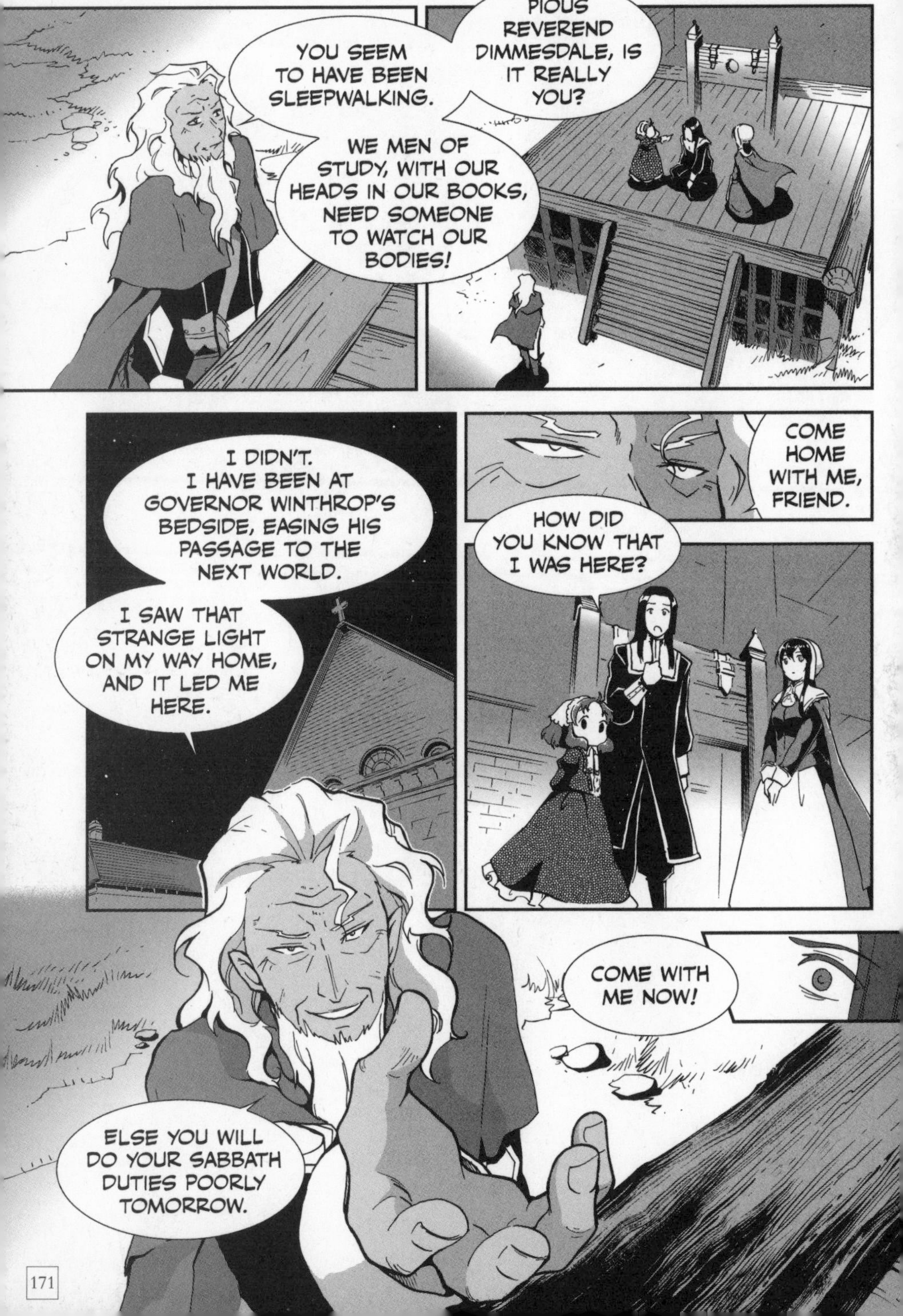
PIOUS REVEREND DIMMESDALE, IS IT REALLY YOU?
YOU SEEM TO HAVE BEEN SLEEPWALKING.
WE MEN OF STUDY, WITH OUR HEADS IN OUR BOOKS, NEED SOMEONE TO WATCH OUR BODIES!
COME HOME WITH ME, FRIEND.
HOW DID YOU KNOW THAT I WAS HERE?
I DIDN'T. I HAVE BEEN AT GOVERNOR WINTHROP'S BEDSIDE, EASING HIS PASSAGE TO THE NEXT WORLD.
I SAW THAT STRANGE LIGHT ON MY WAY HOME, AND IT LED ME HERE.
COME WITH ME NOW!
ELSE YOU WILL DO YOUR SABBATH DUTIES POORLY TOMORROW.

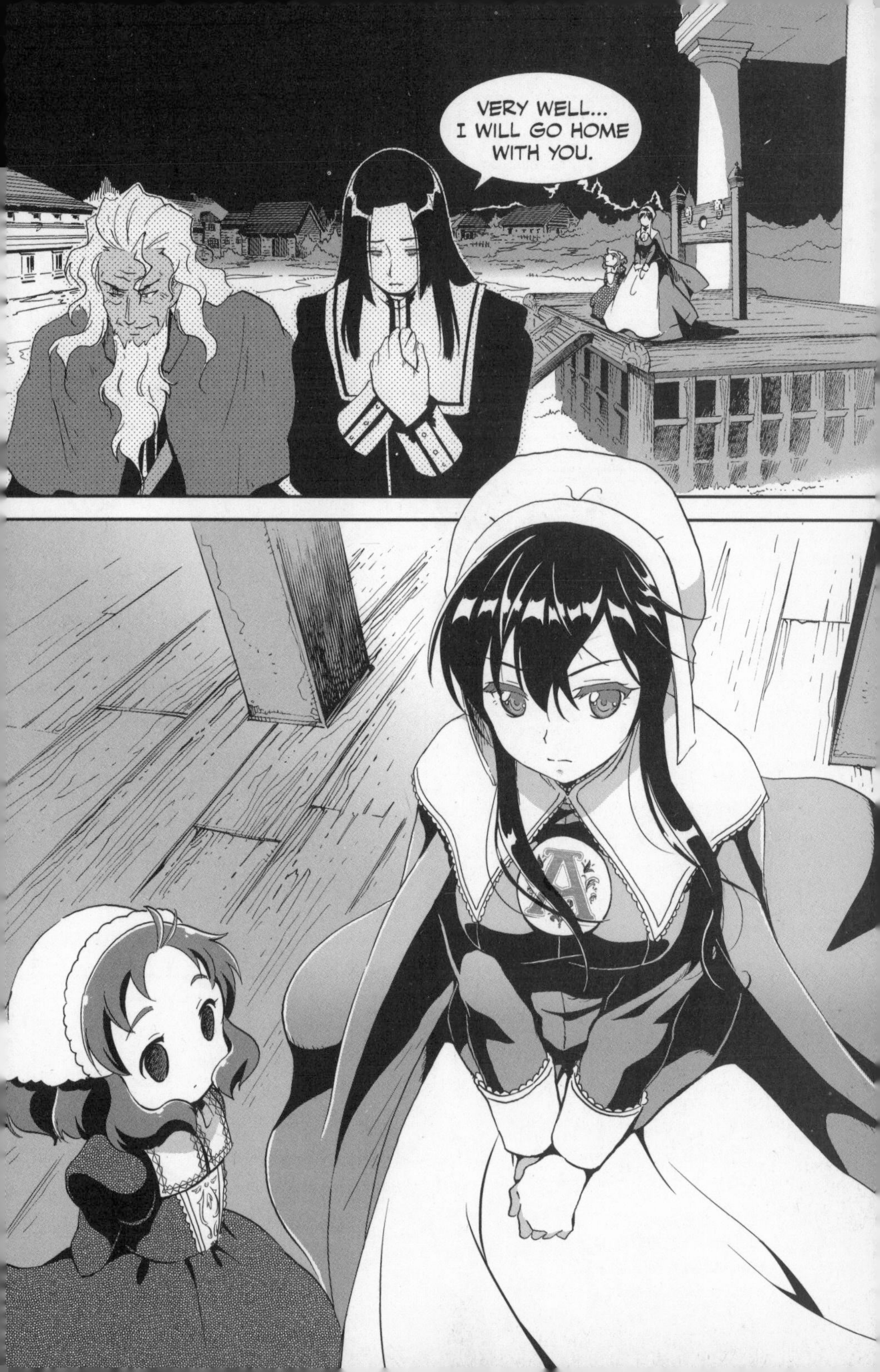
VERY WELL...
I WILL GO HOME
WITH YOU.

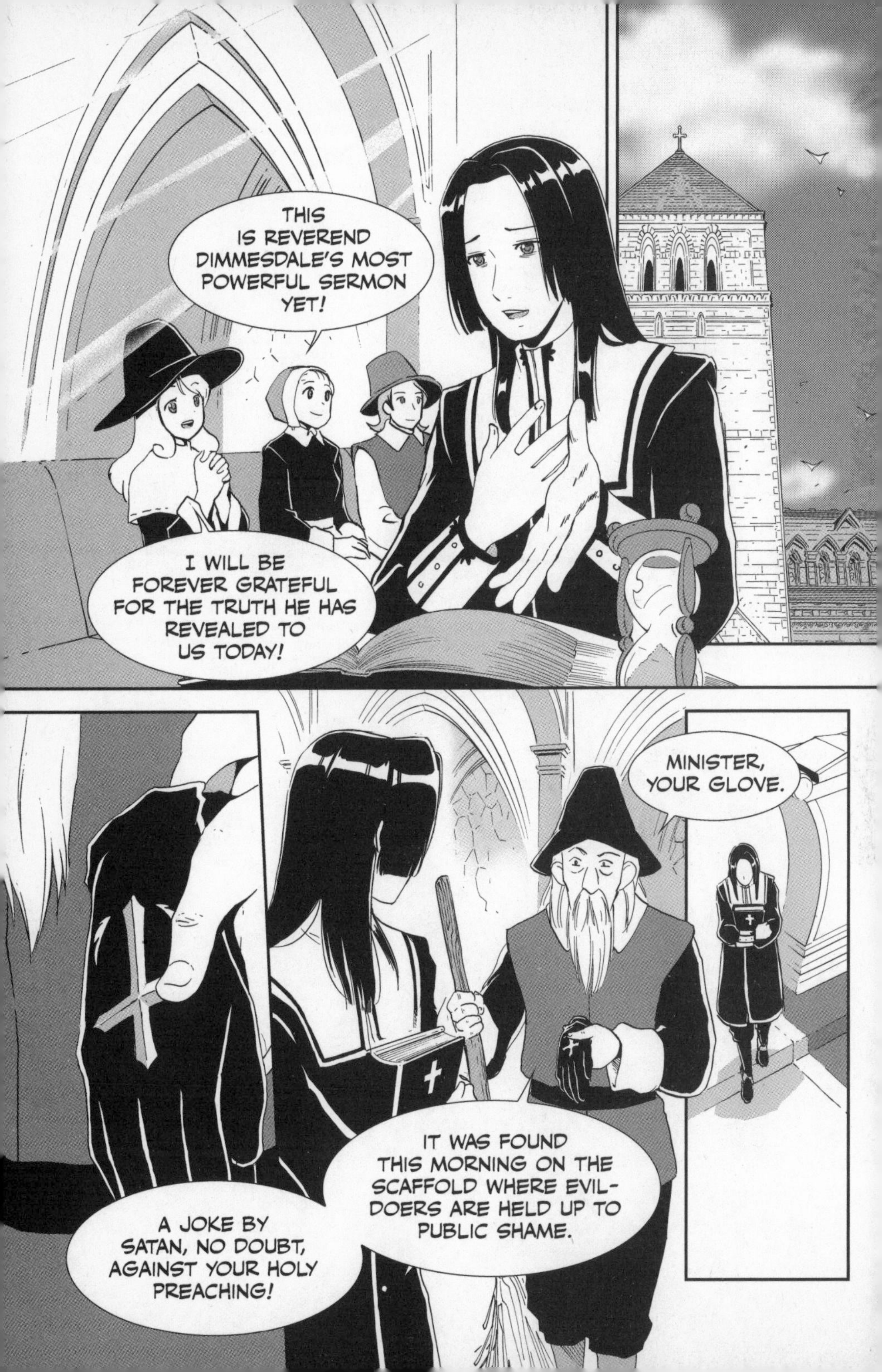
THIS IS REVEREND DIMMESDALE'S MOST POWERFUL SERMON YET!
I WILL BE FOREVER GRATEFUL FOR THE TRUTH HE HAS REVEALED TO US TODAY!
MINISTER, YOUR GLOVE.
IT WAS FOUND THIS MORNING ON THE SCAFFOLD WHERE EVIL-DOERS ARE HELD UP TO PUBLIC SHAME.
A JOKE BY SATAN, NO DOUBT, AGAINST YOUR HOLY PREACHING!

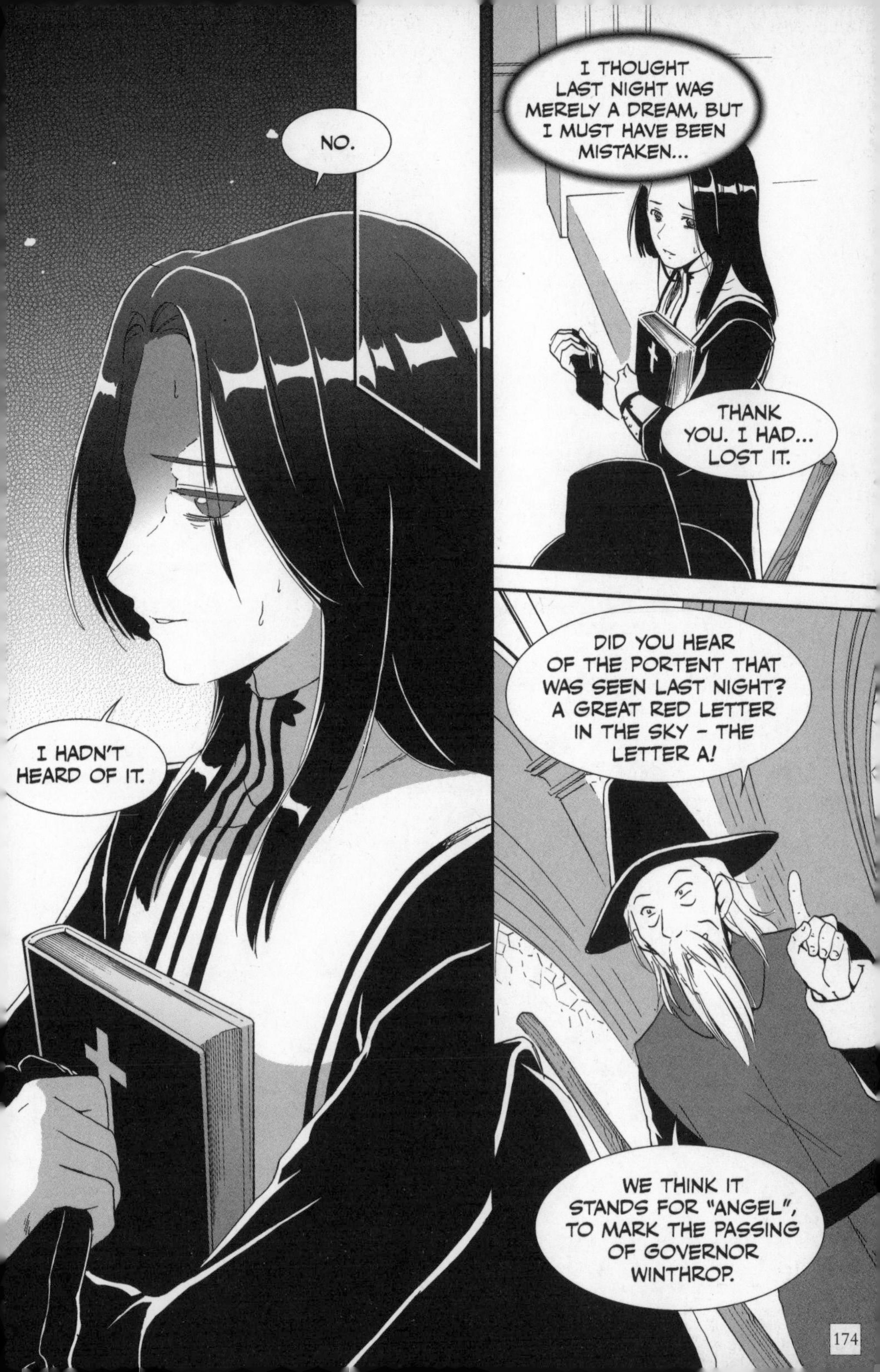
I THOUGHT LAST NIGHT WAS MERELY A DREAM, BUT I MUST HAVE BEEN MISTAKEN...
THANK YOU. I HAD... LOST IT.
DID YOU HEAR OF THE PORTENT THAT WAS SEEN LAST NIGHT? A GREAT RED LETTER IN THE SKY - THE LETTER A!
WE THINK IT STANDS FOR "ANGEL", TO MARK THE PASSING OF GOVERNOR WINTHROP.
NO.
I HADN'T HEARD OF IT.

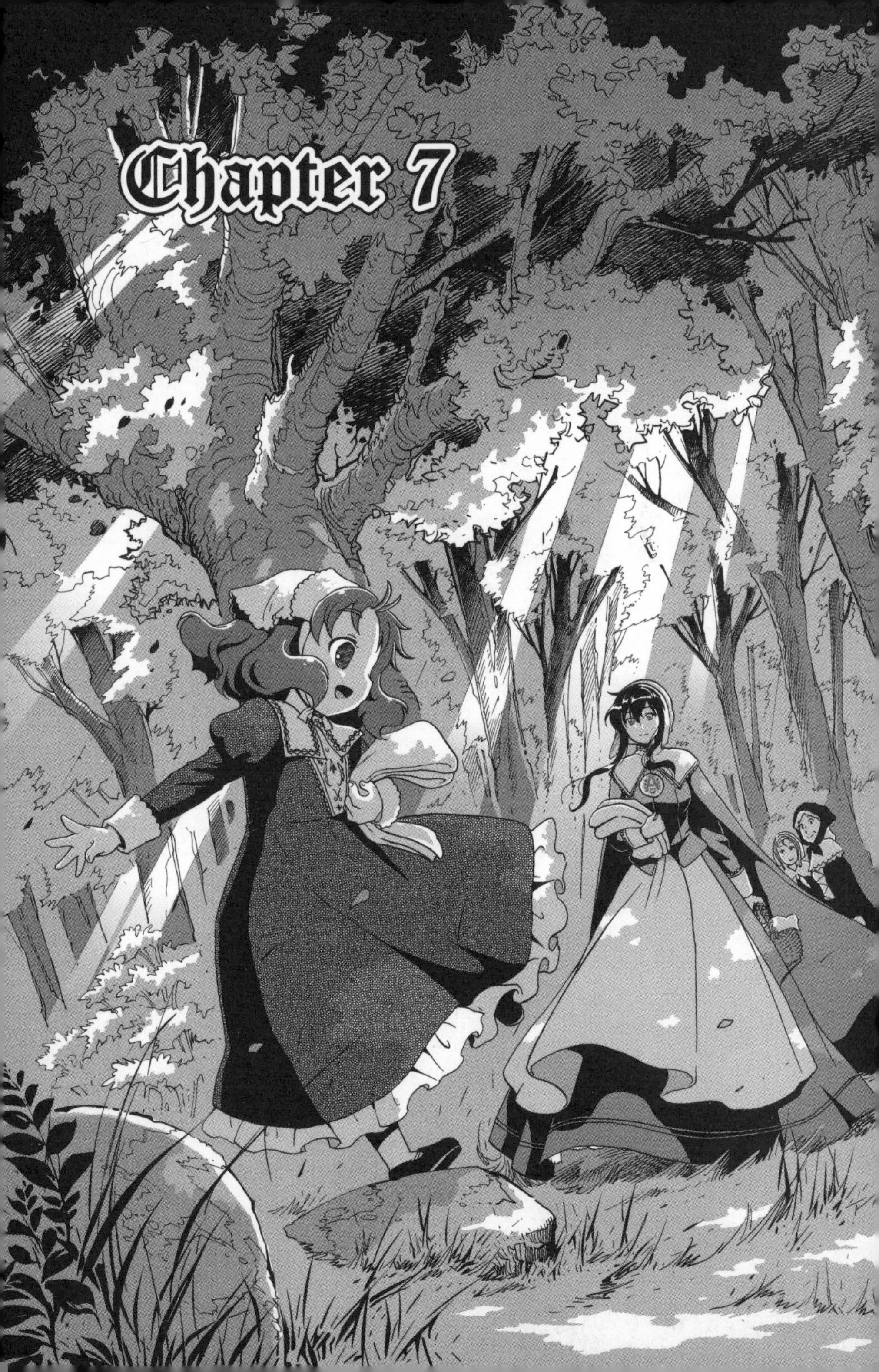
Chapter 7

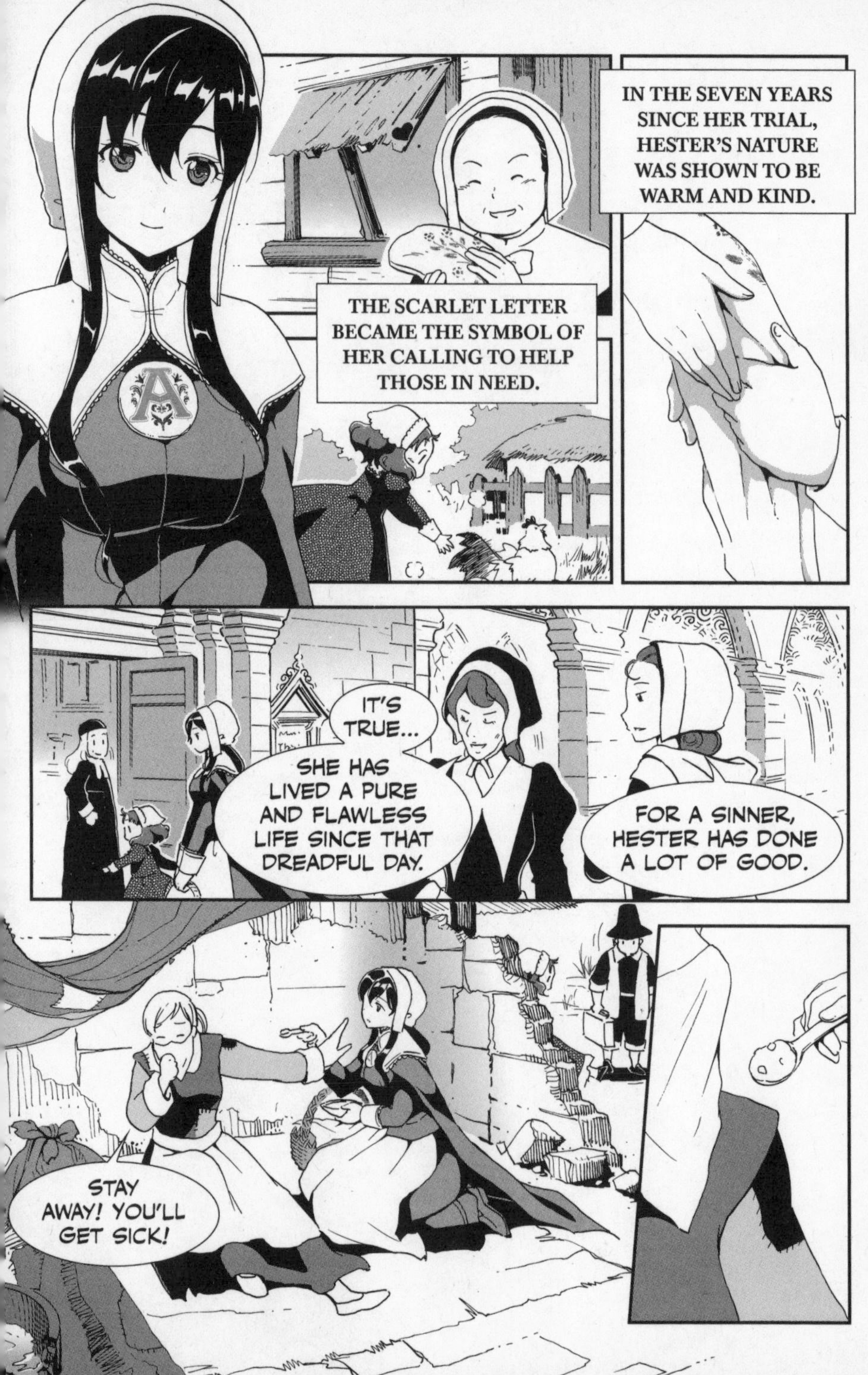
IN THE SEVEN YEARS SINCE HER TRIAL, HESTER'S NATURE WAS SHOWN TO BE WARM AND KIND.
THE SCARLET LETTER BECAME THE SYMBOL OF HER CALLING TO HELP THOSE IN NEED.
FOR A SINNER, HESTER HAS DONE A LOT OF GOOD.
IT'S TRUE...
SHE HAS LIVED A PURE AND FLAWLESS LIFE SINCE THAT DREADFUL DAY.
STAY AWAY! YOU'LL GET SICK!

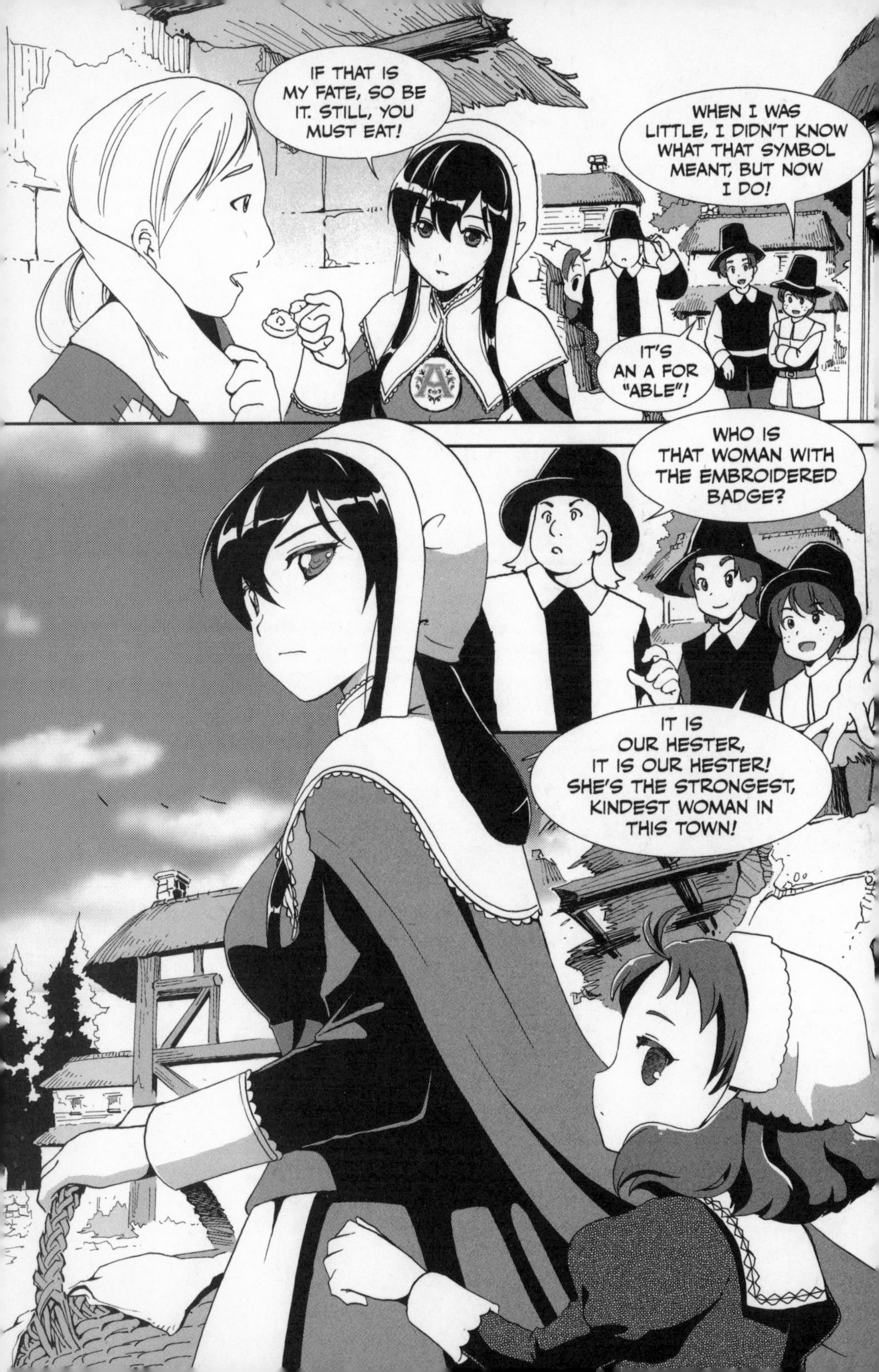
WHEN I WAS LITTLE, I DIDN'T KNOW WHAT THAT SYMBOL MEANT, BUT NOW I DO!
IT'S AN A FOR "ABLE"!
IF THAT IS MY FATE, SO BE IT. STILL, YOU MUST EAT!
WHO IS THAT WOMAN WITH THE EMBROIDERED BADGE?
IT IS OUR HESTER, IT IS OUR HESTER! SHE'S THE STRONGEST, KINDEST WOMAN IN THIS TOWN!

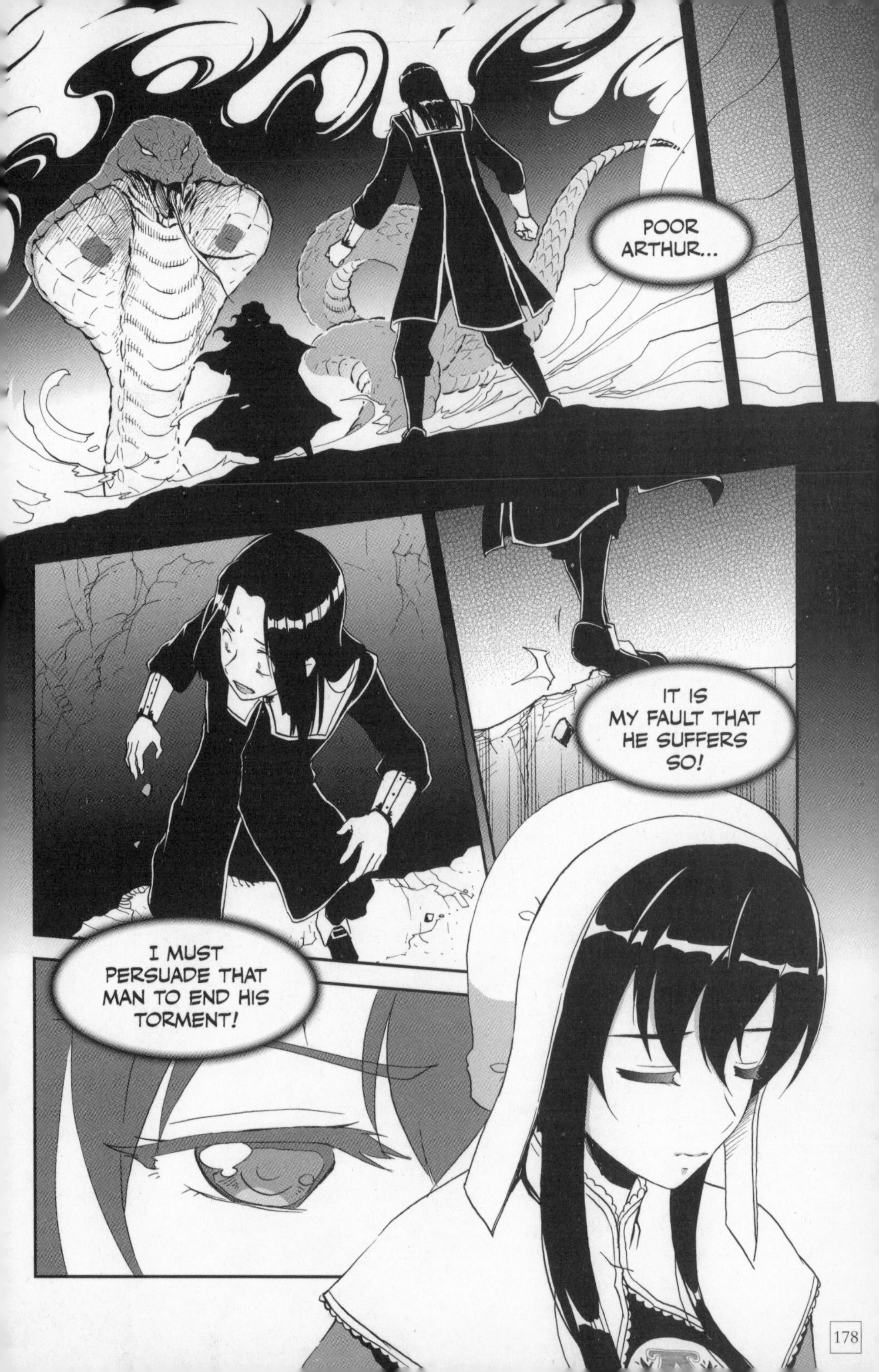
POOR ARTHUR...
IT IS MY FAULT THAT HE SUFFERS SO!
I MUST PERSUADE THAT MAN TO END HIS TORMENT!

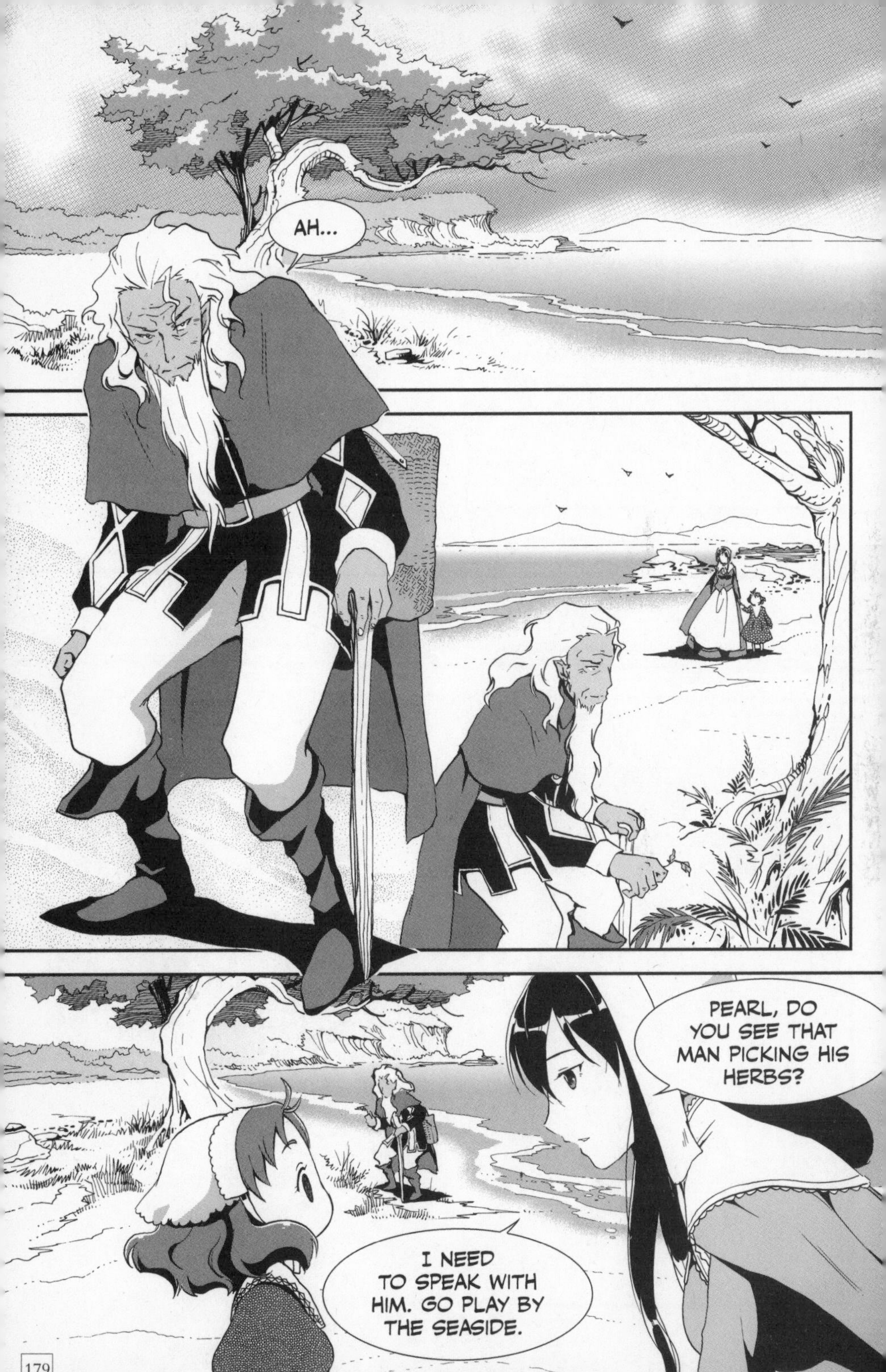
AH...
PEARL, DO YOU SEE THAT MAN PICKING HIS HERBS?
I NEED TO SPEAK WITH HIM. GO PLAY BY THE SEASIDE.

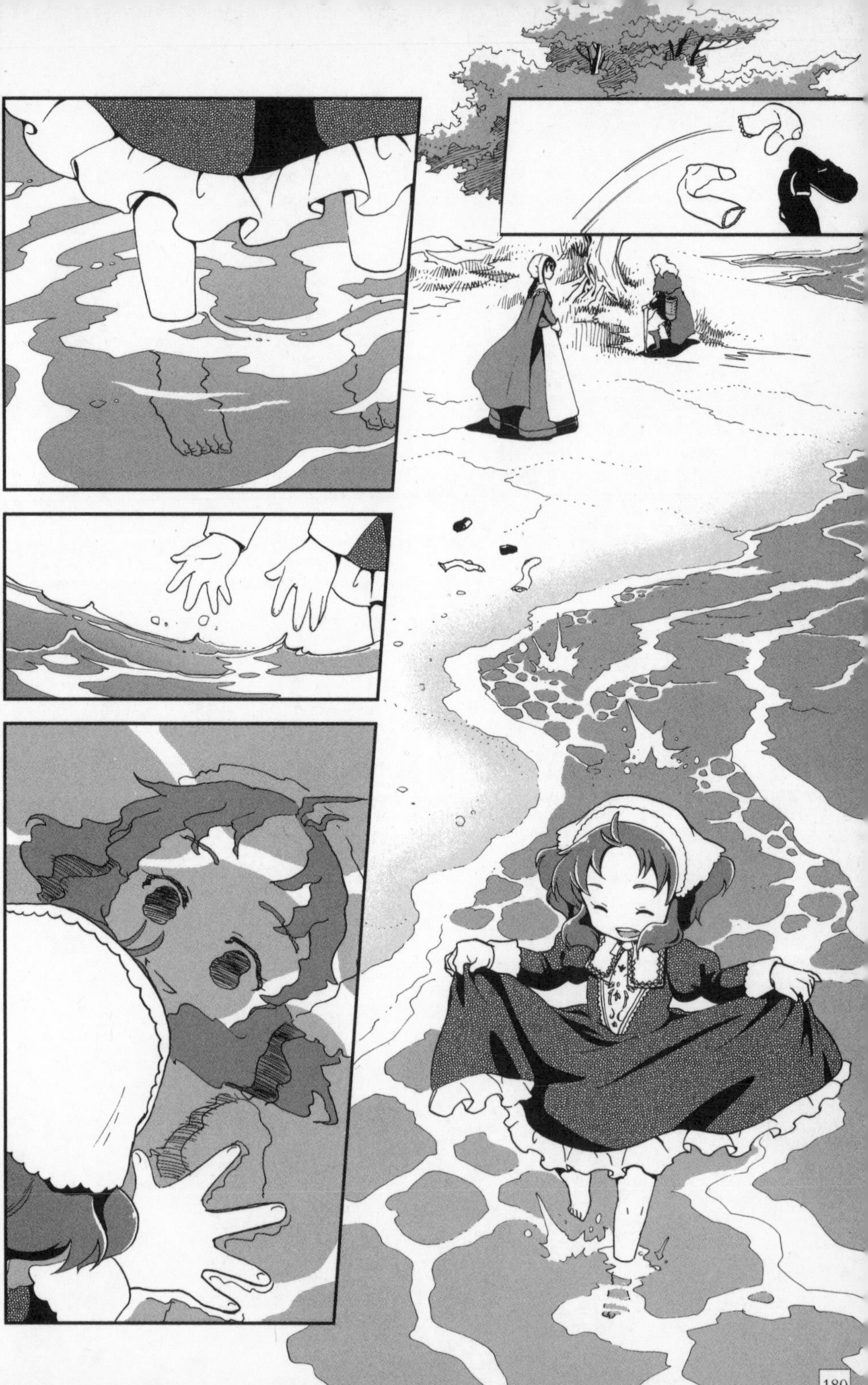

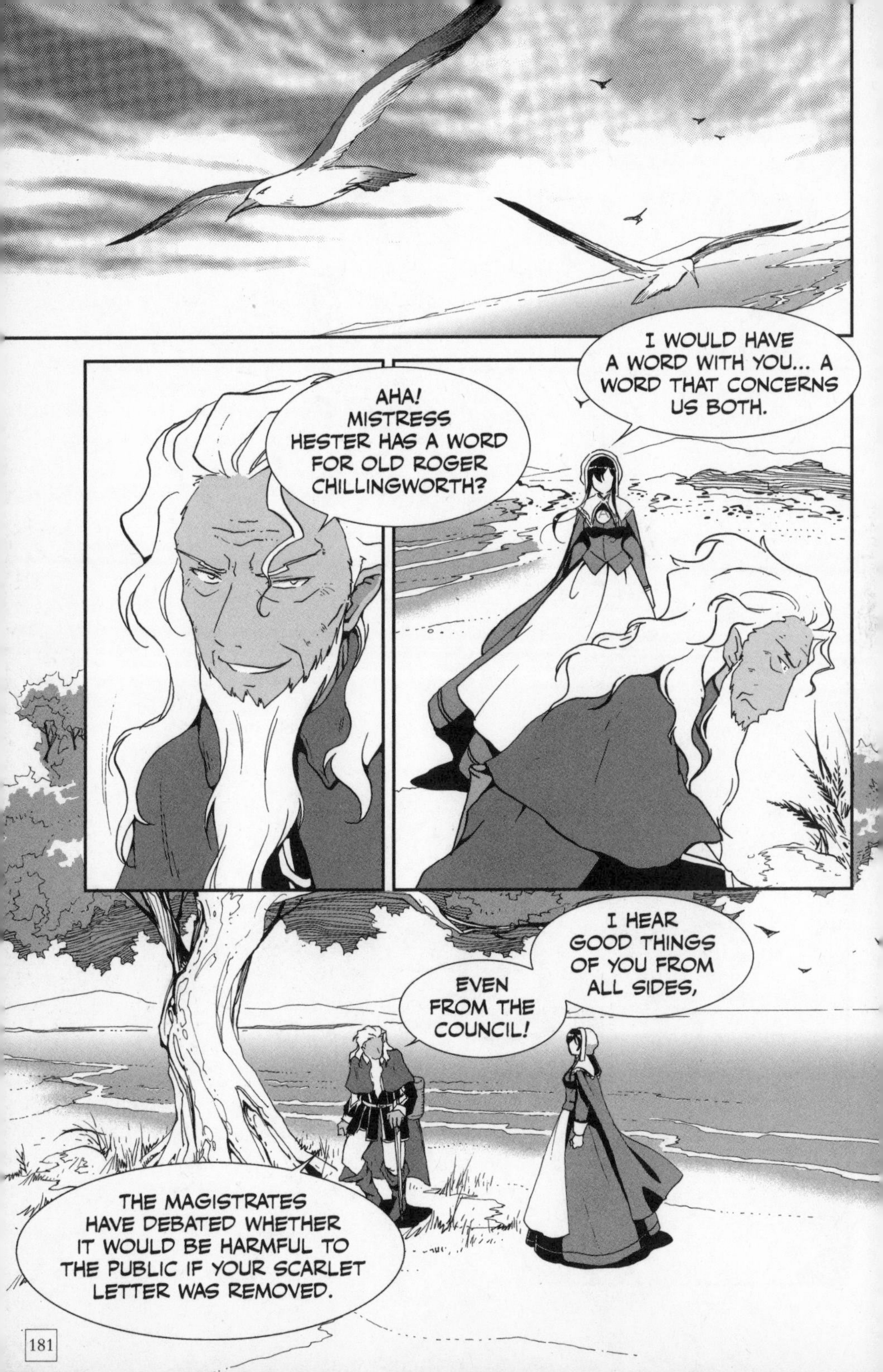
I WOULD HAVE A WORD WITH YOU... A WORD THAT CONCERNS US BOTH.
AHA! MISTRESS HESTER HAS A WORD FOR OLD ROGER CHILLINGWORTH?
I HEAR GOOD THINGS OF YOU FROM ALL SIDES,
EVEN FROM THE COUNCIL!
THE MAGISTRATES HAVE DEBATED WHETHER IT WOULD BE HARMFUL TO THE PUBLIC IF YOUR SCARLET LETTER WAS REMOVED.

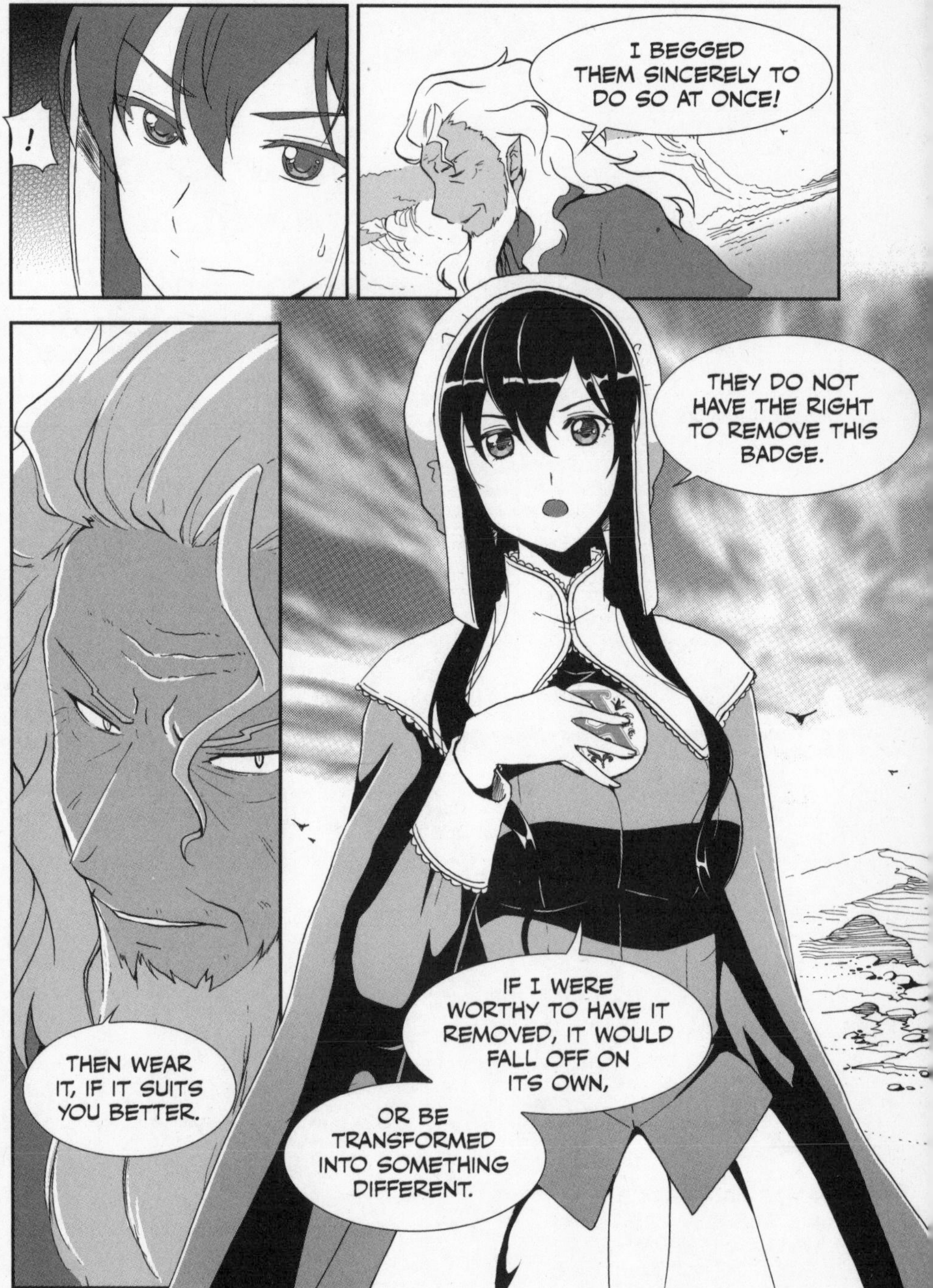
I BEGGED THEM SINCERELY TO DO SO AT ONCE!
!
THEY DO NOT HAVE THE RIGHT TO REMOVE THIS BADGE.
IF I WERE WORTHY TO HAVE IT REMOVED, IT WOULD FALL OFF ON ITS OWN,
OR BE TRANSFORMED INTO SOMETHING DIFFERENT.
THEN WEAR IT, IF IT SUITS YOU BETTER.

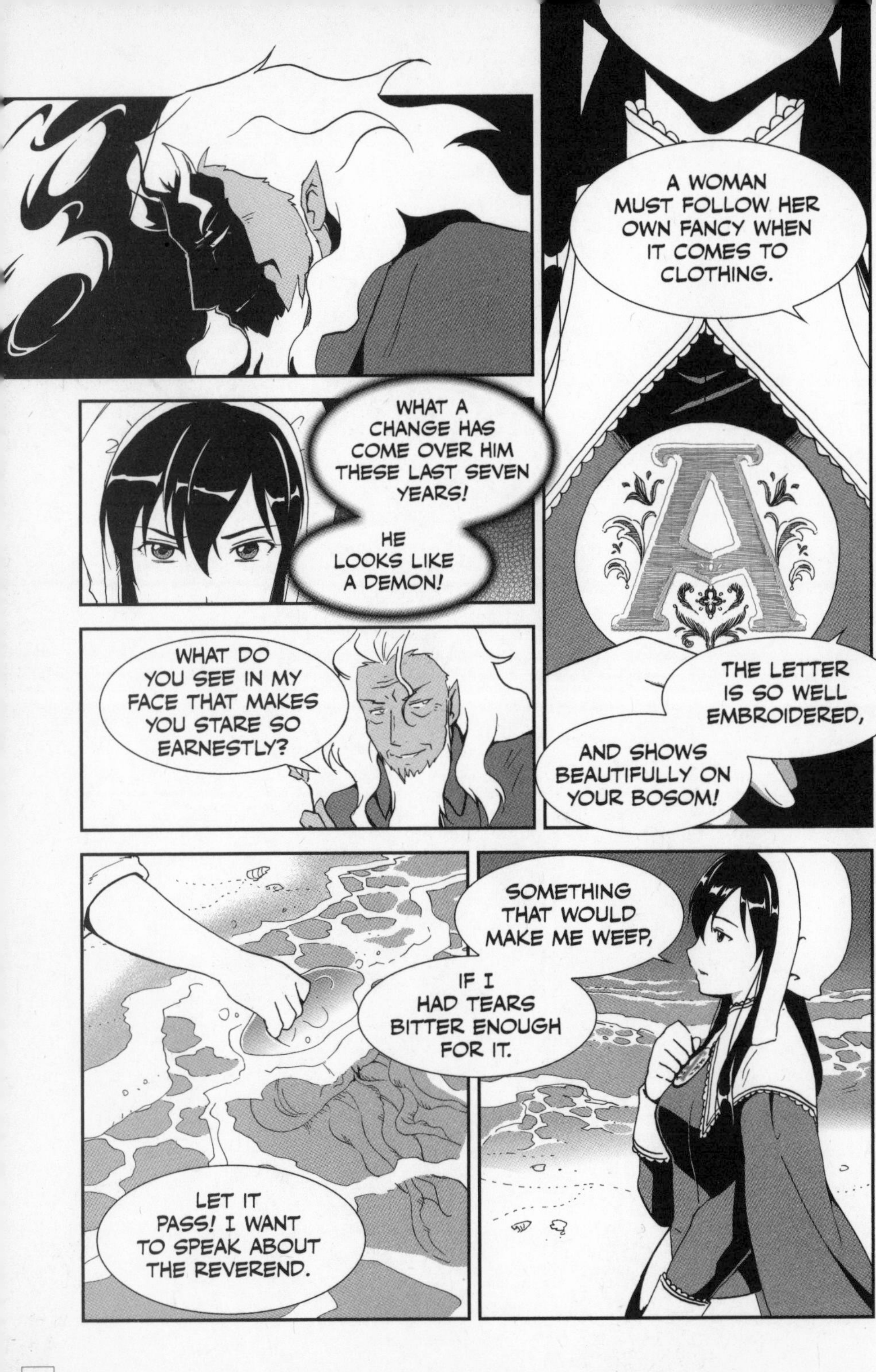
A WOMAN MUST FOLLOW HER OWN FANCY WHEN IT COMES TO CLOTHING.
THE LETTER IS SO WELL EMBROIDERED,
AND SHOWS BEAUTIFULLY ON YOUR BOSOM!
WHAT A CHANGE HAS COME OVER HIM THESE LAST SEVEN YEARS!
HE LOOKS LIKE A DEMON!
WHAT DO YOU SEE IN MY FACE THAT MAKES YOU STARE SO EARNESTLY?
SOMETHING THAT WOULD MAKE ME WEEP,
IF I HAD TEARS BITTER ENOUGH FOR IT.
LET IT PASS! I WANT TO SPEAK ABOUT THE REVEREND.

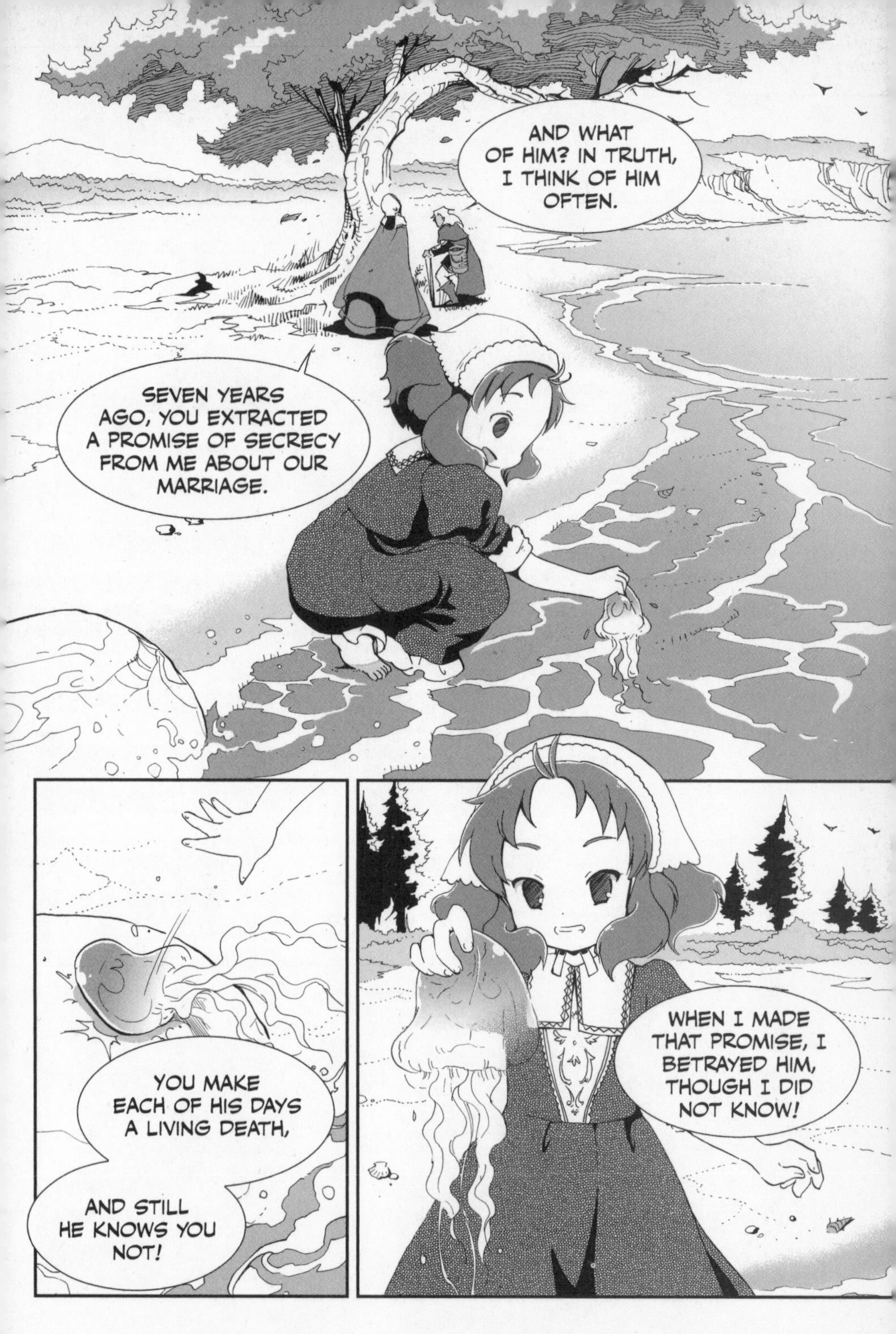
AND WHAT OF HIM? IN TRUTH, I THINK OF HIM OFTEN.
SEVEN YEARS AGO, YOU EXTRACTED A PROMISE OF SECRECY FROM ME ABOUT OUR MARRIAGE.
WHEN I MADE THAT PROMISE, I BETRAYED HIM, THOUGH I DID NOT KNOW!
YOU MAKE EACH OF HIS DAYS A LIVING DEATH,
AND STILL HE KNOWS YOU NOT!

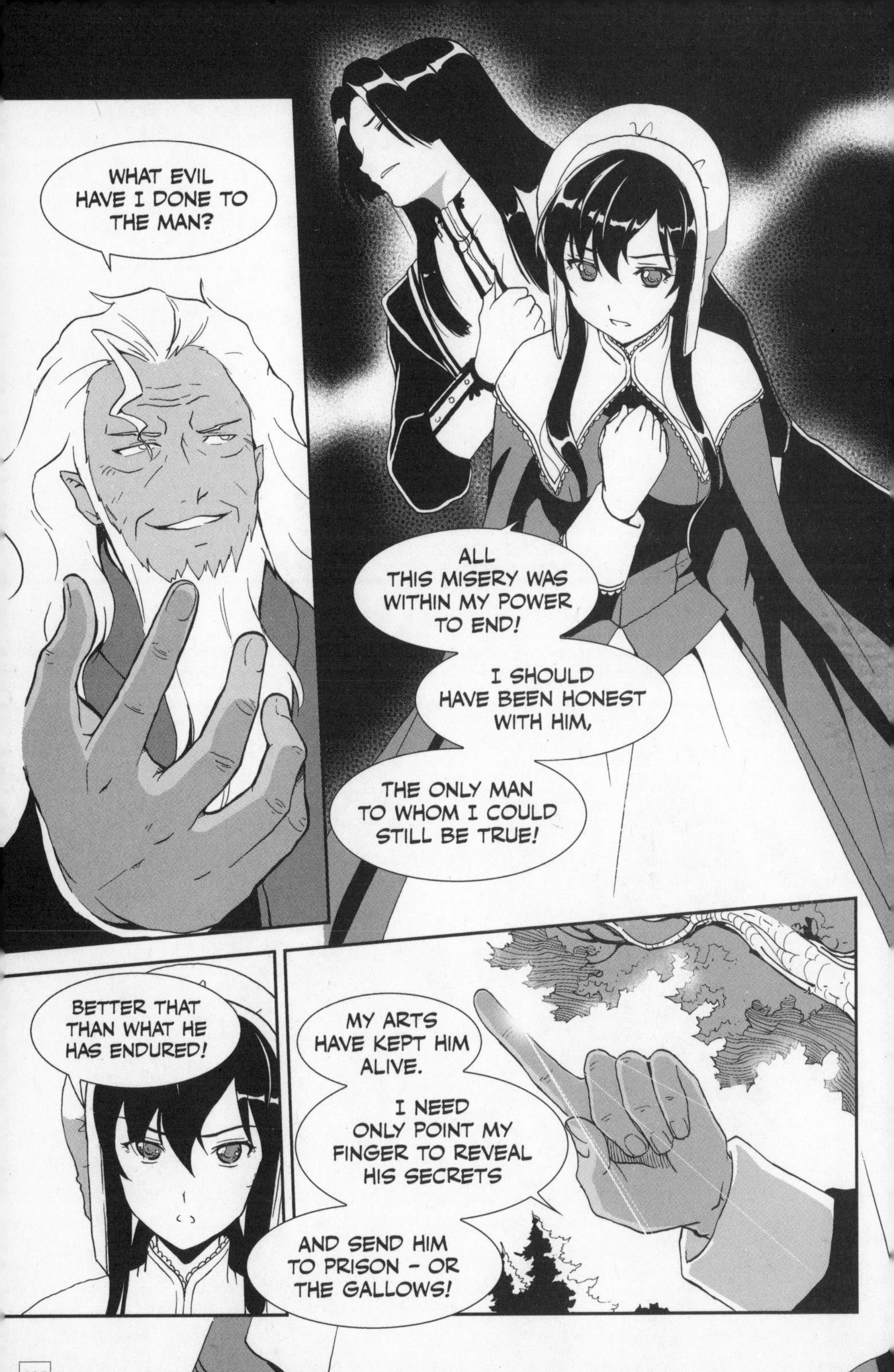
ALL THIS MISERY WAS WITHIN MY POWER TO END!
I SHOULD HAVE BEEN HONEST WITH HIM,
THE ONLY MAN TO WHOM I COULD STILL BE TRUE!
WHAT EVIL HAVE I DONE TO THE MAN?
MY ARTS HAVE KEPT HIM ALIVE.
I NEED ONLY POINT MY FINGER TO REVEAL HIS SECRETS
AND SEND HIM TO PRISON - OR THE GALLOWS!
BETTER THAT THAN WHAT HE HAS ENDURED!

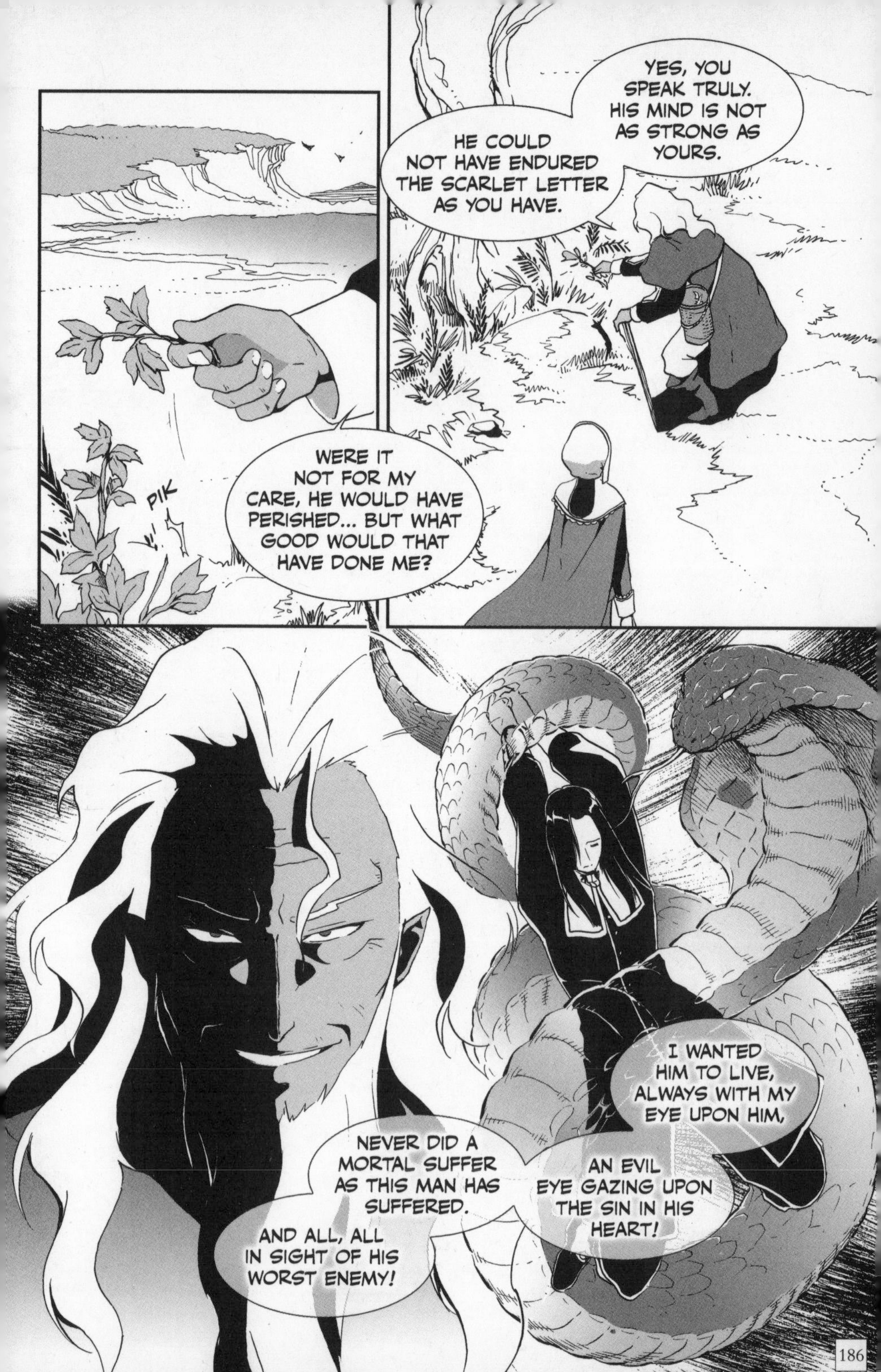
YES, YOU SPEAK TRULY. HIS MIND IS NOT AS STRONG AS YOURS.
HE COULD NOT HAVE ENDURED THE SCARLET LETTER AS YOU HAVE.
PIK
WERE IT NOT FOR MY CARE, HE WOULD HAVE PERISHED... BUT WHAT GOOD WOULD THAT HAVE DONE ME?
I WANTED HIM TO LIVE, ALWAYS WITH MY EYE UPON HIM,
AN EVIL EYE GAZING UPON THE SIN IN HIS HEART!
NEVER DID A MORTAL SUFFER AS THIS MAN HAS SUFFERED.
AND ALL, ALL IN SIGHT OF HIS WORST ENEMY!

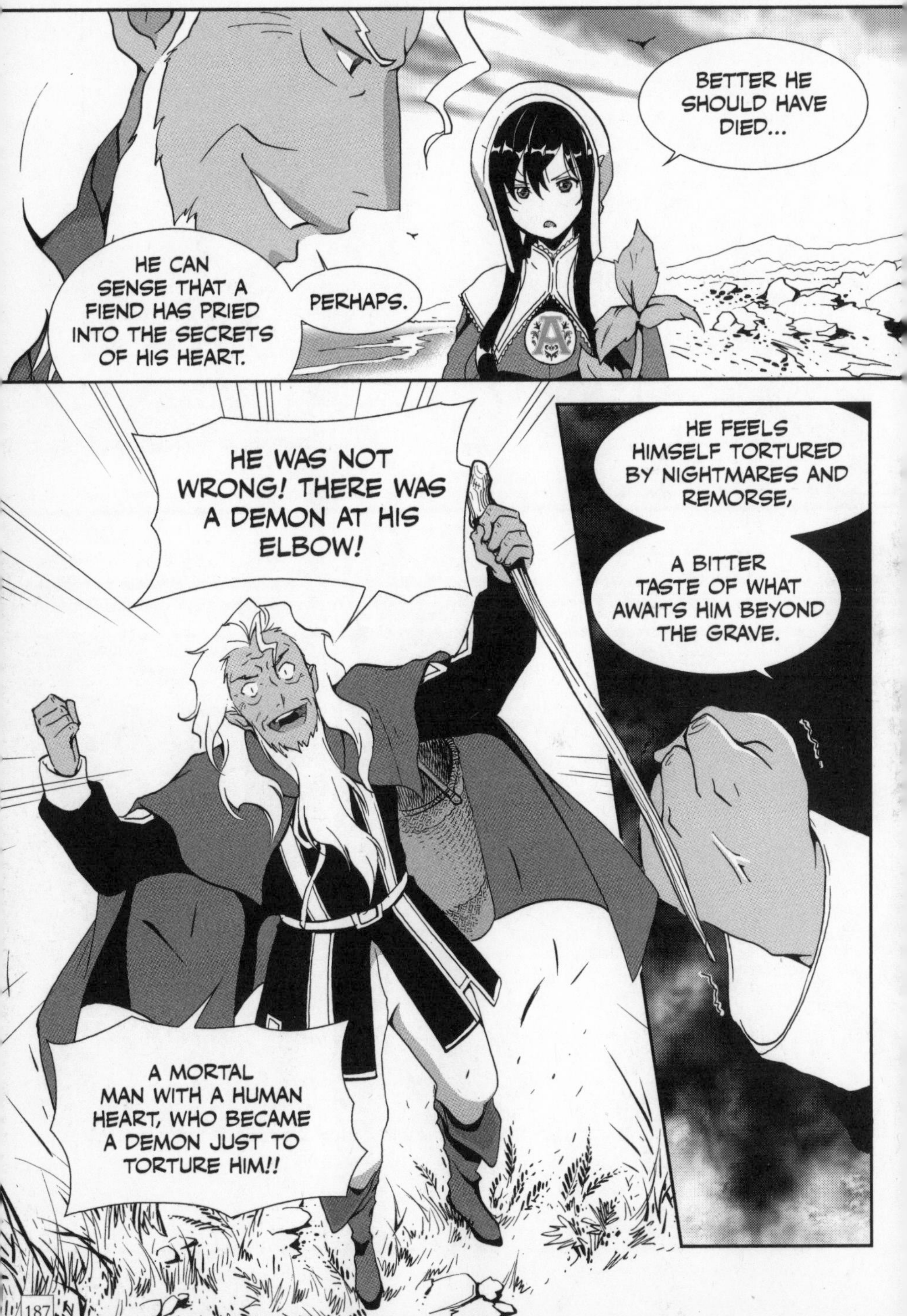
BETTER HE SHOULD HAVE DIED...
PERHAPS.
HE CAN SENSE THAT A FIEND HAS PRIED INTO THE SECRETS OF HIS HEART.
HE FEELS HIMSELF TORTURED BY NIGHTMARES AND REMORSE,
A BITTER TASTE OF WHAT AWAITS HIM BEYOND THE GRAVE.
HE WAS NOT WRONG! THERE WAS A DEMON AT HIS ELBOW!
A MORTAL MAN WITH A HUMAN HEART, WHO BECAME A DEMON JUST TO TORTURE HIM!!

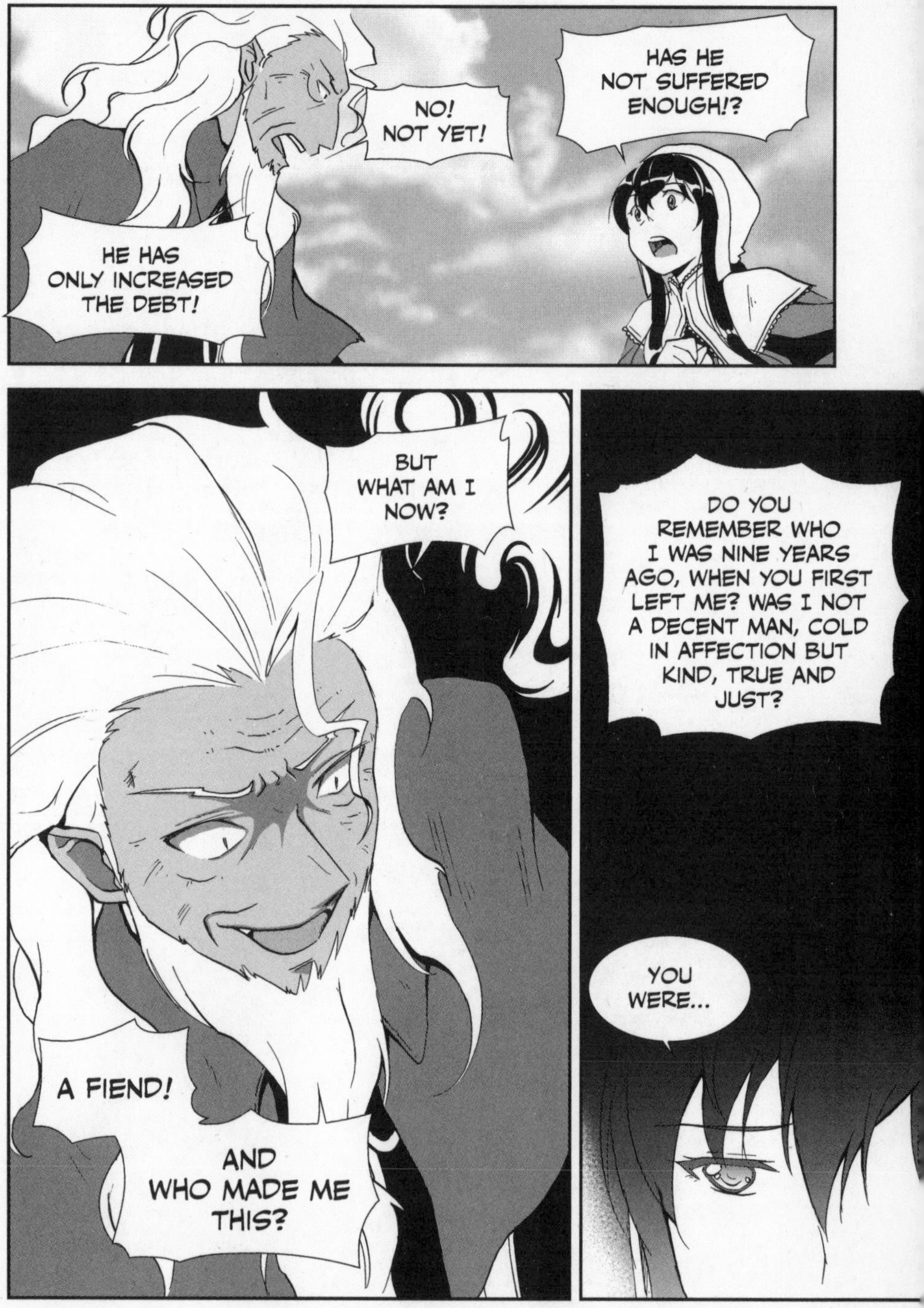
HAS HE NOT SUFFERED ENOUGH!?
NO! NOT YET!
HE HAS ONLY INCREASED THE DEBT!
DO YOU REMEMBER WHO I WAS NINE YEARS AGO, WHEN YOU FIRST LEFT ME? WAS I NOT A DECENT MAN, COLD IN AFFECTION BUT KIND, TRUE AND JUST?
YOU WERE...
BUT WHAT AM I NOW?
A FIEND!
AND WHO MADE ME THIS?

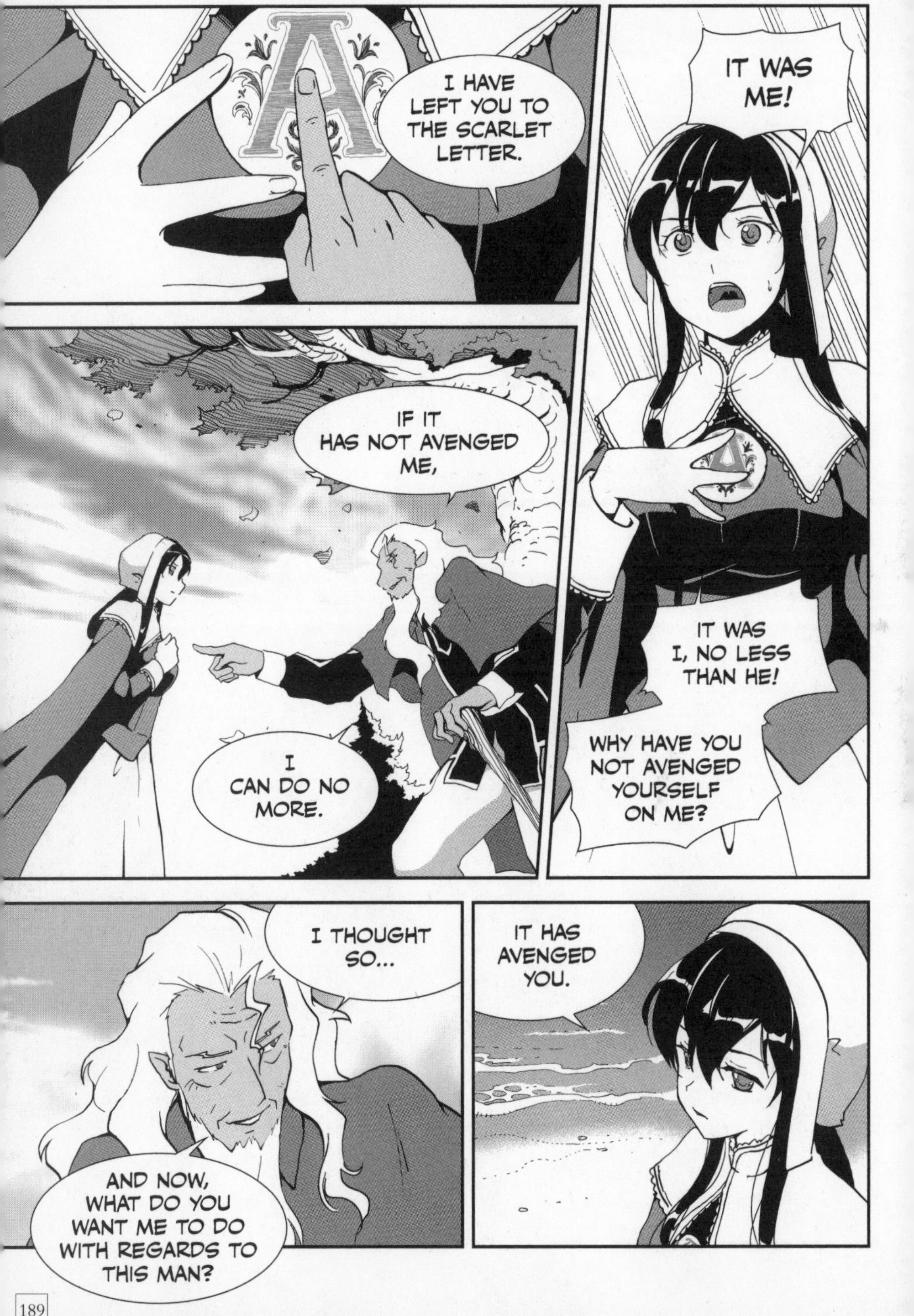
IT WAS ME!
IT WAS I, NO LESS THAN HE!
WHY HAVE YOU NOT AVENGED YOURSELF ON ME?
I HAVE LEFT YOU TO THE SCARLET LETTER.
IF IT HAS NOT AVENGED ME,
I CAN DO NO MORE.
IT HAS AVENGED YOU.
I THOUGHT SO...
AND NOW, WHAT DO YOU WANT ME TO DO WITH REGARDS TO THIS MAN?

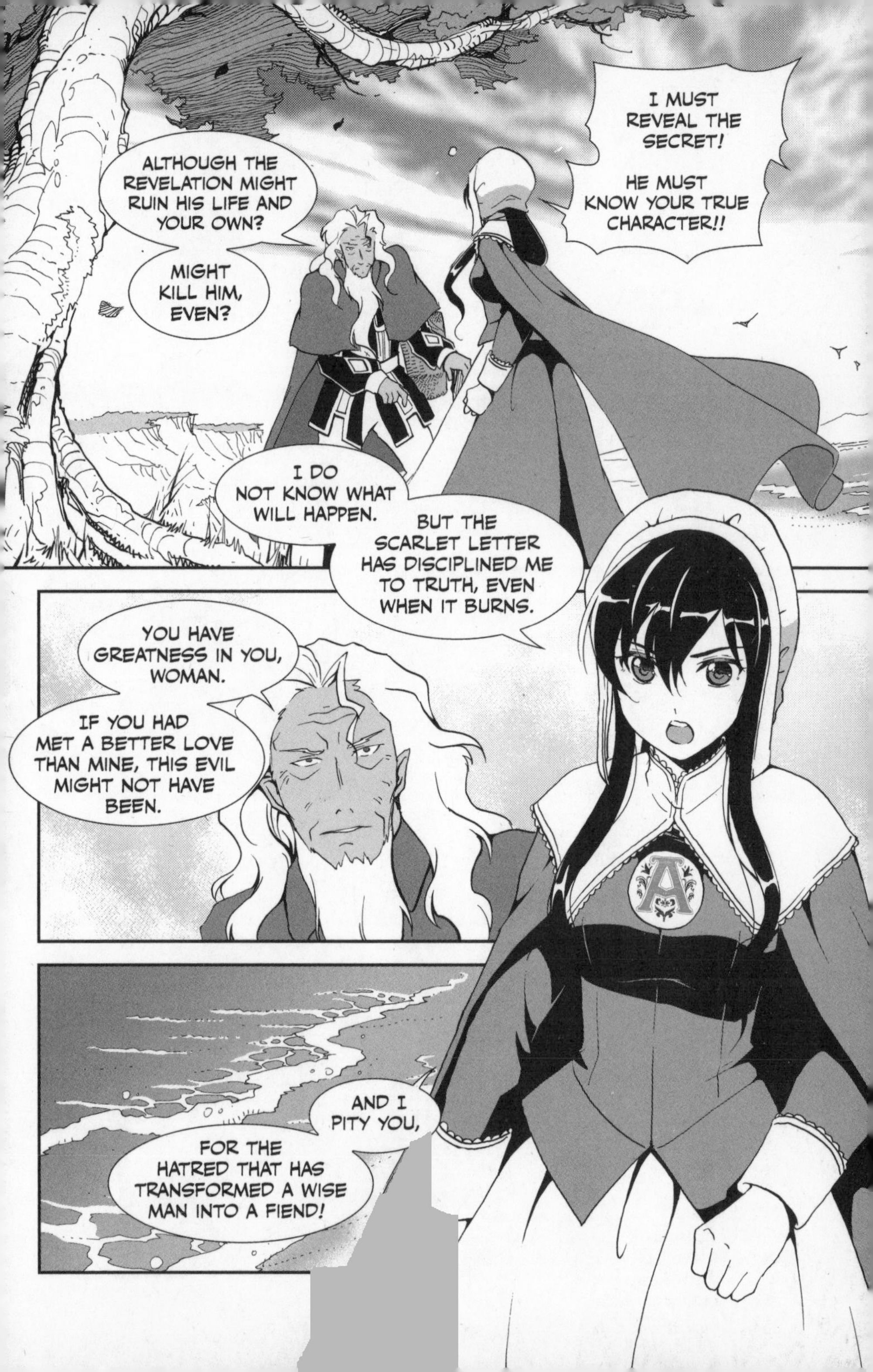
I MUST REVEAL THE SECRET!
HE MUST KNOW YOUR TRUE CHARACTER!!
ALTHOUGH THE REVELATION MIGHT RUIN HIS LIFE AND YOUR OWN?
MIGHT KILL HIM, EVEN?
I DO NOT KNOW WHAT WILL HAPPEN.
BUT THE SCARLET LETTER HAS DISCIPLINED ME TO TRUTH, EVEN WHEN IT BURNS.
YOU HAVE GREATNESS IN YOU, WOMAN.
IF YOU HAD MET A BETTER LOVE THAN MINE, THIS EVIL MIGHT NOT HAVE BEEN.
AND I PITY YOU,
FOR THE HATRED THAT HAS TRANSFORMED A WISE MAN INTO A FIEND!

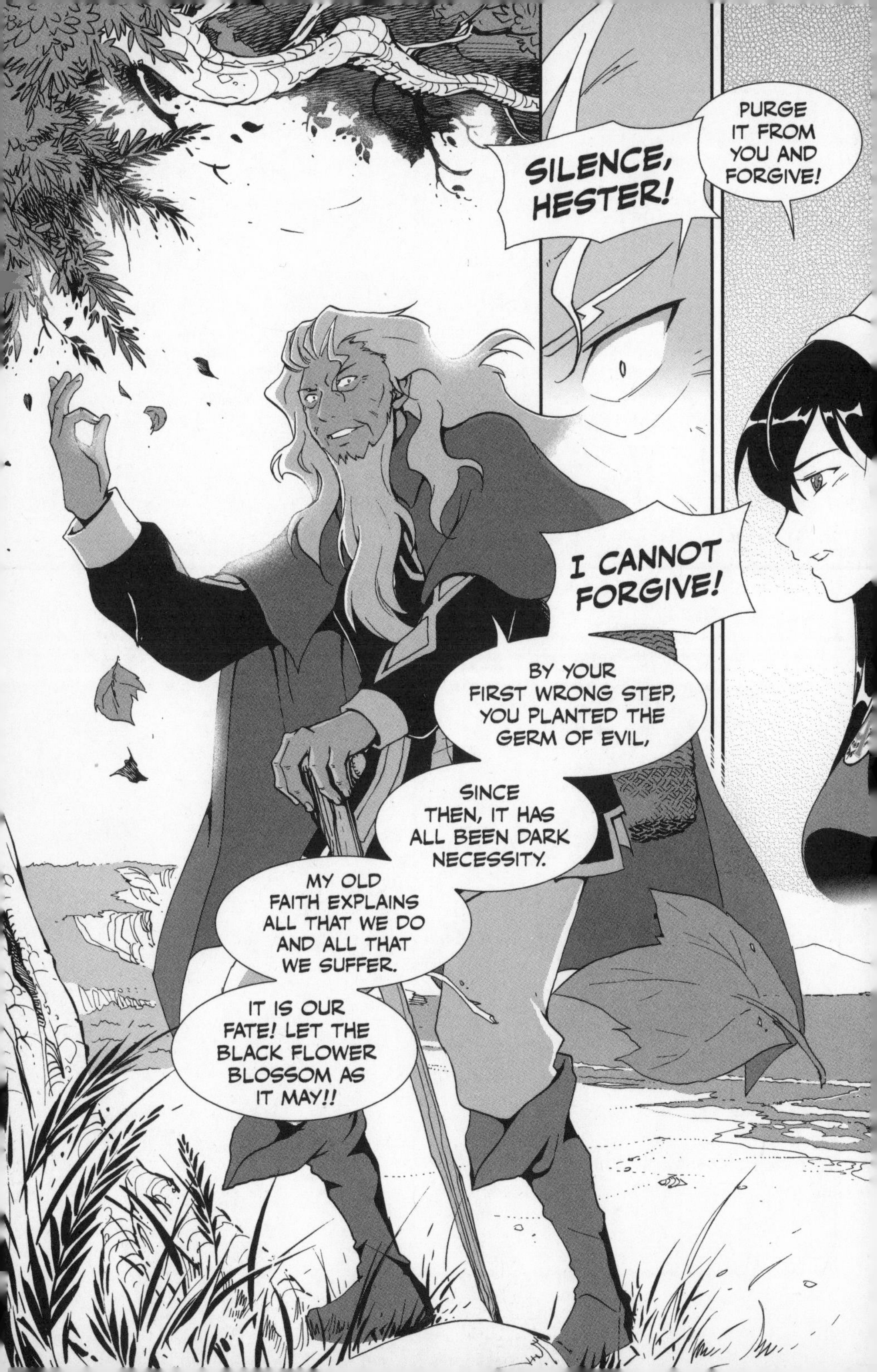
PURGE IT FROM YOU AND FORGIVE!
SILENCE, HESTER!
I CANNOT FORGIVE!
BY YOUR FIRST WRONG STEP, YOU PLANTED THE GERM OF EVIL,
SINCE THEN, IT HAS ALL BEEN DARK NECESSITY.
MY OLD FAITH EXPLAINS ALL THAT WE DO AND ALL THAT WE SUFFER.
IT IS OUR FATE! LET THE BLACK FLOWER BLOSSOM AS IT MAY!!

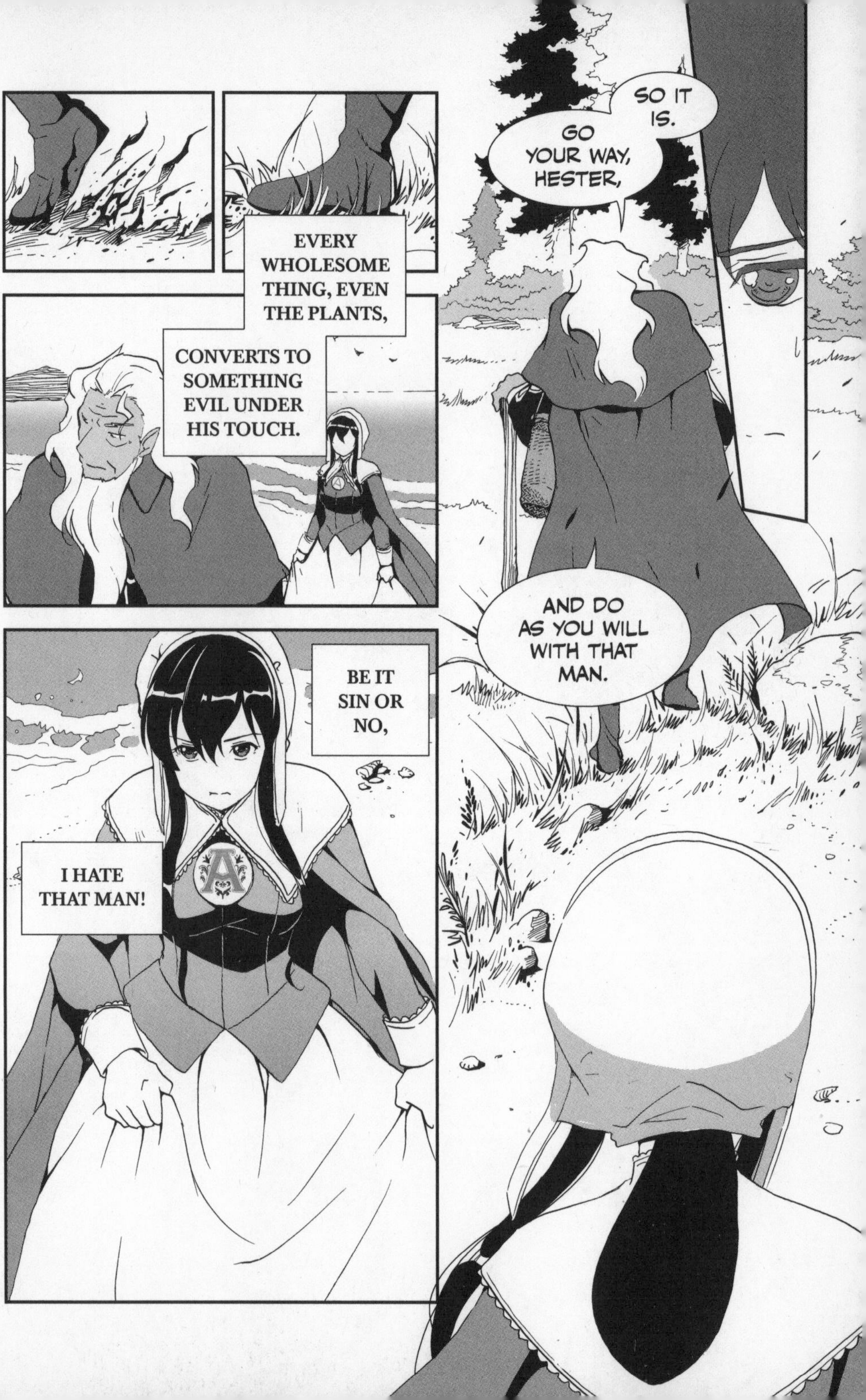
SO IT IS.
GO YOUR WAY, HESTER,
AND DO AS YOU WILL WITH THAT MAN.
EVERY WHOLESOME THING, EVEN THE PLANTS,
CONVERTS TO SOMETHING EVIL UNDER HIS TOUCH.
BE IT SIN OR NO,
I HATE THAT MAN!

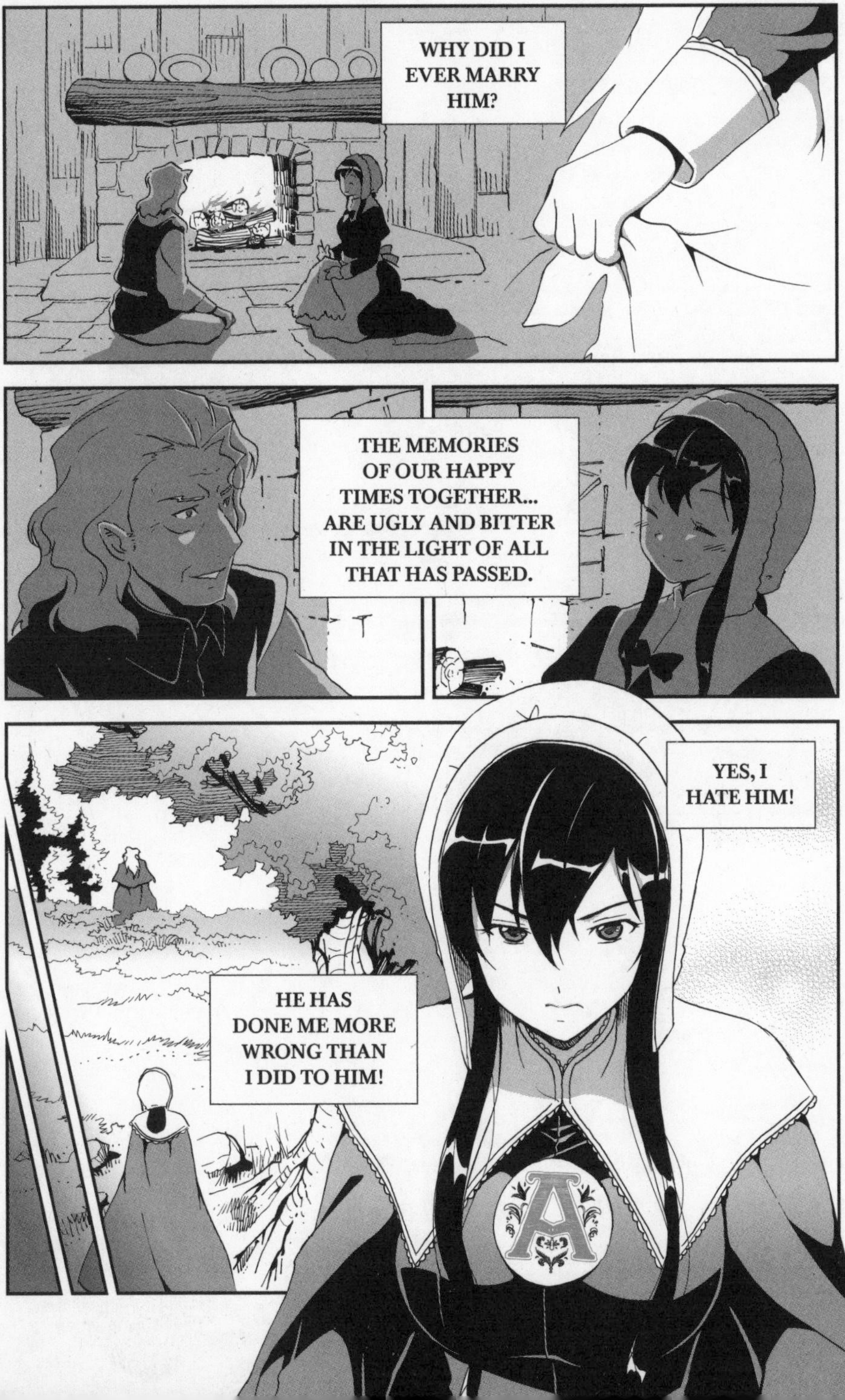
WHY DID I EVER MARRY HIM?
THE MEMORIES OF OUR HAPPY TIMES TOGETHER... ARE UGLY AND BITTER IN THE LIGHT OF ALL THAT HAS PASSED.
YES, I HATE HIM!
HE HAS DONE ME MORE WRONG THAN I DID TO HIM!

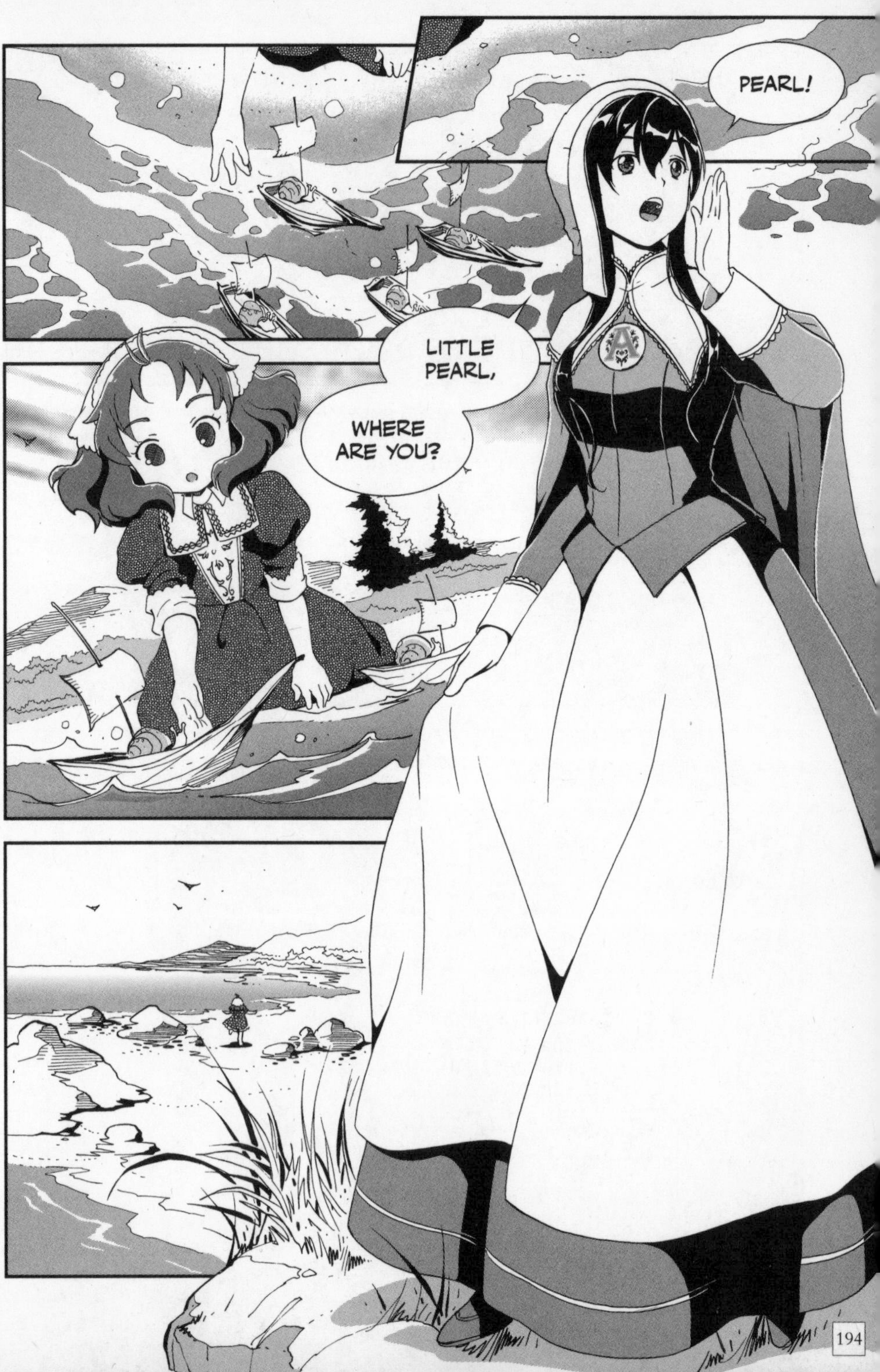
PEARL!
LITTLE PEARL,
WHERE ARE YOU?

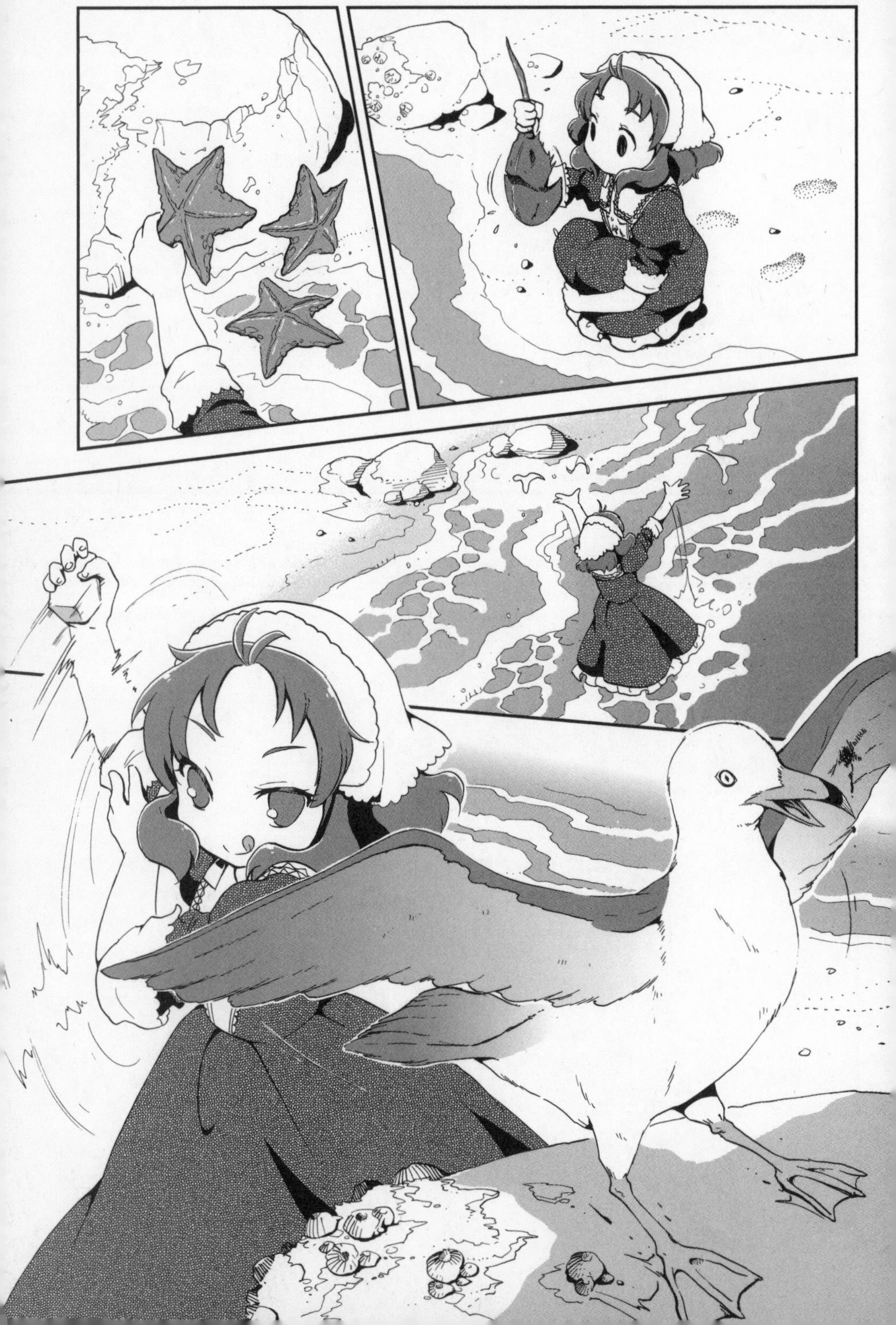

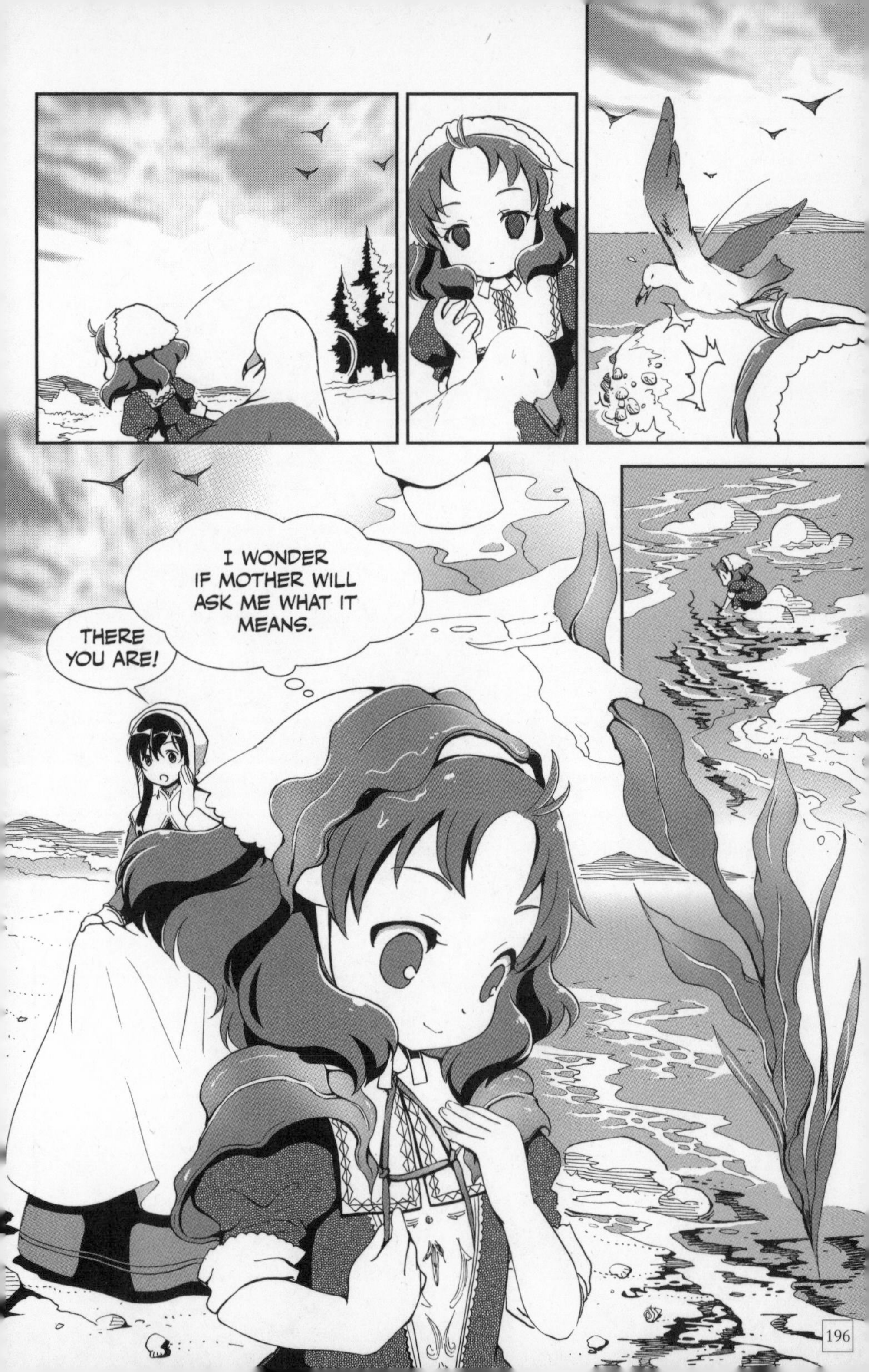
I WONDER IF MOTHER WILL ASK ME WHAT IT MEANS.
THERE YOU ARE!

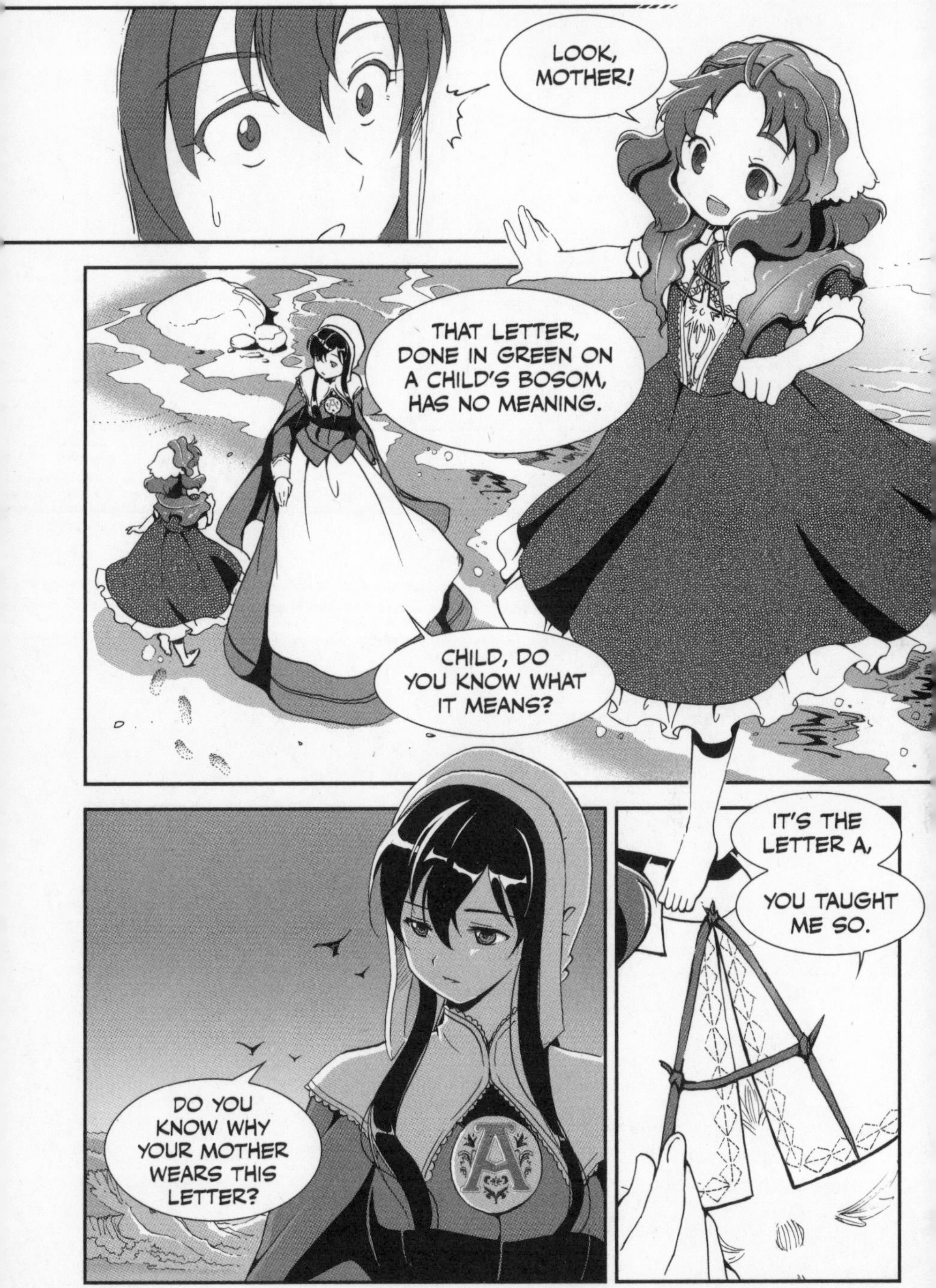
LOOK, MOTHER!
THAT LETTER, DONE IN GREEN ON A CHILD'S BOSOM, HAS NO MEANING.
CHILD, DO YOU KNOW WHAT IT MEANS?
IT'S THE LETTER A,
YOU TAUGHT ME SO.
DO YOU KNOW WHY YOUR MOTHER WEARS THIS LETTER?

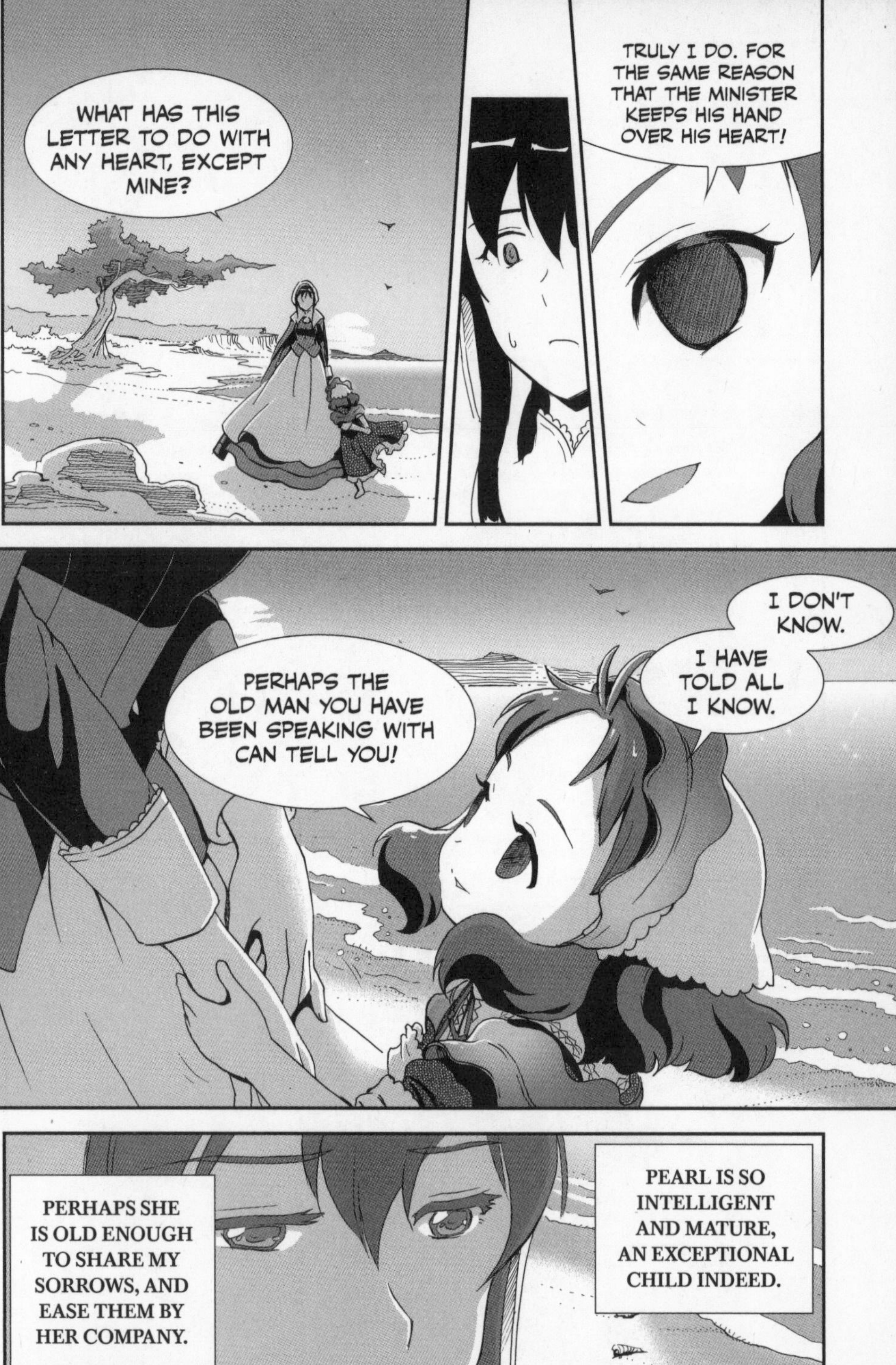

TRULY I DO. FOR THE SAME REASON THAT THE MINISTER KEEPS HIS HAND OVER HIS HEART!
WHAT HAS THIS LETTER TO DO WITH ANY HEART, EXCEPT MINE?
I DON'T KNOW.
I HAVE TOLD ALL I KNOW.
PERHAPS THE OLD MAN YOU HAVE BEEN SPEAKING WITH CAN TELL YOU!
PEARL IS SO INTELLIGENT AND MATURE, AN EXCEPTIONAL CHILD INDEED.
PERHAPS SHE IS OLD ENOUGH TO SHARE MY SORROWS, AND EASE THEM BY HER COMPANY.

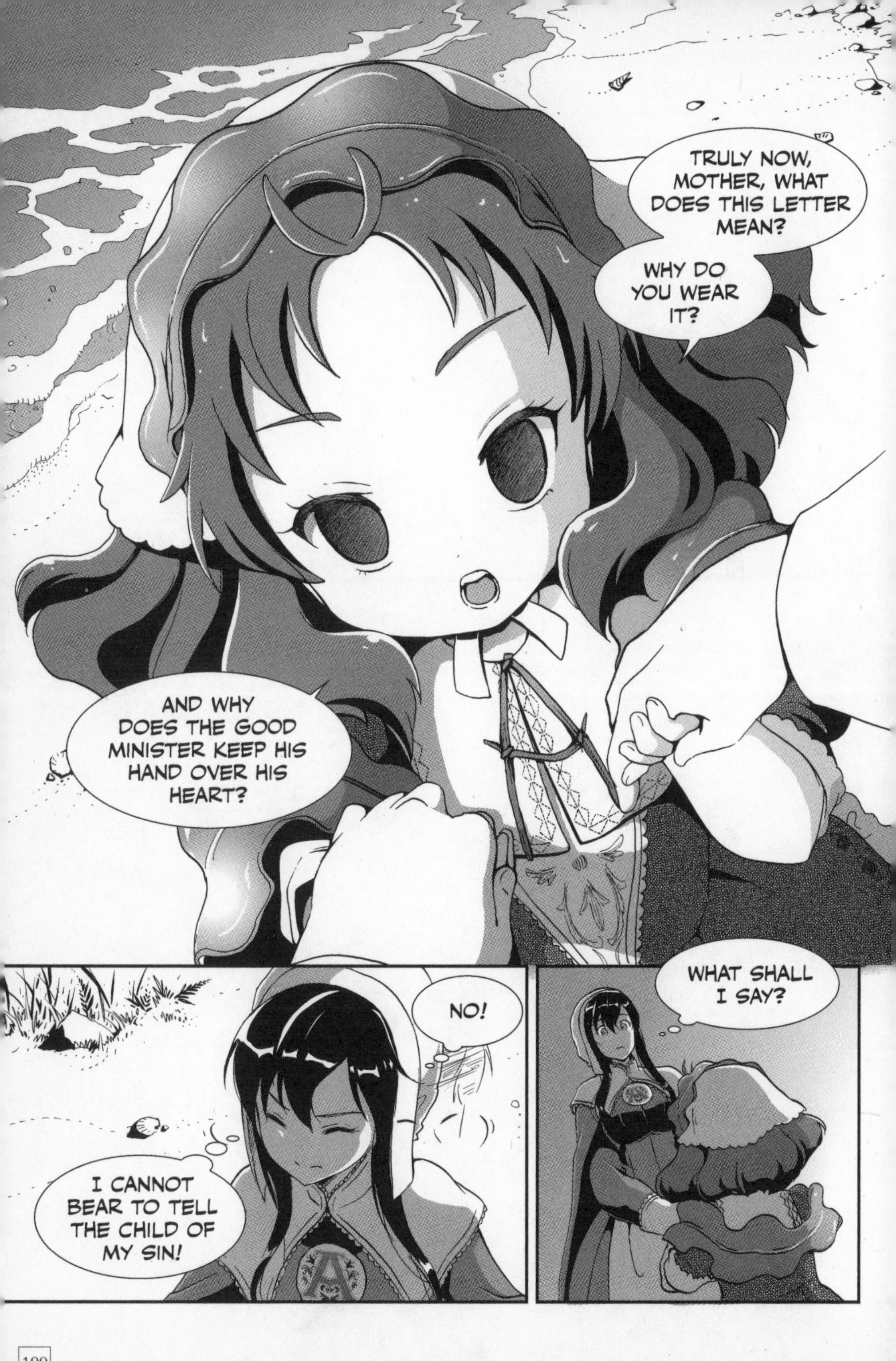
TRULY NOW, MOTHER, WHAT DOES THIS LETTER MEAN?
WHY DO YOU WEAR IT?
AND WHY DOES THE GOOD MINISTER KEEP HIS HAND OVER HIS HEART?
WHAT SHALL I SAY?
NO!
I CANNOT BEAR TO TELL THE CHILD OF MY SIN!

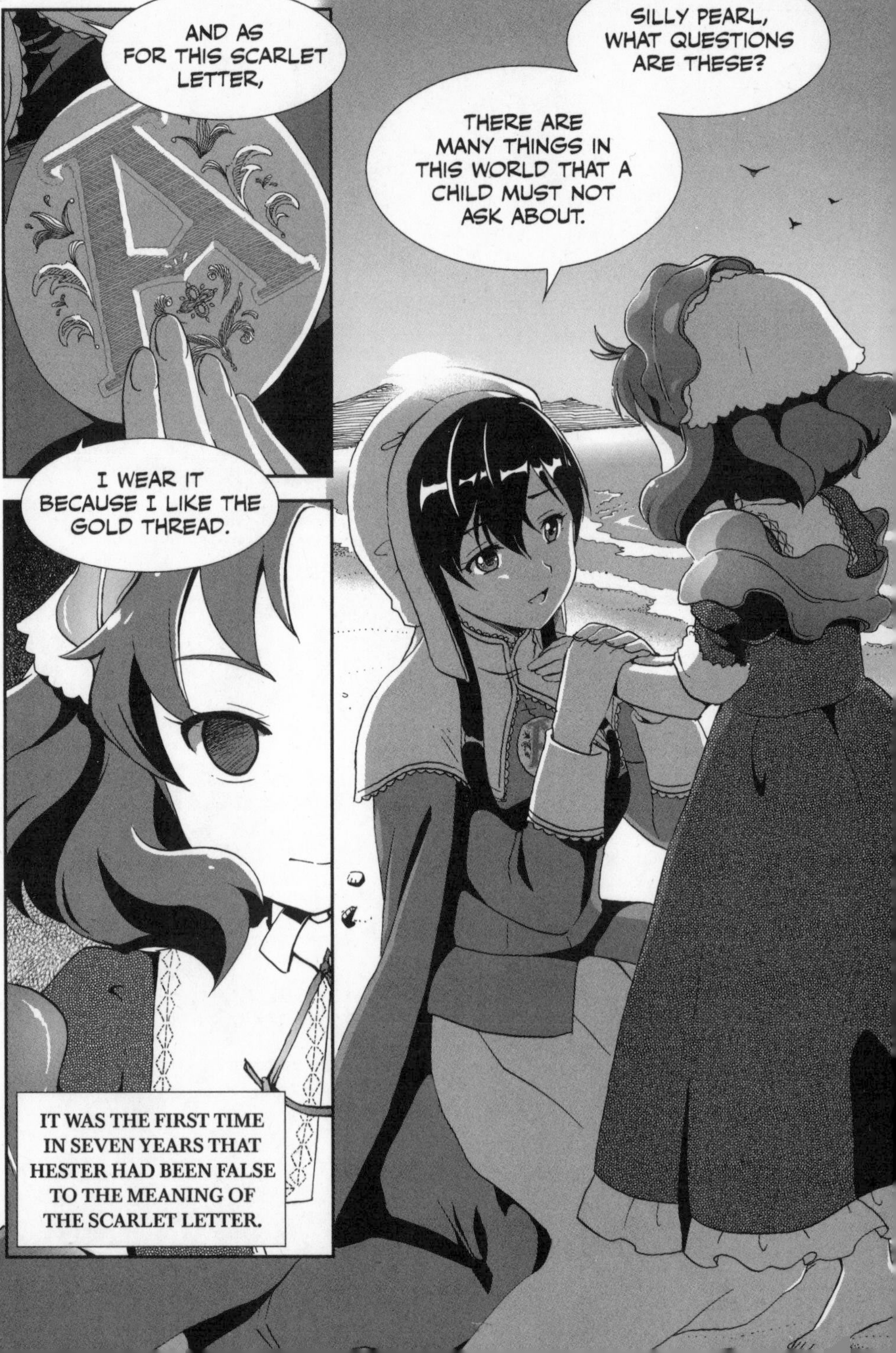
SILLY PEARL, WHAT QUESTIONS ARE THESE?
THERE ARE MANY THINGS IN THIS WORLD THAT A CHILD MUST NOT ASK ABOUT.
AND AS FOR THIS SCARLET LETTER,
I WEAR IT BECAUSE I LIKE THE GOLD THREAD.
IT WAS THE FIRST TIME IN SEVEN YEARS THAT HESTER HAD BEEN FALSE TO THE MEANING OF THE SCARLET LETTER.

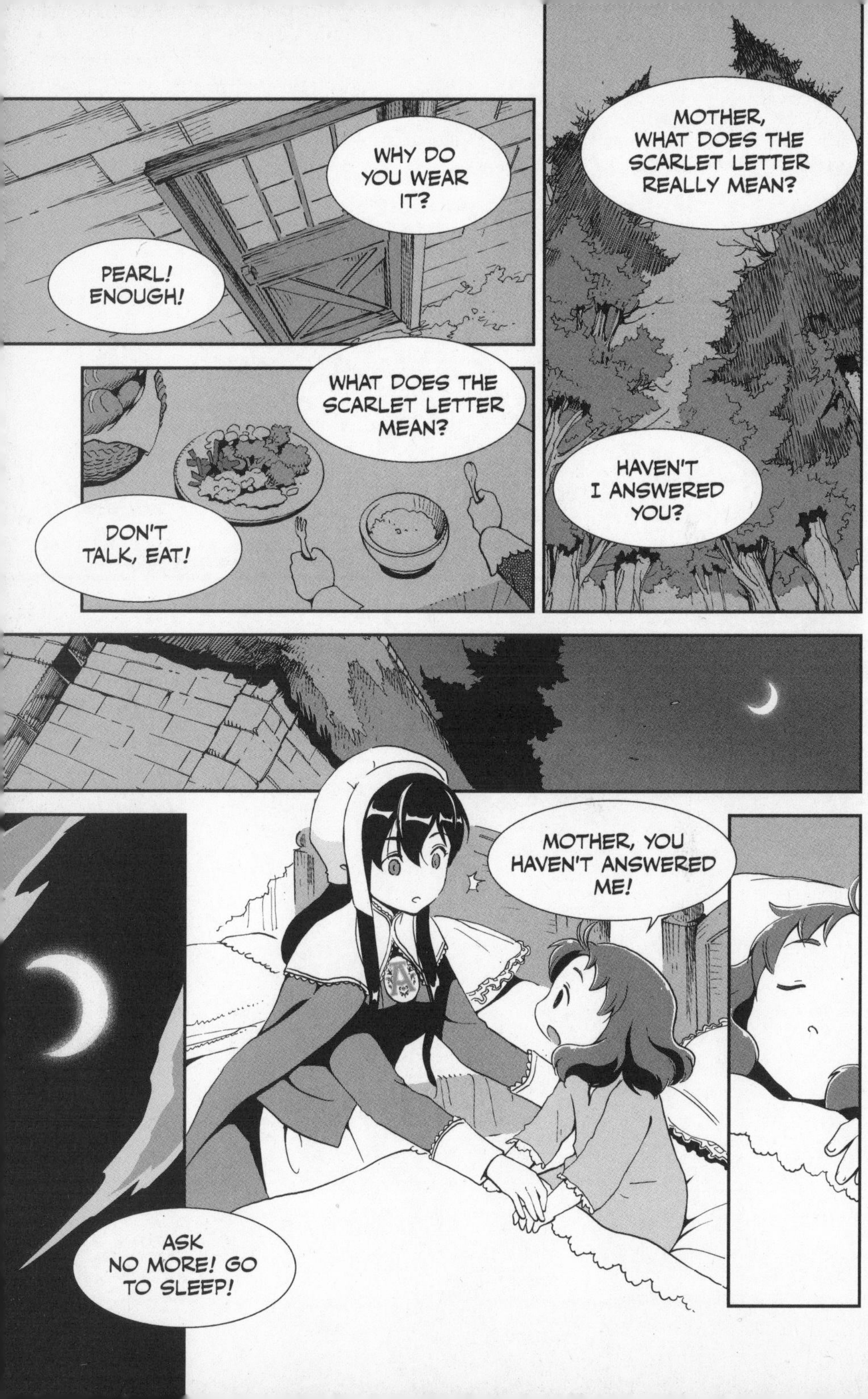
MOTHER, WHAT DOES THE SCARLET LETTER REALLY MEAN?
HAVEN'T I ANSWERED YOU?
WHY DO YOU WEAR IT?
PEARL! ENOUGH!
WHAT DOES THE SCARLET LETTER MEAN?
DON'T TALK, EAT!
MOTHER, YOU HAVEN'T ANSWERED ME!
ASK NO MORE! GO TO SLEEP!

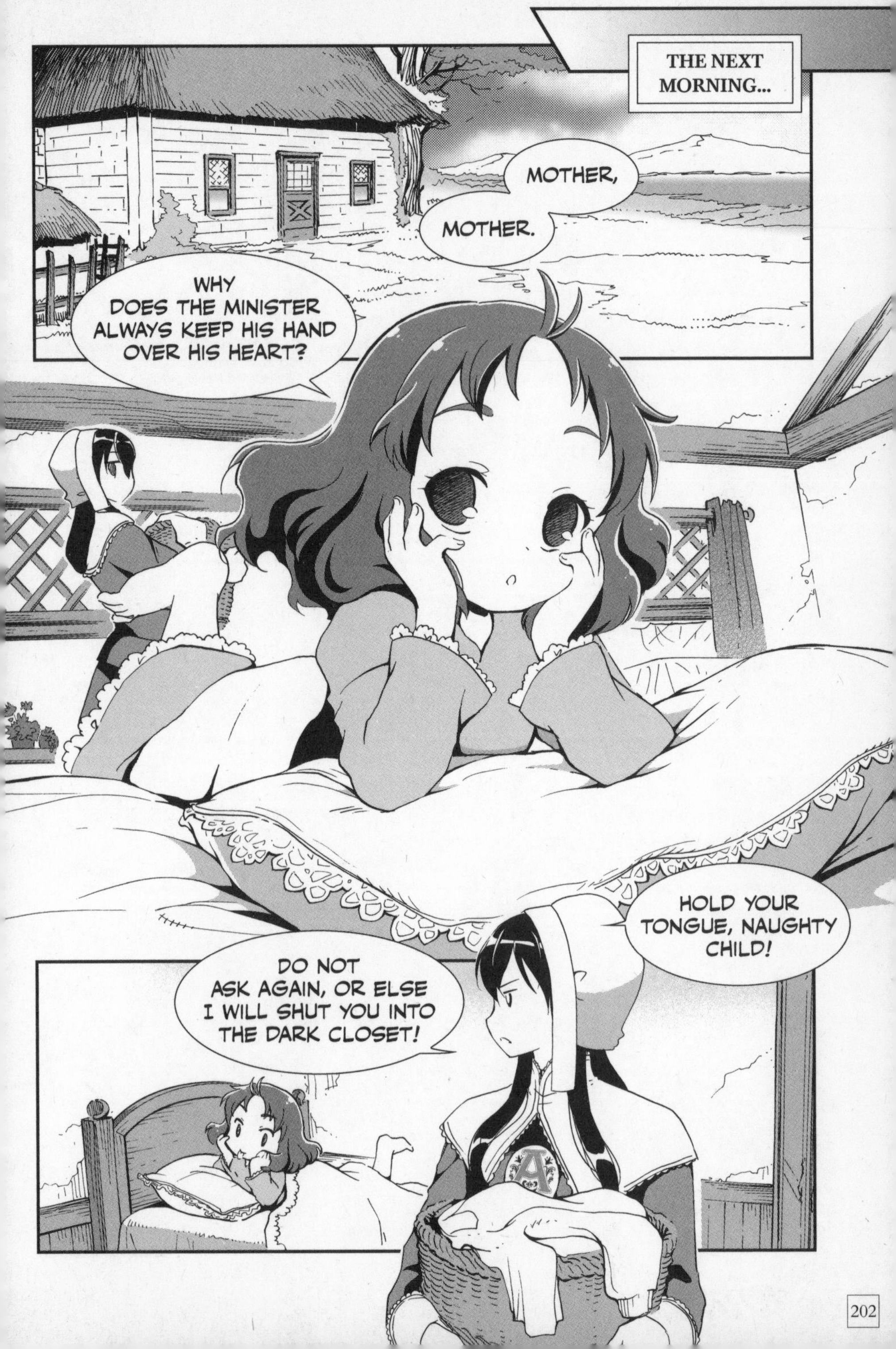
THE NEXT MORNING...
MOTHER,
MOTHER.
WHY DOES THE MINISTER ALWAYS KEEP HIS HAND OVER HIS HEART?
HOLD YOUR TONGUE, NAUGHTY CHILD!
DO NOT ASK AGAIN, OR ELSE I WILL SHUT YOU INTO THE DARK CLOSET!

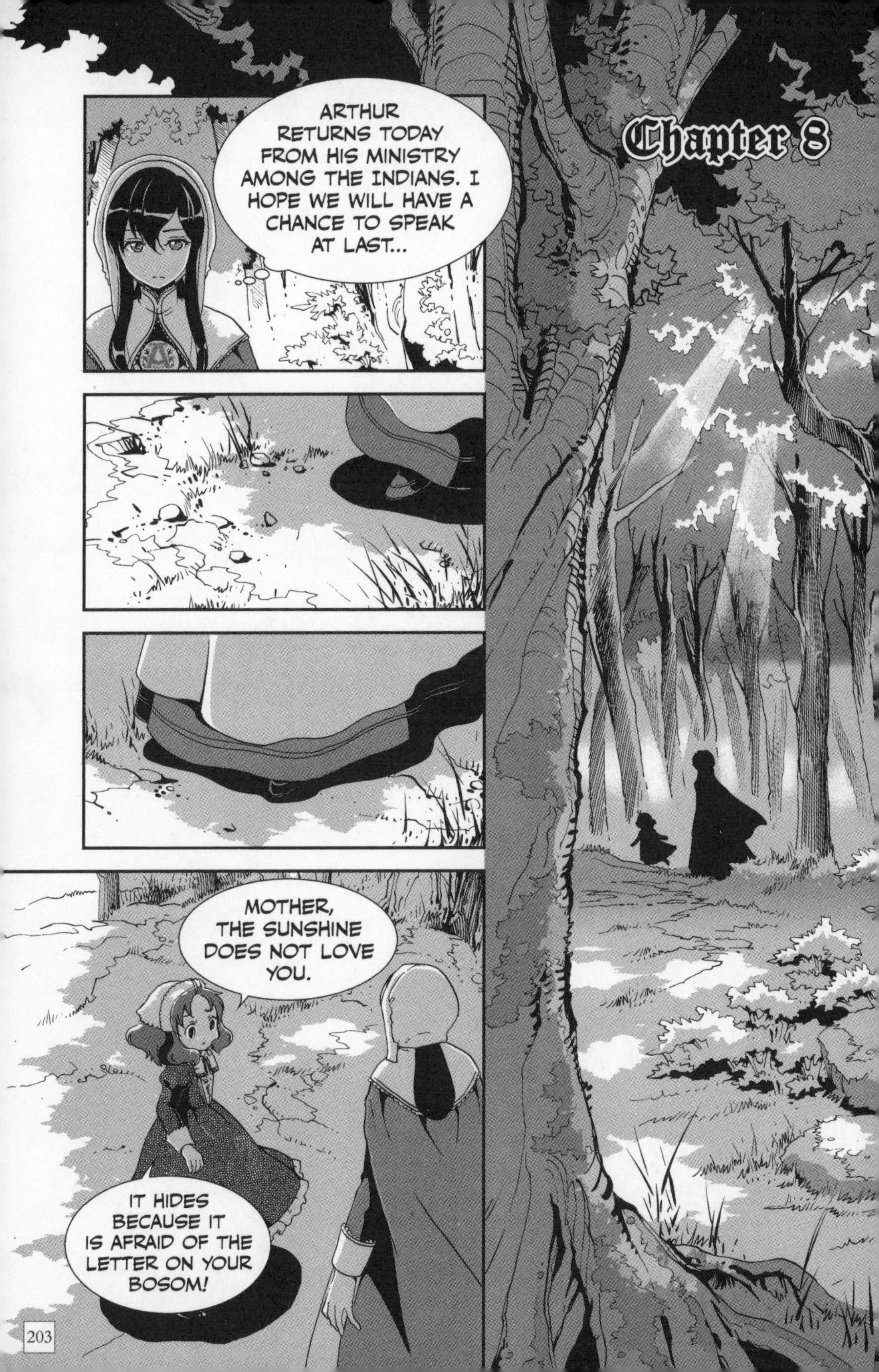
Chapter 8
ARTHUR RETURNS TODAY FROM HIS MINISTRY AMONG THE INDIANS. I HOPE WE WILL HAVE A CHANCE TO SPEAK AT LAST...
MOTHER, THE SUNSHINE DOES NOT LOVE YOU.
IT HIDES BECAUSE IT IS AFRAID OF THE LETTER ON YOUR BOSOM!

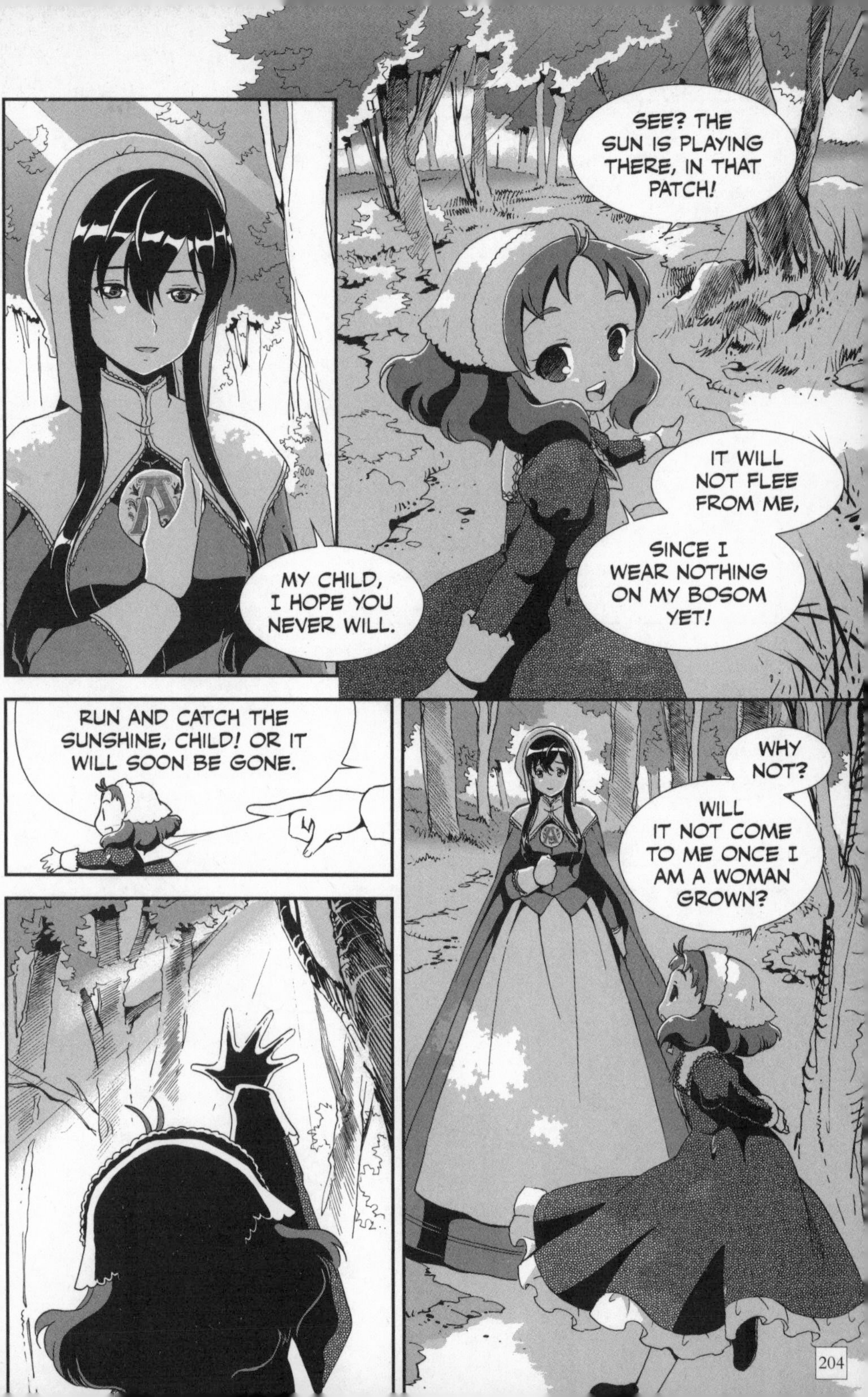

SEE? THE SUN IS PLAYING THERE, IN THAT PATCH!
IT WILL NOT FLEE FROM ME,
SINCE I WEAR NOTHING ON MY BOSOM YET!
MY CHILD, I HOPE YOU NEVER WILL.
WHY NOT?
WILL IT NOT COME TO ME ONCE I AM A WOMAN GROWN?
RUN AND CATCH THE SUNSHINE, CHILD! OR IT WILL SOON BE GONE.

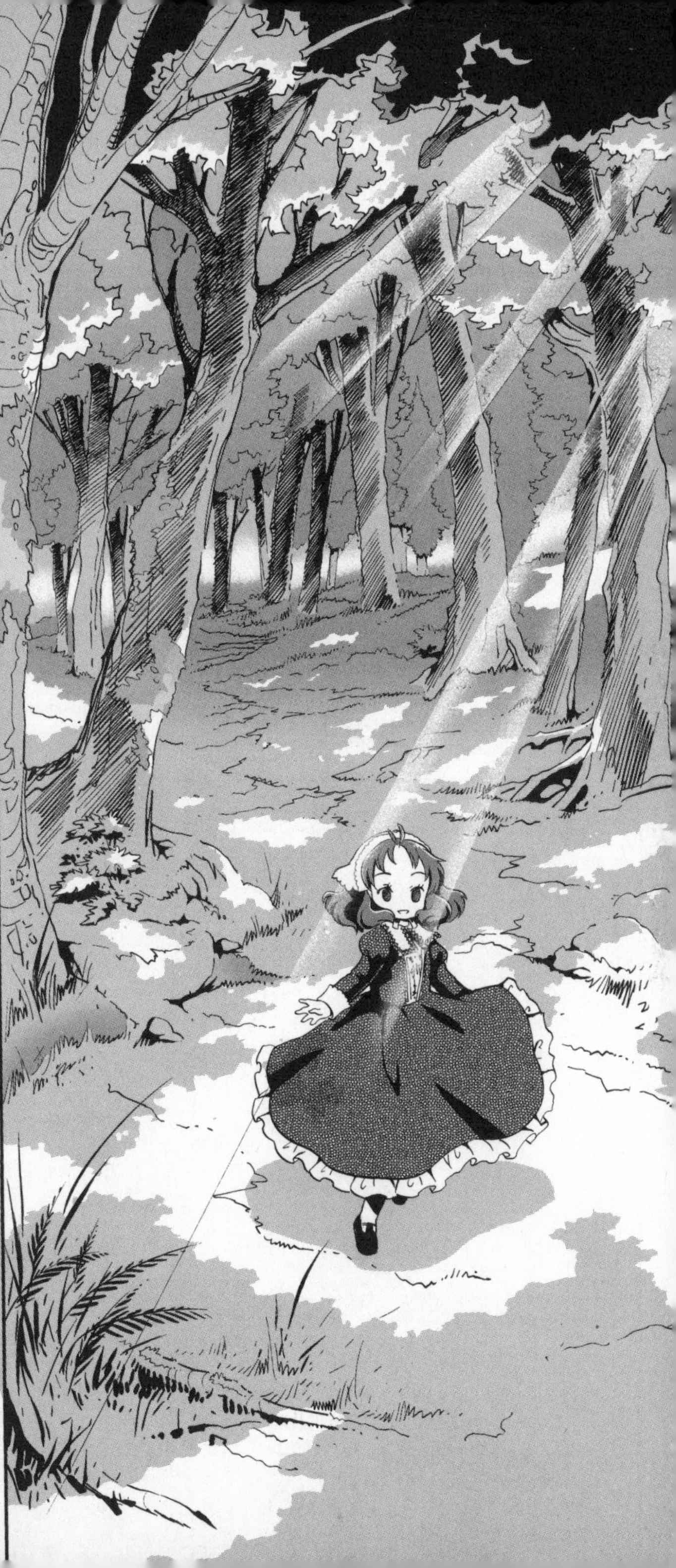
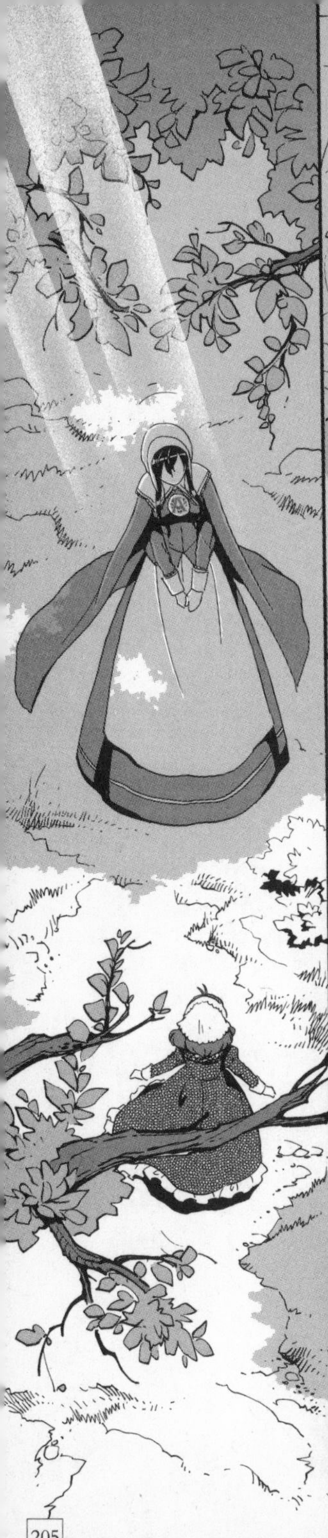

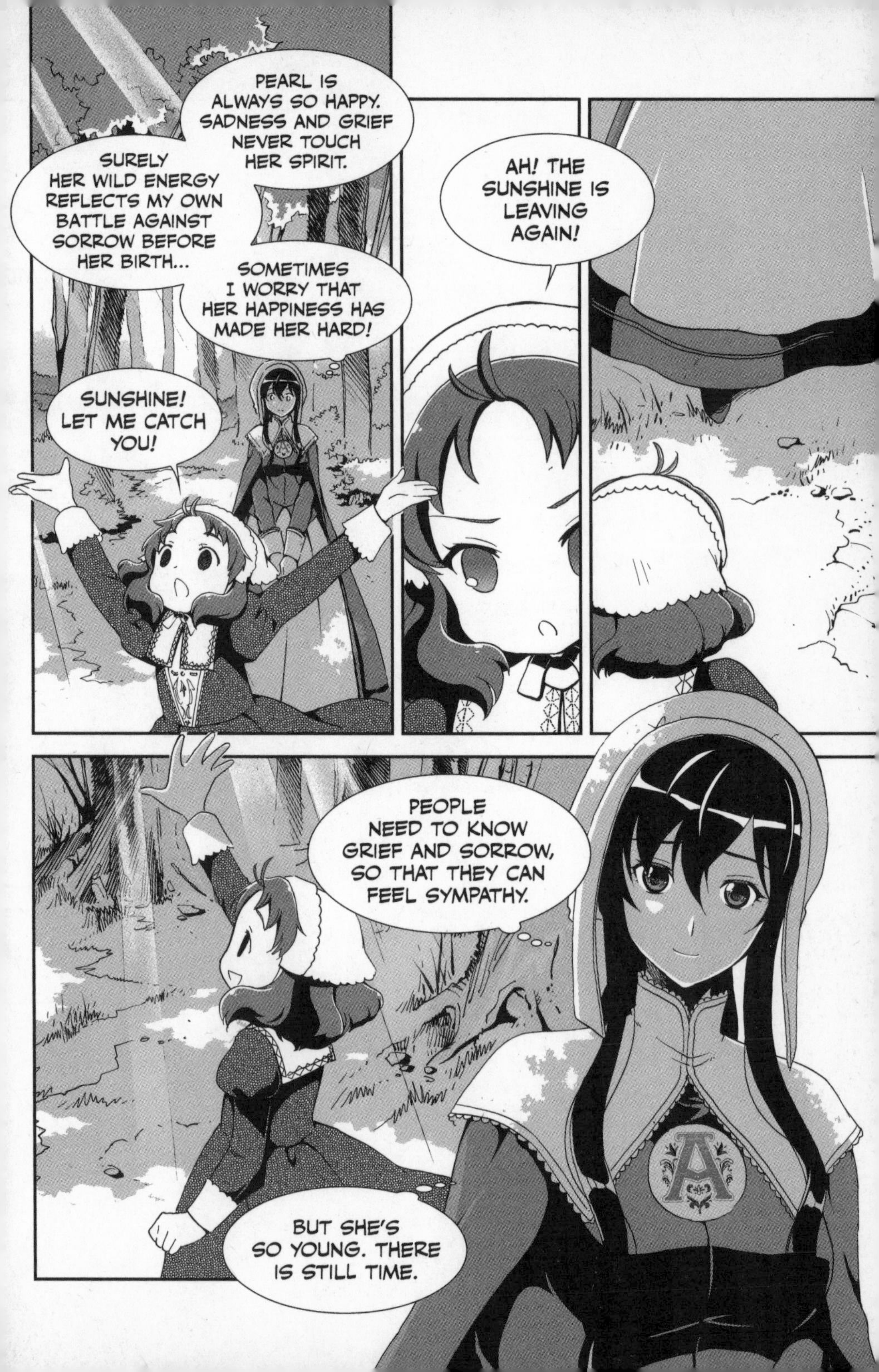
AH! THE SUNSHINE IS LEAVING AGAIN!
PEARL IS ALWAYS SO HAPPY. SADNESS AND GRIEF NEVER TOUCH HER SPIRIT.
SURELY HER WILD ENERGY REFLECTS MY OWN BATTLE AGAINST SORROW BEFORE HER BIRTH...
SOMETIMES I WORRY THAT HER HAPPINESS HAS MADE HER HARD!
SUNSHINE! LET ME CATCH YOU!
PEOPLE NEED TO KNOW GRIEF AND SORROW, SO THAT THEY CAN FEEL SYMPATHY.
BUT SHE'S SO YOUNG. THERE IS STILL TIME.

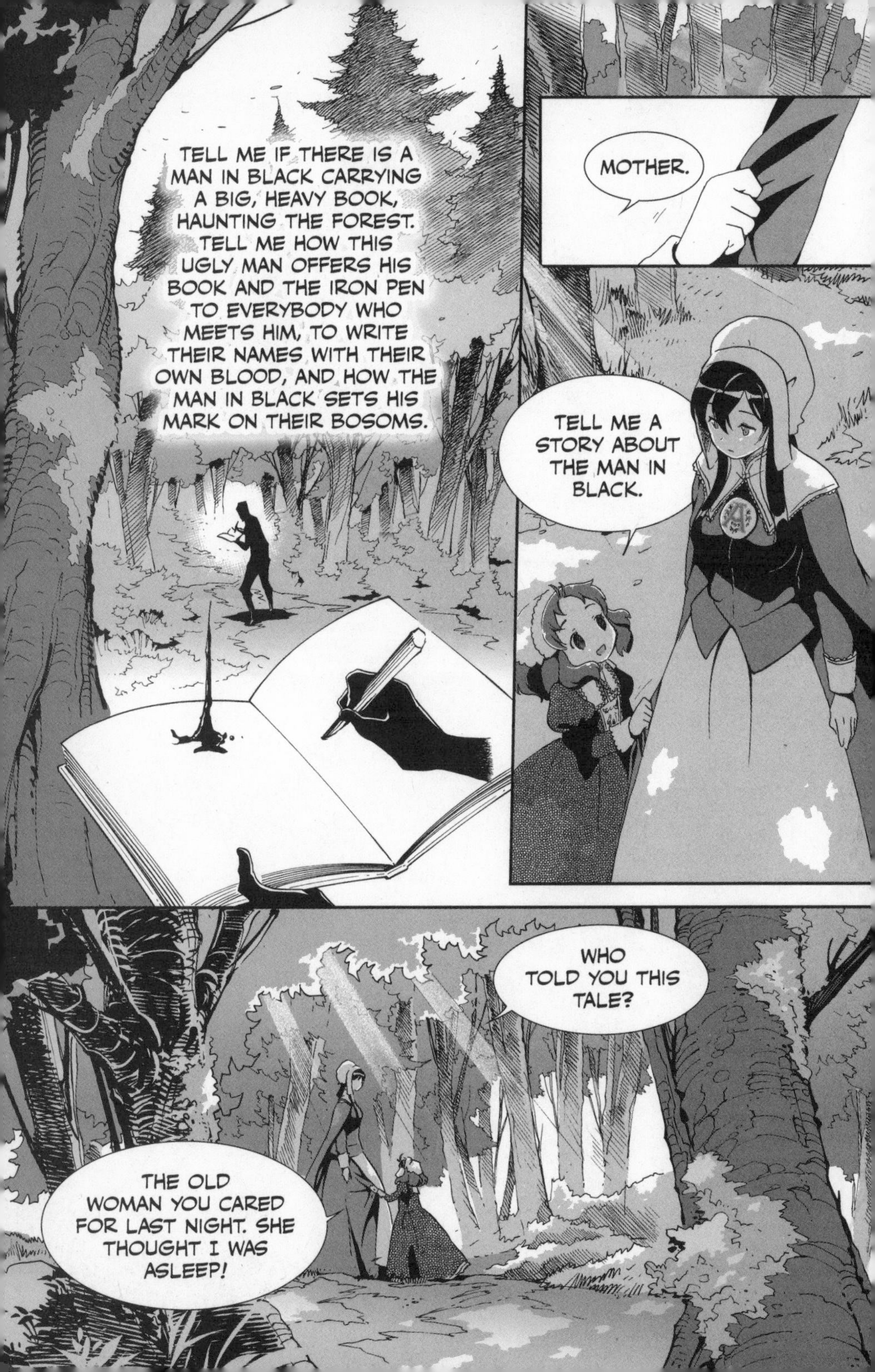
MOTHER.
TELL ME A STORY ABOUT THE MAN IN BLACK.
TELL ME IF THERE IS A MAN IN BLACK CARRYING A BIG, HEAVY BOOK, HAUNTING THE FOREST. TELL ME HOW THIS UGLY MAN OFFERS HIS BOOK AND THE IRON PEN TO EVERYBODY WHO MEETS HIM, TO WRITE THEIR NAMES WITH THEIR OWN BLOOD, AND HOW THE MAN IN BLACK SETS HIS MARK ON THEIR BOSOMS.
WHO TOLD YOU THIS TALE?
THE OLD WOMAN YOU CARED FOR LAST NIGHT. SHE THOUGHT I WAS ASLEEP!

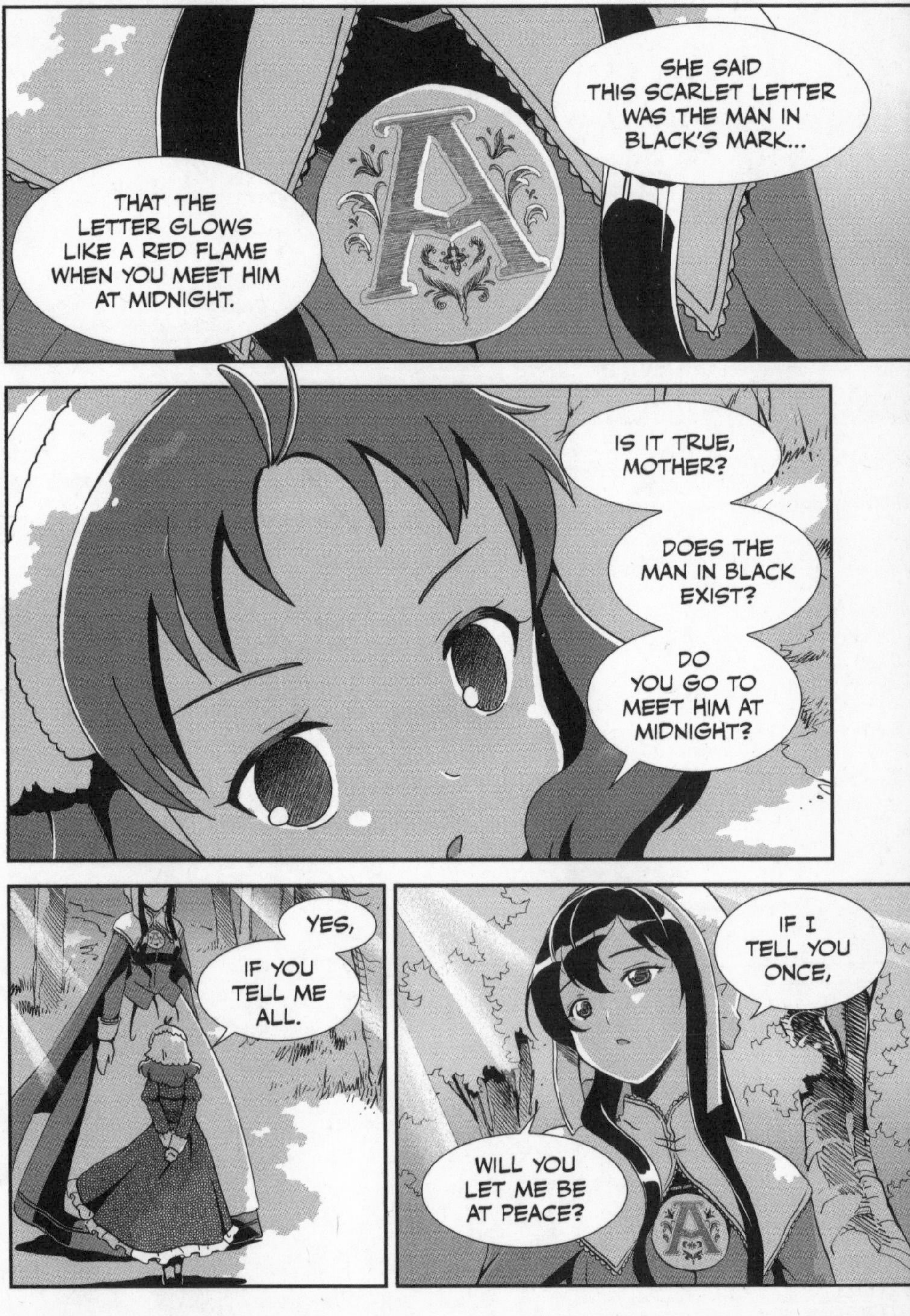
SHE SAID THIS SCARLET LETTER WAS THE MAN IN BLACK'S MARK...
THAT THE LETTER GLOWS LIKE A RED FLAME WHEN YOU MEET HIM AT MIDNIGHT.
IS IT TRUE, MOTHER?
DOES THE MAN IN BLACK EXIST?
DO YOU GO TO MEET HIM AT MIDNIGHT?
IF I TELL YOU ONCE,
WILL YOU LET ME BE AT PEACE?
YES,
IF YOU TELL ME ALL.

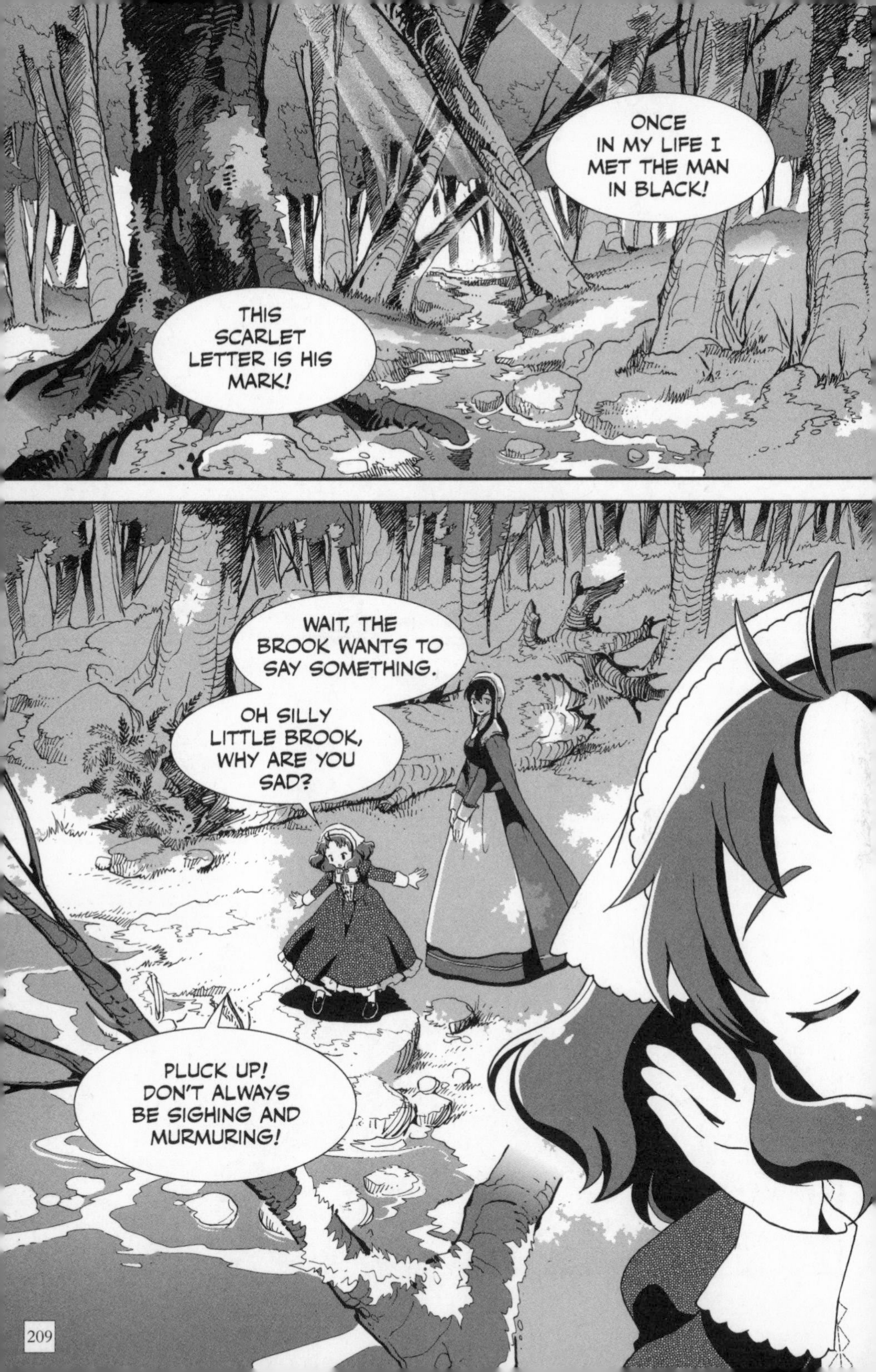
ONCE IN MY LIFE I MET THE MAN IN BLACK!
THIS SCARLET LETTER IS HIS MARK!
WAIT, THE BROOK WANTS TO SAY SOMETHING.
OH SILLY LITTLE BROOK, WHY ARE YOU SAD?
PLUCK UP! DON'T ALWAYS BE SIGHING AND MURMURING!

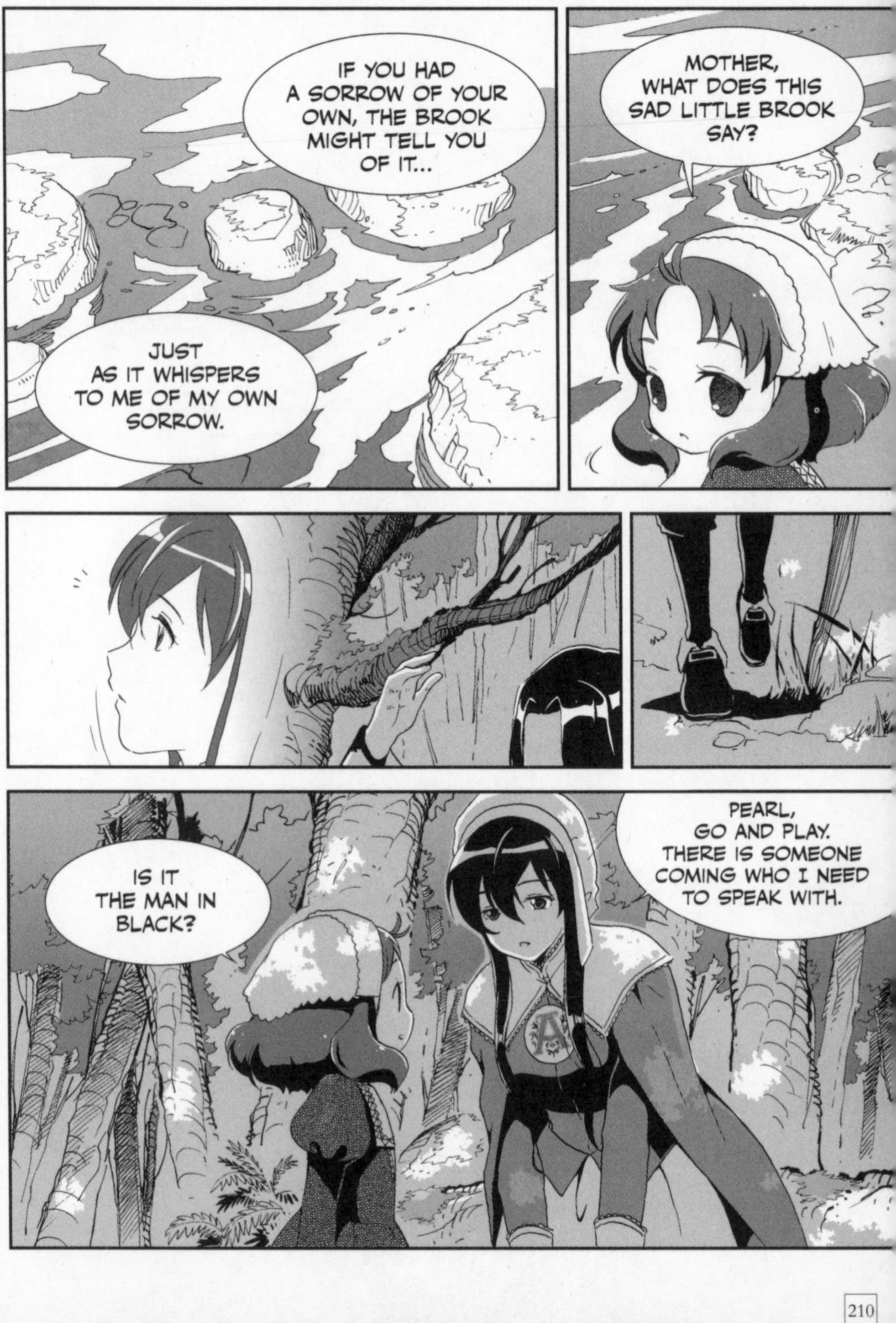
MOTHER, WHAT DOES THIS SAD LITTLE BROOK SAY?
IF YOU HAD A SORROW OF YOUR OWN, THE BROOK MIGHT TELL YOU OF IT...
JUST AS IT WHISPERS TO ME OF MY OWN SORROW.
PEARL, GO AND PLAY. THERE IS SOMEONE COMING WHO I NEED TO SPEAK WITH.
IS IT THE MAN IN BLACK?

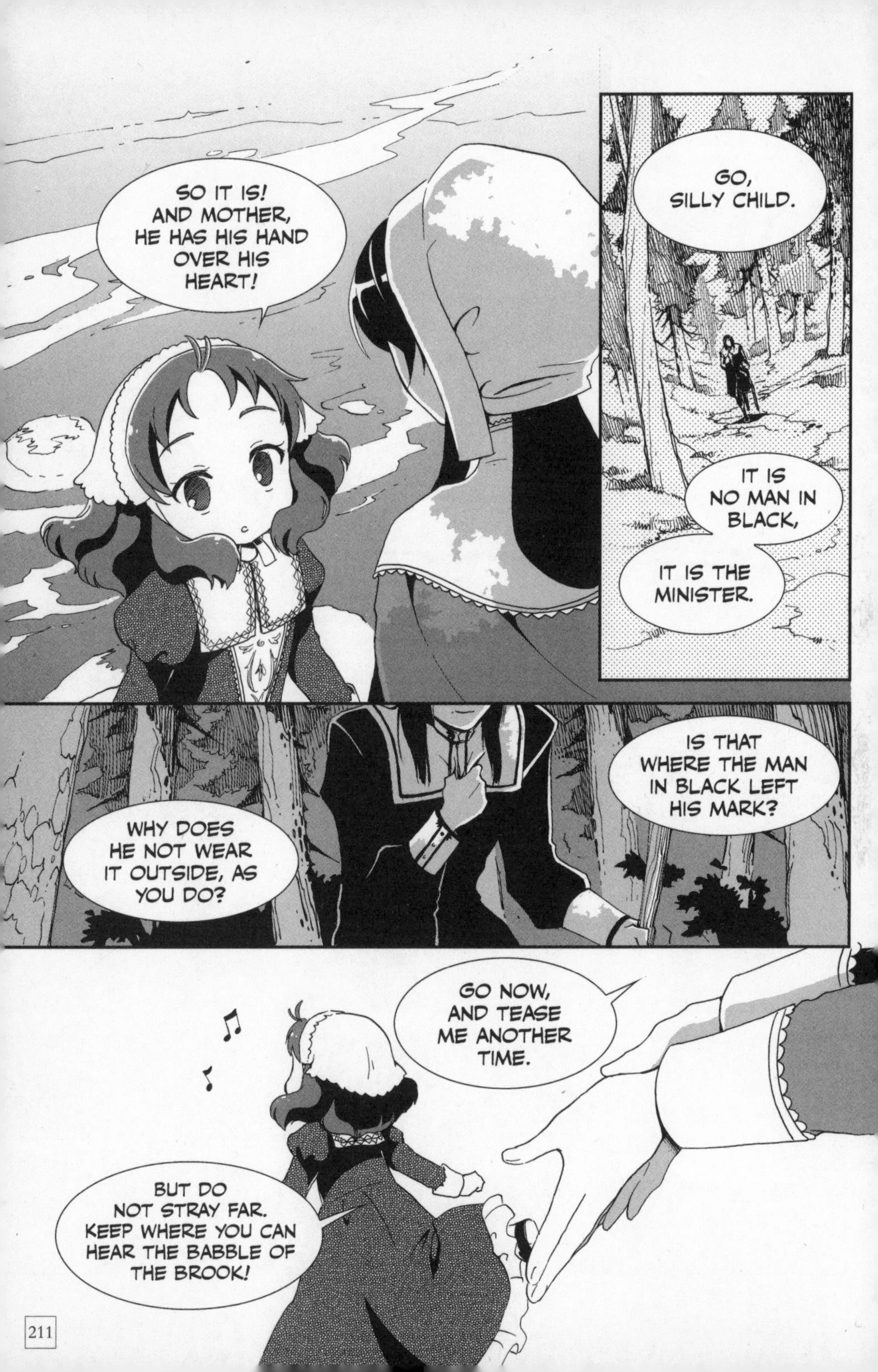
GO, SILLY CHILD.
IT IS NO MAN IN BLACK,
IT IS THE MINISTER.
SO IT IS! AND MOTHER, HE HAS HIS HAND OVER HIS HEART!
IS THAT WHERE THE MAN IN BLACK LEFT HIS MARK?
WHY DOES HE NOT WEAR IT OUTSIDE, AS YOU DO?
GO NOW, AND TEASE ME ANOTHER TIME.
BUT DO NOT STRAY FAR. KEEP WHERE YOU CAN HEAR THE BABBLE OF THE BROOK!

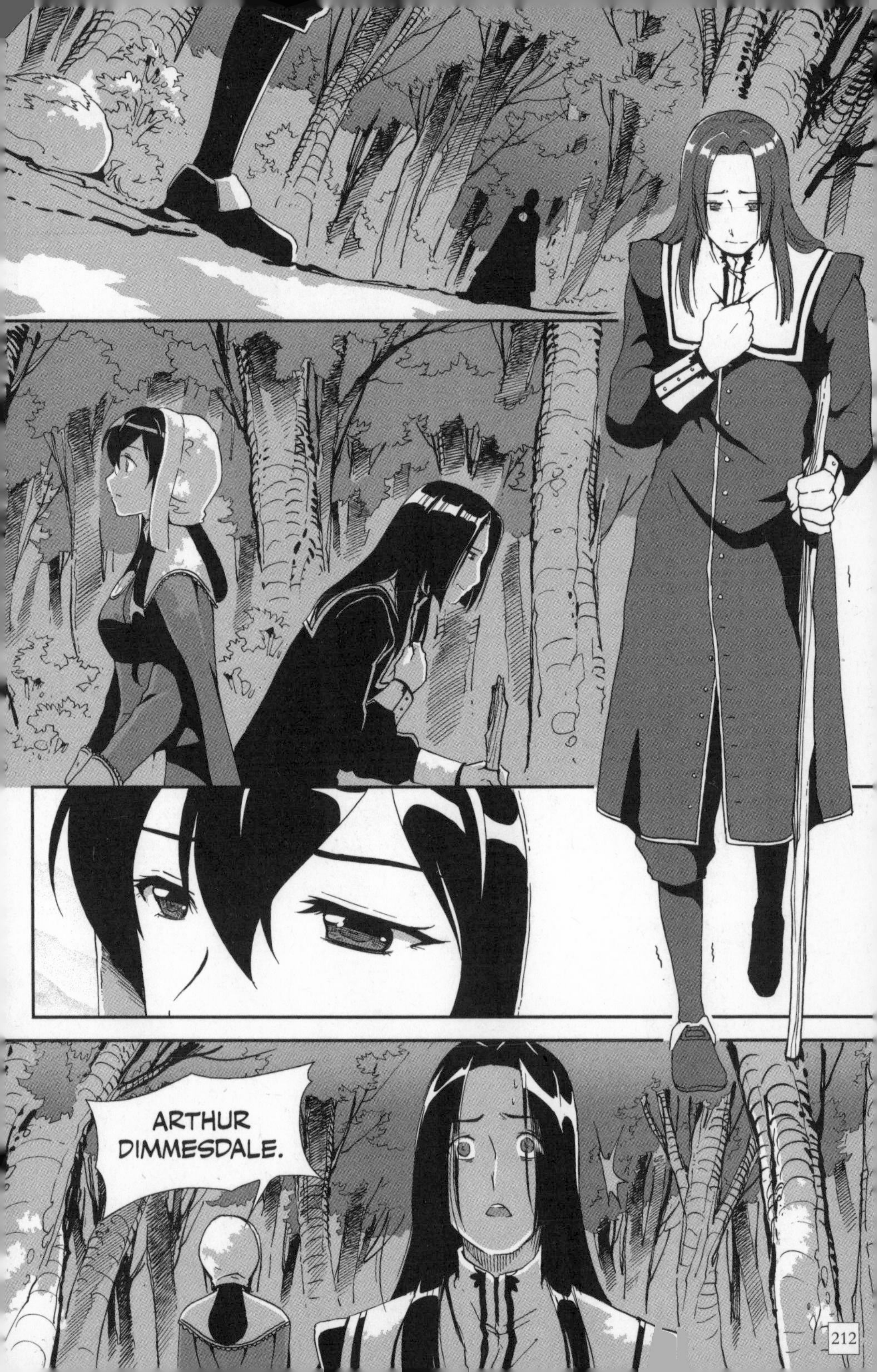
ARTHUR DIMMESDALE.

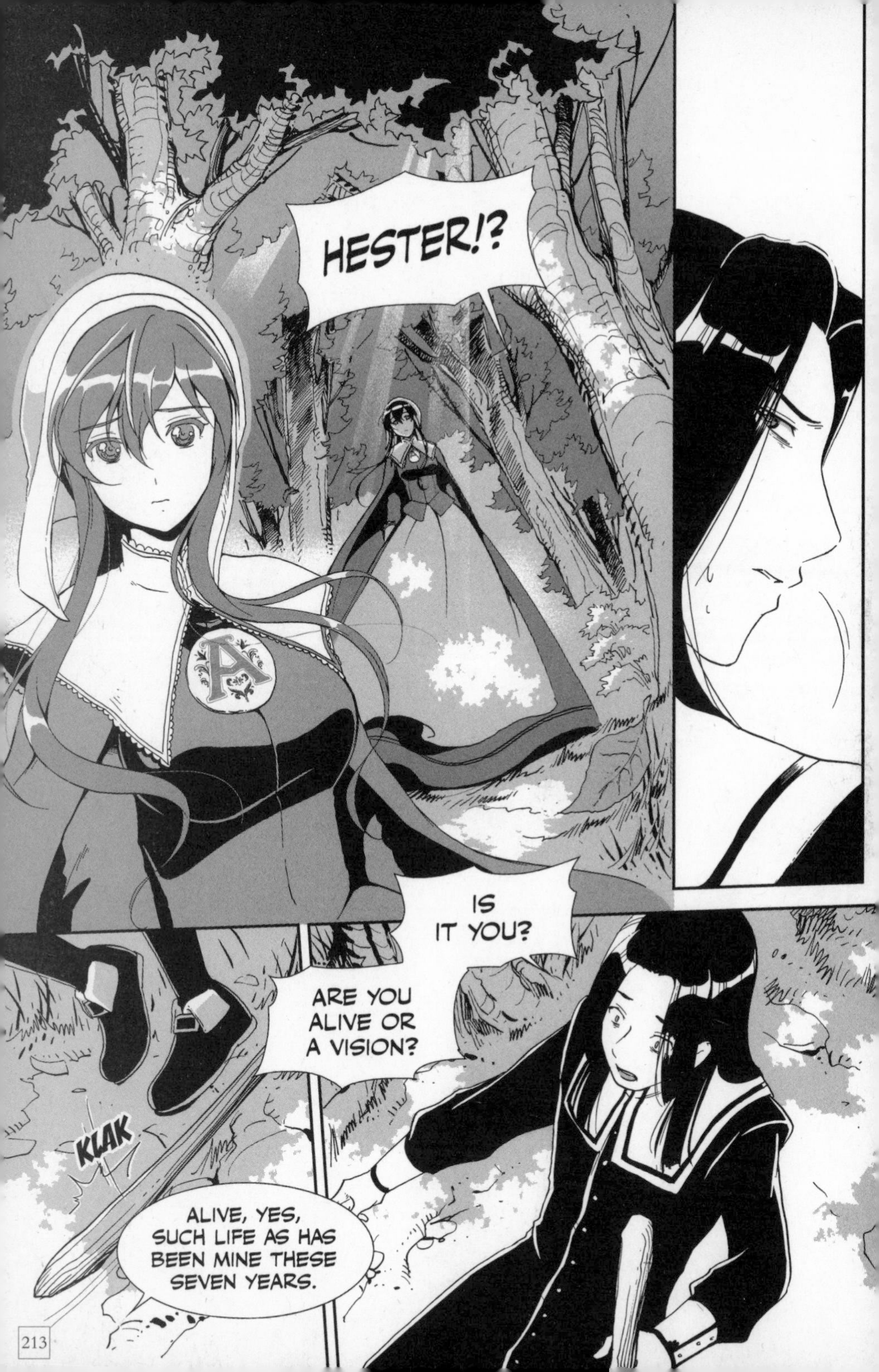
HESTER!?
IS IT YOU?
ARE YOU ALIVE OR A VISION?
KLAK
ALIVE, YES, SUCH LIFE AS HAS BEEN MINE THESE SEVEN YEARS.

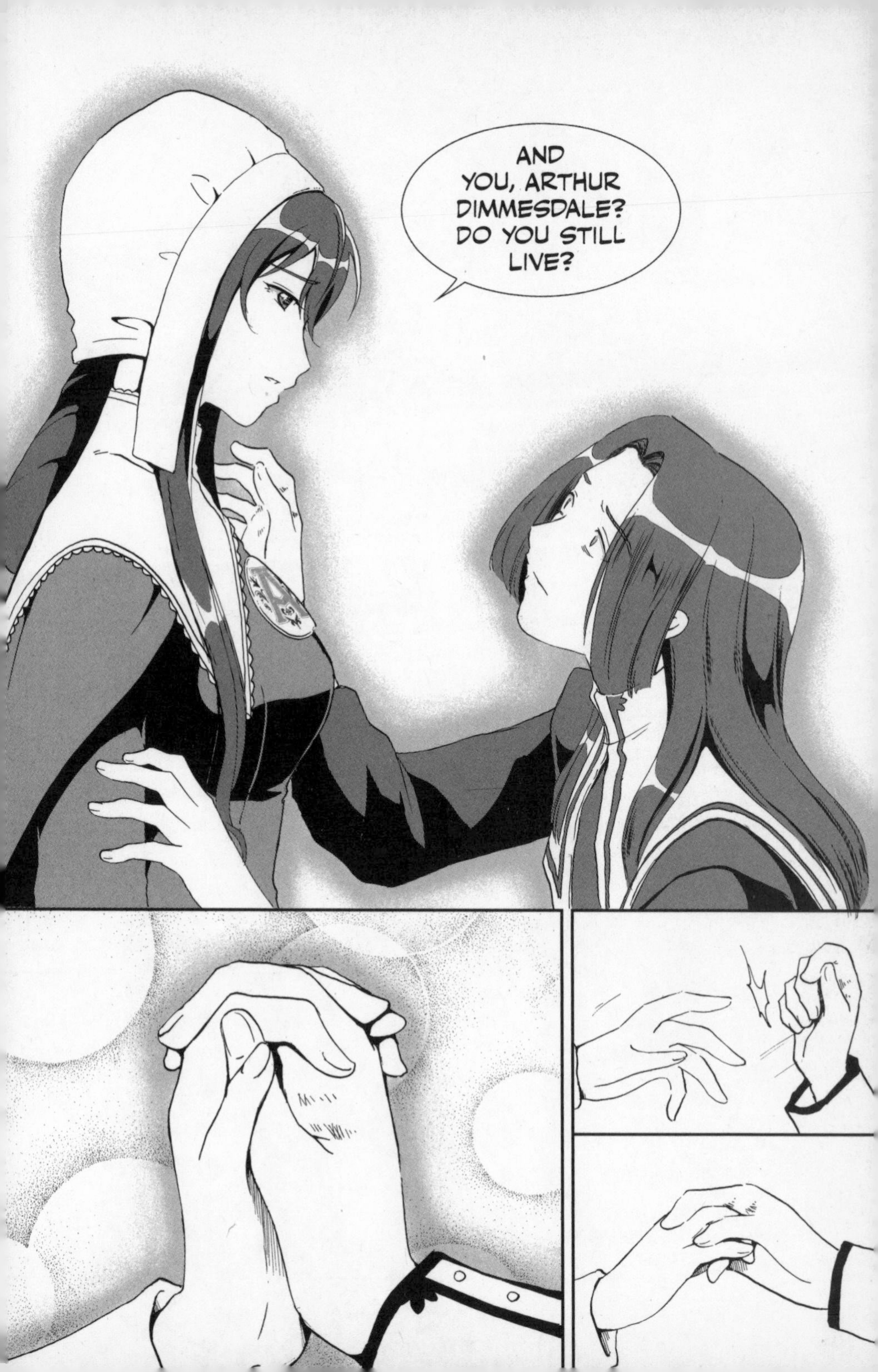
AND YOU, ARTHUR DIMMESDALE? DO YOU STILL LIVE?

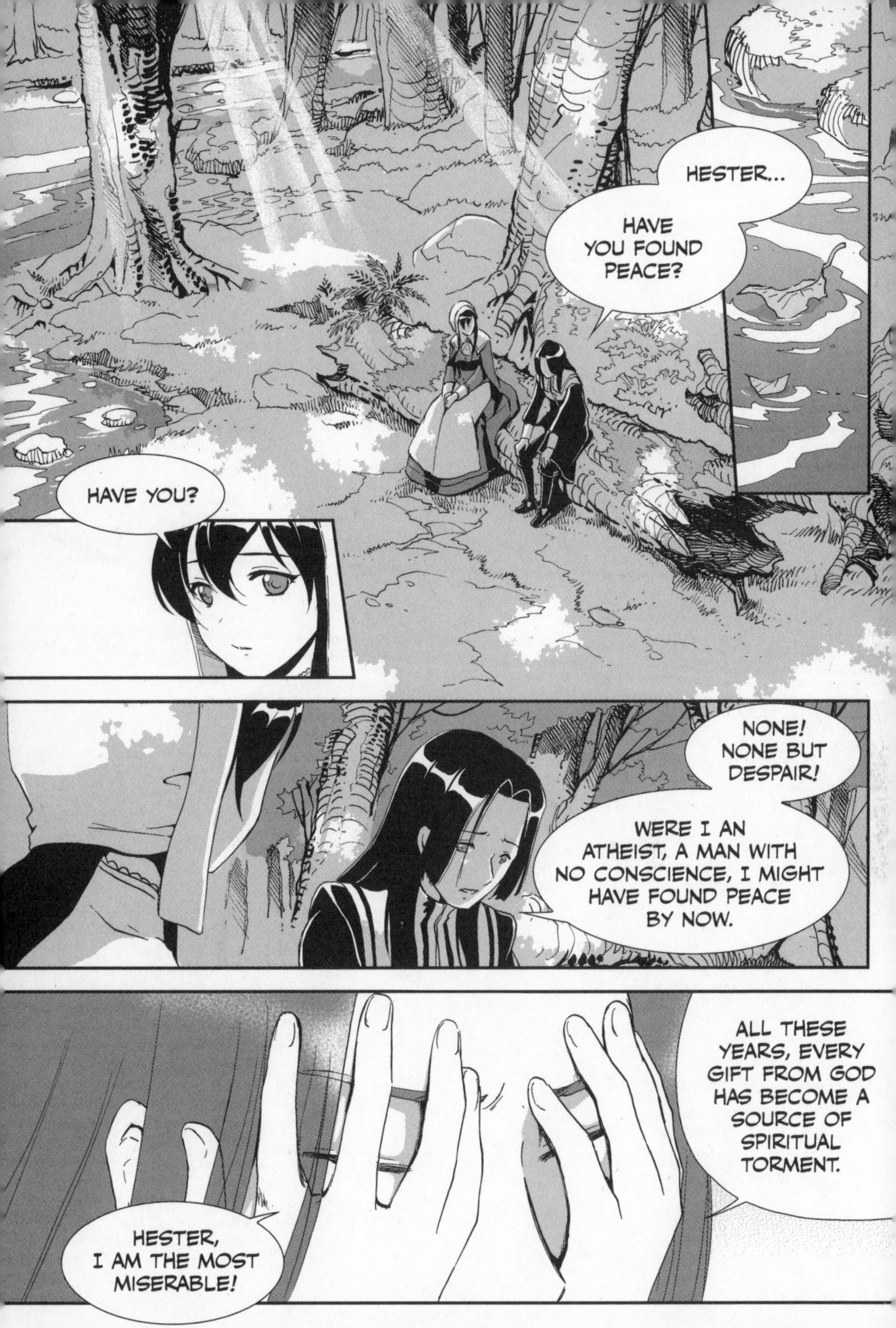
HESTER...
HAVE YOU FOUND PEACE?
HAVE YOU?
NONE! NONE BUT DESPAIR!
WERE I AN ATHEIST, A MAN WITH NO CONSCIENCE, I MIGHT HAVE FOUND PEACE BY NOW.
ALL THESE YEARS, EVERY GIFT FROM GOD HAS BECOME A SOURCE OF SPIRITUAL TORMENT.
HESTER, I AM THE MOST MISERABLE!

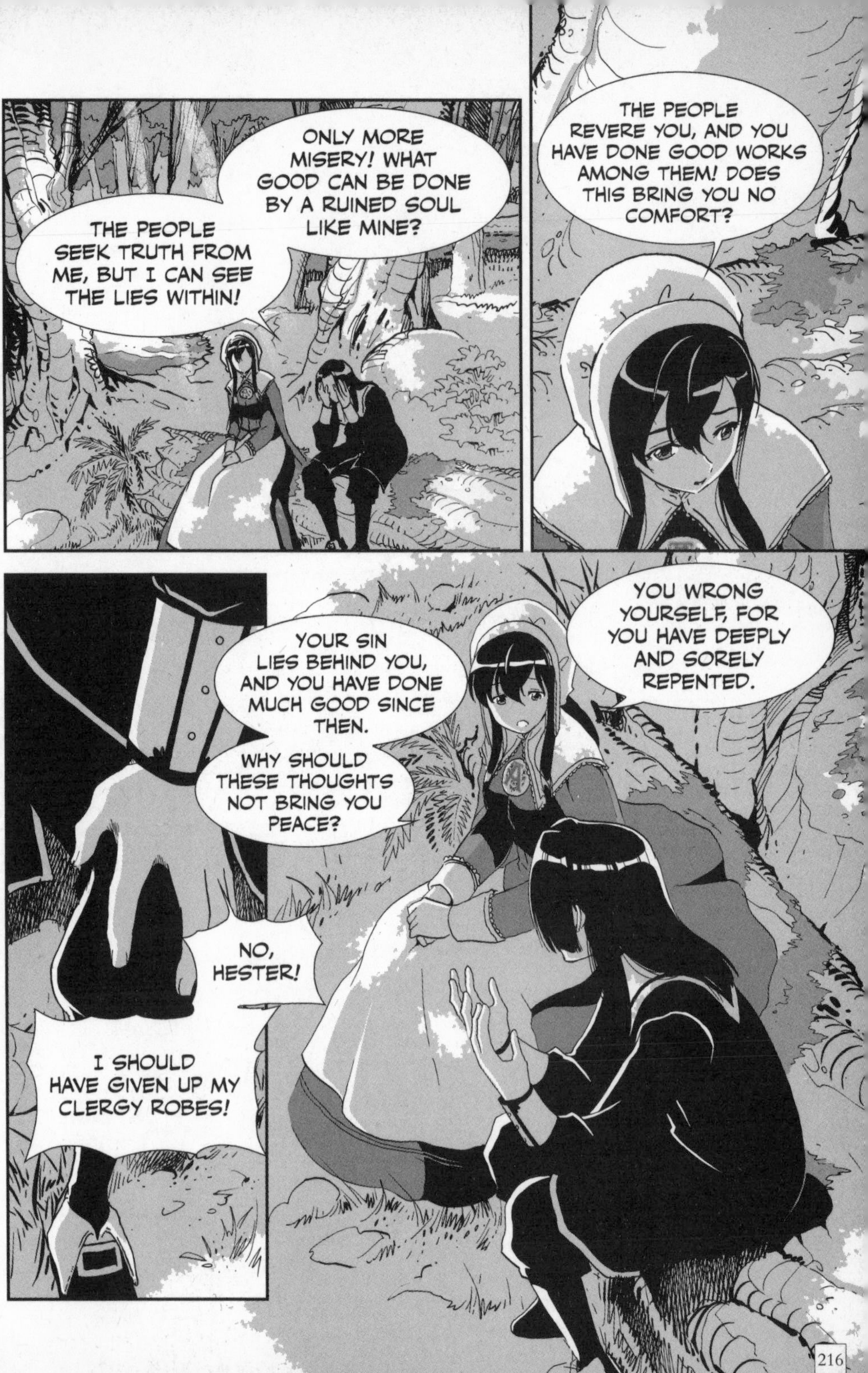
THE PEOPLE REVERE YOU, AND YOU HAVE DONE GOOD WORKS AMONG THEM! DOES THIS BRING YOU NO COMFORT?
ONLY MORE MISERY! WHAT GOOD CAN BE DONE BY A RUINED SOUL LIKE MINE?
THE PEOPLE SEEK TRUTH FROM ME, BUT I CAN SEE THE LIES WITHIN!
YOU WRONG YOURSELF, FOR YOU HAVE DEEPLY AND SORELY REPENTED.
YOUR SIN LIES BEHIND YOU, AND YOU HAVE DONE MUCH GOOD SINCE THEN.
WHY SHOULD THESE THOUGHTS NOT BRING YOU PEACE?
NO, HESTER!
I SHOULD HAVE GIVEN UP MY CLERGY ROBES!

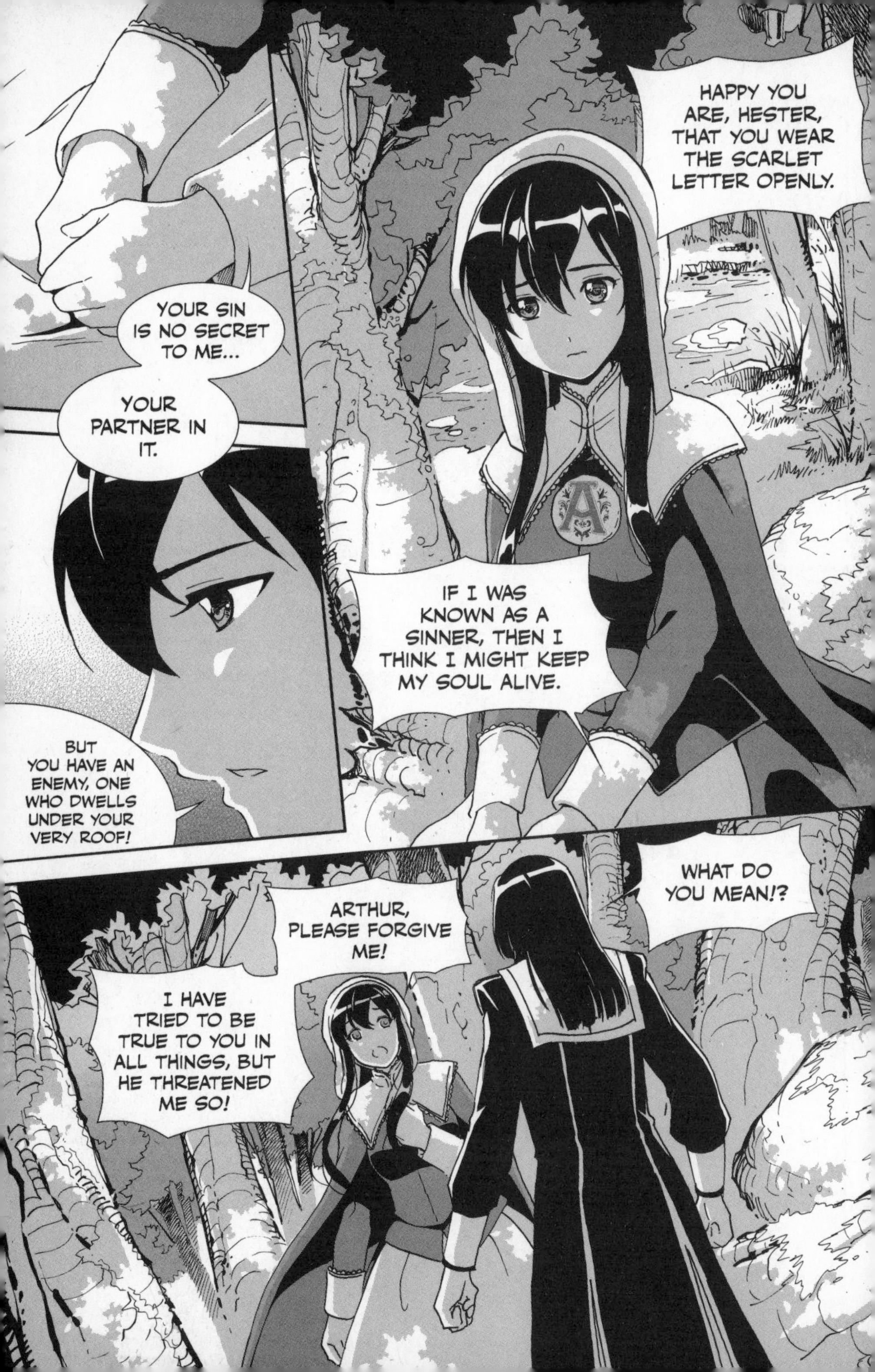
HAPPY YOU ARE, HESTER, THAT YOU WEAR THE SCARLET LETTER OPENLY.
IF I WAS KNOWN AS A SINNER, THEN I THINK I MIGHT KEEP MY SOUL ALIVE.
YOUR SIN IS NO SECRET TO ME...
YOUR PARTNER IN IT.
BUT YOU HAVE AN ENEMY, ONE WHO DWELLS UNDER YOUR VERY ROOF!
WHAT DO YOU MEAN!?
ARTHUR, PLEASE FORGIVE ME!
I HAVE TRIED TO BE TRUE TO YOU IN ALL THINGS, BUT HE THREATENED ME SO!

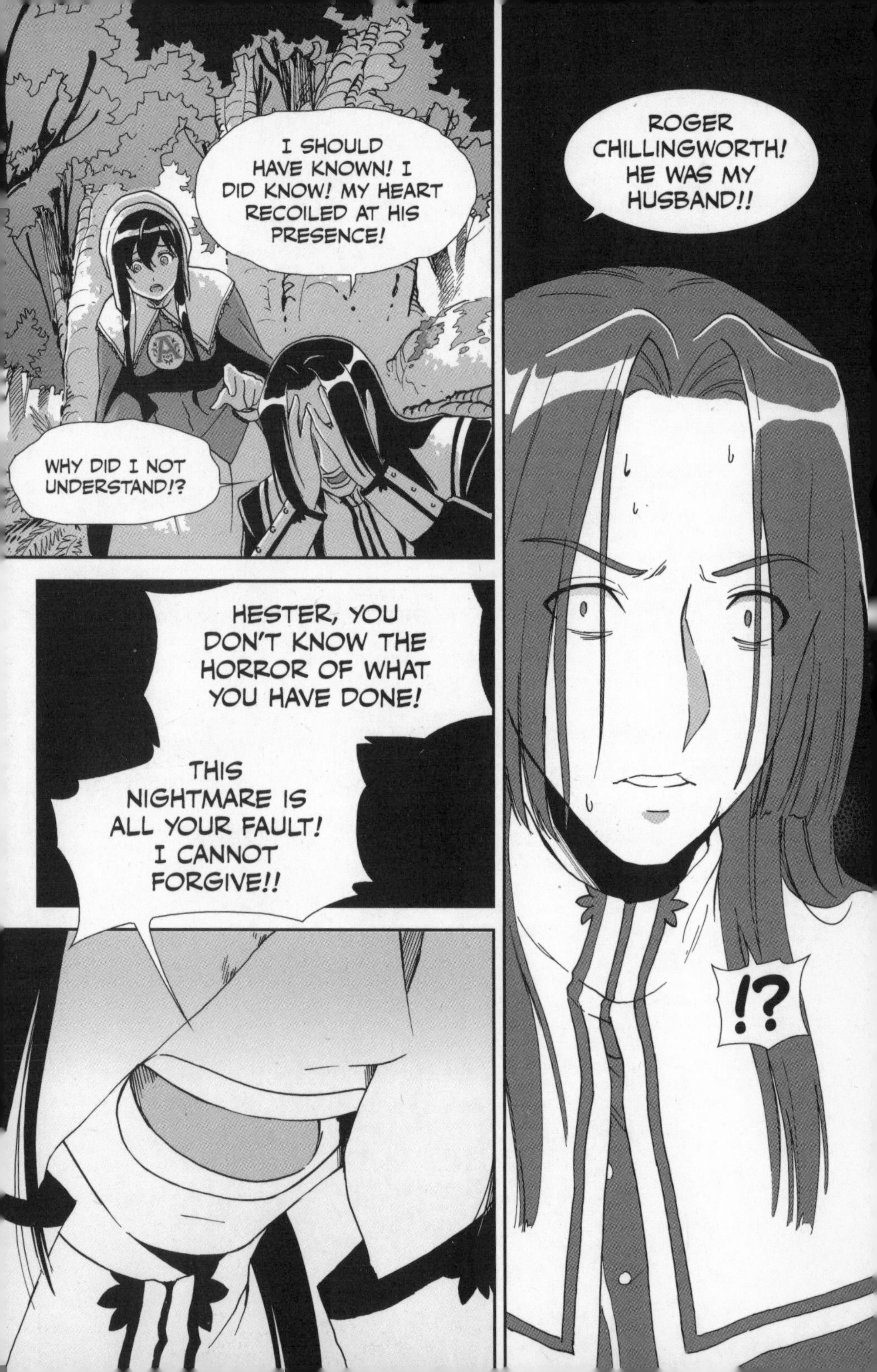
ROGER CHILLINGWORTH! HE WAS MY HUSBAND!!
!?
I SHOULD HAVE KNOWN! I DID KNOW! MY HEART RECOILED AT HIS PRESENCE!
WHY DID I NOT UNDERSTAND!?
HESTER, YOU DON'T KNOW THE HORROR OF WHAT YOU HAVE DONE!
THIS NIGHTMARE IS ALL YOUR FAULT! I CANNOT FORGIVE!!

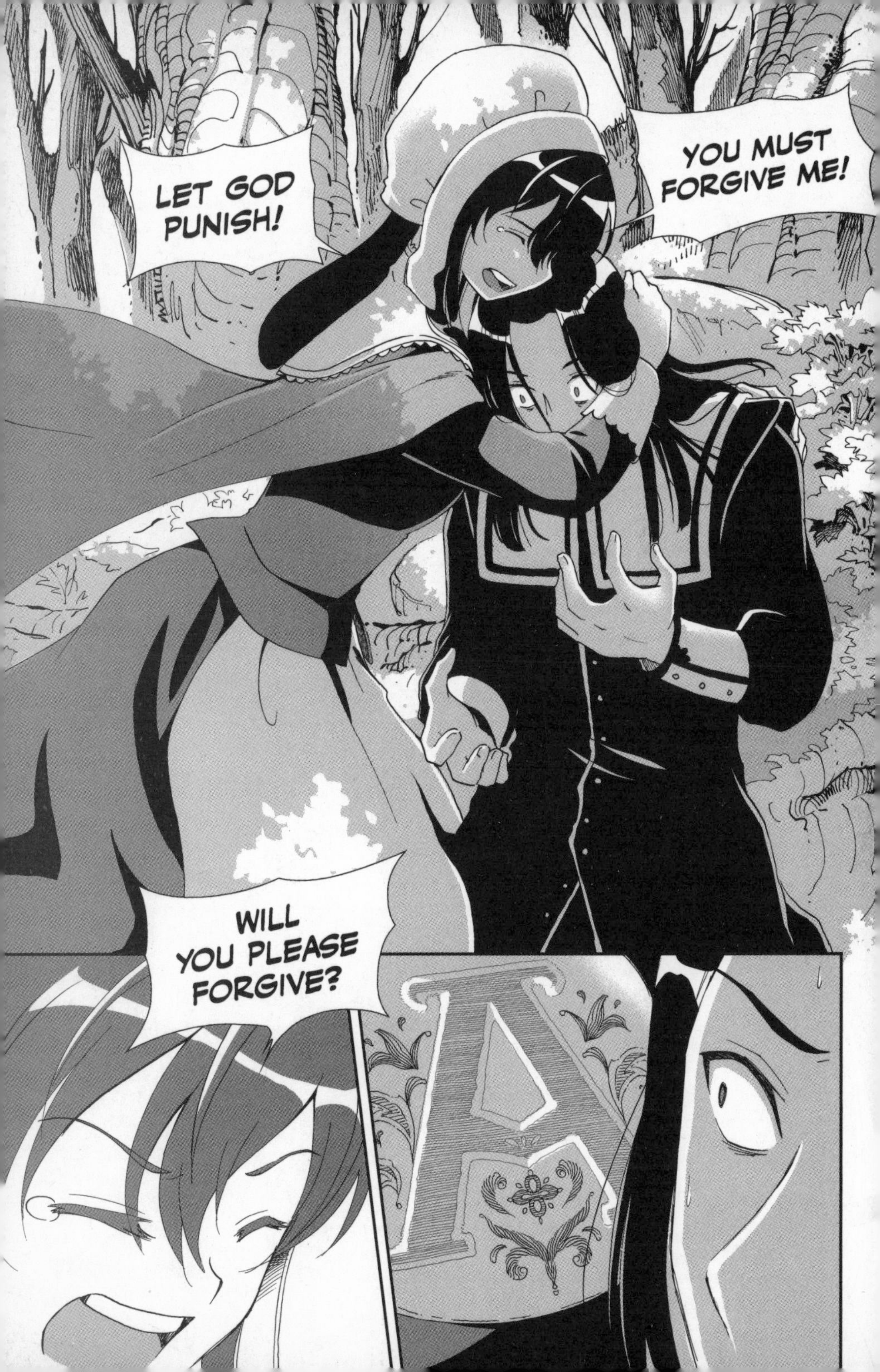
YOU MUST FORGIVE ME!
LET GOD PUNISH!
WILL YOU PLEASE FORGIVE?

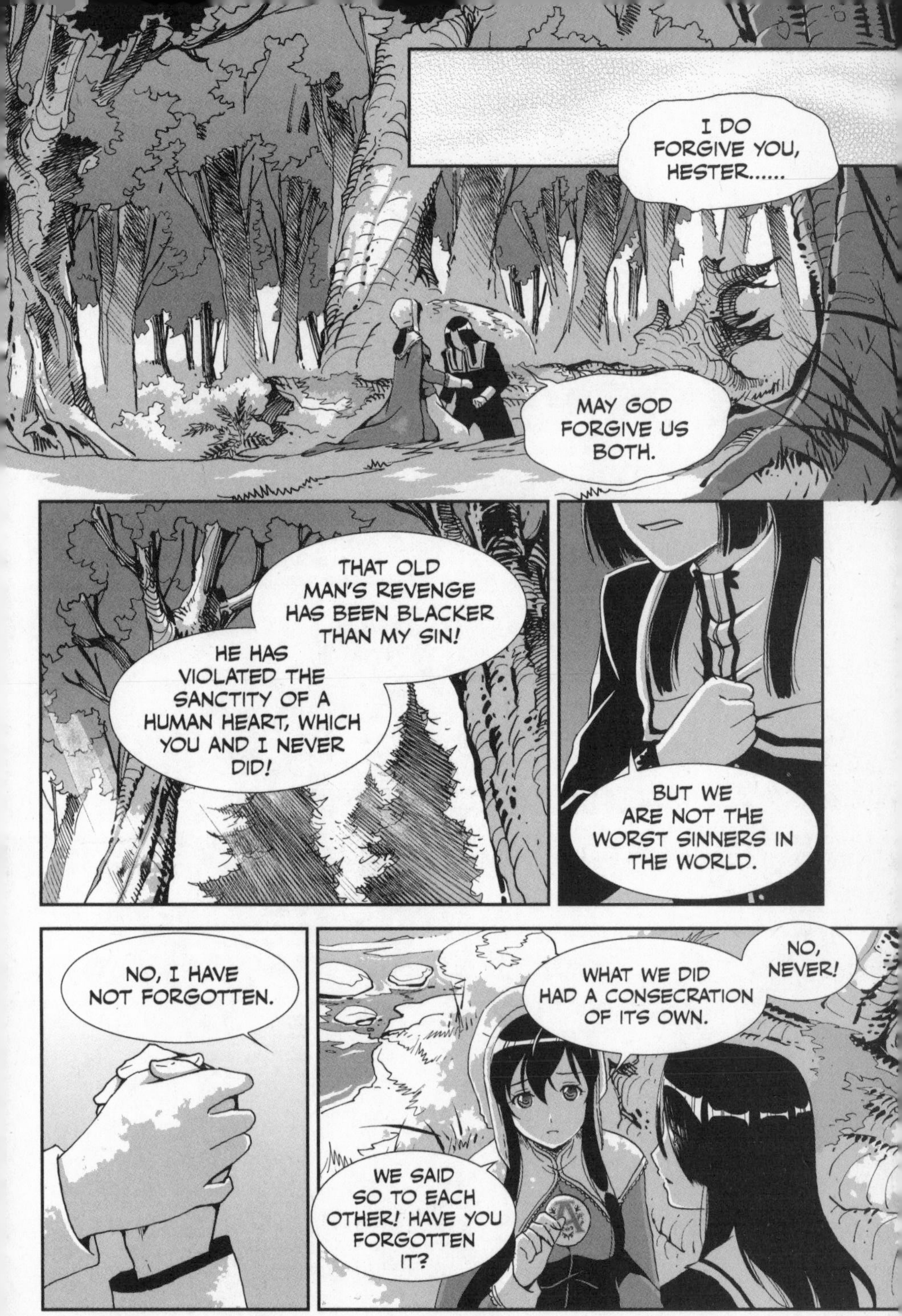
I DO FORGIVE YOU, HESTER......
MAY GOD FORGIVE US BOTH.
BUT WE ARE NOT THE WORST SINNERS IN THE WORLD.
THAT OLD MAN'S REVENGE HAS BEEN BLACKER THAN MY SIN!
HE HAS VIOLATED THE SANCTITY OF A HUMAN HEART, WHICH YOU AND I NEVER DID!
NO, NEVER!
WHAT WE DID HAD A CONSECRATION OF ITS OWN.
WE SAID SO TO EACH OTHER! HAVE YOU FORGOTTEN IT?
NO, I HAVE NOT FORGOTTEN.

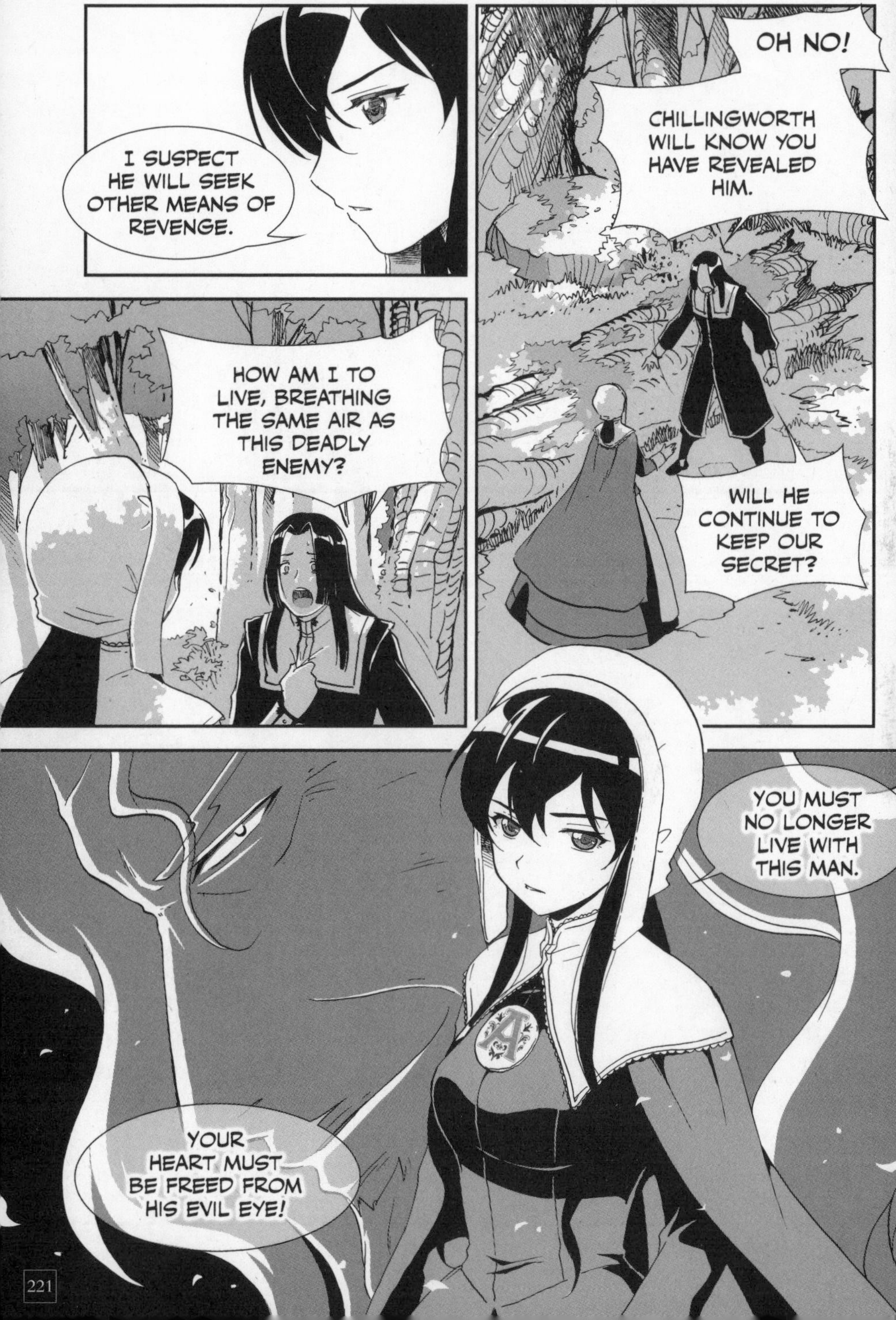
OH NO!
CHILLINGWORTH WILL KNOW YOU HAVE REVEALED HIM.
WILL HE CONTINUE TO KEEP OUR SECRET?
I SUSPECT HE WILL SEEK OTHER MEANS OF REVENGE.
HOW AM I TO LIVE, BREATHING THE SAME AIR AS THIS DEADLY ENEMY?
YOU MUST NO LONGER LIVE WITH THIS MAN.
YOUR HEART MUST BE FREED FROM HIS EVIL EYE!

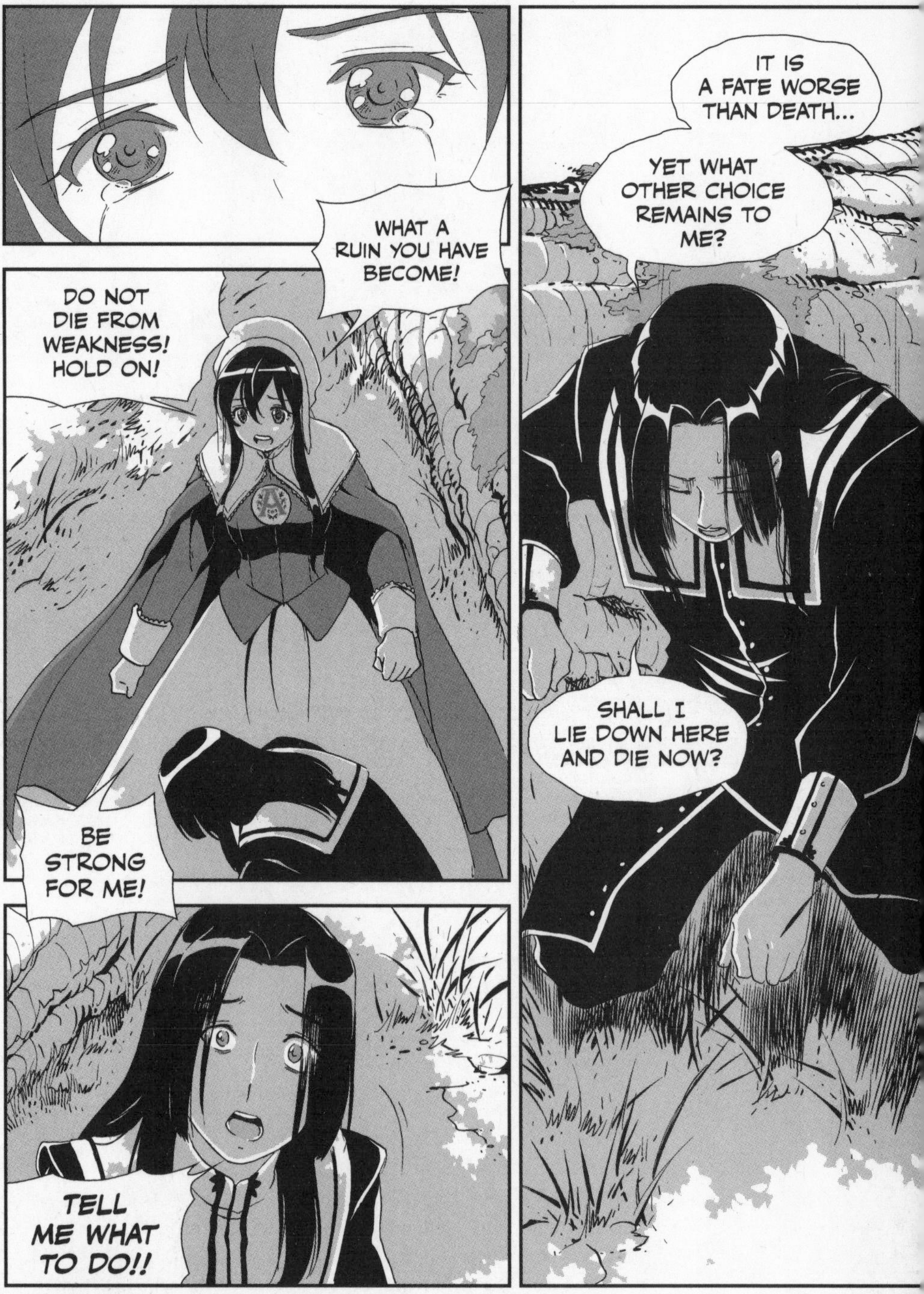
IT IS A FATE WORSE THAN DEATH...
YET WHAT OTHER CHOICE REMAINS TO ME?
SHALL I LIE DOWN HERE AND DIE NOW?
WHAT A RUIN YOU HAVE BECOME!
DO NOT DIE FROM WEAKNESS! HOLD ON!
BE STRONG FOR ME!
TELL ME WHAT TO DO!!

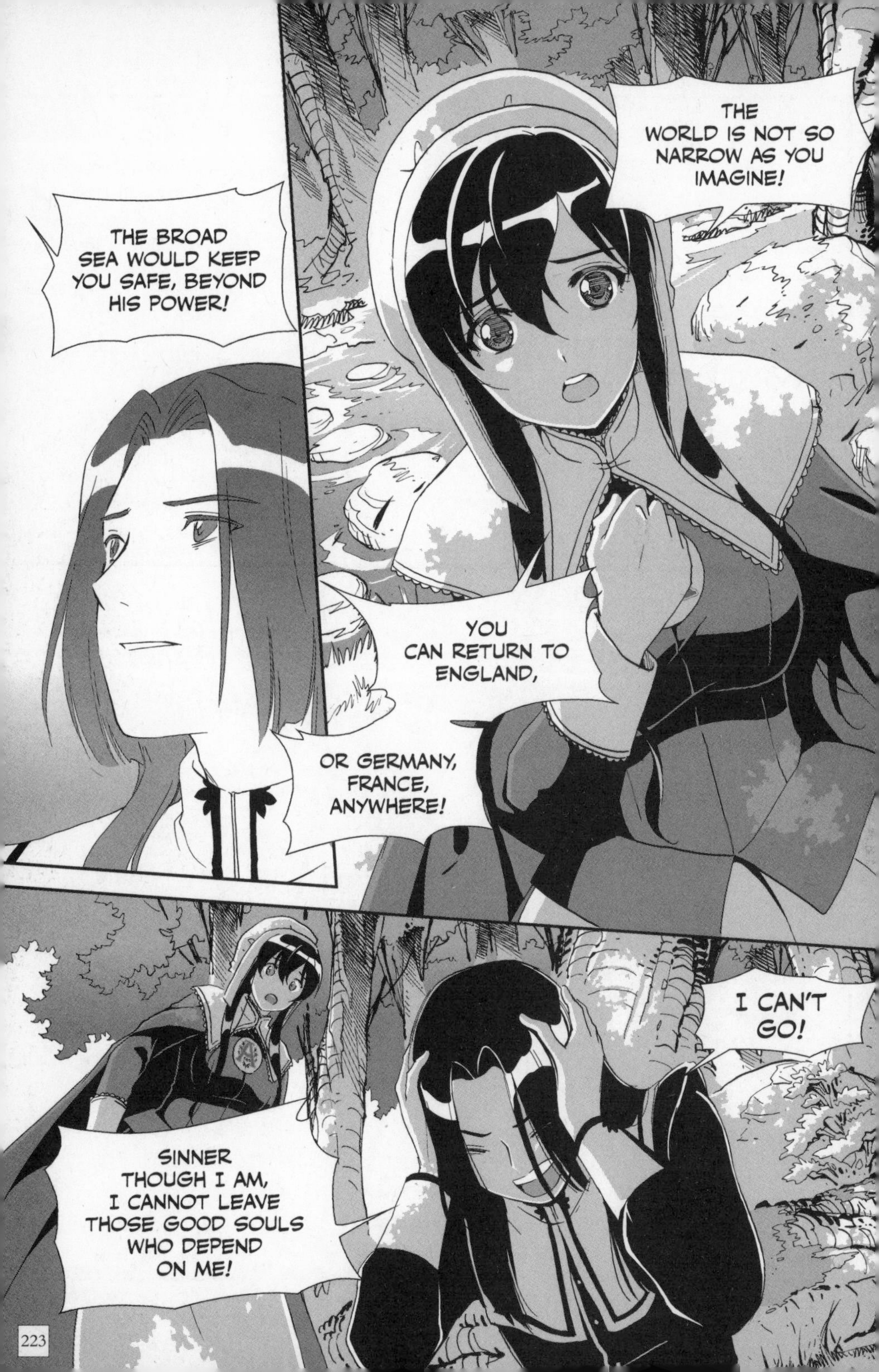
THE WORLD IS NOT SO NARROW AS YOU IMAGINE!
YOU CAN RETURN TO ENGLAND,
OR GERMANY, FRANCE, ANYWHERE!
THE BROAD SEA WOULD KEEP YOU SAFE, BEYOND HIS POWER!
I CAN'T GO!
SINNER THOUGH I AM, I CANNOT LEAVE THOSE GOOD SOULS WHO DEPEND ON ME!

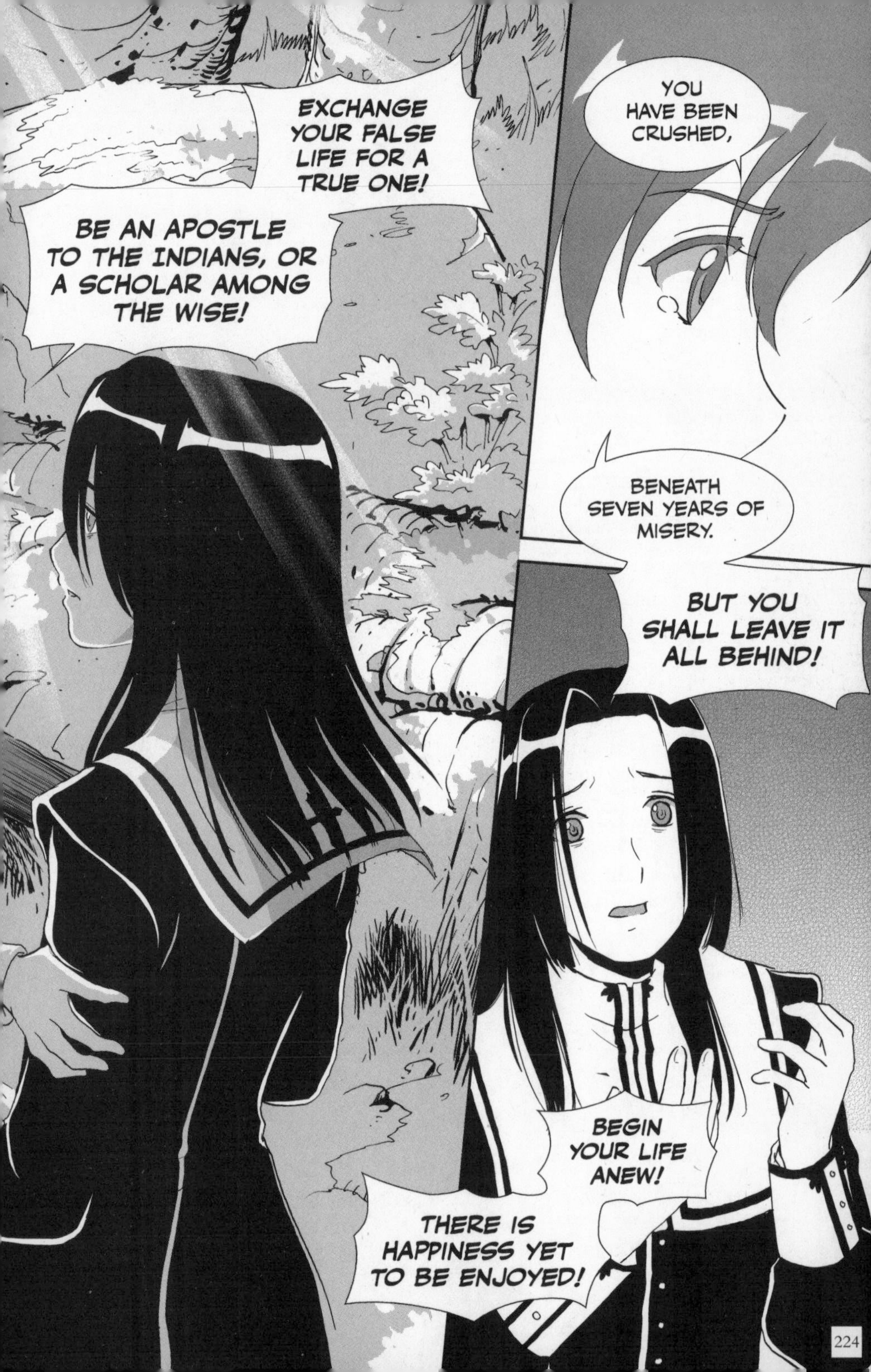
YOU HAVE BEEN CRUSHED,
BENEATH SEVEN YEARS OF MISERY.
BUT YOU SHALL LEAVE IT ALL BEHIND!
BEGIN YOUR LIFE ANEW!
THERE IS HAPPINESS YET TO BE ENJOYED!
EXCHANGE YOUR FALSE LIFE FOR A TRUE ONE!
BE AN APOSTLE TO THE INDIANS, OR A SCHOLAR AMONG THE WISE!

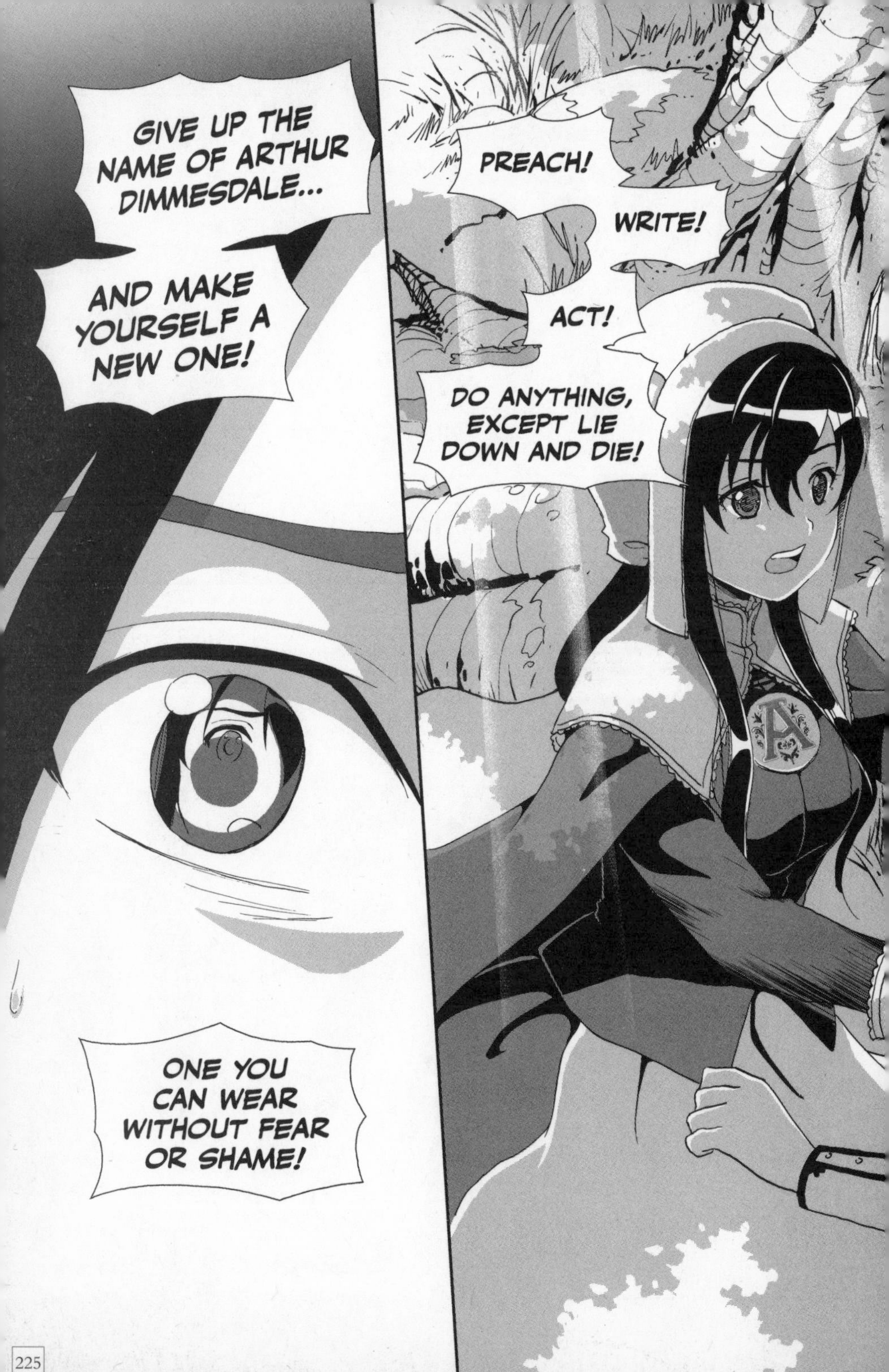
PREACH!
WRITE!
ACT!
DO ANYTHING, EXCEPT LIE DOWN AND DIE!
GIVE UP THE NAME OF ARTHUR DIMMESDALE...
AND MAKE YOURSELF A NEW ONE!
ONE YOU CAN WEAR WITHOUT FEAR OR SHAME!

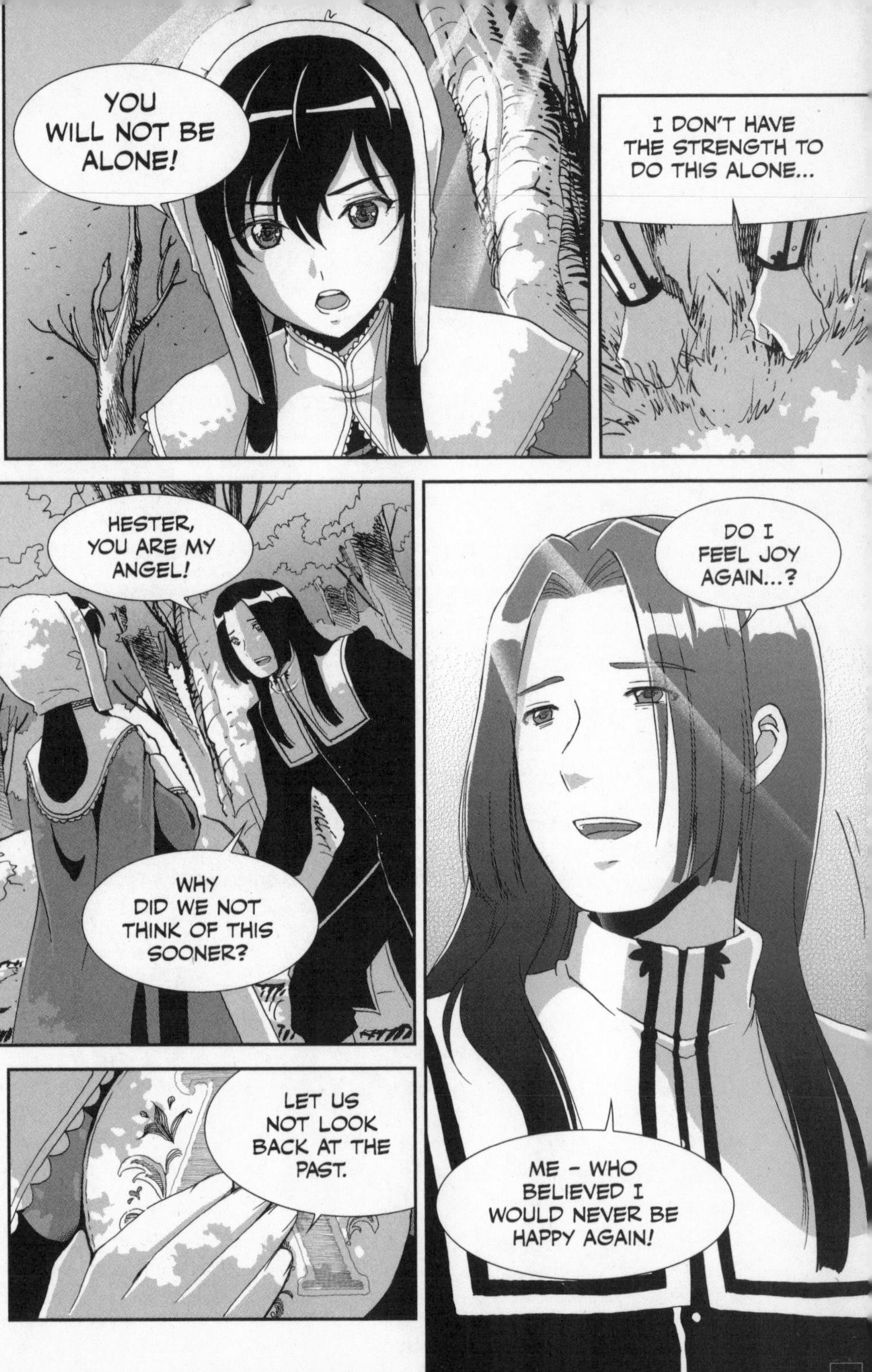
I DON'T HAVE THE STRENGTH TO DO THIS ALONE...
YOU WILL NOT BE ALONE!
DO I FEEL JOY AGAIN...?
ME - WHO BELIEVED I WOULD NEVER BE HAPPY AGAIN!
HESTER, YOU ARE MY ANGEL!
WHY DID WE NOT THINK OF THIS SOONER?
LET US NOT LOOK BACK AT THE PAST.

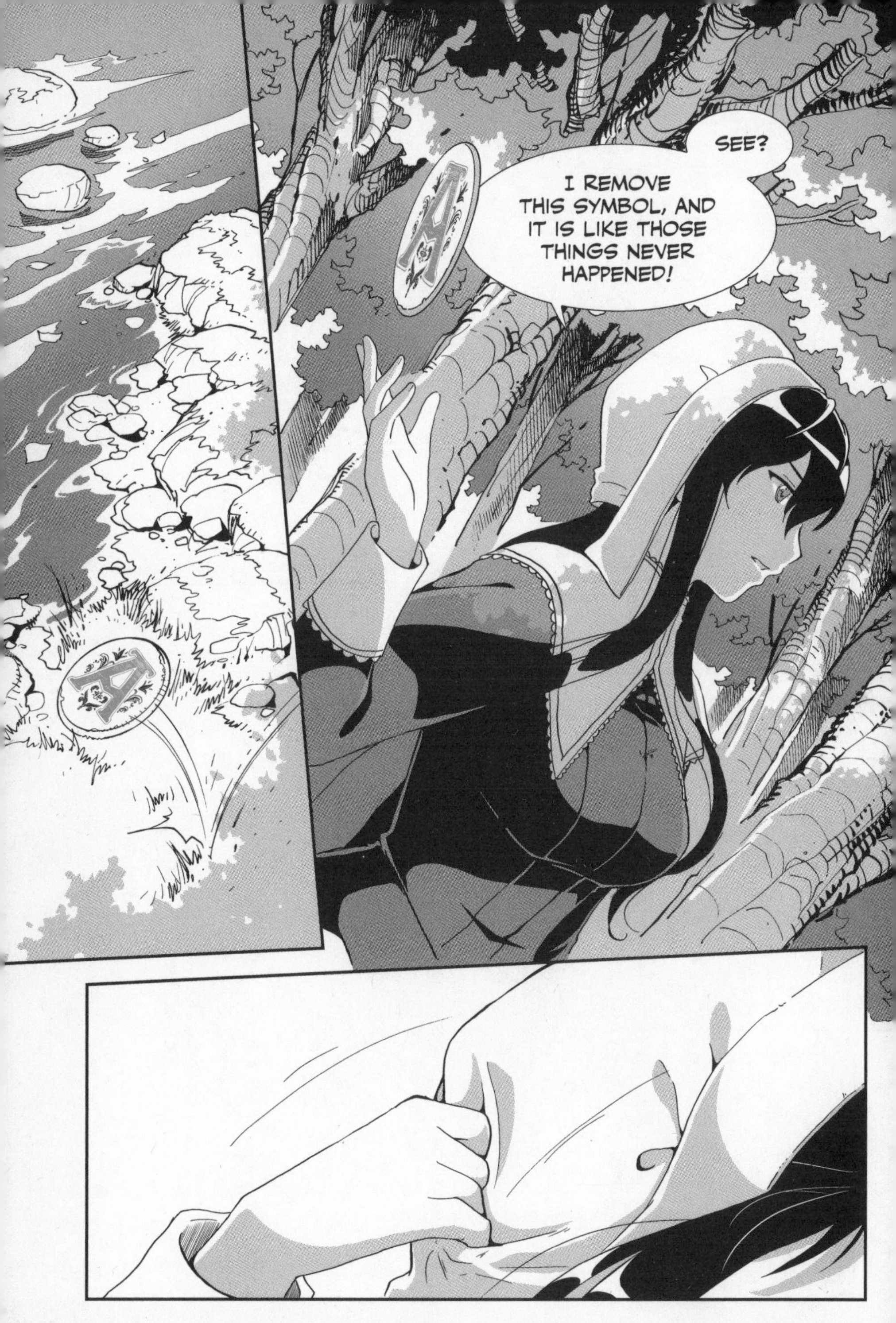
SEE?
I REMOVE THIS SYMBOL, AND IT IS LIKE THOSE THINGS NEVER HAPPENED!

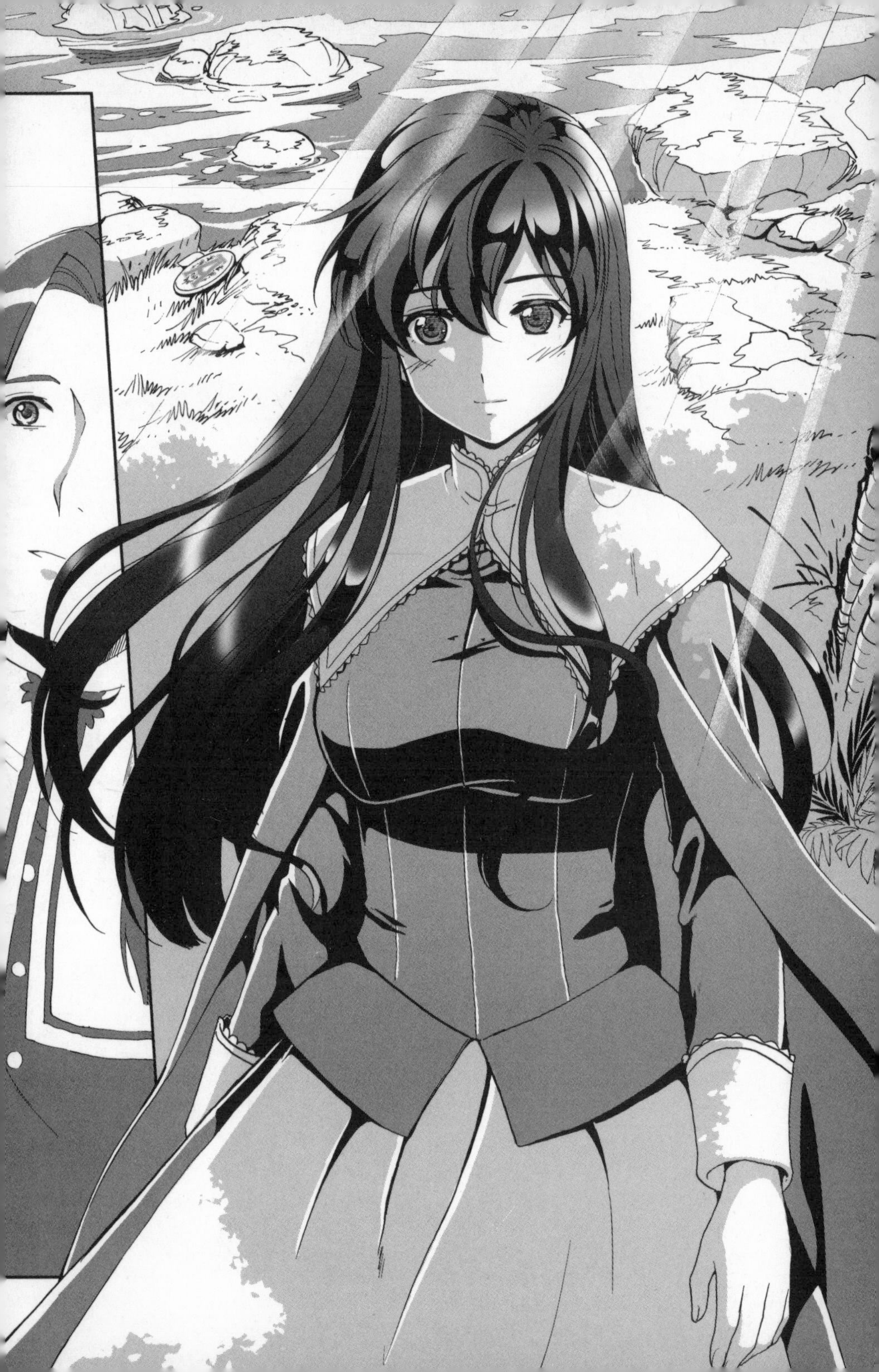

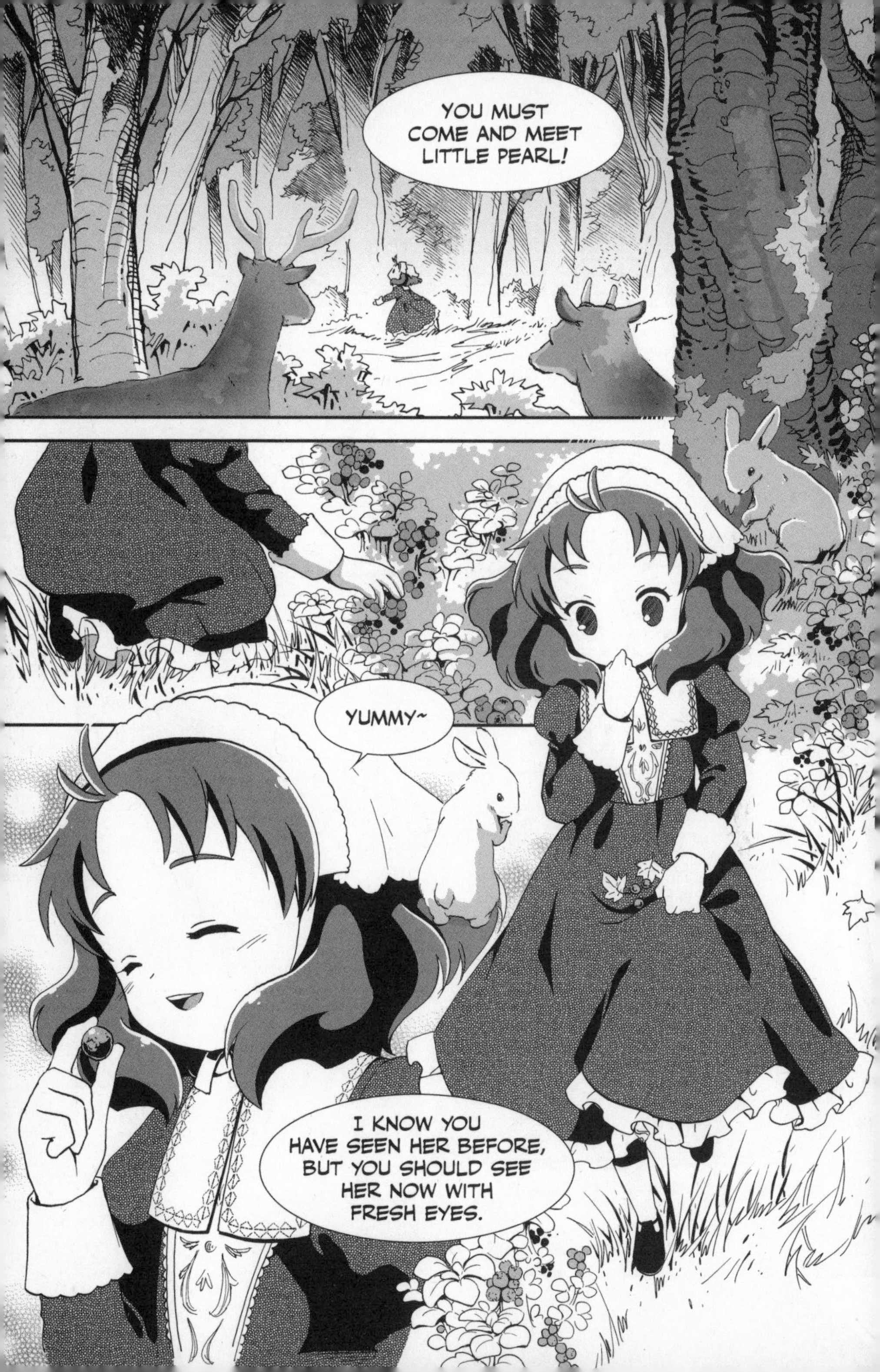
YOU MUST COME AND MEET LITTLE PEARL!
YUMMY~
I KNOW YOU HAVE SEEN HER BEFORE, BUT YOU SHOULD SEE HER NOW WITH FRESH EYES.

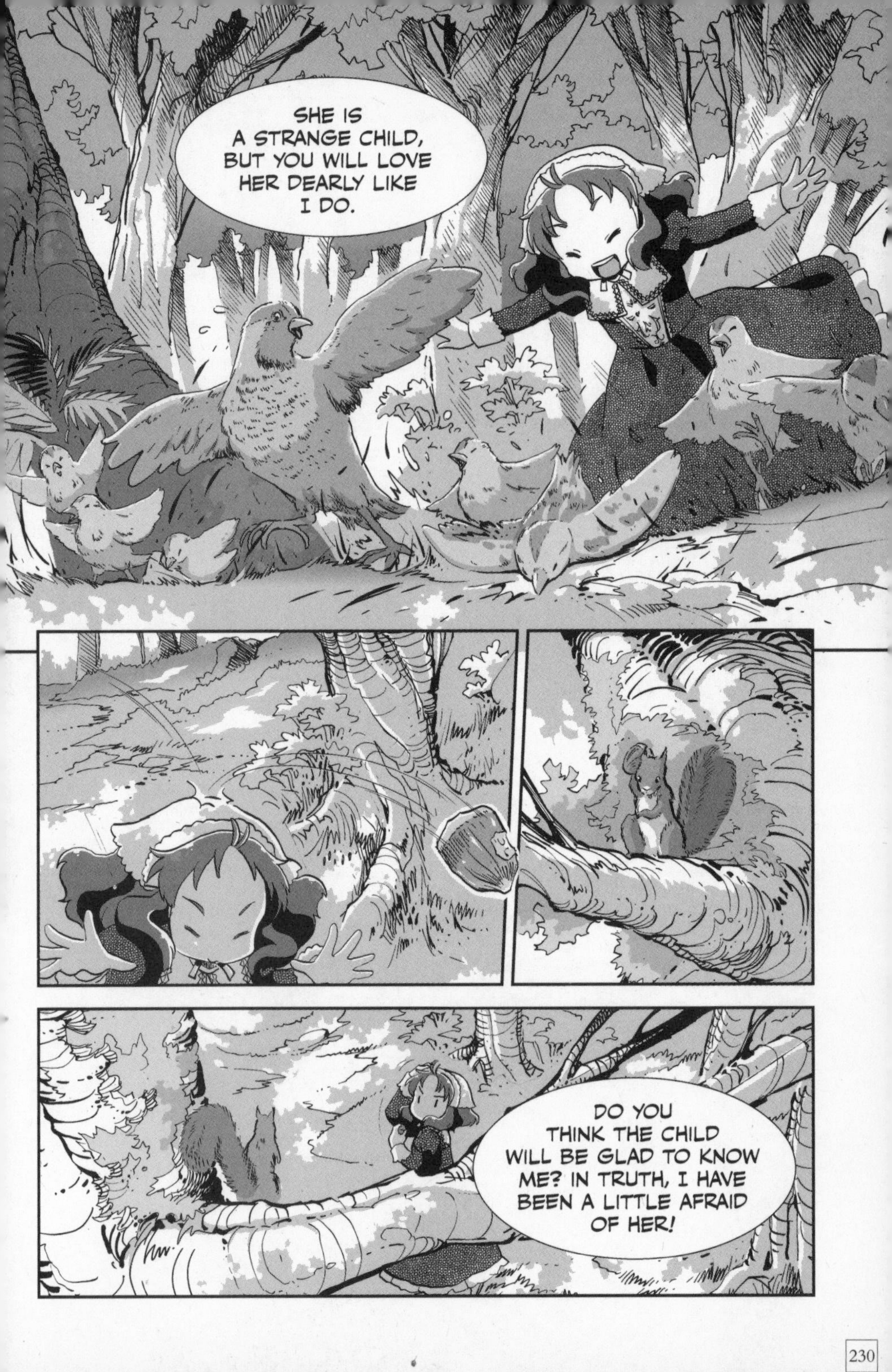
SHE IS A STRANGE CHILD, BUT YOU WILL LOVE HER DEARLY LIKE I DO.
DO YOU THINK THE CHILD WILL BE GLAD TO KNOW ME? IN TRUTH, I HAVE BEEN A LITTLE AFRAID OF HER!

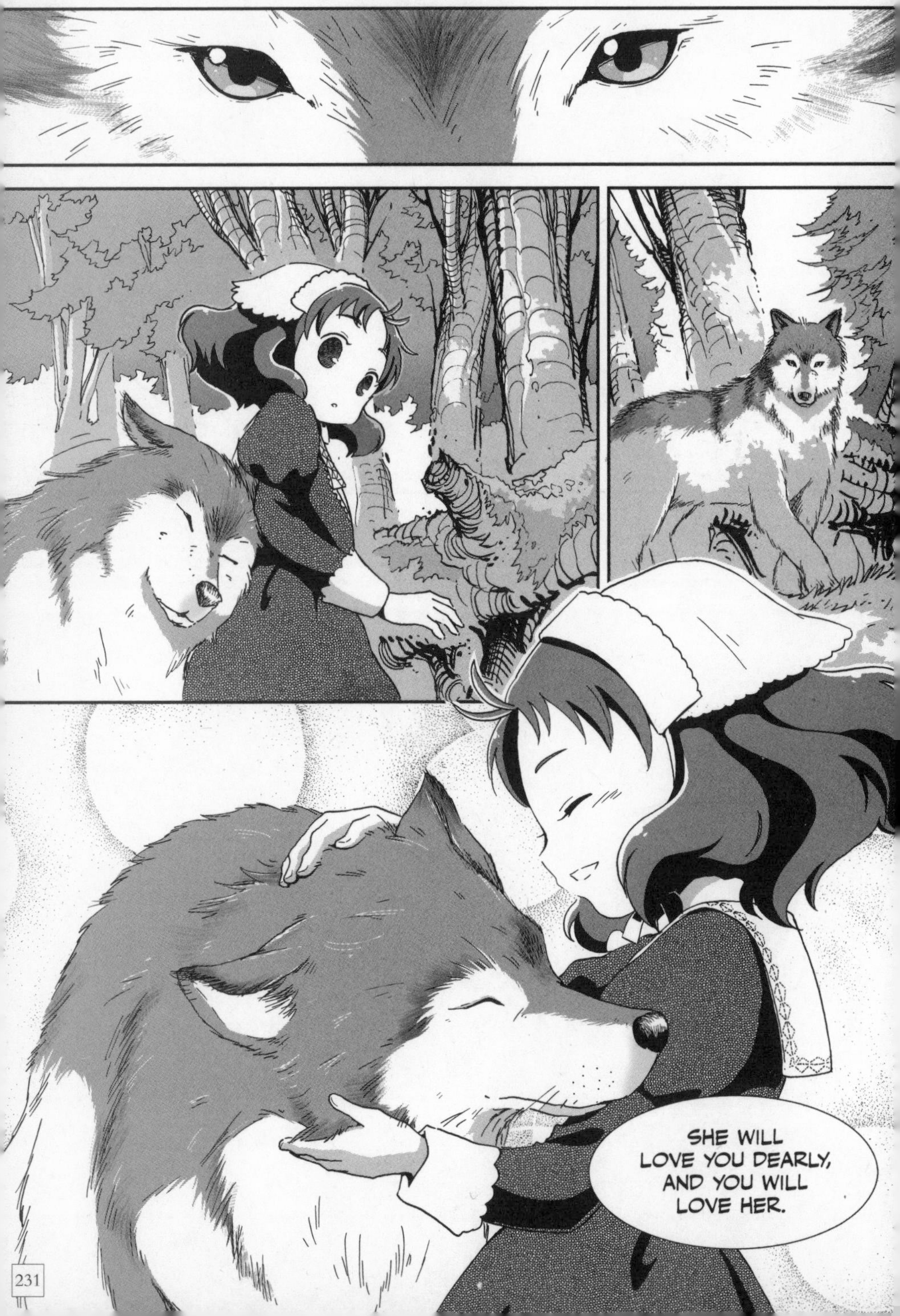
SHE WILL LOVE YOU DEARLY, AND YOU WILL LOVE HER.

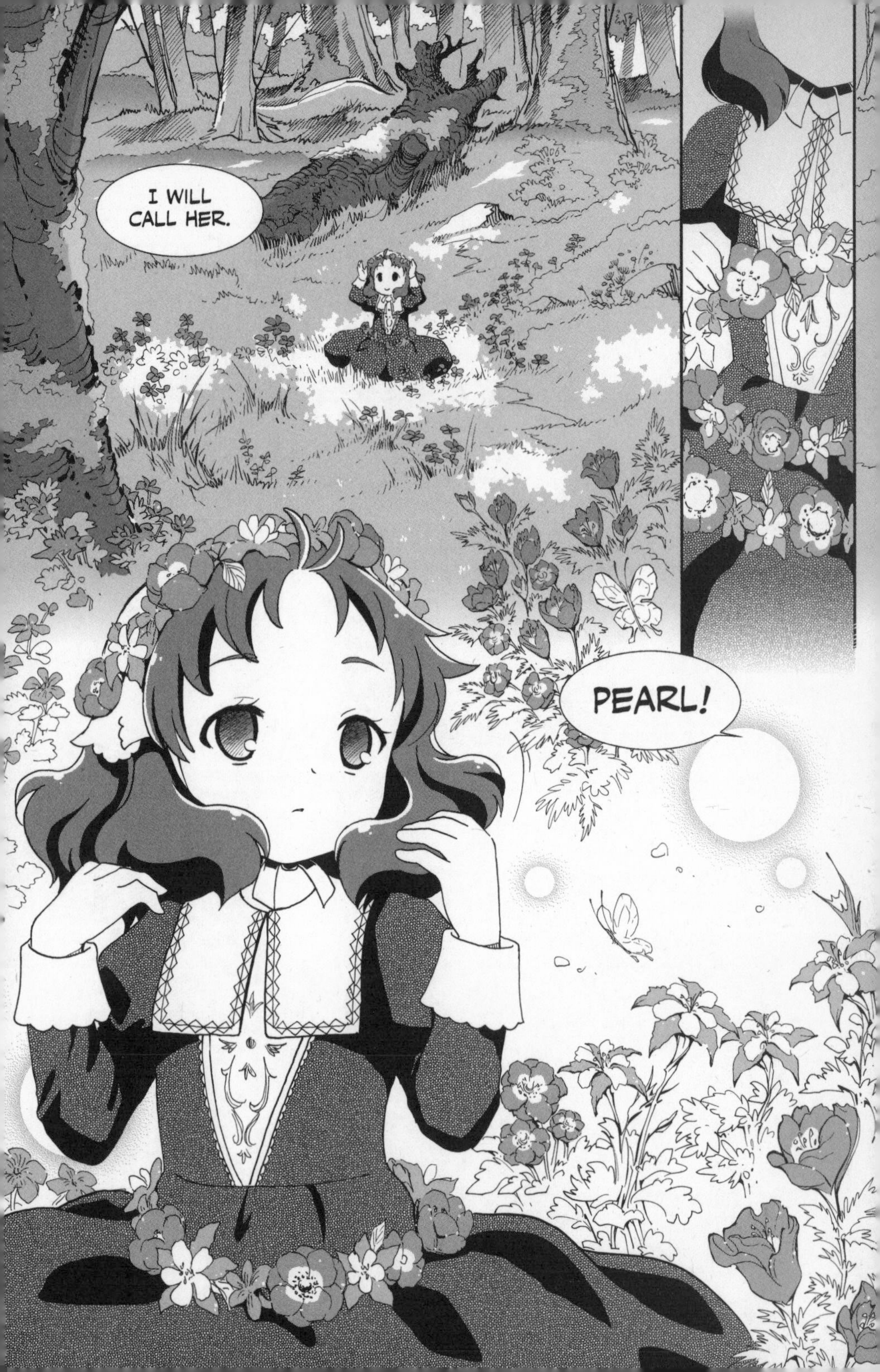
I WILL CALL HER.
PEARL!

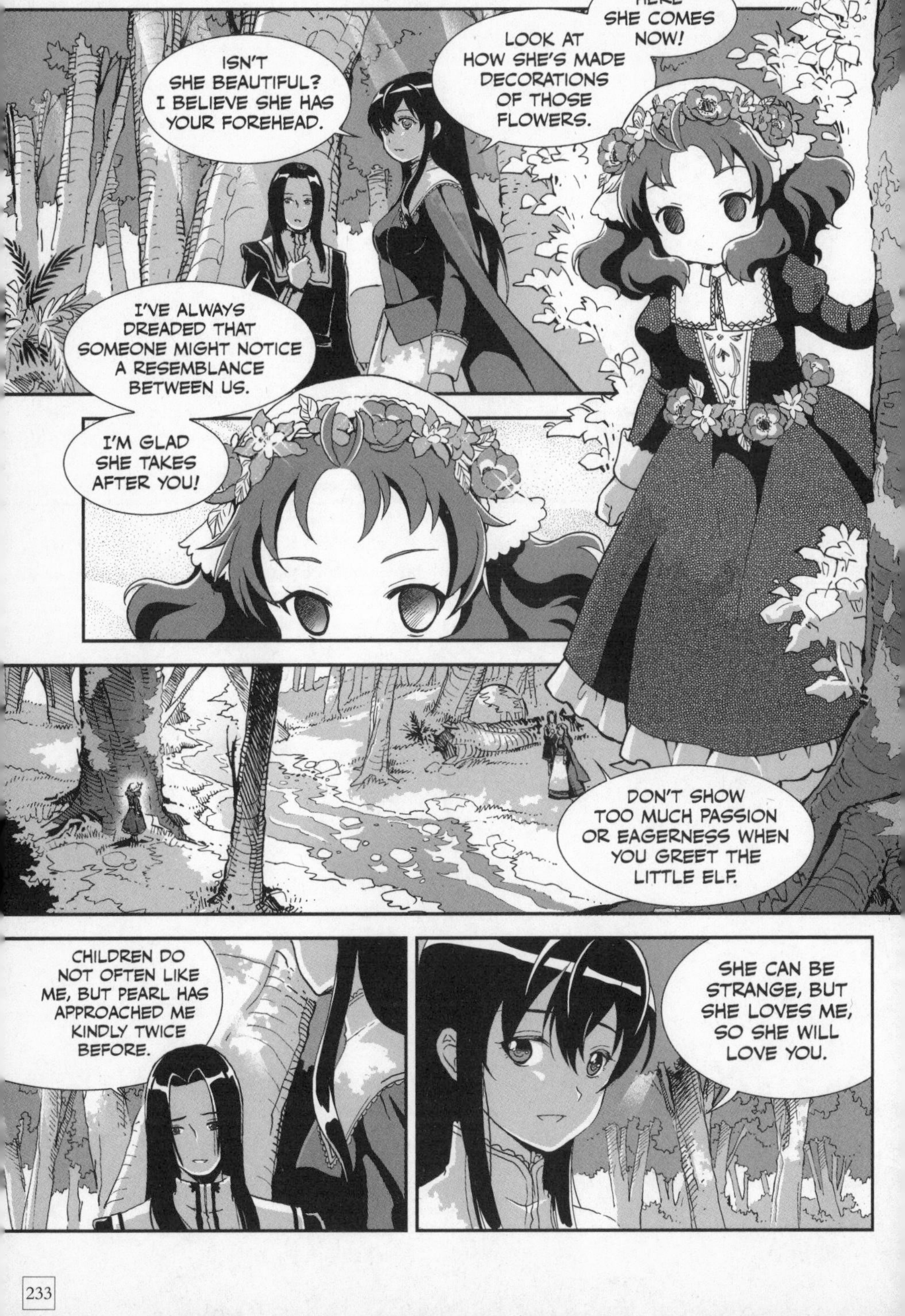
HERE SHE COMES NOW!
LOOK AT HOW SHE'S MADE DECORATIONS OF THOSE FLOWERS.
ISN'T SHE BEAUTIFUL? I BELIEVE SHE HAS YOUR FOREHEAD.
I'VE ALWAYS DREADED THAT SOMEONE MIGHT NOTICE A RESEMBLANCE BETWEEN US.
I'M GLAD SHE TAKES AFTER YOU!
DON'T SHOW TOO MUCH PASSION OR EAGERNESS WHEN YOU GREET THE LITTLE ELF.
SHE CAN BE STRANGE, BUT SHE LOVES ME, SO SHE WILL LOVE YOU.
CHILDREN DO NOT OFTEN LIKE ME, BUT PEARL HAS APPROACHED ME KINDLY TWICE BEFORE.

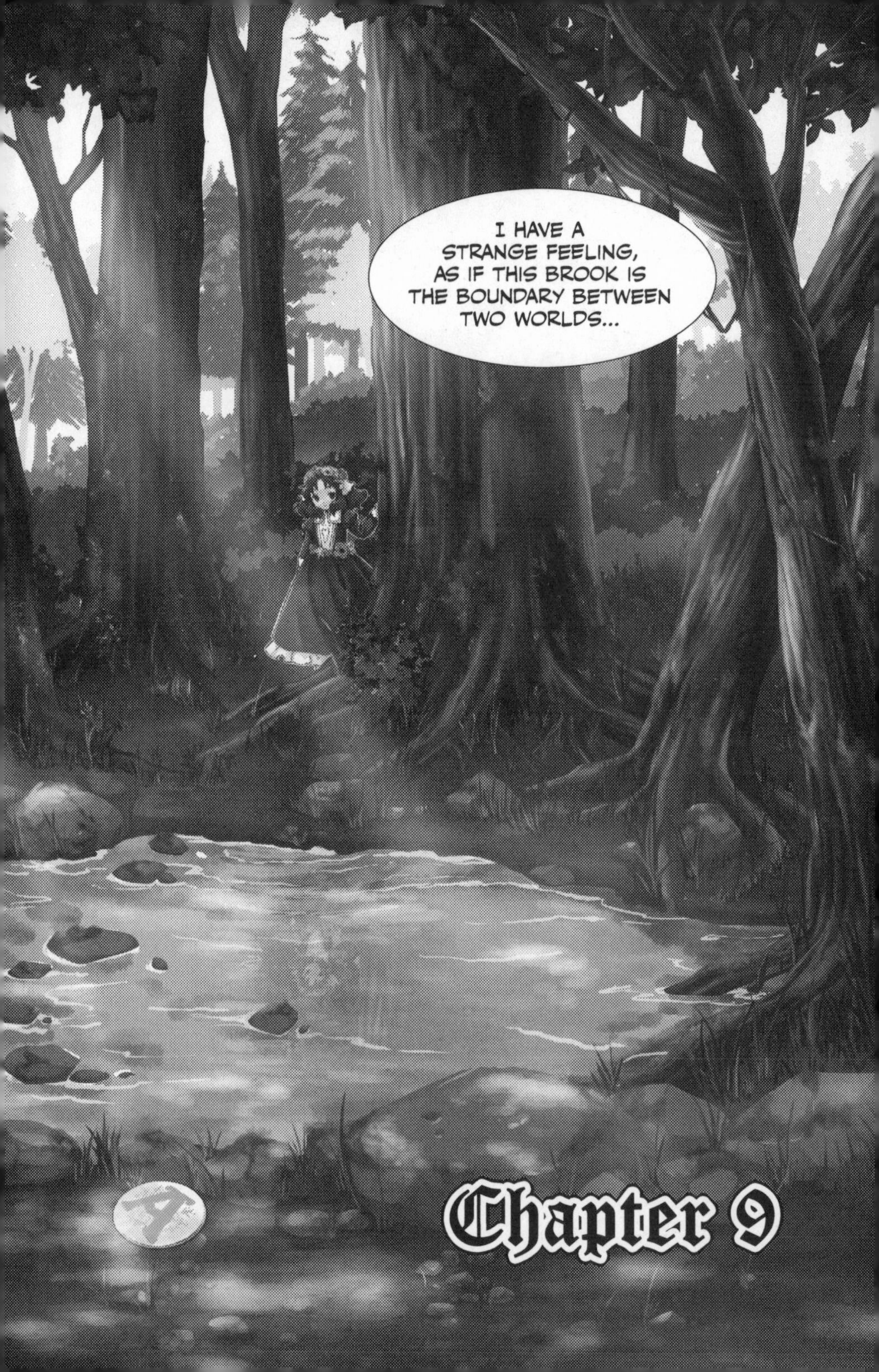
I HAVE A STRANGE FEELING, AS IF THIS BROOK IS THE BOUNDARY BETWEEN TWO WORLDS...
Chapter 9

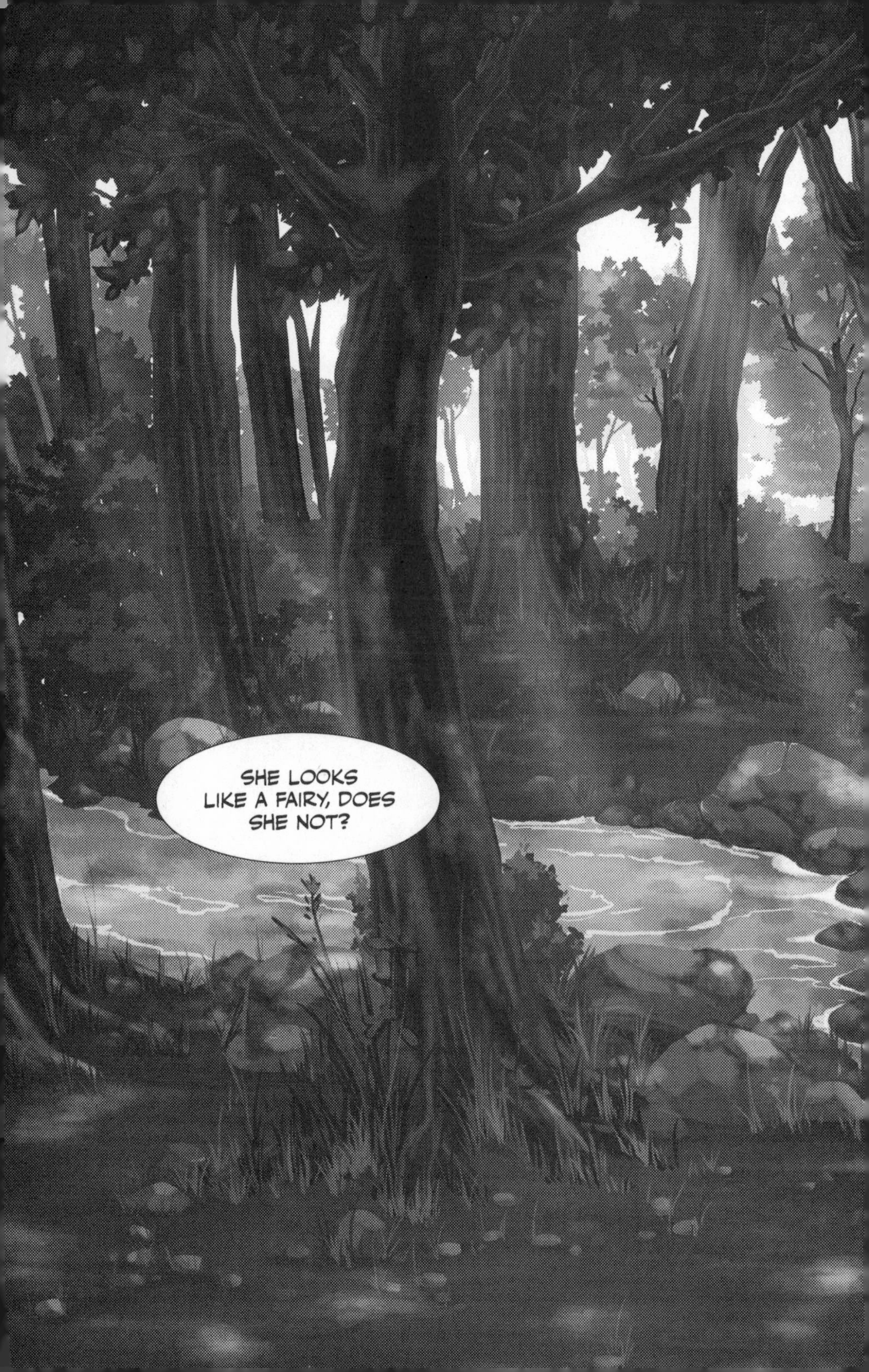
SHE LOOKS LIKE A FAIRY, DOES SHE NOT?

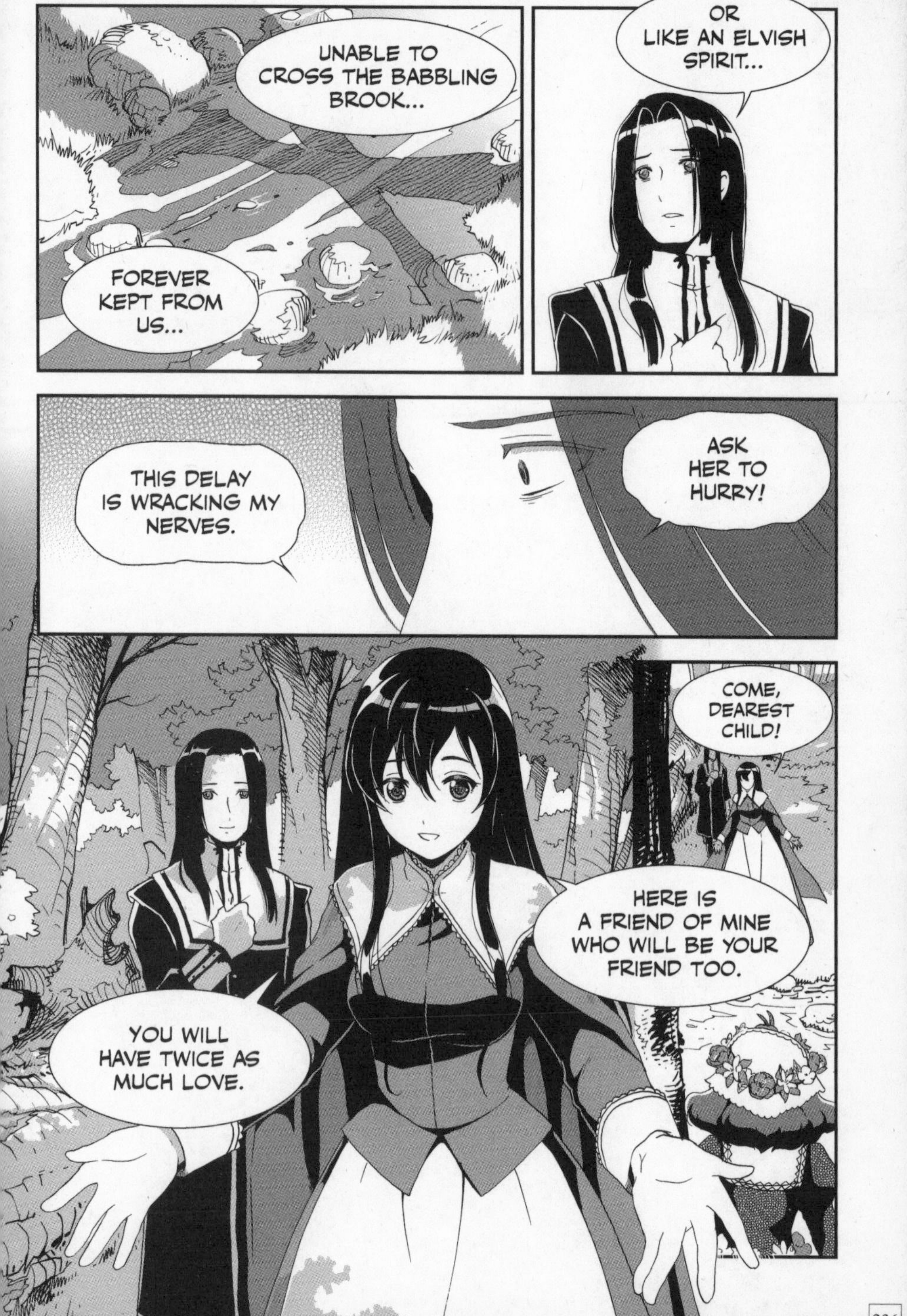
OR LIKE AN ELVISH SPIRIT...
UNABLE TO CROSS THE BABBLING BROOK...
FOREVER KEPT FROM US...
ASK HER TO HURRY!
THIS DELAY IS WRACKING MY NERVES.
COME, DEAREST CHILD!
HERE IS A FRIEND OF MINE WHO WILL BE YOUR FRIEND TOO.
YOU WILL HAVE TWICE AS MUCH LOVE.

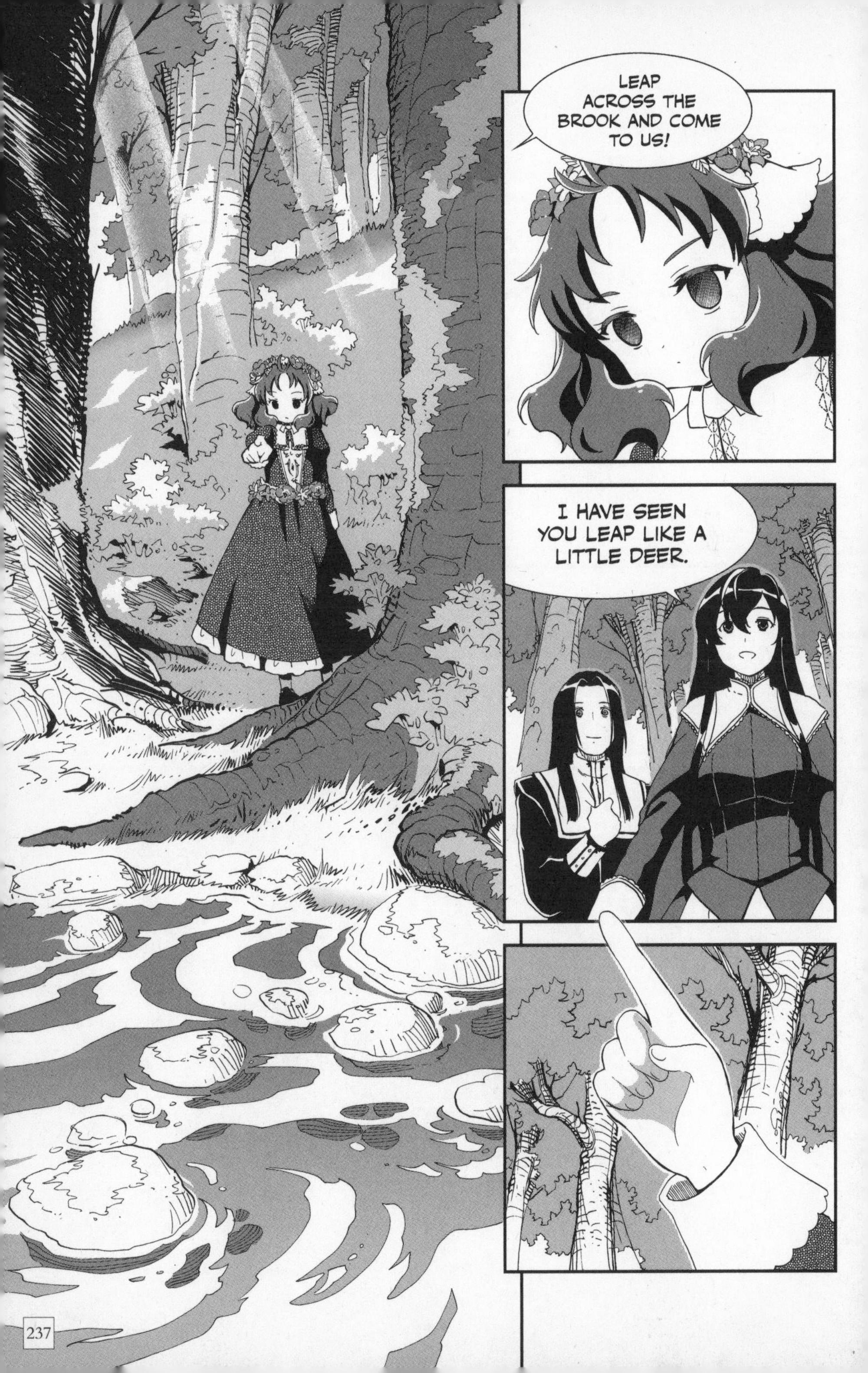
LEAP ACROSS THE BROOK AND COME TO US!
I HAVE SEEN YOU LEAP LIKE A LITTLE DEER.

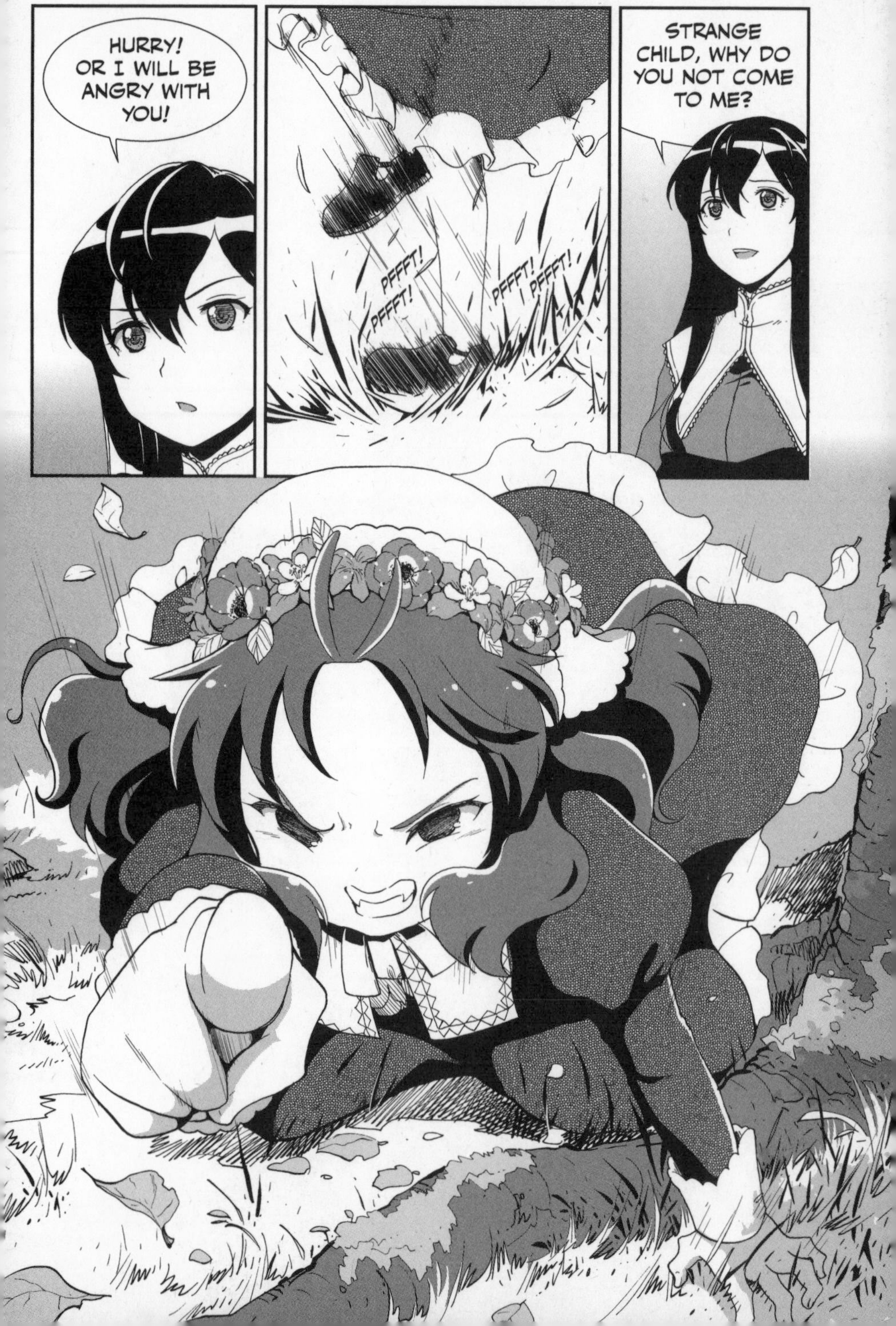
STRANGE CHILD, WHY DO YOU NOT COME TO ME?
PFFFT! PFFFT!
PFFFT! PFFFT!
HURRY! OR I WILL BE ANGRY WITH YOU!

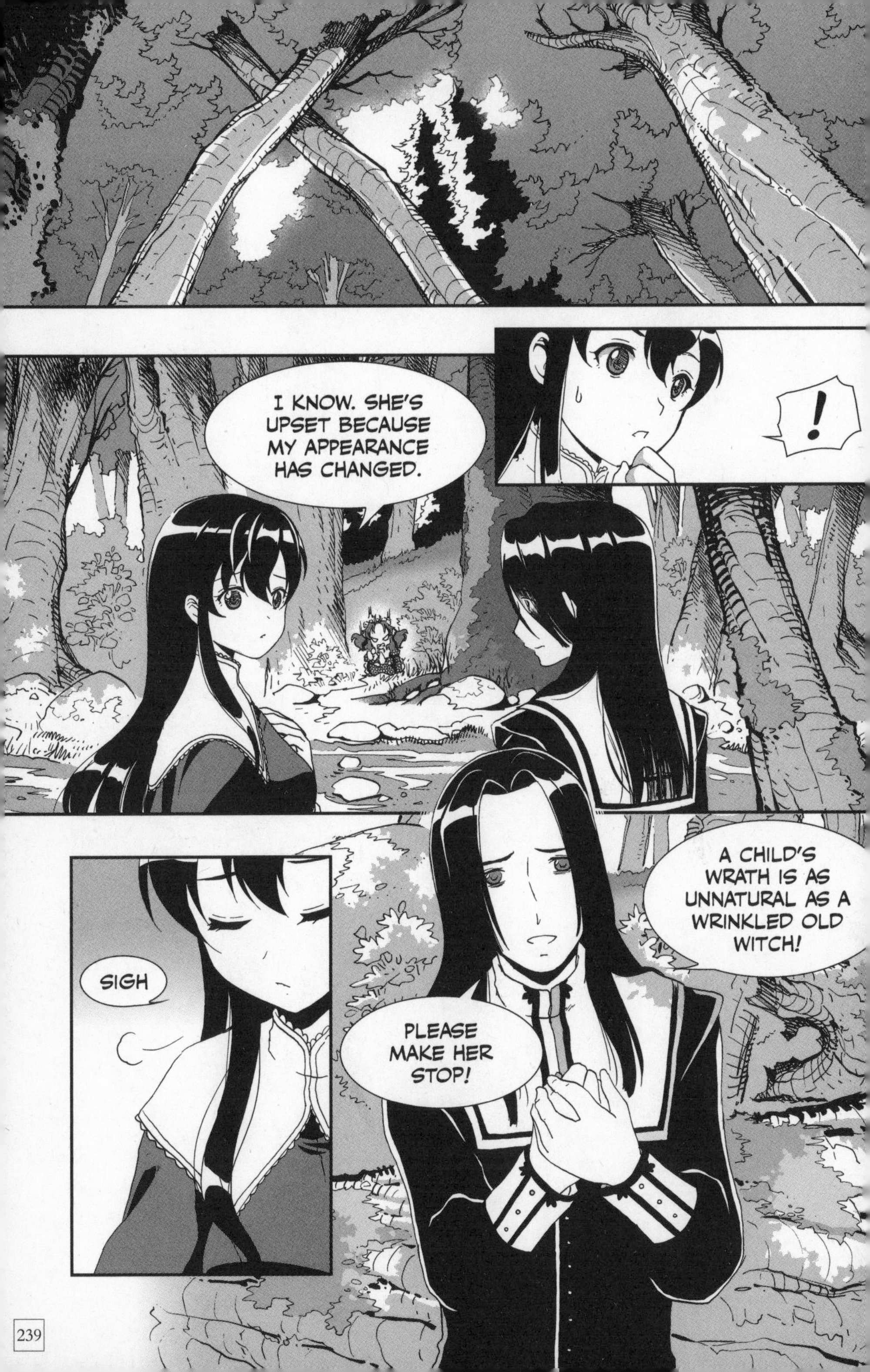
!
I KNOW. SHE'S UPSET BECAUSE MY APPEARANCE HAS CHANGED.
A CHILD'S WRATH IS AS UNNATURAL AS A WRINKLED OLD WITCH!
PLEASE MAKE HER STOP!
SIGH

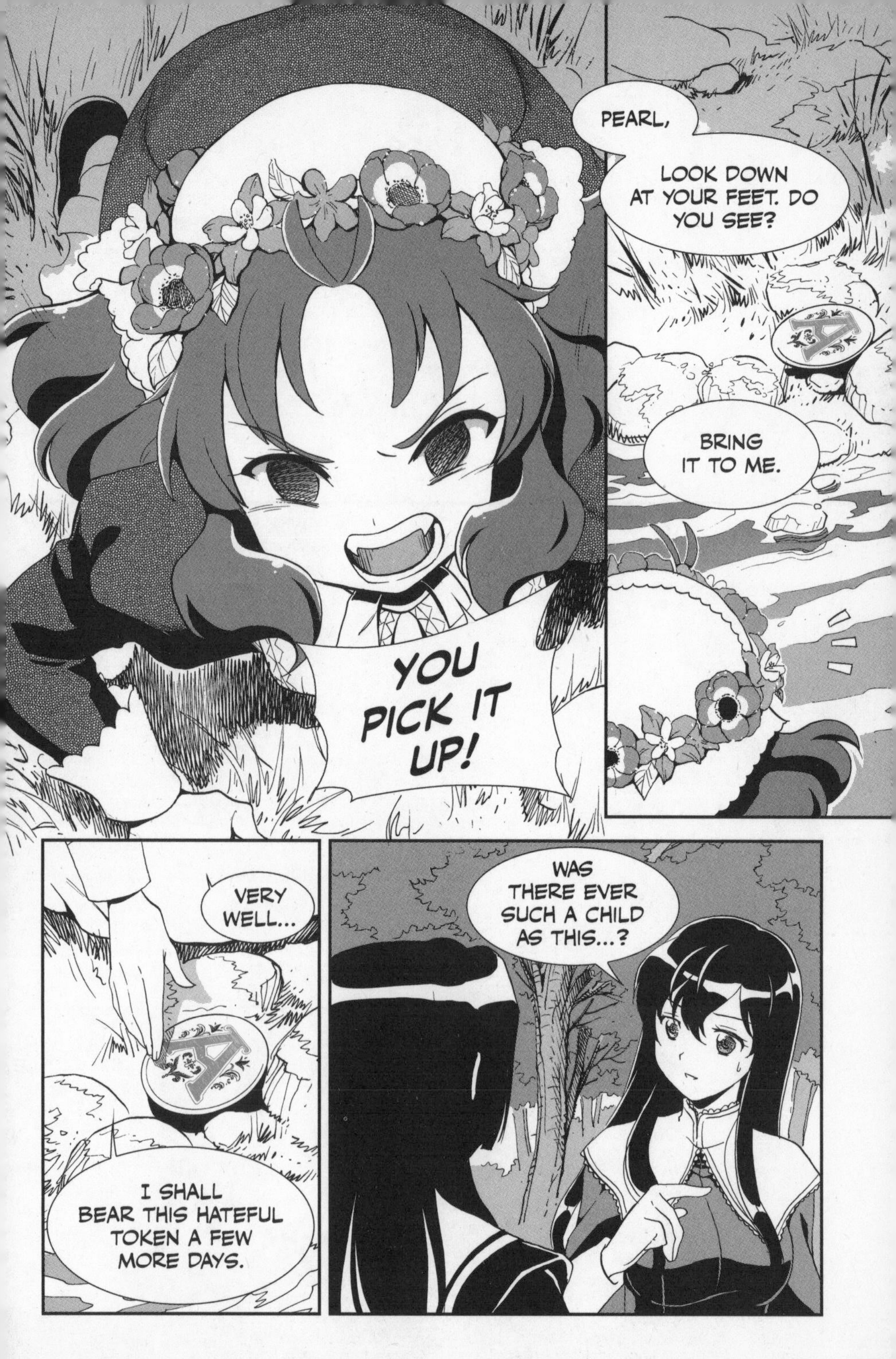
PEARL,
LOOK DOWN AT YOUR FEET. DO YOU SEE?
BRING IT TO ME.
YOU PICK IT UP!
WAS THERE EVER SUCH A CHILD AS THIS...?
VERY WELL...
I SHALL BEAR THIS HATEFUL TOKEN A FEW MORE DAYS.

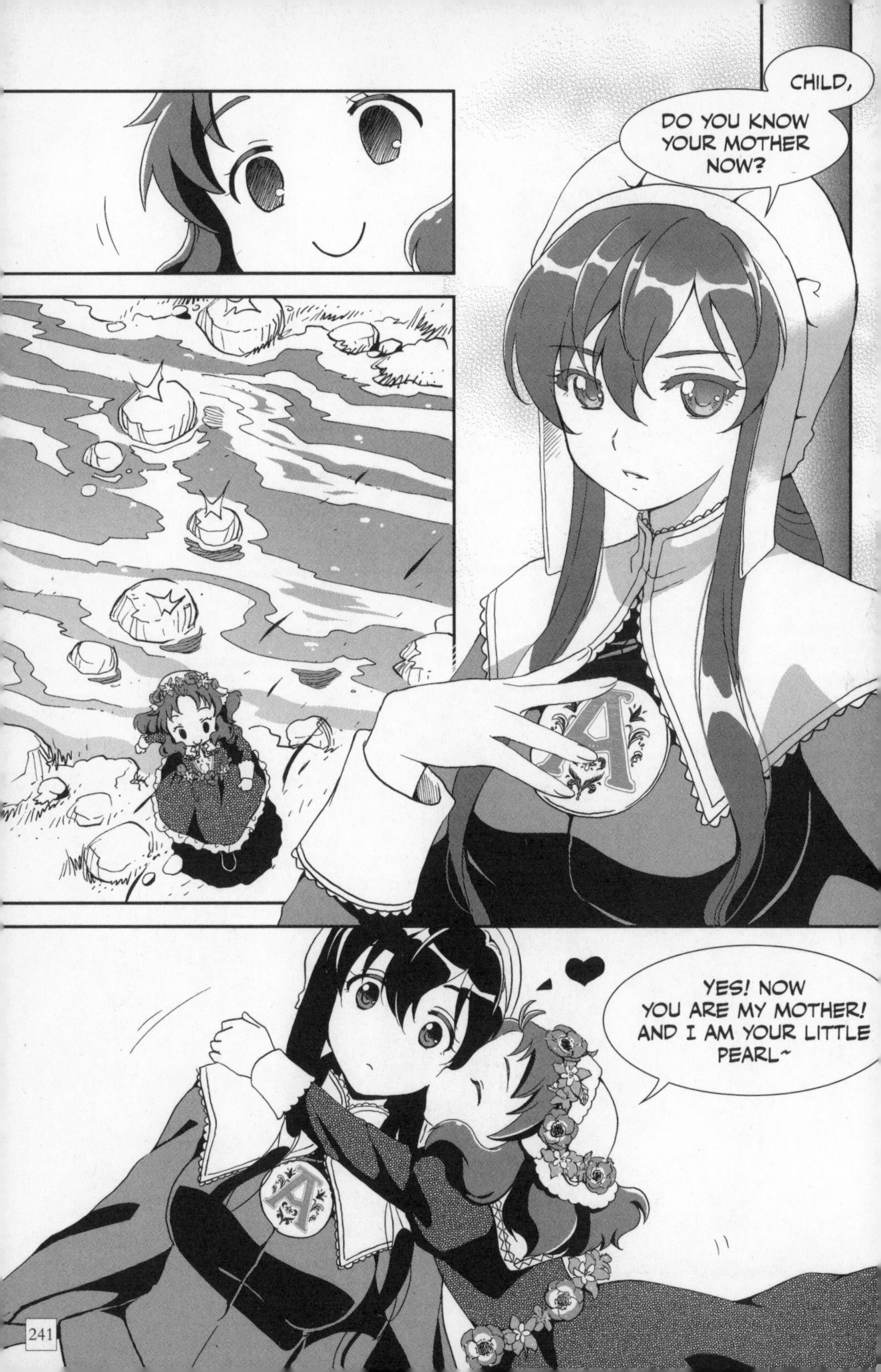
CHILD,
DO YOU KNOW YOUR MOTHER NOW?
YES! NOW YOU ARE MY MOTHER! AND I AM YOUR LITTLE PEARL~

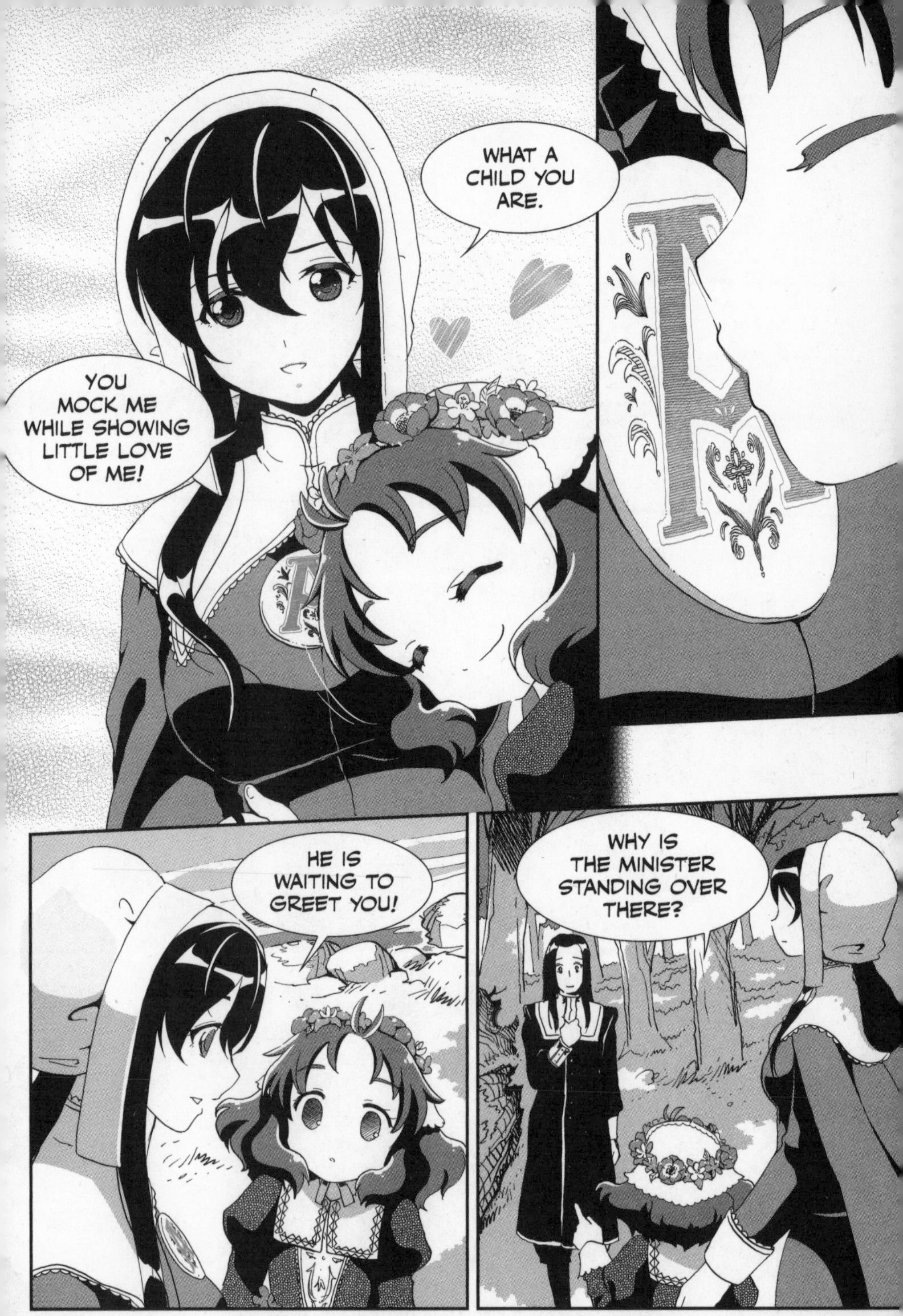
WHAT A CHILD YOU ARE.
YOU MOCK ME WHILE SHOWING LITTLE LOVE OF ME!
WHY IS THE MINISTER STANDING OVER THERE?
HE IS WAITING TO GREET YOU!

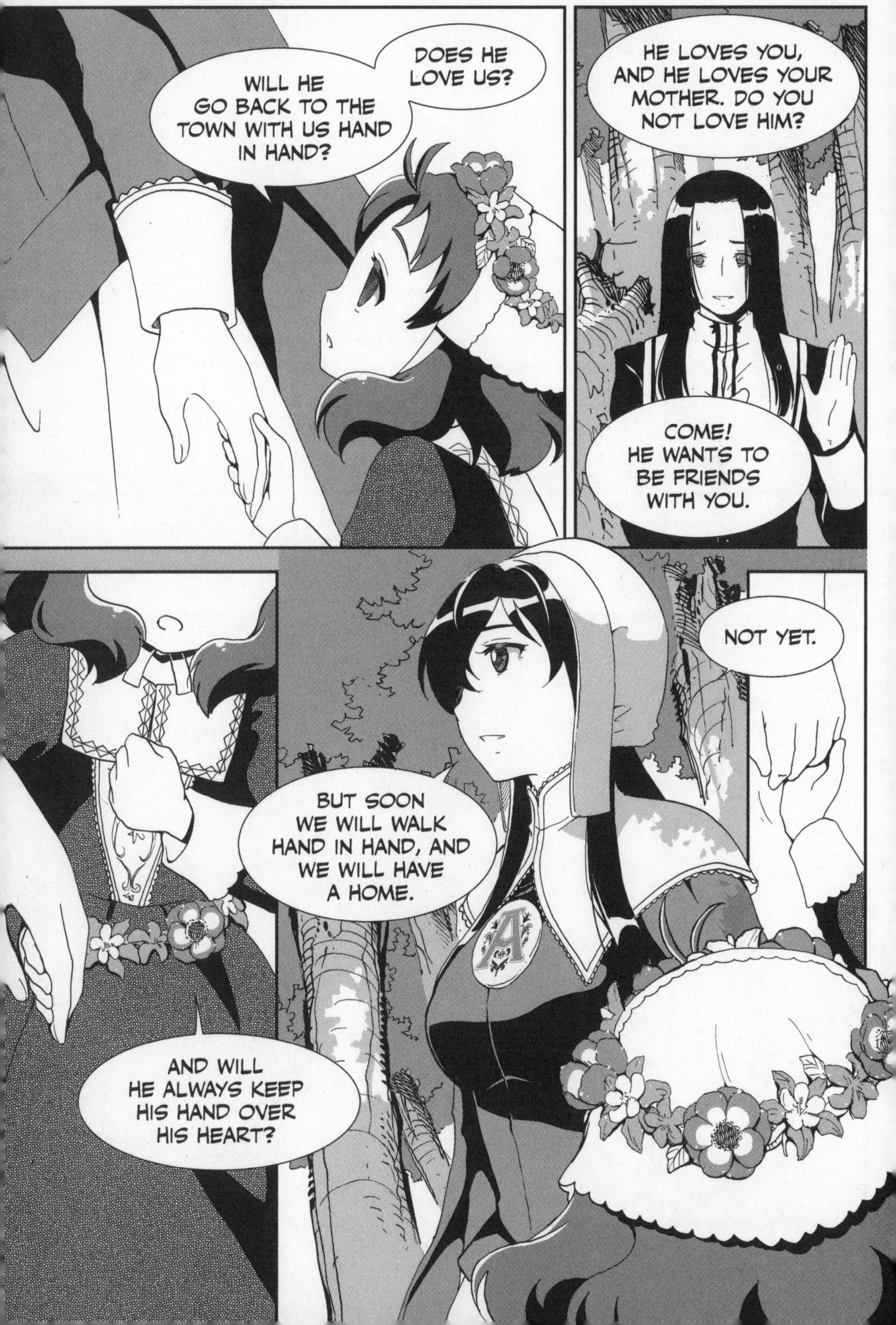
HE LOVES YOU, AND HE LOVES YOUR MOTHER. DO YOU NOT LOVE HIM?
COME! HE WANTS TO BE FRIENDS WITH YOU.
DOES HE LOVE US?
WILL HE GO BACK TO THE TOWN WITH US HAND IN HAND?
NOT YET.
BUT SOON WE WILL WALK HAND IN HAND, AND WE WILL HAVE A HOME.
AND WILL HE ALWAYS KEEP HIS HAND OVER HIS HEART?

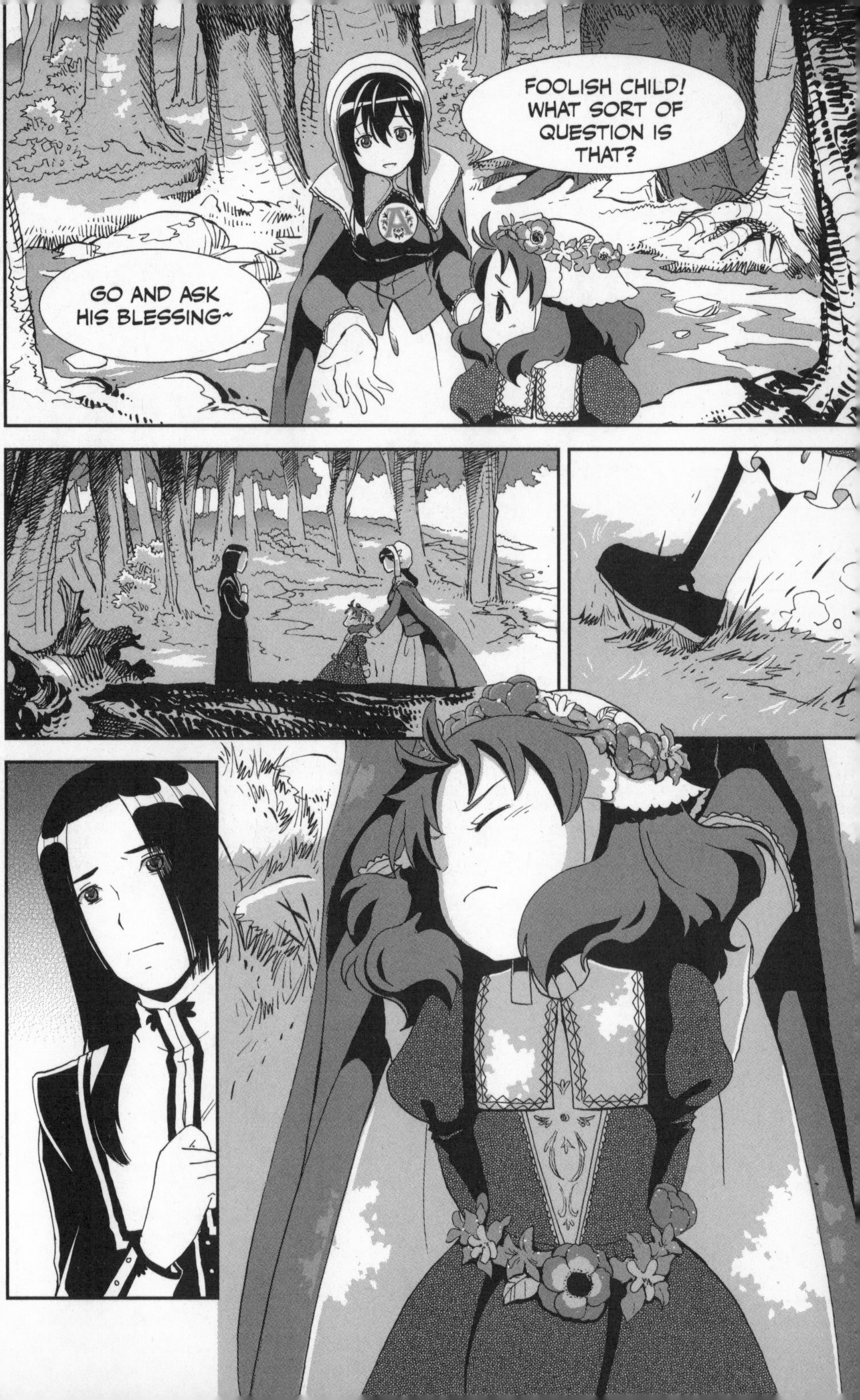
FOOLISH CHILD! WHAT SORT OF QUESTION IS THAT?
GO AND ASK HIS BLESSING~

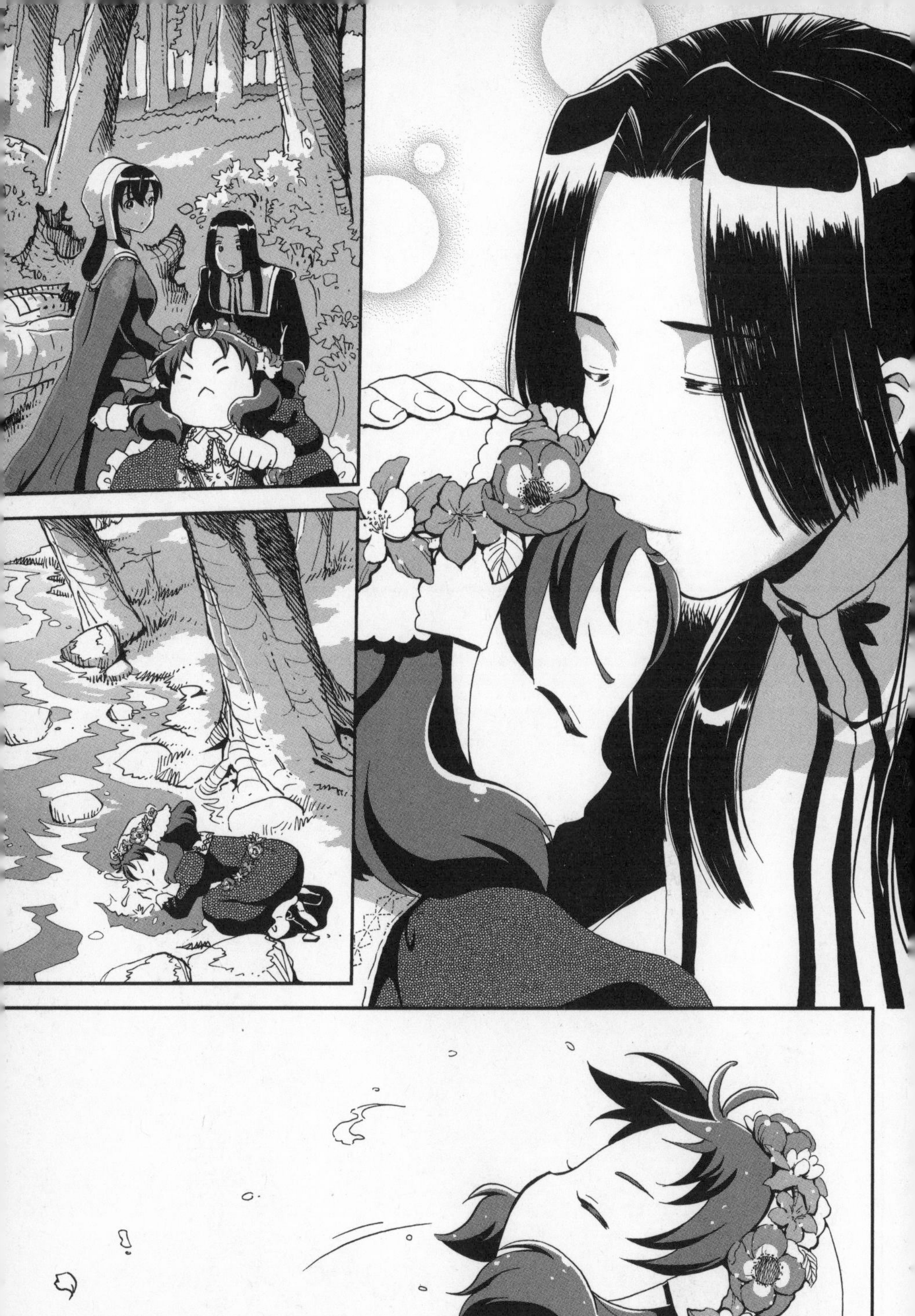

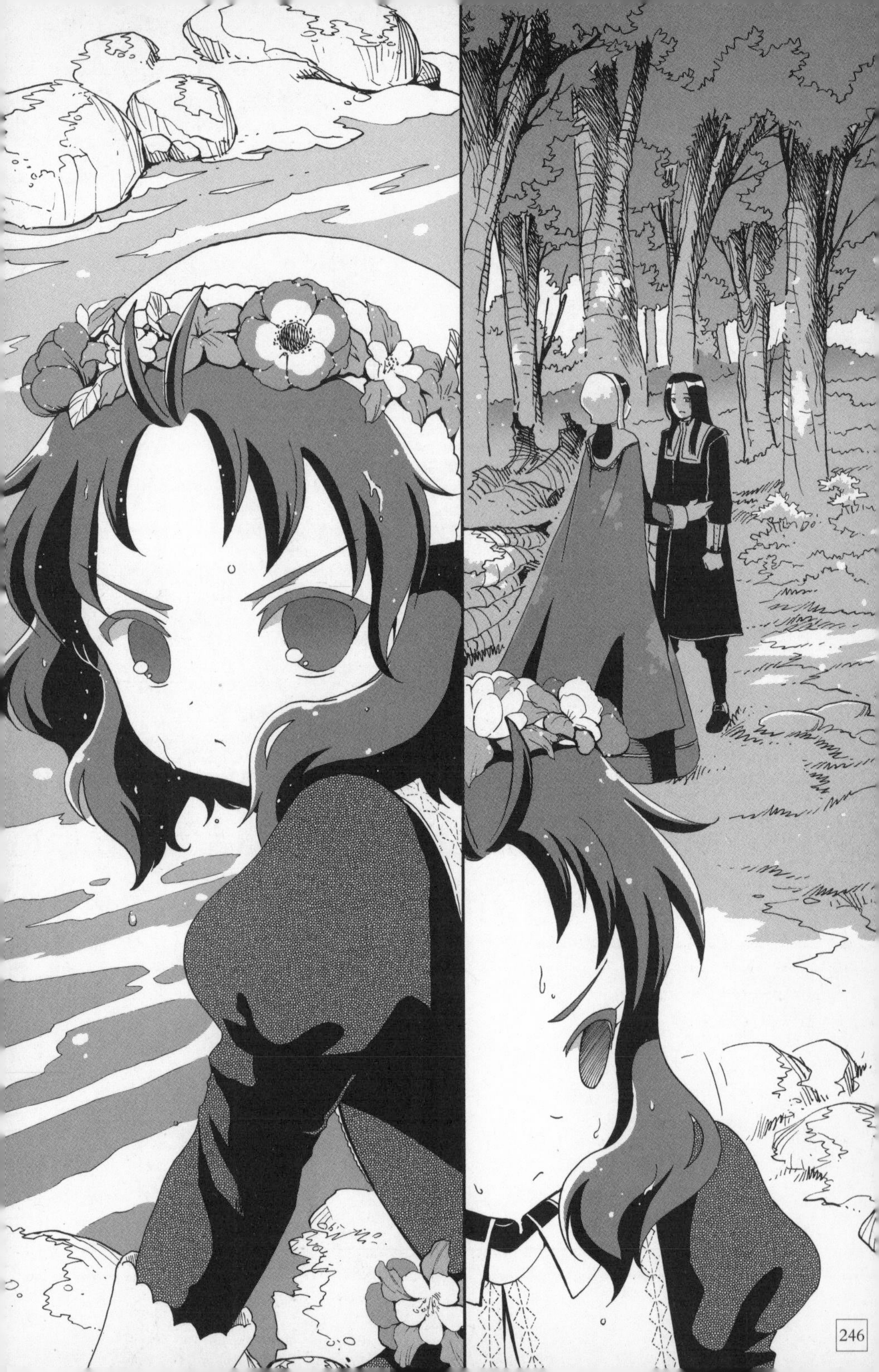

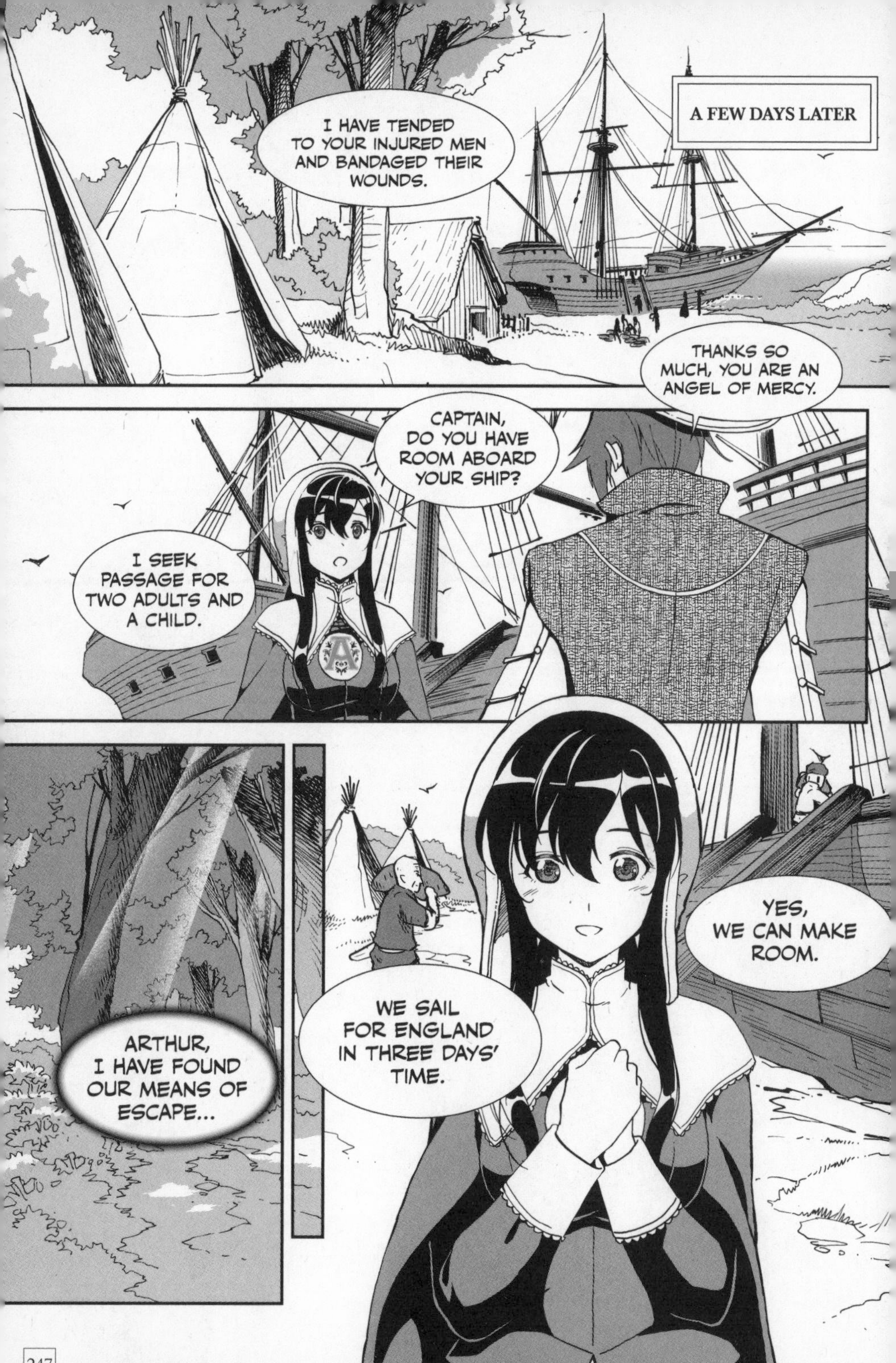
A FEW DAYS LATER
I HAVE TENDED TO YOUR INJURED MEN AND BANDAGED THEIR WOUNDS.
THANKS SO MUCH, YOU ARE AN ANGEL OF MERCY.
CAPTAIN, DO YOU HAVE ROOM ABOARD YOUR SHIP?
I SEEK PASSAGE FOR TWO ADULTS AND A CHILD.
YES, WE CAN MAKE ROOM.
WE SAIL FOR ENGLAND IN THREE DAYS' TIME.
ARTHUR, I HAVE FOUND OUR MEANS OF ESCAPE...

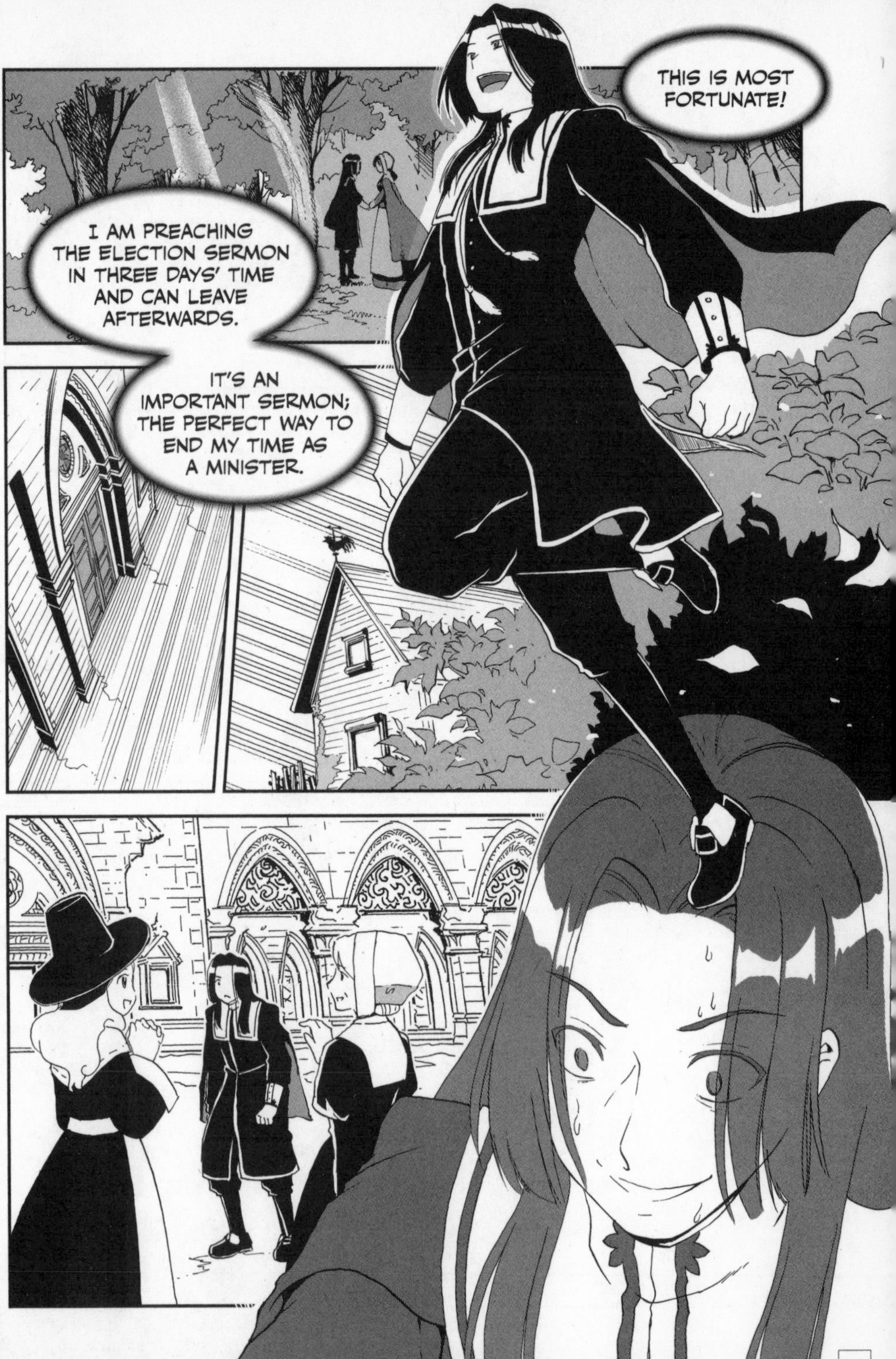
THIS IS MOST FORTUNATE!
I AM PREACHING THE ELECTION SERMON IN THREE DAYS' TIME AND CAN LEAVE AFTERWARDS.
IT'S AN IMPORTANT SERMON; THE PERFECT WAY TO END MY TIME AS A MINISTER.

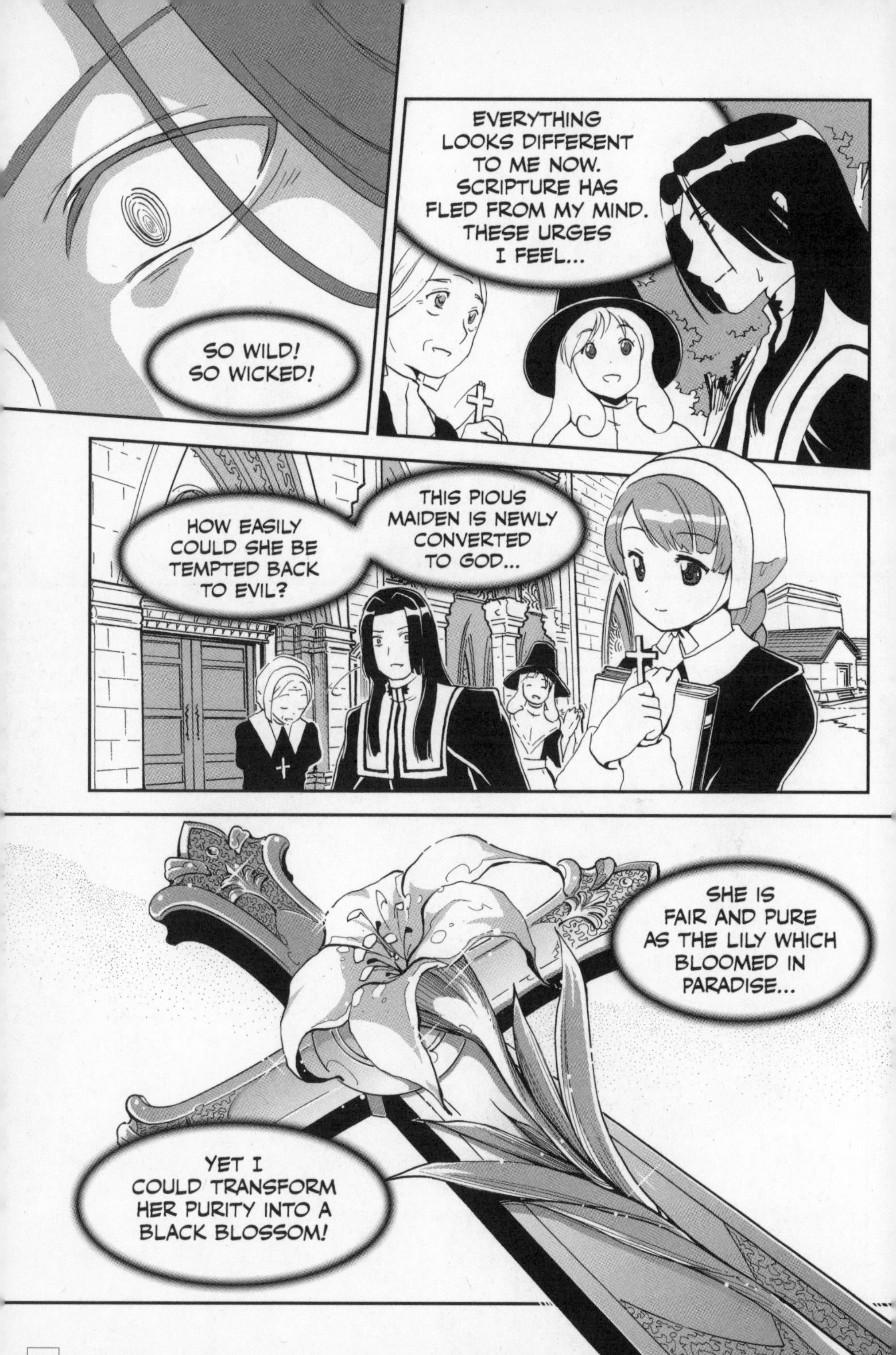
EVERYTHING LOOKS DIFFERENT TO ME NOW. SCRIPTURE HAS FLED FROM MY MIND. THESE URGES I FEEL...
SO WILD! SO WICKED!
THIS PIOUS MAIDEN IS NEWLY CONVERTED TO GOD...
HOW EASILY COULD SHE BE TEMPTED BACK TO EVIL?
SHE IS FAIR AND PURE AS THE LILY WHICH BLOOMED IN PARADISE...
YET I COULD TRANSFORM HER PURITY INTO A BLACK BLOSSOM!

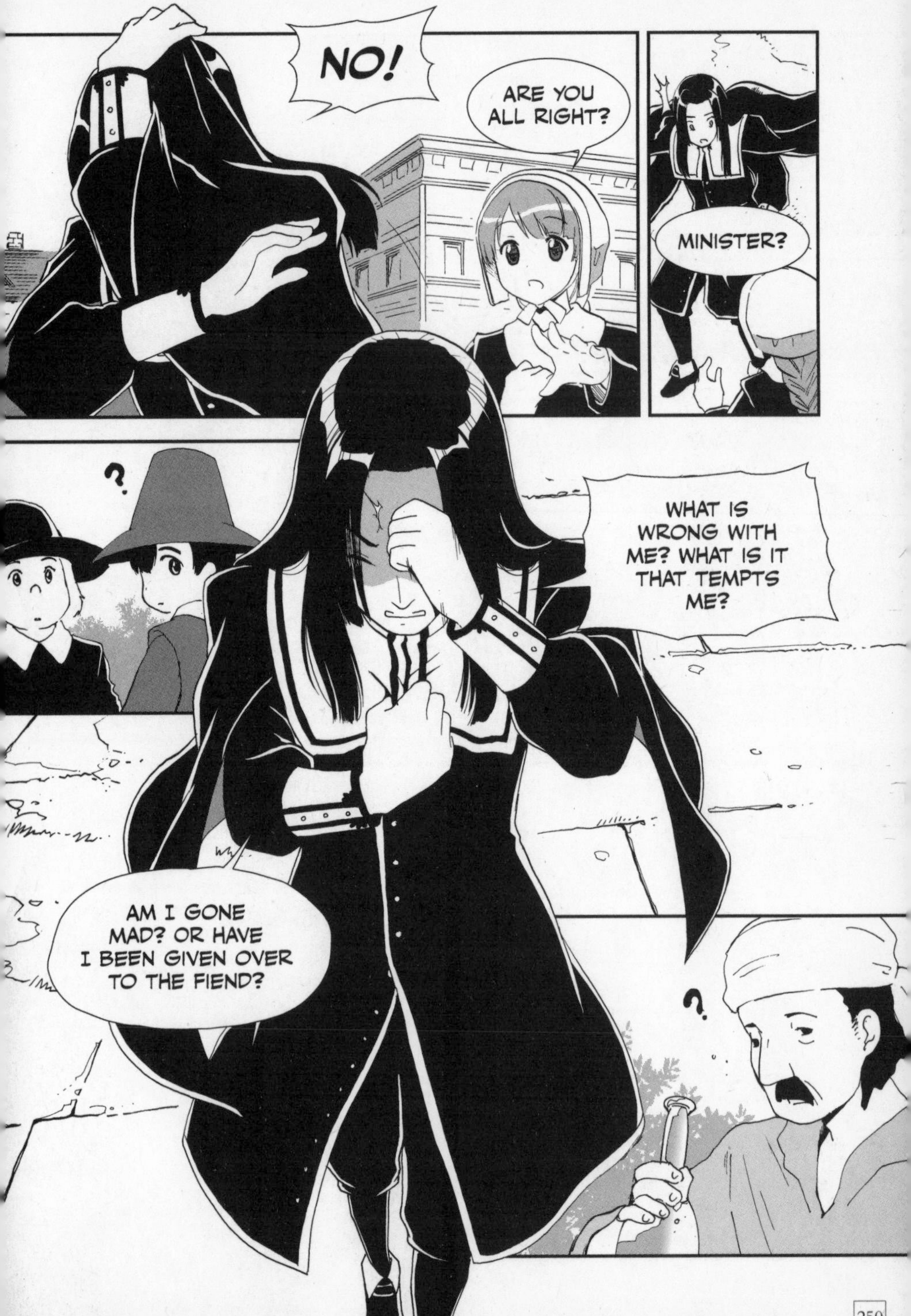
MINISTER?
NO!
ARE YOU ALL RIGHT?
WHAT IS WRONG WITH ME? WHAT IS IT THAT TEMPTS ME?
AM I GONE MAD? OR HAVE I BEEN GIVEN OVER TO THE FIEND?

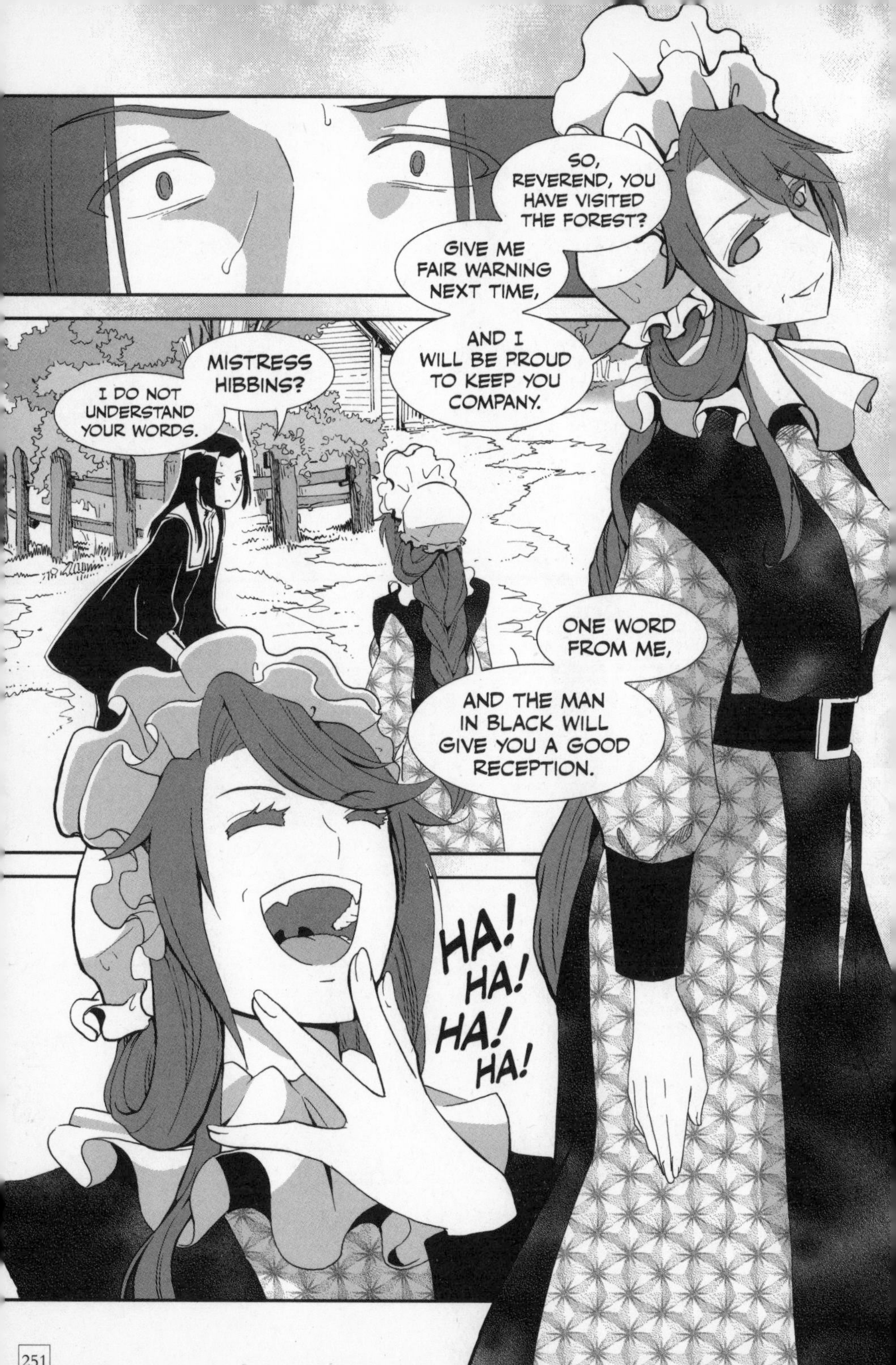
SO, REVEREND, YOU HAVE VISITED THE FOREST?
GIVE ME FAIR WARNING NEXT TIME,
AND I WILL BE PROUD TO KEEP YOU COMPANY.
MISTRESS HIBBINS?
I DO NOT UNDERSTAND YOUR WORDS.
ONE WORD FROM ME,
AND THE MAN IN BLACK WILL GIVE YOU A GOOD RECEPTION.
HA! HA! HA! HA!

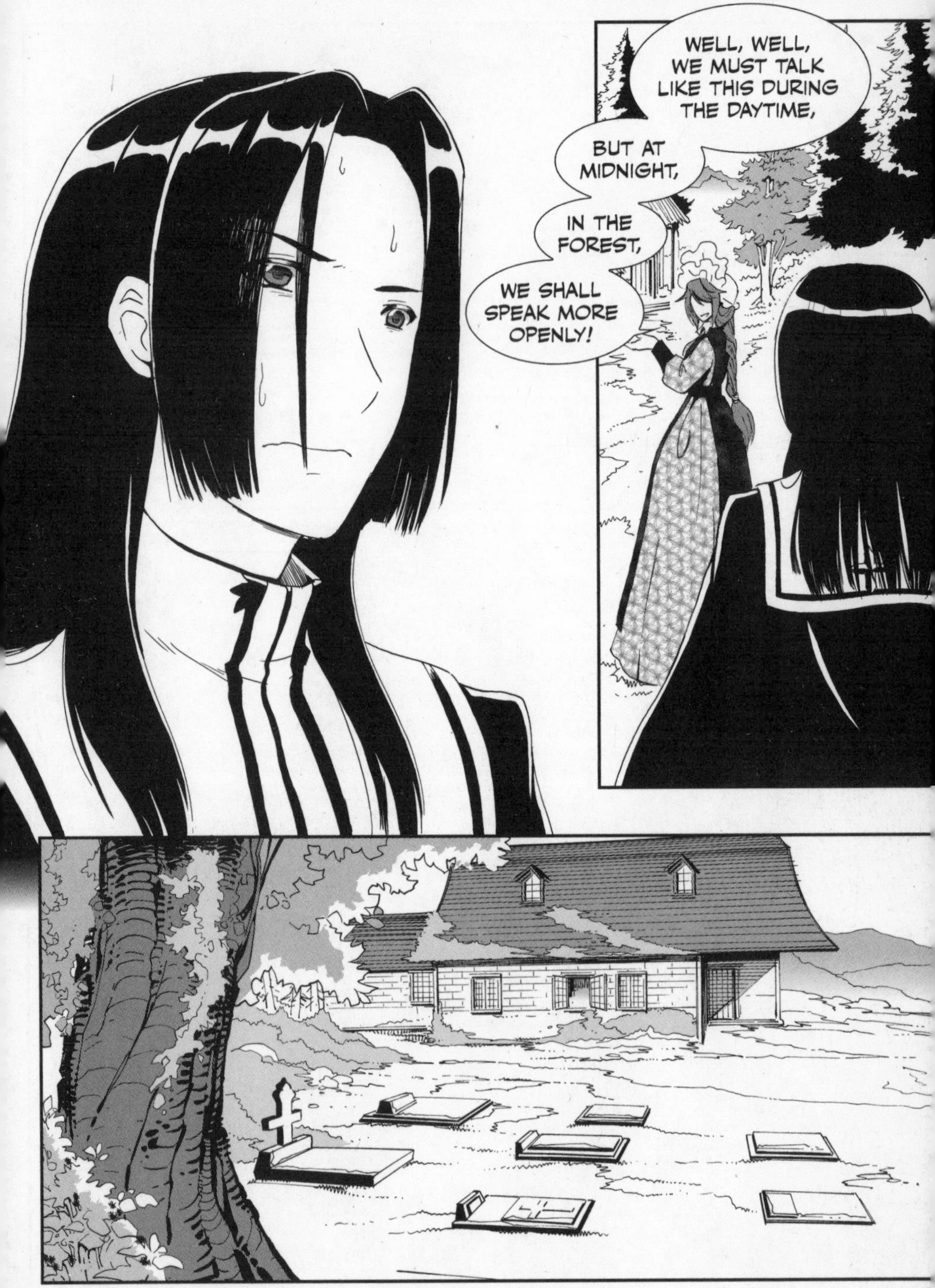
WELL, WELL, WE MUST TALK LIKE THIS DURING THE DAYTIME,
BUT AT MIDNIGHT,
IN THE FOREST,
WE SHALL SPEAK MORE OPENLY!

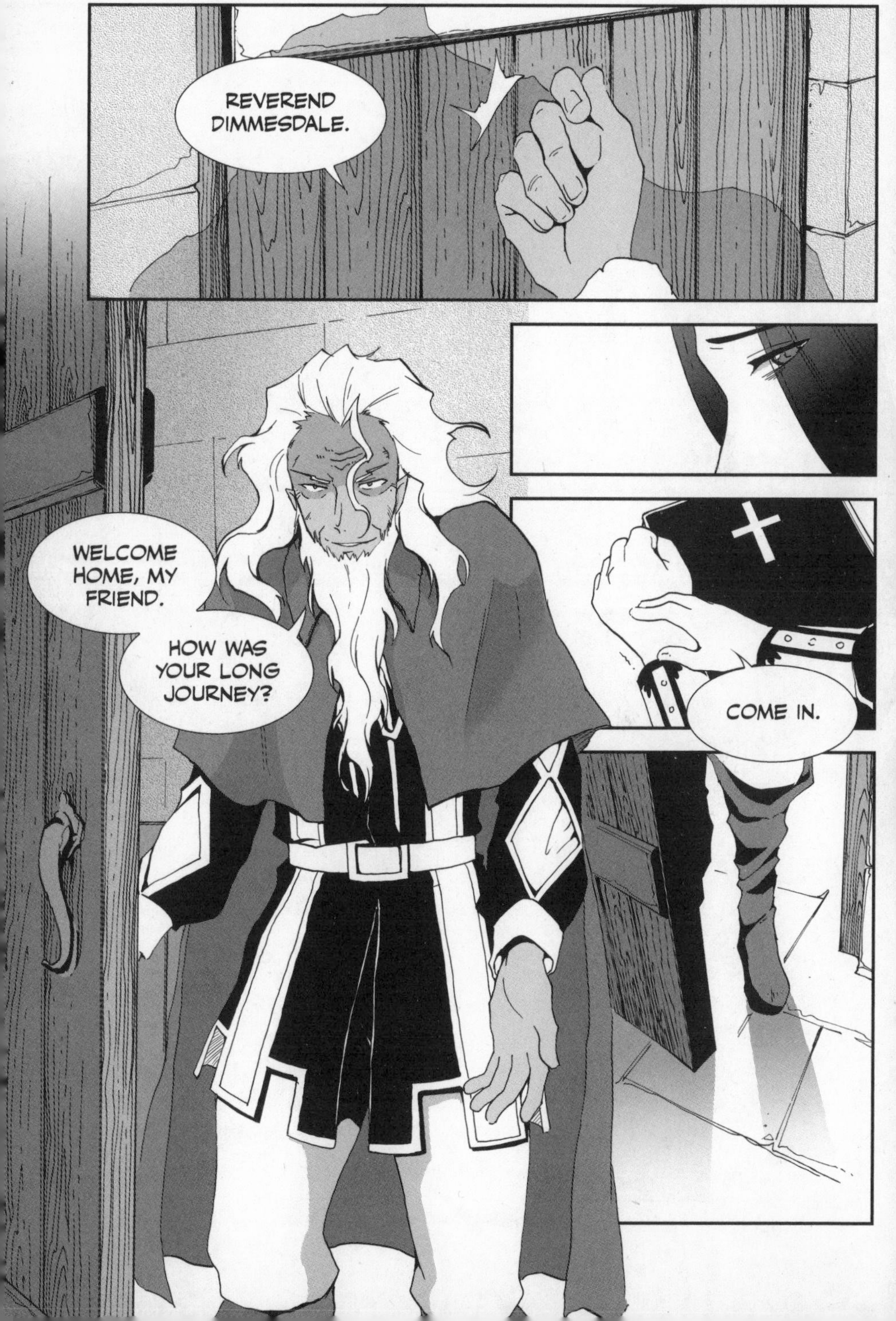
REVEREND DIMMESDALE.
COME IN.
WELCOME HOME, MY FRIEND.
HOW WAS YOUR LONG JOURNEY?

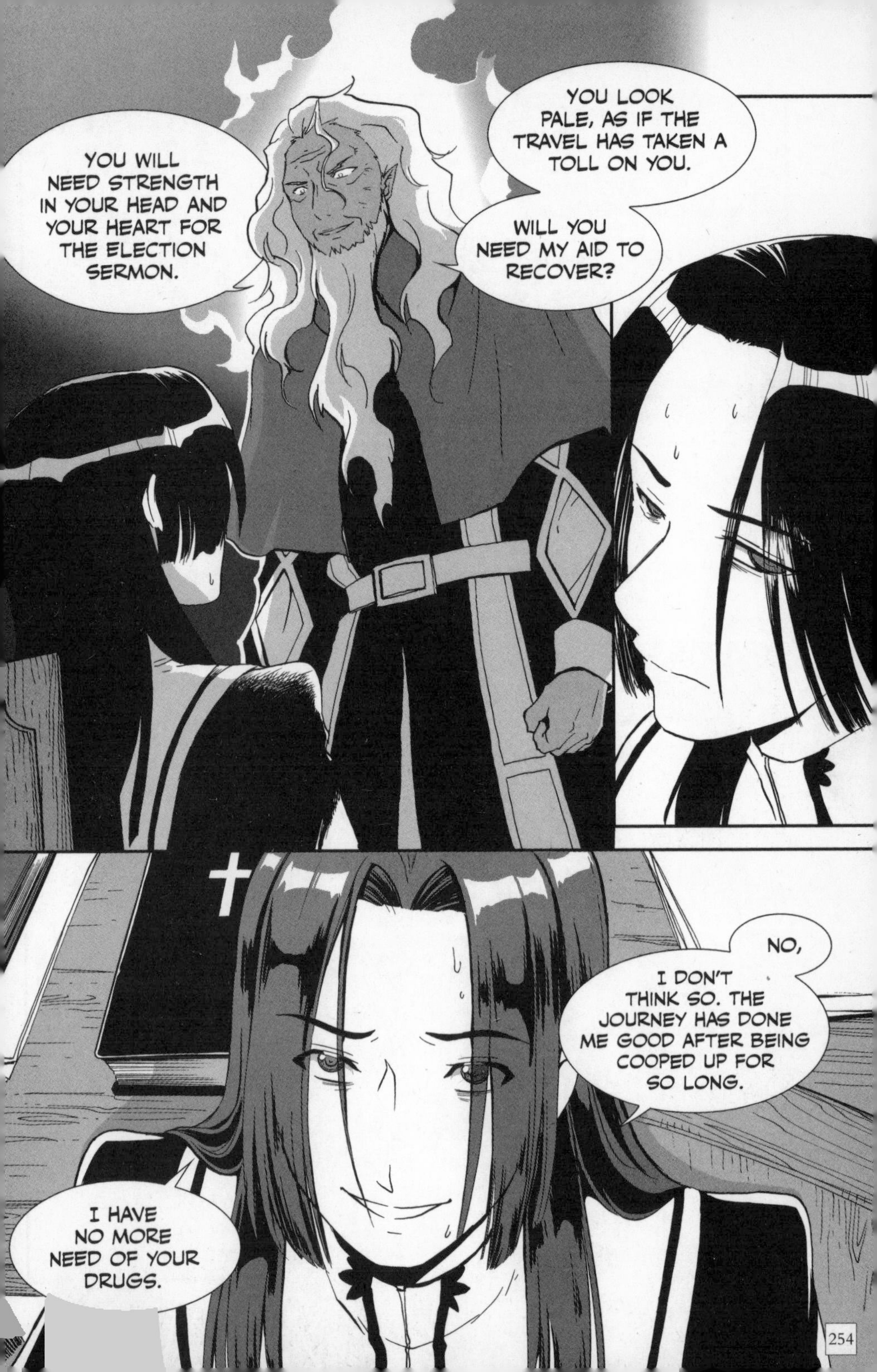
YOU LOOK PALE, AS IF THE TRAVEL HAS TAKEN A TOLL ON YOU.
WILL YOU NEED MY AID TO RECOVER?
YOU WILL NEED STRENGTH IN YOUR HEAD AND YOUR HEART FOR THE ELECTION SERMON.
NO,
I DON'T THINK SO. THE JOURNEY HAS DONE ME GOOD AFTER BEING COOPED UP FOR SO LONG.
I HAVE NO MORE NEED OF YOUR DRUGS.

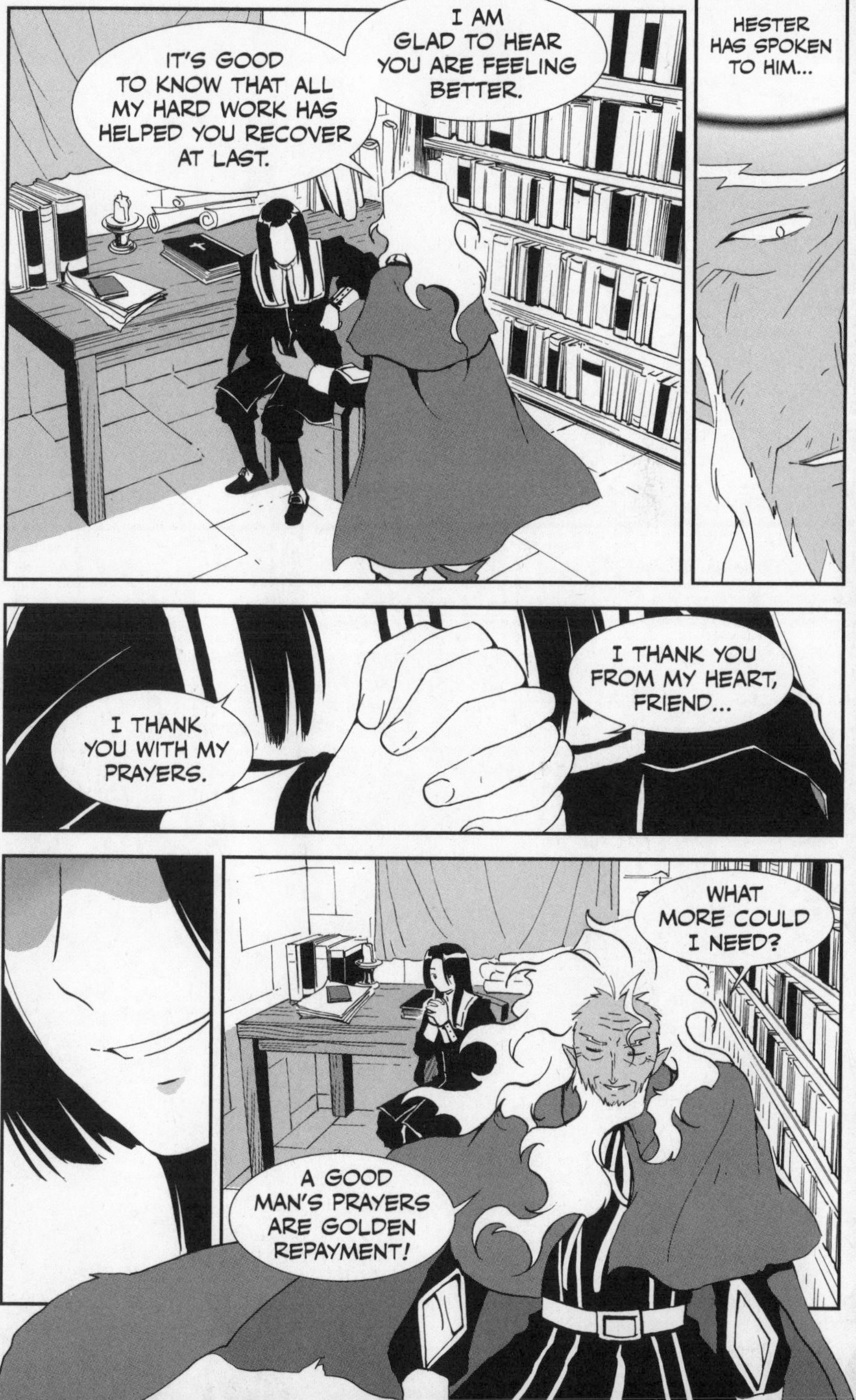
HESTER HAS SPOKEN TO HIM...
I AM GLAD TO HEAR YOU ARE FEELING BETTER.
IT'S GOOD TO KNOW THAT ALL MY HARD WORK HAS HELPED YOU RECOVER AT LAST.
I THANK YOU FROM MY HEART, FRIEND...
I THANK YOU WITH MY PRAYERS.
WHAT MORE COULD I NEED?
A GOOD MAN'S PRAYERS ARE GOLDEN REPAYMENT!

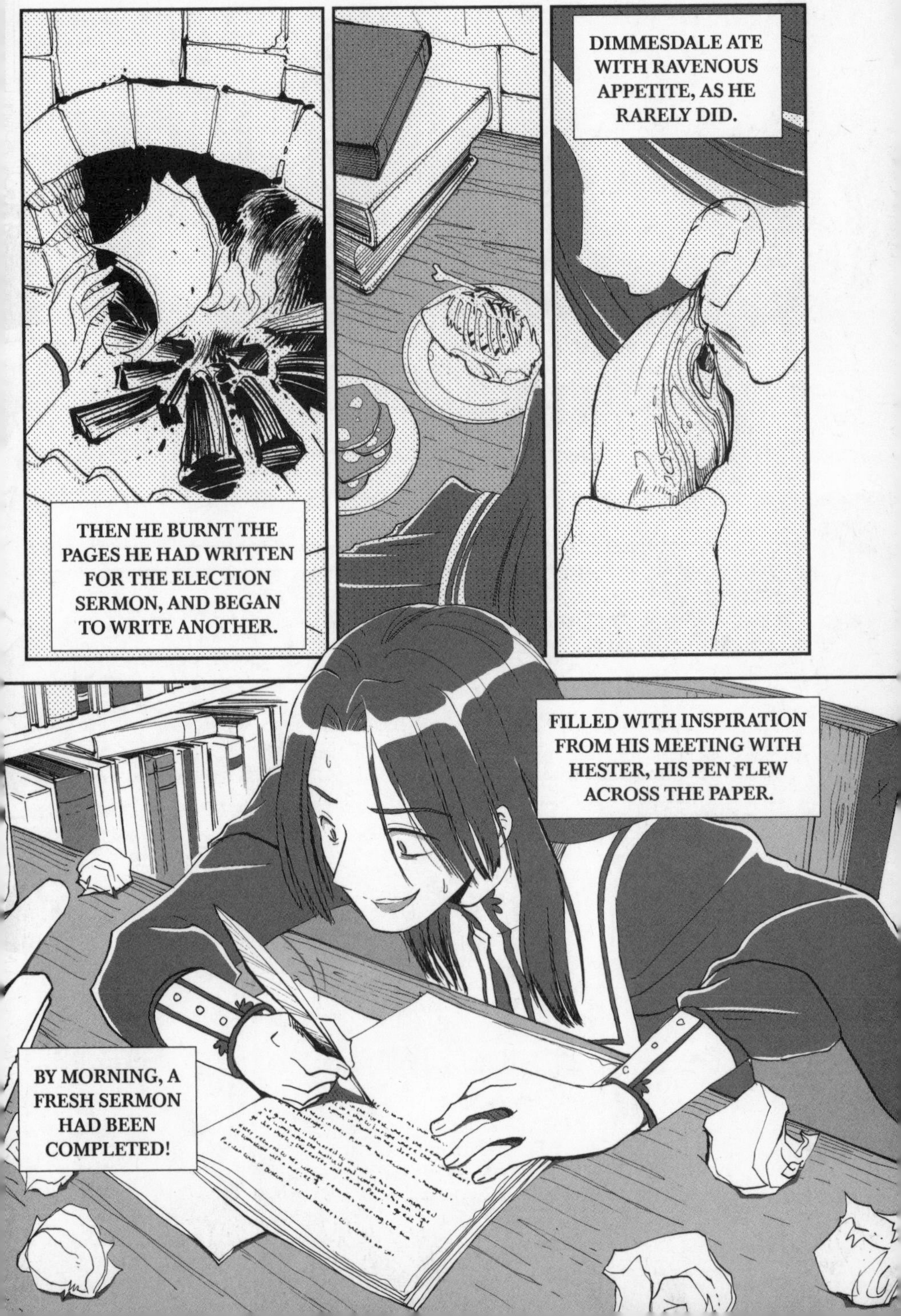
DIMMESDALE ATE WITH RAVENOUS APPETITE, AS HE RARELY DID.
THEN HE BURNT THE PAGES HE HAD WRITTEN FOR THE ELECTION SERMON, AND BEGAN TO WRITE ANOTHER.
FILLED WITH INSPIRATION FROM HIS MEETING WITH HESTER, HIS PEN FLEW ACROSS THE PAPER.
BY MORNING, A FRESH SERMON HAD BEEN COMPLETED!

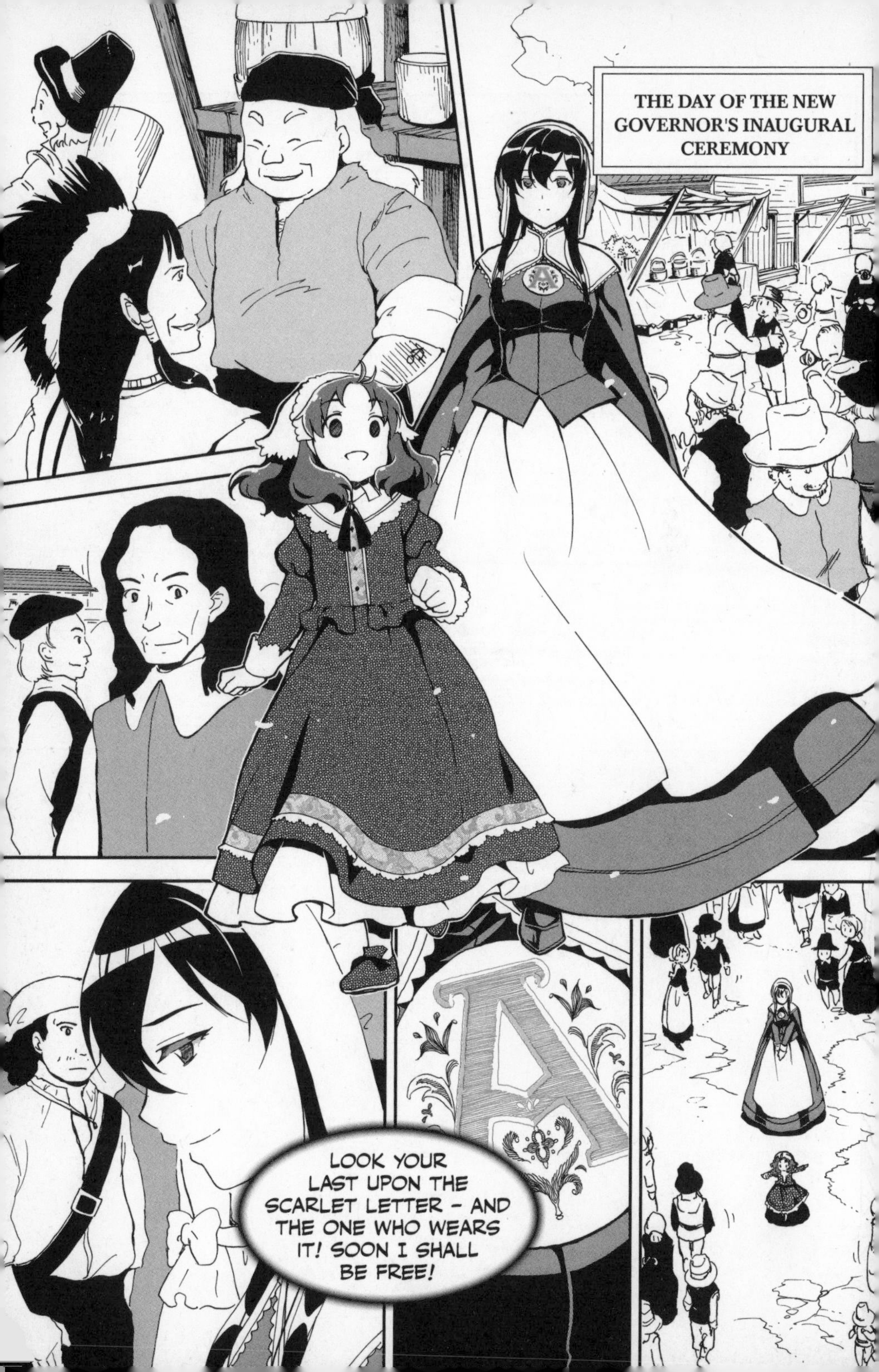
THE DAY OF THE NEW GOVERNOR'S INAUGURAL CEREMONY
LOOK YOUR LAST UPON THE SCARLET LETTER - AND THE ONE WHO WEARS IT! SOON I SHALL BE FREE!

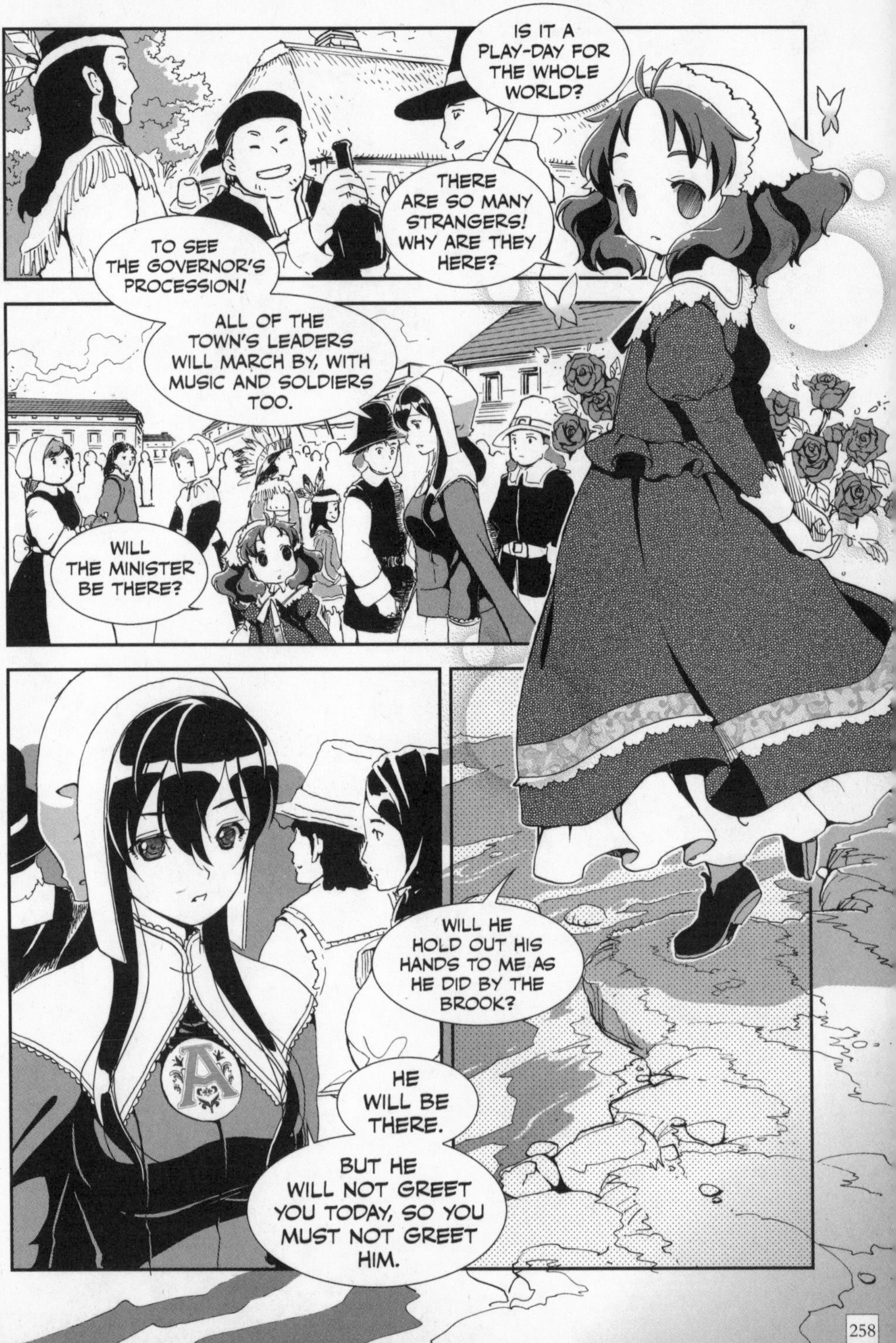
IS IT A PLAY-DAY FOR THE WHOLE WORLD?
THERE ARE SO MANY STRANGERS! WHY ARE THEY HERE?
TO SEE THE GOVERNOR'S PROCESSION!
ALL OF THE TOWN'S LEADERS WILL MARCH BY, WITH MUSIC AND SOLDIERS TOO.
WILL THE MINISTER BE THERE?
WILL HE HOLD OUT HIS HANDS TO ME AS HE DID BY THE BROOK?
HE WILL BE THERE.
BUT HE WILL NOT GREET YOU TODAY, SO YOU MUST NOT GREET HIM.

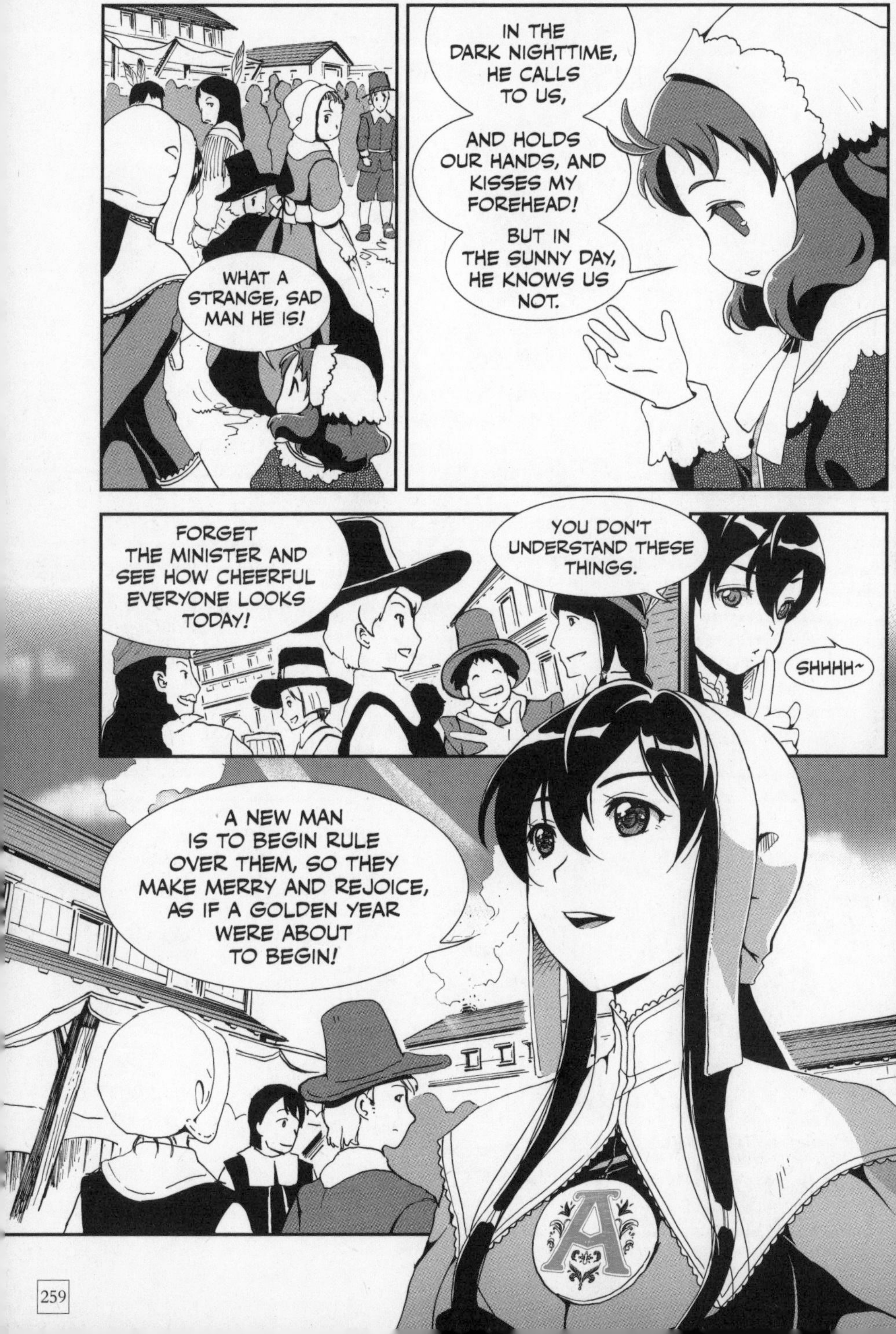
IN THE DARK NIGHTTIME, HE CALLS TO US,
AND HOLDS OUR HANDS, AND KISSES MY FOREHEAD!
BUT IN THE SUNNY DAY, HE KNOWS US NOT.
WHAT A STRANGE, SAD MAN HE IS!
SHHHH~
YOU DON'T UNDERSTAND THESE THINGS.
FORGET THE MINISTER AND SEE HOW CHEERFUL EVERYONE LOOKS TODAY!
A NEW MAN IS TO BEGIN RULE OVER THEM, SO THEY MAKE MERRY AND REJOICE, AS IF A GOLDEN YEAR WERE ABOUT TO BEGIN!
A

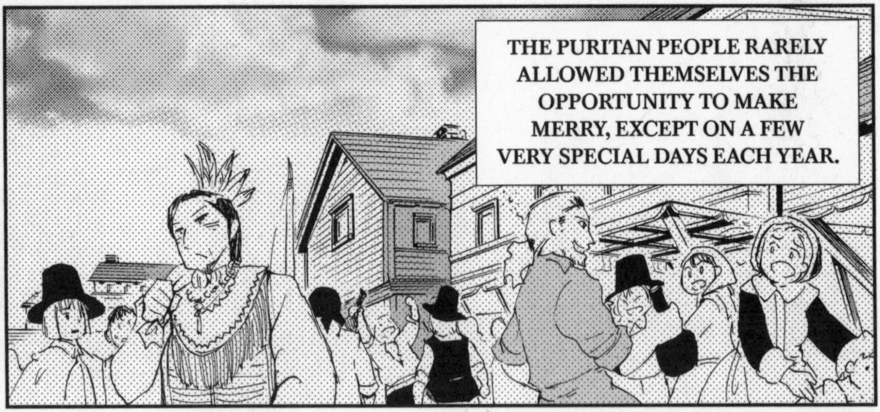
THE PURITAN PEOPLE RARELY ALLOWED THEMSELVES THE OPPORTUNITY TO MAKE MERRY, EXCEPT ON A FEW VERY SPECIAL DAYS EACH YEAR.

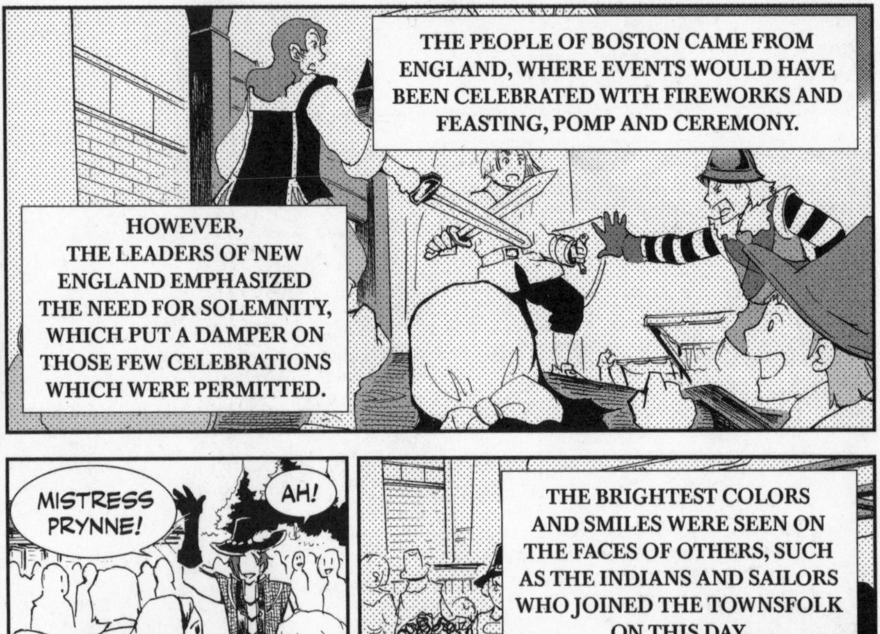
THE PEOPLE OF BOSTON CAME FROM ENGLAND, WHERE EVENTS WOULD HAVE BEEN CELEBRATED WITH FIREWORKS AND FEASTING, POMP AND CEREMONY.
HOWEVER, THE LEADERS OF NEW ENGLAND EMPHASIZED THE NEED FOR SOLEMNITY, WHICH PUT A DAMPER ON THOSE FEW CELEBRATIONS WHICH WERE PERMITTED.

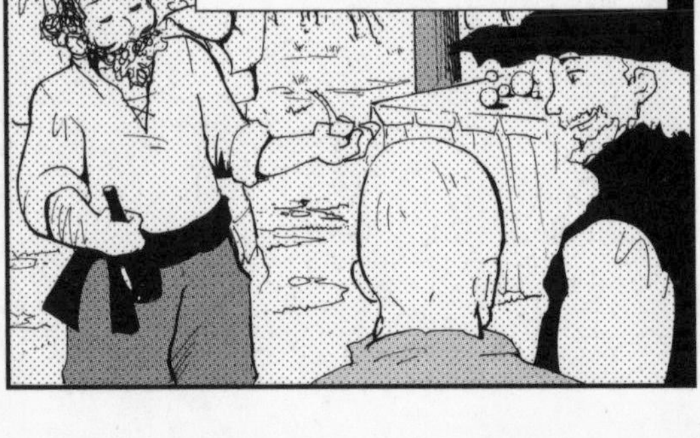
THE BRIGHTEST COLORS AND SMILES WERE SEEN ON THE FACES OF OTHERS, SUCH AS THE INDIANS AND SAILORS WHO JOINED THE TOWNSFOLK ON THIS DAY.

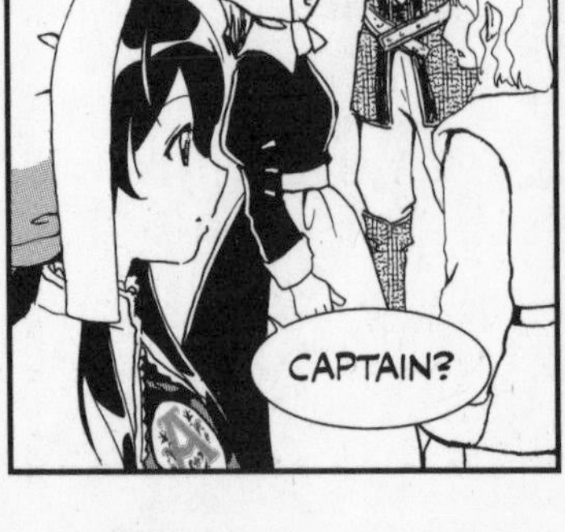
AH!
MISTRESS PRYNNE!
CAPTAIN?

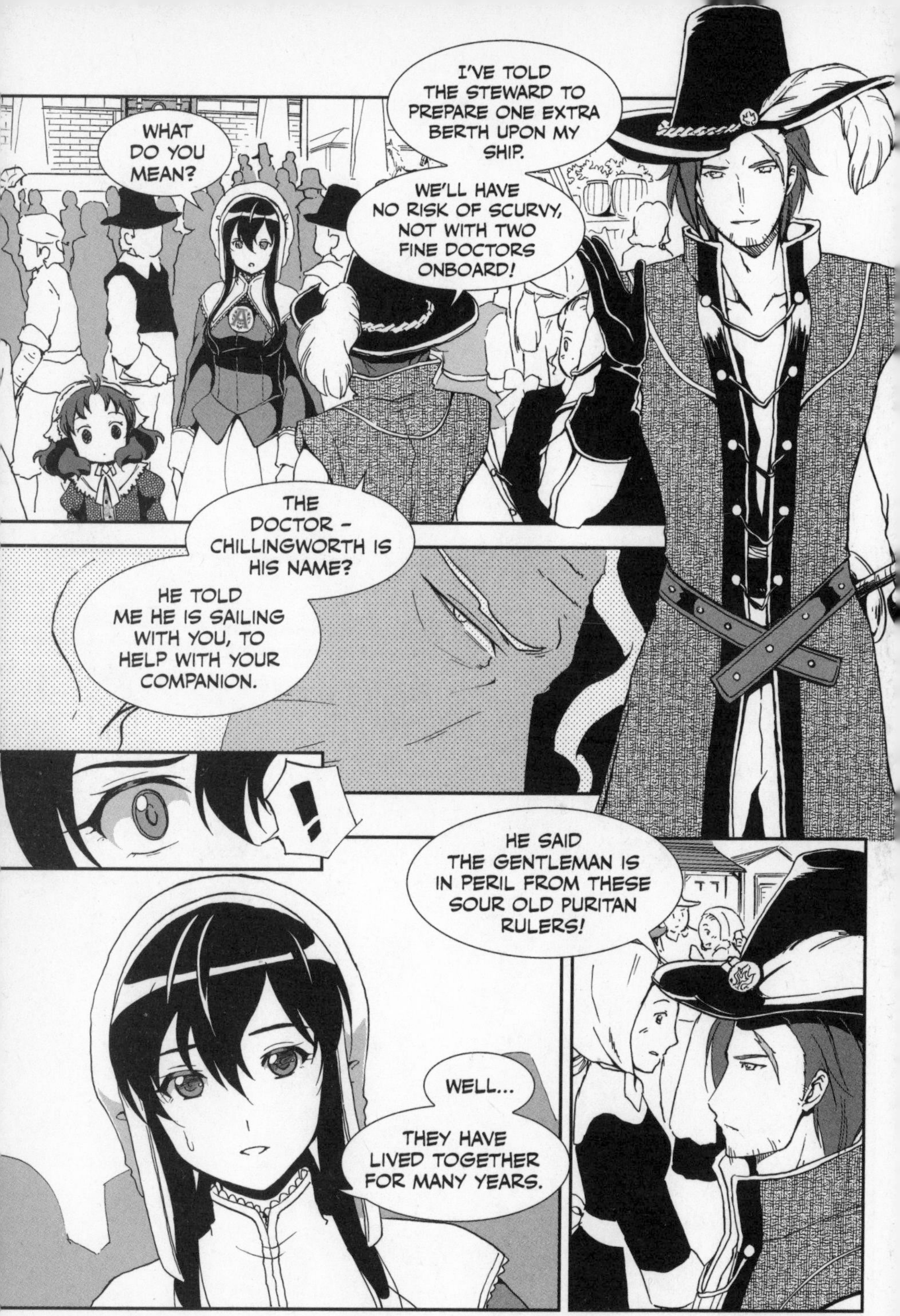
I'VE TOLD THE STEWARD TO PREPARE ONE EXTRA BERTH UPON MY SHIP.
WE'LL HAVE NO RISK OF SCURVY, NOT WITH TWO FINE DOCTORS ONBOARD!
WHAT DO YOU MEAN?
THE DOCTOR - CHILLINGWORTH IS HIS NAME?
HE TOLD ME HE IS SAILING WITH YOU, TO HELP WITH YOUR COMPANION.
!
HE SAID THE GENTLEMAN IS IN PERIL FROM THESE SOUR OLD PURITAN RULERS!
WELL...
THEY HAVE LIVED TOGETHER FOR MANY YEARS.

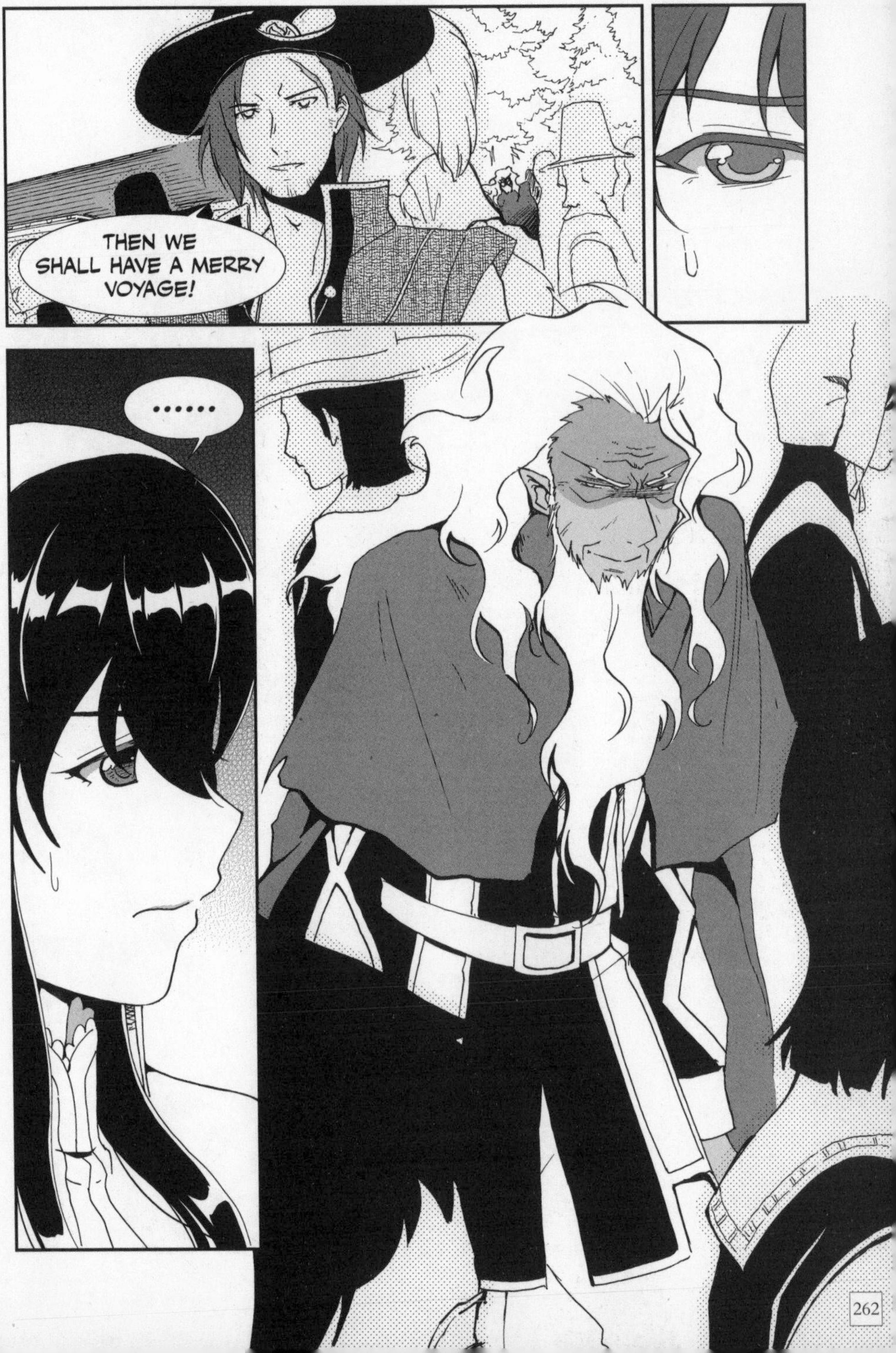
THEN WE SHALL HAVE A MERRY VOYAGE!
......

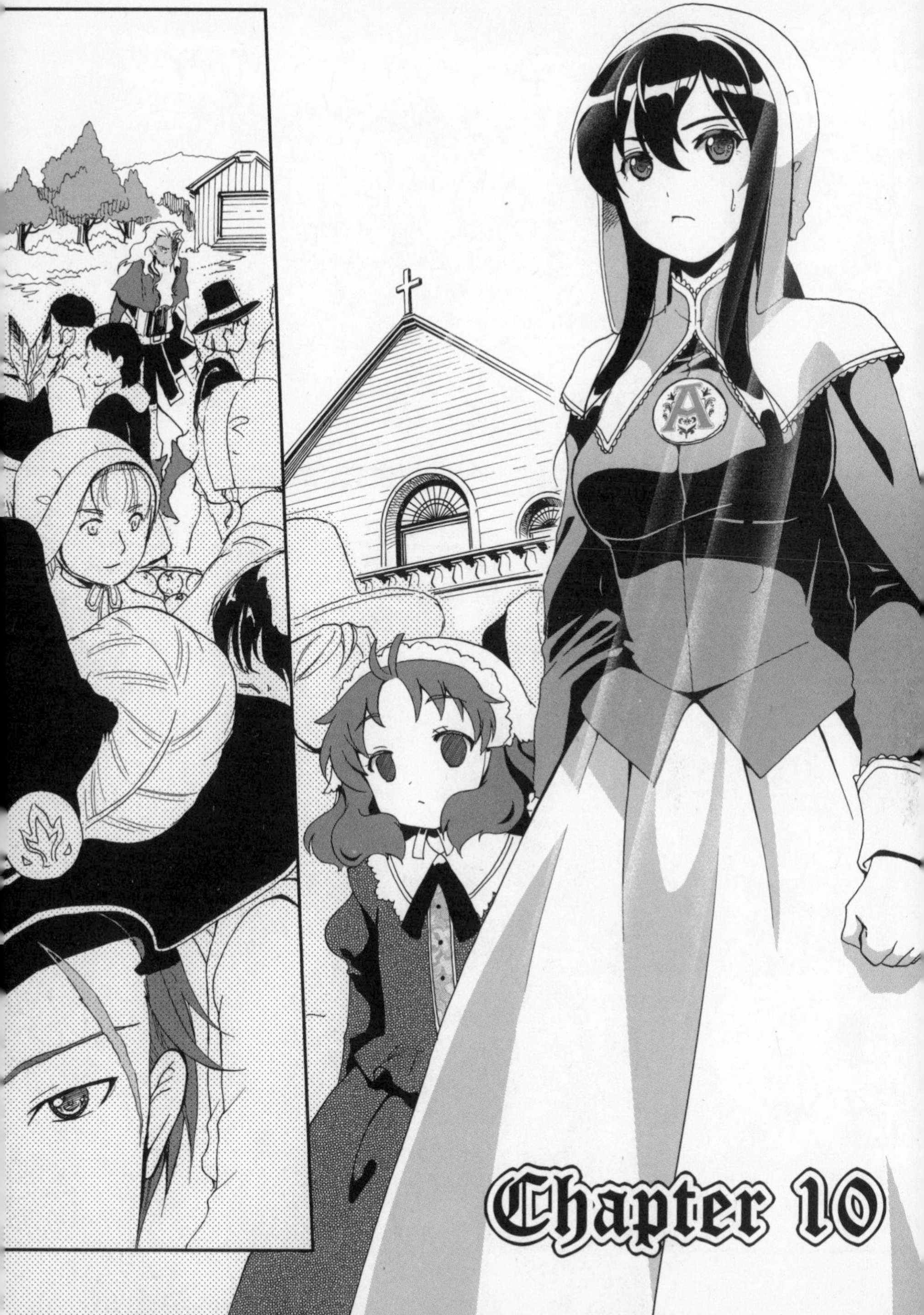
Chapter 10

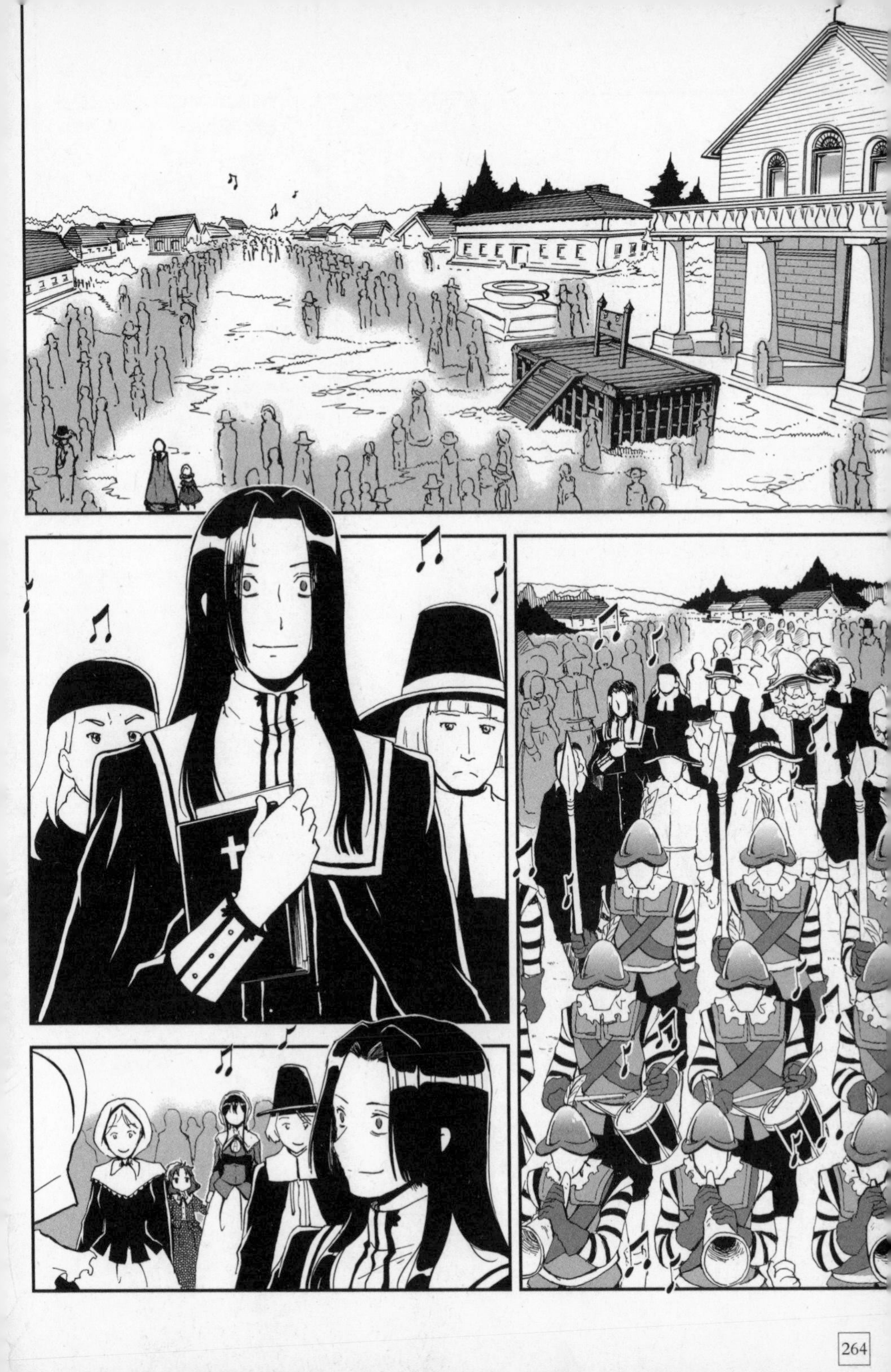

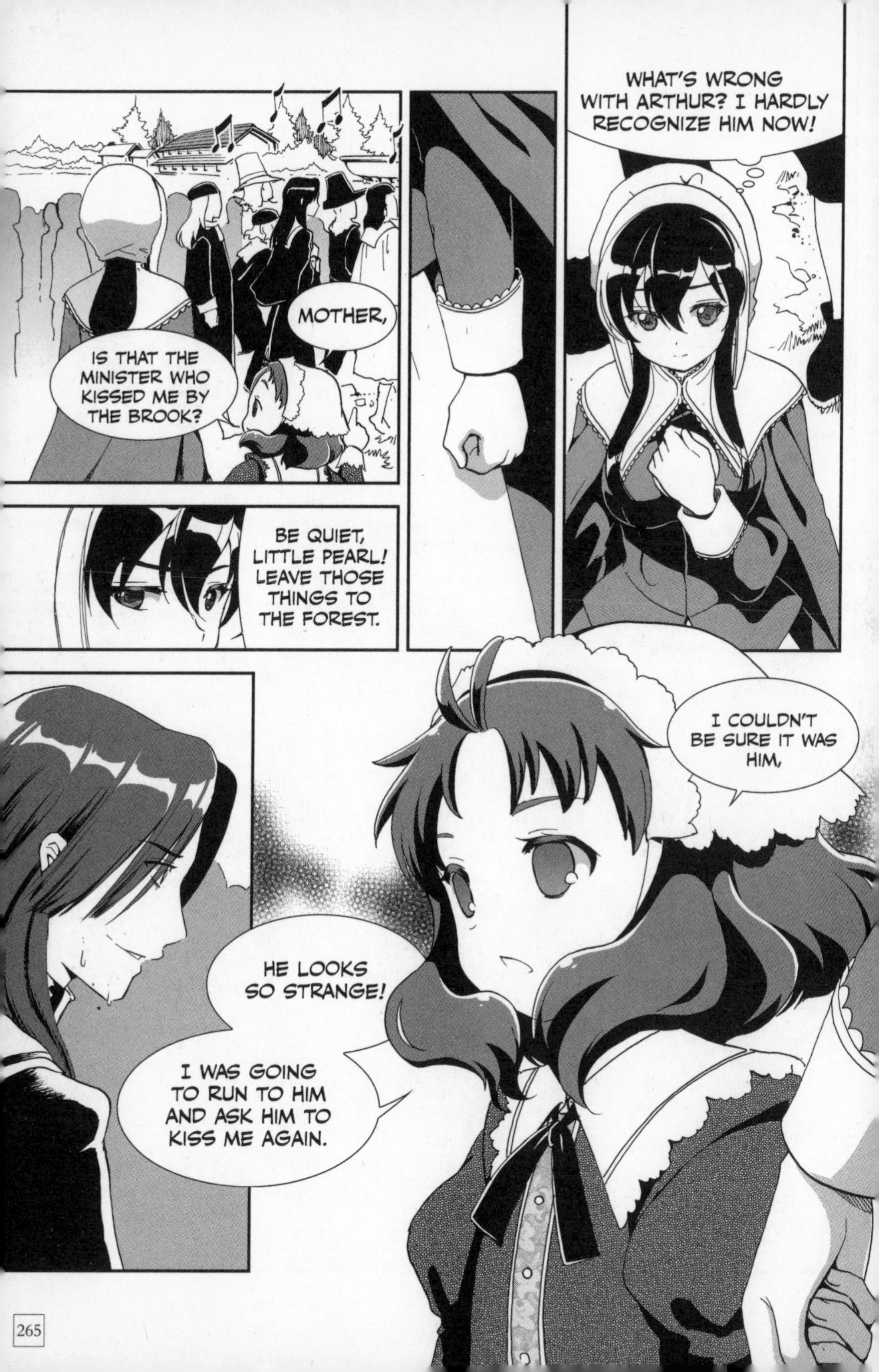
WHAT'S WRONG WITH ARTHUR? I HARDLY RECOGNIZE HIM NOW!
MOTHER,
IS THAT THE MINISTER WHO KISSED ME BY THE BROOK?
BE QUIET, LITTLE PEARL! LEAVE THOSE THINGS TO THE FOREST.
I COULDN'T BE SURE IT WAS HIM,
HE LOOKS SO STRANGE!
I WAS GOING TO RUN TO HIM AND ASK HIM TO KISS ME AGAIN.

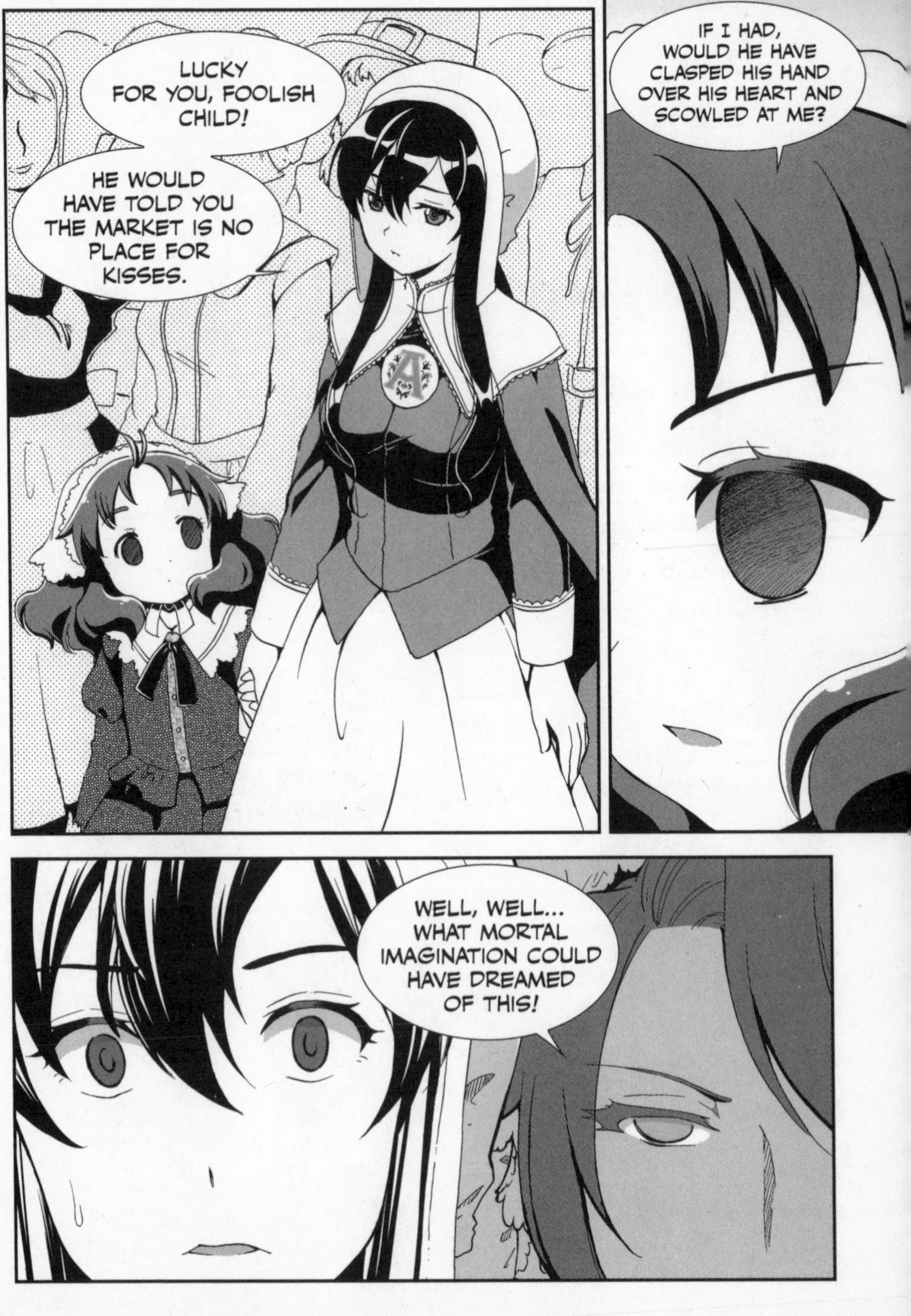
IF I HAD, WOULD HE HAVE CLASPED HIS HAND OVER HIS HEART AND SCOWLED AT ME?
LUCKY FOR YOU, FOOLISH CHILD!
HE WOULD HAVE TOLD YOU THE MARKET IS NO PLACE FOR KISSES.
WELL, WELL... WHAT MORTAL IMAGINATION COULD HAVE DREAMED OF THIS!

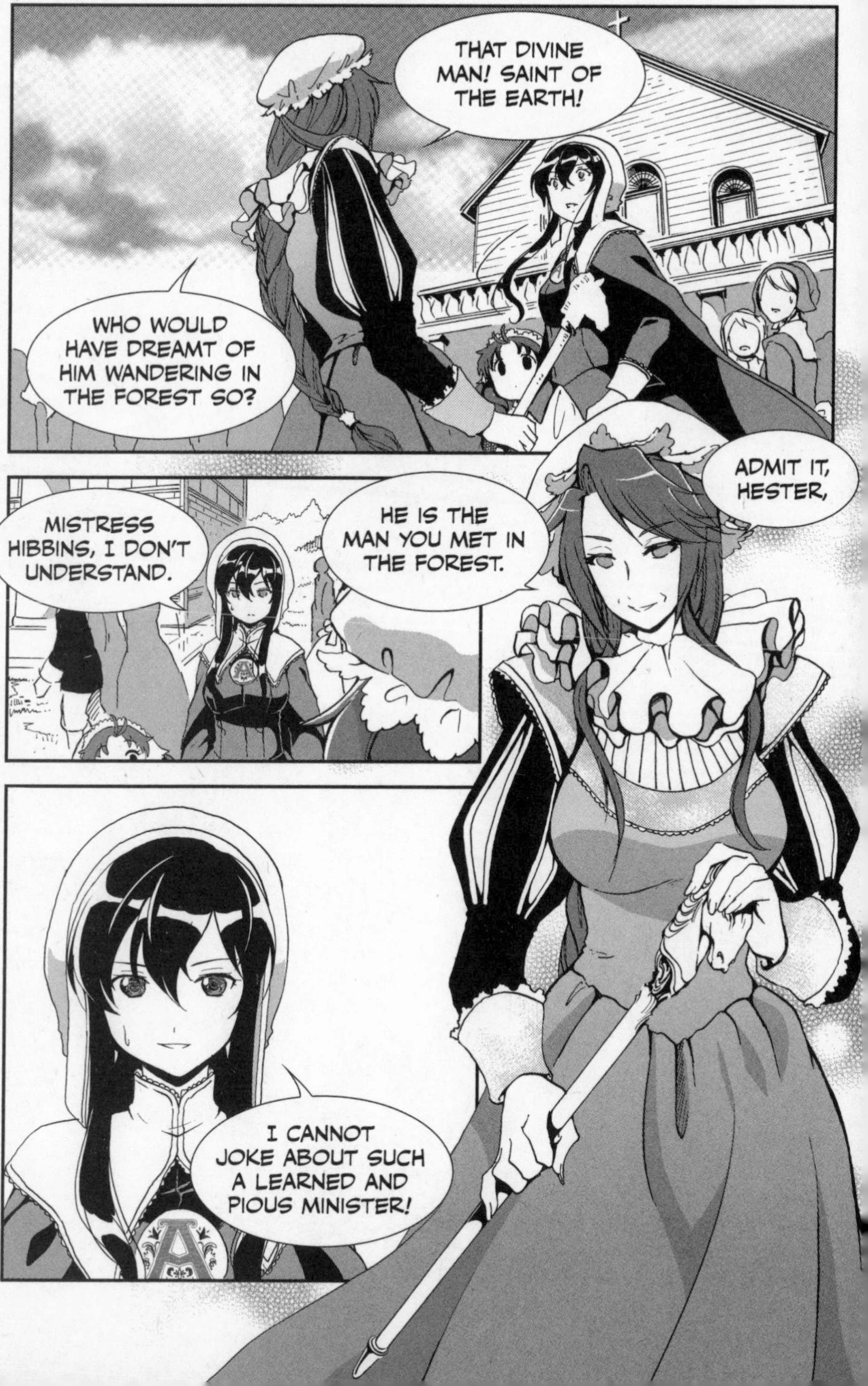
THAT DIVINE MAN! SAINT OF THE EARTH!
WHO WOULD HAVE DREAMT OF HIM WANDERING IN THE FOREST SO?
ADMIT IT, HESTER,
HE IS THE MAN YOU MET IN THE FOREST.
MISTRESS HIBBINS, I DON'T UNDERSTAND.
I CANNOT JOKE ABOUT SUCH A LEARNED AND PIOUS MINISTER!

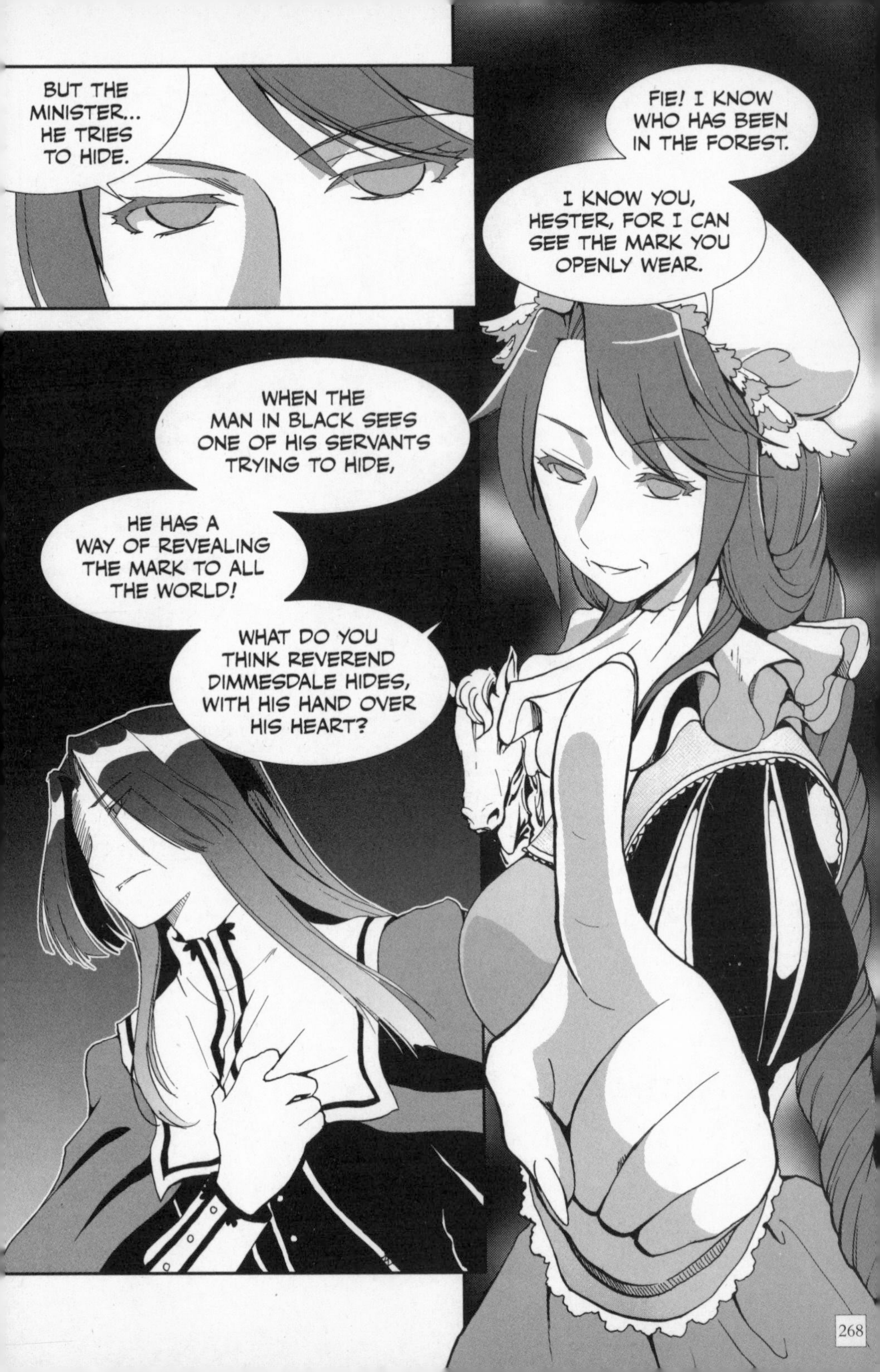
FIE! I KNOW WHO HAS BEEN IN THE FOREST.
I KNOW YOU, HESTER, FOR I CAN SEE THE MARK YOU OPENLY WEAR.
BUT THE MINISTER... HE TRIES TO HIDE.
WHEN THE MAN IN BLACK SEES ONE OF HIS SERVANTS TRYING TO HIDE,
HE HAS A WAY OF REVEALING THE MARK TO ALL THE WORLD!
WHAT DO YOU THINK REVEREND DIMMESDALE HIDES, WITH HIS HAND OVER HIS HEART?

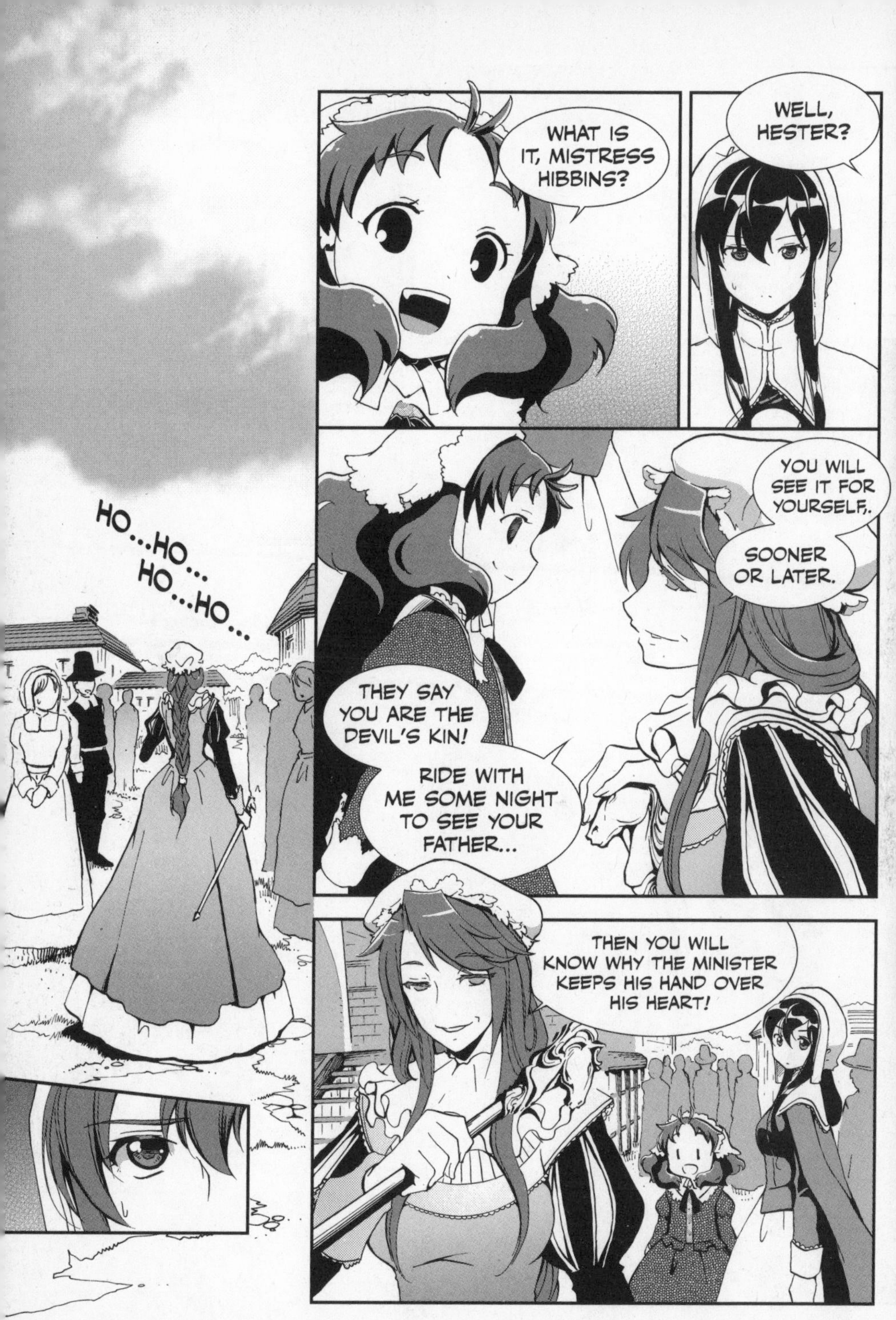
WELL, HESTER?
WHAT IS IT, MISTRESS HIBBINS?
YOU WILL SEE IT FOR YOURSELF.
SOONER OR LATER.
THEY SAY YOU ARE THE DEVIL'S KIN!
RIDE WITH ME SOME NIGHT TO SEE YOUR FATHER...
THEN YOU WILL KNOW WHY THE MINISTER KEEPS HIS HAND OVER HIS HEART!
HO...HO... HO...HO...

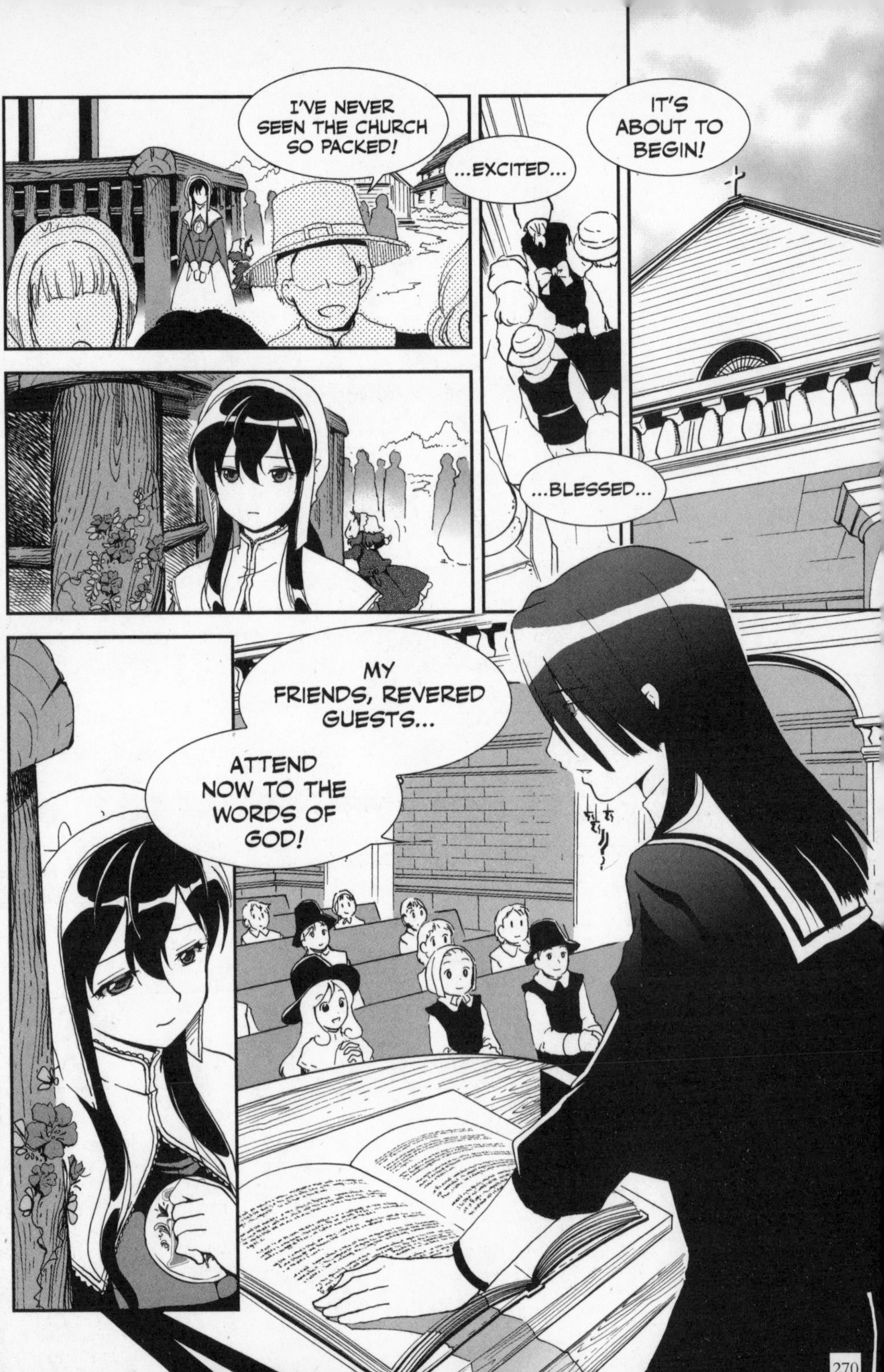
IT'S ABOUT TO BEGIN!
...EXCITED...
...BLESSED...
I'VE NEVER SEEN THE CHURCH SO PACKED!
MY FRIENDS, REVERED GUESTS...
ATTEND NOW TO THE WORDS OF GOD!

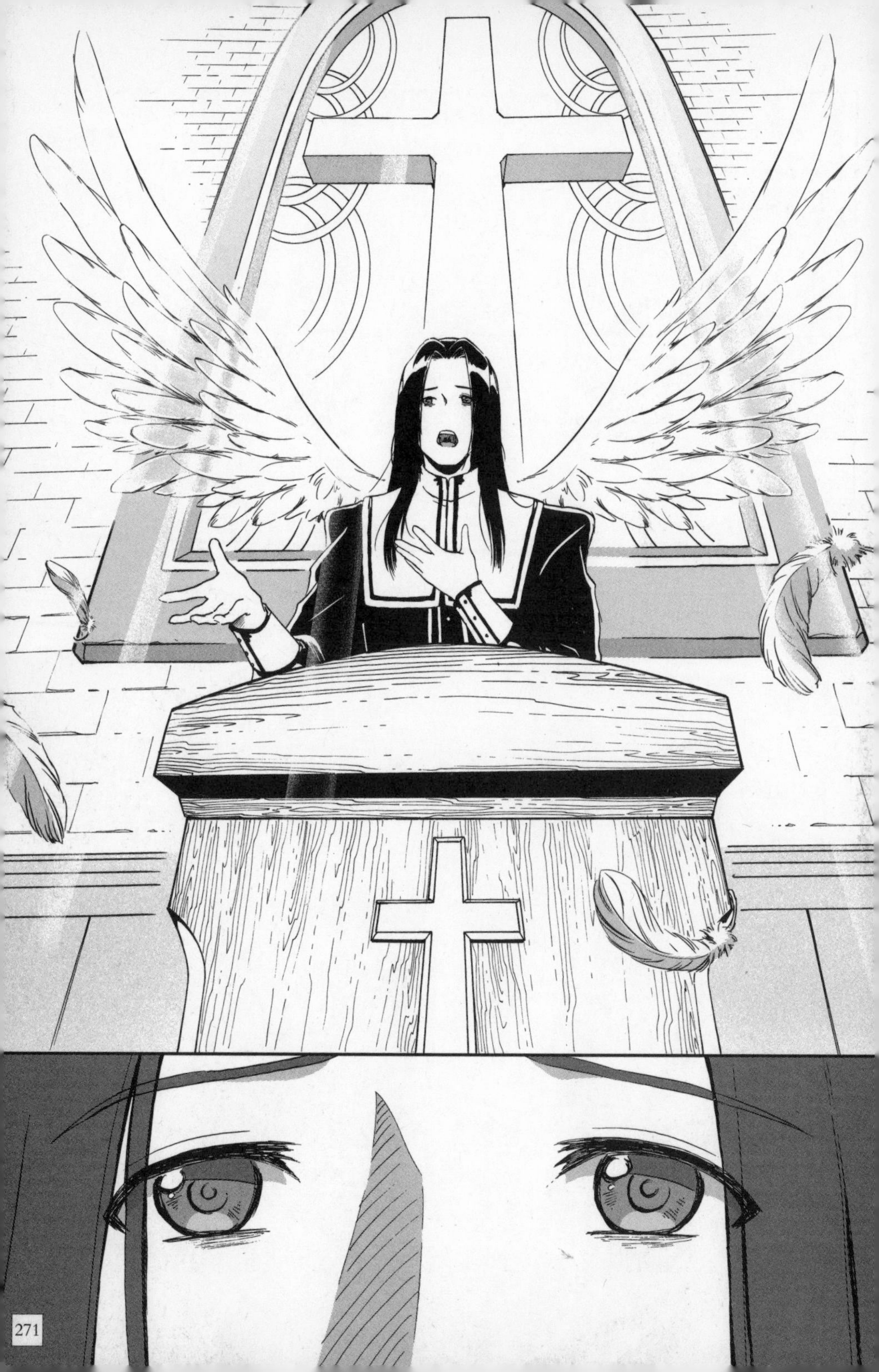

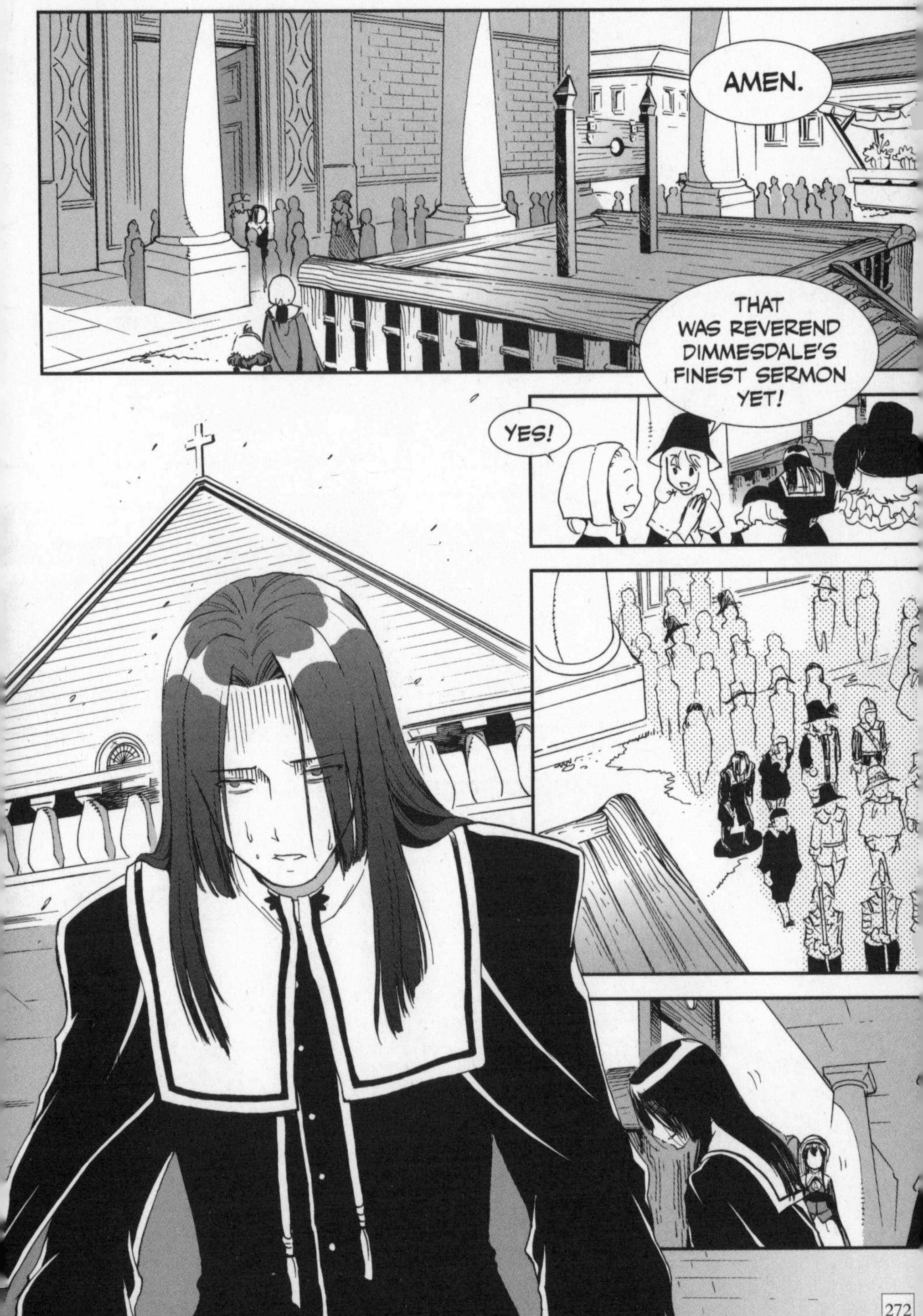
AMEN.
THAT WAS REVEREND DIMMESDALE'S FINEST SERMON YET!
YES!

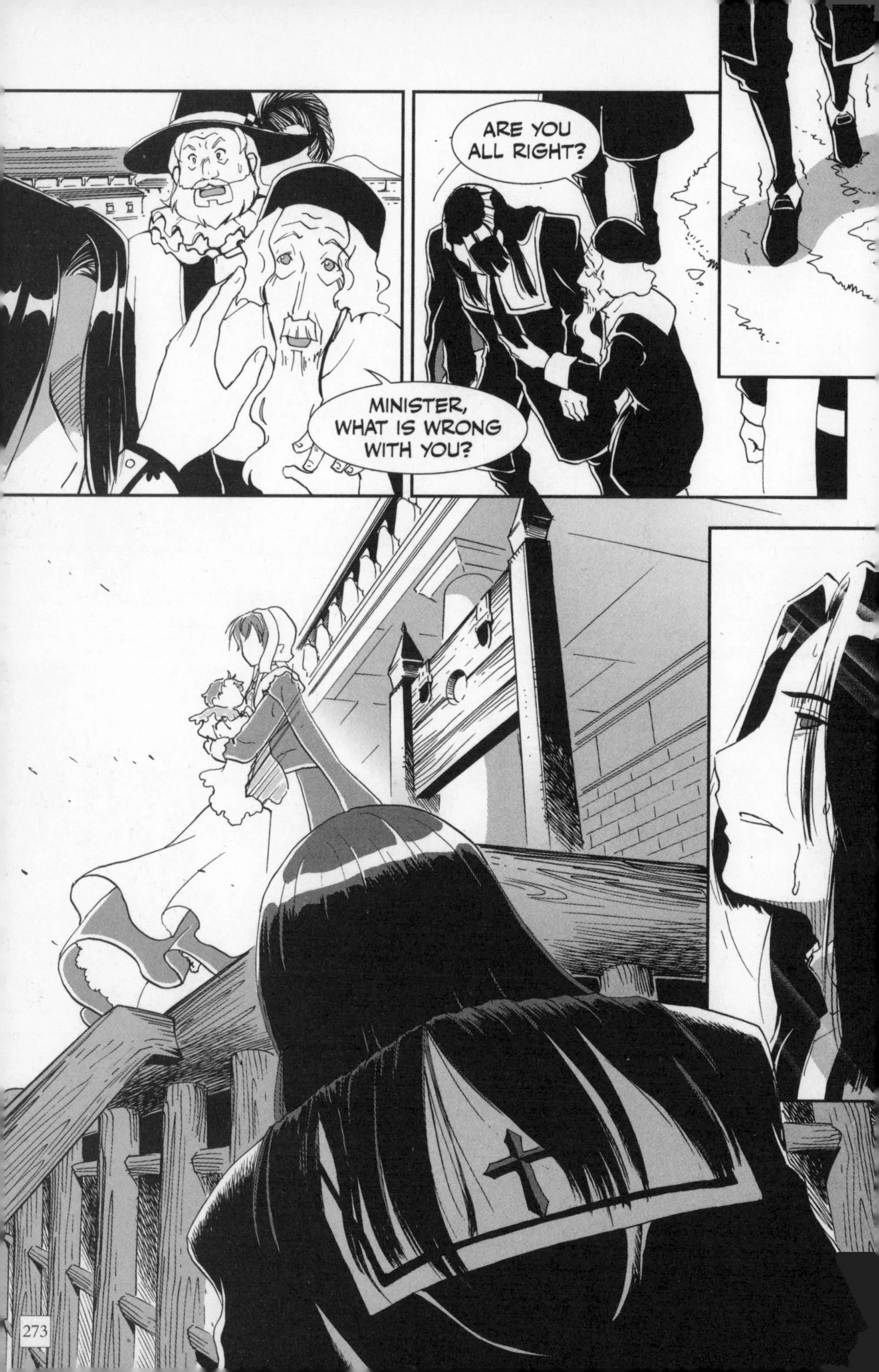
ARE YOU ALL RIGHT?
MINISTER, WHAT IS WRONG WITH YOU?

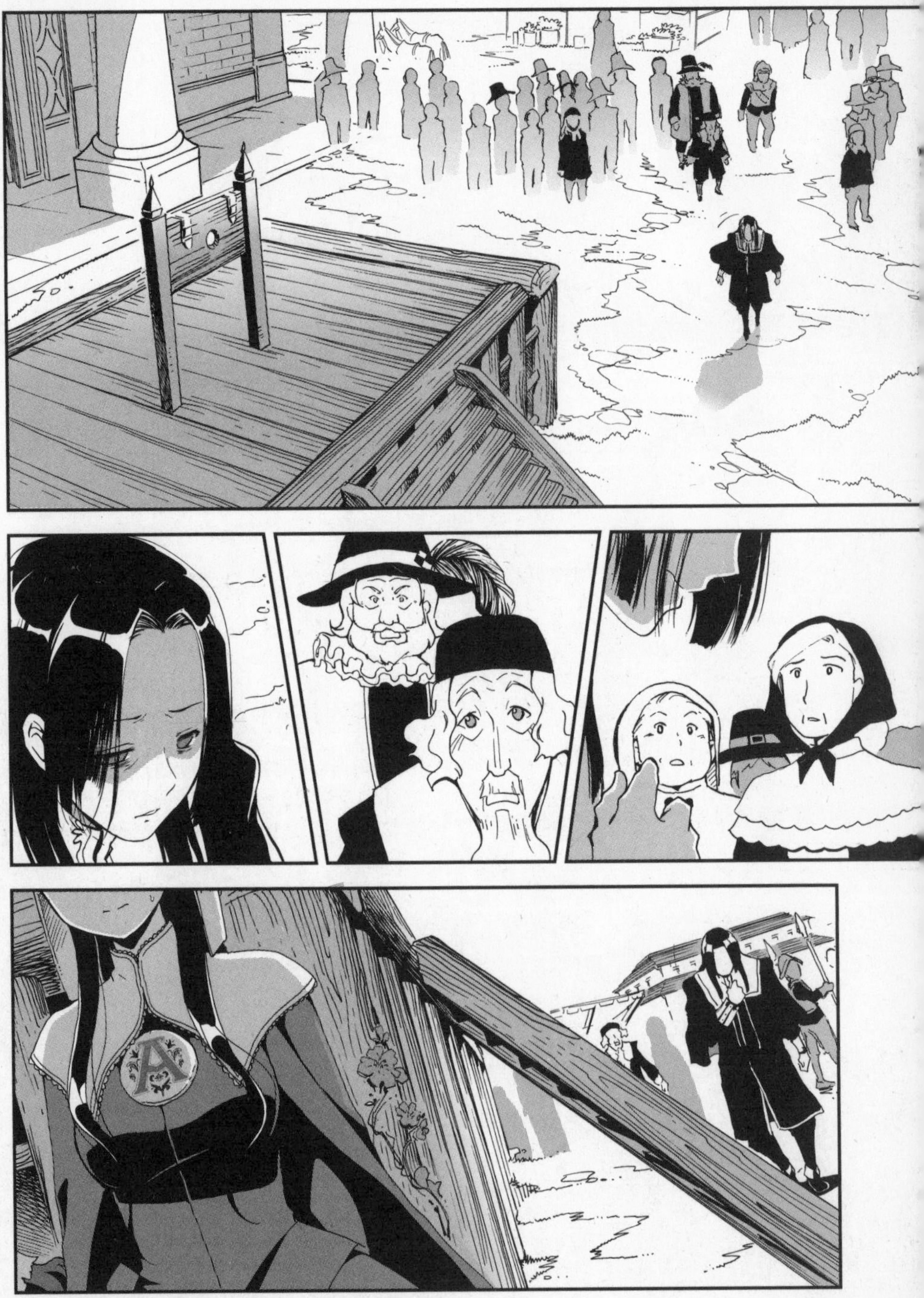

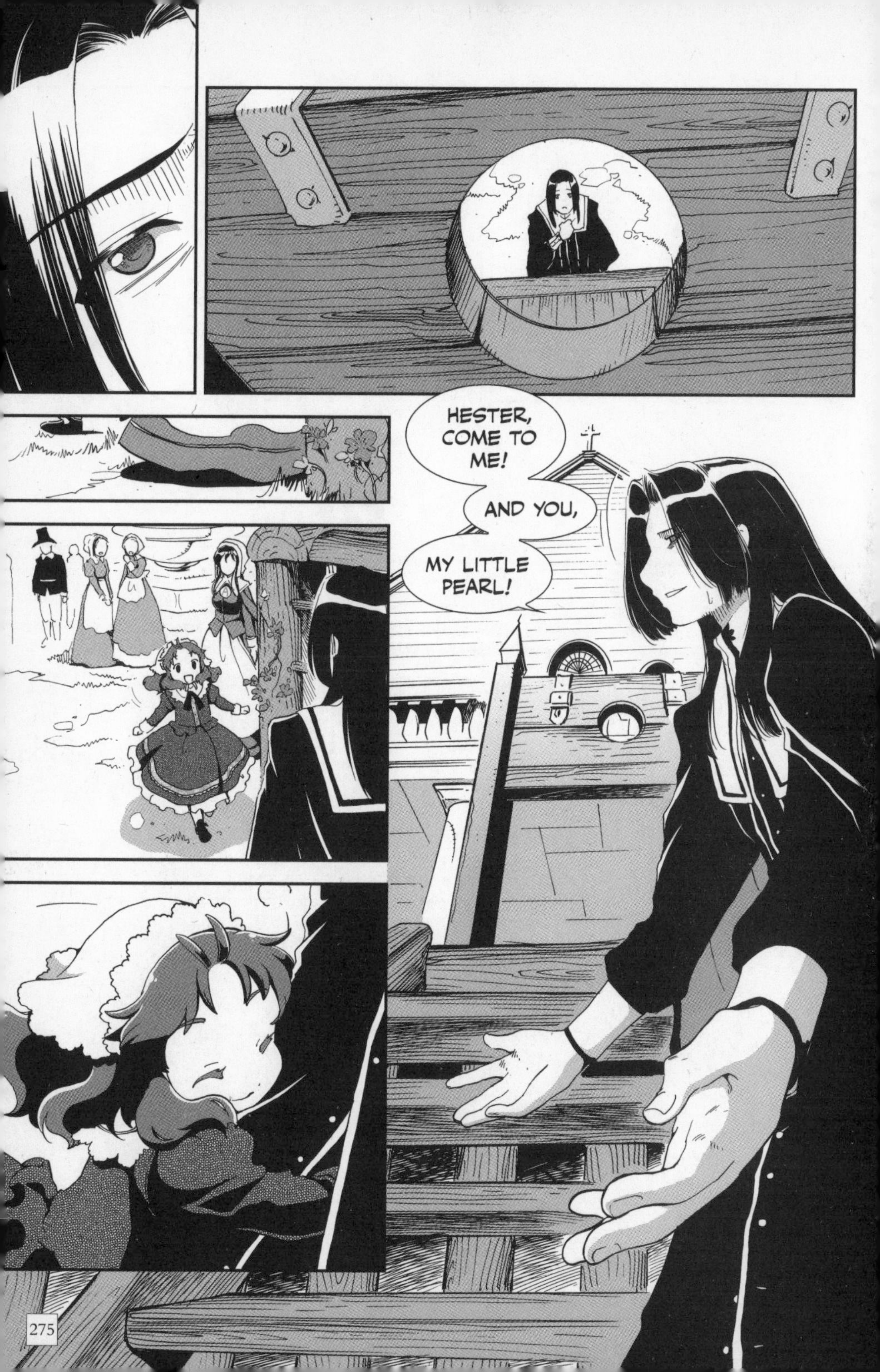
HESTER, COME TO ME!
AND YOU,
MY LITTLE PEARL!

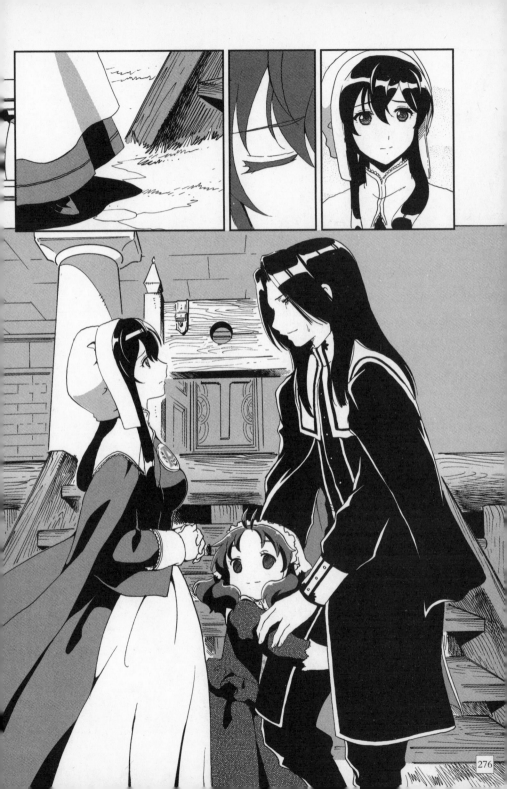

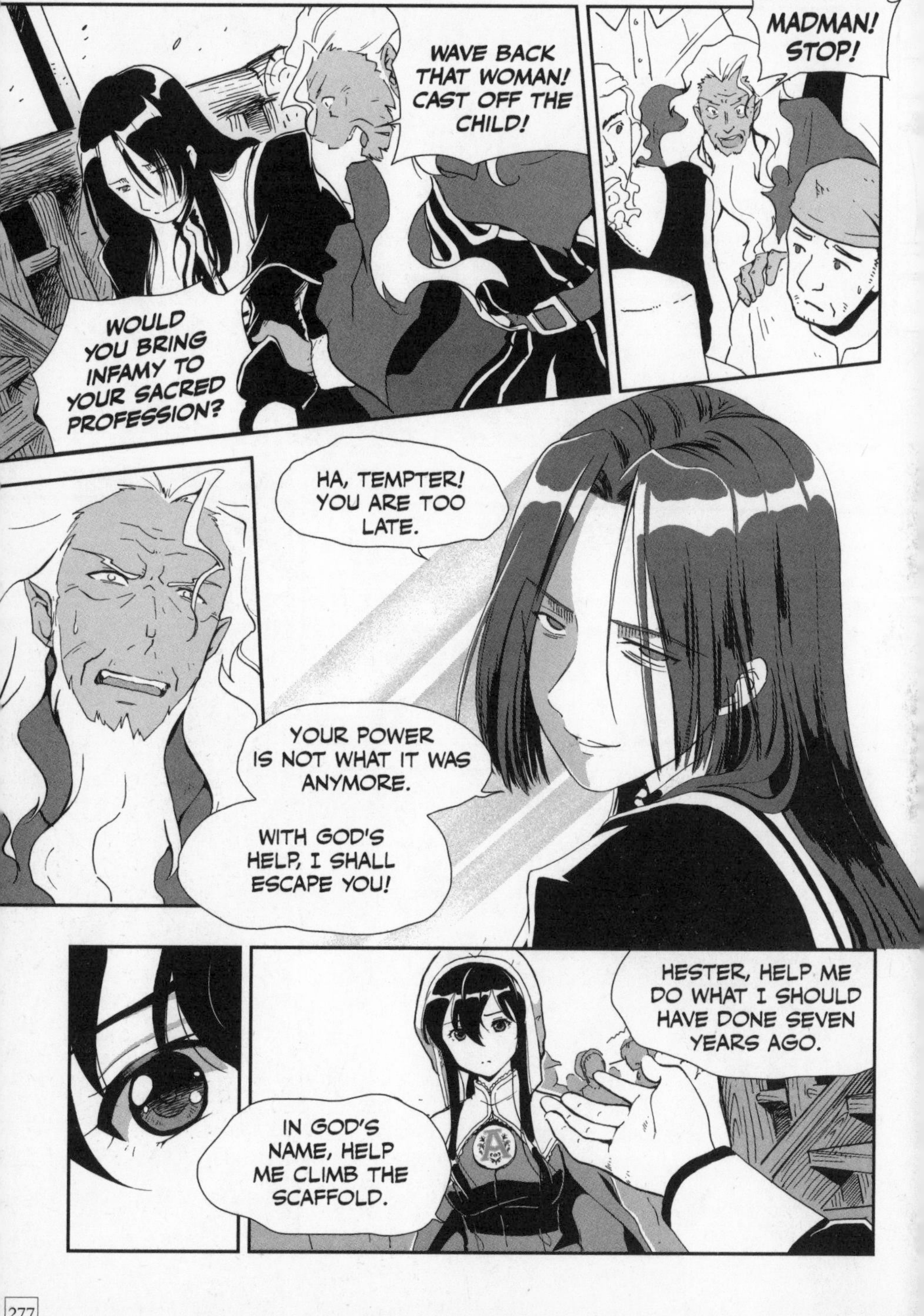
MADMAN! STOP!
WAVE BACK THAT WOMAN! CAST OFF THE CHILD!
WOULD YOU BRING INFAMY TO YOUR SACRED PROFESSION?
HA, TEMPTER! YOU ARE TOO LATE.
YOUR POWER IS NOT WHAT IT WAS ANYMORE.
WITH GOD'S HELP, I SHALL ESCAPE YOU!
HESTER, HELP ME DO WHAT I SHOULD HAVE DONE SEVEN YEARS AGO.
IN GOD'S NAME, HELP ME CLIMB THE SCAFFOLD.

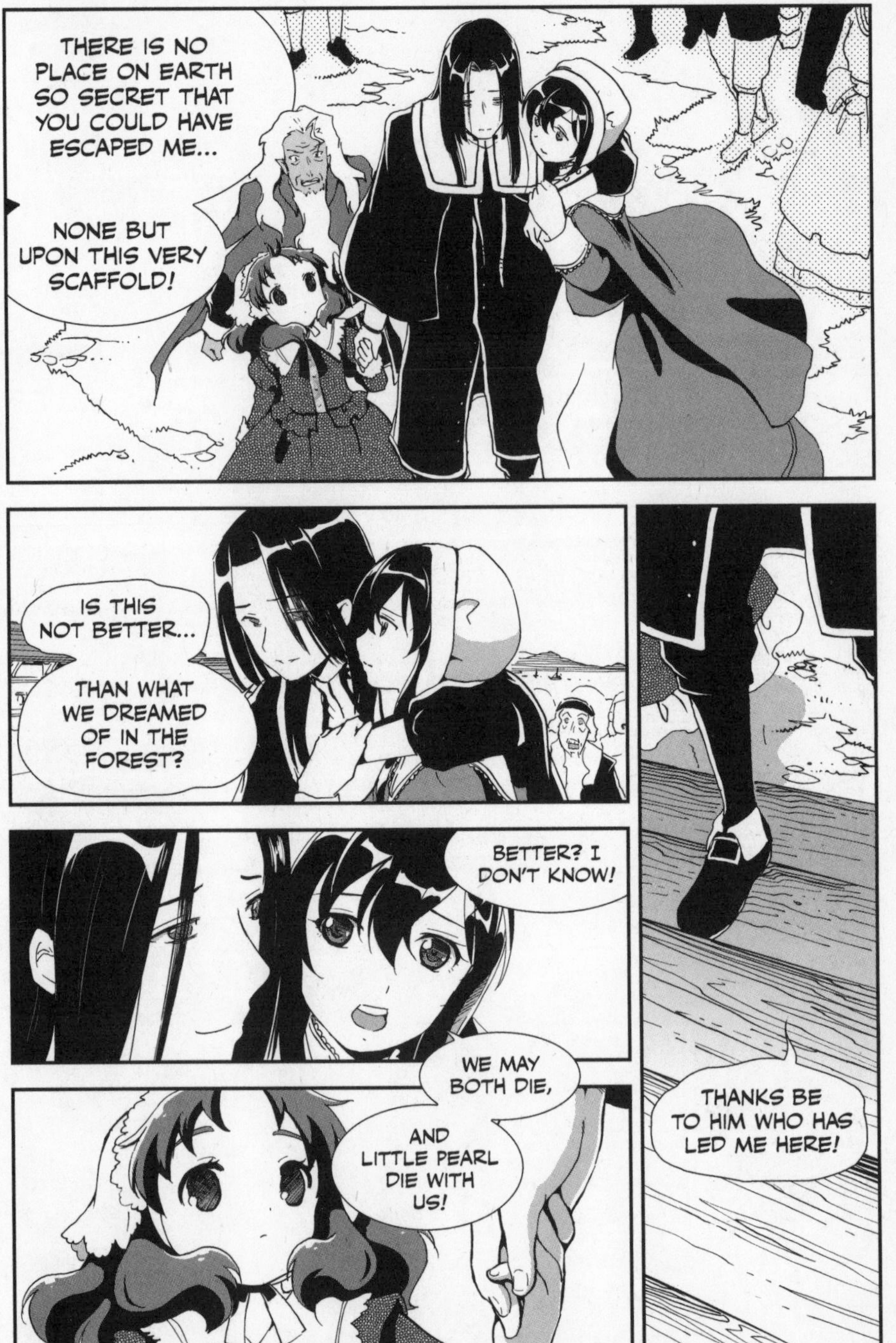
THERE IS NO PLACE ON EARTH SO SECRET THAT YOU COULD HAVE ESCAPED ME...
NONE BUT UPON THIS VERY SCAFFOLD!
THANKS BE TO HIM WHO HAS LED ME HERE!
IS THIS NOT BETTER...
THAN WHAT WE DREAMED OF IN THE FOREST?
BETTER? I DON'T KNOW!
WE MAY BOTH DIE,
AND LITTLE PEARL DIE WITH US!

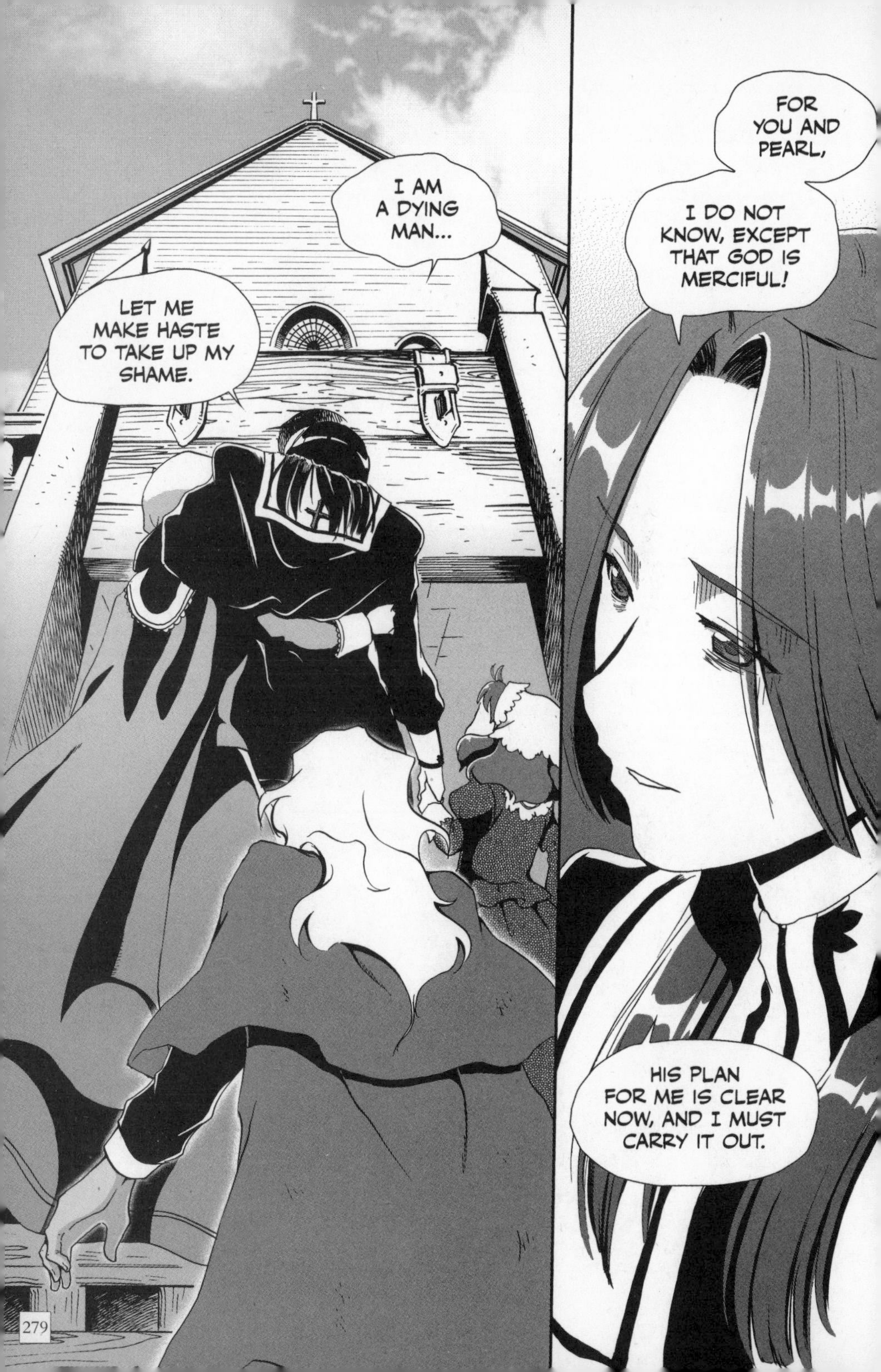
FOR YOU AND PEARL,
I DO NOT KNOW, EXCEPT THAT GOD IS MERCIFUL!
HIS PLAN FOR ME IS CLEAR NOW, AND I MUST CARRY IT OUT.
I AM A DYING MAN...
LET ME MAKE HASTE TO TAKE UP MY SHAME.

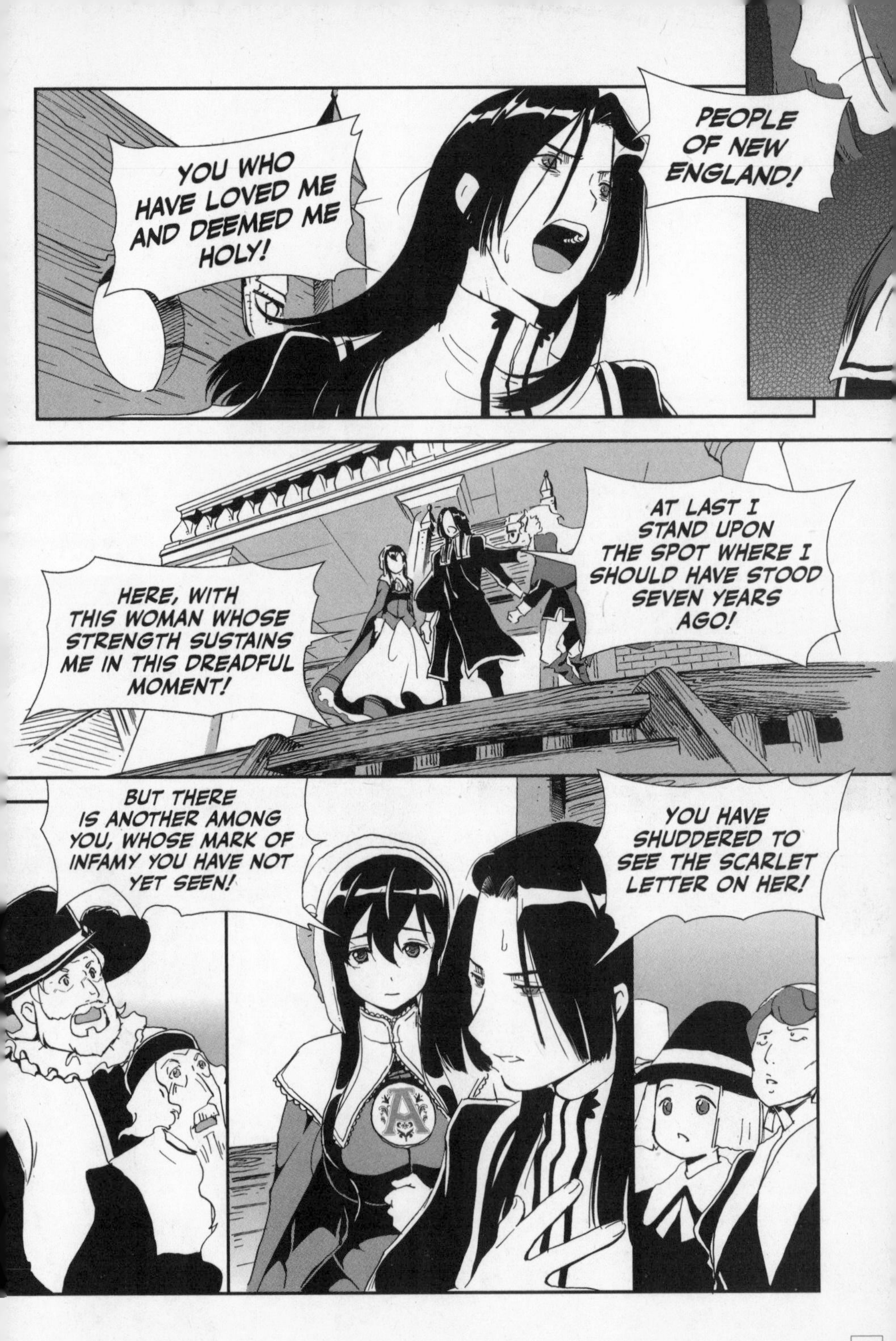
PEOPLE OF NEW ENGLAND!
YOU WHO HAVE LOVED ME AND DEEMED ME HOLY!
AT LAST I STAND UPON THE SPOT WHERE I SHOULD HAVE STOOD SEVEN YEARS AGO!
HERE, WITH THIS WOMAN WHOSE STRENGTH SUSTAINS ME IN THIS DREADFUL MOMENT!
YOU HAVE SHUDDERED TO SEE THE SCARLET LETTER ON HER!
BUT THERE IS ANOTHER AMONG YOU, WHOSE MARK OF INFAMY YOU HAVE NOT YET SEEN!

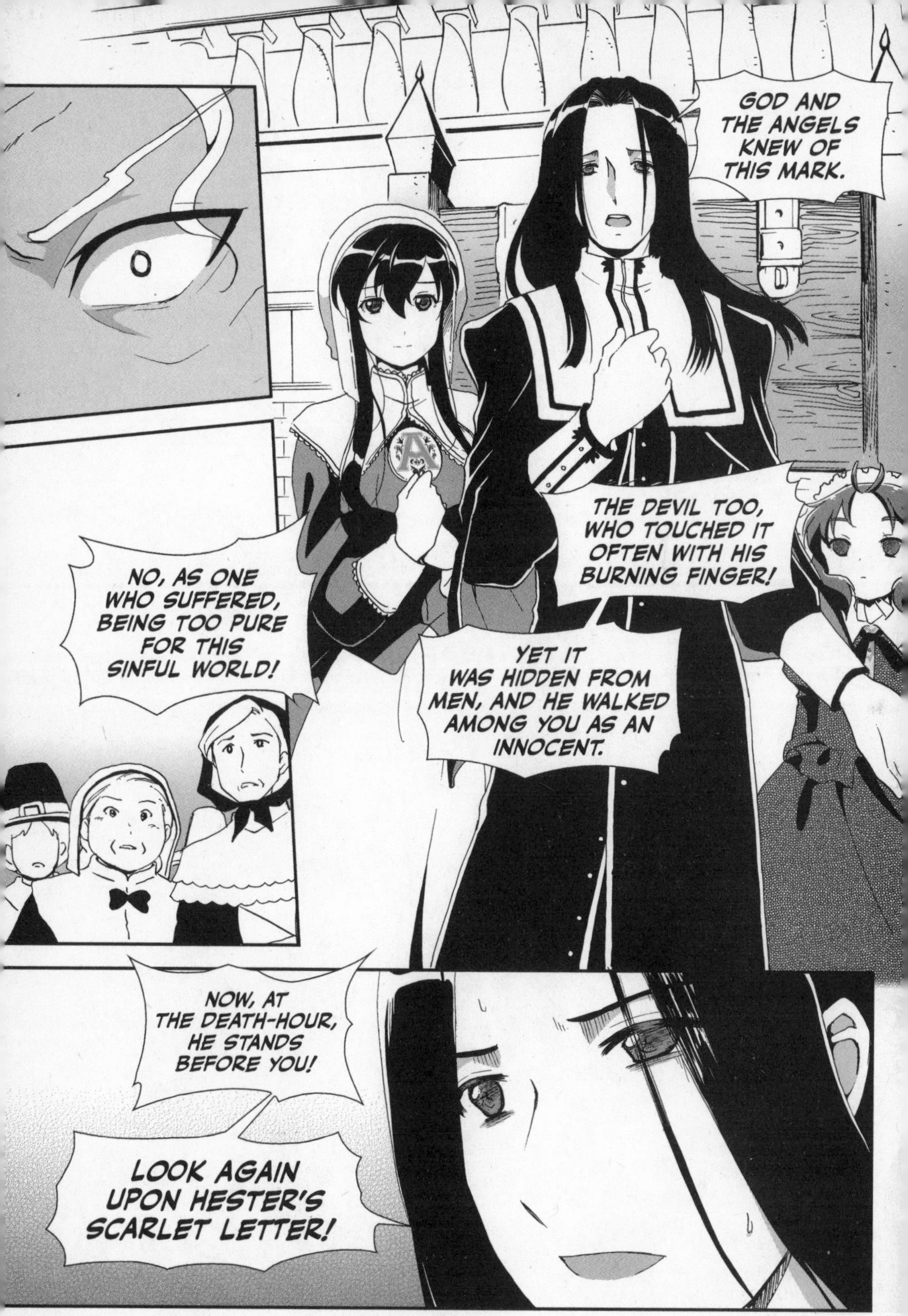
GOD AND THE ANGELS KNEW OF THIS MARK.
THE DEVIL TOO, WHO TOUCHED IT OFTEN WITH HIS BURNING FINGER!
YET IT WAS HIDDEN FROM MEN, AND HE WALKED AMONG YOU AS AN INNOCENT.
NO, AS ONE WHO SUFFERED, BEING TOO PURE FOR THIS SINFUL WORLD!
NOW, AT THE DEATH-HOUR, HE STANDS BEFORE YOU!
LOOK AGAIN UPON HESTER'S SCARLET LETTER!

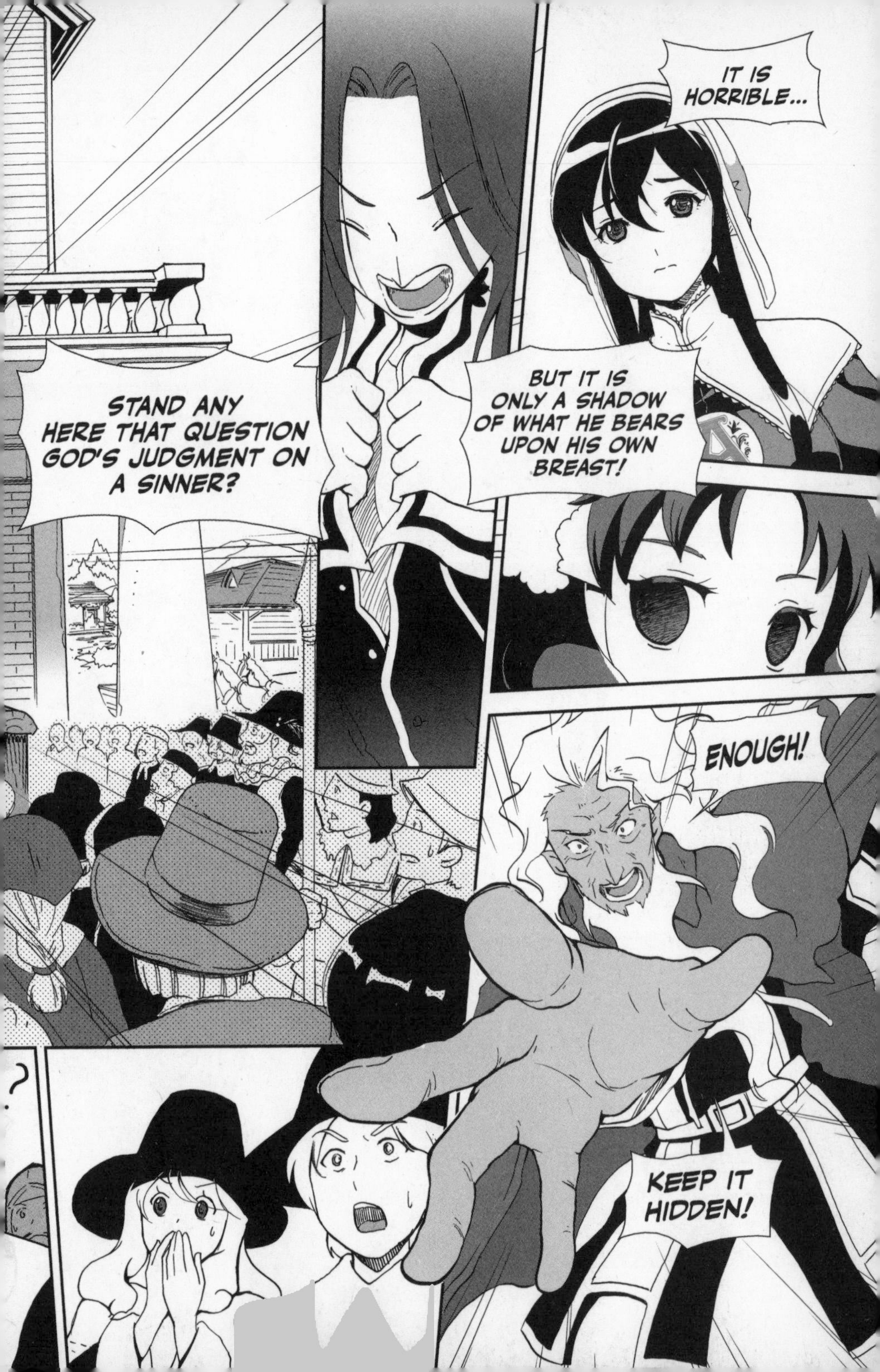
IT IS HORRIBLE...
BUT IT IS ONLY A SHADOW OF WHAT HE BEARS UPON HIS OWN BREAST!
STAND ANY HERE THAT QUESTION GOD'S JUDGMENT ON A SINNER?
ENOUGH!
KEEP IT HIDDEN!
?

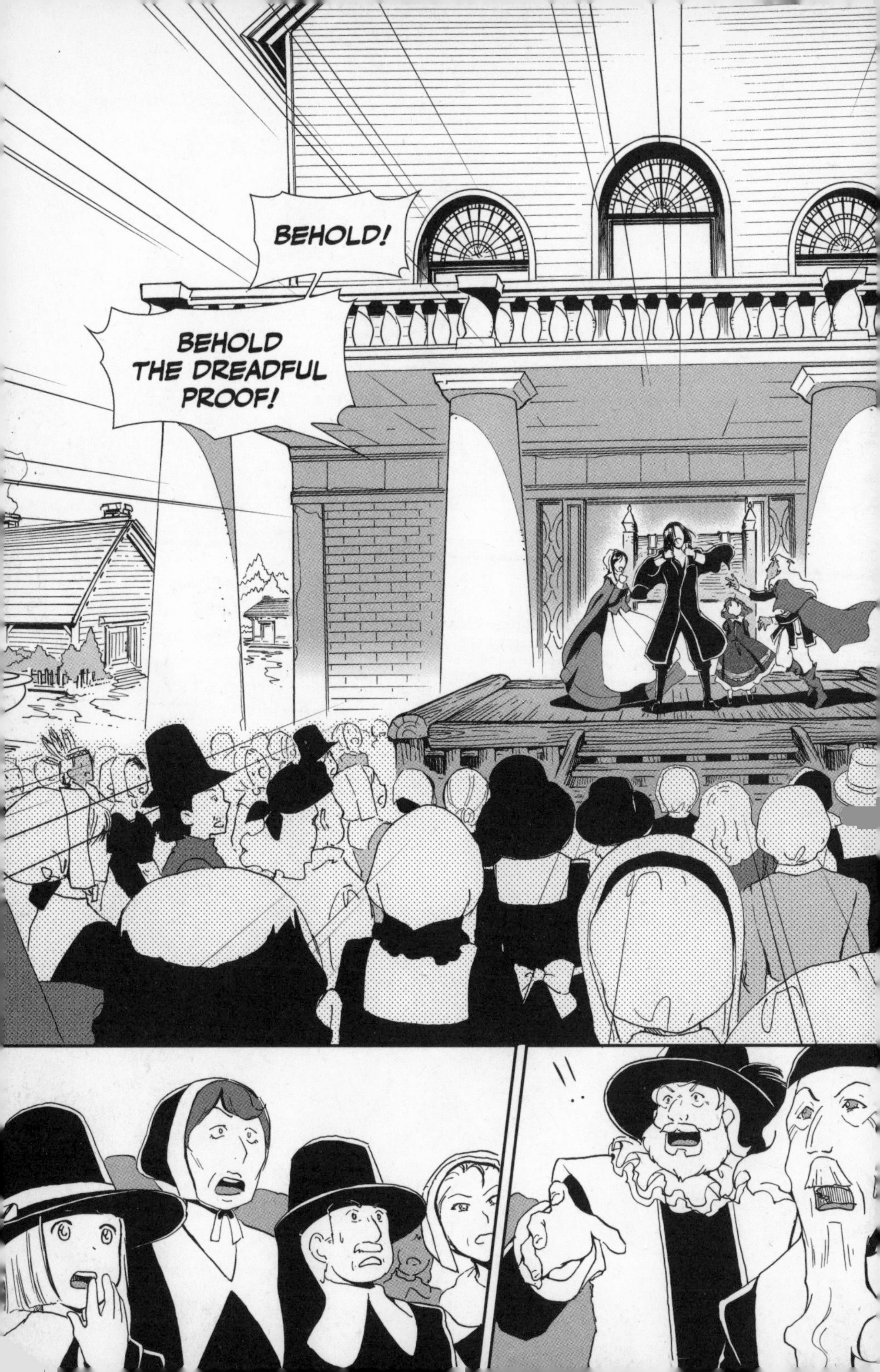
BEHOLD!
BEHOLD THE DREADFUL PROOF!

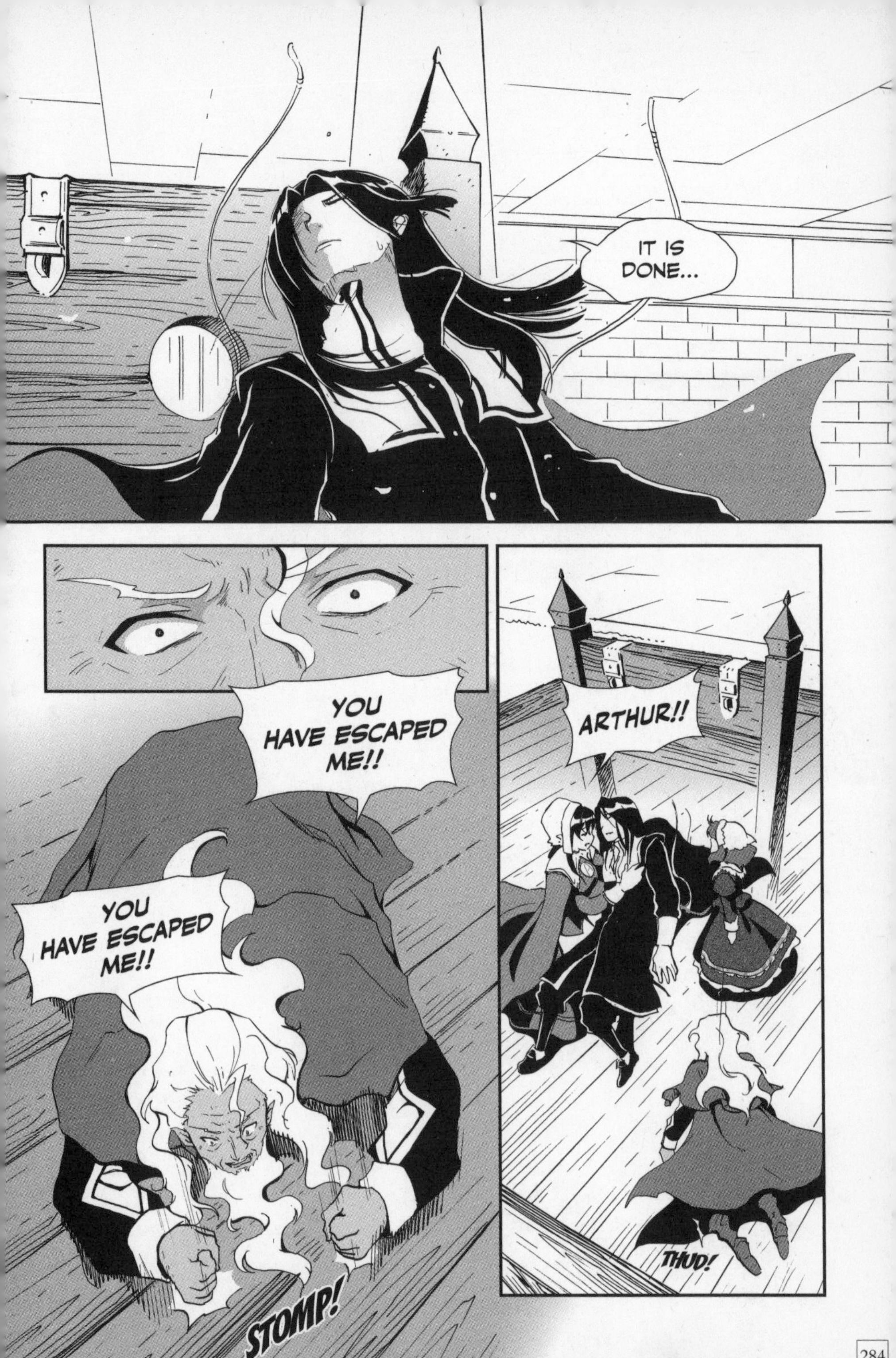
IT IS DONE...
ARTHUR!!
THUD!
YOU HAVE ESCAPED ME!!
YOU HAVE ESCAPED ME!!
STOMP!

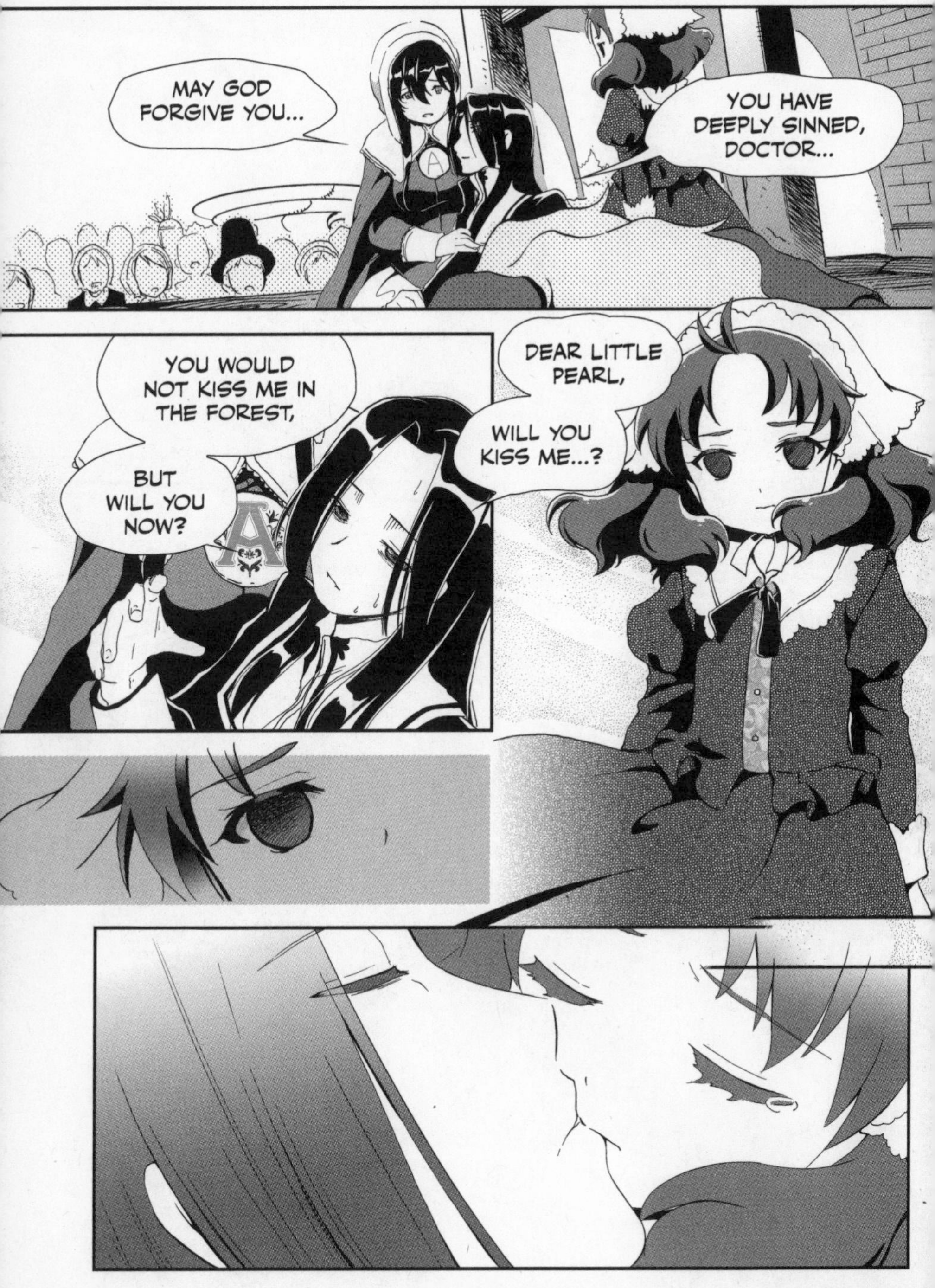
YOU HAVE DEEPLY SINNED, DOCTOR...
MAY GOD FORGIVE YOU...
DEAR LITTLE PEARL,
WILL YOU KISS ME...?
YOU WOULD NOT KISS ME IN THE FOREST,
BUT WILL YOU NOW?

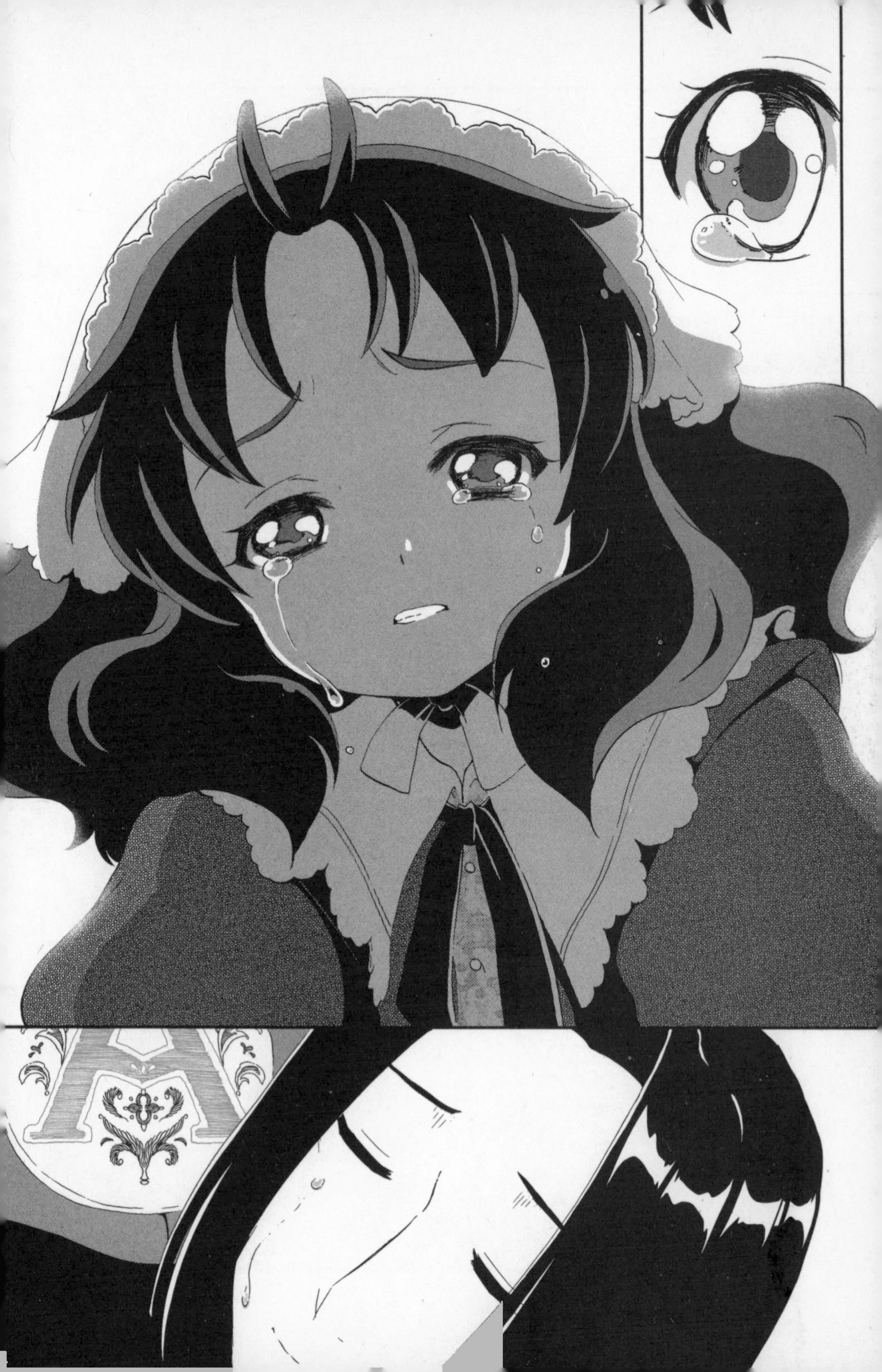

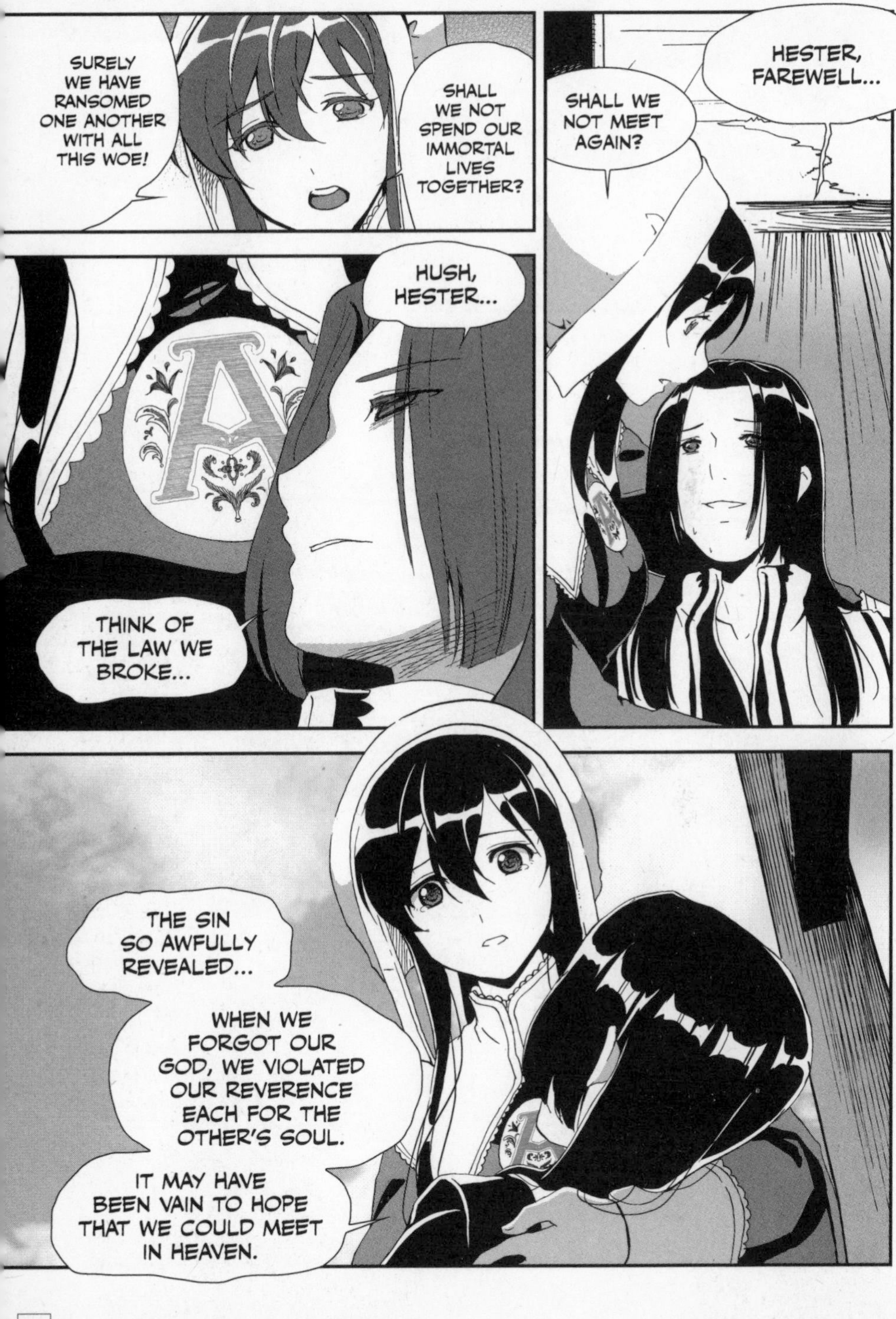
HESTER, FAREWELL...
SHALL WE NOT MEET AGAIN?
SHALL WE NOT SPEND OUR IMMORTAL LIVES TOGETHER?
SURELY WE HAVE RANSOMED ONE ANOTHER WITH ALL THIS WOE!
HUSH, HESTER...
THINK OF THE LAW WE BROKE...
THE SIN SO AWFULLY REVEALED...
WHEN WE FORGOT OUR GOD, WE VIOLATED OUR REVERENCE EACH FOR THE OTHER'S SOUL.
IT MAY HAVE BEEN VAIN TO HOPE THAT WE COULD MEET IN HEAVEN.

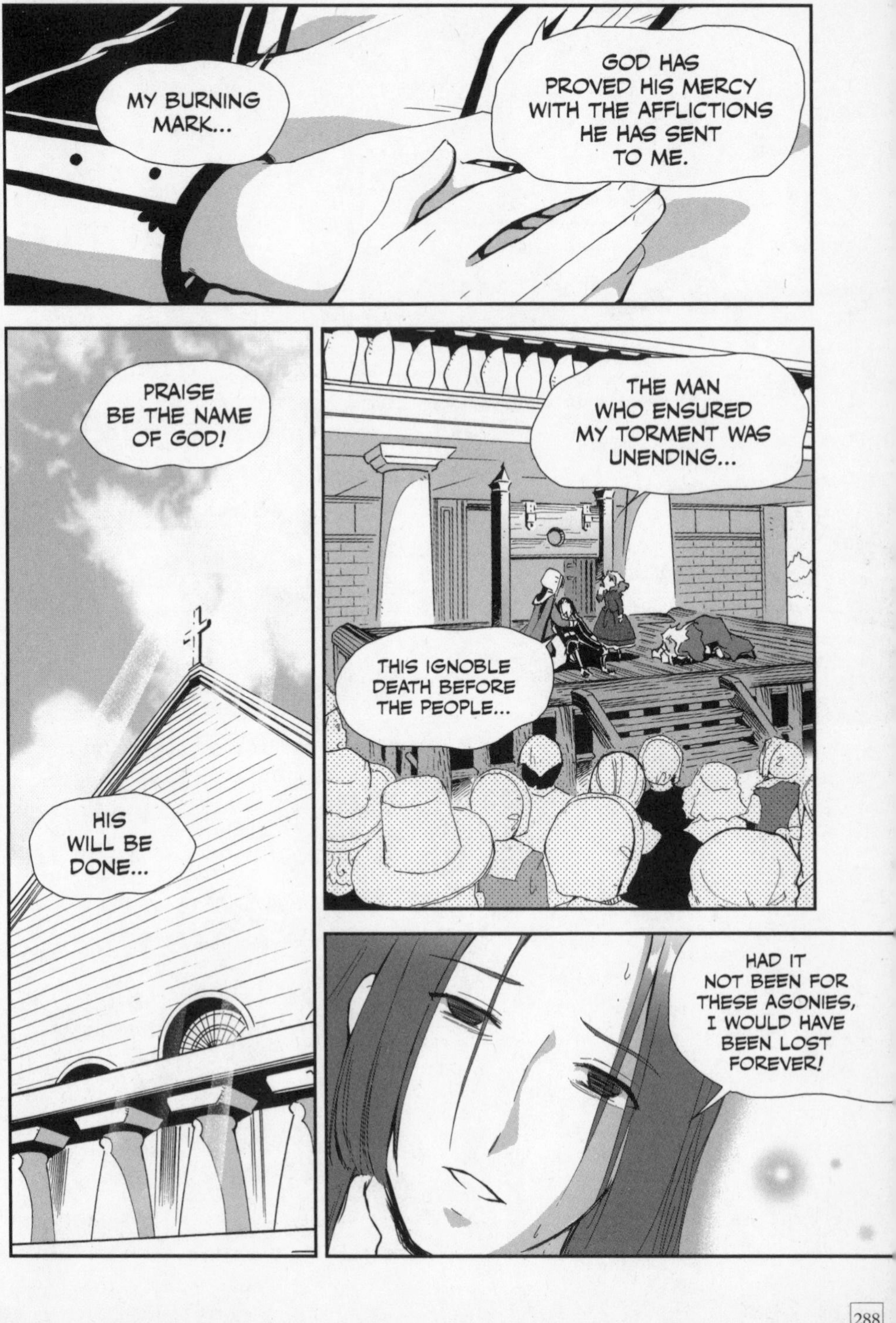
GOD HAS PROVED HIS MERCY WITH THE AFFLICTIONS HE HAS SENT TO ME.
MY BURNING MARK...
THE MAN WHO ENSURED MY TORMENT WAS UNENDING...
THIS IGNOBLE DEATH BEFORE THE PEOPLE...
HAD IT NOT BEEN FOR THESE AGONIES, I WOULD HAVE BEEN LOST FOREVER!
PRAISE BE THE NAME OF GOD!
HIS WILL BE DONE...

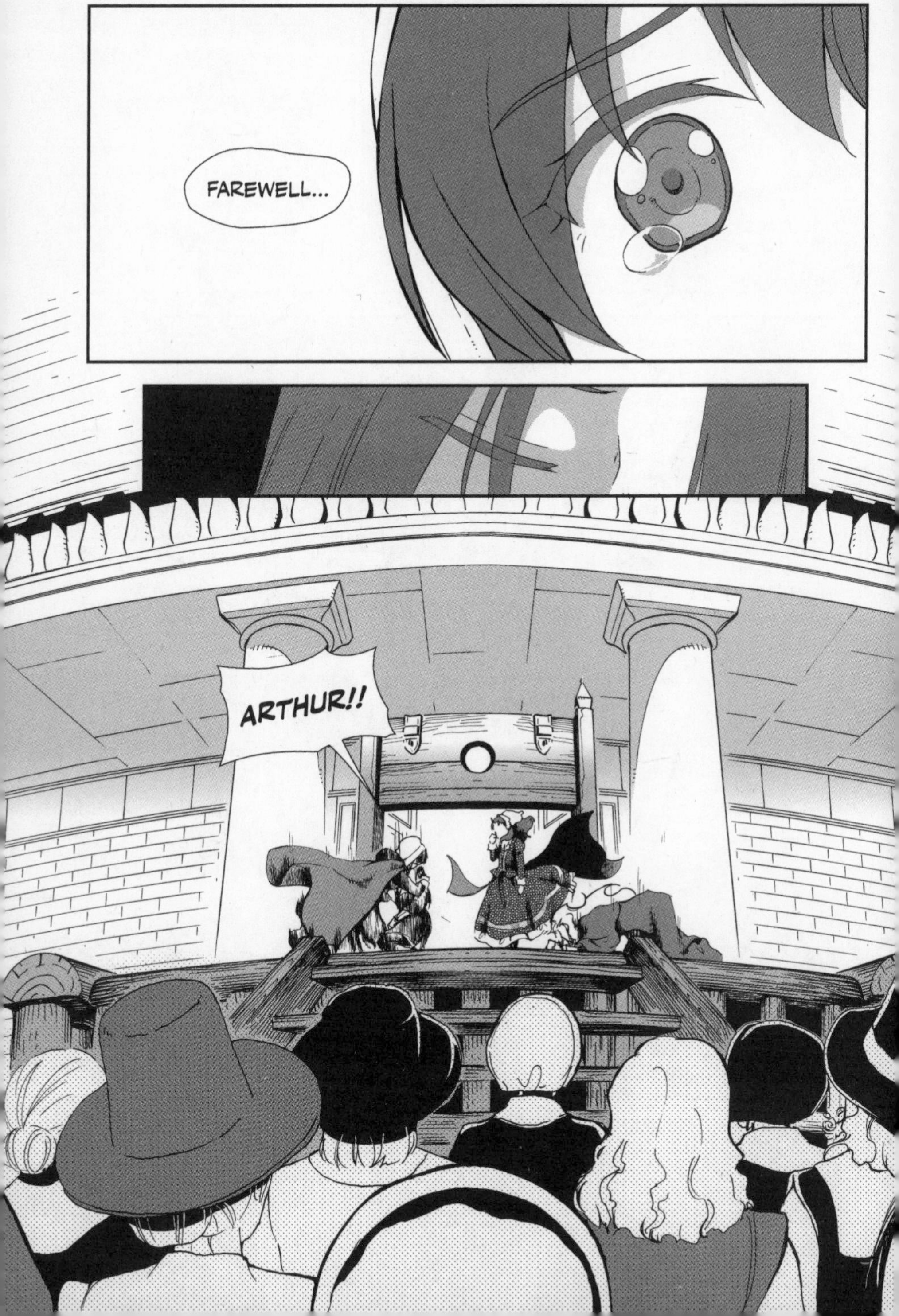
FAREWELL...
ARTHUR!!

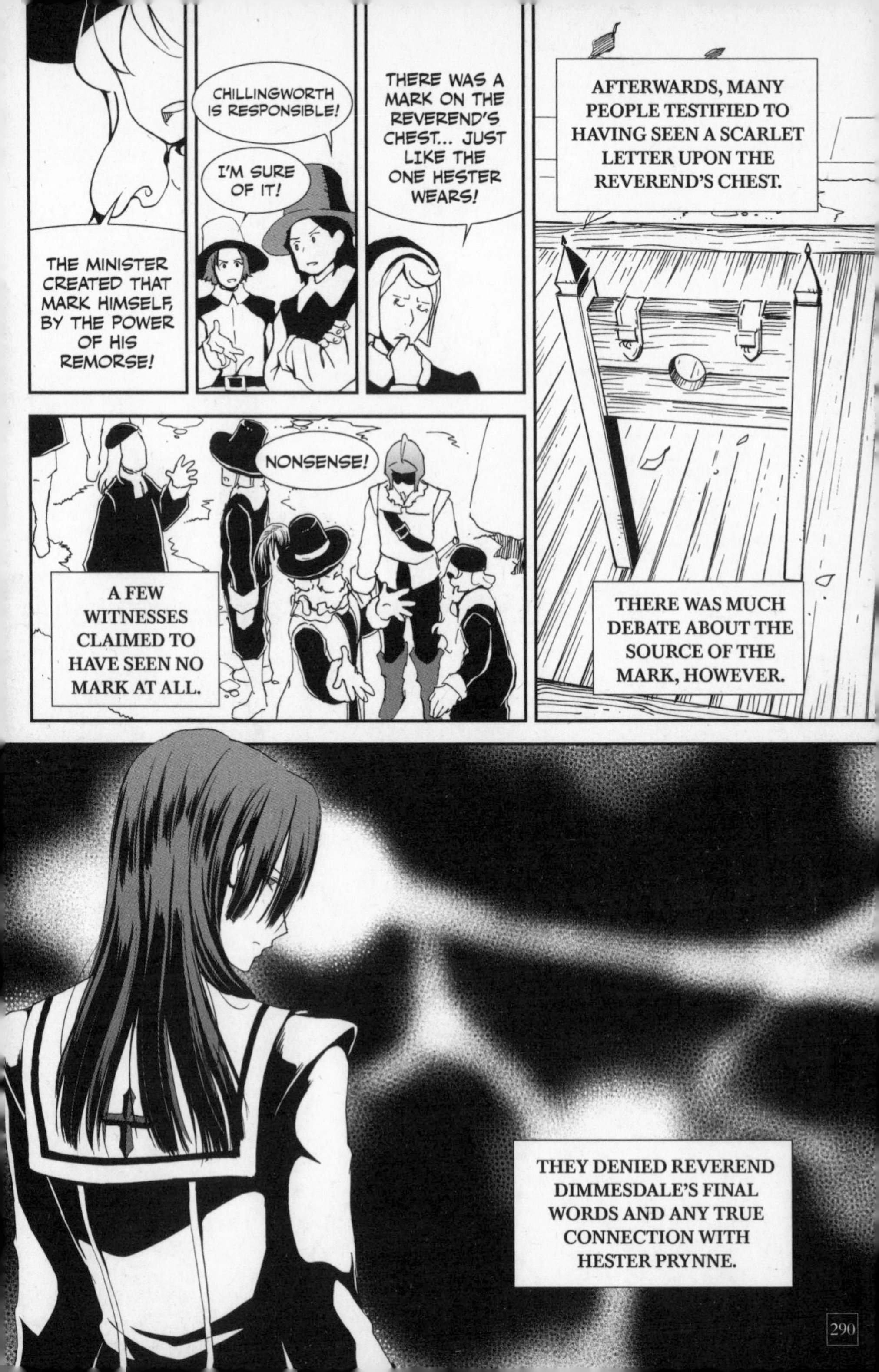
AFTERWARDS, MANY PEOPLE TESTIFIED TO HAVING SEEN A SCARLET LETTER UPON THE REVEREND'S CHEST.
THERE WAS MUCH DEBATE ABOUT THE SOURCE OF THE MARK, HOWEVER.
THERE WAS A MARK ON THE REVEREND'S CHEST... JUST LIKE THE ONE HESTER WEARS!
CHILLINGWORTH IS RESPONSIBLE!
I'M SURE OF IT!
THE MINISTER CREATED THAT MARK HIMSELF, BY THE POWER OF HIS REMORSE!
NONSENSE!
A FEW WITNESSES CLAIMED TO HAVE SEEN NO MARK AT ALL.
THEY DENIED REVEREND DIMMESDALE'S FINAL WORDS AND ANY TRUE CONNECTION WITH HESTER PRYNNE.

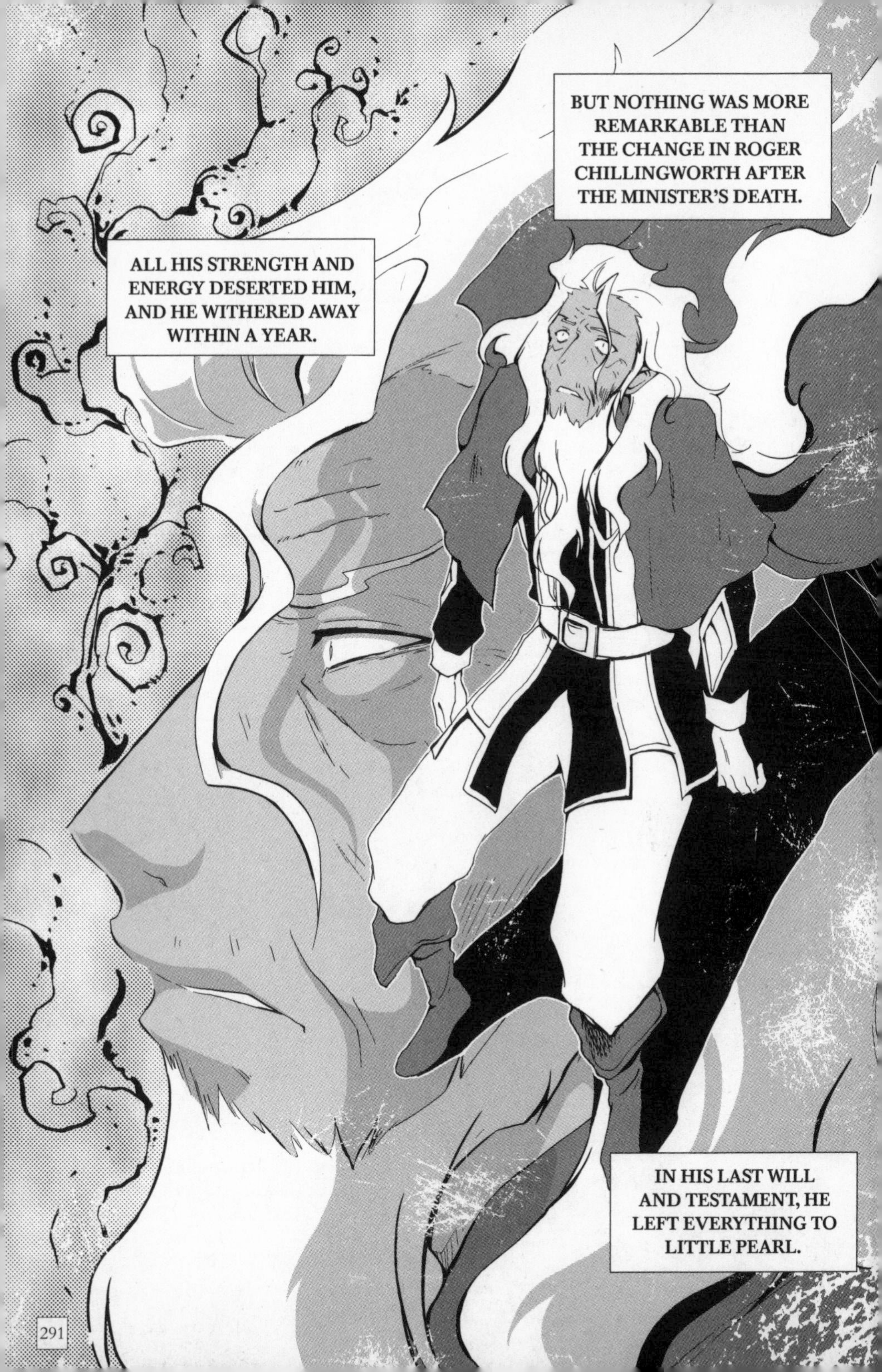
BUT NOTHING WAS MORE REMARKABLE THAN THE CHANGE IN ROGER CHILLINGWORTH AFTER THE MINISTER'S DEATH.
ALL HIS STRENGTH AND ENERGY DESERTED HIM, AND HE WITHERED AWAY WITHIN A YEAR.
IN HIS LAST WILL AND TESTAMENT, HE LEFT EVERYTHING TO LITTLE PEARL.

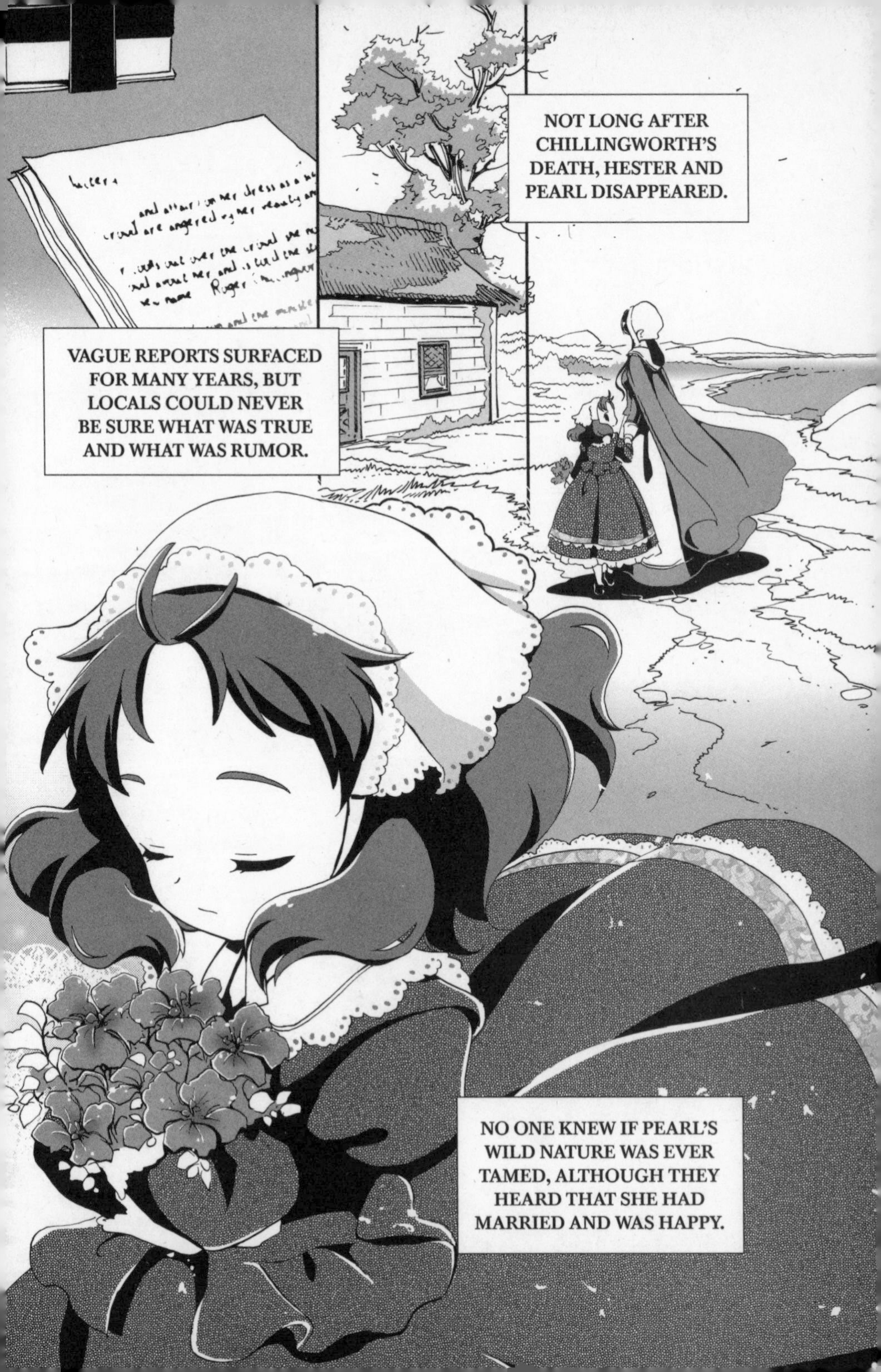
NOT LONG AFTER CHILLINGWORTH'S DEATH, HESTER AND PEARL DISAPPEARED.
VAGUE REPORTS SURFACED FOR MANY YEARS, BUT LOCALS COULD NEVER BE SURE WHAT WAS TRUE AND WHAT WAS RUMOR.
NO ONE KNEW IF PEARL'S WILD NATURE WAS EVER TAMED, ALTHOUGH THEY HEARD THAT SHE HAD MARRIED AND WAS HAPPY.

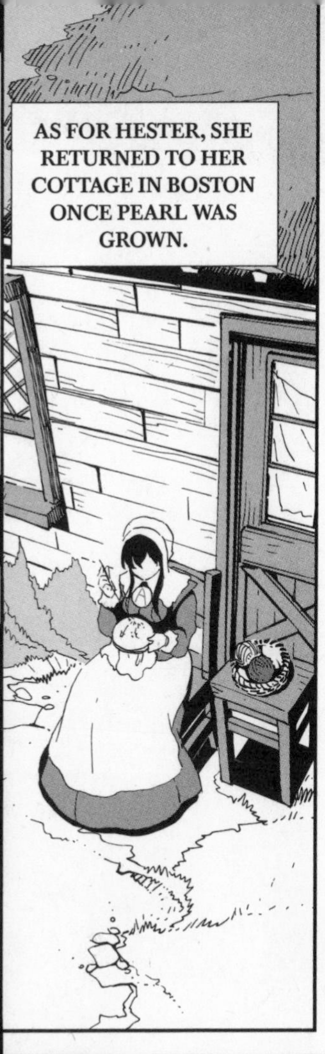
AS FOR HESTER, SHE RETURNED TO HER COTTAGE IN BOSTON ONCE PEARL WAS GROWN.

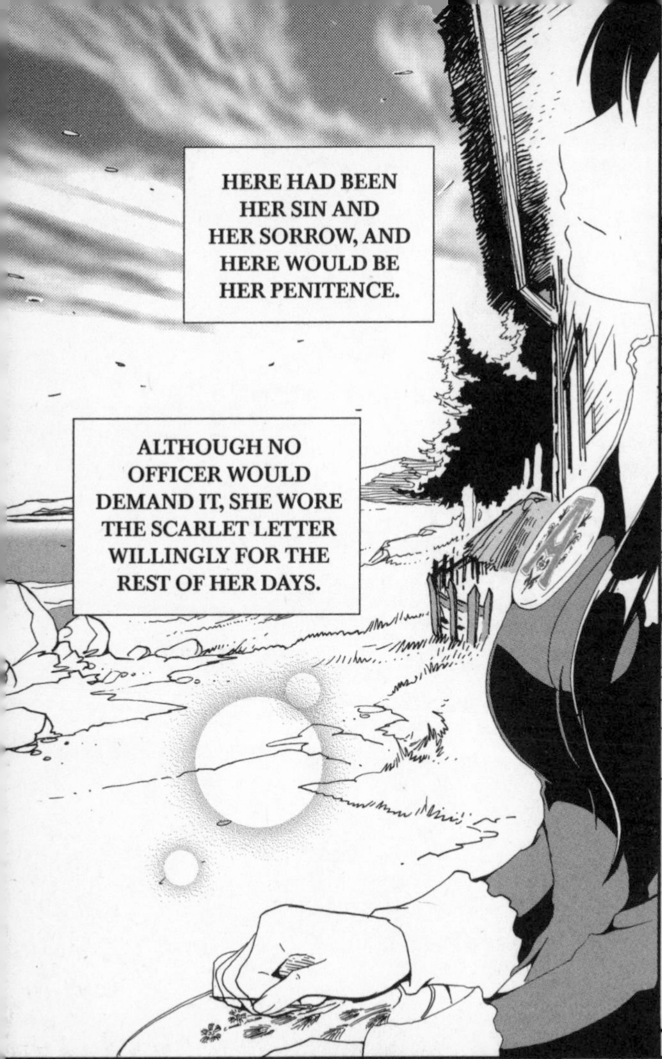
HERE HAD BEEN HER SIN AND HER SORROW, AND HERE WOULD BE HER PENITENCE.
ALTHOUGH NO OFFICER WOULD DEMAND IT, SHE WORE THE SCARLET LETTER WILLINGLY FOR THE REST OF HER DAYS.

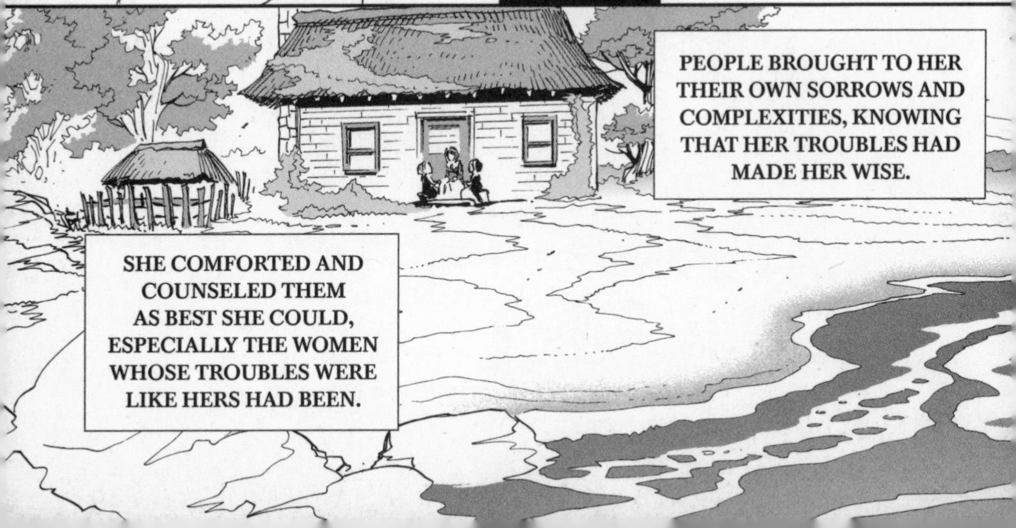
PEOPLE BROUGHT TO HER THEIR OWN SORROWS AND COMPLEXITIES, KNOWING THAT HER TROUBLES HAD MADE HER WISE.
SHE COMFORTED AND COUNSELED THEM AS BEST SHE COULD, ESPECIALLY THE WOMEN WHOSE TROUBLES WERE LIKE HERS HAD BEEN.

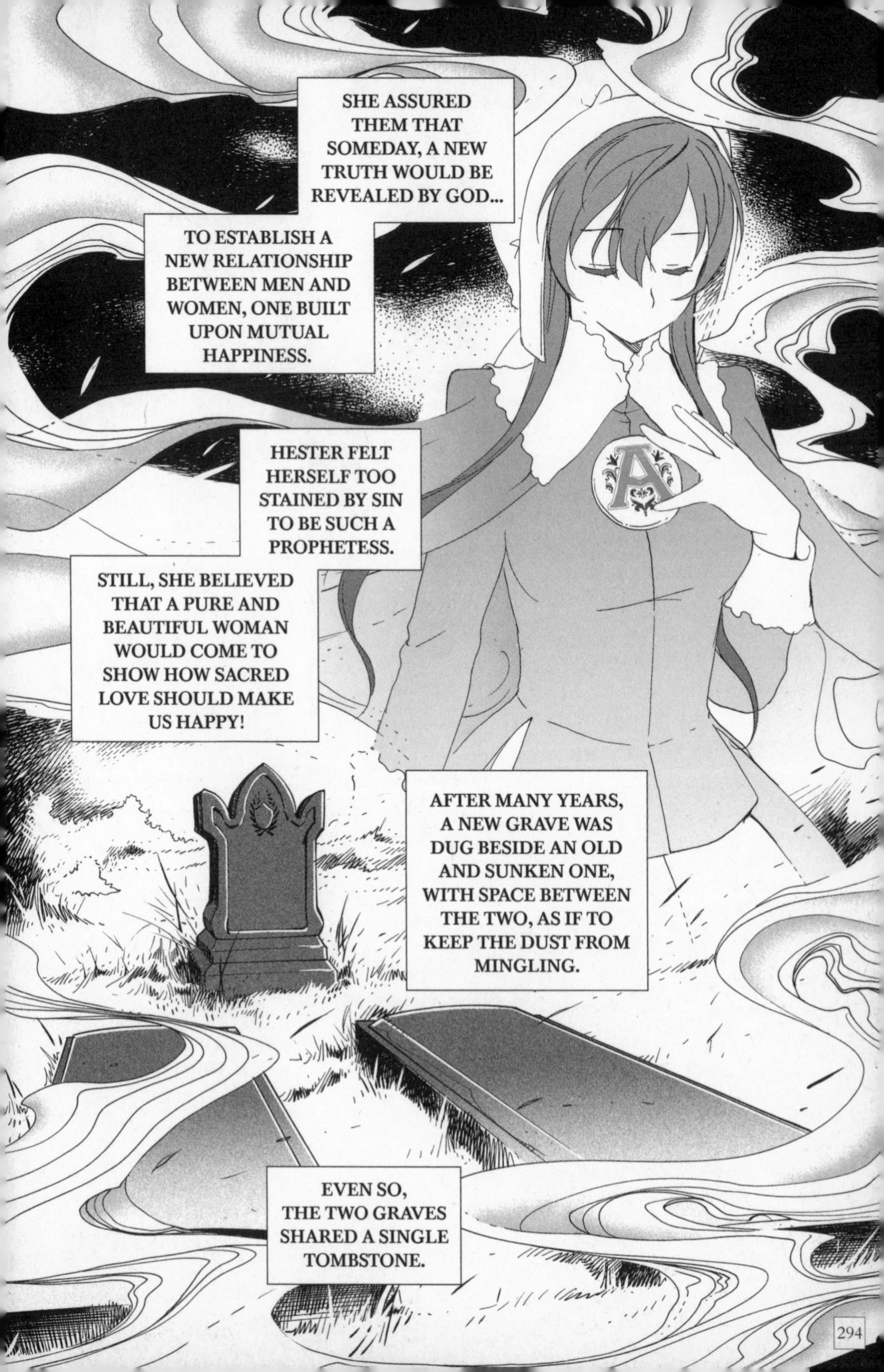
SHE ASSURED THEM THAT SOMEDAY, A NEW TRUTH WOULD BE REVEALED BY GOD...
TO ESTABLISH A NEW RELATIONSHIP BETWEEN MEN AND WOMEN, ONE BUILT UPON MUTUAL HAPPINESS.
HESTER FELT HERSELF TOO STAINED BY SIN TO BE SUCH A PROPHETESS.
STILL, SHE BELIEVED THAT A PURE AND BEAUTIFUL WOMAN WOULD COME TO SHOW HOW SACRED LOVE SHOULD MAKE US HAPPY!
AFTER MANY YEARS, A NEW GRAVE WAS DUG BESIDE AN OLD AND SUNKEN ONE, WITH SPACE BETWEEN THE TWO, AS IF TO KEEP THE DUST FROM MINGLING.
EVEN SO, THE TWO GRAVES SHARED A SINGLE TOMBSTONE.

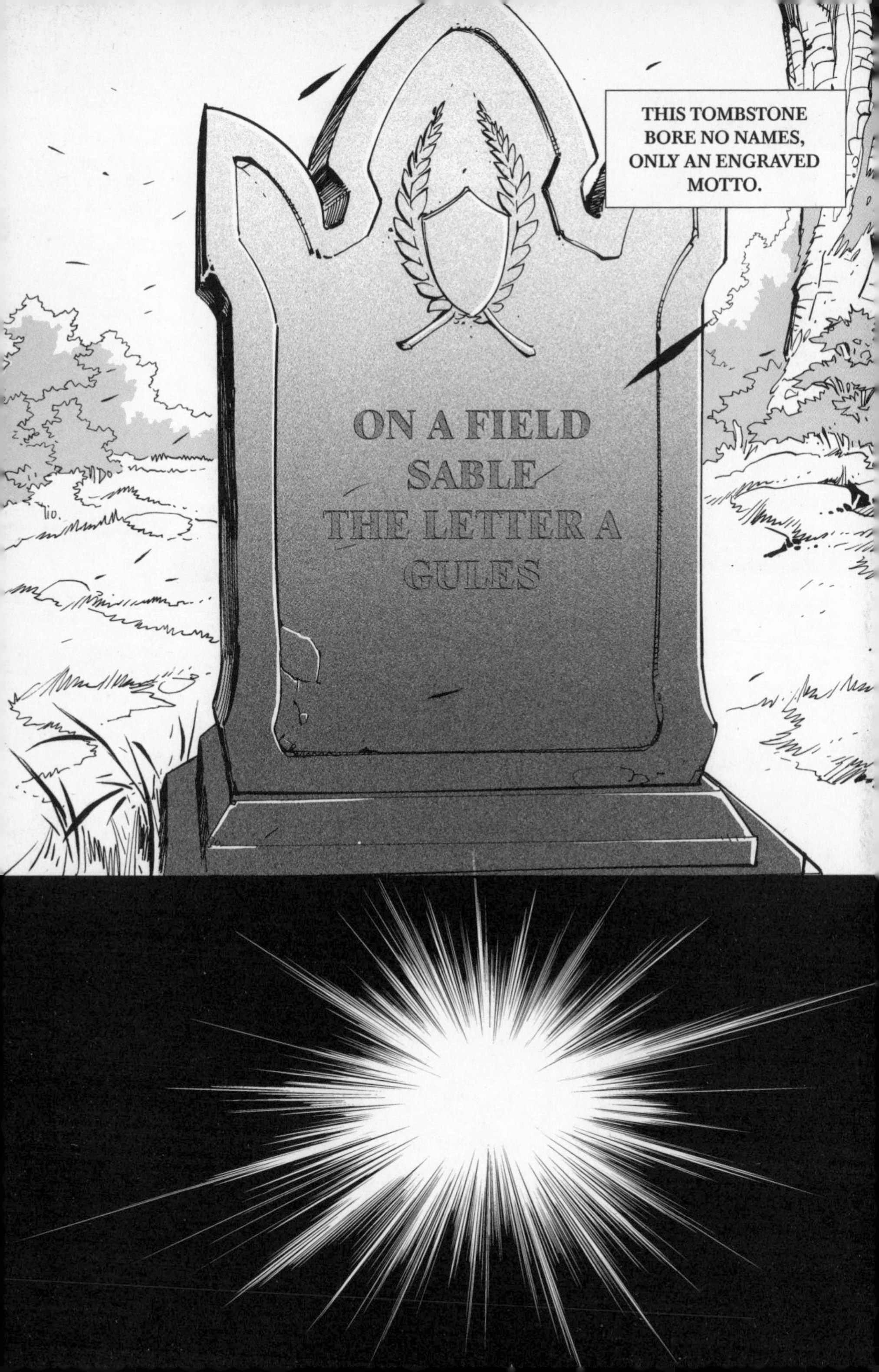
THIS TOMBSTONE BORE NO NAMES, ONLY AN ENGRAVED MOTTO.
ON A FIELD SABLE THE LETTER A GULES

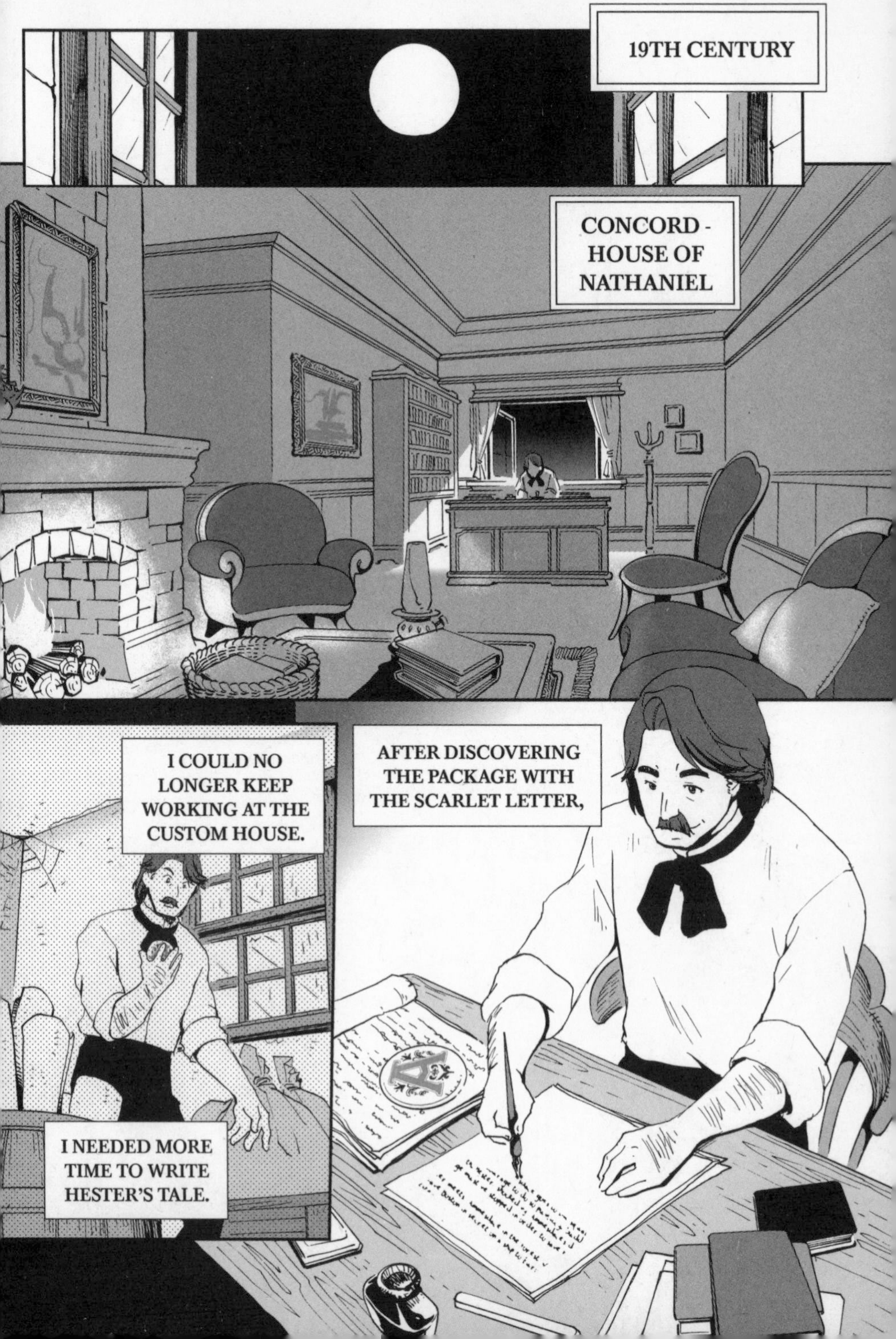

19TH CENTURY
CONCORD - HOUSE OF NATHANIEL
AFTER DISCOVERING THE PACKAGE WITH THE SCARLET LETTER,
I COULD NO LONGER KEEP WORKING AT THE CUSTOM HOUSE.
I NEEDED MORE TIME TO WRITE HESTER'S TALE.

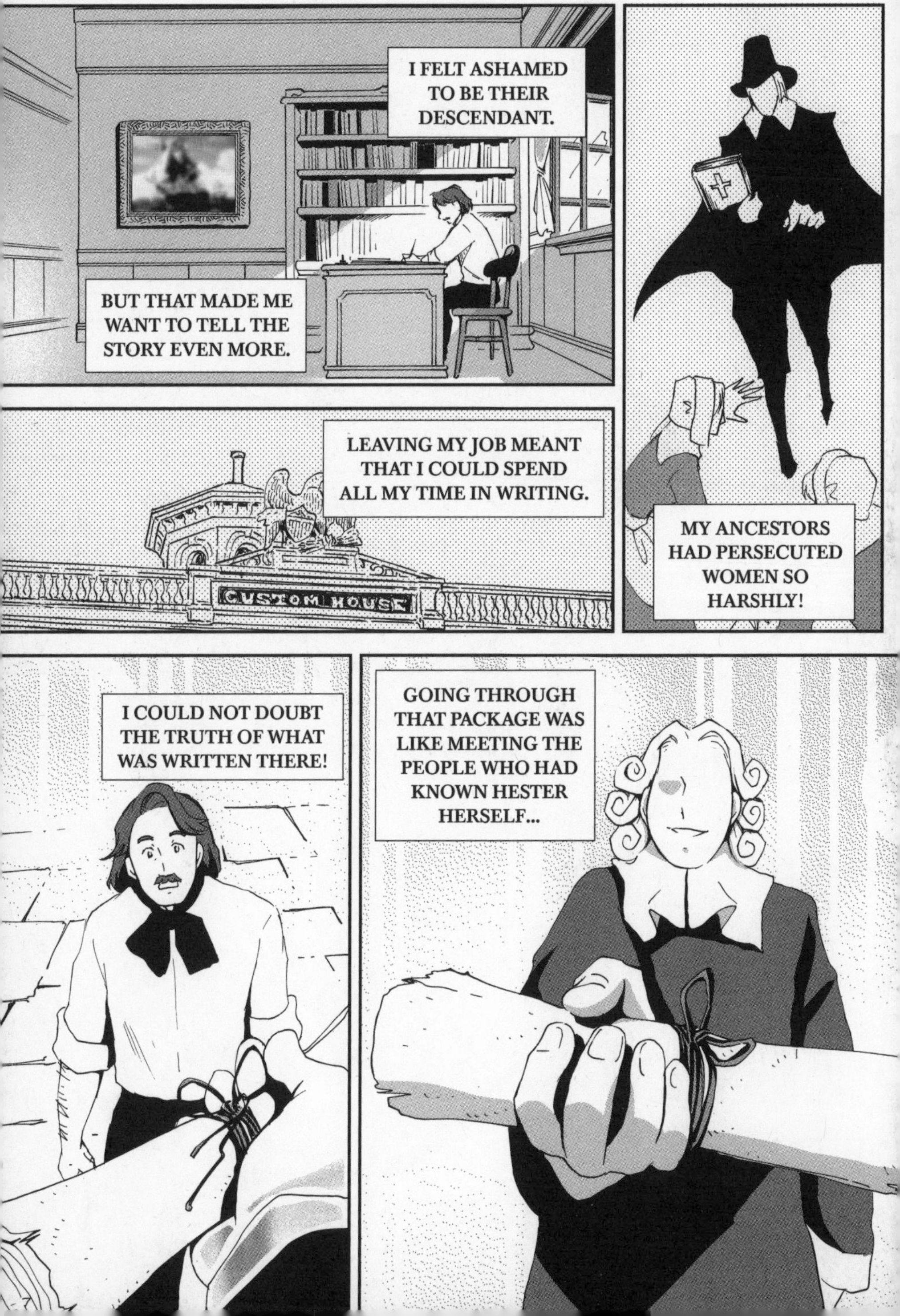
MY ANCESTORS HAD PERSECUTED WOMEN SO HARSHLY!
I FELT ASHAMED TO BE THEIR DESCENDANT.
BUT THAT MADE ME WANT TO TELL THE STORY EVEN MORE.
LEAVING MY JOB MEANT THAT I COULD SPEND ALL MY TIME IN WRITING.
CUSTOM HOUSE
GOING THROUGH THAT PACKAGE WAS LIKE MEETING THE PEOPLE WHO HAD KNOWN HESTER HERSELF...
I COULD NOT DOUBT THE TRUTH OF WHAT WAS WRITTEN THERE!

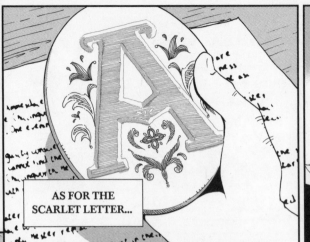

AS FOR THE SCARLET LETTER...

HESTER'S GOOD WORKS AND KINDNESS CHANGED THE MEANING OF THAT MARK DURING HER LIFETIME.

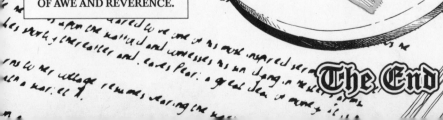

NO LONGER WAS IT SOMETHING TO MOCK OR FEAR, BUT A SYMBOL OF AWE AND REVERENCE.

The End

About the Author and Artist

Crystal S. Chan
(aka Crystal Silvermoon)

SunNeko Lee

Crystal has won an Award for Teen Literature and earned a degree in language and literature. She was a professional screenplay writer for TV drama before working as an adapter for the Manga Classics series. She accepts the challenge because of her love in literature and comic. Her background allows her to always find the right balance between preserving the depth of the original piece while keeping up with the taste of the younger generation.

Crystal is a big fan of Sailor Moon. She loves it so much that she once made her alias as Crystal Silvermoon to pay tribute to the author.

SunNeko is an amphibian who thrives in both comic and animation. She debuts as a comic strip artist for magazine before moving on to become a character designer and storyboard artist. SunNeko joins the Manga Classics project to re-live her passion in comic.

SunNeko is obsessed with cats, glasses, and anything related to the maid culture. Bringing joy to people with her works is what's been driving her to keep moving forward each day. Lee picks her alias because she loves the warmth of the Sun and the elegance of cats (Neko is cat in Japanese)

Metaphors:

Metaphors are another important characteristic of the original book, but the meanings behind them are not easy to understand. One of the biggest challenges I faced was presenting the book's metaphors such that readers would be able to figure them out. Mainly, there are three cases in the book that I would like to specifically point out.

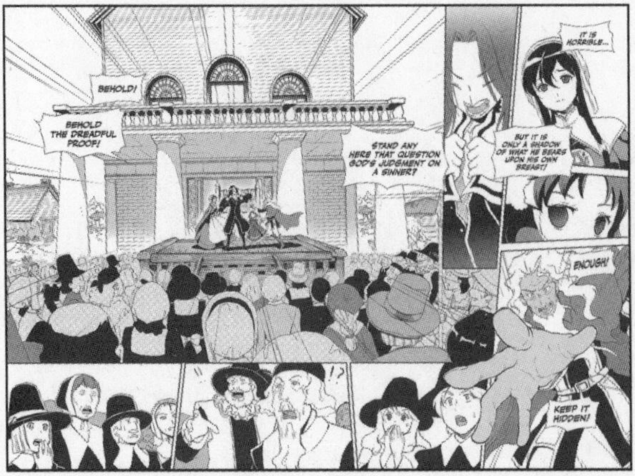
IT IS HORRIBLE...
BUT IT IS ONLY A SHADOW OF WHAT HE BEARS UPON HIS OWN BREAST!
ENOUGH!
STAND ANY HERE THAT QUESTION GOD'S JUDGMENT ON A SINNER?
BEHOLD!
BEHOLD THE DREADFUL PROOF!
KEEP IT HIDDEN!
!?
!!

First, the original book implies that there was a "scarlet letter" on Dimmesdale's chest just like the one Hester wears, and the crowd discusses this in chapter ten, with some people saying they saw his scarlet letter and others insisting they did not. So did Dimmesdale's scarlet letter actually exist, and in what form? The original book doesn't take a clear position on this either, so I wanted to leave that for the readers to decide. After discussing it with the manga artist, we decided to avoid drawing his chest and mirror the original book by leaving the existence and nature of Dimmesdale's scarlet letter up to the reader's imagination.

Next, Pearl's presence in the book is a considerably strange and mysterious. She often comes across as more elf-like than human, and I needed to think carefully about how to express this quality in the manga. I decided to have other characters commenting on her to describing her oddness: "That little creature has witchcraft in her, I say. She needs no broomstick to fly!" There are also some minor details to show just how different Pearl is. For example, Pearl does not act like a normal kid when playing in the woods; she befriends various forest animals, and even the wild wolf is kind to her. And most importantly, Pearl's eyes stand out from those of the other characters as being different and almost inhuman for most of the story, and her eyes only become "normal" again after her father dies, implying that she has regained her humanity at that point. Emphasizing a character's unique qualities via graphics and dialogue is something manga does particularly well, and it helps those qualities blend into the story more naturally.

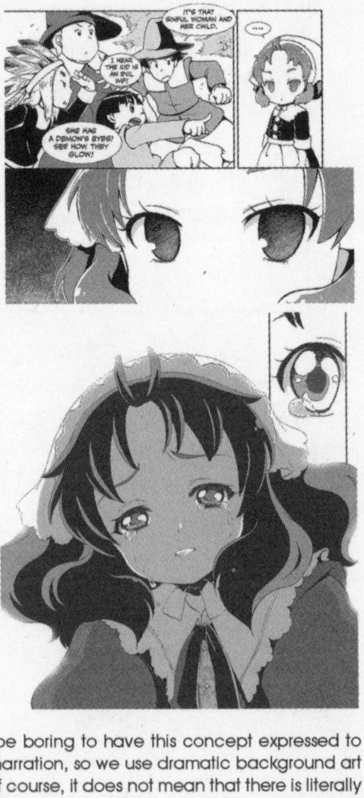
....
IT'S THAT SINFUL WOMAN AND HER CHILD.
I HEAR THE KID IS AN EVIL IMP!
SHE HAS A DEMON'S EYES! SEE HOW THEY GLOW!

And what's with the giant snake that is always behind Chillingworth? This is actually one of the more common visual metaphors commonly used in manga storytelling. The original book mentions that "A writhing horror twisted itself across his features, like a snake gliding swiftly over them, and making one little pause, with all its wreathed intervolutions in open sight." The snake, of course, serves as a symbol of the Devil in traditional Christian lore, and Chillingworth admits to Hester that he turned himself into a demon over his obsession with taking revenge on Dimmesdale. The snake seen behind him so often is a symbol showing the darkness or evil in his heart. It would be boring to have this concept expressed to the reader through mere narration, so we use dramatic background art to emphasize it instead. Of course, it does not mean that there is literally a snake behind him! Also, although Chillingworth's irises are drawn to be like a snake's, this does not mean his eyes are actually mutating; this is actually a general example of artistry in manga.

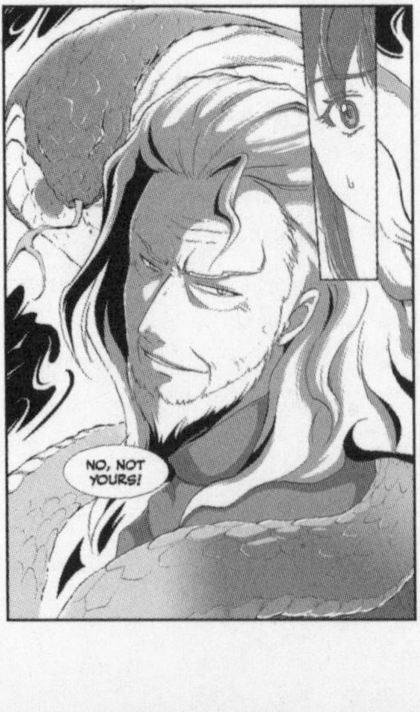
NO, NOT YOURS!

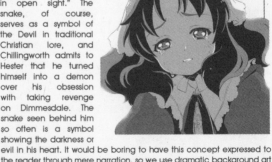

CRYSTAL S. CHAN:

ADAPTING THE SCARLET LETTER

The idea of two pious Puritans engaging in a forbidden love affair is an excellent basis for a romance novel, and Nathaniel Hawthorne explores this risqué topic in a thorough and chilling manner in the extraordinary "The Scarlet Letter." And I want to take the chance here to share with you my experience on adapting this story into manga format.

In general, my goal was to leverage the unique strengths of manga to recreate the essence of the original book. I strived to present an adaptation that included all of the book's most important characteristics while never losing focus on the main plot and characters. The original book focuses more on the story's artistic elements, with the drama being relatively weak by comparison. The book also includes many emotional scenes and scenes described through narration, while there are relatively few scenes in which characters have actual dialogue. Therefore, in this adaptation, I focused on using the manga style to present artistry while using the graphics to present the original book's romance. At the same time, I preserved as many plot details as possible in order to recreate the dialogue and emotions of the characters and visually represented the book's various metaphors in order to achieve the overall direction of this adaptation.

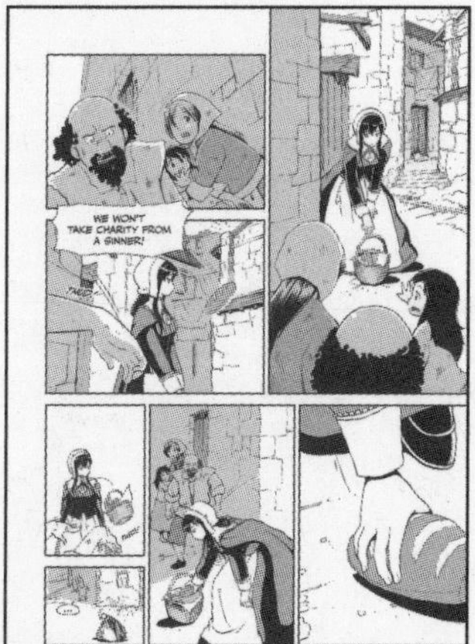
WE WON'T TAKE CHARITY FROM A SINNER!

First, let me explain how I translate the book's many descriptive scenes into the manga format. For example, chapter five mainly describes Hester's life after being released from prison. The entire chapter is composed of bits and pieces of scenes without one important event linking everything together. In order to make the story more cohesive, I pick the scenes that can be somewhat related and linked them together, and I also try to more fully express scenes that were only narrated in the original book (i.e. the two scenes quoted directly from the original book, "Hester bestowed all her superfluous means in charity, on wretches less miserable than herself, and who not unfrequently insulted the hand that fed them," and "The poor, as we have already said, whom she sought out to be the objects of her bounty, often reviled the hand that was stretched forth to succor them." I imagine these descriptions as scenes with characters and dialogue, and thus they became the scene where some poor people reject Hester after she tries to give them bread. Witnessing Hester and her plight directly in this manner makes it easier for readers to understand and empathize with her and engages them in a more memorable way than simply using narration ever could.

Background characters:

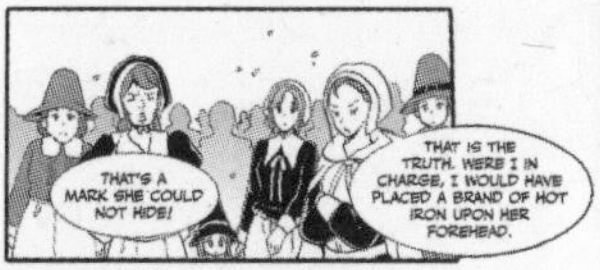
THAT IS THE TRUTH. WERE I IN CHARGE, I WOULD HAVE PLACED A BRAND OF HOT IRON UPON HER FOREHEAD.
THAT'S A MARK SHE COULD NOT HIDE!

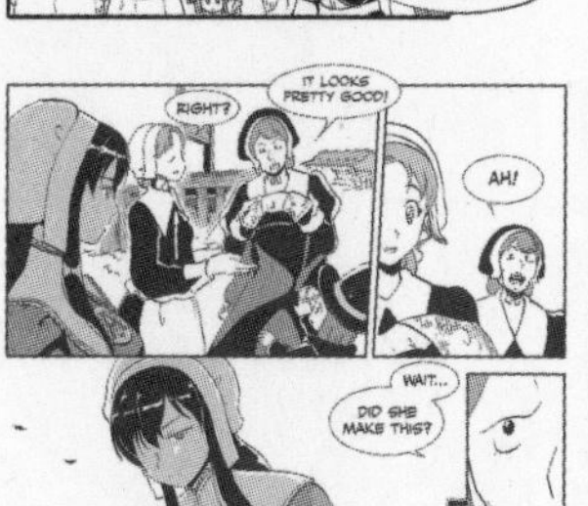
AH!
IT LOOKS PRETTY GOOD!
RIGHT?
WAIT... DID SHE MAKE THIS?

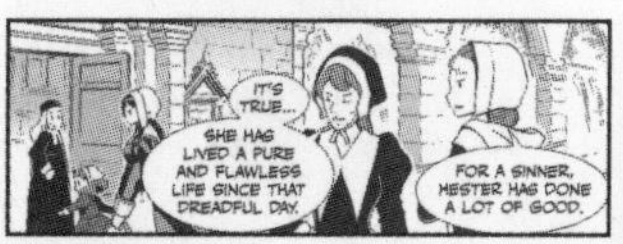
FOR A SINNER, HESTER HAS DONE A LOT OF GOOD.
IT'S TRUE...
SHE HAS LIVED A PURE AND FLAWLESS LIFE SINCE THAT DREADFUL DAY.

Certainly it is best to try and use the original lines from the book when adapting a scene; sometimes, however, we have to be a little creative in certain scenes to express some of the original book's vaguer details. In this story, we took some liberties to connect the continuity of the insignificant background characters in scenes that feature crowds or random townsfolk. Precisely because they are insignificant, giving them my own unique touch in no way affects the essence of the original story. If you had paid attention, we have "recurring cast" showing up throughout the book. The mother and her son who have sympathy for Hester in chapter one, I had them buy clothes from Hester in chapter three to follow through on their sympathetic feelings. The same goes for the woman who despise Hester in chapter one. In chapter three, the same woman still believes that anything touched by Hester is dirty. Six years later in chapter seven is when she finally comes around and changes her mind. This way, I expressed that this woman who once despised Hester is later moved by her and agrees that Hester has lived a pure life. The locals who see their fellow villagers slowly changing their minds about Hester invariably follow suit, leading to a gradual but consistent shift in their attitudes toward her over the course of the story – a shift I consciously tried to express by establishing the aforementioned continuity in some of the background characters. Of course, missing these details won't affect a reader's ability to understand and enjoy the core story, but noticing them might add a little extra enjoyment.

The Tapestry of King David:

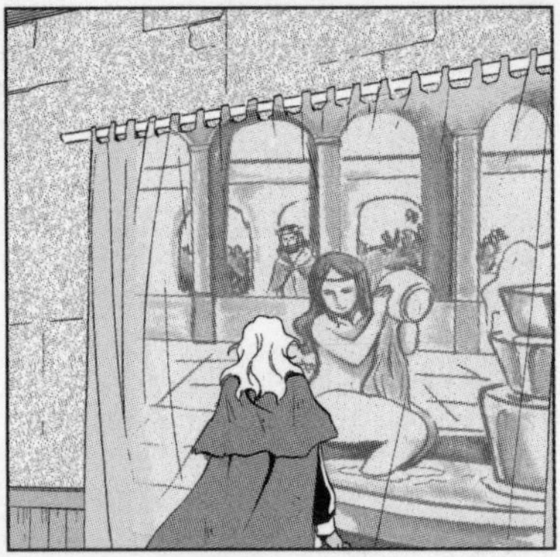

There are some minor details in the original book that was mentioned, but because of the flow of the manga story, we have to omit. But we still try to incorporate them in our book somehow. One example I wish to point out is that in chapter five, in the house Dimmesdale and Chillingworth move into together, there is a piece of textile hanging on the wall telling the story of King David of Israel. This story actually comes from the Bible's Old Testament. Back in 10th century B.C., King David had a good relationship with God. One day, however, he saw the beautiful young woman Bathsheba bathing, and is tempted by his desire for her. Even though he already knew she was the wife of Uriah, he still slept with her. Bathsheba eventually is pregnant with King David's child, and in order to conceal his sin he summoned Uriah from the army, planning to have Uriah sleep with Bathsheba. Uriah refused to return home, however, as the war was not over. King David did not expect this, so instead he sends Uriah to the battle's front lines so that he would be killed in battle. King David's plan works and he later made Bathsheba his wife. This is one of the famous stories in the Bible about a powerful man taking another's wife for himself. This picture hanging on the wall of their house has different meaning to Chillingworth and Dimmesdale. Now you can imagine why Chillingworth's feelings of vengeance would grow stronger – and why Dimmesdale's guilt would consume him even more – after seeing the textile describing this story. Although we do not have time to dive into the back story of this item, we still want to put this important detail in our book so that the readers will be able to reference it to the original story.

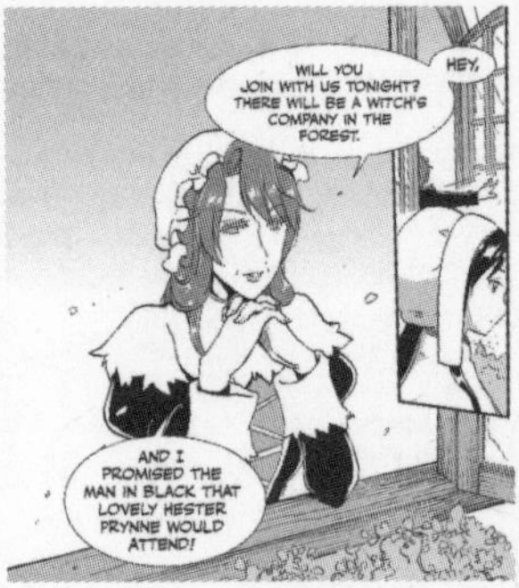
HEY,
WILL YOU JOIN WITH US TONIGHT? THERE WILL BE A WITCH'S COMPANY IN THE FOREST.
AND I PROMISED THE MAN IN BLACK THAT LOVELY HESTER PRYNNE WOULD ATTEND!

The "Man in Black":

There is the lingering question of who is the "man in black" mentioned by the characters? Why was Pearl so interested in him? He never actually appears, does he? This is an ongoing mystery that was never truly explained in the book, but the author dropped a lot of hints especially through the character Mrs. Hibbins. Mrs. Hibbins seems to be close to the man in black and mentions him every time she appears. Although not showing up regularly in the story, she is indeed a key character! It was written in the original book that "A few years later, [she] was executed as a witch." She claimed that she knows how to fly, and even Hester thought Mrs. Hibbins had some mental problems! You can imagine how the local Puritans felt about her. It is said that witches are the Devil's minions, and because Mrs. Hibbins was eventually executed for being a witch, can we speculate that the man in black she appears to be close to may be the Devil or Satan? Another hint this is the fact that Dimmesdale conceals his sin until the end of the story, and Mrs. Hibbins points out that Dimmesdale does not admit publicly that he was once the servant of the man in black… and who traditionally leads men astray and causes them to commit crimes. Pearl is the product of the crime that Hester and Dimmesdale committed together. This child is the symbol of sin, but because she did not commit any crime herself, she only knows about the man in black in passing and is merely curious about him. Pearl is not acutely aware of the man in black like Hester is, but neither does she outright deny the man in black's existence like Dimmesdale does.

The Dialogue:

After reading the entire manga, did you find some dialogue to be a bit odd and unnatural? Actually, those are old dialogues that were in the original book and I intentionally kept it in for the manga adaptation, hoping the readers would think about it. For example, Hester does not see Dimmesdale for several years, and when they meet again in the woods she asks him, "And you, Arthur Dimmesdale? Do you still live?" You might wonder why Hester would ask such a thing when she sees Dimmesdale alive and standing right in front of her, but if you think about it more deeply you will understand the true reason: She is not asking if he is physically alive, but if his soul still exists after being crushed under the weight of his guilt all those years. This plot point and the dialogue in this scene may be hard to understand the first time you read this part, but I decided not to rewrite the scene to make its subtext easier to figure out. After all, that scene was an important part in the original book, and it is more fun to let readers experience it the way it was intended and let them figure it out for themselves.

Hopefully you now have a greater understanding of just how complex the original book was, especially in terms of its characters, their different motivations, and the subtext in many of the scenes they share. It is a new level of challenge for me to try to preserve the details of the original book and worked closely with SunNeko Lee to present our ideal manga version that is also faithful to source material. I hope this will be one of your favorite adaptations of "The Scarlet Letter"!

Crystal (Silvermoon) Chan

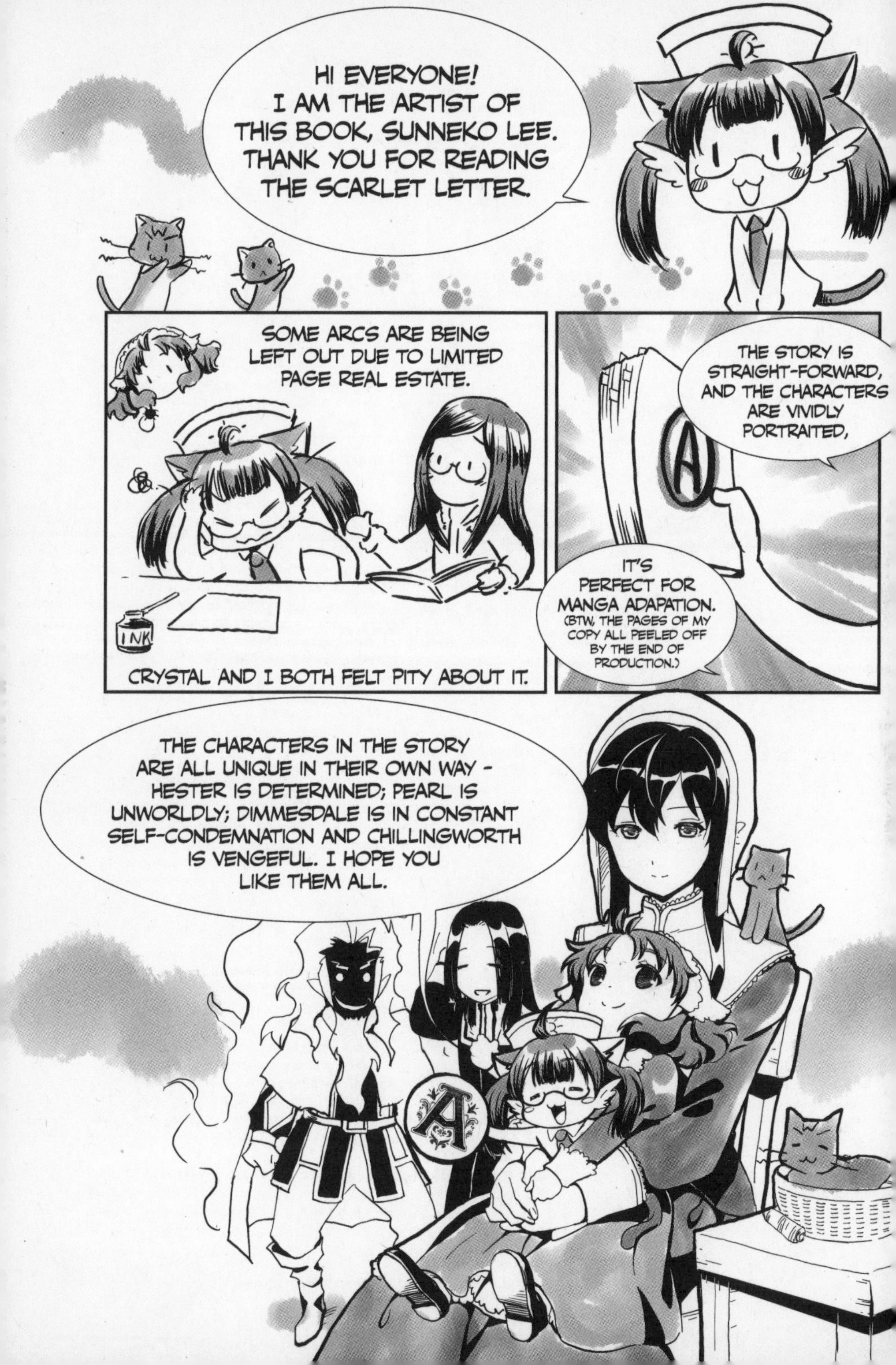
HI EVERYONE! I AM THE ARTIST OF THIS BOOK, SUNNEKO LEE. THANK YOU FOR READING THE SCARLET LETTER.
THE STORY IS STRAIGHT-FORWARD, AND THE CHARACTERS ARE VIVIDLY PORTRAITED,
IT'S PERFECT FOR MANGA ADAPATION.
(BTW, THE PAGES OF MY COPY ALL PEELED OFF BY THE END OF PRODUCTION.)
SOME ARCS ARE BEING LEFT OUT DUE TO LIMITED PAGE REAL ESTATE.
INK
CRYSTAL AND I BOTH FELT PITY ABOUT IT.
THE CHARACTERS IN THE STORY ARE ALL UNIQUE IN THEIR OWN WAY - HESTER IS DETERMINED; PEARL IS UNWORLDLY; DIMMESDALE IS IN CONSTANT SELF-CONDEMNATION AND CHILLINGWORTH IS VENGEFUL. I HOPE YOU LIKE THEM ALL.
A

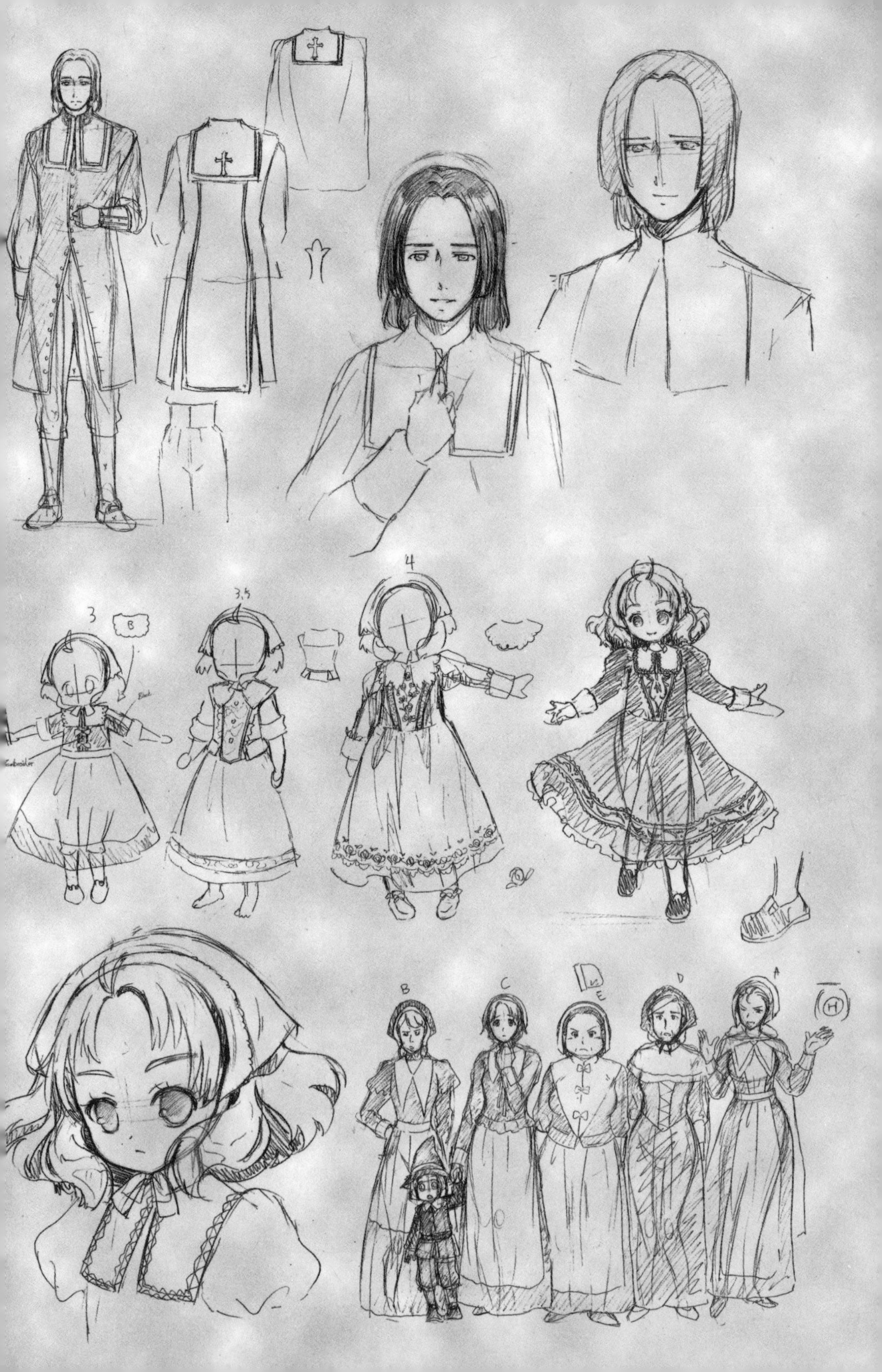
3
B
3.5
4
B
C
D
E
D
A
H

CHARACTER DESIGN SKETCH BOOK

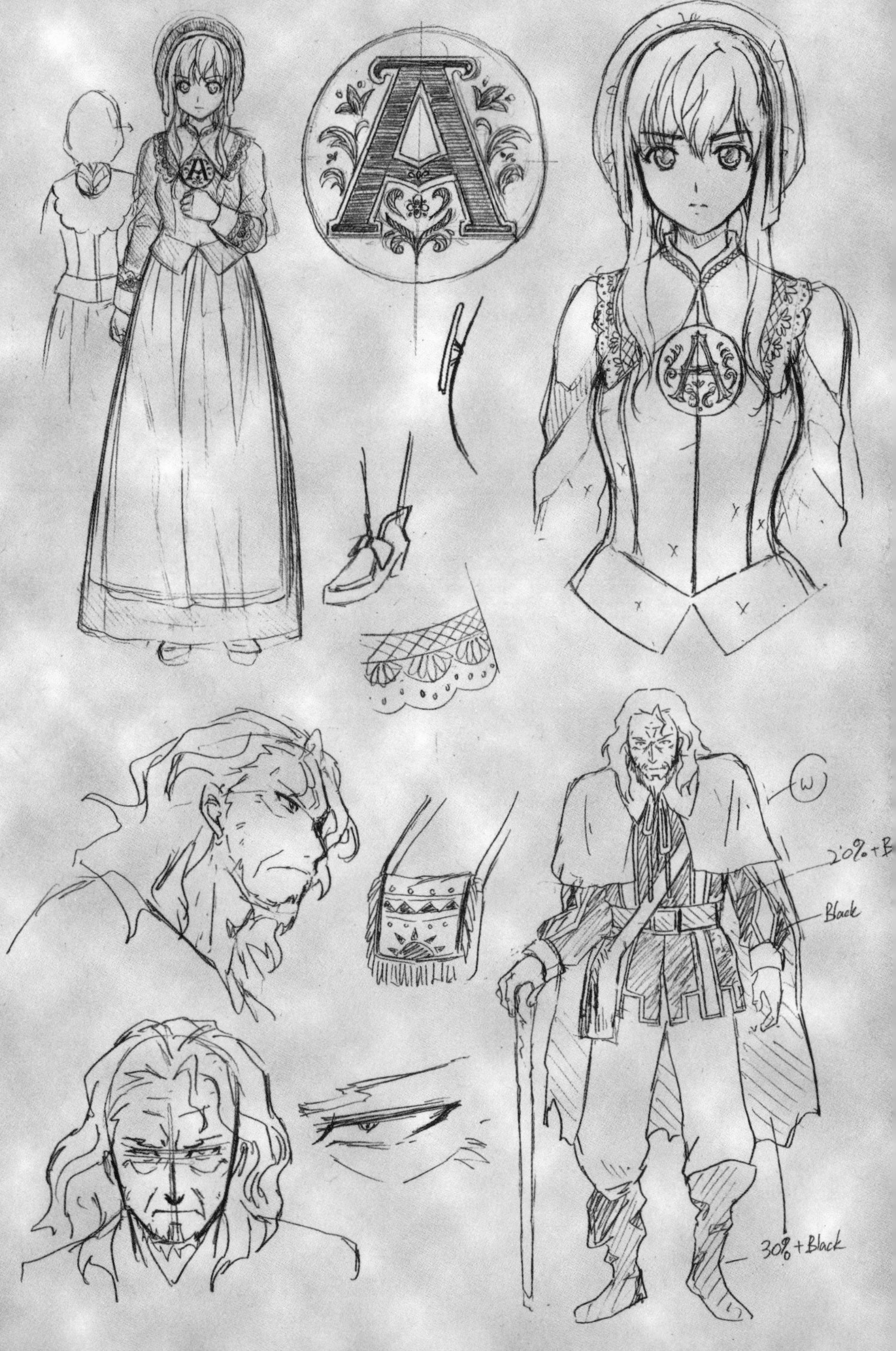
W
20%+B
Black
30%+Black

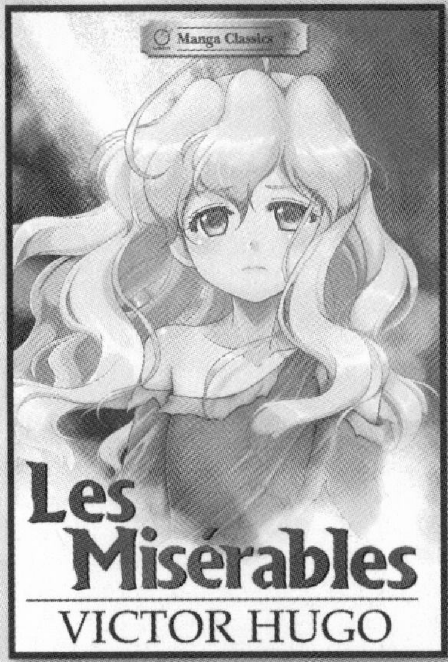
Manga Classics
Les Misérables
VICTOR HUGO

Manga Classics: Les Miserables
Hard Cover $24.99
ISBN #978-1927925157
Soft Cover $19.99
ISBN #978-1927925164

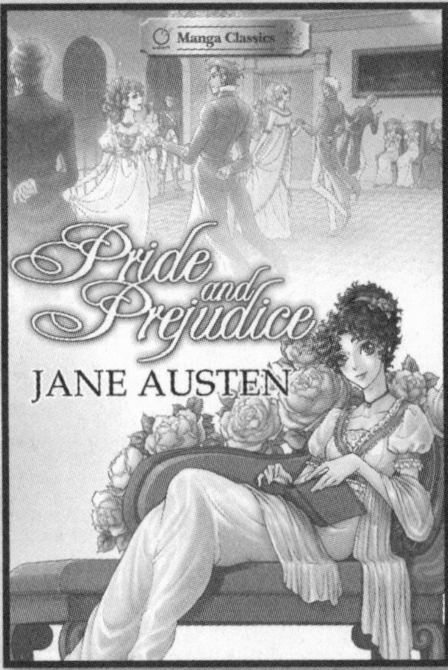
Manga Classics
Pride and Prejudice
JANE AUSTEN

Manga Classics: Pride & Prejudice
Hard Cover $24.99
ISBN #978-1927925171
Soft Cover $19.99
ISBN #978-1927925188

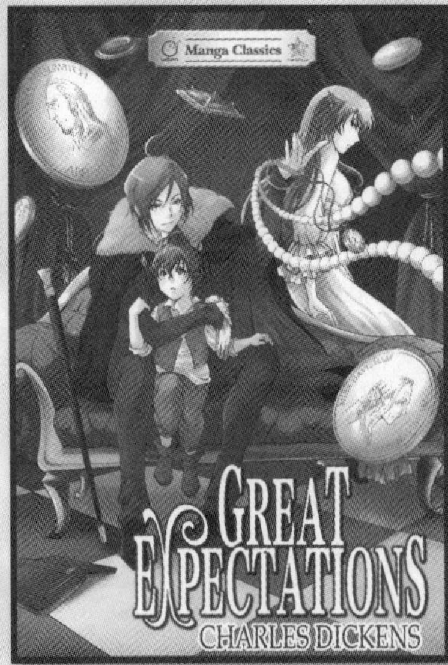
Manga Classics
GREAT EXPECTATIONS
CHARLES DICKENS

Manga Classics: Great Expectations
Hard Cover $24.99
ISBN #978-1927925324
Soft Cover $19.99
ISBN #978-1927925317

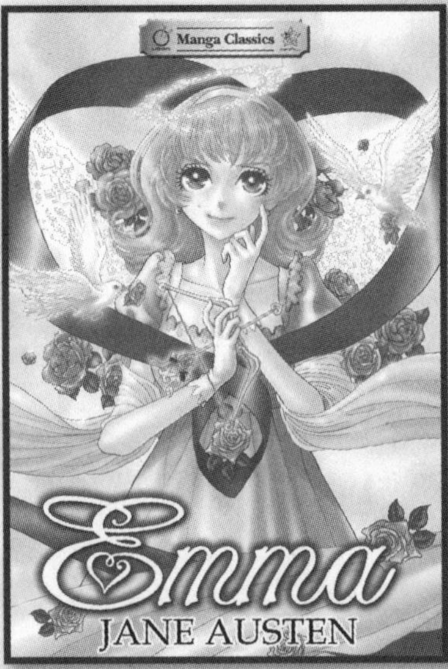
Manga Classics
Emma
JANE AUSTEN

Manga Classics: Emma
Hard Cover $24.99
ISBN #978-1927925362
Soft Cover $19.99
ISBN #978-1927925355

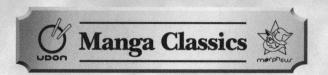

Manga Classics

UDON Entertainment proudly presents: **Manga Classics**!

The finest name in adaptations of great, classic literature!

Manga Classics
THE SCARLET LETTER
NATHANIEL HAWTHORNE

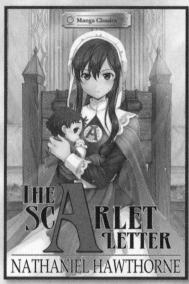

UDON is proud to bring you this very special new line of books, adapting classic literature with the same attention to detail and quality as our fantastic graphic novels, art books, and manga releases! UDON's Manga Classics is an international partnership with Asian comics and animation studio Morpheus, to bring the highest-quality adaptations of these works to the North American market!

UDON and Morpheus have worked very hard to fully realize the world of these classic works of literature. The artists have done extensive research on the settings of these works, to give the costumes and architecture a real weight and accuracy, expertly executed thanks to the studio's animation background. This high quality work has been coupled with a generous page count of over 300 pages per book, more than double the average comics-format adaptation! This allows for a more thorough, accurate, and natural adaptation of the source material, with the artists' vision given as much space as it needs to be properly realized. In short, these look and read like great commercial manga, while being faithful adaptations of literary classics!

Intended for a young adult audience, UDON's Manga Classics are just as likely to be enjoyed in the reader's free time as in the classroom. The gripping story and the lush art place them easily alongside today's bestselling popular manga, with strong and accurate adaptations that will please even the toughest teacher or librarian! UDON's Manga Classics are also a great way for adult readers to rediscover their favorite classics, or experience them for the first time!

Now that you have read The Scarlet Letter, look for UDON's Manga Classics adaptations of Victor Hugo's Les Misérables, Jane Austen's Pride and Prejudice, and Emma, plus Charles Dickens' Great Expectations in stores!

Recommended Age: Young Adult
Genre: Literature / Manga
BISAC Code: CGN004050
BISAC Code 2: CGN004140
BISAC Code 3: FIC014000

Check out more MANGA CLASSICS titles !!

! WHOOPS !

This is the back of the book!

UDON's Manga Classics books follow the Japanese comic (aka Manga!) reading order. Traditional manga is read in a "reversed" format starting on the right and heading towards the left. The story begins where English readers expect to find the last page because the spine of the book is on the opposite side. Flip to the other end of the book and start reading your Manga Classics!

THE SCARLET LETTER

—NATHANIEL HAWTHORNE—

Art by: SunNeko Lee
Story Adaptation by: Crystal S. Chan

English Dialogue Adapted by: Stacy King
Lettering: Morpheus Studios
Lettering Assist: W.T. Francis

UDON STAFF:
UDON Chief: Erik Ko
Managing Editor: Matt Moylan
Marketing Manager: Jenny Myung
Senior Editor: Ash Paulsen
Production Manager: Janice Leung
Copy Editing Assistant: Michelle Lee
Japanese Liaisons: Steven Cummings

MORPHEUS STAFF:
Morpheus Chief: Andy Hung
Production Manager: Tai
Art Assistants: KK, Ashton Touyu, VIP96neko, Mingsin Song, Stoon

Manga Classics: The Scarlet Letter. Published by UDON Entertainment Inc. 118 Tower Hill Road, PO Box 20008, Richmond Hill, Ontario, L4K 0K0, Canada. **Printed in Canada**

First Printing March 2015.

Hard Cover Edition ISBN # 978-1-927925-34-8 Soft Cover Edition ISBN # 978-1-927925-33-1

Recommended Age: Young Adult Genre: Manga BISAC Code: CGN004050 / CGN004140 / FIC014000

www.mangaclassics.com

An UDON Entertainment Production, in association with Morpheus Publishing Limited.
www.udonentertainment.com www.morpheuspublishing.com